TWELFTH EDITION

INVESTMENTS

Principles and Concepts

International Student Version

Charles P. Jones, Ph.D., CFA

WILEY

To Kay and Kathryn
For making every year special
and to
Georgie,
Who continues to be there during working hours

Brief Contents

Contents

Preface

This book is designed to provide a good understanding of the field of investments while stimulating interest in the subject. This understanding is valuable because each of us must make various investment decisions during our lifetimes—definitely as individuals, and possibly in our chosen careers. If we try to avoid making these decisions, they will likely be made for us, and often to our detriment.

My goal in this text is to help readers gain an appreciation of what is involved in (1) understanding what is involved when it comes to investing, (2) making good investment decisions, and (3) recognizing where investment problems and controversies arise and knowing how to deal with them.

This book is designed as an appropriate guide to investments for everyone wanting to learn, being neither too basic nor too advanced. Descriptive material must be—and is—thoroughly covered. Equally important, however, the analytics of investments are presented throughout the discussion to help students reason out investment issues for themselves and thus be better prepared when making real-world investment decisions. Terminology and trading mechanisms may change, but learning to carefully analyze and evaluate investment opportunities will pay off under any circumstances.

The book is written for the first course in investments, generally taught at the junior/ senior level. Standard prerequisites include basic accounting, economics, and financial management. A course in statistics is very useful but not absolutely essential. I have sought to minimize formulas and to simplify difficult material, consistent with a presentation of the subject that takes into account current ideas and practices. Relevant, state-of-the-art material has been simplified and structured specifically for the benefit of the beginning student. The emphasis in this text is on readability—making *Investments*' material readily accessible, as well as interesting and entertaining, so that the reader who has modest prerequisites can follow the entire discussion and hopefully be motivated to delve further into the subject.

Organization Of The Text

The text is divided into seven parts for organizational purposes—organized around background, returns and basic portfolio theory, the analysis of different types of securities (four parts), and portfolio management.

Part 1 provides the needed background for students before encountering the specifics of security analysis and portfolio management. The goal of this introductory set of chapters is to acquaint beginners with an overview of what investing is all about. After a general discussion of the subject in Chapter 1, the next four chapters describe the variety of securities available when investing directly, investing indirectly (investment companies), the markets in which they are traded, and the mechanics of securities trading.

Part 2 is concerned with an analysis of returns and risk, along with the basics of portfolio theory and capital market theory. Chapter 6 contains a careful analysis of the important concepts of risk and return that dominate any discussion of investments. Chapter 7 contains a complete discussion of expected return and risk for both individual securities and portfolios. The primary emphasis is on the essentials of Markowitz portfolio theory. Chapter 8 completes portfolio theory and then covers asset allocation, one of the most important decisions that any investor makes. Beta and the CAPM are introduced in Chapter 9 so these important concepts can be used throughout the course. This illustrates one of the primary characteristics of this text—introducing material only at the point it is needed, and only in the detail needed by beginning students. I believe this improves the flow of the material greatly, and keeps students from becoming mired in needless, and often tedious, details.

Parts 3 and 4 focus on the basics of the valuation and management of stocks by analyzing "how-to" tools and techniques for understanding stocks as well as issues and techniques in their management.

Part 3 examines the analysis, valuation, and management of stocks, a logical starting point in learning how to value securities. It emphasizes the analysis, valuation, and management of common stocks. Chapter 12 explains the efficient market hypothesis and provides some insights into the controversy surrounding this topic.

Part 4 is devoted to security analysis, a reasonable allocation given investor interest in common stocks. It also covers fundamental analysis, the heart of security analysis, as well as technical analysis. Because of its scope and complexity, three chapters are required to adequately cover the fundamental approach. The sequencing of these chapters—market, industry, and company—reflects the author's belief that the top-down approach to fundamental analysis is the preferable one for students to learn, although the bottom-up approach is also discussed. Part 4 also discusses technical analysis, a well-known technique for analyzing stocks which goes back many years. It is not unusual for beginners to have heard of one or more technical analysis tools.

Part 5 is devoted to bonds. Chapter 17 covers the basics of bonds as far as prices and yields are concerned. It includes such topics as the term structure of interest rates and yield spreads. All important calculations regarding prices and yields are explained and illustrated. Other issues include bond price changes in response to interest rate changes. Chapter 18 focuses on the management of bonds, and covers topics such as duration and immunization. As always, the emphasis is on the basics—the important topics that students need to know to understand the world of fixed income investing.

Part 6 discusses the other major securities available to investors, derivative securities. Chapter 19 analyzes options (puts and calls), a popular investment alternative in recent years. Stock index options are also covered. Chapter 20 is devoted to financial futures, an important topic for investors when it comes to hedging their positions and reducing the risk of investing.

Finally, Part 7 concludes the text with a discussion of financial planning in general and portfolio management in particular, and the issue of evaluating portfolio performance. Chapter 21 is structured around an individual investor's approach to financial planning and managing a portfolio. Chapter 22 is a logical conclusion to the entire book because all investors are keenly interested in how well their investments have performed. Mutual funds are used as examples of how to apply these portfolio performance measures and how to interpret the results.

The 12th edition contains exactly the same set of chapters, in the same order, as the 11th edition. Therefore, the transition to this new edition should be painless.

Special Features

This text offers several important features.

1. *The sequence of chapters has been carefully structured and streamlined* in each edition, reflecting considerable experimentation over the years and a continuing search for the most effective organizational structure. I believe that this arrangement is very satisfactory

for many students in a beginning investments course. However, those who prefer a different order—such as covering portfolio theory and capital market theory later in the course—can do so with no loss of continuity at all.

2. I have diligently sought to ensure that *the text length is reasonably manageable* in the standard undergraduate investments course. Although it requires a very tight schedule, the entire text could be covered in a typical three-hour course. However, many instructors choose to omit chapters, depending on preferences and constraints; doing so will cause no problems in terms of teaching a satisfactory investments course. For example, the chapters on fundamental analysis and technical analysis (Part 4) could be omitted, because the valuation and management of common stocks is fully covered in Part 3. Alternatively, the chapters on options and futures could be omitted if necessary. Another alternative is assigning some chapters, or parts of chapters, to be read by students with little or no class discussion (for example, Part 4).

3. *The pedagogy is specifically designed for the student's benefit.*
   - Each chapter begins with a set of specific *learning objectives*, which will aid the reader in determining what is to be accomplished in a particular chapter.
   - Each chapter contains *key words* in boldface, carefully defined as marginal definitions; they also are included in the glossary. Other important words are italicized.
   - Each chapter contains a *detailed summary* of bulleted points for quick and precise reading.
   - Each chapter contains an *extensive set of numbered examples*, designed to clearly illustrate important concepts.
   - Most chapters contain a designated feature called *Concepts in Action* which illustrates the use of one or more of the important items in that chapter.
   - Throughout the text, as appropriate, *Investments Intuition* sections are set off from the regular text for easy identification. These discussions are designed to help the reader quickly grasp the intuitive logic of, and therefore better understand, particular investing issues.
   - Each chapter has a set of questions titled "Checking Your Understanding" spaced throughout the chapter, as appropriate. These questions, with answers at the end of chapters, give students a chance to see if they understand critical issues as they progress through the text.
   - Throughout the text, as appropriate, *Some Practical Advice* is given in a clearly designated format.
   - Each chapter contains an *extensive set of questions* keyed specifically to the chapter material and designed to thoroughly review the concepts in each chapter.
   - Many chapters have a *separate set of problems* designed to illustrate the quantitative material in the chapters. Some of these problems can be solved in the normal manner, and some are best solved with available software. Included as part of some problem sets are demonstration problems that show the reader how to solve the most important types of problems.
   - Where appropriate, chapters have *spreadsheet exercises* and *computational problems* which are more complex.
   - Many chapters contain *multiple questions and problems* taken from the chartered financial analyst examinations. This allows students to see that the concepts and problem-solving processes they are studying in class are exactly the same as those asked on professional examinations for people in the money-management business.
   - A few *boxed inserts* continue to be included in the text. These inserts provide timely and interesting material from the popular press, enabling the student to see the real-world side of issues and concepts discussed in the text. Space limitations and difficulties with permissions have necessitated a reduction in this material.

Changes In The Twelfth Edition

The 12th edition has been thoroughly updated using the latest information and numbers available. Most of the data are through year-end 2011 and some extend into 2012.

Important features in the 12th edition include the following:

- Pedagogy has been enhanced. For example, some chapters have lead-in questions or problems to illustrate an important issue that will be discussed in that chapter. In other chapters, this may be done later in the chapter.
- Features such as "Concepts in Action" and "Investments Intuition" have been increased in number to illustrate important issues with interesting, real-world, current examples.
- Computational problems and spreadsheet exercises have been significantly increased relative to the 11th edition.
- Part 1 contains the latest information available on newer concepts such as ETFs (exchange-traded funds) and ECNs (electronic communications networks) and the most current information on important trends such as discount/Internet brokers. Also included are items like BATS, algorithmic trading, and high-frequency trading. The section on market indexes has been expanded and improved.
- Chapter 6 is continually being improved to facilitate the understanding of important calculations like the geometric mean. These calculations are important in finance, and in general, and the more examples and practice available to students, the better.
- Chapter 10, on the valuation of common stocks, places somewhat less emphasis on the dividend discount model and more on relative valuation techniques and other discounted cash flow approaches. The uses of the P/E ratio model are better explained and illustrated.
- Chapter 8 contains a more extended discussion of asset allocation.
- Some of the material in Chapters 17 and 18 has been reoriented to improve the flow. Chapter 17 contains the discussion of the term structure of interest rates and yield spreads as well as discussion of bond yields and prices. Concepts such as duration and immunization are in Chapter 18.
- Chapter 21 has been reoriented to have a personal financial planning flavor while still considering portfolio management and strategy issues.
- Chapter 22 has more real-world connections, pointing out what others have to say about this issue.
- Appendices have been removed from the text itself and are available on the website to students and users of the text. These appendices can be easily accessed as necessary.

Supplements

The 12th edition includes a complete set of supplements for instructors and students. Resources can be found on the book's companion site, www.wiley.com/college/jones.

- **Instructor's manual.** For each chapter, chapter objectives, lecture notes, a listing of tables and figures, and additional material relevant to the particular chapter are included. Answers to all questions and problems in the text are provided. The instructor's manual was carefully prepared by the author.
- **Test bank.** The test bank includes numerous multiple choice and true-false questions for each chapter as well as short discussion questions and problems. These are carefully

checked; most have also been class-tested. The test bank is also available in a computerized format.

- **PowerPoint files.** PowerPoint presentation materials are available. A presentation file for each chapter includes outline material as well as all figures and tables from the text.
- **List of equations.** A comprehensive list of all equations found in the text.
- **Appendices.** As noted above, appendices containing additional material in select chapters can be found on the companion site.
- **Excel templates.** This online collection of Excel templates allow students to complete select end-of-chapter questions and problems identified by a spreadsheet icon in the textbook. Solution files are available to instructors.
- **Student practice quizzes** contain at least 10—15 multiple choice questions per chapter. With instant feedback, questions of varying difficulty help students evaluate individual progress through a chapter.

Acknowledgments

A number of individuals have contributed to this project. I am particularly indebted to the late Jack W. Wilson, North Carolina State University, a highly valued friend and colleague who offered many useful comments, provided material for some of the tables, figures and appendices, and worked out many of the problems (including the extended problems) for the text. Over the years he supplied data, graphs, suggestions, and insights. Some of the material used in this book and the accompanying supplements is based on Jack's groundbreaking work in the area of asset returns. Jack was always most generous with his time and efforts for this project. He is greatly missed.

A text does not achieve multiple editions unless it has met the needs of a large number of instructors who find it to be a useful tool in assisting their teaching. The earlier editions of this text benefited substantially from the reviews of many instructors whose suggestions for improvements are found on many pages of this text. I owe a debt of gratitude to those teachers and colleagues who, after 12 editions, are too numerous to name here. Their criticisms and suggestions have substantially affected the evolution of this text and made it a better book. Most recently, I received valuable feedback for the 12th edition from Jay T. Brandi, University of Louisville; Laura Seery Cole, University of Tennessee, Knoxville; William P. Dukes, Texas Tech University; Rodrigo Hernandez, Radford University; Nancy Jay, Mercer University; Iqbal Mansur, Widener University; Kerri D. McMillan, Clemson University; and Tanja Steigner, Emporia State University.

I would also like to thank a number of my former editors at Wiley: Rich Esposito, Joe Dougherty, and John Woods. John Woods worked hard to enhance the supplementary material to the 3rd edition of the text and to provide the overall support necessary to substantially revise the material and improve the book in numerous ways. Whitney Blake was most helpful in developing a top-of-the-line 4th and 5th editions, always displaying a "can-do" attitude. Melissa Ryan significantly aided in developing the 7th edition. Cindy Rhoads was a large part of the 8th and 9th editions, as was Leslie Kraham. For the 10th and 11th editions, I thank Judy Joseph, Emily Horowitz, and Emily McGee. Brian Kamins also played a valuable role for the 10th edition. Sarah Vernon was a major asset in helping to bring about the 11th edition. For the 12th edition, I'd like to thank my editorial team, Joel Hollenbeck, Jennifer Manias, Courtney Luzzi, and Erica Horowitz, as well as my production team, especially Elaine Chew, and Greg Chaput.

Finally, I continue to thank my family, who have always put up with the interruptions caused by writing a book. Without their support, a project such as this is difficult at best. I thank in particular my wife, Kay, who has helped me tremendously in the preparation of various editions of this text. She did much additional work for the 12th edition, involving the difficult jobs of coordinating and checking the numerous details involved in a project such as this. Kay and Kathryn make a difficult job bearable, and worth doing. For this edition they provided strong support and encouragement when I needed it most.

Charles P. Jones
North Carolina State University
August 2012

chapter 1

Investing is an Important Activity Worldwide

Suppose you are fortunate enough to receive an inheritance of $1 million from a relative. She specifies only that you must invest this money intelligently in financial assets within the next six months, and not spend it on consumption, and that you must be answerable to a trustee who has the final say if you fail to make reasonable decisions. You now face an enviable task—building a portfolio of stocks, bonds, and so forth—and you quickly realize that not only do you not know all the answers, you don't even know some of the questions.

Having had a finance course in college, you learned about return and risk, but now you must really understand what these variables mean. You have heard some people talk about making a "killing in the market," but common sense tells you it can't be all that easy. Like the prospective investor asked the broker when the latter was showing him the yachts belonging to other brokers, "Where are the customers' yachts?" Also, you have on several occasions read about fraudulent investment schemes leaving people broke, but wiser. And so you realize you have your work cut out for you. You need to identify the important issues, ask the right questions, and learn the basics about successful investing.

You can, in fact, construct and manage your portfolio, as the following chapters will show. With a little tenacity, you can be on your way to an intelligent investing program, because basic knowledge can go a long way. Let's get started.

Chapter 1 provides the foundation for the study of Investments by analyzing what investing is all about. The critically important tradeoff between expected return and risk is explained, and the major issues that every investor must deal with in making investment decisions are analyzed. An organizational structure for the entire text is provided.

AFTER READING THIS CHAPTER YOU WILL BE ABLE TO:

▶ Understand why return and risk are the two critical components of all investing decisions.

▶ Appreciate the scope of investment decisions and the operating environment in which they are made.

▶ Follow the organization of the investment decision process as we progress through the text.

An Overall Perspective on Investing

- In less than two years, from its peak in March 2000, the S&P 500 Index, a measure of large stocks, subsequently lost about 50 percent of its value, while the NASDAQ Stock Market lost about 75 percent of its value. In less than two years during 2000–2002, investors lost $5 trillion, or 30 percent of their wealth in stocks. In 2008–2009 stock market volatility was even greater. In only two months in 2011, $3 trillion in stock market wealth disappeared in the United States, and $8 trillion globally. With volatility like this, should most investors avoid stocks, particularly for their retirement plans?

- Following the financial crisis of 2008, interest rates on U.S. Treasury securities dropped to record lows, in some cases close to zero. In early 2012, Germany sold six-month Treasury securities with a negative yield. Why would investors continue to invest in these debt securities, sometimes stampeding to invest in them?

- Almost everyone says stocks have always outperformed Treasury bonds over long periods of time, such as 30 years. Is this an accurate statement?

- Many company employees with self-directed retirement plans have none of their funds invested in stocks, although over the years stocks have significantly outperformed the alternative assets they did hold. Is this smart?

- About two-thirds of all affluent Americans use financial advisors, a percentage that has been increasing? Will you need one?

- For a recent 10-year period, only one-fourth of professionally managed stock portfolios were able to outperform the overall stock market. Why?

- How can futures contracts, with a reputation for being extremely risky, be used to reduce an investor's risk?

- What is the historical average annual rate of return on common stocks and bonds? What can an investor reasonably expect to earn from stocks in the future?

The objective of this text is to help you understand the investments field as it is currently understood, discussed, and practiced so that you can intelligently answer questions such as the preceding and make sound investment decisions that will enhance your economic welfare. To accomplish this objective, key concepts are presented to provide an appreciation of the theory and practice of investments.

Both descriptive and quantitative materials on investing are readily available. Some of this material is very enlightening; much of it is entertaining but debatable because of the many controversies in investments; and some of it is worthless. This text seeks to cover what is particularly useful and relevant for today's investment climate. It offers some ideas about what you can reasonably expect to accomplish by using what you learn, and therefore what you can realistically expect to achieve as an investor in today's investment world. Many investors have unrealistic expectations, and this will ultimately lead to disappointments in results achieved from investing—or, worse, the loss of all of their funds in a fraud or scam.

Just Say NO! Prepare yourself to say NO! Learning how to avoid the many pitfalls awaiting you as an investor—in particular, investing scams and frauds—by clearly understanding what you can reasonably expect from investing your money may be the single most important benefit to be derived from this text. For example, would you entrust your money to someone offering 36 percent annual return on riskless Treasury securities? Some 600 investors did, and lost some $10 million to a former Sunday school teacher.

In February 2009, the SEC filed a complaint alleging that R. Allen Stanford and James Davis operated a massive Ponzi scheme, misappropriating billions of dollars of investors' money. According to the complaint, the $8 billion fraud involved certificates of deposit promising overly high rates of return. The size of this alleged fraud pales in comparison to the

Madoff scandal reported in December 2008, involving a very large Ponzi scheme. According to a criminal complaint, Bernard Madoff admitted that his investment advisor business was a fraud and had been insolvent for years. Supposedly, returns were being paid to certain investors out of the principal received from other investors.

Intelligent investors quickly learn to say no, thereby avoiding many of the pitfalls that await investors daily. At the very least, you must be prepared to carefully investigate the investment alternatives that will be offered to you.

✓ Remember, there are many financial scams and frauds awaiting the unwary. However, you can easily learn to avoid them.

Establishing a Framework for Investing

SOME DEFINITIONS

The term *investing* can cover a wide range of activities. It often refers to investing money in certificates of deposit, bonds, common stocks, or mutual funds. More knowledgeable investors would include other "paper" assets, such as warrants, puts and calls, futures contracts, and convertible securities, as well as tangible assets, such as gold, real estate, and collectibles. Investing encompasses very conservative positions as well as aggressive speculation. Whether your perspective is that of a college graduate starting out in the workplace or that of a senior citizen concerned with finances after retirement, investing decisions are critically important to most people sometime in their life.

Investment The commitment of funds to one or more assets that will be held over some future period

Investments The study of the investment process

An **investment** can be defined as the commitment of funds to one or more assets that will be held over some future time period. **Investments** is concerned with the management of an investor's wealth, which is the sum of current income and the present value of all future income. (This is why present value and compound interest concepts have an important role in the investment process.) Although the field of investments encompasses many aspects, it can be thought of in terms of two primary functions: analysis and management—hence the title of this text.

Financial Assets Pieces of paper evidencing a claim on some issuer

Marketable Securities Financial assets that are easily and cheaply traded in organized markets

Financial Assets and Marketable Securities   In this text, the term investments refers in general to financial assets and in particular to marketable securities. **Financial assets** are paper (or electronic) claims on some issuer, such as the federal government or a corporation; on the other hand, real assets are tangible, physical assets such as gold, silver, diamonds, art, and real estate. **Marketable securities** are financial assets that are easily and cheaply tradable in organized markets. Technically, the word investments includes both financial and real assets, and both marketable and nonmarketable assets. Because of the vast scope of investment opportunities available to investors, our primary emphasis is on marketable securities; however, the basic principles and techniques discussed in this text are applicable to real assets.

Even when we limit our discussion primarily to financial assets, it is difficult to keep up with the proliferation of new products. Two such assets that did not exist a few years ago are the many new Exchange Traded Funds and Direct Access Notes (corporate bonds designed for the average investor), both of which are discussed in a later chapter.

A Perspective on Investing

WHY DO WE INVEST?

We invest to make money! Although everyone would agree with this statement, we need to be more precise. (After all, this is a college textbook and anyone helping to pay for your education expects more.) We invest to improve our welfare, which for our purposes can be defined as monetary wealth, both current and future. We assume that investors are interested only in the monetary benefits to be obtained from investing, as opposed to such factors as the psychic income to be derived from impressing one's friends with one's financial prowess.

Funds to be invested come from assets already owned, borrowed money, and savings or foregone consumption. By foregoing consumption today and investing the savings, investors expect to enhance their future consumption possibilities by increasing their wealth. Don't underestimate the amount of money many individuals can accumulate. A 2004 survey found that more than 8 million U.S. households had a net worth of more than $1 million (excluding their primary residence). That represented a one-third increase over 2003 alone, and amounted to 7 percent of all U.S. households. Much of this success was attributed to ownership of stocks and bonds. Of course, things can change. Americans' net worth declined a record 18 percent in 2008.

Investors also seek to manage their wealth effectively, obtaining the most from it while protecting it from inflation, taxes, and other factors. To accomplish both objectives, people invest.

TAKE A PORTFOLIO PERSPECTIVE

This text assumes that investors have established their overall financial plan and are now interested in managing and enhancing their wealth by investing in an optimal combination of financial assets. The idea of an "optimal combination" is important because our wealth, which we hold in the form of various assets, should be evaluated and managed as a unified whole. Wealth should be evaluated and managed within the context of a **portfolio**, which consists of the asset holdings of an investor. For example, if you own four stocks and three mutual funds, that is your portfolio. If your parents own 23 stocks, some municipal bonds, and some CDs, that is their portfolio of financial assets.

Portfolio The securities held by an investor taken as a unit

The Importance of Studying Investments

THE PERSONAL ASPECTS

It is important to remember that all individuals have wealth of some kind; if nothing else, this wealth may consist of the value of their services in the marketplace. Most individuals must make investment decisions sometime in their lives. For example, many employees today must decide whether their retirement funds are to be invested in stocks or bonds or some other alternative. And many people try to build some wealth during their working years by investing.

Retirement Decisions Estimates suggest that more than 40 percent of households headed by someone between 47 and 62 will be unable to replace half their pre-retirement income when they cease working. Even more worrisome, many will have retirement income below the poverty line.

A major revolution in personal finance is to provide employees with self-directed retirement plans (defined contribution plans rather than defined benefit plans). Whereas traditional defined-benefit retirement plans guarantee retirees an amount of money each month, the new emphasis on self-directed retirement plans means that you will have to choose among stock funds, bond funds, guaranteed investment contracts, and other alternatives.

✓ In 1979, more than 85 percent of workers in the private sector were covered with a pension; by 2012, less than 20 percent.

Your choices are many, and your success—or lack thereof—will directly affect your retirement benefits. Therefore, while employees in the past typically did not have to concern themselves much with investing decisions relative to their company's retirement plan, future employees will have to do so. This is a very important personal reason for studying the subject of investments!

A good example of this revolution in retirement programs is a 401(k) plan offered by many employers, whereby employees contribute a percentage of salary to a tax-deferred plan, and the employer often matches part of the contribution. Tens of millions of American workers contribute to 401(k) plans. At the end of 2011, these plans held approximately $3 trillion in assets. The bulk of 401(k) assets are invested in stocks; therefore, it is important to know something about stocks.[1]

To illustrate the critical importance of making good investment decisions, consider yet another self-directed retirement vehicle, the Individual Retirement Account (IRA). IRAs are a primary method that Americans use to provide for their retirement. IRA assets totaled approximately $5 trillion by 2011, which was roughly 30 percent of the total U.S. retirement market.

The annual maximum IRA contribution was $5,000 in 2012 ($6,000 for those age 50 and above). IRA funds can be invested in a wide range of assets, from the very safe to the quite speculative. IRA owners are allowed to have self-directed brokerage accounts, which offer a wide array of investment opportunities. Since these funds may be invested for as long as 40 or more years, good investment decisions are critical, as shown in Example 1-1.

Example 1-1

Consider the amount of retirement wealth that can be accumulated by one individual contributing $5,000 annually to a tax sheltered account if returns are compounded annually. Over many years of investing, the differences in results that investors realize, owing solely to the investment returns earned, can be staggering. Note that in the case of a $5,000 annual contribution for 40 years, the payoff at a compound earnings rate of 15 percent is almost $9 million, whereas at an earnings rate of 10 percent the payoff is $2.21 million, a great retirement fund but significantly less than almost $9 million. Similarly, if a 10 percent rate of return can be obtained instead of a 5 percent rate of return, over a period of 40 years the difference approaches a fourfold multiple. Clearly, good investment decisions leading to higher returns can make a tremendous difference in the wealth that you can accumulate.

Amount Invested per Year	Number of Years	Final Dollar Wealth if Funds Are Compounded at		
		5%	10%	15%
$5000	20	165,330	286,375	512,218
$5000	30	332,194	822,470	2,173,726
$5000	40	603,999	2,212,963	8,895,452

Building Wealth Over Your Lifetime   Beyond the retirement issue, the study of investments is more important than ever in the 21st century. After being net sellers of stocks for many years, individual investors swarmed into the financial markets, either by force (becoming part of a self-directed retirement plan) or by choice (seeking higher returns than those available from financial institutions). In the late 1990s individuals increased their direct ownership of stocks, reversing the earlier trend. Approximately 52 million households in the United States own mutual funds.

---

[1] The maximum 401(k) contribution for 2012 was $16,500.

Individual investor interest in the stock market is best expressed by the power of mutual funds (explained in Chapter 3), a favorite investment vehicle of small investors. Mutual funds are a driving force in the stock market. With so much individual investor money flowing into mutual funds, and with individual investors owning a large percentage of all stocks outstanding, the study of investments is as important as ever, or more so.

In the final analysis, we study investments in the hope of earning better returns in relation to the risk we assume when we invest. A careful study of investment analysis and portfolio management principles can provide a sound framework for both managing and increasing wealth. Furthermore, a sound study of this subject matter will allow you to obtain maximum value from the many articles on investing that appear daily in newspapers and magazines, which in turn will increase your chances of reaching your financial goals. Popular press articles cover many important topics, such as the following examples:

1. Financial assets available to investors
2. Should a mutual fund investor use a financial advisor?
3. Compounding effects and terminal wealth
4. Realized returns vs. expected returns
5. How to compare taxable bonds to municipal (tax-exempt) bonds
6. Index funds and ETFs
7. How diversification works to reduce risk
8. The asset allocation decision
9. Active vs. passive investing

All of these issues are covered in the text, and learning about them will make you a much smarter investor.

INVESTMENTS AS A PROFESSION

In addition to the above reasons for the importance of studying investments, the world of investments offers several rewarding careers, both professionally and financially. A study of investments is an essential part of becoming a professional in this field.

Investment Bankers and Traders   Investment bankers, who arrange the sale of new securities as well as assist in mergers and acquisitions, enjoyed phenomenal financial rewards in the booming 1980s and 1990s. Given the turmoil of 2000–2002, investment banking business dropped off sharply, and by mid-2002 was the slowest part of Wall Street's business. In 2008 the financial crisis saw the demise of Bear Stearns and Lehman Brothers, and the merger of Merrill Lynch with Bank of America. Furthermore, signaling the end of an era on Wall Street, Goldman Sachs and Morgan Stanley, the last two major investment banks at the time, became bank holding companies in order to stay in business.

Security Analysts and Portfolio Managers   A range of financial institutions, including brokerage firms and investment bankers as well as banks and insurance companies, need the services of **security analysts** (also called investment analysts). Brokerage houses need them to support their registered representatives who in turn serve the public—for example, preparing the research reports provided to customers. Investment bankers need analysts to assist in the sale of new securities and in the valuation of firms as possible merger or acquisition candidates. Banks and insurance companies own portfolios of securities that must be evaluated in order to be managed. Mutual funds need analysts to evaluate securities for possible purchase or sale.

Financial firms need portfolio managers to manage the portfolios of securities handled by these organizations. Portfolio managers are responsible for making the actual portfolio buy

Security Analysts Market professionals whose job it is to study, evaluate and recommend stocks to investors, either institutions or individuals

and sell decisions—what to buy and sell, when to buy and sell, and so forth. Portfolio performance is calculated for these managers, and their jobs may depend on their performance relative to other managed portfolios and to market averages.

Stockbrokers and Financial Advisors   What about the registered representatives (stockbrokers) employed in cities across the country? A few superbrokers earn $1 million or more per year. Of course, the average broker earns much less, but still the compensation can be quite rewarding. More will be said about brokers in Chapter 5.

The employment and pay for the various job types associated with Wall Street tend to be cyclical. While the late 1990s were great years for investors and investment firms and employees, the market declines of 2000–2002 brought a new reality, as did the financial crisis of 2008. Given the tremendous turmoil in the financial markets in 2008, we have entered a new era of banking, financial institutions, and trading practices, and the exact structure will take time to unfold.

Finally, the number of financial advisors continues to grow. This area has employment opportunities for people interested in the Investments field. The Bureau of Labor Statistics expects this job category to expand significantly out to 2016. Roughly two-thirds of all affluent Americans now use one. For a typical $1 million portfolio, a financial advisor will charge $10,000 a year. Some charge by the hour, with the hourly rate in the $115 to $150 range.

Standard credentials do not exist for financial advisors. Most advisors must register with their local state securities commission and with the Securities and Exchange Commission as a Registered Investment Advisor (RIA) when they manage more than $25 million. Otherwise, financial advisors are bound only by the job requirements of professional organizations to which they belong.[2] According to one survey, planners gross a little over $100,000 per year, primarily from selling products for commissions and from managing clients' assets for a percentage of the assets under management.

Exhibit 1-1 lists three designations that financial advisors and planners may hold and indicates how they are compensated. Those interested in this field as a career should seriously consider obtaining one (or more) of these professional designations.

EXHIBIT 1-1

Professional Designations Held by Financial Advisors and Planners

☐ Certified Financial Planner (CFP), awarded by the Certified Financial Planning Board of Standards, an industry group, requires course work and an examination on financial planning. Holders of the CFP must have three years experience and adhere to a code of ethics.
☐ Chartered Financial Consultant (ChFC) requires a comprehensive examination and often involves those with an insurance background;
☐ Personal Financial Specialist (PFS), awarded by the American Institute of Certified Public Accountants to CPAs only, requires experience in personal financial planning and a comprehensive examination.

Financial advisors are compensated by four methods:

- Fee-based—may involve a comprehensive financial plan, or specific issues.
- Commission-based—plan and recommendations are provided at no charge, with compensation derived from commissions earned from products sold to implement the plan.
- Fee-and-commission based—commissions are often greater than the fees.
- Salaried—banks, credit unions, and so forth often offer planning services by salaried financial planners.

[2] In order to sell securities, financial planners and advisors may need to pass what are called Series 66 and Series 7 exams.

Chartered Financial
Analyst (CFA)
A professional designation
for people in the
investments field

The CFA Designation   Individuals interested in careers in the investments field, as opposed to financial planning, should consider studying to receive the **Chartered Financial Analyst (CFA)** designation. This is a professional designation for people in the investments area, not unlike the CPA designation for accountants. The CFA designation is widely recognized in the investments industry today. It serves as an indication that areas of knowledge relevant to investing have been studied and that high ethical and professional standards have been recognized and accepted. Details of the CFA program are included in Appendix 1-A. Throughout this text, we will use some questions and problems from previous CFA exams.

Understanding the Investment Decision Process

An organized view of the investment process involves analyzing the basic nature of investment decisions and organizing the activities in the decision process.

Common stocks have produced, on average, significantly larger returns over the years than savings accounts or bonds. Should not all investors invest in common stocks and realize these larger returns? The answer to this question is: To pursue higher returns, investors must assume larger risks. Underlying all investment decisions is the tradeoff between expected return and risk.

Investments Intuition

The stock market suffered sharp declines during 2000–2002 because of the collapse of technology stocks. However, if investors had bought Apple and Amazon during that time, they would have done extremely well over the next decade. Why didn't more investors buy these stocks? The reason is that at the time the risk was thought to be too great, not only for these stocks, but for stocks in general. And therein lies the story of investing. There are great opportunities, but there are also large risks.

THE BASIS OF INVESTMENT DECISIONS—RETURN AND RISK

Return   Why invest? Stated in simplest terms, investors wish to earn a return on their money. Cash has an opportunity cost: By holding cash, you forego the opportunity to earn a return on that cash. Furthermore, in an inflationary environment, the purchasing power of cash diminishes, with high rates of inflation (such as that in the early 1980s) bringing a relatively rapid decline in purchasing power.

Investments Intuition

Investors buy, hold, and sell financial assets to earn returns on them. Within the spectrum of financial assets, why do some people buy common stocks instead of safely depositing their money in an insured savings account or a U.S. savings bond with a guaranteed minimum return? The answer is that they are trying to earn returns larger than those available from such safer (and lower-yielding) assets. They know they are taking a greater risk of losing some of their money by buying common stocks, but they expect to earn a greater return.

Expected Return   The ex
ante return expected by
investors over some future
holding period

Expected Return vs. Realized Return   In investments it is critical to distinguish between an **expected return** (the anticipated return for some future period) and a

Realized Return Actual return on an investment for some previous period of time

realized return (the actual return over some past period). Investors invest for the future—for the returns they expect to earn—but when the investing period is over, they are left with their realized returns. What investors actually earn from their holdings may turn out to be more or less than what they expected to earn when they initiated the investment. This point is the essence of the investments process: Investors should always consider the risk involved in investing.

Properly stated, investors seek to maximize their returns from investing, subject to the risk they are willing to incur. Therefore, we must consider the other side of the coin from return, which is risk.

Risk   Investors would like their returns to be as large as possible; however, this objective is subject to constraints, primarily risk.[3] The stock market enjoyed the five greatest consecutive years of returns in its history during 1995–1999, with total returns each year in excess of 21 percent on a broad cross-section of common stocks. Nevertheless, several professionally managed funds performed poorly relative to the market, and some managed to lose money in one or more of those years. As this example shows, marketable securities offering variable returns across time are risky. The investment decision, therefore, must always be considered in terms of both risk and return. The two are inseparable.

Risk The chance that the actual return on an investment will be different from the expected return

There are different types, and therefore different definitions, of risk. **Risk** is defined here as the uncertainty about the actual return that will be earned on an investment. When we invest, we may do so on the basis of an expected return, but there is a risk that what we in fact end up with when we terminate the investment—the actual (realized) return—will be different.

Using the term risk in this manner, we find that the nominal (current dollar) return on a Treasury bill has no practical risk, because there is little chance that the U.S. government will fail to redeem these obligations as they mature in 13 or 26 weeks. On the other hand, there is some risk, however small, that General Electric, a company in business for more than 100 years, will be unable to redeem an issue of 30-year bonds when they mature. And there is a very substantial risk of not realizing the expected return on any particular common stock over some future holding period, such as one year, six months, one month, or even one day.

Concepts in Action

Returns and Risk

Investors enjoyed the best five consecutive years in stock market history over the period 1995–1999. They thought they were truly in the golden age of money making, and in fact they were—during that period. This great performance came to an end with negative returns in 2000, and 2001 and 2002 also showed negative returns. Such is the nature of stock market returns and risk!

Or consider an individual company and its risk to investors. Cisco, the router company, was the world's most valuable company during some part of 2000. It had a market cap of $550 billion. It's stock price climbed 35-fold in five years (more than $80/share) as annual sales growth averaged 40 percent. Then the Internet crash occurred. Revenues declined 18 percent, while stock price declined 90 percent, an incredible loss for such a company. By mid-2004 annual sales were $22 billion, and net income was $3.6 billion in 2003 (higher than in the bubble). Stock price, however, had recovered to only $25 or so. Such is the nature of stock risk!

---

[3] Although risk is the most important constraint on investors, other risks clearly exist. Taxes and transaction costs are often viewed as constraints. Some institutional investors may face legal constraints on the types of securities they can purchase or the amount they can hold.

As we shall see in Chapter 7, Harry Markowitz changed the study of Investments in a significant manner by quantifying risk as a statistical measure, the variance or standard deviation. This allows us to measure the risk of various assets and compare them.

Risk-Averse Investor An investor who will not assume a given level of risk unless there is an expectation of adequate compensation for having done so

Investors Are Risk-Averse!

It is easy to say that investors dislike risk, but more precisely, we should say that investors are risk-averse. A **risk-averse investor** is one who will not assume risk simply for its own sake and will not incur any given level of risk unless there is an expectation of adequate compensation for having done so.

✓ Note carefully that it is not irrational to assume risk, even very large risk, as long as we expect to be compensated for it.

Investors cannot reasonably expect to earn larger returns without assuming larger risks. Furthermore, it is possible that some investors, perhaps unwittingly, act in a manner that is too risk-averse, thereby severely diminishing the final wealth they will accumulate over a long period of time.

Example 1-2

A 2007 study of 401(k) retirement plan participants found that 16 percent of participants under age 30 had none of their funds invested in stocks. Given that stocks have almost always outperformed other asset classes *over long periods*, is this a case of being too risk-averse?

Risk Tolerance An investor's willingness to accept risk when investing

Investor's Risk Tolerance

Investors deal with risk by choosing (implicitly or explicitly) the amount of risk they are willing to incur—that is, they decide their **risk tolerance**. Some investors choose to incur high levels of risk with the expectation of high levels of return. Other investors are unwilling to assume much risk, and they should not typically expect to earn large returns.

Can we say that investors, in general, will choose to minimize their risks? No! The reason is that there are costs to minimizing the risk, specifically a lower expected return. Taken to its logical conclusion, the minimization of risk would result in everyone holding risk-free assets such as savings accounts and Treasury bills. The intelligent way to think about return and risk is this:

✓ Investors decide on their risk tolerance—how much risk they are willing to assume when investing. They then seek to maximize their returns subject to this risk tolerance constraint and any other constraints that might apply (for example, taxes).

Of course, investors' risk tolerance changes as conditions (real or perceived) change. In today's world, with all the instant communications available to most people, this can happen quickly.

Example 1-3

During 2011, investors' risk tolerance shifted as they reacted to a variety of events in both the United States and abroad. The European sovereign debt crisis (Greece, etc.) and banking crisis, and the confrontation over raising the U.S. debt limit, along with the downgrade in the rating of U.S. debt, led to significant shifts in risk tolerance as many investors lost their appetite for stocks.

To put these two criteria for making investment decisions together, we need to think in terms of the expected return-risk tradeoff that results from the direct relationship between the risk and the expected return of an investment. We will do this below.

The Expected Risk-Return Tradeoff Within the realm of financial assets, investors can achieve virtually any position on an expected return-risk spectrum such as that depicted in Figure 1-1. The line RF to B is the assumed tradeoff between *expected* return and risk that exists for all investors interested in financial assets. This tradeoff always slopes upward, because the vertical axis is expected return, and rational investors will not assume more risk unless they expect to be compensated. The expected return should be large enough to compensate for assuming the additional risk; however, there is no guarantee that the additional returns will be realized.

RF in Figure 1-1 is the return on a risk-free asset such as Treasury bills. This position has zero risk (on a practical basis, in the sense of default) and an expected return equal to the current rate of return available on risk-free assets such as Treasury bills. This **risk-free rate of return**, which is available to all investors, will be designated as RF throughout the text.

Risk-Free Rate of Return The return on a riskless asset, often proxied by the rate of return on Treasury securities

Figure 1-1 shows approximate relative positions for some of the financial assets that will be discussed in Chapter 2. As we move from risk-free Treasury securities to more risky corporate bonds, equities, and so forth, we assume more risk in the expectation of earning a larger return. Common stocks are quite risky, in relation to bonds, but they are not as risky as a speculative purchase of options (puts and calls) or futures contracts. (All these terms are defined in Chapter 2.)

Obviously, Figure 1-1 depicts broad categories. Within a particular category, such as common stocks, a wide range of expected return and risk opportunities exists at any time.

The important point in Figure 1-1 is the tradeoff between expected return and risk that should prevail in a rational environment. Investors unwilling to assume risk must be satisfied with the risk-free rate of return, RF. If they wish to try to earn a larger rate of return, they must be willing to assume a larger risk as represented by moving up the expected return-risk

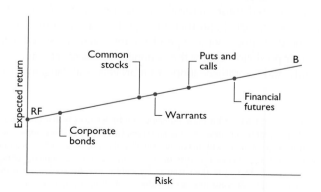

Figure 1-1

The Expected Return-Risk Tradeoffs Available to Investors.

tradeoff into the wide range of financial assets available to investors. In effect, investors have different risk tolerances, and, therefore, they should have differing return expectations.[4]

Ex Post vs. Ex Ante   Always remember that the risk-return tradeoff depicted in Figure 1-1 is ex ante, meaning "before the fact." That is, before the investment is actually made, the investor expects higher returns from assets that have a higher risk. This is the only sensible expectation for risk-averse investors, who are assumed to constitute the majority of all investors.

Ex post means "after the fact" or when it is known what has occurred. For a given period of time, such as a month or a year or even several years, the tradeoff may turn out to be flat or even negative. Such is the nature of risky investments!

Example 1-4   The years 2000–2002 each showed negative returns for the major stock indexes, as did 2008. While investors may have expected the returns for those years to be positive at the outset, they turned out to be years with negative returns.

Checking Your Understanding

1. Historically, stocks on average have outperformed other asset classes such as bonds. Should all intelligent investors own stocks?
2. Rational investors always attempt to minimize their risks. Agree or disagree, and explain your reasoning.
3. Investors should always seek to maximize their returns from investing. Agree or disagree.
4. The following is a correct statement: "The tradeoff between return and risk can be, and has been, both upward-sloping and downward-sloping." How is this possible?

Structuring the Decision Process

Traditionally, investors have analyzed and managed securities using a broad two-step process: security analysis and portfolio management.

Security Analysis   The first part of the investment decision process involves the valuation and analysis of individual securities, which is referred to as **security analysis**. The valuation of securities is a time-consuming and difficult job. First of all, it is necessary to understand the characteristics of the various securities and the factors that affect them. Second, a valuation model is applied to these securities to estimate their price, or value. Value is a function of the expected future returns on a security and the risk attached. Both of these parameters must be estimated and then brought together in a model.

Security Analysis The first part of the investment decision process, involving the valuation and analysis of individual securities

Despite the difficulties, some type of security analysis is performed by most investors serious about their portfolios. Unless this is done, one has to rely on personal hunches, suggestions from friends, and recommendations from brokers—all dangerous to one's financial health.

---

[4] In economic terms, the explanation for these differences in preferences is that rational investors strive to maximize their utility, the perception of which varies among investors. Utility theory is a complex subject, but for our purposes we can equate maximization of utility with maximization of welfare. Because welfare is a function of present and future wealth, and wealth in turn is a function of current and future income discounted (reduced) for the amount of risk involved, in effect, investors maximize their welfare by optimizing the expected return-risk tradeoff. In the final analysis, expected return and risk constitute the foundation of all investment decisions.

Portfolio Management   The second major component of the decision process is portfolio management. After securities have been evaluated, a portfolio should be constructed. Concepts on why and how to build a portfolio are well known. Much of the work in this area is in the form of mathematical and statistical models, which have had a profound effect on the study of investments in this country in the last 30 years.

Having built a portfolio, the astute investor must consider how and when to revise it. And, of course, portfolios must be managed on a continuing basis.

Finally, all investors are interested in how well their portfolio performs. This is the bottom line of the investment process. Measuring portfolio performance is an inexact procedure, even today, and needs to be carefully considered.

Important Considerations in the Investment Decision Process for Today's Investors

Intelligent investors should be aware of the fact that the investment decision process as just described can be lengthy and involved. Regardless of individual actions, however, certain factors in the investment environment affect all investors. These factors are relevant to investors as they work through the investment decision process.

THE GREAT UNKNOWN

"You have to understand that being wrong is part of the process," according to Peter Bernstein, one of the most prominent investment experts.

The first, and paramount, factor that all investors must come to grips with is uncertainty. Investors buy various financial assets, expecting to earn various returns over some future holding period. These returns, with few exceptions, may never be realized.

✓   The simple fact that dominates investing, although many investors never seem to appreciate it fully, is that the realized return on any risky asset will often differ from what was expected—sometimes quite dramatically.

At best, estimates are imprecise; at worst, they are completely wrong. The best one can do is make the most informed return and risk estimates possible, act on them, and be prepared for shifting circumstances. Regardless of how careful and informed investors are, the future is uncertain, and mistakes will be made.

✓   All investors, individuals as well as professionals, make investing mistakes.

Someone can always tell you what you should have bought or sold in the past. No one, however, can guarantee you a successful portfolio for next year or any other specified period of time because no one can consistently forecast what will happen in the financial markets, including those professionals who are paid to make recommendations. Uncertainty affects the financial markets. Consider the following quote on the *Morningstar* (a well-known provider of investment information) website around September 2011:[5]

> *Uncertainty Causes Investors to Bid Up Safe Stocks*
> Apparently uncertainty has carried over to investors, who are now bidding up the more defensive portion of our stock investing universe and seeking stocks that provide income in addition to capital gains.

[5] Robert Johnson, "Outlook for the Economy," *Morningstar* website, September 27, 2011.

Although the future is uncertain, it is manageable, and a thorough understanding of the basic principles of investing will allow investors to cope intelligently.

A GLOBAL PERSPECTIVE

Now more than ever, investors must think of investments in a global context. The investing environment has changed dramatically as the world's economies have become more integrated. The United States no longer accounts for a majority of stock market capitalization globally, as it did in the past.

✓ U.S. stocks now account for considerably less than half of the world's total stock market capitalization.

A global marketplace of round-the-clock investing opportunities is emerging. Approximately two-thirds of U.S. investors now own the securities of foreign companies.

Why should today's investors be actively interested in international investing? We should first note that European and Asian companies have adopted a more shareholder-friendly attitude in recent years. Also, the dividend yields on these stocks have improved dramatically. In early 2008, European stocks had an average dividend yield of about 3 percent, considerably above that of the S&P 500 Index (less than 2 percent). Even Asian stocks were yielding more than U.S. stocks.

Many U.S. companies now derive a very large percentage of their revenues from abroad. Consider some of the 100 largest multinational corporations headquartered in the United States. ExxonMobil and Hewlett Packard earned about 70 percent of their revenues from abroad, while some 75 percent of Coca-Cola's revenues came from abroad. Google was getting about half of its revenue outside the Americas. Thus, U.S. investors investing in what traditionally are thought of as classic American companies are vitally affected by what happens abroad. Of course, not all large corporations are affected this much. Walmart receives only about one-fourth of its revenues from abroad.

From an investing standpoint, the real importance of adding foreign securities is that investors can achieve beneficial risk reduction if some foreign markets move differently than do U.S. markets. For example, when U.S. stocks are doing poorly, some foreign stocks may be doing well, which would help offset the poor U.S. performance. This risk reduction in a portfolio is a result of diversification, a very important concept in investing analyzed in Chapter 7. Over the last 35 years, a portfolio consisting of a major U.S. stock index and a major foreign stock index would have outperformed either index slightly, but with less risk.

Some Practical Advice

U.S. investors are regularly advised to diversify their portfolios by investing globally. Such activity can be heavily influenced by what the dollar is doing relative to other currencies. Net purchases by U.S. investors of foreign shares has been heavy in recent years. Such activity by U.S. investors was heavily influenced by the dollar's decline in recent years, which increased returns to U.S. investors in dollar terms (as explained in Chapter 6). Intelligent investors must pay attention to what is happening in the investing world on a global basis, and not simply what is happening in the United States.

Thus, we should consider foreign markets as well as the U.S. financial environment. We will do so throughout this text as an integral part of the discussion, rather than as a separate chapter. Although the technical details may vary, the principles of investing are applicable to financial assets and financial markets wherever they exist.

While it may be a smart play, foreign investing does not ensure our success as investors because of the first issue we discussed—the great unknown. As in any other area of investing, the experts are often wrong. Furthermore, as economies around the world become more integrated, markets become more similar than dissimilar.

Example 1-5 Investors have often sought out emerging markets as an investing opportunity on the basis that these economies may act differently from the industrialized economies, thereby providing some offset in case of market declines in the latter. However, this view is now less certain. Consider the following quote from the head of global credit at a firm managing more than $200 billion in fixed-income investments: "People often make the argument about decoupling (that emerging markets can rise as developed markets fall), but then they start to realize—*wait a second, it's one big interconnected world.*"[6]

THE IMPORTANCE OF THE INTERNET

Any discussion of the investment decision process today must focus on the role of the Internet, which in a short time has significantly changed the investments environment. Now, all investors can access a wealth of information about investing, trade cheaply and quickly in their brokerage accounts, obtain real-time quotes throughout the day, and track their portfolios.

This is a true revolution—the Internet has democratized the flow of investment information. Any investor, at home, at work, or on vacation, can download an incredible array of information, trade comments with other investors, do security analysis, manage portfolios, check company filings with government agencies, and carry out numerous other activities not thought possible for a small investor only a few years ago. While some of these information sources and/or services carry a fee, most of it is free.

INDIVIDUAL INVESTORS VS. INSTITUTIONAL INVESTORS

There are two broad categories of investors: individual investors and institutional investors. The latter group, consisting of bank trust departments, pension funds, mutual funds, insurance companies, and so forth, includes the professional money managers, who are often publicized in the popular press. Institutional investors in the United States hold trillions in assets.

Institutional investors have a dual relationship with individual investors. On the one hand, individuals are the indirect beneficiaries of institutional investor actions, because they own or benefit from these institutions' portfolios. On a daily basis, however, they are "competing" with these institutions in the sense that both are managing portfolios of securities and attempting to do well financially by buying and selling securities.

Institutional investors are indeed the "professional" investors, with vast resources at their command. In the past, they were often treated differently from individual investors, because companies often disclosed important information selectively to some institutional investors. However, this situation changed significantly in October 2000 when Regulation FD (Full Disclosure) took place.

Regulation FD Regulates communications between public companies and investment professionals

Regulation FD, which applies to almost all public companies, attempts to regulate communications between public companies and investment professionals. Companies are now prohibited from (intentionally) disclosing material, nonpublic information to specific types of investment professionals unless the company simultaneously publicly discloses the information.

[6] Neil Shah, "Institutions Hit By Emerging Bets," *The Wall Street Journal,* September 26, 2011, p. c2.

If a non-intentional disclosure is made of such information, the company must publicly disclose the information promptly.

Some individual investors do even better either by superior skill and insight, or luck. Furthermore, some opportunities can more easily be exploited by individual investors than by institutional investors.

Example 1-6

Individual investors can exploit a spin-off (defined as a division of a company that is turned into a separate publicly held company), better than institutional investors in some cases. Some institutional investors will not purchase the new companies because they often pay no dividends immediately after spin-off, and they may be too small to be held by some institutions. Furthermore, unless the spin-off is unusually large, it is often ignored by security analysts.

These companies often look unattractive at the time of spin-off because they had problems as a division. However, these problems tend to be solved by a new, proactive management, and these companies become attractive as take-over candidates.

A study of 150 spin-offs found that the average three-year total return was about 75 percent, 30 percentage points higher than a comparable group of companies. In fact, several studies have found that over a period of one to three years, these stocks generally do well. In contrast, initial public offerings, which may enjoy great success on their first day of trading, generally track the overall market. In 2009, 50 spin-offs were completed, and in 2010, 74. 2011 had 60+ spin-offs.

Investors are advised to defer purchases of spin-offs until they have been trading for a few weeks, because some institutions may sell the shares they received in the spin-off, and prices are often lower weeks later than at the time trading begins in the new companies. With a newly energized management team who have stock options, these companies often take off and do very well.

Individual investors are now on a more competitive basis with institutional investors, given the information they can access from the Internet. We should expect the market to be more efficient today relative to the past, because information is even more quickly and freely available.

The question of how well individual investors do relative to institutional investors raises the issue of market efficiency, which we consider in Chapter 12. All intelligent investors who seek to do well when investing must ultimately come to grips with the issue of market efficiency.

ETHICS IN INVESTING

Today, perhaps more than ever, investors need to stop and think about ethical issues as they apply to investing. Recent corporate scandals involving Enron, WorldCom, HealthSouth, and so forth were prominently in the news as executives from these firms went on trial, charged with possible fraud in connection with the companies' financial activities. Other recent negative headlines involving ethical issues include the conflicts of interest with security analysts and the role of some mutual funds in providing a few investors with unfair trading advantages.

Financial markets depend on integrity in the process, whether it be from CEOs, brokers, stock exchange employees, security analysts, managers of mutual funds, or so forth. If investors lose confidence in the overall honesty of the investing environment, financial markets could be severely damaged, and this in turn could adversely impact the capital formation process which is so vital to the success of the U.S. economy.

Because of the overall importance of ethics in the investing process, we will examine some ethical issues in various chapters. In some cases, as in the next example, we will not provide a clear answer to the issue raised. In other examples we will offer some guidance on the issue. This is consistent with the real-life nature of ethical issues, which, while extremely important, is not always easy to address in the process of deciding on the correct course of action.

Ethics in Investing

The Case of Martha Stewart

The SEC filed securities fraud charges against Martha Stewart and her stockbroker in 2003. Stewart became entangled in this matter as a result of selling her stock in ImClone Systems after allegedly receiving an unlawful tip from her broker. The SEC also alleged that Stewart and her broker created an alibi for Stewart's sales and concealed important facts during the investigation into the matter. An SEC official stated that "[t]he Commission simply cannot allow corporate executives or industry professionals to profit illegally from their access to nonpublic information. The coordinated action announced today by the U.S. Attorney's Office shows that the consequences for those individuals will be even greater if we uncover evidence that they obstructed our investigation."

Stewart was forced to resign as an officer and director of her company, and was sentenced to five months in prison and two years' probation, in addition to a fine of $30,000. Contrary to popular belief, Stewart was not charged with insider trading, but rather with obstruction of justice.

Although many people seem to believe otherwise, she maintained throughout the proceedings that she had done nothing wrong. In this situation, when many believe her guilty while she maintains her innocence, would it have been appropriate for her to admit guilt in exchange for a reduced sentence?

Checking Your Understanding

5. Individual investors make investing decisions under conditions of uncertainty, while professional investors make such decisions under conditions of controlled risk taking, thereby eliminating the uncertainty. Agree or disagree and explain your reasoning.
6. A chance for larger returns than those available domestically is the primary reason U.S. investors should hold foreign securities. Agree or disagree and explain your reasoning.

Organizing the Text

Four chapters of background material follow this introductory chapter to form Part I, which covers background. The financial assets available to investors—both from direct investing and indirect investing—are examined in separate chapters, followed by a discussion of the securities markets in which they trade. This, in turn, is followed by an analysis of how securities are actually traded.

Part II deals with the important issues of return and risk, which underlie all investment decisions. Chapter 6 covers returns that investors have earned in the financial markets in the past, along with the risk involved, because investors must have an understanding of the results of investing in major assets such as stocks and bonds if they are to make intelligent estimates of the future. Chapter 7, in turn, deals with the estimation of return and risk, and involves the important principles of Markowitz portfolio theory that all investors should understand as they choose portfolios of securities to hold for the future. Chapter 8 continues the discussion of portfolio theory, explaining how an efficient portfolio is selected. Chapter 9 discusses capital market theory.

Nine chapters of the text, involving Parts III, IV, and V, are devoted to evaluating the primary financial assets, stocks and bonds, and explaining the basics of asset valuation. Common stocks are analyzed in Part III. For both stocks and bonds, valuation techniques are discussed in the first of the two chapters, and analysis and management in the second. For stocks, a chapter on market efficiency is included because this important concept affects the strategies followed in selecting and managing stocks.

Because of the complexity of common stocks, four additional chapters are needed to describe the basics of security analysis, the most popular method for analyzing stocks. Part IV is purposefully sequenced from market to industry to company analysis, followed by a discussion of technical analysis.

Part V covers bonds, using the same format as Part III. Chapter 17 covers the principles of bond valuation, and Chapter 18 covers the analysis and management of bonds.

Part VI contains a complete basic analysis of alternative investment opportunities involving derivative securities. Separate chapters cover options and futures.

Part VII contains two chapters involving the portfolio management process. Chapter 21 describes some of the issues that investors face in their financial planning and how they can proceed to manage their financial assets. The text concludes with the logical capstone to a study of investments, the measurement of portfolio performance, in Chapter 22.

Summary

▶ An investment is the commitment of funds to one or more assets that will be held over some future period. The field of investments involves the study of the investment process.

▶ The investment opportunities considered in this text consist primarily of a wide array of financial assets (primarily marketable securities), which are financial claims on some issuer.

▶ The basic element of all investment decisions is the tradeoff between expected return and risk. Financial assets are arrayed along an upward-sloping expected return-risk tradeoff, with the risk-free rate of return as the vertical axis intercept.

▶ Expected return and risk are directly related; the greater (smaller) the expected return, the greater (smaller) the risk.

▶ Investors seek to maximize expected returns subject to constraints, primarily risk.

▶ Risk is defined as the chance that the actual return on an investment will differ from its expected return.

▶ Rational investors are risk-averse, meaning that they are unwilling to assume risk unless they expect to be adequately compensated. The study of Investments is based on the premise that investors act rationally.

▶ Investors deal with risk by choosing (implicitly or explicitly) the amount of risk they are willing to incur—that is, they decide their risk tolerance.

▶ For organizational purposes, the investment decision process has traditionally been divided into two broad steps: security analysis and portfolio management.

▶ Security analysis is concerned with the valuation of securities. Valuation, in turn, is a function of expected return and risk.

▶ Portfolio management encompasses building an optimal portfolio for an investor. Considerations include initial portfolio construction, revision, and the evaluation of portfolio performance.

▶ Major factors affecting the decision process include uncertainty in investment decisions, the global nature of investing, the increasing importance of the Internet, the role of institutional investors in the marketplace, and ethical issues in investing. As they study investments, evaluate information and claims, and make decisions, investors should consider these factors carefully.

Questions

1-1 Define the term "investments."

1-2 Describe the broad two-step process involved in making investment decisions.

1-3 Is the study of investments really important to most individuals?

1-4 Distinguish between a financial asset and a real asset.

1-5 Carefully describe the risk-return tradeoff faced by all investors.

1-6 In terms of Figure 1-1, when would an investor expect to earn the risk-free rate of return?

1-7 "A risk-averse investor will not assume risk." Agree or disagree with this statement, and explain your reasoning.

1-8 Summarize the basic nature of the investment decision in one sentence.

1-9 Distinguish between expected return and realized return.

1-10 Define risk. How many specific types can you think of?

1-11 What other constraints besides risk do investors face?

1-12 Are all rational investors risk-averse? Do they all have the same degree of risk-aversion?

1-13 What is meant by an investor's risk tolerance? What role does this concept play in investor decision making?

1-14 What external factors affect the decision process? Which do you think is the most important?

1-15 What are institutional investors? How are individual investors likely to be affected by institutional investors?

1-16 Why should the rate of return demanded by investors be different for a corporate bond and a Treasury bond?

1-17 Discuss three reasons why U.S. investors should consider international investing. Do you think the exchange rate value of the dollar will have a significant effect on the decision to invest internationally?

1-18 What should the long-run ex ante tradeoff between expected return and risk look like in a graph? What about the long-run ex post tradeoff?

1-19 Rational investors always attempt to minimize their risks! Agree or disagree, and explain your reasoning.

1-20 Investors should always seek to maximize their returns from investing. Agree or disagree.

Spreadsheet Exercises

1-1 Assume that when you are 25 years old you plan to aggressively save for your retirement by contributing $6,000 a year to a tax-sheltered account. A relative of yours tells you to forget about earning 10 percent or more a year, because that is very unlikely to happen (which is true). He also tells you that you should not worry too much about whether you earn, for example, 6 or 7 percent, because it won't make a lot of difference in your final wealth. You decide to see for yourself the various results that could occur by doing some calculations.

a. Fill in the spreadsheet below with the combinations indicated. Determine the difference in outcomes between 8 percent for 40 years and 9 percent for 40 years.

b. Calculate the difference between earning 6 percent and earning 7 percent for 20, 30, and 40 years. How would you respond to your relative?

	5%	6%	7%	8%	9%	10%
20 yrs						
25 yrs						
30 yrs						
35 yrs						
40 yrs						

Checking Your Understanding

1-1   Investors should select assets consistent with their risk tolerance. Some investors may not be able to deal with the risk of common stocks. Therefore, it is not correct to argue that all intelligent investors should own common stocks.

1-2   Disagree. If rational investors always minimized their investing risk, they would likely own nothing but Treasury bills. The correct statement is that rational investors assume risk if they expect to be compensated adequately for doing so.

1-3   Disagree. In this case investors would seek the assets expected to return the most regardless of their risk. The correct statement is that investors should seek to maximize their returns for a given level of risk.

1-4   "The tradeoff between return and risk can be, and has been, both upward-sloping and downward-sloping." This is possible because the tradeoff is always upward-sloping for rational investors before one invests—that is, ex ante. However, for various periods that have occurred, the tradeoff can be downward-sloping, because the returns on the risk-free asset are positive while the returns on stocks may be lower, or even negative. A vivid example is 2000–2002, when stocks dropped sharply, and most investors holding stocks lost money—in many cases, a lot of money. Another example of a very sharp market drop is 2008.

1-5   Uncertainty cannot be eliminated, only reduced. For example, no one, whether professional investor or not, can know what the stock market will do with certainly next year, next month, or even tomorrow.

1-6   The primary reason for holding foreign securities is to diversify one's portfolio. Diversification is a major tenet of portfolio management.

chapter 2

Investment Alternatives: Generic Principles All Investors Must Know

Continuing our scenario from Chapter 1 wherein you inherit $1 million dollars from a relative, with the stipulation that you must invest it under the general supervision of a trustee, let's consider our investing opportunities. You know generally about stocks and bonds, but you are not really sure about the specific details of each. For example, you do not know what a BBB rating on a bond indicates. Furthermore, you are unaware of zero coupon bonds, you have never heard the term securitization, and when your broker suggests that you consider ADRs for international exposure, you are really at a loss. For sure, you are not ready to explain to your trustee why you might consider derivative securities for your portfolio. It is clear that an investor in today's world should be prepared to deal with these issues, because they, and similar issues, will come up as soon as you undertake any type of investing program.

Fortunately, you can learn to evaluate your investing opportunities, both current and prospective, by learning some basics about the fundamental types of securities as outlined in this chapter.

Chapter 2 explains the most important investment alternatives available to investors, ranging from money market securities to capital market securities—primarily, bonds and stocks—to derivative securities. The emphasis is on the basic features of these securities, providing the reader with the knowledge needed to understand the investment opportunities of interest to most investors. Financial market innovations such as securitization are considered.

Changes in the securities field occur so rapidly that investors are regularly confronted with new developments. Investors in the twenty-first century have a wide variety of investment alternatives available, and it is reasonable to expect that this variety will only increase. However, if investors understand the basic characteristics of the major existing securities, they will likely be able to understand new securities as they appear.

AFTER READING THIS CHAPTER YOU WILL BE ABLE TO:

▶ Identify money market and capital market securities and understand the important features of these securities.

▶ Recognize important terms such as asset-backed securities, stock splits, bond ratings, and ADRs.

▶ Understand the basics of two derivative securities, options and futures, and how they fit into the investor's choice set.

Organizing Financial Assets

The emphasis in this chapter (and in the text in general) is on *financial assets*, which, as explained in Chapter 1, are financial claims on the issuers of the *securities*. These claims are marketable securities that are saleable in the various marketplaces discussed in Chapter 4.

Basically, households have three choices with regard to savings options:

1. Hold the liabilities of traditional intermediaries, such as banks, thrifts, and insurance companies. This means holding savings accounts and other financial assets well known to many individual investors.
2. Hold securities directly, such as stocks and bonds, purchased directly through brokers and other intermediaries. This option can also include self-directed retirement plans involving IRAs, 401(k)s, Keoghs, and so forth.
3. Hold securities indirectly, through mutual funds and pension funds. In this case, households leave the investing decisions to others by investing indirectly rather than directly.

Indirect Investing
The buying and selling of the shares of investment companies which, in turn, hold portfolios of securities

A pronounced shift has occurred in these alternatives over time. Households have decreased the percentage of direct holdings of securities and the liabilities of traditional intermediaries and increased their indirect holdings of assets through mutual funds and pension funds. **Indirect investing**, discussed in Chapter 3, refers to investors owning securities indirectly through investment companies such as mutual funds and exchange traded funds. This method of investing has become tremendously popular in the last few years with individual investors. For example, the assets of mutual funds, the most popular type of investment company, now total approximately $12 trillion.

Households also own a large, and growing, amount of pension fund reserves. Most of this amount is being invested by pension funds, on behalf of households, in equity and fixed-income securities, the primary securities of interest to most individual investors. Pension funds (both public and private) are the largest single institutional owner of common stocks. Investors have $3 trillion + in 401(k) plans.

DIRECT INVESTING

Direct Investing
Investors buy and sell securities themselves, typically through brokerage accounts

This chapter concentrates on investment alternatives available through **direct investing**, which involves securities that investors not only buy and sell themselves but also have direct control over. Investors who invest directly in financial markets, either using a broker or by other means, have a wide variety of assets from which to choose.

Nonmarketable investment opportunities, such as savings accounts at thrift institutions, are discussed briefly since investors often own, or have owned, these assets and are familiar with them. However, our emphasis will be on marketable securities. Such securities may be classified into one of three categories: the money market, the capital market, and the derivatives market.

Investors should understand money market securities, particularly Treasury bills, but they typically will not own these securities directly, choosing instead to own them through the money market funds explained in Chapter 3. Within the capital market, securities can be classified as either fixed-income or equity securities. Finally, investors may choose to use derivative securities in their portfolios. The market value of these securities is derived from an underlying security such as common stock.

Exhibit 2-1 organizes the types of financial assets to be analyzed in this chapter and in Chapter 3 using the above classifications. Although for expositional purposes we cover direct investing and indirect investing in separate chapters, it is important to understand that

EXHIBIT 2-1

Major types of financial assets

DIRECT INVESTING

Nonmarketable
- Savings deposits
- Certificates of deposit
- Money market deposit accounts
- U.S. savings bonds

Money market
- Treasury bills
- Negotiable certificates of deposit
- Commercial paper
- Eurodollars
- Repurchase agreements
- Banker's acceptances

Capital market
- Fixed income
  - *Treasuries*
  - *Agencies*
  - *Municipals*
  - *Corporates*
- Equities
  - *Preferred stock*
  - *Common stock*

Derivatives market
- Options
- Future contracts

INDIRECT INVESTING

Investment companies
- Unit investment trust
- Open end
  - *Money market mutual fund*
  - *Stock, bond, and income funds*
- Closed end
- Exchange-traded funds

investors can do both, and often do, investing directly through the use of a brokerage account and investing indirectly in one or more types of investment company. Furthermore, brokerage accounts can accommodate the ownership of investment company shares, thereby combining direct and indirect investing into one account.

✔ Today's investors often engage in both direct and indirect investing in their portfolios. Brokerage accounts can accommodate both.

A GLOBAL PERSPECTIVE

As noted in Chapter 1, investors should adopt a global perspective in making their investment decisions. The investment alternatives analyzed in this chapter, in particular some money market assets, bonds, and stocks, are available from many foreign markets to U.S. investors. Thus, the characteristics of these basic securities are relevant whether investors own domestic or foreign stocks, or both. Furthermore, investors must recognize that securities traditionally thought of as U.S. securities are, in reality, heavily influenced by global events. To illustrate, in 2010, GE had profits of $14 billion, only $5 billion of which came from U.S. operations. Clearly, GE is heavily influenced by global events.

Example 2-1

Coca-Cola is justifiably famous for its brand name and its global marketing efforts. Its success, however, is heavily dependent on what happens in the foreign markets it has increasingly penetrated. If foreign economies slow down, Coke's sales may be hurt. Furthermore, Coke must be able to convert its foreign earnings into dollars at favorable rates and repatriate them. Therefore, investing in Coke involves betting on a variety of foreign events.

U.S. investors can choose to purchase foreign stocks directly. Alternatively, many U.S. investors invest internationally by turning funds over to a professional investment organization, the investment company, which makes all decisions on behalf of investors who own shares of the company.[1] Regardless, investors today must understand we live in a global environment that will profoundly change the way we live and invest. The simple fact is that while the United States is and will continue to be a major player in the financial markets, it no longer dominates as it once did.

Nonmarketable Financial Assets

We begin our discussion of investment alternatives with those that are nonmarketable simply because most individuals will own one or more of these assets regardless of what else they do in the investing arena. For example, approximately 15 percent of total financial assets of U.S. households are in the form of deposits, including checkable deposits and currency, and time and savings deposits. Furthermore, these assets serve as a good contrast to the marketable securities we will concentrate on throughout the text.

A distinguishing characteristic of these assets is that they represent personal transactions between the owner and the issuer. That is, you as the owner of a savings account at a credit union must open the account personally, and you must deal with the credit union in maintaining the account or in closing it. In contrast, marketable securities trade in impersonal markets—the buyer (seller) does not know who the seller (buyer) is, and does not care.

Liquidity The ease with which an asset can be bought or sold quickly with relatively small price changes

These are "safe" investments, occurring at (typically) insured financial institutions or issued by the U.S. government. At least some of these assets offer the ultimate in **liquidity**, which can be defined as the ease with which an asset can be converted to cash. Thus, we know we can get all of our money back from a savings account, or a money market deposit account, very quickly.

Exhibit 2-2 describes the four major nonmarketable assets held by investors. Innovations have occurred in this area. For example, the Treasury now offers *I bonds*, or inflation-indexed savings bonds. The yield on these bonds is a combination of a fixed rate of return and a semiannual inflation rate.[2]

---

[1] We will discuss the first alternative in this chapter and the second in Chapter 3.

[2] *I bonds* are purchased at face value. Earnings grow inflation-protected for maturities up to 30 years. Face values range from $50 to $10,000. Federal taxes on earnings are deferred until redemption.

EXHIBIT 2-2

Important Nonmarketable Financial Assets

1. *Savings accounts.* Undoubtedly the best-known type of investment in the United States, savings accounts are held at commercial banks or at "thrift" institutions such as savings and loan associations and credit unions. Savings accounts in insured institutions (and your money should not be in a noninsured institution) offer a high degree of safety on both the principal and the interest earned on that principal. Liquidity is taken for granted and, together with the safety feature, probably accounts substantially for the popularity of savings accounts. Most accounts permit unlimited access to funds although some restrictions can apply. Rates paid on these accounts are stated as an Annual Percentage Yield (APY).

2. *Nonnegotiable certificates of deposit.* Commercial banks and other institutions offer a variety of savings certificates known as certificates of deposit (CDs). These certificates are available for any amount and for various maturities, with higher rates offered as maturity increases. (Larger deposits may also command higher rates, holding maturity constant.) These CDs are meant to be a buy-and-hold investment. Although some CD issuers have now reduced the stated penalties for early withdrawal, and even waived them, penalties for early withdrawal of funds can be imposed.

3. *Money market deposit accounts (MMDAs).* Financial institutions offer money market deposit accounts (MMDAs) with no interest rate ceilings. Money market "investment" accounts have a required minimum deposit to open, pay competitive money market rates and are insured up to $100,000 by the Federal Deposit Insurance Corporation (FDIC), if the bank is insured. Six pre-authorized or automatic transfers are allowed each month, up to three of which can be by check. As many withdrawals as desired can be made in person or through automated teller machines (ATMs), and there are no limitations on the number of deposits.

4. *U.S. government savings bonds.* The nontraded debt of the U.S. government, savings bonds, are nonmarketable, nontransferable, and nonnegotiable, and cannot be used for collateral. They are purchased from the Treasury, most often through banks and savings institutions. Series EE bonds in paper form are sold at 50 percent of face value, with denominations of $50, $75, $100, $200, $500, $1,000, $5,000, and $10,000. Electronic EE bonds are sold at face value and now earn a fixed rate of return.

    A second series of savings bonds is the *I bond*, sold in both electronic and paper form. A comparison of these two savings bonds is available at http://www.savingsbonds.gov/indiv/research/indepth/ebonds/res_e_bonds_eecomparison.htm.

Money Market Securities

Money Markets The market for short-term, highly liquid, low-risk assets such as Treasury bills and negotiable CDs

Money markets include short-term, highly liquid, relatively low-risk debt instruments sold by governments, financial institutions, and corporations to investors with temporary excess funds to invest. This market is dominated by financial institutions, particularly banks, and governments. The size of the transactions in the money market typically is large ($100,000 or more). The maturities of money market instruments range from one day to one year and are often less than 90 days.

Some of these instruments are negotiable and actively traded, and some are not. Investors may choose to invest directly in some of these securities, but more often they do so indirectly through money market mutual funds (discussed in Chapter 3), which are investment companies organized to own and manage a portfolio of securities and which in turn are owned by investors. Thus, many individual investors own shares in money market funds that, in turn, own one or more of these money market certificates. Exhibit 2-3 describes the major money market securities of most interest to individual investors.[3]

---

[3] Other money market securities exist, such as federal funds, but most individual investors will never encounter them.

EXHIBIT 2-3

Important Money Market Securities

1. *Treasury bills.* The premier money market instrument, a fully guaranteed, very liquid IOU from the U.S. Treasury. They are sold on an auction basis every week at a discount from face value in denominations starting at $10,000; therefore, the discount determines the yield. The greater the discount at time of purchase, the higher the return earned by investors. Typical maturities are 13 and 26 weeks, although maturities range from a few days to 52 weeks. New bills can be purchased by investors on a competitive or non-competitive bid basis. Outstanding (i.e., already issued) bills can be purchased and sold in the secondary market, an extremely efficient market where government securities dealers stand ready to buy and sell these securities.

2. *Negotiable certificates of deposit (CDs).* Issued in exchange for a deposit of funds by most American banks, the CD is a marketable deposit liability of the issuer, who usually stands ready to sell new CDs on demand. The deposit is maintained in the bank until maturity, at which time the holder receives the deposit plus interest. However, these CDs are negotiable, meaning that they can be sold in the open market before maturity. Dealers make a market in these unmatured CDs. Maturities typically range from 14 days (the minimum maturity permitted) to one year. The minimum deposit is $100,000.

3. *Commercial paper.* A short-term, unsecured promissory note issued by large, well-known, and financially strong corporations (including finance companies). Denominations start at $100,000, with a maturity of 270 days or less (average maturity is about 30 days). Commercial paper is usually sold at a discount either directly by the issuer or indirectly through a dealer, with rates comparable to CDs. Although a secondary market exists for commercial paper, it is weak and most of it is held to maturity. Commercial paper is rated by a rating service as to quality (relative probability of default by the issuer).

4. *Repurchase agreement (RPs).* An agreement between a borrower and a lender (typically institutions) to sell and repurchase U.S. government securities. The borrower initiates an RP by contracting to sell securities to a lender and agreeing to repurchase these securities at a pre-specified price on a stated date. The effective interest rate is given by the difference between the two prices. The maturity of RPs is generally very short, from three to 14 days, and sometimes overnight. The minimum denomination is typically $100,000.

5. *Banker's acceptance.* A time draft drawn on a bank by a customer, whereby the bank agrees to pay a particular amount at a specified future date. Banker's acceptances are negotiable instruments because the holder can sell them for less than face value (i.e., discount them) in the money market. They are normally used in international trade. Banker's acceptances are traded on a discount basis, with a minimum denomination of $100,000. Maturities typically range from 30 to 180 days, with 90 days being the most common.

THE TREASURY BILL

Treasury Bill A short-term money market instrument sold at discount by the U.S. government

The **Treasury bill** (T-bill) is the most prominent money market security because it is the safest asset available and because it serves as a benchmark asset. Although in some pure sense there is no such thing as a risk-free financial asset, on a practical basis the Treasury bill is risk-free on a nominal basis (ignoring inflation). There is little practical risk of default by the U.S. government, despite the debt ceiling "crisis" in the summer of 2011.

✓ The Treasury bill rate, denoted RF, is used throughout the text as a proxy for the nominal (today's dollars) *risk-free rate of return* available to investors (e.g., the RF that was shown in Figure 1-1).

Treasury bills are auctioned weekly at a discount from face value, which is a minimum $10,000.[4]

---

[4] Individuals can purchase bills directly from the Treasury using so called TreasuryDirect accounts. They can also purchase them through banks and brokers on either a competitive or noncompetitive basis.

T-bills are redeemed at face value, thereby providing investors with an effective rate of return that can be calculated at time of purchase. Obviously, the less investors pay for these securities, the larger their return.[5,6] Treasury bill rates are determined at auction each week, and therefore reflect current money market conditions. If T-bill rates are rising (falling), this generally reflects an increased (decreased) demand for funds. In turn, other interest rates will be affected.

MONEY MARKET RATES

Money market rates tend to move together, and most rates are very close to each other for the same maturity. Treasury bill rates are less than the rates available on other money market securities because of their presumed risk-free nature.[7]

Some Practical Advice

Most investors will never own any money market security directly other than Treasury bills because of the unfamiliarity and the large face value of these instruments. On the other hand, many investors will own them indirectly sometime in their investing lifetime in the form of money market mutual funds, discussed in Chapter 3. By buying shares in this type of fund, an investor gets the benefits of these securities without having to worry about the details and the large face value.

Checking Your Understanding

1. Why are money market securities referred to as impersonal assets, while the non-marketable financial assets are not?
2. Holding maturity constant, would you expect the yields on money market securities to be within a few tenths of a percent of each other?
3. Why does the Treasury bill serve as a benchmark security?

Capital Market Securities

Capital Markets The market for long-term securities such as bonds and stocks

Capital markets encompass fixed-income and equity securities with maturities greater than one year. Risk is generally much higher than in the money market because of the time to maturity and the very nature of the securities sold in the capital markets. Marketability is poorer in some cases.

---

[5] The convention in the United States for many years is to state the yield on Treasury bills with six month maturities or less on a discount yield basis, using a 360-day year. The discount yield is calculated as follows:

Discount yield = [(Face value − Pur. price)/Face value] × [360/Maturity of the bill in days]

[6] The discount yield understates the investor's actual yield because it uses a 360-day year and divides by the face value instead of the purchase price. The investment yield method (also called the bond equivalent yield and the coupon equivalent rate) can be used to correct for these deficiencies, and for any given Treasury bill the investment yield will be greater than the discount yield. The investment yield is calculated as follows:

Investment yield = [(Face value − Pur. price)/Pur. price] × [365/Maturity of the bill in days]

[7] Note that in this text we use the term "money market rates" to refer to the rates on T-bills, commercial paper, negotiable CDs, etc. Several websites and other sources use the term to refer to the rates on money market accounts and other accounts at financial institutions.

✓ The capital market includes both debt and equity securities, with equity securities having no maturity date.

Fixed-Income Securities

Fixed-Income Securities Securities with specified payment dates and amounts, primarily bonds

We begin our review of the principal types of capital market securities typically owned directly by individual investors with **fixed-income securities**. All of these securities have a specified payment schedule. In most cases, such as with a traditional bond, the amount and date of each payment are known in advance. Some of these securities deviate from the traditional-bond format, but all fixed-income securities have a specified payment or repayment schedule—they must mature at some future date.

Technically, fixed-income securities include Treasury bonds, agency bonds, municipal bonds, corporate bonds, asset-backed securities, mortgage-related bonds, and money market securities.[8] We covered money market securities in the previous section.

BONDS

Bonds Long-term debt instruments representing the issuer's contractual obligation

Bonds can be described simply as long-term debt instruments representing the issuer's contractual obligation, or IOU.[9]

Bonds are *fixed-income securities* because the interest payments (for coupon bonds) and the principal repayment for a typical bond are specified at the time the bond is issued and fixed for the life of the bond. At the time of purchase, the bond buyer knows the future stream of *cash flows* to be received from buying and holding the bond to maturity. Barring default by the issuer, these payments will be received at specified intervals until maturity, at which time the principal will be repaid. However, if the buyer decides to sell the bond before maturity, the price received will depend on the level of interest rates at that time.

✓ From an investor's viewpoint a bond is typically a "safe" asset, at least relative to stocks and derivative securities. Principal and interest are specified and the issuer must meet these obligations or face default, and possibly bankruptcy.[10]

Par Value (Face Value) The redemption value of a bond paid at maturity, typically $1,000

Bond Characteristics   The **par value (face value)** of most bonds is $1,000, and we will use this number as the amount to be repaid at maturity.[11] The typical bond matures (terminates) on a specified date and is technically known as a *term bond*.[12] Most bonds are coupon bonds, where *coupon* refers to the periodic interest that the issuer pays to the holder of the bonds.[13] Interest on bonds is typically paid semiannually.

---

[8] This is the definition used by the Bond Market Association.

[9] The buyer of a newly issued coupon bond is lending money to the issuer who, in turn, agrees to pay interest on this loan and repay the principal at a stated maturity date.

[10] A bond has clearly defined legal ramifications. Failure to pay either interest or principal on a bond constitutes default for that obligation. Default, unless quickly remedied by payment or a voluntary agreement with the creditor, leads to bankruptcy.

[11] The par value is almost never less than $1,000, although it easily can be more.

[12] The phrase *term-to-maturity* denotes how much longer the bond will be in existence. In contrast, a serial bond has a series of maturity dates. One issue of *serial bonds* may mature in specified amounts year after year, and each specified amount could carry a different coupon.

[13] The terms *interest income* and *coupon income* are interchangeable.

Example 2-2 A 10-year, 10 percent coupon bond has a dollar coupon of $100 (10 percent of $1,000); therefore, knowing the percentage coupon rate is the same as knowing the coupon payment in dollars.[14] This bond would pay interest (the coupons) of $50 on a specified date every six months. The $1,000 principal would be repaid 10 years hence on a date specified at the time the bond is issued. Similarly, a 5.5 percent coupon bond pays an annual interest amount of $55, payable at $27.50 every six months. Note that all the characteristics of a bond are specified exactly when the bond is issued.

Bond Prices By convention, corporations and Treasuries use 100 as par rather than $1,000, which is the actual par value of most bonds. Therefore, a price of 90 represents $900 (90 percent of the $1,000 par value), and a price of 55 represents $550 using the normal assumption of a par value of $1,000. Each "point," or a change of "1," represents 1 percent of $1,000, or $10. The easiest way to convert quoted bond prices to actual prices is to remember that they are quoted in percentages, with the common assumption of a $1,000 par value.

Example 2-3 A closing price of 101.375 on a particular day for an IBM bond represents 101.375 percent of $1,000, or 1.01375 × $1,000 = $1,013.75. Treasury bond prices are quoted in 32nds and may be shown as fractions, as in 100 14/32.

✓ Bond prices are quoted as a percentage of par value, which is typically $1,000.

Accrued Interest Example 2-3 suggests that an investor could purchase the IBM bond for $1,013.75 on that day. Actually, bonds trade on an *accrued interest* basis. That is, the bond buyer must pay the bond seller the price of the bond as well as the interest that has been earned (accrued) on the bond since the last semiannual interest payment. This allows an investor to sell a bond any time between interest payments without losing the interest that has accrued. Bond buyers should remember this additional "cost" when buying a bond because prices are quoted to investors without the accrued interest.[15]

Discounts and Premiums The price of the IBM bond in Example 2-3 is above 100 (i.e., $1,000) because market yields on bonds of this type declined after this bond was issued.
The coupon on the IBM bond became more than competitive with the going market interest rate for comparable newly issued bonds, and the price increased to reflect this fact. At any point in time some bonds are selling at *premiums* (prices above par value), reflecting a decline in market rates after that particular bond was sold. Others are selling at *discounts* (prices below par value of $1,000), because the stated coupons are less than the prevailing interest rate on a comparable new issue.

✓ While a bond will be worth exactly its face value (typically $1,000) on the day it matures, its price will fluctuate around $1,000 until then, depending on what interest rates do. Interest rates and bond prices move inversely.

[14] The coupon rate on a traditional, standard bond is fixed at the bond's issuance and cannot vary.
[15] The *invoice price*, or the price the bond buyer must pay, will include the accrued interest.

Call Provision Gives the issuer the right to call in a security and retire it by paying off the obligation

Callable Bonds The **call provision** gives the issuer the right to "call in" the bonds, thereby depriving investors of that particular fixed-income security.[16] Exercising the call provision becomes attractive to the issuer when market interest rates drop sufficiently below the coupon rate on the outstanding bonds for the issuer to save money.[17] Costs are incurred to call the bonds, such as a "call premium" and administrative expenses.[18] However, issuers expect to sell new bonds at a lower interest cost, thereby replacing existing higher interest-cost bonds with new, lower interest-cost bonds.

Investments Intuition

The call feature is a disadvantage to investors who must give up the higher-yielding bonds. The wise bond investor will note the bond issue's provisions concerning the call, carefully determining the earliest date at which the bond can be called and the bond's yield if it is called at the earliest date possible. (This calculation is shown in Chapter 17.) Some investors have purchased bonds at prices above face value and suffered a loss when the bonds were unexpectedly called in and paid off at face value.[19]

An example of a surprise call occurred when New York City initiated a redemption of $430 million of their bonds, saddling some bondholders with losses of 15 percent or more. Many of these investors had paid more than face value for these bonds the year before in the secondary market, attracted by their high yields. Virtually no one expected a call, because the city was prohibited from refinancing the bonds with new tax-exempts. The city, however, issued taxable bonds and called these in.

Some bonds are not callable. Most Treasury bonds cannot be called, although some older Treasury bonds can be called within five years of the maturity date. About three-fourths of municipal bonds being issued today are callable.

Zero Coupon Bond A bond sold with no coupons at a discount and redeemed for face value at maturity

The Zero Coupon Bond A radical innovation in the format of traditional bonds is the **zero coupon bond**, which is issued with no coupons, or interest, to be paid during the life of the bond. The purchaser pays less than par value for zero coupons and receives par value at maturity. The difference in these two amounts generates an effective interest rate, or rate of return. As in the case of Treasury bills, which are sold at discount, the lower the price paid for the coupon bond, the higher the effective return.

Issuers of zero coupon bonds include corporations, municipalities, government agencies, and the U.S. Treasury. Since 1985 the Treasury has offered STRIPS, or Separate Trading of Registered Interest and Principal of Securities.[20]

---

[16] Unlike the call provision, the *sinking fund* provides for the orderly retirement of the bond issue during its life. The provisions of a sinking fund vary widely. For example, it can be stated as a fixed or variable amount and as a percentage of the particular issue outstanding or the total debt of the issuer outstanding. Any part or all of the bond issue may be retired through the sinking fund by the maturity date. One procedure for carrying out the sinking fund requirement is simply to buy the required amount of bonds on the open market each year. A second alternative is to call the bonds randomly. Again, investors should be aware of such provisions for their protection.

[17] There are different types of call features. Some bonds can be called any time during their life, given a short notice of 30 or 60 days. Many callable bonds have a "deferred call" feature, meaning that a certain time period after issuance must expire before the bonds can be called. Popular time periods in this regard are 5 and 10 years.

[18] The call premium often equals one year's interest if the bond is called within a year; after the first year, it usually declines at a constant rate.

[19] A bond listed as "nonrefundable" for a specified period can still be called in and paid off with cash in hand. It cannot be refunded through the sale of a new issue carrying a lower coupon.

[20] Under this program, all new Treasury bonds and notes with maturities greater than 10 years are eligible to be "stripped" to create zero coupon Treasury securities that are direct obligations of the Treasury.

TYPES OF BONDS

There are four major types of bonds in the United States based on the issuer involved (U.S. government, federal agency, municipal, and corporate bonds), and variations exist within each major type.

Treasury Securities   The U.S. government, in the course of financing its operations through the Treasury Department, issues numerous notes and bonds with maturities greater than one year. The U.S. government is considered the safest credit risk because of the overall stability and economic power of the U.S. economy and because of the government's power to print money.

✓   For practical purposes, investors do not consider the possibility of risk of default for U.S. Treasury securities.

Treasury Bonds Long-term bonds sold by the U.S. government

     Treasury bonds have been rated since 1917, and always received a triple-A rating until 2011, when Standard & Poor's lowered the rating one notch in a controversial move. The other two rating agencies did not follow suit.

     Most investors still consider U.S. Treasury securities the safest securities in the world. Investors purchase these securities with the expectation of earning a steady stream of interest payments and with full assurance of receiving the par value of the bonds when they mature. This was made clear following the unprecedented rating cut by Standard & Poor's. Long-term Treasury returns for 2011 were at near record levels because investors were worried about the European debt crisis, and the slow economic growth in the United States indicated no inflationary pressures, which harm bond returns.

Treasury Notes Treasury securities with maturities up to 10 years

Treasury Bonds   traditionally have had maturities of 10 to 30 years, although a bond can be issued with any maturity.[21] The Treasury also sells **Treasury notes**, issued for a term of two, five, or 10 years.[22] Interest is paid every six months. Notes can be held to maturity or sold.[23]

---

[21] U.S. securities with maturities greater than one year and less than 10 years technically are referred to as Treasury notes. See www.publicdebt.treas.gov for information about Treasury bonds, including inflation-indexed bonds. For a nominal fee and some simple paperwork, investors can join in TreasuryDirect. This program allows investors to buy Treasury securities directly by Internet or over the phone. Participants put in a "noncompetitive" bid which means they receive the average successful bid of the professionals. Payments are deducted from, or credited to, each participant's banking account.

[22] These notes exist in electronic form only, not in paper form.

[23] To buy a note, investors place a bid at auction (either competitive or noncompetitive), where the interest rate is determined. Bids may be placed in multiples of $1,000.

Treasury Inflation-
Indexed Securities
(TIPS) Treasury
securities fully indexed for
inflation

TIPS   Since 1997 the Treasury has sold **Treasury Inflation-Indexed Securities (TIPS)** which protect investors against losses resulting from inflation. TIPS pay a fixed rate of interest twice a year, but this rate is applied to the inflation-adjusted principal.[24] Each six-month interest payment is determined by multiplying the principal, which has been adjusted for inflation, by one-half the fixed annual interest rate. Therefore, with inflation occurring on a regular basis, the inflation-adjusted principal rises, and the dollar amount of each interest payment rises.

TIPS are sold at auction by the Treasury, with the interest rate determined at the auction. Therefore, at the time you buy a new TIPS you do not know what the interest rate will be.[25] They can be held to maturity or sold. At maturity, the investor receives the higher of the adjusted principal or the original principal (with deflation, the adjusted principal could be less than face value).

Taxes must be paid each year on both the interest and the inflation adjustments, although the actual cash for the latter is not received until maturity. This is often referred to as a phantom tax—the investor owes tax each year on the increased value of the principal but does not receive this money until the bond is sold or matures. Therefore, many investors may prefer to hold these securities in a tax-deferred retirement account.

Some Practical Advice

An investor can buy Treasury securities through a financial institution, bank or broker. Alternatively, investors can open a TreasuryDirect account with the Treasury. This account allows investors to buy, reinvest, and sell Bills, Notes, Bonds, Treasury Inflation-Protected Securities (TIPS), and savings bonds 24 hours a day, seven days a week. All account information is readily available online.

GOVERNMENT AGENCY SECURITIES

Since the 1920s, the federal government has created various federal agencies designed to help certain sectors of the economy, through either direct loans or guarantee of private loans. These credit agencies compete for funds in the marketplace by selling **government agency securities**.

Government Agency
Securities Securities
issued by federal credit
agencies (fully guaranteed)
or by government-
sponsored agencies (not
guaranteed)

Two types of government agencies have existed in the U.S. financial system: federal agencies and government-sponsored enterprises (GSEs).

1. Federal agencies are part of the federal government, and their securities are fully guaranteed by the Treasury. The most important "agency" for investors is the Government National Mortgage Association (often referred to as "Ginnie Mae").
2. Government Sponsored Enterprises (GSEs) are publicly held, for-profit corporations created by Congress to help lower and middle income people buy houses. They sell their own securities in the marketplace in order to raise funds for their specific purposes. Although these agencies have access to credit lines from the government, their securities are not explicitly guaranteed by the government as to principal or interest. GSEs include the Federal Home Loan Bank and the Farm Credit System.[26]

---

[24] Based on the CPI, the value of the bond is adjusted upwards every six months by the amount of inflation.

[25] The minimum purchase amount is $1,000, and bids must be placed in multiples of $1,000. TIPS are being sold with terms of five, 10, and 20 years.

[26] Some GSEs transition from being a government sponsored enterprise to a completely private company. Sallie Mae, the country's leading provider of student loans, began privatizing its operations in 1997, and by the end of 2004, it ended all ties to the federal government.

The Federal National Mortgage Association ("Fannie Mae") and the Federal Home Loan Mortgage Corporation ("Freddie Mac") started as federal agencies and later offered stock to the public, becoming GSEs.[27] They buy mortgages from financial institutions, freeing them to make more mortgage loans to Americans. Because of their Congressional charters, the financial markets always believed that the government would not allow these GSEs to default. In September 2008, a Federal takeover of Fannie Mae and Freddie Mac occurred.

Mortgage-Backed Securities   A part of the market of fixed-income securities is known as asset-backed securities, which includes **Mortgage-Backed Securities (MBSs)**. These securities are simply shares of home loans (mortgages) sold to investors in various security forms. Traditionally, investors in mortgage-backed securities expected to minimize default risk because most mortgages were guaranteed by one of the government agencies. Nevertheless, these securities present investors with uncertainty, because they can receive varying amounts of monthly payments depending on how quickly homeowners pay off their mortgages.

By now, almost everyone knows of the recent horrific difficulties associated with subprime mortgages and mortgage-backed securities. In mid-2007, a pair of hedge funds managed by Bear Stearns collapsed because of heavy losses in subprime mortgages. By 2008, a large amount of home loans had been packaged and sold to investors, and repackaged and sold again, and so on. As good borrowers dwindled in number, the loan originators made more and more loans to less creditworthy borrowers. Sometime in 2008, the rate of house foreclosures started to increase sharply as many borrowers could no longer keep up on their mortgages. With MBSs widely held throughout the economy, the foreclosures and declining house prices lead to larger and larger losses for many investment banks and other financial institutions.

Municipal Securities   Bonds sold by states, counties, cities, and other political entities (e.g., airport authorities, school districts) other than the federal government and its agencies are called **municipal bonds**. This is a vast market, roughly $3 trillion in size, with tens of thousands of different issuers and more than one million different issues outstanding. Roughly one-third of municipal bonds outstanding are owned by households, and roughly one-third by mutual funds.

While we typically think of long-term bonds as those with maximum maturities of about 30 years, exceptions do occur. In late 2011, the California Institute of Technology (Caltech) sold $350 million of debt maturing in 100 years. These bonds, rated AA+, were sold at a record low yield of 4.744 percent, which was 1.8 percentage points higher than 30-year Treasuries.

Credit ratings range from very good to very suspect. Thus, risk varies widely, particularly given the recent financial crisis, as does marketability. Overall, however, the default rate on municipal bonds historically has been very favorable. This may change, however, in this new era of deficits for many municipal bond issuers.

Two basic types of municipals are *general obligation bonds*, which are backed by the "full faith and credit" of the issuer, and *revenue bonds*, which are repaid from the revenues generated by the project they were sold to finance (e.g., a toll road or airport improvement).[28] In the case of general obligation bonds, the issuer can tax residents to pay for the bond interest and principal. In the case of revenue bonds, the project must generate enough revenue to service the issue.

Mortgage-Backed Securities (MBSs) Securities whose value depends upon some set of mortgages

Municipal Bonds Securities issued by political entities other than the federal government and its agencies, such as states and cities

---

[27] These two GSEs have always been widely referred to in the press and any discussions as "Fannie Mae", or Fannie, and "Freddie Mac," or Freddie.

[28] Municipalities also issue short-term obligations. Some of these qualify for money market investments because they are short-term and of high quality.

Some Practical Advice

A new free online municipal bond information service is now available, Electronic Municipal Market Access, nicknamed EMMA, at emma.msrb.org. It shows real-time trade data as well as the issuer's prospectus, which contains the official information about the issue. To use this service effectively, you will generally need the Cusip number, which is a unique identification code for each issue.

Most long-term municipals are sold as *serial bonds*, which means that a specified number of the original issue matures each year until the final maturity date. For example, a 10-year serial issue might have 10 percent of the issue maturing each year for the next 10 years.

A majority of municipals sold are insured by one of the major municipal bond insurers. By having the bonds insured, the issuers achieve a higher rating for the bond, and therefore a lower interest cost. Investors trade some yield for protection. However, the financial viability of the bond insurers themselves came under strong scrutiny in 2008 as the subprime crisis deepened.

The Taxable Equivalent Yield (TEY) The distinguishing feature of most municipals is their exemption from federal taxes. Because of this feature, the stated interest rate on these bonds will be lower than that on comparable nonexempt bonds because, in effect, it is an after-tax rate. The higher an investor's tax bracket, the more attractive municipals become.

✓ The *taxable equivalent yield* (TEY) shows the before-tax interest rate on a municipal bond that is equivalent to the stated (after-tax) interest rate on that bond, given any marginal tax rate.

The TEY for any municipal bond return and any marginal tax bracket can be calculated using the following formula:

$$\text{Taxable equivalent yield} = \frac{\text{Tax-exempt municipal yield}}{1 - \text{Marginal tax rate}} \qquad (2\text{-}1)$$

Example 2-4 An investor in the 28 percent marginal tax bracket who invests in a 5 percent municipal bond would have to receive

$$\frac{0.05}{(1 - 0.28)} = 6.94\%$$

from a comparable taxable bond to be as well off.

In some cases, the municipal bondholder can also avoid state and/or local taxes. For example, a North Carolina resident purchasing a bond issued by the state of North Carolina would escape all taxes on the interest received.[29] In 2008, the Supreme Court reaffirmed that

---

[29] To calculate the TEY in these cases, first determine the effective state rate:

$$\text{Effective state rate} = \text{Marginal state tax rate} \times (1 - \text{Federal marginal rate})$$

Then, calculate the combined effective federal/state tax rate as:

$$\text{Combined effective tax rate} = \text{Effective state rate} + \text{Federal rate}$$

Use Equation 2-1 to calculate the combined TEY, substituting the combined effective tax rate for the federal marginal tax rate shown in Equation 2-1.

states can exempt interest on their own bonds for residents while taxing interest on bonds issued by other states.

✓ Bond yields are typically stated on a before-tax basis except in the case of municipal bonds, which are stated on an after-tax basis. The TEY puts the municipal bond yield on a before tax basis, allowing investors to compare bond yields across the board.

Corporates

Corporate Bonds Long-term debt securities of various types sold by corporations

Most of the larger corporations, several thousand in total, issue **corporate bonds** to help finance their operations. Many of these firms have more than one issue outstanding.

Although an investor can find a wide range of maturities, coupons, and special features available from corporates, the typical corporate bond matures in 20 to 40 years, pays semi-annual interest, is callable, carries a sinking fund, and is sold originally at a price close to par value, which is almost always $1,000. Credit quality varies widely.

Senior Securities Securities, typically debt securities, ahead of common stock in terms of payment or in case of liquidation

Corporate bonds are **senior securities**. That is, they are senior to any preferred stock and to the common stock of a corporation in terms of priority of payment and in case of bankruptcy and liquidation. However, within the bond category itself there are various degrees of security.

Debenture An unsecured bond backed by the general worthiness of the firm

✓ The most common type of unsecured bond is the **debenture**, a bond backed only by the issuer's overall financial soundness.[30]

Debentures can be subordinated, resulting in a claim on income that stands below (subordinate to) the claim of the other debentures.

New Types of Corporate Bonds

In an attempt to make bonds more accessible to individuals, high credit-quality firms have begun selling direct access notes (DANs). These notes eliminate some of the traditional details associated with bonds by being issued at par ($1,000), which means no discounts, premiums, or accrued interest. Coupon rates are fixed, and maturities range from nine months to 30 years. The company issuing the bonds typically "posts" the maturities and rates it is offering for one week, allowing investors to shop around.

One potential disadvantage of DANs is that they are best suited for the buy-and-hold investor. A seller has no assurance of a good secondary market for the bonds, and therefore no assurance as to the price that would be received.

Responding to the success of TIPS, explained earlier, some companies have begun offering corporate inflation-protected notes. These bonds feature monthly payments that immediately reflect the effects of inflation. These payments consist of a fixed base rate plus the year-to-year change in the CPI.[31] Unlike Treasury bonds, corporate bonds are subject to credit risk, because a corporation can go bankrupt.

Convertible Bonds

Some bonds have a built-in conversion feature. The holders of these bonds have the option to convert the bonds into common stock whenever they choose. Typically, the bonds are turned in to the corporation in exchange for a specified number of common shares, with no cash payment required. Convertible bonds are two securities simultaneously: a fixed-income security paying a specified interest payment and a claim on the common stock that will become increasingly valuable as the price of the underlying common

[30] Bonds that are "secured" by a legal claim to specific assets of the issuer in case of liquidation are called *mortgage bonds*.

[31] These bonds are being issued with maturities of five, seven, and 10 years, and at maturity the $1,000 principal is repaid to investors. Unlike TIPS, investors must pay state taxes on the corporate bonds.

stock rises. Thus, the prices of convertibles may fluctuate over a fairly wide range, depending on whether they currently are trading like other fixed-income securities or are trading to reflect the price of the underlying common stock.

Investments Intuition

Investors should not expect to receive the conversion option free. The issuer sells convertible bonds at a lower interest rate than would otherwise be paid, resulting in a lower interest return to investors.

Bond Ratings   Corporate and municipal bonds, unlike Treasury securities, carry the risk of default by the issuer. Rating agencies such as Standard & Poor's (S&P) Corporation and Moody's Investors Service, Inc., provide investors with **bond ratings**—that is, current opinions on the *relative* quality of most large corporate and municipal bonds, as well as commercial paper. By carefully analyzing the issues in great detail, the rating firms, in effect, perform the *credit analysis* for the investor.

Bond Ratings Letters assigned to bonds by rating agencies to express the relative probability of default

Example 2-5   In September 2011, with the European crisis regularly in the news, it was reported that Moody's Investors Services was expected to cut the ratings of three large French banks because of their large holdings of Greek government debt. A move such as this would lower investor confidence in French banks.

Standard & Poor's bond ratings consist of letters ranging from AAA, AA, A, BBB, and so on, to D. (Moody's corresponding letters are Aaa, Aa, A, Baa, . . . , to D.) Plus or minus signs can be used to provide more detailed standings within a given category.[32] Exhibit 2-4 shows Standard & Poor's rating definitions and provides a brief explanation of the considerations on which the ratings are based.

EXHIBIT 2-4

Standard & Poor's Debt-Rating Definitions

AAA	Extremely strong capacity to pay interest and repay principal
AA	Strong capacity to pay interest and repay principal
A	Strong capacity to pay interest and repay principal but more vulnerable to an adverse change in conditions than in the case of AA
BBB	Adequate capacity to pay interest and repay principal. Even more vulnerable to adverse change in conditions than A-rated bonds
	Debt rated BB and below is regarded as having predominantly speculative characteristics.
BB	Less near-term risk of default than lower rated issues. These bonds are exposed to large ongoing uncertainties or adverse change in conditions.
B	A larger vulnerability to default than BB but with the current capacity to pay interest and repay principal
CCC	A currently identifiable vulnerability to default and dependent on favorable conditions to pay interest and repay principal
CC	Applied to debt subordinated to senior debt rated CCC
C	Same as CC
D	A debit that is in default
+ or −	May be used to show relative standings within a category

---

[32] Moody's uses numbers (i.e., 1, 2, and 3) to designate quality grades further. For example, bonds could be rated Aa1 or Aa2. Major rating categories for Moody's include: Aaa, Aa, A, Baa, Ba, B, Caa, Ca, and C.

The first four categories, AAA through BBB, represent *investment grade* securities. AAA securities are judged to have very strong capacity to meet all obligations, whereas BBB securities are considered to have adequate capacity. Typically, institutional investors must confine themselves to bonds in these four categories. Other things being equal, bond ratings and bond coupon rates are inversely related.

Bonds rated BB, B, CCC, and CC are regarded as speculative securities in terms of the issuer's ability to meet its contractual obligations. These securities carry significant uncertainties, although they are not without positive factors. Bonds rated C are currently not paying interest, and bonds rated D are in default.

Of the large number of corporate bonds outstanding, traditionally more than 80 percent have been rated A or better (based on the value of bonds outstanding). Utilities and finance companies have the fewest low-rated bonds, and transportation companies the most (because of problems with bankrupt railroads). Of course, the financial crisis has had a major impact on the corporate bond market.

Despite their widespread acceptance and use, bond ratings have some limitations. The rating agencies may disagree on their evaluations. Furthermore, because most bonds are in the top four categories, it seems safe to argue that not all issues in a single category (such as A) can be equally risky. It is extremely important to remember that *bond ratings are a reflection of the relative probability of default*, which says little or nothing about the absolute probability of default. Finally, it is important to remember that, like most people and institutions in life, rating agencies aren't perfect. Sometimes, for various reasons, they really fail.

Example 2-6 In December 2001, Enron was rated investment grade on a Friday. On Sunday, it filed for bankruptcy. S&P continued to rate Tyco bonds as investment grade (BBB), although the market clearly priced Tyco bonds in the junk category. And by the time the rating services downgraded WorldCom to junk status, the market had reflected that fact for some time.

Junk Bonds Bonds that carry ratings of BB or lower, with correspondingly higher yields

Junk Bonds The term **junk bonds** refers to high-risk, high-yield bonds that carry ratings of BB (S&P) or Ba (Moody's) or lower, with correspondingly higher yields. An alternative, and more reassuring, name used to describe this area of the bond market is the *high-yield debt market*. Default rates on junk bonds vary each year. The default rate in 2001 was almost 9 percent, the highest level since 1991. It was over 6 percent in 2000. In contrast, the global default rate in 2007 was approximately at its lowest level in 25 years, reflecting several years of easy credit conditions. The financial crisis, starting in 2008, may dramatically impact default rates.

ASSET-BACKED SECURITIES

The money and capital markets are constantly adapting to meet new requirements and conditions. This has given rise to new types of securities that were not previously available.

Asset-Backed Securities (ABS) Securities issued against some type of asset-linked debts bundled together, such as credit card receivables or mortgages

Securitization refers to the transformation of illiquid, risky individual loans into more liquid, less risky securities referred to as **Asset-Backed Securities (ABS)**. An asset-backed security is a securitized interest in a pool of non-mortgage assets (conceptually, the structure of ABS is similar to the mortgage-backed securities discussed earlier). To create an ABS, a corporation creates a trust and sells it a group of assets. The trust, in turn, sells securities to investors. Legal safeguards are established to protect investors from possible bankruptcy of the corporation.

Example 2-7

Citicorp, a major bank, has a large Visa operation. In the past, it regularly took the cash flows from the monthly payments that customers make on their Visa accounts, securitized them, and sold the resulting bonds to investors.

Marketable securities have been backed by car loans, credit-card receivables, railcar leases, small-business loans, photocopier leases, aircraft leases, and so forth. The assets that can be securitized seem to be limited only by the imagination of the packagers, as evidenced by the fact that by 1996 new asset types included royalty streams from films, student loans, mutual fund fees, tax liens, monthly electric utility bills, and delinquent child support payments.

As a result of the trend to securitization, asset-backed securities proliferated prior to 2008 as financial institutions rushed to securitize various types of loans. ABS and MBS volume was down substantially in 2008 because of the onset of the financial crisis. By early 2009, the issuance of ABS and MBS securities was down 90 percent.

ABSs can be structured into "tranches," or different classes, which are priced according to the degree of risk. Different classes can have different credit ratings, and tranches may by structured with different average maturities. As for risks, securitization works best when packaged loans are homogeneous, so that income streams and risks are more predictable. This is not the case for some of the newer loans being considered for packaging, such as loans for boats and motorcycles; the smaller amount of information results in a larger risk from unanticipated factors.

Concepts in Action

Do You Want a Tailor-Made Fixed Income Security?

Structured products are the recent "in" thing in investing. Basically, a structured product combines a Treasury or corporate bond with a play (an option) on a stock or stock index. Investors earn income while sharing in some equity gains, if they occur, while insuring against market losses on equities.

The number and variety of structured products have increased rapidly. Hundreds are aimed at individual investors. These notes can serve a wide variety of investor objectives, such as protecting retirement money, insuring against stock market losses, allowing investors to pursue possible large returns, and so forth.

Let's consider one popular structured product, the Principal Protection Note. Part of your money is invested in a zero coupon bond, which locks in a return. The remainder is invested in options contracts on a stock market index. If the index rises strongly, the investor shares in part, but not all, of the gain. If the market declines over the life of the note, the option expires worthless, but the investor still has the return from the zero coupon bond.

Like any investing opportunity, there are risks involved. Generally, investors must hold these products to maturity because there is no market for them. Commissions can be expensive. And the notes are being backed by a bank, which could experience significant financial problems or failure. Certainly, the wild events involving financial institutions in 2008 should give investors pause as to the absolute safety of some of our financial institutions.

RATES ON FIXED-INCOME SECURITIES

Interest rates on fixed-income securities fluctuate widely over the years as inflationary expectations change as well as demand and supply conditions for long-term funds. As we would expect on the basis of the return-risk tradeoff explained in Chapter 1, corporate bond rates exceed Treasury rates because of the possible risk of default, and lower-rated corporates yield more than do higher-rated bonds. The municipal bond rate as reported is below all other rates, but we must remember that this is an after-tax rate. To make it comparable, municipal bond yields should be adjusted to a taxable equivalent yield using Equation 2-1. When this is done, the rate will be much closer to the taxable rates. Investors can obtain daily information on the rates available on fixed-income securities in the "Credit Markets" section of *The Wall Street Journal*.

Checking Your Understanding

4. Consider a corporate bond rated AAA versus another corporate bond rated only BBB. Could you say with confidence that the first bond will not default while for the second bond there is some reasonable probability of default?
5. Municipal bond yields are stated on an after-tax basis while corporate bond yields are stated on a before-tax basis. Agree or disagree, and state your reasoning.
6. Should risk-averse investors avoid junk bonds?

Equity Securities

Unlike fixed-income securities, equity securities represent an ownership interest in a corporation. These securities provide a residual claim—after payment of all obligations to fixed-income claims—on the income and assets of a corporation. There are two forms of equities, preferred stock, and common stock. Investors are primarily interested in common stocks.

PREFERRED STOCK

Preferred Stock An equity security with an intermediate claim (between the bondholders and the stockholders) on a firm's assets and earnings

Although technically an equity security, **preferred stock** is known as a hybrid security because it resembles both equity and fixed-income instruments. As an equity security, preferred stock has an infinite life and pays dividends. Preferred stock resembles fixed-income securities in that the dividend is fixed in amount and known in advance, providing a stream of income very similar to that of a bond. The difference is that the stream continues forever, unless the issue is called or otherwise retired (most preferred is callable). The price fluctuations in preferreds often exceed those in bonds.

Preferred stockholders are paid after the bondholders but before the common stockholders in terms of priority of payment of income and in case the corporation is liquidated. However, preferred stock dividends are not legally binding, but must be voted on each period by a corporation's board of directors. If the issuer fails to pay the dividend in any year, the unpaid dividend(s) will have to be paid in the future before common stock dividends can be paid if the issue is cumulative. (If noncumulative, dividends in arrears do not have to be paid.)[33]

Types of Preferred Stocks   A large amount of the total preferred outstanding is variable-rate preferred; that is, the dividend rate is tied to current market interest rates. More than one-third of the preferred stock sold in recent years is convertible into common stock at

---

[33] In the event of omitted dividends, preferred stock owners may be allowed to vote for the directors of the corporation.

the owner's option.[34] Hybrid securities combining features of preferred stock and corporate bonds are available from brokerage houses.[35] For individual investors, these securities are an alternative to corporate bonds and traditional preferred stocks.

Most of the new hybrids are traded on the NYSE, offer fixed monthly or quarterly dividends considerably higher than investment-grade corporate bond yields, are rated as to credit risk, and have maturities in the 30–49-year range. Hybrids are sensitive to interest rate changes and can be called, although a fixed dividend is paid for five years.[36]

COMMON STOCK

Common Stock An equity security representing the ownership interest in a corporation

Common stock represents the ownership interest of corporations, or the equity of the stockholders, and we can use the term *equity securities* interchangeably. If a firm's shares are held by only a few individuals, the firm is said to be "closely held." Most companies choose to "go public"; that is, they sell common stock to the general public. This action is taken primarily to enable the company to raise additional capital more easily. If a corporation meets certain requirements, it may, if it chooses to, be listed on an exchange.

As a purchaser of 100 shares of common stock, an investor owns $100/n$ percent of the corporation (where n is the number of shares of common stock outstanding). As the residual claimants of the corporation, stockholders are entitled to income remaining after the fixed-income claimants (including preferred stockholders) have been paid; also, in case of liquidation of the corporation, they are entitled to the remaining assets after all other claims (including preferred stock) are satisfied.

As owners, the holders of common stock are entitled to elect the directors of the corporation and vote on major issues.[37] Most stockholders vote by *proxy*, meaning that the stockholder authorizes someone else (typically management) to vote his or her shares.[38]

Stockholders also have *limited liability*, meaning that they cannot lose more than their investment in the corporation. In the event of financial difficulties, creditors have recourse only to the assets of the corporation, leaving the stockholders protected. This is perhaps the greatest advantage of the corporation and the reason why it has been so successful.

Characteristics of Common Stocks   The *par value* (stated or face value) for a common stock, unlike a bond or preferred stock, is generally not a significant economic variable. Corporations can make the par value any number they choose—for example, the par value of Coca-Cola is $0.25 per share. A typical par value is $1. Some corporations issue no-par stock.[39]

Book Value The accounting value of the equity as shown on the balance sheet

The **book value** of a corporation is the accounting value of the equity as shown on the books (i.e., balance sheet). It is the sum of common stock outstanding, capital in excess of par

---

[34] A recent innovation is mandatory convertible preferreds, which automatically convert to the common stock in a few years at a ratio specified at time of issuance. These mandatory convertibles pay above-market yields, for which investors give up roughly 20 percent of any upside potential.

[35] These include MIPS and QUIPS (*monthly income preferred securities* and *quarterly income preferred securities*), issued by Goldman Sachs, and TOPrS, or *trust originated preferred security*, originated by Merrill Lynch.

[36] Unlike a traditional preferred stock, hybrids can suspend dividend payments no longer than five years.

[37] The *voting rights* of the stockholders give them legal control of the corporation. In theory, the board of directors controls the management of the corporation, but in many cases the effect is the opposite. Stockholders can regain control if they are sufficiently dissatisfied.

[38] Most shareholders do not attend, often allowing management to vote their proxy. Therefore, although technically more than 50 percent of the outstanding shares are needed for control of a firm, effective control can often be exercised with considerably less, because not all of the shares are voted.

[39] With a stock split, the book value and par value of the equity are changed; for example, each would be cut in half with a two-for-one split.

value, and retained earnings. Dividing this sum, or total book value, by the number of common shares outstanding produces the *book value per share*. In effect, book value is the accounting value of the stockholders' equity. Book value per share can play a role in making investment decisions.

Example 2-8   The Coca-Cola Company reported $31.003 billion as total stockholders' equity for fiscal year-end 2010. This is the book value of the equity. Based on average shares outstanding of 2.308 billion for that year (a figure typically obtained for a company from its annual report), the book value per share was $13.43.

The market value (i.e., price) of the stock is the variable of concern to investors. The *aggregate market value* for a corporation, calculated by multiplying the market price per share of the stock by the number of shares outstanding, represents the total value of the firm as determined in the marketplace. The market value of one share of stock, of course, is simply the observed current market price.

Cash Dividends   The only cash payments regularly made by corporations *directly* to their stockholders are dividends. They are decided on and declared by the board of directors and can range from zero to virtually any amount the corporation can afford to pay (typically, up to 100 percent of present and past net earnings).

✓ The common stockholder has no specific promises to receive any cash from the corporation since the stock never matures, and dividends do not have to be paid.

Common stocks involve substantial risk, because the dividend is at the company's discretion and stock prices typically fluctuate sharply, which means that the value of investors' claims may rise and fall rapidly over relatively short periods of time.

Investment Intuition

Companies may choose to repurchase their stocks as an alternative way to affect their stockholders. In effect, cash is paid out by the company and the number of shares of its stock is reduced. Typically, companies repurchase their shares in the open market.

Note that with repurchases, companies make the decision as to when to buy their stock and affect their stockholders. With cash dividends, on the other hand, investors are in control. They can choose to reinvest in the paying company, in other companies, or use the cash elsewhere. Many companies have made poor timing decisions when repurchasing their own shares.

For example, J. P. Morgan Chase spent over $4 billion in the first seven months of 2011 repurchasing its shares, only to show a $600 million paper loss at the end of that time.

✓ Dividends are extremely important to investors. Over the last 80 plus years, 44 percent of the total return on the S&P 500 Index, a major index measuring the performance of 500 large companies, came from dividends.

The following two dividend terms are important:

Dividend Yield Dividend divided by current stock price

■ The **dividend yield** is the income component of a stock's return stated on a percentage basis. It is one of the two components of total return, discussed in Chapter 6. Dividend yield typically is calculated as the most recent 12-month dividend divided by the current market price.

Payout Ratio Dividends divided by earnings

☐ The **payout ratio** is the ratio of dividends to earnings. It indicates the percentage of a firm's earnings paid out in cash to its stockholders. The complement of the payout ratio, or $(1.0 - \text{payout ratio})$, is the *retention ratio*, and it indicates the percentage of a firm's current earnings retained by it for reinvestment purposes.

Example 2-9

Coca-Cola's 2011 earnings were $3.84 per share, and it paid an annual dividend per share that year of $1.88. Assuming a price for Coca-Cola of $67.94 (early February 2012), the dividend yield would be 2.77 percent. The payout ratio was $1.88/$3.84, or 49 percent.[40]

How Dividends Are Paid   Dividends traditionally are declared and paid quarterly, although a few firms, such as Disney, have moved to annual dividend payments. To receive a declared dividend, an investor must be a *holder of record* on the specified date that a company closes its stock transfer books and compiles the list of stockholders to be paid. However, to avoid problems the brokerage industry has established a procedure of declaring that the right to the dividend remains with the stock until four days before the holder-of-record date. On this fourth day, the right to the dividend leaves the stock; for that reason this date is called the *ex-dividend* date.

Example 2-10

Assume that the board of directors of Coca-Cola meets on May 24 and declares a quarterly dividend, payable on July 2. May 24 is called the *declaration date*. The board will declare a *holder-of-record date*—say, June 7. The books close on this date, but Coke goes *ex-dividend* on June 5. To receive this dividend, an investor must purchase the stock by June 4. The dividend will be mailed to the stockholders of record on the *payment date*, July 2.

Stock Dividend A payment by the corporation in shares of stock rather than cash

Stock Dividends and Stock Splits   Dividends other than cash, as well as splits in the stock itself, continue to attract investor attention. A **stock dividend** is a payment by the corporation in shares of stock instead of cash. A **stock split** involves the issuance of a larger number of shares in proportion to the existing shares outstanding. On a practical basis, there is little difference between a stock dividend and a stock split.[41]

Example 2-11

A 5 percent stock dividend would entitle an owner of 100 shares of a particular stock to an additional five shares. A 2-for-1 stock split would double the number of shares of the stock outstanding, double an individual owner's number of shares (e.g., from 100 shares to 200 shares), and cut the price in half at the time of the split.

Stock Split The issuance by a corporation of shares of common stock in proportion to the existing shares outstanding

The important question to investors is the value of the distribution, whether a dividend or a split. It is clear that the recipient has more shares (i.e., more pieces of paper), but has anything of real value been received? Other things being equal, these additional shares do not represent additional value, because proportional ownership has not changed. Quite simply, the pieces of

---

[40] The dividend and earnings numbers used here are as reported in *The Value Line Investment Survey*.

[41] With a stock split, the book value and par value of the equity are changed; for example, each would be cut in half with a 2-for-1 split.

paper, stock certificates, have been repackaged.[42] For example, if you own 1,000 shares of a corporation that has 100,000 shares of stock outstanding, your proportional ownership is 1 percent; with a 2-for-1 stock split, your proportional ownership is still 1 percent, because you now own 2,000 shares out of a total of 200,000 shares outstanding. If you were to sell your newly distributed shares, however, your proportional ownership would be cut in half.

P/E Ratio (Earnings Multiplier) The ratio of stock price to earnings, using historical, current or estimated data

P/E Ratio (Earnings Multiplier) The **P/E Ratio**, also referred to as the *earnings multiplier*, can be calculated as the ratio of the current market price to the firm's most recent 12-month earnings. As reported daily in newspapers, and in most other sources, it is an *identity*, because it is calculated simply by dividing the current price by the latest 12-month earnings. However, variations of this ratio are often used in the valuation of common stocks. In fact, the P/E ratio in its various forms is one of the best-known and most often cited variables in security analysis and is familiar to almost all investors.[43]

✓ Because the price of a stock, which is determined in the marketplace, is divided by its earnings, the P/E ratio shows how much the market as a whole is willing to pay per dollar of earnings.

It is standard investing practice to refer to stocks as selling at, say, 10 times earnings, or 25 times earnings. Investors have traditionally used such a classification to categorize stocks. Growth stocks, for example, typically sell at high multiples, compared to the average stock, because investors are willing to pay more for their expected higher earnings growth.

The P/E ratio is a widely reported variable, appearing in daily newspapers carrying stock information, in brokerage reports covering particular stocks, in magazine articles recommending various companies, and so forth.

Example 2-12   The price of Coca-Cola in early February 2012 was $67.94. The most recent 12-month trailing earnings per share for the company at the time was $5.44. The P/E ratio, therefore, was 12.9.

INVESTING INTERNATIONALLY IN EQUITIES

U.S. investors, like investors in many other countries, invest today in the securities of other countries as they seek higher returns, and possibly lower risks. Furthermore, changes in the value of the dollar can greatly increase interest in owning foreign securities. Such was the case in 2004 and early 2005 as the dollar continued its drop against other currencies. While U.S. investors typically choose to use investment companies—the mutual funds, closed-end funds, and exchange-traded funds—discussed in Chapter 3 to pursue international investing, they also buy individual foreign securities.

---

[42] Stock data, as reported to investors in most investment information sources and in the company's reports to stockholders, typically are adjusted for all stock dividends and stock splits. Obviously, such adjustments must be made when stock splits or stock dividends occur in order for legitimate comparisons to be made for the data.

[43] In calculating P/E ratios, on the basis of either the latest reported earnings or the expected earnings, problems can arise when comparing P/E ratios among companies if some of them are experiencing, or are expected to experience, abnormally high or low earnings. To avoid this problem, some market participants calculate a *normalized* earnings estimate. Normalized earnings are intended to reflect the "normal" level of a company's earnings; that is, transitory effects are presumably excluded, thus providing the user with a more accurate estimate of "true" earnings.

American Depository Receipts (ADRs)
Securities representing an ownership interest in the equities of foreign companies

American Depository Receipts (ADRs) A popular way to buy foreign companies is to purchase **American Depository Receipts (ADRs)**. ADRs represent indirect ownership of a specified number of shares of a foreign company. These shares are held on deposit in a bank in the issuing company's home country, and the ADRs are issued by U.S. banks called depositories. In effect, ADRs are tradable receipts issued by depositories that have physical possession of the foreign securities through their foreign correspondent banks or custodian.[44] The bank (or its correspondent) holding the securities collects the dividends, pays any applicable foreign withholding taxes, converts the remaining funds into dollars, and pays this amount to the ADR holders.[45]

ADRs are an effective way for an American investor to invest in specific foreign stocks without having to worry about currency problems, bank accounts, and brokerage issues. At the beginning of 2012 there were hundreds of ADRs listed on U.S. exchanges and markets. Examples of well-known companies that trade as ADRs include De Beers Consolidated, Toyota, Volvo, Sony, and Glaxo. The prices of ADRs are quoted in dollars, and dividends are paid in dollars. Note that while some companies in developing countries have issued ADRs, some prominent foreign companies have no ADR that trades in the United States. The only realistic alternative in this situation is to purchase portfolios of foreign securities by purchasing mutual funds, closed-end funds, or exchange-traded funds (as explained in Chapter 3) specializing in foreign securities.

Example 2-13 Petrobras, a large energy company in Brazil, has an ADR listed on the NYSE. On the other hand, Samsung, a major producer of consumer products, has no ADR traded in the United States. However, an investor could buy the South Korea exchange-traded fund which has Samsung as one of its major holdings (exchange-traded funds are explained in Chapter 3).

Checking Your Understanding

7. Why might investors opt to hold preferred stocks rather than bonds in their portfolios?
8. Distinguish between the D/P, the D/E, and the P/E.
9. Assume you wish to take advantage of an expected change in exchange rates. Would ADRs be an effective way for you to do this?

Derivative Securities

Derivative Securities
Securities that derive their value in whole or in part by having a claim on some underlying security

Warrant A corporate-created option to purchase a stated number of common shares at a specified price within a specified time (typically several years)

We will focus our attention here on the two types of derivative securities that are of interest to most investors. Options and futures contracts are **derivative securities**, so named because their value is derived from their connected underlying security. Numerous types of options and futures are traded in world markets. Furthermore, there are different types of options other than the puts and calls discussed here. For example, a **warrant** is a corporate-created long-term option on the underlying common stock of the company. It gives the holder the right to buy the stock from the company at a stated price within a stated period of time, typically several years.

Options and futures contracts share some common characteristics. Both have standardized features that allow them to be traded quickly and cheaply on organized exchanges. In

---

[44] ADRs are initiated by the depository bank, assuming the corporation does not object.

[45] The securities are to be held on deposit as long as the ADRs are outstanding. Holders can choose to convert their ADRs into the specified number of foreign shares represented by paying a fee.

addition to facilitating the trading of these securities, the exchange guarantees the performance of these contracts and its clearinghouse allows an investor to reverse his or her original position before maturity. For example, a seller of a futures contract can buy the contract and cancel the obligation that the contract carries. The exchanges and associated clearinghouses for both options and futures contracts have worked extremely well.

Options and futures contracts have important differences in their trading, the assets they can affect, their riskiness, and so forth. Perhaps the biggest difference to note now is that a futures contract is an obligation to buy or sell, but an options contract is only the right to do so, as opposed to an obligation. The buyer of an option has limited liability, but the buyer of a futures contract does not.

Options and futures contracts are important to investors because they provide a way for investors to manage portfolio risk. For example, investors may incur the risk of adverse currency fluctuations if they invest in foreign securities, or they may incur the risk that interest rates will adversely affect their fixed-income securities. Options and futures contracts can be used to limit some, or all, of these risks, thereby providing risk-control possibilities. Thus, options and futures are useful to hedgers who wish to limit price fluctuations. On the other hand, speculators can use options and futures to try to profit from price fluctuations.

OPTIONS

Options Rights to buy or sell a stated number of shares of a security within a specified period at a specified price

Puts An option to sell a specified number of shares of stock at a stated price within a specified period

Calls An option to buy a specified number of shares of stock at a stated price within a specified period

LEAPs Puts and calls with longer maturity dates, typically up to two years

In today's investing world, the word **options** refers to **puts** and **calls**. Options are created not by corporations but by investors seeking to trade in claims on a particular common stock. A call (put) option gives the buyer the right, but not the obligation, to purchase (sell) 100 shares of a particular stock at a specified price (called the exercise price) within a specified time. The maturities on most new puts and calls are available up to several months away, although one form of puts and calls called **LEAPs** has maturity dates typically up to two years. Several exercise prices are created for each underlying common stock, giving investors a choice in both the maturity and the price they will pay or receive. Equity options are available for many individual stocks, but LEAPs are available for only about 450 stocks.

Buyers of calls are betting that the price of the underlying common stock will rise, making the call option more valuable. Put buyers are betting that the price of the underlying common stock will decline, making the put option more valuable. Both put and call options are written (created) by other investors who are betting the opposite of their respective purchasers. The sellers (writers) receive an option premium for selling each new contract while the buyer pays this option premium.

Once the option is created and the writer receives the premium from the buyer, it can be traded repeatedly in the secondary market. The premium is simply the market price of the contract as determined by investors. The price will fluctuate constantly, just as the price of the underlying common stock changes. This makes sense, because the option is affected directly by the price of the stock that gives it value. In addition, the option's value is affected by the time remaining to maturity, current interest rates, the volatility of the stock, and the price at which the option can be exercised.

Using Puts and Calls Puts and calls allow both buyers and sellers (writers) to speculate on the short-term movements of certain common stocks. Buyers obtain an option on the common stock for a small, known premium, which is the maximum that the buyer can lose. If the buyer is correct about the price movements on the common, gains are magnified in relation to having bought (or sold short) the common because a smaller investment is required. However, the buyer has only a short time in which to be correct. Writers (sellers) earn the premium as income, based on their beliefs about a stock. They win or lose, depending on whether their beliefs are correct or incorrect.

Options can be used in a variety of strategies, giving investors opportunities to manage their portfolios in ways that would be unavailable in the absence of such instruments. For example, since the most a buyer of a put or call can lose is the cost of the option, the buyer is able to truncate the distribution of potential returns. That is, after a certain point, no matter how much the underlying stock price changes, the buyer's position does not change.

FUTURES CONTRACTS

Futures contracts have been available on commodities such as corn and wheat for a long time. They are also available on several financial instruments, including stock market indexes, currencies, Treasury bills, Treasury bonds, bank certificates of deposit, and GNMAs.

Futures Contract
Agreement providing for the future exchange of a particular asset at a currently determined market price

A **futures contract** is an agreement that provides for the future exchange of a particular asset between a buyer and a seller. The seller contracts to deliver the asset at a specified delivery date in exchange for a specified amount of cash from the buyer. Although the cash is not required until the delivery date, a "good faith deposit," called the margin, is required to reduce the chance of default by either party. The margin is small compared to the value of the contract.

A long position represents a commitment to purchase the asset on the delivery date, while a short position represents a commitment to deliver the asset at contract maturity. Although the words "buy" and "sell" are used in conjunction with futures contracts, these words are figurative only because a futures contract is not actually bought or sold. Instead, each party enters into the contract by mutual agreement, and no money changes hands at this time.

Most futures contracts are not exercised. Instead, they are "offset" by taking a position opposite to the one initially undertaken. For example, a purchaser of a May Treasury bill futures contract can close out the position by selling an identical May contract before the delivery date, while a seller can close out the same position by purchasing that contract.

The person holding a long position will profit from an increase in the price of the asset, while a person holding a short position will profit from a decrease. Every long position is offset by a short position; therefore, when all futures participants are taken into account, the aggregate profits must also be zero. This is what is meant when we say the futures contract is a zero-sum game.

Using Futures Contracts   Most participants in futures are either hedgers or speculators. Hedgers seek to reduce price uncertainty over some future period. For example, by purchasing a futures contract, a hedger can lock in a specific price for the asset and be protected from adverse price movements. Similarly, sellers can protect themselves from downward price movements. Speculators, on the other hand, seek to profit from the uncertainty that will occur in the future. If prices are expected to rise (fall), contracts will be purchased (sold). Correct anticipations can result in very large profits because only a small margin is required.

A Final Note

There are, of course, other financial assets that an investor could consider. Exchange-traded funds are often cited today for investors to consider. Hedge funds are often in the news. Both of these will be discussed in Chapter 3.

Summary

- Important investment alternatives for investors include nonmarketable assets, money market instruments, capital market securities (divided into fixed-income and equity securities), derivative securities, and indirect investments in the form of investment company shares.

- Nonmarketable financial assets, widely owned by investors, include savings deposits, nonnegotiable certificates of deposit, money market deposit accounts, and U.S. savings bonds.

- Money market investments, characterized as short-term, highly liquid, very safe investments, include (but are not limited to) Treasury bills, negotiable certificates of deposit (CDs), commercial paper, and banker's acceptances. The first three are obligations (IOUs) of the federal government, banks, and corporations, respectively.

- Capital market investments have maturities in excess of one year.

- Fixed-income securities, one of the two principal types of capital market securities, have a specified payment and/or repayment schedule. They include

four types of bonds: U.S. government, federal agency, municipal, and corporate bonds.

- Equity securities include preferred stock and common stock.

- Preferred stock, while technically an equity security, is often regarded by investors as a fixed-income type of security because of its stated (and fixed) dividend. Preferred has no maturity date, but may be retired by call or other means.

- Common stock (equity) represents the ownership of the corporation. The stockholder is the residual claimant in terms of both income and assets.

- Derivative securities include options and futures.

- Options allow both buyers and sellers (writers) to speculate on and/or hedge the price movements of stocks for which these claims are available. Calls (puts) are multiple-month rights to purchase (sell) a common stock at a specified price.

- Futures contracts provide for the future exchange of a particular asset between a buyer and a seller. A recent innovation is options on futures.

Questions

2-1 What is meant by "indirect" investing?

2-2 What does it mean for Treasury bills to be sold at a discount?

2-3 Distinguish between a negotiable certificate of deposit and the certificate of deposit discussed in the section "Nonmarketable Securities."

2-4 Name the four issuers of bonds discussed in this chapter. Which do you think would be most risky as a general proposition?

2-5 From an issuer standpoint, what is the distinction between Fannie Mae and Ginnie Mae?

2-6 Name and explain the difference between the two types of municipal securities.

2-7 What does it mean to say that investors in Ginnie Maes face the risk of early redemption?

2-8 What are the advantages and disadvantages of Treasury bonds?

2-9 Is there any relationship between a savings bond and a U.S. Treasury bond?

2-10 Why is preferred stock referred to as a "hybrid" security?

2-11 Why is the common stockholder referred to as a "residual claimant"?

2-12 Do all common stocks pay dividends? Who decides?

2-13 What is meant by the term *derivative security*?

2-14 What is meant by the term *securitization*?

2-15 Give at least two examples of asset-backed securities.

2-16 Why should we expect 6-month Treasury bill rates to be less than 6-month CD rates or six-month commercial paper rates?

2-17 Why is the call provision on a bond generally a disadvantage to the bondholder?

2-18 Is a typical investor more likely to hold zero coupon bonds in a taxable account or a nontaxable account? Why?

2-19 What are the potential advantages and disadvantages of DANs (Direct Access Notes) to investors compared to conventional bonds?

2-20 What is an ADR? What advantages do they offer investors?

2-21 Of what value to investors are stock dividends and splits?

2-22 What are the advantages and disadvantages of being a holder of the common stock of IBM as opposed to being a bondholder?

2-23 Assume that a company in whose stock you are interested will pay regular quarterly dividends soon. You determine that a dividend of $3.20 is indicated for this stock. The board of directors has declared the dividend payable on September 1, with a holder-of-record date of August 15. When must you buy the stock to receive this dividend, and how much will you receive if you buy 150 shares?

2-24 With regard to bond ratings, which of the following statements is INCORRECT?

  a. The first four categories represent investment grade securities.

  b. Ratings reflect the absolute probability of default.

  c. Both corporates and municipals are rated.

  d. Ratings are current opinions on the relative quality of bonds.

2-25 Preferred stocks and common stocks are similar in that

  a. both are equity securities

  b. both pay a stated and fixed dividend

  c. the expected return for each can be estimated with precision for the next period

  d. both have an equal claim on the income stream of the company

2-26 The common stockholder

  a. is guaranteed a specified dividend return

  b. is senior to (that is, ranks above) debt-holders in terms of payment

  c. takes relatively small risk in any given year

  d. can best be described as the residual claimant

2-27 Why does the Treasury bill serve as a benchmark security?

2-28 Consider a corporate bond rated AAA versus another corporate bond rated only BBB. Could you say with complete confidence that the first bond will not default, while for the second bond there is some reasonable probability of default?

2-29 Municipal bond yields are stated on an after-tax basis, while corporate bond yields are stated on a before-tax basis. Agree or disagree, and state your reasoning.

Problems

2-1 Assuming an investor is in the 25 percent tax bracket, what taxable equivalent must be earned on a security to equal a municipal bond yield of 7.5 percent?

2-2 Assume an investor is in the 15 percent tax bracket? Other things equal, after taxes are paid would this investor prefer a corporate bond paying 8 percent or a municipal bond paying 6.5 percent?

2-3 Assume an investor is in the 15 percent federal tax bracket and faces a 6 percent marginal state tax rate. What is the combined TEY for a municipal bond paying 5.5 percent?

CFA

2-4   Given the information in the first and third columns, complete the table in the second and fourth columns:

Quoted Price	Price per $1 of Par Value	Par Value	Dollar Price
98 1/6		$1,000	
102 7/8		$5,000	
109 9/16		$10,000	
86 11/32		$100,000	

CFA

2-5   For each of the following issues, indicate whether the price of the issue should be par value, above par value, or below par value:

	Issue	Coupon Rate	Yield Required by Market
a.	A	7 ¼%	7.25%
b.	B	8 3/8%	7.15%
c.	C	0%	6.20%
d.	D	5 7/8%	5.00%
e.	E	4 ½ %	4.50%

Spreadsheet Exercises

2-1   Solve for the taxable equivalent yields given the following yields on municipal bonds and marginal tax rates. Once you set up the cell correctly for the first yield in any tax rate column, you should be able to copy this cell down the column, thereby solving for all yields in that column. Note that you may want to use the absolute address for one of these cells.

a.   For an investor in the 28 percent tax bracket, what is the approximate point of indifference between a corporate bond yield and a municipal bond yielding 4.75 percent (ignore state taxes).

b.   For an investor in the 33 percent tax bracket, what must she earn on a municipal bond to be equivalent to a corporate bond yielding 9.7 percent?

Marginal tax rates					
Munc.	**0.15**	**0.25**	**0.28**	**0.33**	**0.35**
Yld.					
4					
4.25					
4.5					
4.75					
5					
5.25					
5.5					
5.75					
6					
6.25					
6.5					
6.75					
7					

2-2 Using a spreadsheet, determine what a $3,000 investment in a CD would be worth after one year if the stated interest rate is 1.5 percent and the interest is compounded monthly, quarterly, and annually.

2-3 Using the spreadsheet below, calculate the dollar dividend for each of the five companies and place your answers in the "Dividend" column. Then calculate the dividend yield and place results in the "Yield" column.

  a. Which stock had the highest dividend yield? Why do you think this is?

  b. Which stock had the highest P/E ratio?

	Price	Earnings	Payout	Dividend	Yield	P/E
Microsoft	28.95	2.00	0.38			
Verizon	38.26	2.2	0.75			
Duke Energy	21.07	1.38	0.70			
Wells Fargo	35.18	3.02	0.23			
Pfizer	21.97	1.3	0.55			

Checking Your Understanding

2-1 Money market securities can be sold in financial markets, where neither the buyer or seller is identified to each other. Nonmarketable financial assets must be handled by the owner of the asset.

2-2 You should expect the yields on money market securities to be within a few tenths of a percent of each other because they are very short-term, very high quality assets with little risk of default.

2-3 The Treasury bill is the benchmark security for the economy because bills are auctioned off every week, and the rates offered on them reflect current demand and supply conditions for short-term funds without credit risk. Other interest rates are scaled up from this short-term, riskless rate by adding time and risk premiums.

2-4 No, because bond ratings are a measure of the relative probability of default. There is some absolute probability, although it is extremely small, that an AAA bond will default.

2-5 Agree. Municipal bond yields must be adjusted to a before-tax basis to make them comparable to corporate bond yields. This is done by calculating the TEY.

2-6 Risk-averse investors can buy junk bonds, or any financial asset, if they expect to be adequately compensated for the risk. The greater the risk, the greater the expected return should be.

2-7 Preferred stocks could have higher expected returns and have no maturity date. Also, preferred stocks can be much easier to buy and sell than individual bonds.

2-8 D/P is the dividend yield, dividend divided by current price; D/E is the payout ratio, dividends divided by earnings. The P/E is price divided by earnings and indicates the multiple of earnings that investors pay for a stock.

2-9 No. ADRs do not involve foreign currencies, but rather are stated on a dollar basis.

chapter 3

Indirect Investing: A Global Activity

As you consider your investing alternatives, given your inheritance, you decide to seriously consider mutual funds and Exchange Traded Funds (ETFs) as a significant part of your strategy. Why? Like many people, you hear a lot about them because they are so widely owned by individual investors. Furthermore, the financial press is continually touting how well one or more funds did last quarter or last year. Some of your family or friends own mutual funds and/or ETFs and have been pleased with them. Moreover, you understand that investing in funds will relieve you of the day-to-day investment decision making that you would otherwise be faced with. So, what's the catch? If mutual funds and ETFs have all these pluses, why don't most people opt for them and minimize or even forego direct investing altogether? It's a good question, and one you decide you need an answer to.

Like many others, you have been hearing a lot lately about ETFs, and you feel that you need to learn about them. They are currently viewed as an increasingly popular alternative to mutual funds, and you do not want to be left out. Finally, in order to impress your friends with your knowledge, you want to know at least a little about hedge funds, which are frequently in the news these days.

As we will see, you can make a strong case for using index (passive) mutual funds and/or ETFs as your complete portfolio, saving the cost of a financial advisor as well as the cost of actively managed mutual funds. On a $1 million portfolio, such savings could easily amount to $20,000 or more. Could you use a windfall of $20,000 per year you were not expecting? Nah, probably not.

Chapter 2 was primarily concerned with direct investing, meaning investors make decisions to buy various securities, typically in a brokerage account, and eventually sell them. The investor makes the decisions and controls the actions involving the investments. Chapter 3, in contrast, discusses the very important alternative of indirect investing used by many investors—buying and selling mutual funds, closed-end funds, and ETFs.

The key point about indirect investing is that the investor turns his or her money over to one of these types of funds, thereby relinquishing direct control of the securities in the portfolio. In contrast, an investor with a portfolio of 10 stocks in his or her brokerage account can decide exactly how long to hold each one before selling, when to realize capital losses for tax purposes, or what to do with any dividends generated by the portfolio, as examples.

Investing Indirectly

Indirect investing in this discussion refers to the buying and selling of the shares of investment companies that, in turn, hold portfolios of securities.

Rather than buy and sell securities themselves, investors can purchase some type of investment company fund which then relieves them from making decisions about that portfolio. As shareholders with an ownership interest in that portfolio, they are entitled to their pro rata share of the dividends, interest, and capital gains generated, and they pay their pro rata share of the company's expenses and its management fee.

Figure 3-1

Direct versus Indirect Investing.

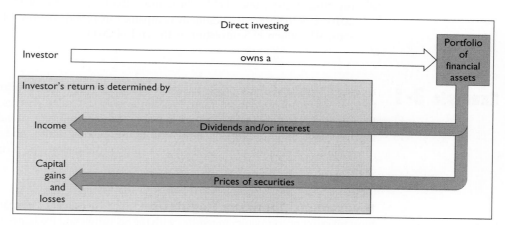

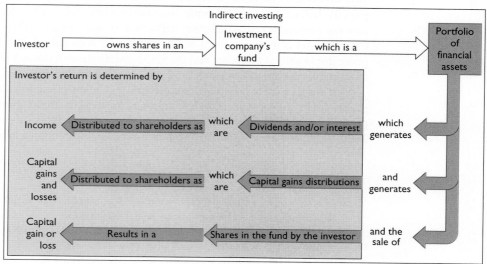

The contrast between direct and indirect investing is illustrated in Figure 3-1 using investment companies, which shows that indirect investing essentially accomplishes the same thing as direct investing. The primary difference is that the investment company stands between the investors and the portfolio of securities.

What is an Investment Company?

Investment Company A company engaged primarily in the business of investing in, and managing, a portfolio of securities

In general, an **investment company** is a company that is engaged primarily in the business of investing in, and managing, a portfolio of securities.[1] By pooling the funds of thousands of investors, an investment company can offer its owners (shareholders) a portfolio with a specific objective as well as offer them a variety of services in addition to diversification, including professional management and liquidity.

HOW IMPORTANT ARE INVESTMENT COMPANIES TO INVESTORS?

Registered investment companies manage almost a quarter of households' financial assets. Households are the largest group of investors in funds offered by investment companies.

✓   Investment companies held a little more than one-fourth of U.S. corporate equities in 2010. U.S. registered investment companies managed roughly \$12 trillion in assets for some 91 million U.S. investors at the end of 2011.[2]

Example 3-1

Fidelity Investments traditionally has been one of the very largest investment companies in the United States, offering more than 175 funds with no sales charges to investors. Fidelity Investments is the fund company, or sponsor, of these multitude of individual mutual funds. Fidelity offers among its many funds the Equity-Income Fund, and we will use this fund throughout the chapter to illustrate mutual funds (the major type of investment company).

Investment Company Regulation   The Investment Company Act of l940 requires most investment companies to register with the Securities and Exchange Commission (SEC), the primary federal agency regulating investment companies. This detailed regulatory statute contains numerous provisions designed to protect shareholders.[3] (The SEC and the Investment Company Act of 1940 are discussed in Chapter 5.) Both federal and state laws require appropriate disclosures to investors, and the SEC's major role with this Act is to ensure full disclosure of fund information to investors, both prospective investors and current shareholders.[4]

It is important to note that despite federal regulation, *investment companies are not insured or guaranteed by any government agency*, or by any financial institution from which an investor may obtain shares. These are risky investments—losses to investors can and do occur (such as in 2000–2002 and 2008)—and investment companies' promotional materials state this clearly.

---

[1] It can be a corporation, a business trust, a partnership, or a limited liability company.

[2] *2011 Fact Book*, Investment Company Institute, various pages.

[3] Investment companies are also regulated under the Securities Acts of 1933, the Securities Exchange Act of 1934, and the Investment Advisers Act of 1940. These acts are discussed in Chapter 5.

[4] Most states also regulate investment companies selling shares within the state.

Investment Company Taxation Most regulated investment companies pass on their earnings each year in the form of dividends, interest, and realized capital gains to their shareholders.[5] The investment company acts as a conduit, "flowing through" these distributions to stockholders who pay their own marginal tax rates on them.[6] In effect, fund shareholders are treated as if they personally held the securities in the fund's portfolio and therefore pay the same taxes they would pay if they owned the securities directly.[7]

✓ Note that a fund's shareholders are responsible each year for paying taxes on the distributions they receive from an investment company whether they receive the distributions in cash or have them reinvested in additional shares.[8]

Organizational Structures for Investment Companies Technically, there are four distinct types of investment company: the UIT (unit investment trust), the ETF (exchange traded fund), the closed-end fund, and the mutual fund (open-end fund). However, because of the (relatively) tiny amount of assets held by UITs, we essentially ignore them in our discussion and discuss the other three, but with emphasis on mutual funds and ETFs, because closed-end funds are much less important than the other two types.[9]

Three Major Types of Investment Companies

We begin our discussion with the oldest form of investment company, the closed-end company, and then contrast it with the newest form of investment company, the exchange traded fund. However, we focus in detail on the third type of investment company, mutual funds, by far the most popular of the three for the typical individual investor. The reason for emphasizing mutual funds when discussing types of investment companies is evident from Table 3-1, which shows the assets of each of the three major types of investment companies. Mutual funds totally dominate the investment company industry in terms of assets held, *and there is no remotely close second*. The attention spent on mutual funds in this chapter is justified by their dominance in terms of both number of funds and assets held, although we must also take note of the rise of the ETFs.

✓ Traditionally, mutual funds have served as the core investment asset for millions of Americans, and despite new products and technologies, they will continue to do so for the indefinite future.

---

[5] To qualify as a regulated investment company, a fund must earn at least 90 percent of all income from security transactions and distribute at least 90 percent of its investment company taxable income each year. Furthermore, the fund must diversify its assets. For at least 50 percent of the portfolio, no more than 5 percent of the fund's assets can be invested in the securities of any one issuer, and a position in any one security cannot exceed 25 percent of the fund's assets.

[6] Investment companies pay taxes only on annual earnings retained and not paid out to shareholders.

[7] A fund's short-term gains and other earnings are taxed to shareholders as ordinary income, while its long-term capital gains are taxed to shareholders as long-term capital gains. Tax-exempt income received by a fund is generally tax-exempt to the shareholder.

[8] Note that for investors who choose to receive their distributions in additional shares, their basis (cost of shares) changes over time. Therefore, when they sell their shares, they typically will have a smaller capital gain than otherwise because their basis (cost) will have risen over time.

[9] The typical unit investment trust is an unmanaged portfolio of tax-exempt securities put together by a sponsor and handled by an independent trustee. All interest (or dividends) and principal repayments are distributed to the holders of the certificates. The assets are almost always kept unchanged, and the trust ceases to exist when the bonds mature.

In general, unit investment trusts are designed to be bought and held, with capital preservation as a major objective. They provide investors with diversification, professional management, and minimum operating costs. If conditions change, however, investors lose the ability to make rapid, inexpensive, or costless changes in their positions.

Table 3-1 Assets for Each of the Three Major Types of Investment Company as of January 1, 2012

Mutual Funds	$11.6 trillion
Closed End Funds	237 billion
Exchange Traded Funds	1.05 trillion

CLOSED-END INVESTMENT COMPANIES

Closed-End Investment Company An investment company with a fixed capitalization whose shares trade on exchanges and OTC

The oldest form of the three major types of investment companies, a **closed-end investment company** offers investors an actively managed portfolio of securities. A fixed number of shares of a closed-end fund trade on a stock exchange exactly like any other stock.[10] To buy and sell, investors use their brokerage firms, paying (receiving) the current price at which the shares are selling plus (less) brokerage commissions.

✓ Because shares of closed-end funds trade on stock exchanges, their prices are determined by investors.

Closed-end funds were a popular investment before the great stock market crash of 1929, and then lost favor with investors for many years.[11] There are approximately 625 closed-end stock and bond funds that trade daily. Total assets were only $237 billion in 2011, with municipal bond funds accounting for more than half of all closed-end funds.

EXCHANGE TRADED FUNDS (ETFs)

Exchange Traded Fund (ETF) Generally an index fund priced and traded on exchanges like any share of stock

The newest form of the three major types of investment companies is the **Exchange Traded Fund (ETF)**, which began trading in 1993. The typical ETF is a basket of stocks that tracks a particular sector, investment style, geographical area, or the market as a whole. From their inception until 2008, ETFs were passive (unmanaged) portfolios that simply held a basket of stocks. Starting in 2008, some actively managed ETFs are available.[12]

✓ ETFs are typically unmanaged portfolios that offer investors equity indexes ranging from a broad market index such as the S&P 500 to targeted indexes such as energy stocks or Chinese stocks. There are also bond ETFs, currency ETFs, sector and industry ETFs, commodity ETFs, and foreign market ETFs. And there are managed portfolios.

Like closed-end funds, ETFs trade on exchanges like individual stocks. Therefore, they can be bought on margin, and sold short (both concepts are explained in Chapter 5) anytime the exchanges are open. Like open-end funds, ETF shares are created and extinguished in response to the demand for them.[13] Because ETF portfolios are typically unmanaged portfolios, they have much lower annual expense ratios than actively managed mutual funds.

---

[10] Its capitalization (the number of fund shares outstanding) is fixed unless a new public offering is made.

[11] The first closed-end fund in the United States was started in 1893, and the number of these funds grew rapidly prior to the great market crash of 1929.

[12] Invesco PowerShares is one example of a group of actively managed ETFs.

[13] A brokerage firm can put together a basket of the stocks in a particular ETF and turn them in to the ETF sponsor, receiving ETF shares in exchange.

Well-Known ETFs   Let's consider some equity ETFs. Most ETFs have three letters as their ticker symbol (used to obtain quotes and place orders), and some have popular "nicknames." Probably the best-known ETF is the "Spider" (Standard & Poor's Depositary Receipts), introduced in 1993 to track the S&P 500 Index. Other ETFs include "Diamonds" (the DJIA), "Cubes" (NASDAQ-100 Index Tracking Stock), and "iShares" (S&P 500 as well as other S&P indexes for small cap, mid-cap, and growth and value indexes, various Russell Indexes, various Dow Jones Sector funds, and various country funds). Vanguard, one of the largest investment companies, has created multiple ETFs to track the entire stock market as well as various segments of both domestic and foreign markets.

Example 3-2   One of Vanguard's ETFs, Vanguard Total Stock Market ETF, seeks to provide long-term growth of capital and income by investing in more than 3,000 stocks representative of the entire U.S. market. These shares carry a 0.07 percent expense ratio.

Some Practical Advice

On the Trail of the ETFs

Given the popularity of ETFs, numerous informational sources are available. A few examples will be mentioned, but there are many more. An ETF center can be found at finance.yahoo.com. Invesco Power-Shares features more than 120 domestic and international ETFs. PowerShares seek to outperform traditional benchmark indexes with a wide range of focused ETFs (www.invescopowershares.com). Morningstar has an entire section devoted to ETFs at its website, www.morningstar.com. A large amount of information about ETFs can be found at etf.about.com.

ETF Tax Efficiency   A particularly appealing feature of ETFs to investors is their tax efficiency. Many ETFs report little or no capital gains over the years. Shareholders in mutual funds, in contrast, have no control over the amount of distributions their fund may make in a given year. In 2007, for example, many mutual funds made large capital gains distributions to shareholders based on performance results from prior years. In 2008, their shareholders faced large tax bills (for the tax year 2007) while watching the shares of their funds decline as the stock market sharply declined.[14] Note, however, that capital gains distributions can occur with ETFs. Also, ETFs holding the shares of companies that pay dividends or interest make distributions to their shareholders. Regardless of these exceptions, in general ETFs are highly tax-efficient and are now appreciated more and more by investors for this reason.

ETF Growth Trends   Until Summer 2002, all ETFs involved equity securities. Currently, ETFs are available covering various bond segments as well as currencies, gold and other commodities. As of year-end 2011, there were approximately 1,130 ETFs, with approximately $1 trillion in assets. Although this is small compared to the assets in mutual funds, the growth rate in assets for ETFs has been very rapid, as more and more investors discover the advantages that ETFs can offer them.

---

[14] The same thing happened in 2001, based on large distributions for the tax year 2000. Taxpayers faced large tax bills for capital gains distributions even as the value of their fund shares was declining.

✓ ETFs are serious competition for mutual funds despite their much smaller amount of aggregate assets, and are expected to continue their rapid growth both in the number of funds and in assets held.

Investments Intuition

Given the rapid growth in the number of ETFs, and the narrow specialization that many pursue, it may come as no surprise to realize that a number of these funds may go out of business. Although there is no precise number, it is believed that funds with assets of less than $50 million may not be profitable to operate. In one recent year slightly less than half of all ETFs and ETNs had assets less than $50 million. To dissolve itself, a fund can liquidate and return money to shareholders at net asset value. Alternatively, it can merge with another fund.

MUTUAL FUNDS (OPEN-END INVESTMENT COMPANIES)

The following facts about mutual funds illustrate their importance to investors:

- Approximately 52 million U.S. households own mutual funds.
- More than two in five households in the United States own mutual funds.
- In 1990, mutual funds comprised roughly 7 percent of the total financial assets held by households. By 1996, this had grown to 13 percent; by the beginning of 2012, it was about 23 percent.
- Mutual funds owned approximately 29 percent of U.S. stocks at the end of 2011, and since they are simply intermediaries between households and equities, this represents a significant household investment in equities.
- One-third of U.S. households hold mutual funds in employer-sponsored retirement plans.
- The 401(k) plan is a popular type of defined-contribution (DC) plan, and mutual funds managed more than half of the assets in 401(k) and DC plans in 2011.
- Mutual funds managed about 45 percent of the total assets in IRAs in 2011.

Clearly, the fact that so many people have chosen to invest using mutual funds, documents their overall importance when it comes to indirect investing.

The potential benefits of mutual funds to investors are illustrated in Figure 3-2.

Diversification may be the most important reason for buying a typical mutual fund. As we will see in Chapter 7, diversification of your portfolio is the one rule of portfolio management. Many investors cannot build a diversified portfolio on their own because of the amount of money involved to do so. Most mutual funds provide instant diversification.

Mutual funds provide professional managers to handle the portfolios. It seems logical that they should be able to do a good job since that is their full time focus. Whether in fact active managers perform all that well will be considered later.

Convenience refers to the fact that the investor does not have to do the analysis and work involved in managing the portfolio. The investor is, in effect, hiring someone to do this, thereby saving the investor a lot of time and effort.

Mutual funds provide a number of services, including in some cases check-writing on the account, record keeping, preparing information for tax purposes, wiring money as directed by the investor, serving as the fiduciary for retirement accounts, and so forth. They strive to serve their shareholders.

The cost involved can span a range, but in general buying a mutual funds with no sales charge, and paying a low annual expense fee for having the fund managed, is cost-effective.

Figure 3-2

Possible Benefits to Investors of Owning a Mutual Fund.

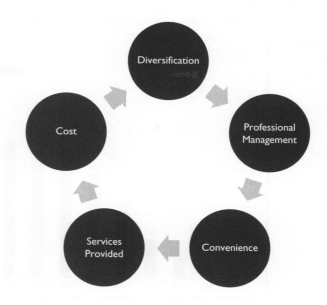

Open-End Investment Company An investment company whose capitalization constantly changes as new shares are sold and outstanding shares are redeemed

Defining a Mutual Fund Technically, a mutual fund is an **open-end investment company**, the most familiar type of investment company. Unlike closed-end funds and ETFs, mutual funds do not trade on stock exchanges. Investors buy mutual funds shares from investment companies, and sell their shares back to the companies.

Example 3-3

As stated in its prospectus (which is designed to describe a particular fund's objectives, policies, operations, and fees), "Equity-Income is a mutual fund: an investment that pools shareholders' money and invests it toward a specified goal. . . . The fund is governed by a Board of Trustees, which is responsible for protecting the interests of shareholders. . . . The fund is managed by FMR, which chooses the fund's investments and handles its business affairs."

✓ The number of shares outstanding of an open-end investment company (mutual fund) is continually changing—that is, it is open-ended—as new investors buy additional shares from the company and some existing shareholders cash in by selling their shares back to the company. Thus, the fund's capitalization is said to be open-ended.

Multiple Funds Managed by One Company Individual investment companies are often referred to as "fund complexes" or "fund families" because one company manages multiple funds. Well-known fund families (complexes) include Fidelity, Vanguard, T. Rowe Price, American Funds, Janus, and Dreyfus. At the beginning of 2012, the top 10 complexes controlled 53 percent of industry assets, while the largest 25 fund complexes controlled three-fourths of fund assets. There were approximately 600 fund complexes.

Given the economies of scale in managing portfolios, expenses rise as assets under management increase, but revenues rise more quickly. Investment companies seek to increase the size of the fund(s) being managed as well as operate several different funds simultaneously. The name of the game in the investment company industry is to get more assets under management. Why?

Figure 3-3

Assets of Mutual Funds for Selected Years.

SOURCE: Investment Company Institute, *2012 Investment Company Fact Book.*

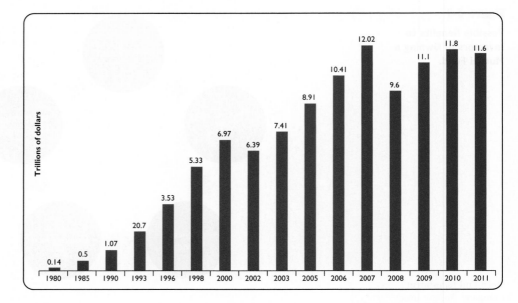

✓ Investment companies are compensated as a percentage of assets under management. The more assets being managed, the more money the companies make. Therefore, companies strive to gain investors.

The Growth in Mutual Funds   The growth in the number of mutual funds and the assets they hold is an incredible story. The number of mutual funds has grown rapidly in recent years. In 1980, there were 564 funds; at the beginning of 1997, there were approximately 7,000 funds, and in January 2012, there were approximately 7,600 domestic funds. The reasons for this great growth include investor demand for funds and low barriers to entry into the business. Consider this fact: More than 80 percent of all equity and hybrid funds, and 60 percent of all bond funds, were started after 1991.

Asset growth has also been dramatic, as shown in Figure 3-3. Assets of mutual funds were relatively small for many years, but exploded in the 1990s. Total assets of mutual funds first exceeded $1 trillion in 1990, were almost $9 trillion in 2005, and were approximately $11.6 trillion at the end of 2011. Most of today's mutual funds were created after 1991.

✓ As of early 2012, there were approximately 7,600 distinct domestic mutual funds with assets of approximately $11.6 trillion.[15]

Keep in mind that mutual funds can disappear. This is accomplished by merging a fund with another fund within the same company. It is typically done for poorly performing funds—the fund, and its record of bad performance, disappear forever. Between 2001 and 2007, almost 1,550 mutual funds were merged out of existence.

Checking Your Understanding

1. ETFs and closed-end funds both trade on exchanges. Why, then, are ETFs having a big negative impact on closed-end funds?
2. Why do you think mutual funds are by far the most popular type of investment company with investors as measured by assets under management?

---

[15] This does not count those mutual funds with different share classes, such as A, B, and C shares.

Types of Mutual Funds

Figure 3-4 shows the general range of mutual funds arrayed along a return-risk spectrum. As we can see, money market funds are on the lower end, and bond funds and balanced funds (which hold both bonds and stocks) are in the middle. Stock funds are on the upper-end of the risk-return spectrum.

There are four basic types of mutual funds:

- ❑ Money market mutual funds
- ❑ Equity (also called stock) funds
- ❑ Bond funds
- ❑ Hybrid or balanced funds (hold a combination of stocks and bonds)

These types of funds parallel our discussion in Chapter 2 of money markets and capital markets. Money market funds concentrate on short-term investing by holding portfolios of money market assets, whereas equity funds, bond funds, and hybrid funds concentrate on longer term investing by holding mostly capital market assets. We will discuss money market funds first, and then consider the other three types together.

The distribution of total mutual fund assets among these four basic types is shown in Figure 3-5.

Figure 3-4

Types of Mutual Funds Based on the Potential Risk-Reward Spectrum.

SOURCE: Adapted Loosely from the Vanguard Web Site.

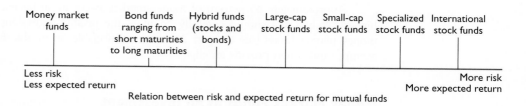

Figure 3-5

Percentage of Mutual Fund Assets by Type of Mutual Fund, 2010.

SOURCE: Investment Company Institute, *2011 Investment Company Fact Book*

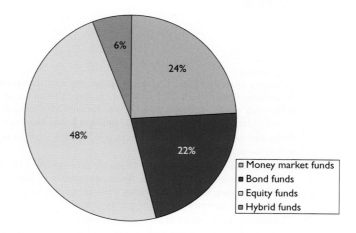

✓   Of the roughly $11.6 trillion mutual fund assets at the beginning of 2012, about half was invested in equity funds, and about a quarter was in money market funds. This asset distribution among types of funds is fairly typical.[16]

MONEY MARKET FUNDS

Money Market Funds (MMFs) are open-end investment companies whose portfolios consist of money market instruments. Created in 1974, by the beginning of 2012 money market mutual fund assets approximated $2.7 trillion.

> **Money Market Funds (MMFs)** A mutual fund that invests in money market instruments

- Investors in money market funds pay neither a sales charge nor a redemption charge, but they do pay a management fee (unless temporarily waived to attract business).
- The average maturity of money market portfolios ranges from approximately one month to two months. SEC regulations limit the maximum average maturity of money funds to 90 days.
- Interest is earned and credited daily.
- The shares can be redeemed at any time by phone or wire.
- The shares of money market funds are held constant at $1.00; therefore, there are no capital gains or losses on money market shares under normal circumstances.
- Many funds offer check-writing privileges for checks of $250 or more, with the investor earning interest until the check clears.[17]

Approximately 85 percent of money market assets are in taxable funds.[18] Investors in higher tax brackets should carefully compare the taxable equivalent yield on tax-exempt money market funds (see Chapter 2) with that available on taxable funds because the tax-exempt funds often provide an edge.[19]

Money Market Funds as an Investment   Money market funds (MMFs) provide investors with a chance to earn the going rates in the money market while enjoying broad diversification and great liquidity. These rates have varied widely as market conditions changed. The important point is that their yields quickly correspond to current market conditions.

---

[16] However, the asset composition changes depending on market/economy conditions. For example, at the beginning of 2009 total mutual fund assets had declined to about $9.4 billion because of the financial crisis and the sharp decline in the stock market. Equity funds accounted for only 37 percent of assets at the time, while money market funds accounted for about 41 percent. Hybrid funds and bond funds made up the remaining 22 percent of assets.

[17] Shareholders have made only limited use of the check-writing privilege, however, indicating that they regard money market funds primarily as a way to save.

[18] Taxable funds hold assets such as Treasury bills, negotiable CDs, and prime commercial paper. Some funds hold only bills, whereas others hold various mixtures. Commercial paper typically accounts for 40–50 percent of the total assets held by these funds, with Treasury bills, government agency securities, domestic and foreign bank obligations, and repurchase agreements rounding out the portfolios.

[19] Tax-exempt funds consist of *national* funds which invest in short-term municipal securities of various issuers, and *state tax-exempt money market funds*, which invest only in the issues of a single state, thereby providing additional tax benefits.

Although investors may assume little risk because of the diversification and quality of these instruments, money market funds are not insured. Banks and thrift institutions have emphasized this point in competing with money market funds for the savings of investors.[20] A money market fund is not insured or guaranteed by the FDIC or any other government agency. However, money market funds must invest in fixed income securities with very short maturities, thereby constantly rolling over their holdings.

✓ By convention, money market funds attempt to always maintain a $1 per share price; however, this is not guaranteed and a loss is possible.

In 2008 the oldest money market fund in the United States, Reserve Primary, saw its shares go below $1 because it held some debt of an investment bank, Lehman Brothers, which failed.

EQUITY FUNDS, BOND FUNDS, AND HYBRID FUNDS

Simply stated, equity funds hold primarily stocks, bond funds hold bonds, and *hybrid funds* hold some combination of the two. Within these three broad categories, however, a mutual fund's objectives can vary widely. It is important to consider a fund's stated objectives.

Mutual Fund Objectives The board of directors (trustees) of an investment company must specify the objective that the company will pursue in its investment policy. The companies try to follow a consistent investment policy, according to their specified objective. Investors should be able to count on mutual funds to pursue their stated objectives.

Example 3-4 "Equity-Income seeks reasonable income by investing mainly in income-producing equity securities. In selecting investments, the fund also considers the potential for capital appreciation."

Exhibit 3-1 shows some major categories of investment objectives, most of which are for equity and bond funds. There are two categories for money market funds.[21] Of course, funds within one of these categories, such as capital appreciation funds, may hold quite different securities.

---

[20] Investors searching for safe assets in which to invest got a shock in 2007–2008 when the auction-rate securities market froze up, leaving investors stranded. These securities were touted as cash equivalents but failed as a marketable security.

[21] Current statistics and useful information about investment companies can be found at the Institute's website http://www.ici.org/.

EXHIBIT 3-1

Mutual Fund Investment Objectives

The Investment Company Institute has categorized U.S. mutual funds according to 13 broad investment classifications.

EQUITY FUNDS

- **Capital appreciation funds** seek capital appreciation; dividends are not a primary consideration.
- **Total return funds** seek a combination of current income and capital appreciation.
- **World equity funds** invest primarily in stocks of foreign companies.

HYBRID FUNDS

- **Hybrid funds** may invest in a mix of equity and fixed-income securities.

TAXABLE BOND FUNDS

- **Corporate bond funds** seek current income by investing in high-quality debt securities issued by U.S. corporations.
- **High-yield funds** invest two-thirds or more of their portfolios in lower-rated U.S. corporate bonds (Baa or lower by Moody's and BBB or lower by Standard and Poor's rating services).
- **Government bond funds** invest in U.S. government bonds of varying maturities. They seek high current income.
- **Strategic income funds** invest in a combination of U.S. fixed-income securities to provide a high level of current income.
- **World bond funds** invest in debt securities offered by foreign companies and governments. They seek the highest level of current income available worldwide.

TAX-EXEMPT BOND FUNDS

- **National municipal bond funds** invest primarily in the bonds of various municipal issuers in the United States. These funds seek high current income free from federal tax.
- **State municipal bond funds** invest primarily in municipal bonds issued by a particular state. These funds seek high after-tax income for residents of individual states.

MONEY MARKET FUNDS

- **Taxable money market funds** invest in short-term, high-grade money market securities and must have average maturities of 90 days or less. These funds seek the highest level of income consistent with preservation of capital (i.e., maintaining a stable share price).
- **Tax-exempt money market funds** invest in short-term municipal securities and must have average maturities of 90 days or less. These funds seek the highest level of income—free from federal and, in some cases, state and local taxes—consistent with preservation of capital.

SOURCE: *2004 Mutual Fund Fact Book*, Copyright © 2004 by the Investment Company Institute (www.ici.org). Reprinted with permission.

Some believe it is important to describe a fund's *investment style* and actual portfolio holdings rather than state that the fund is seeking "capital appreciation (as one example)," which could be accomplished in several different ways. Morningstar, Inc., a well-known Chicago mutual fund research firm, pioneered a nine-cell matrix to describe a fund's investing style. For equity funds, for example, the style box uses the categories "large-cap," "mid-cap," "small-cap," "value," "blend," and "growth" to describe investment styles.[22] A red dot called a "fund centroid" represents a weighted average of the domestic stock holdings.

[22] "Cap" refers to capitalization, or market value for a company, calculated as the price of the stock times the total number of shares outstanding. A mutual fund that invests in stocks with a median market cap of $5 billion or more would be considered to be a large-cap fund, while a small-cap fund is one with a median market cap of $1 billion or less.

Exhibit 3-2 shows the investment style for Equity-Income Fund as shown in their prospectus, and as supplied by *Morningstar*. This fund concentrates on large-cap stocks using a value approach.[23]

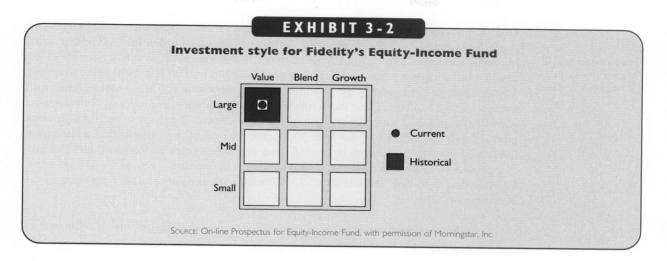

EXHIBIT 3-2

Investment style for Fidelity's Equity-Income Fund

SOURCE: On-line Prospectus for Equity-Income Fund, with permission of Morningstar, Inc.

Value Funds vs. Growth Funds   Many equity funds can be divided into two categories based on their approach to selecting stocks, *value funds* and *growth funds*.

- A value fund generally seeks to find stocks that are cheap on the basis of standard fundamental analysis yardsticks, such as earnings, book value, and dividend yield.
- Growth funds, on the other hand, seek to find companies that are expected to show rapid future growth in earnings, even if current earnings are poor or, possibly, nonexistent.

Value funds and growth funds tend to perform well at different times because value stocks and growth stocks perform well at different times, each having its own cycle. Therefore, value fund investors will have a run when they do well, and growth fund investors will have similar runs.

Example 3-5   In the late 1990s growth funds had a big run. With the strong emphasis on dot.coms and technology stocks, value funds performed poorly. Some growth funds had triple-digit returns, and some value managers quit the business. The situation reversed in 2000, however, with the average equity value fund gaining almost 10 percent for the year while the average growth fund lost almost 12 percent. Value funds outperformed growth funds during the bear market of 2000–2002 by a wide margin.

---

[23] Lipper Inc., an alternative provider of investment company information, announced a new classification system for U.S. diversified equity mutual funds, effective mid-1999, to replace its "General Equity Investment Objectives." Funds are assigned to one of five investment objectives: aggressive equity, growth equity, general equity, value equity, and income equity. The market capitalization of the funds is also recognized—for example, large-cap funds—and a special size category, flexible-cap range, was created for the roughly 1,500 funds that do not fit regularly into size categories. Lipper indexes for mutual fund categories are carried daily in *The Wall Street Journal*.

A more risk-averse investor worrying about a market decline may wish to emphasize value funds, while more aggressive investors seeking good performance in an expected market rise would probably favor growth funds. Given the evidence on efficient markets discussed in Chapter 12, the best strategy is probably to buy both types of funds.

Index Funds   Mutual funds designed to replicate a market index such as the Standard & Poor's 500 Composite Index (explained in Chapter 4) are called **index funds**. The first index fund was started in 1976 by John Bogle (former CEO of Vanguard), and it is now one of the largest mutual funds in terms of assets—Vanguard's 500 Index Fund. In 1990, there were only 15 index mutual funds, and by the beginning of 2012 there were 365 index mutual funds with assets totaling $1 trillion. These index funds covered a wide variety of indexes, both domestic and international, and both debt and equity. However, almost 40 percent of the assets in index mutual funds are indexed to the S&P 500 Index. The majority of index fund assets are in funds sold directly to investors by mutual fund companies (such as Vanguard and Fidelity) as opposed to being sold indirectly through financial advisors such as brokerage firms. Equity index funds now account for about 15 percent of all equity mutual fund assets at the beginning of 2012.

Index Funds Mutual funds holding a bond or stock portfolio designed to match a particular market index

✓ An index fund is an *unmanaged* portfolio of securities designed to match some market index; it typically has a low expense ratio.

Index funds have lower expenses because they are "unmanaged" funds seeking only to duplicate the chosen index. While the typical actively managed equity traditional has operating expenses of approximately 1.5 percent of assets annually, the typical index fund has expenses of only 0.56 percent, and Vanguard's 500 Index Admiral fund has an amazingly low expense rate of 0.05 percent.

How have index funds fared in recent years? Over a recent 20-year period, the average actively managed large-cap fund realized 1.7 percentage points less than the S&P 500 Index on an annual basis. Therefore, S&P 500 index funds outperformed these actively managed funds. Of the actively managed funds in operation since 1976 when the first index fund was created, only one in four has managed to outperform Vanguard's 500 Index Fund.

Some Practical Advice

Investors buying mutual funds have several sources from which to choose, and therein lies the danger. For example, one study found that mutual funds run by insurance companies underperform other funds. On average, shareholders fell behind by 1.5 percentage points a year.[24]

Investors can buy no-load funds from the companies themselves, or buy through a broker. Half of all investment in mutual funds is made through brokers. However, a recent study finds that "[f]unds sold by brokers underperform those sold through the direct channel."[25] Investors in one recent year paid some $15 billion in sales charges and distribution fees alone (management fees were $24 billion).

There are numerous index funds today, and expenses vary widely. Investors need to do due diligence when selecting an index fund to be sure that the expenses are reasonable. After all, if the Vanguard fund can match the S&P 500 Index with an expense ratio of 0.05 percent, why pay 0.50 percent,

---

[24] Tong Yao, Xuanjuan Chen and Tong Yu, "Prudent Man or Agency Problem? On the Performance of Mutual Funds," *Journal of Financial Intermediation,* 86, 3, 2007, pp. 175–203.

[25] Daniel Bergstresser, Peter Tufano, and John Chalmers, "Assessing the Costs and Benefits of Brokers in the Mutual Fund Industry," Social Science Research Network, October 1, 2007.

or 0.70 percent, to do the same thing? In fact, excluding Vanguard, the average S&P 500 index fund charges 0.82 percent. Furthermore, total costs for index funds can be amazingly large. For example, one well-known S&P 500 Index Fund has an expense ratio of 0.60 and also charges a 5.25 percent load charge.

To accomplish the same thing as Vanguard's S&P 500 Index Fund, why would you give up 5.25 percent of your money off the top, and pay an annual expense ratio 12 times as large Vanguard's?

Bottom line: Investors should think carefully about where and how they buy their mutual funds.

Checking Your Understanding

3. Why are money market funds the safest type of mutual fund an investor can hold?
4. Why might investors prefer a hybrid fund to either a stock fund or a bond fund?
5. Why is it reasonable to expect growth funds and value funds to perform well over different periods of time?

The Net Asset Value Per Share

Net Asset Value (NAV) The per share value of the securities in an investment company's portfolio

The **Net Asset Value (NAV)** is the per share value of the securities in the fund's portfolio. It is computed daily after the markets close at 4 p.m. by calculating the total market value of the securities in the portfolio, subtracting any liabilities, and dividing by the number of investment company fund shares currently outstanding.[26]

$$NAV = \frac{\text{Market value of a fund's securities} - \text{Liabilities}}{\text{Number of investor shares outstanding}}$$

Example 3-6   Assume the Titan Fund has a portfolio of stocks valued on a given day at $50,000,000. Its liabilities are $500,000, and shareholders of this fund own five million shares. The NAV is

$$NAV = \frac{\$50,000,000 - \$500,000}{5,000,000} = \$9.90$$

Federal law requires that a fund's NAV be calculated for each business day.

✓ The NAV of any fund—mutual fund, closed-end fund, or ETF—is the per share value of the portfolio of securities held by that fund on a given day. It changes daily as the value of the securities held changes, and as income from the securities held is received and paid out while the expenses for operating the fund are deducted.

Ignoring any sales charges, NAV is the price an investor pays to buy a mutual fund on a given day, or the price an investor receives when selling shares back to the investment company.

---

[26] Total market value of the portfolio is equal to the product of each security's current market price multiplied by the number of shares of that security owned by the fund.

The Details of Indirect Investing

Investors invest indirectly via investment companies by buying, holding, and selling shares of closed-end funds, mutual funds, and ETFs (we ignore UITs here). In this section, we analyze some of the details involved in these transactions.

CLOSED-END FUNDS

Closed-end funds trade on exchanges and markets like any other stocks. Therefore, their prices are determined by investor demand and supply. Historically, the market prices of closed-ends have varied widely from their net asset values (NAVs).

The current price of a closed-end fund, which trades on an exchange, almost always differs from its NAV. Therefore, you will be paying more, or less, than the per share value of the securities in the fund's portfolio.

- If market price < NAV, the fund is selling at a discount.
- If market price > NAV, the fund is selling at a premium.[27]

It is important to remember that the portfolio's return is calculated based on net asset values while the shareholder's return is calculated on the basis of closing prices.[28]

Example 3-7

The John Hancock Bank & Thrift Opportunity Fund had an average discount of about 13.5 percent over one five-year period. At one point the fund sold for a discount of 18 percent, at which time an investor could buy $1 worth of securities in this fund for $0.82. If the discount narrowed to its five-year average of 13.5 percent, the investor would make money even if the portfolio value (its NAV) remained unchanged.

Brokers often support the price of an IPO in the after market temporarily, but then the price drops to NAV, or below. Individual investors should avoid purchasing the newly offered shares of closed-end funds because of the fees involved.

MUTUAL FUNDS

How Mutual Fund Shares Are Distributed

Mutual funds typically are purchased by either of these methods:

1. Directly, from a fund company, using mail or telephone, or at the company's office locations.
2. Indirectly, from a sales agent, including securities firms, banks, life insurance companies, and financial planners.

Mutual funds may be affiliated with an underwriter, which usually has an exclusive right to distribute shares to investors. Most underwriters distribute shares through broker/dealer firms.

Mutual funds are aggressively marketed and discussed in the popular press and they offer numerous conveniences and services. For example, the minimum investment requirements for

---

[27] Although several studies have addressed the question of why these funds sell at discounts and premiums, no totally satisfactory explanation has been widely accepted by all market observers.

[28] Historical discounts can be found at *Morningstar.com* and *closed-endfunds.com*.

most funds are small. Almost two-thirds of all funds require $1,000 or less for investors to get started, and about four out of five require $5,000 or less. For IRA and other retirement accounts, the minimum required is often lower.

Example 3-8 $2,500 is required to open an account in the Equity-Income Fund (only $500 for Fidelity retirement accounts). Minimum balances are $2,000. Minimums to add to the account are $250 in either case, or $100 through an automatic investment plan.

Mutual Fund Share Prices   Owners of fund shares can sell them back to the company (redeem them) any time they choose; the mutual fund is legally obligated to redeem them. Investors purchase new shares and redeem their existing shares at the net asset value (NAV) explained earlier plus or minus any sales charges (for purchases) or redemption fees (for sales) that may apply.

Most funds price the shares in their portfolio at 4 p.m. EST. Orders to buy or sell shares received from investors before 4 p.m. receive the price determined that day at 4 p.m., and orders received after 4 p.m. receive the price determined at 4 p.m. on the next business day.

Fees vs. Expenses   It is important to understand the difference between mutual fund fees and mutual fund expenses. Mutual fund fees and expenses are required by law to be clearly disclosed to investors. They can be found in the fund's prospectus.

✓ Mutual fund expenses are *indirect* expenses, deducted from fund assets before earnings are distributed to shareholders.

Expense Ratio The annual charge by a mutual fund to its shareholders as a percentage of assets under management

A mutual fund's **expense ratio** (its annual operating expenses as a percent of assets) include any or all of the following (a fund may waive some of these expenses from time to time, or charge less than the maximum allowed).

- Management fee—the amount charged by the fund's advisor for managing the fund
- Distribution (12b-1) fee—may or may not be assessed. Compensates sales professionals for service provided, and also used to pay marketing and advertising expenses. This fee is a fraction of a percent of the fund's average assets, and for some funds it has ranged as high as 1.00 percent.
- Other expenses—pays for recordkeeping, printing, mailing, and so on.

✓ Mutual fund *fees* are paid *directly* by the shareholders.

- Sales charge ("load")—either front-end (at time of purchase) or back-end (at time of sale)
- Redemption fee—fee other than sales charge involved with a redemption
- Exchange fee—sometimes charged to transfer funds within the same fund family
- Annual account maintenance fee—may be charged on low-balance accounts

The sales charge, or load fee, applies only to load mutual funds. That is, mutual funds can be subdivided into

- Load funds (those that charge a sales fee)
- No-load funds (those that do not charge a sales fee)

This is an important distinction, and we consider each of these in turn.

Load Funds   Funds that charge investors a sales fee for the costs involved in selling the fund to the investor are known as **load funds**. This front-end sales fee, added to the fund's NAV, currently ranges up to 5.75 percent. On a $1,000 purchase of a load mutual fund, with a 5.75 percent load fee, an investor would pay $57.50 "commission," acquiring only $942.50 in shares. Many load funds now charge less than the maximum they could charge because of market conditions or competition. According to Investment Company Institute data, while the maximum front-end sales charge for most funds in 2010 was 5.3 percent, investors actually incurred a smaller sales load.[29]

Load Funds Mutual funds with a sales charge or load fee, a direct cost to investors

The load or sales charge goes to the marketing organization selling the shares, which could be the investment company itself or brokers. The fee is split between the salesperson and the company employing that person. The load fee percentage usually declines with the size of the purchase. The old adage in the investment company business is that "mutual fund shares are sold, not bought," meaning that the sales force aggressively sells the shares to investors because of the money involved with the sales charge.

Example 3-9

American Funds is one of the largest mutual fund organizations. Rather than advertise extensively as does Fidelity and Vanguard, American sells funds through brokers at a maximum sales charge (load charge) of 5.75 percent. Despite the sales charges, American's funds, such as Investment Company of America and Washington Mutual Investors Fund, have attracted large amounts of money from investors.

Mutual Fund Share Classes   In the 1990s, brokers began to emphasize a new trend in the sale of load mutual funds whereby they offer several classes of shares of a fund, each with a different combination of front-end load (sales charge), annual or 12b-1 fee, and redemption fee. The idea is that if investors are reluctant to pay higher sales charges when they buy shares of a fund, for example, the brokers can do as well by charging less up-front and more in annual and redemption fees. All fees and expenses must be stated in the **prospectus**, and investors should carefully read a fund's prospectus before investing.

Prospectus Provides information about an initial public offering of securities to potential buyers

✓   When share classes exist, there is only one portfolio of securities, and one investment advisor. Each class constitutes the same claim on the portfolio, and has exactly the same NAV per share. The only difference is how the mutual fund charges investors fees and expenses.

Class A shares: Class A shares are what most investors traditionally think of when they buy mutual funds. Class A shares carry a front-end sales charge and may also impose an annual 12b-1 distribution fee which is typically smaller than the distribution fee for other share classes. The annual expense ratio is typically lower than that for Class B shares.

Class B shares: Class B shares impose a redemption fee which declines over time and will disappear if the shares are held long enough (typically, five or six years). When the redemption fee period is over, Class B shares are often converted into Class A shares.[30] The distribution fee (12b-1) is typically 1 percent of assets. Also, the expense ratio charged investors for operating the fund may be larger under this alternative relative to the Class A shares; however, if the shares are converted to Class A shares, a lower expense ratio will apply.

Class C shares: Like Class B shares, Class C shares impose no front-end sales charge and charge the same higher 12b-1 distribution fee (1 percent of assets).[31] However, because these

---

[29] Investment Company Institute, 2011.

[30] This is typically an advantage to the investor, because the annual distribution fee is lower for the A shares than for the B shares.

[31] A small charge may be imposed if the shares are sold within a short period, typically a year.

shares do not eventually convert to Class A shares, the distribution fee is not subsequently reduced as it is with Class B shares but continues on and on. Furthermore, the annual expense ratio is typically higher with Class C shares than for Class A shares, matching that of the Class B shares, or even exceeding it.

Example 3-10 Consider the three classes of shares for the MFS Massachusetts Investors Growth Stock Fund, A, B, and C. Each has a different combination of loads, fees, and total annual expenses as follows:

	Class A	Class B	Class C
Sales Load	6.1%	None	None
Redemption Fee	None	4.2%	1.0%
Annual Distri. Fee	0.35%	1.0%	1.0%
Total Annual Expenses	0.85%	1.50%	1.50%

No-Load Funds Mutual funds with no sales charge

No-Load Funds In contrast to the load funds, **no-load funds** are bought at NAV directly from the fund itself. No sales fee is charged because there is no sales force to compensate. Investors must seek out these funds by responding to advertisements in the financial press, and purchase and redeem shares by Internet, or telephone.

Some giants of the mutual fund industry, such as Fidelity, Vanguard, and T. Rowe Price, advertise no-load funds aggressively in the major financial publications.

Example 3-11 Fidelity's Equity-Income Fund has no sales charge on purchases, no deferred sales charge on redemptions, no exchange fee, and no 12b-1 fee.

The Vanguard Group operates a well-known family of mutual funds, all of which are no-load. Vanguard advertises some of its funds regularly, as do many other investment companies. Investors interested in no-load funds such as these can contact the company for information or purchases.

A question that is often asked is: If the no-load funds charge no sales fee, how is the investment company compensated? The answer is that all funds, open-end or closed-end, load funds or no-load funds, charge the shareholders the expense ratio described earlier. These expenses are paid out of the fund's income, derived from the dividends, interest, and capital gains earned during the year. These annual operating expenses consist of management fees, overhead, and 12b-1 fees, if any, and are typically stated as a percentage of average net assets, which gives us the expense ratio.

✓ The expense ratio is calculated as a percentage of the assets under management by a fund.

Some money market funds charge very low expense ratios, while some equity funds, particularly specialized funds and funds investing in foreign securities, may charge upwards of 2 percent. The asset weighted average expense ratio for equity mutual funds in 2010 was 0.84 percent, and for bonds, 0.64 percent. However, a number of equity mutual funds may charge more than the asset weighted average, between 1 and 1.5 percent.

Example 3-12   The Equity-Income Fund has an expense ratio of approximately 0.69 percent, consisting of a management fee of 0.48 percent and other expenses of 0.21 percent. The Fund calculates that if its operating expenses are 0.69 percent, for every $10,000 invested an investor would pay $70, $221, $384, and $859 if the account was closed after one, three, five, and 10 years.

How do sales of load and no-load funds compare? Consider load and no-load fund assets as a percentage of total fund assets for the last 20 years or so for both equity funds and bond funds. In both cases the trend over time is clear: load fund sales declined while no-load fund sales increased. For long-term mutual funds, no-load shares now have twice the net assets that load shares have.

Ethics In Investing

Those Who Live in Glass Houses

In late 2003, Edward D. Jones & Co., a large retail brokerage firm, took out ads criticizing the "anything goes" approach that led to abuses in the mutual fund industry. In late 2004 the Securities and Exchange Commission finalized a $75 million settlement agreement with the company. The company was charged with accepting tens of millions of dollars secretly from seven preferred mutual fund groups, which could lead its brokers to favor those funds with their clients even if it were not in the best interest of the clients. Brokers received bonuses and other incentives to sell these particular funds. It was also found that the brokerage firm did not have in place the proper systems to prevent late trading of mutual funds from taking place. Late trading occurs when fund buyers are able to execute mutual fund orders after 4 p.m. using the 4 p.m. closing price. Thus, favorable market-moving developments after 4 p.m. could cause a fund's value to go up the next day, and buying the shares at the same day 4 p.m. price can allow favored clients to earn profits at the expense of long-term fund shareholders.

EXCHANGE TRADED FUNDS

Why buy an ETF when you could buy an index mutual fund (explained earlier)? After all, as one example, Vanguard offers the S&P 500 Index Fund, with operating expenses of 0.05 percent.

- An investor can buy ETFs, or sell them, anytime during the trading day at the current price. Mutual funds are priced once a day, and you can only enter and exit accordingly.
- ETFs can be bought on margin (borrowed funds) or sold short if prices are expected to decline (both concepts are explained in Chapter 5).
- When investors sell their mutual fund shares back to the company, the fund may have to sell securities to purchase the shares. If enough redemptions occur, the fund could generate a capital gains liability for the remaining shareholders. In contrast, the ETF manager does not have to sell shares to pay for redemptions; therefore, redemptions do not create capital gains which must be distributed to the shareholders.[32]

We know that index funds have much lower operating expenses than do actively managed funds because they are passively managed. ETFs also have low expenses, although on average they have been rising. Some ETFs have incredibly low expenses; for example, Vanguard's Total Stock Market ETF has an expense ratio of 0.06 percent.

---

[32] ETF redemptions do not involve the ETF fund at all, but rather one investor selling to another.

An interesting issue with ETFs is how they weight their indexes. Typically, ETFs have been market-capitalization weighted. However, this results in larger companies being a bigger percentage of the index, which leads to certain biases and strongly affects the fund's total return. One solution, offered by Rydex, is to have an equally weighted index. WisdomTree, on the other hand, weights by dividends or earnings. It appears so far that the equal-weighted approach is outperforming both the market-capitalization weighted ETFs and those of WisdomTree, although with higher expenses in some cases.

Some Practical Advice

Investors Need to Use Caution When It Comes to ETFs

With assets of roughly $1 trillion, ETFs are obviously popular. As more are created, investors need to ask some hard questions. Should they really be investing in ETFs concentrating on palladium, or Belgium, or small stocks in Hong Kong? Even worse, leveraged ETFs and inverse leveraged ETFs have been created to magnify movements two and three times. For complex technical reasons, these funds are intended to be used as very short-term hedging devices, but some investors have held them for weeks and months, with large losses. Investors can expect to see more new ETF products with, at best, only marginal value.

Checking Your Understanding

6. Given the wide availability of no-load funds, why do many investors choose to buy load funds and pay sales charges?
7. What is the rationale for buying class B shares? Class C shares?
8. Why would a closed-end fund trade at a premium?

Investment Company Performance

Few topics in investments are as well reported on a regular basis as is the performance of investment companies, and in particular mutual funds. *Business Week*, *Forbes*, *Money Magazine*, *U.S. News & World Report*, and *The Wall Street Journal*, among other popular press publications, regularly cover the performance of mutual funds, emphasizing their returns and risks.[33]

MEASURES OF FUND PERFORMANCE

Consider the 10-year period ending in November 2011. The iShares Russell 2000 Index, a small stock ETF, showed a price increase of 61 percent. Meanwhile, the Utilities Select Sector SPDR, a utilities ETF, had a much more modest price increase of 29 percent.[34] Did the former outperform the latter by almost two to one? If you could go back in time and choose one to hold, which would it be?

Given a choice, you should have picked the Utilities Select Sector SPDR. Why? When dividends are included, as we know from Chapter 6 are part of the investor's total, the utilities ETF returned 84 percent versus 81 percent for the small stock ETF. There is a big difference between price performance and total return.

---

[33] We will discuss the calculation of investment returns in much more detail in Chapter 6, but the primary focus in that chapter is on individual securities or market indexes and the actual mechanics involved. Furthermore, we will discuss the evaluation of portfolio performance in Chapter 22, and therefore we do not consider the evaluation of fund performance in detail now.

[34] This example is based on Simon Constable, "Price Charts Can Mislead," *The Wall Street Journal*, December 5, 2011, p. C8.

Throughout this text we will use *total return* (explained in detail in Chapter 6) to measure the return from any financial asset, including a mutual fund or ETF. Total return for a fund includes both cash distributions and capital gains/losses, and therefore includes all of the ways investors make money from financial assets. It is stated as a percentage or a decimal, and can cover any time period—one month, one year, or multiple years.

✓ Total return measures both the income component of an investment, and any price change, for a specified period of time.[35]

Average Annual Return

Average Annual Total Return A hypothetical rate of return used by mutual funds that, if achieved annually, would have produced the same cumulative total return if performance had been constant over the entire period

Standard practice in the investment company industry is to calculate and present the **average annual total return**, a hypothetical rate of return that, if achieved annually, would have produced the same cumulative total return if performance had been constant over the entire period. The average annual total return is another name for the *geometric mean* and reflects the *compound* rate of growth at which money grew over time. As noted in the Equity-Income prospectus, "Average annual total returns smooth out variations in performance; they are not the same as actual year-by-year results."

Note that in making this calculation we are asking at what compound rate of return does an initial investment grow over time? Although any period of time can be used, we typically are talking about annual returns. Therefore, the average annual total return for a fund shows the compound annual rate of return at which money grew over time. Given some initial investment (e.g., $1, $10,000, $100,000, and so forth) and the average annual total return for a mutual fund or ETF, we can easily determine the ending wealth would one have as a result of investing in that particular fund for a specified number of years.

Example 3-13

The average annual total returns for the Titan Equity Fund and its corresponding market benchmark for several recent years were as follows:

	1 Year	3 Year	5 Years	10 Years
Titan Equity Fund	11.29%	6.21%	4.31%	11.94%
Market Benchmark	16.94	9.16	6.10	13.84

Therefore, investing $10,000 in the Titan Fund and compounding at the rate of 11.94 percent each year for 10 years would produce a final wealth of $30,893 (rounded). To make the calculation, convert 11.94 percent to a decimal, add 1.0, and raise 1.1194 to the 10th power.[36] Finally, multiply this result, 3.08925, by the $10,000 to obtain $30,892.50.

$$(1.1194)^{10} \times \$10,000 = \$30,892.50^{[37]}$$

---

[35] As shown in Chapter 6,

$$TR = \frac{\text{Cash payments received}}{\text{Purchase price}} + \frac{\text{Price change over the period}}{\text{Purchase price}}$$

[36] This procedure is used many times in finance, and all finance students and anyone interested in investing should be thoroughly comfortable with it.

[37] Note that if we subtract the initial investment of $10,000 from the $30,893 (rounded), we have $20,893, which is the cumulative total dollar return, not counting the initial investment.

Using the Calculator:

1 enter *1.1194*
2 press the y^x key (may be an upper key on some calculators)
3 enter *10*
4 press "="

An answer of 3.08952 is obtained. Multiply by $10,000 to get $30,892.50.

Alternative method of calculation:

Using the	N	I/YR	PV	PMT	FV	buttons
Enter the values	10	11.94	10,000	0	?	

(NOTE: enter 10, press N, enter 11.94, press I/YR, etc., finally press FV)
Pressing the FV button produces the answer, $30,892.50.

Average annual total returns allow investors to make direct comparisons among funds as to their performance, assuming they do so legitimately, as explained in Chapter 22 when we discuss the evaluation of performance. This means that the risk of the funds being compared should be considered, and the funds should have the same general objectives. We expect, on average, for equity funds to outperform bond funds and money market funds.

While average returns are important, they don't tell you everything. Many investors want to know how a fund performs when there is a sharp market decline because of the possible difficulty in recovering from such a decline. A fund that is said to be defensive should hold up as well as similar funds. Clearly, a fund should fit well with an investor's objectives and other portfolio holdings. Costs are very important in affecting a fund's performance, and should be carefully considered.

Tax Efficiency   The question of tax efficiency has become an important issue in recent years. Shareholders can end up paying significant taxes in a particular year regardless of the performance of the fund. In fact, a fund's performance in one year can be negative while shareholders received large distributions on which they must pay taxes.

Example 3-14   Janus Venture Fund, an equity fund with strong performance over the last several years, had a return of −45 percent for the year 2000. However, it paid out $16.38 per share as a result of selling securities which had appreciated substantially. Therefore, shareholders in this fund faced a significant tax liability for 2000 while suffering a 45 percent loss for the year.

MORNINGSTAR RATINGS

One of the best-known assessments of fund performance among investors is the rating system developed by Morningstar, the well-known provider of information about investment companies. *Morningstar* uses a 5-star rating system, with five stars the highest rating and one star the lowest. The "star" system has become very well known among investors. Many investment companies run advertisements to tout any funds they manage that achieve high ratings, particularly five stars.

Morningstar ratings have been widely used by investors as a quick screening device, believing that the rating is a likely predictor of future success. However, it is important to note that this rating system is measuring *historical* risk-adjusted performance for funds that have at least a three-year history. The ratings take into account both a fund's risk relative to its category as a whole, and its returns, taking out the sales charge on a monthly basis. In effect, the ratings assess how the fund has balanced return and risk (volatility) in the past.

When both the risk and return measure are put together, a rating can be determined for all funds in a set. The top 10 percent receive five stars, the next 22.5 percent receive four stars, and the middle 35 percent receive three stars.[38] *Morningstar* ranks funds against comparable funds. This means that large-company value funds are ranked against other large-company value funds, and so forth.[39]

✓ Morningstar's star ratings are not intended to predict future performance or a fund's quality.

In November 2011 Morningstar announced a forward-looking ranking system for mutual funds that will supplement the star-ratings system. While the latter measures past performance, the new system attempts to predict which funds will outperform in the future. It incorporates not only past performance but also the expense ratio, the fund's investing strategy, and other information concerning the fund's manager and parent company. New rating designations are gold, silver, bronze, neutral, and negative.

Investments Intuition

Morningstar's star ratings, calculated once a month, are simply quantitative measures of historical performance, showing how funds have balanced return and risk in the past. Although a sound, well-regarded tool for investors if used properly, a fund's future performance may be different from its past performance. *Morningstar* itself has always urged investors to use its star system of rankings as a starting point in selecting funds, not as the bottom line. This is good advice to heed.

BENCHMARKS

Investors need to relate the performance of a mutual fund to some benchmark in order to judge relative performance with (hopefully) a comparable investment alternative. Fidelity's Equity-Income Fund, presented above, was compared to the S&P 500 Composite Index. Other firms make different comparisons and claims, as one will quickly discover by looking at their ads. For example, T. Rowe Price, in noting that its Dividend Growth Fund had a 5-star Morningstar rating for overall risk-adjusted performance, compared this fund to the Lipper Growth & Income Funds Average.[40] The Kaufmann Fund, on the other hand, a well-known small company aggressive growth fund, compared its performance to the Russell 2000, an index of small companies, and (in one ad) only for a 10-year period.

---

[38] Additional information about the *Morningstar* rating system can be found at its website.

[39] Note that the *Morningstar* ranking system takes into account a fund's load charges by calculating a load-adjusted return. Because each share class of a fund with share classes has to be rated separately, one class of shares can have a different rating than another class of shares although the same mutual fund is being evaluated.

[40] As mentioned earlier, Lipper, Inc., is a well-known provider of fund rankings and performance.

HOW IMPORTANT ARE EXPENSES IN AFFECTING PERFORMANCE?

An important issue for all fund investors is that of expenses. Should they be overly concerned about the load charges, given the large number of no-load funds? What about annual operating expenses? Investors need to pay attention to fund expenses because net performance can be dramatically affected. The annual expenses deducted for operating the fund can have a big impact on an investor's net return.

Example 3-15 The State Street High Income Fund has share classes. The B shares have no up-front sales charge. This fund had a return of 2.6 percent one year when the expense ratio was 2.17 percent. Therefore, before expenses the owner of the B shares earned 4.77 percent, but after expenses this share class, with no up-front charge for a new buyer, netted a shareholder only 2.6 percent for the year.

John Bogle, founder of Vanguard and a well-known critic of many mutual fund practices, estimates that the average actively managed mutual fund actually costs investors approximately 2.5 percentage points in expenses when all expenses are properly accounted for.[41] Obviously, that contrasts sharply with the expenses for ETFs and index funds, which perform on average as well as the actively managed funds.

✓ Several studies have shown that expenses are the best indicator of a fund's performance.

SOME CONCLUSIONS ABOUT FUND PERFORMANCE

The consistency of performance of mutual funds has long been a controversy, and this continues to be true. Earlier studies tended to find a lack of consistency of fund performance, while some recent studies find some persistence in fund performance. Overall, however, the evidence is not encouraging when it comes to consistent fund performance across time. For example, less than 25 percent of mutual funds outperformed their benchmarks.

✓ Typically, over a period such as five years, about 75 percent of mutual fund managers fail to outperform the market.

Survivorship Bias The bias resulting from the fact that analyzing a sample of investment companies at a point in time reflects only those companies that survived, ignoring those that did not

Survivorship Bias An important issue concerning mutual fund performance arises out of what is called **survivorship bias.** The financial press media, which reports widely on the performance of funds, typically use databases that erase funds which are merged into other funds or which are liquidated. Thus, by removing funds that close or merge, the reported record consists only of surviving funds, and the average return increases relative to the true return for all funds. How big an impact can this bias produce?

Estimates of the bias suggest it is approximately 1.6 percentage points of the average annual return. This is the amount by which the average annual return is overstated.

Such a bias can make a big difference when investors consider the benefits of actively managed mutual fund portfolios. Consider the results for annualized excess returns versus the U.S. stock market for actively managed U.S. equity mutual funds. For 10-, 15-, and 20-year periods, the percentage of funds underperforming without adjusting for the bias was

---

[41] Included here are sales charges, annual expense ratios, and trading costs.

50 percent, 53 percent, and 53 percent respectively. Adjusting for the bias, the percentages are 62 percent, 67 percent, and 72 percent.[42]

Some Practical Advice

Much of the disappointment suffered by shareholders in mutual funds centers around performance. They examine the rankings and ratings of mutual funds which appear regularly in the popular press. They often form their expectations of what they should earn from what the fund did earn. The end result is that mutual fund investors are often chasing historical performance, and they end up disappointed. Most funds don't continue to perform well year after year for a variety of reasons. Growth stocks fall out of favor, and value stocks gain favor for awhile, only to reverse later. Large stocks are in favor for awhile, and then small stocks are. Some sectors are hot this year and cold next year.

Chasing the Hot Funds   One of the enduring aspects of mutual funds is the tendency of investors to chase those funds with recent strong performance. Such funds are hyped in the financial press on a regular basis. Clearly, different funds will perform well for different periods of time. Many investors react to the most current strong performances and invest accordingly. Subsequently, many of these funds fail to perform well as performance leadership rotates to a new group of funds which happens to be positioned correctly relative to what the market is now emphasizing—for example, oil, foreign securities, dividend payers, and so forth.

As David Dreman, who writes a column for *Forbes* magazine, states: "Many investors flock to funds with sizzling short-term performance. The media and the fund-ranking services fan the misbegotten enthusiasm by hyping current star performers and ranking these funds atop weekly lists."[43]

If most mutual funds do not outperform their corresponding benchmark, it seems that many mutual fund shareholders would opt for index mutual funds because of their low expenses and guaranteed performance relative to their respective indexes. However, this appears not to be the case. Equity index fund assets accounted for only about 16 percent of total equity mutual fund assets at the end of 2011. ETFs now contribute a few percentage points or so to equity index assets.

Investing Internationally Through Investment Companies

The mutual fund industry has become a global industry. Open-end funds around the world have grown rapidly, including emerging market economies. Worldwide assets by the beginning of 2012 were $23.8 trillion, with the United States accounting for about half the total at $11.6 trillion. About half of worldwide mutual fund assets were invested in equity funds. The mutual fund industry is truly a worldwide industry.[44]

The decline of the dollar in recent years contributed to the growth in many countries in assets of mutual funds reported in U.S. dollars. As we will see in Chapter 6, a drop in the dollar's value benefits U.S. investors.

---

[42] Christopher B. Philips, "The Case for Indexing," The Vanguard Group, February 2011, p. 6.

[43] David Dreman, "The Curse of the Hot Hand," *Forbes*, October 18, 2004, p. 146. © 2004 Forbes, Inc.

[44] All of this information can be found at the website for the Investment Company Institute, www.ici.org.

One of the potential problems with international investing is the higher costs involved. According to Morningstar, the costs of international index mutual funds average almost 2.3 percent when sales, redemption, and marketing charges are included.

FUND CATEGORIES FOR INTERNATIONAL INVESTING

U.S. investors can invest internationally by buying and selling mutual funds, ETFs, or closed-end funds. Funds that specialize in international securities have become both numerous and well known in recent years.

International Funds Mutual funds that concentrate primarily on international stocks

Global Funds Mutual funds that keep a minimum of 25 percent of their assets in U.S. securities

Single-Country Funds Investment companies, primarily closed-end funds, concentrating on the securities of a single country

Most mutual funds that offer "international" investing invest primarily in non-U.S. stocks, thereby exposing investors to foreign markets, which may behave differently from U.S. markets. However, investors may also be exposed to currency risks. An alternative approach to international investing is to seek international exposure by investing in U.S. companies with strong earnings abroad, which is a natural extension of the globalization concept. If an investor believes that the best-managed global companies tend to be based in the United States, this is a safer strategy.

International funds tend to concentrate primarily on international stocks. In contrast, **global funds** tend to keep a minimum of 25 percent of their assets in the United States. Closed-end **single-country funds** concentrate on the securities of a single country.

Some ETFs concentrate on foreign country and international indexes. Together they offer exposure to various foreign sectors, regions, countries, and global benchmarks. For example, investors could choose ETFs concentrating on the global energy sector, the Pacific region, countries such as Austria, South Korea, Italy, and Japan, and indexes such as the Nikkei 225 index. Note that international ETFs are unhedged for currency risk, and therefore U.S. investors benefit when the foreign currency appreciates relative to the dollar.

Concepts in Action

So You Want to Invest Internationally?

Most investment advisors recommend that investors put at least some percentage of their assets in international securities for the reasons listed in Chapter 1. Let's assume you want to do so. What are your options?

First, you could build your own portfolio, choosing from stocks that trade on foreign markets. It is relatively easy to find foreign stocks that are either listed on U.S exchanges or trade as American Depository Receipts (ADRs). However, buying numerous stocks can be expensive, and understanding foreign companies' financial statements and operations can be challenging. Therefore, most investors opt for indirect investing.

Most investors seeking foreign investments naturally think of mutual funds. Americans in 2004 had some $300 billion invested in international funds. Foreign funds with good performance and reasonable expense ratios include Vanguard International Value,

Fidelity International Growth and Income, Harbor International Investments, and T. Rowe Price International Discovery. The average expense ratio for international funds is 1.75 percent, so paying attention to this number can be very important.

Samsung, a South Korean company, has been a very profitable tech company. What if you wanted to invest in Samsung, but with some diversification in case things slow down? An ETF, iShares MSCI South Korea, makes this possible. Samsung is one of the stocks in its portfolio. If you want to invest in emerging markets, you could try iShares MSCI Emerging Markets Index.

Finally, what if you want to concentrate on India, an emerging economy that is now receiving considerable attention? You can buy a closed-end fund, Morgan Stanley India Investment, or one of four mutual funds, or an ETF.

The Future of Indirect Investing

FUND SUPERMARKETS

Fund Supermarkets Offered by brokerage firms, these allow the firm's customers to choose from a large set of mutual funds through their brokerage accounts

A popular trend concerning indirect investing is the mutual fund "supermarket"—indeed, a number of observers feel that fund supermarkets are the future of mutual funds sold directly to investors. **Fund supermarkets** are a mechanism by which investors can buy, own, and sell the funds of various mutual fund families through one source, such as a brokerage firm. "Supermarket" refers to the fact that an investor has hundreds of choices available through one source, and does not have to go to each mutual fund company separately to buy one of their funds.

Example 3-16   Fidelity Investments has a fund supermarket known as FundsNetwork. Over 70 companies participate, offering over 1,200 funds.

The discount brokerages of Schwab and Fidelity have been pioneers in making funds available to investors through brokerage accounts offered by them. Schwab and Fidelity are two of the largest supermarkets, but many other discount brokerage firms and fund firms have smaller programs.

Fund supermarkets have two tracks, or "aisles": a no-fee aisle, where investors can buy various mutual funds without paying a sales charge or transaction fee, and a transaction-fee aisle, where they do pay a fee. The mutual funds participating in the fund supermarket which want to offer their shares with no fees to investors pay the supermarkets an annual charge of 0.35 percent of the assets that the fund has acquired at the supermarket. As a result, the typical new fund being sold without fees will establish expense charges that are enough to cover the supermarket fees.

Hedge Funds

We close our discussion of investment companies by considering an offshoot, an unregulated investment company. The Investment Company Act of 1940 gave primacy to the open-end investment company (or mutual fund) as the way to protect investors from the excesses of the unregulated companies of the 1920s. The key was that such companies would be heavily regulated as to investor protections. However, the Act also left open the possibility of a money manager handling funds for a small group of sophisticated investors in an unregulated format. In 1949 a fund was started to "hedge" market risk by both buying and selling short, thus initiating the hedge fund industry. Today there are many hedge funds and a lot of notoriety about them, for better or worse.

Hedge Funds Unregulated companies that seek to exploit various market opportunities and thereby earn larger returns than are ordinarily available to investment companies

Hedge funds are unregulated companies that seek to exploit various market opportunities and thereby earn larger returns than are ordinarily available. For example, they may use leverage or derivative securities, or invest in illiquid assets, strategies not generally available to the typical mutual fund. They require a substantial initial investment from investors, and may have restrictions on how quickly investors can withdraw their funds. Unlike mutual funds, they traditionally do not disclose information to their investors about their investing activities. Hedge funds charge substantial fees, and take a percentage of the profits earned, typically at least 20 percent.

Over time, the performance of hedge funds has been thought to be good, with larger returns and less risk than the typical mutual fund. Part of this is a result of some funds that perform strongly for a period receiving a lot of publicity. In Chapter 12 we examine some evidence suggesting average performance has not been very good. Furthermore, there have been some well-known failures, such as Bayou in 2005, whereby the principals are alleged to have drained investor monies for their own purposes. The most spectacular failure was Long Term Capital in 1998, which got in trouble as a result of Russia's defaulting on its debt. In this case the Federal Reserve had to step in to calm the waters.

Today there are thousands of hedge funds with large sums under management. A legitimate issue to consider is whether there are enough talented managers to run thousands of funds, all looking for opportunities to exploit. Many hedge funds, like other investors, cannot overcome a financial crisis year such as 2008 when the financial markets underwent tremendous turmoil. A number of hedge funds went out of business.

Hedge funds do close when conditions change. For example, in late 2011 Goldman Sachs closed the Global Alpha Fund LP which had about $1 billion in assets, down from $12 billion in 2007. This fund was down about 40 percent in 2007, and as of late Fall 2011 it was down about 12 percent for the year.

A revolutionary move has now started whereby a hedge fund, in addition to its portfolios designed for institutional clients, is offering its skills to individual investors in the form of mutual funds. AQR, a highly successful hedge fund, has made available several mutual funds using techniques developed for its hedge fund clients. These funds will rely heavily on momentum investing.

Summary

▶ As an alternative to purchasing financial assets themselves, all investors can invest indirectly, which involves the purchase of shares of some type of investment company.

▶ Investment companies are financial intermediaries that hold a portfolio of securities on behalf of their shareholders.

▶ Investment companies are classified as either open-end or closed-end, depending on whether their own capitalization (number of shares outstanding) is constantly changing or fixed.

▶ ETFs bundle together a basket of stocks based on some index or grouping of stocks and trade as one security on an exchange. They resemble closed-end funds but generally sell close to NAV and have certain tax advantages.

▶ Open-end investment companies, commonly called mutual funds, can be divided into four categories, money market funds and stock, bond, and hybrid funds.

▶ Money market mutual funds concentrate on portfolios of money market securities, providing investors with a way to own these high face value securities indirectly.

▶ Stock, bond, and hybrid funds own portfolios of stocks and/or bonds, allowing investors to participate in these markets without having to purchase these securities directly.

▶ Investors transacting indirectly in closed-end funds encounter discounts and premiums, meaning that the price of these funds is unequal to their net asset values.

▶ Mutual funds can be load funds or no-load funds, where the load is a sales charge calculated as a percentage of the amount invested in the fund.

▶ All investment companies typically charge a fee (called the annual expense ratio or simply "expense ratio") to shareholders to pay for the operating costs and the management fee.

▶ Total return for a mutual fund includes reinvested dividends and capital gains. A cumulative total return measures the actual performance over a stated period of time, such as the past three, five, or 10 years. The average annual return is a hypothetical rate of return that, if achieved annually, would have produced the same cumulative total return if performance had been constant over the entire period.

▶ International funds tend to concentrate primarily on international stocks while global funds tend to keep a minimum of 25 percent of their assets in the United States.

▶ Single-country funds, which traditionally have been closed-end funds, concentrate on the securities of a single country.

▶ Fund supermarkets are a mechanism by which investors can buy, own, and sell the funds of various mutual fund families through one source, such as a brokerage firm.

▶ Hedge funds are unregulated companies that seek to exploit various market opportunities and thereby earn larger returns than are ordinarily available.

Questions

3-1 What is meant by "indirect" investing?

3-2 What is an investment company? Distinguish between an open-end and a closed-end company.

3-3 What does the term "open-end" mean with regard to an investment company's capitalization? What about the term "closed-end?"

3-4 List some reasons an investor might prefer an ETF to an open-end fund.

3-5 It has been said that many closed-end funds are "worth more dead than alive." What is meant by this expression?

3-6 How similar is an ETF to a closed-end fund?

3-7 What does it mean for an investment company to be regulated?

3-8 What is meant by an investment company's "objective"? What are some of the objectives pursued by equity, bond, and income funds?

3-9 How is the net asset value for a mutual fund calculated?

3-10 What is a money market fund? Why would it appeal to investors?

3-11 List the benefits of a money market fund for investors? List the disadvantages. What alternative investment is a close substitute?

3-12 Distinguish between a value fund and a growth fund.

3-13 Distinguish between a global fund and an international fund.

3-14 What is the difference between the average annual return for a fund and the geometric mean return for that fund?

3-15 What is the value to investors of *Morningstar* ratings? What is the weakness of these ratings?

3-16 Distinguish between the direct and indirect methods by which mutual fund shares are typically purchased.

3-17 How would the owner of some shares of Fidelity's Equity-Income Fund "cash out" when she was ready to sell the shares?

3-18 What does it mean to say an index fund is related to passive investing?

3-19 What percentage of equity mutual fund assets are accounted for by index equity mutual funds? Should a typical investor pay 75 or 100 basis points in annual expenses for an index equity mutual fund?

3-20 What is survivorship bias? How does it affect investors in judging mutual fund performance?

3-21 What is the difference between a load fund and a no-load fund?

3-22 What are passively managed country funds? Give an example.

3-23 What is meant by the exchange privilege within a "family of funds"?

3-24 How does a hedge fund differ from a mutual fund?

3-25 What is a fund supermarket?

3-26 John Bogle started the first equity index fund in 1976. It struggled at first, and the fund met with overt hostility from most of the industry, which wanted to see it fail. Why do you think this happened?

Computational Problems

3-1 A mutual fund has the following returns for three consecutive years: −8%, 5%, and 12%.

   a. What is the cumulative wealth per $1 invested?

   b. What is the geometric mean return for this three-year period.

3-2 For a recent 10-year period, T. Rowe Price, a mutual fund company, reported performance (average annual total return) for two of its funds as follows:

Equity-Income Fund	12.48%
Personal Strategy Growth Fund	12.26%

Assume you invested $5,000 in each fund at the beginning of this 10-year period. How much difference would there be in the ending wealth between the two funds?

3-3 For the same two funds discussed in 3-2, the ending wealth after five years was $1.2438 per dollar invested at the beginning for the Equity-Income Fund, and $1.0492 per dollar invested at the beginning for the Personal Strategy fund. What were the annual average total returns for each fund for this five-year period?

3-4 The net asset value per share for the T. Rowe Price Global Stock Fund at the beginning of one recent year was $15.07. During the year the fund earned $.04 in net investment income and $1.82 in "net gains or losses on securities." It distributed $.03 in dividends and $.02 in capital gains. What was the net asset value for this fund at the end of the year?

3-5 As of December 31, 2012, the 10-year annualized rate of return (geometric mean) for the Wall Street Emerging Growth Fund was −8.45 percent. Assume an investor invested $10,000 in this fund on January 1, 2003. How much would this investment be worth on December 31, 2012, a 10-year period?

3-6 For the period ending July 2012, Vanguard's Prime Money Market Fund Investor Shares earned .03 percent. What was the ending wealth given a $1,000 investment.

Spreadsheet Exercises

3-1 The years 1995−1999 were the five greatest consecutive years in the stock market in terms of performance. They were followed by three years of significant declines, and a recovery in 2003. The data below show the percentage annual returns for two Fidelity funds, Fidelity Growth (symbol = FDGRX) and Fidelity Aggressive Growth (symbol = FDEGX). Note that the performance of both funds mirrored that of the market, showing strong positive returns the first five years, followed by three years of negative returns, and then positive performance in 2003.

	FDGRX	FDEGX
1995	39.6	35.9
1996	16.8	15.8
1997	18.9	19.5
1998	27.2	43.3
1999	79.5	103
2000	−6.3	−27.1
2001	−25.3	−47.3
2002	−33.5	−41.2
2003	41.4	33.4

a. Calculate the average performance for each fund for the nine-year period. Use the spreadsheet function { = Average(B2:B9)} where B2:B9 represents the cells with the first fund's annual returns.

b. Now calculate how much $10,000 invested in each fund at the beginning of 1995 would have grown to by the end of 1999, when the market was booming. To do this, construct two new columns, one for each fund, showing the decimal equivalent of the fund's return added to 1.0 (call this the *return relative*—to find it, divide each return by 100 and add 1.0). For example, for FDGRX, the first entry would be 1.396. Then for each fund multiply $10,000 by each of the first five return relatives in turn. How much money would an investor in each fund have at the end of 1999? Which fund performed better up to that point?

c. Using the answer determined in (b), calculate the amount of money an investor would have in each fund at the end of 2003. Do this in a manner similar to (b), compounding the result you found at the end of 1999 by each of the four remaining return relatives.

d. What is the difference in ending wealth between the two funds, having started with $10,000 in each fund?

e. Now calculate the average annual total return (geometric mean) for each fund using the spreadsheet function { = geomean (D2:D9) } assuming for example that the return relatives for one fund are in the cells D2:D9.

f. How does the difference in the average annual total returns for each fund compare to the arithmetic averages for each over the nine-year period?

3-2   Fill in the missing data in the spreadsheet below to calculate the net asset value of this mutual fund for each of the years shown.

Years ended December 31,	2012	2011	2010	2009	2008
Selected Per Share Data					
Net asset value, beginning of period	$ 45.26		$ 65.21		$ 56.34
Income from Investment Operations					
Net investment income (loss)[B]	.12	.23		.41	
Net realized and unrealized gain (loss)		(27.22)	12.34	6.92	8.95
Total from investment operations	13.22		12.82		9.22
Distributions from net investment income		(.21)	(.46)	(.39)	(.23)
Distributions from net realized gain	(.09)				
Total distributions	(.20)	(.86)	(4.92)	(6.88)	(1.20)
Net asset value, end of period	$ 58.28	$ 45.26		$ 64.71	

Checking Your Understanding

3-1   Mutual funds are by far the most popular type of investment company because they have existed for many years, as have closed-end funds, but the latter fell out of favor with investors a long time ago. ETFs are relatively new and while growing rapidly, have a long way to go to catch up with mutual funds. Very heavy promotion and publicity also accounts for the popularity of mutual funds.

3-2 ETFs have largely eliminated the issue of discounts and premiums which plague closed-end funds. They typically offer targeted diversification while closed-ends often resemble mutual funds.

3-3 Money market funds by definition hold money market assets, the safest financial assets because of their high credit quality and very short maturity. Therefore, they are simply a reflection of the type of assets they hold.

3-4 A hybrid fund holds both bonds and stocks, thereby offering a combination to investors in one fund. Typically, such funds should have higher returns, on average, than bond funds while offering lower risk than stock funds.

3-5 Investor tend to favor value stocks for certain periods of time, and growth stocks at other times based on perceived economic conditions. Therefore, growth funds and value funds will reflect these varying expectations.

3-6 Investors may choose to buy load funds and pay sales charges because of ignorance about the alternatives available, or carelessness in seeking out the lower-cost alternative of no-load funds. Of course, if investors believe that a particular fund/manager offers better opportunities than the alternatives, and such a fund charges a sales charge, they will be willing to pay the load fees.

3-7 Some investors simply wish to avoid paying an up-front sales charge, which can be avoided by buying B or C class shares. Of course, what really matters is what an investor pays in total in fees during the period the shares are owned; therefore, investors in mutual funds with share classes should do some calculations to try to determine which class of shares will be least expensive during the time period the shares are owned.

3-8 A closed-end fund typically trades at a premium when investors are convinced that the future performance of the fund will be so strong that paying a premium for the shares is warranted. For example, a closed-end fund might concentrate on a single country expected to perform very strongly over the future, and other readily available alternatives for participating in this particular country are not available.

chapter *4*

Securities Markets Matter to All Investors

A s you prepare to invest your inheritance, you realize that like most people you have certainly heard of the New York Stock Exchange as well as NASDAQ because their activities are reported daily, but you really don't know how they work. Why should you care where the stocks you buy and sell trade? Having heard of the bubble in the NASDAQ market that burst in 2000, causing investors spectacular losses, you also wonder if you should even consider NASDAQ stocks. And someone has mentioned that Electronic Communications Networks (ECNs) may be the future of investing, but you do not know what these are. Even more basic, despite listening to the national news each night and hearing how the Dow Jones Index and NASDAQ Index closed for the day, you clearly realize that this doesn't tell you much. Does a 75-point gain in the Dow in one day constitute a great day, or could it be less significant in today's world than in the past? Even more confusing, in 2011 the stock market was up 5.5 percent for the year, although it was also unchanged—how is this possible? Finally, what about bonds—where do they trade, and how will you handle their purchase and sale?

Chapter 4 outlines the structure of the markets where investors buy and sell securities. Although primary markets, including the role of investment bankers, are considered, the emphasis is on secondary markets where most investors are active. We focus in particular on equity markets because most investors are primarily interested in stocks; bond markets and derivative markets are outlined. Market indexes are analyzed in some detail because of their universal everyday use by investors.

The structure and operating mechanisms of the securities markets in the United States have changed drastically in the last 10 years. Given the financial crisis starting in 2008, more changes can be expected.

AFTER READING THIS CHAPTER YOU WILL BE ABLE TO:

▶ Distinguish between primary and secondary markets.

▶ Outline where the three major types of securities discussed in Chapter 2—bonds, equities, and derivatives—are traded.

▶ Understand how the equity markets, where stocks are traded, are organized, how they operate, and how they differ from each other.

▶ Recognize and understand the various stock market indexes typically encountered by investors.

The Importance of Financial Markets

In order to finance as well as expand their operations, business firms must invest capital in amounts that are beyond their capacity to save in any reasonable period of time. Similarly, governments must borrow large amounts of money to provide the goods and services that people demand of them. The financial markets permit both business and government to raise the needed funds by selling securities. Simultaneously, investors with excess funds are able to invest and earn a return, enhancing their welfare.

Financial markets are absolutely vital for the proper functioning of capitalistic economies, since they serve to channel funds from savers to borrowers. Furthermore, they provide an important allocative function by channeling the funds to those who can make the best use of them—presumably, the most productive. In fact, the chief function of a capital market is to allocate resources optimally.[1]

The existence of well-functioning secondary markets, where investors come together to trade existing securities, assures the purchasers of new securities that they can quickly sell their securities if the need arises. Of course, such sales may involve a loss, because there are no guarantees in the financial markets. A loss, however, may be much preferred to having no cash at all if the securities cannot be sold readily.

In summary, in the United States secondary markets are indispensable to the proper functioning of the primary markets, where new securities are sold. The primary markets, in turn, are indispensable to the proper functioning of the economy.

The Primary Markets

Primary Market The market for new issues of securities, typically involving investment bankers

A **primary market** is one in which an issuer seeking new funds sells additional securities in exchange for cash from an investor (buyer). New sales of Treasury bonds, or Apple stock, or California bonds all take place in the primary markets. The issuers of these securities—the U.S. government, IBM, and the state of California, respectively—receive cash from the buyers of these new securities, who in turn receive new financial claims on the issuer.

Sales of common stock of a publicly traded company are called *seasoned new issues*. On the other hand, if the issuer is selling securities for the first time, they are referred to as **Initial Public Offering (IPO)**. Once the original purchasers sell the securities, they trade in secondary markets. New securities may trade repeatedly in the secondary market, but the original issuers will be unaffected in the sense that they receive no additional cash from these transactions.

Initial Public Offering (IPO) Common stock shares of a company being sold for the first time

Primary markets can be illustrated as (for publicly traded securities):

---

[1] A securities market with this characteristic is said to be *allocationally efficient*. An *operationally efficient* market, on the other hand, is one with the lowest possible prices for transactions services.

INITIAL PUBLIC OFFERINGS (IPOs)

The year 2000 set a record for equity issuance of $223 billion in U.S. common stock underwriting when 391 IPOs raised $61 billion. In contrast, there were only 107 IPOs in 2001, with $39 billion raised, and in 2002, the number dropped to 97 domestic IPOs, with approximately $27 billion raised. 2007 was the strongest year for IPOs since 2000, with more than 230 offerings involving in excess of $53 billion. 2008, on the other hand, was a year of financial crisis. In 2010, approximately $36 billion was raised, and in 2011, $34 billion.

Although some years have seen relatively small amounts of IPOs, the United States must clearly be the world leader in IPOs, having essentially pioneered and developed this concept. Correct? Not any longer. In 2010 China was the new world leader in IPOs, with $125 billion raised. Once again, we see the impact of the global economy.

When the IPO market is very active, and investors are clamoring for shares of new companies, the prices of these stocks often soar on the first day of trading. Those investors lucky enough to receive an initial allocation of these stocks at the price set by the investment banker can see the value of their shares increase dramatically in a short time. However, the average investor typically cannot receive any of the initial allocation of "hot" stocks because the investment bankers reward favored clients with shares.

What if you wish to know more about a company that is planning to go public—Facebook in early 2012, for example? A company must file a registration statement with the Securities and Exchange Commission before it goes public. This statement, called an S-1, often contains useful information about the company. In particular, investors may spot warning signals or troublesome issues that will affect the company's performance.

IPOs tend to run in cycles of investor interest. For example, the IPO market was very active in the late 1990s because of the dot.com craze and technology boom. In the severe market downturn of 2000–2002, on the other hand, investors had little interest in assuming the risk of new issues. In 2008, during the financial crisis, only 21 operating companies in the United States went public.

Example 4-1

Unlike the late 1990s, when IPOs tended to soar indefinitely, in 2000 they often did well on the first day, but suffered thereafter. Almost 70 percent of IPOs traded below their issue price at the end of the year. In 2004 an IPO doubled in value on the first day of trading, the first time that had happened since 2000. In 2010, with 152 IPOs, the average increase for the year was about 25 percent. However, in Fall 2011 a count showed that more than 60 percent of new offerings for the year were below the offer price. On February 1, 2012, Facebook filed for an initial public offering, a highly anticipated event. It was expected to be one of the biggest IPOs in U.S. history.

THE INVESTMENT BANKER

Investment Banker Firm specializing in the sale of new securities to the public, typically by underwriting the issue

In the course of selling new securities, issuers often rely on an **investment banker** for the necessary expertise as well as the ability to reach widely dispersed suppliers of capital. Along with performing activities such as helping corporations in mergers and acquisitions, *investment banking firms* specialize in the design and sale of securities in the primary market while operating simultaneously in the secondary markets. For example, Merrill Lynch offers investment banking services while operating a large retail brokerage operation throughout the country. Other investment banking names have included J. P. Morgan, Goldman Sachs, and Morgan Stanley.

Concepts in Action

LinkedIn, a Successful IPO, and the Wealth It Generated

In May 2011, LinkedIn, the professional social networking company, went public, selling almost 8 million shares. The underwriters were led my J. P. Morgan, Bank of America Merrill Lynch, and Morgan Stanley. Shortly before it went public, the company suggested a valuation for the IPO of about $3 billion. The IPO price was set at $45. On the day of the IPO, the stock opened at $83, about 84 percent higher than the IPO price. At one point during that first day, the stock price was up about 170 percent, and it closed at $94.25.

The company did not expect to be profitable in 2011. Nevertheless, the demand for shares was such that numerous institutional investors were unable to buy shares at the IPO price. Some feared that such a high valuation for an Internet company could be a sign of a bubble for web valuations.

An interesting point is what happens when LinkedIn employees are able to sell their shares. Typically, with an IPO employees have a six-month lockup period, meaning they can't sell their shares for six months after the company goes public. LinkedIn's lockup period ended on November 19, 2011, and 50 million shares became saleable, with another 44 million becoming available over time. Prior to November 19, merchants and sellers of a wide range of expensive products were gearing up for the event, with the expectation of making sales to these newly minted wealthy people.

Investment bankers act as intermediaries between issuers and investors. Typically, the issuer sells its securities to investment bankers, who in turn sell the securities to investors. For firms seeking to raise long-term funds, the investment banker can provide important advice to their clients during the planning stage preceding the issuance of new securities. This advice includes providing information about the type of security to be sold, the features to be offered with the security, the price, and the timing of the sale.

Underwrite The process by which investment bankers purchase an issue of securities from a firm and resell it to the public

Selling the New Issue Investment bankers **underwrite** new issues by purchasing the securities (once the details of the issue have been negotiated) and assuming the risk of reselling them to investors. Investment bankers provide a valuable service to the issuers at this stage. The issuer receives its check and can spend the proceeds for the purposes for which the funds are being raised. The investment bankers own the securities until they are resold. Although many issues are sold out quickly (e.g., the first day they are offered to the public), others may not be sold for days or even weeks. Investment bankers are compensated for their efforts by a spread, which is the difference between what they pay the issuer for the securities and what they sell them for to the public (i.e., the securities are purchased from the issuer at a discount).

Investment Banking Syndicates In addition to having expertise in these matters and closely scrutinizing any potential issue of securities, investment bankers can protect themselves by forming a *syndicate*, or group of investment bankers. This allows them to diversify their risk. One or more investment bankers oversee the underwriting syndicate. This syndicate becomes part of a larger group that sells the securities.

Prospectus Provides information about an initial public offering of securities to potential buyers

Figure 4-1 illustrates a primary offering of securities through investment bankers, a process referred to as a syndicated offering. The issuer (seller) of the securities works with the originating investment banker in designing the specific details of the sale.[2] A **prospectus**,

---

[2] All documents are prepared to satisfy federal laws. In particular, the issuer files a registration statement, which contains financial and other information about the company, with the appropriate government agency.

Figure 4-1

A Primary Offering of Securities.

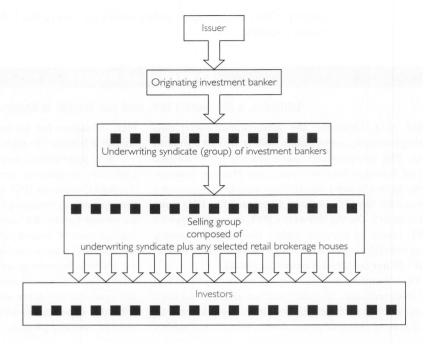

which summarizes this information, officially offers the securities for sale.[3] The lead underwriter forms a syndicate of underwriters who are willing to undertake the sale of these securities once the legal requirements are met.[4] The selling group consists of the syndicate members and, if necessary, other firms affiliated with the syndicate. The issue may be fully subscribed (sold out) quickly, or several days (or longer) may be required to sell it.[5]

Automatic Shelf Registration   Securities and Exchange rules since the end of 2005 allow "well-known seasoned issuers" to file shelf registration statements with the SEC which become effective immediately. This means that an issuer can make a primary offering immediately upon the statement becoming effective; alternatively, having filed the "base prospectus," they can choose to sell the securities at a later time quickly and easily. Large issuers may find this procedure to be the most efficient when selling both debt and equity issues.

A GLOBAL PERSPECTIVE

In today's global economy, companies in various countries can raise new capital in amounts that would have been impossible only a few years earlier because these companies often were limited in selling new securities.

✓   China is an increasingly important player in the IPO market.

---

[3] However, the selling group can send out a preliminary prospectus to investors describing the new issue. No offering date or price is shown, and the prospectus is identified clearly as an informational sheet and not a solicitation to sell the securities. For this reason, the preliminary prospectus is often referred to as a "red herring."

[4] New issues must be registered with the SEC at least 20 days before being publicly offered. Upon approval from the SEC, the selling group begins selling the securities to the public.

[5] During this time, the underwriting manager can legally elect to stabilize the market by placing purchase orders for the security at a fixed price. Underwriters believe that such stabilization is sometimes needed to provide for an orderly sale (thereby helping the issuer) and reduce their risk (thereby helping themselves).

For example, Beijing Jingdong Century Trading Company, which runs 360buy.com, an online shopping site similar to Amazon, hoped to raise as much as $5 billion in an IPO during the first half of 2012. Qunar.com Information Technology, a travel-search company, planned to list its shares in the United States in 2012.

Private Placements   In recent years an increasing number of corporations have executed *private placements*, whereby new securities issues (typically, debt securities) are sold directly to financial institutions, such as life insurance companies and pension funds, bypassing the open market. One advantage is that the firm does not have to register the issue with the SEC, thereby saving both time and money.[6] Investment bankers' fees also are saved because they are not typically used in private placements, and even if they are used as managers of the issue, the underwriting spread is saved. The disadvantages of private placements include a higher interest cost, because the financial institutions usually charge more than would be offered in a public subscription, and possible restrictive provisions on the borrower's activities.[7]

Example 4-2   In 2008, the brokerage firm Merrill Lynch sold $6.6 billion of its own preferred shares through private placements to long-term investors. This sale was intended to enhance its capital position.

Checking Your Understanding

1. In a typical underwriting, the procedure is referred to as a firm commitment. What do you think this means?
2. It is said that IPOs are often underpriced relative to the price at which they could be marketed. What are some possible reasons for this?

The Secondary Markets

Secondary Markets
Markets where existing securities are traded among investors

Once new securities have been sold in the primary market, an efficient mechanism must exist for their resale if investors are to view securities as attractive opportunities. **Secondary markets** provide investors with a mechanism for trading existing securities.

Secondary markets exist for the trading of common and preferred stock, warrants, bonds, and derivative securities. Exhibit 4-1 diagrams the structure of the secondary markets, which is discussed below in the following order: equities, bonds, and derivative securities.

---

[6] The savings in time can sometimes be important, because market conditions can change rapidly between the time an issue is registered and sold.

[7] In addition, a lack of marketability exists, because the issue is unregistered. Therefore, the buyer may demand additional compensation from the lender in the form of a higher yield.

EXHIBIT 4-1

Structure of the Secondary Markets

Type of Securities	Where Traded
EQUITY SECURITIES	Three Major Stock Exchanges
	NYSE (including NYSE MKT)
	NASDAQ Stock Market
	BATS
	ECNs
Unlisted Equities	Over-the-Counter
BONDS	Mostly Over-the-Counter
	NYSE and Amex Bond Markets (very small amounts of corporates)
PUTS AND CALLS	Various Options Exchanges
FUTURES CONTRACTS	Various Futures Exchanges

U.S. SECURITIES MARKETS FOR THE TRADING OF EQUITIES

U.S. equity markets lead the world in the trading of securities. In 2011 the U.S. stock market volume was almost 8 billion shares daily, down from 2010 and 2009.

Currently, equities trade in the United States on two well-known major exchanges: The New York Stock Exchange/Euronext and the NASDAQ Stock Market (NASDAQ).[8] In addition, there is a newer exchange known as BATS as well as Electronic Communication Networks (ECNs), a relatively recent innovation for the trading of securities. Competition between markets benefits investors and the economy as a whole.

Listed Securities The securities of companies meeting specified requirements of exchanges and marketplaces

Each major exchange trades **listed securities**. Companies that issue stock for public trading must choose where their shares will be listed for trading, and then apply for listing. They must also meet the listing requirements of the respective marketplace, and agree to abide by the investor protection rules of that market. Additionally, each listing company must pay a listing fee to the market where their securities are traded.

What about companies not listed on any market? In most cases these companies fail to qualify for trading on an exchange or market, but in some cases they simply choose not to apply for listing for whatever reason. These securities are considered to be over-the-counter (OTC) securities, a term which refers to an equity security not listed or traded on a national securities exchange or market.

Exhibit 4-2 shows where both listed and unlisted stocks are traded in the secondary markets. Although relatively new, BATS is now the third largest stock exchange.

Broker An intermediary who represents buyers and sellers in securities transactions and receives a commission

The NYSE involves a physical location in New York, while the NASDAQ stock market is an electronic market of dealers who make a market in each of the NASDAQ stocks. In either case, investors are represented by **brokers**, intermediaries who represent both buyers and sellers and attempt to obtain the best price possible for either party in a transaction.

---

[8] NYSE Euronext acquired the American Stock Exchange® (Amex®) and has now renamed it the NYSE MKT.

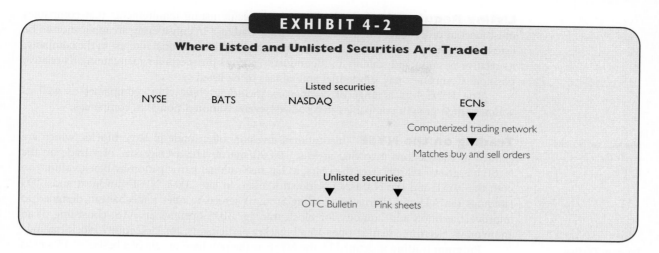

EXHIBIT 4-2

Where Listed and Unlisted Securities Are Traded

Listed securities

NYSE   BATS   NASDAQ   ECNs

Computerized trading network

Matches buy and sell orders

Unlisted securities

OTC Bulletin   Pink sheets

✓ Brokers collect commissions for their efforts and generally have no vested interest in whether a customer places a buy order or a sell order, or, in most cases, in what is bought or sold (holding constant the value of the transaction).

THE NEW YORK STOCK EXCHANGE

New York Stock Exchange (NYSE) The major secondary market for the trading of equity securities

Tracing its history back to 1792, the **New York Stock Exchange (NYSE)** is the oldest and most prominent secondary market in the United States, and the world's largest and most valuable equity market. An historic change occurred in 2005 when the NYSE announced that it and the Archipelago Exchange (ArcaEx) had entered a definitive merger agreement (which closed in April 2006). The combined entity, called the NYSE Group, Inc., represented a merger of the world's leading equity market with the most successful, totally open, fully electronic exchange (an ECN). Furthermore, for the first time in its long and storied history, the NYSE became a publicly owned company.

An additional major change occurred in 2007 with the merger of the NYSE Group with Euronext N.V. to form NYSE Euronext. According to its website, "Euronext operates the world's largest and most liquid exchange group and offers the most diverse array of financial products and services.[9] NYSE Euronext, which brings together six cash equities exchanges in five countries and six derivatives exchanges, is a world leader for listings, trading in cash equities, equity and interest rate derivatives, bonds and the distribution of market data." NYSE Euronext's equities markets represent nearly 40 percent of the world's equities trading, the most liquidity of any global exchange group. However, in early 2012 the European Commission blocked a $17 billion merger between NYSE Euronext and Deutsche Borse.

Individual investors can think of the NYSE as the traditional stock exchange that has existed for over 200 years. NYSE Euronext acquired the American Stock Exchange in 2008, now referred to as NYSE MKT, and it specializes in the efficient trading of small companies. These two exchanges combine the latest in technology with the human element—Designated Market Makers—who provide deeper liquidity and improved prices. NYSE Arca is an all electronic market offering anonymous market access and rapid execution of orders. NYSE Euronext is the European regulated market of the NYSE Euronext group, with over 1,700 companies listed in Europe. It integrated the marketplaces of five countries to create the first transnational exchange in Europe.

[9] www.nyse.com.

Listing Requirements The NYSE has specific listing requirements that companies must meet in order to be listed (i.e., accepted for trading). In considering an application to be listed, the exchange pays particular attention to the degree of national interest in the company, its relative position and stability in the industry, and its prospects for maintaining its relative position. Companies pay substantial annual fees to be listed.

The NYSE lists a range of companies, including "blue chip" companies as well as younger, high-growth companies. It also lists several hundred non-U.S. companies.

Blocks Transactions involving at least 10,000 shares

Trading on the NYSE Institutional investors often trade in large **blocks**, which are defined as transactions involving at least 10,000 shares. The average size of a trade on the NYSE has grown sharply over the years, as has institutional participation by block volume on both the NYSE and the NASDAQ National Market. In late 2007, NYSE Euronext and BIDS Holdings (an ATS, or Alternative Trading System) agreed to offer a mechanism designed to improve execution and liquidity for block trading. BIDS operates an ATS, consisting of an anonymous electronic market open to all market participants, for U.S. equity block trading.

Program Trading Involves the use of computer-generated orders to buy and sell securities based on arbitrage opportunities between common stocks and index futures and options

Program trading is defined by the NYSE as the purchase or sale of a basket of 15 stocks or more and valued at $1 million or more. It is used to accomplish certain trading strategies, such as arbitrage against futures contracts and portfolio accumulation and liquidation strategies. Program trading volume often accounts for approximately 30 percent of total NYSE volume.

For January 2012, the NYSE share of U.S. stock trading fell to approximately 24 percent, an all time low up to that time. This reflected a shift of more trading to private electronic markets.

THE NASDAQ STOCK MARKET

NASDAQ Stock Market (NASDAQ) An electronic marketplace providing instantaneous transactions as its market makers compete for investor orders.

The **NASDAQ Stock Market** has called itself "the largest electronic screen-based equity securities market in the United States." This electronic trading system provides instantaneous transactions as its market makers compete for investor orders. NASDAQ is the primary market for trading NASDAQ-listed stocks. In addition, it claims that it routes more share volume to the floor of the NYSE than any other member.

Market Makers (Dealers) An individual (firm) who makes a market in a stock by buying from and selling to investors

Orders on NASDAQ come from **market makers (dealers)** who make markets in NASDAQ stocks, ECNs, and online brokers such as E*Trade. These participants compete freely with each other through an electronic network of terminals. Dealers conduct transactions directly with each other and with customers. In effect, NASDAQ links together all of the liquidity providers for a particular stock, allowing them to efficiently compete with each other. The NASDAQ market gathers the quotes and orders from these participants and consolidates them into one tape (which is, effectively, the NASDAQ market).

The sharp market decline of 2000–2002 dramatically affected this market. The NASDAQ index went from an all-time high of 5,048 in March 2000 to levels such as 1,200 in 2002, and trading in technology stocks, a prominent feature of NASDAQ, plunged sharply. For example, the telecommunications companies—Global Crossing, WorldCom, etc.—were completely devastated, and many technology/Internet companies went bankrupt.

NASDAQ is well known as the home of numerous prominent technology companies. For example, on NASDAQ's Global Market are Apple (AAPL), Google (GOOG), Adobe Systems (ADBE), and Intel (INTL). Note that each of these stock symbols (in parentheses) consists of 4 letters.

NASDAQ is now part of the NASDAQ OMX Group, which claims to be the world's largest exchange company. Like the NYSE, it is publicly traded. Its trading and technology reach across six continents. As of late 2011, it owned and operated six U.S. markets and 18 European markets. NASDAQ OMX, with over 3,900 companies, states that it is number one in worldwide listings among major markets.

NYSE VS. NASDAQ

The NYSE and NASDAQ have carried on a running battle for stock listings. Each of the two tries to attract companies being listed for the first time while also attempting to lure the other's established listings away. The NYSE argues that its well-known brand and global reach are very important to companies. NASDAQ points to its electronic trading. Both markets are now offering a variety of services to companies in an attempt to persuade companies to list with them.

Example 4-3

In November 2011, Viacom announced it was moving from the New York Stock Exchange, after 40 years, to the NASDAQ Global Select Market. The opposite also occurs. In 2010, Charles Schwab, the large discount broker, moved from NASDAQ to the NYSE EuroNext. Visibility plays a major role in such decisions today. When Groupon went public in late 2011, it selected NASDAQ because of a promise to promote its visibility and what it offers.

THE OVER-THE-COUNTER (OTC) MARKET

The Over-The-Counter (OTC) market is not an organized marketplace or exchange. Instead, it indicates a forum for equity securities not listed on a U.S. exchange. OTC securities are issued by companies that either are unable to meet the standards for listing or that, for whatever reason, choose not to be listed on an exchange.

Many OTC issuers are small companies facing financial difficulties, or perhaps have a limited operating record. It is safe to say that many of these companies are high-risk investments, and often lead to a complete loss for the investor.

OTC equity securities can be quoted on the *Pink Sheets Electronic Quotation Service*, and/or, if the securities are registered with the SEC and their issuers are current in their reporting obligation, on the OTC Bulletin Board.

BATS

Most investors are not familiar with the newest security exchange known as the Better Alternative Trading System (BATS). Only a few years old, BATS was designed as an alternative to the NYSE and NASDAQ. It is now the third largest securities exchange in the world (the NYSE and NASDAQ are the two largest). BATS accounts for about 11 percent of daily trading in U.S. listed shares. BATS appeals to hedge funds and others who trade often, and for whom speed of trading is critically important.

BATS operates two stock exchanges in the United States as well as a U.S. equities options market and BATS Europe. In mid-2011, BATS applied to the SEC to be able to list securities on one of its U.S. exchanges. In early 2012, it reached an agreement to list eight new ETFs, its first primary listings.

ELECTRONIC COMMUNICATION NETWORKS (ECNs)

The traditional ways of trading equity securities—agency auction markets and the fully computerized NASDAQ market—have been significantly changed by new advances in electronic trading. Electronic Communication Networks (ECNs) have clearly had an effect on the traditional markets such as NASDAQ and the NYSE. They compete for customers with the more traditional NASDAQ market makers, and NYSE Euronext is now a hybrid market with the addition of Arca.

An **Electronic Communication Network (ECN)** is a computerized trading network that matches buy and sell orders that come from their own subscribers as well as customer

Electronic Communication Network (ECN) A computerized trading network for buying and selling securities electronically

orders routed from other brokerage firms. Each order received is displayed by the ECN in its computer system. Paying subscribers can see the entire order book, and ECNs display their best bid and ask quotes in the NASDAQ quotation system for all market participants to see. An investor wishing to transact at one of the prices displayed on the computer system electronically submits an order to the ECN. ECNs offer automation, lower costs, and anonymity as to who is doing the buying or selling. There are no spreads, or conflicts of interest with a broker. ECNs earn their fees from those who trade on their systems.

✓ The role of the ECN is to match buy and sell orders, thereby completing trades. Basically, ECNs are simply order-matching systems.

Instinet is the original electronic trading network, started in 1969, long before the term ECN, a relatively recent innovation. Today Instinet is a global securities broker catering to institutional customers by allowing them to trade securities in global markets. By offering an electronic securities order matching system among its clients, Instinet provides anonymous trading, allowing large traders to bypass brokers with their often attendant leaks on who is transacting. Trades are often less than 10,000 shares each, and an institution can do multiple trades to get into or out of a position in a stock without others knowing.

ECNs have both grown and consolidated. For example, Instinet and Island merged in 2002. The NYSE merged with Arca.

After-Hours Trading   Normal stock exchange hours are 9:30 A.M. to 4 P.M. ECNs allow investors to trade after regular exchange hours, which primarily means 4 P.M. to 8 P.M. EST, and sometimes early morning. However, Instinet, one of the largest ECNs, usually operates around the clock.

Online brokerage firms offer their clients access to after-hours trading using the computerized order matching systems of the ECNs. It is important to note that such trading is completely independent from the standard trading during market hours. Investors must, in effect, find someone willing to fill their orders at an acceptable price. Liquidity may be thin, although heavily traded NYSE stocks are good candidates for trading, as are most NASDAQ 100 stocks. Limitations may exist on the types of orders that can be placed and the size of the orders.

Stocks can have sharp price movements during after-hours trading. Therefore, investors may be shocked by the opening price the following day, based on the closing price of the previous day, if they are unaware of what happened after hours.

Example 4-4

Netflix, the DVD and streaming video company, enjoyed a stock price above $100 for many months. However, it tried to change its pricing policy and lost subscribers. In announcing 2011 third-quarter earnings, which were strong, the company noted on October 24, 2011 that the fourth quarter would be weaker than analysts expected. Netflix closed at $118.84 on October 24 when the markets closed at 4 P.M. It then fell 27 percent to $87 in after-hours trading. It opened the next day at $77.37.

FOREIGN MARKETS

Investors have become increasingly interested in equity markets around the world because the United States now accounts for a decreasing part of the world's stock market capitalization. Many equity markets exist, including both developed countries and emerging markets. As explained earlier, both the NYSE Euronext and NASDAQ OMX offer trading on multiple exchanges in multiple countries.

Western Europe has well-developed markets which are now electronic. The London Stock Exchange (LSE) is an important equity market. Europe's emerging markets include the Czech Republic, Hungary, and Poland, where potential profits are large, but risks are also large: illiquidity is great, corporate information can be difficult to obtain, and political risk of a type unknown to U.S. investors still exists.

The Far East has been a fast-growing region. Some of these markets have been very volatile, with large gains and losses because of illiquidity (a scarcity of buyers at times) as well as currency risks and political risks.

Japan, the traditional Asian economic power (China being the new economic power), has one of the largest stock markets in the world, although the Japanese markets have been severely battered since 1989. While Japan has several stock exchanges, the Tokyo Stock Exchange (TSE) dominates that country's equity markets. Both domestic and foreign stocks are listed on the TSE, and among domestic issues a relatively few are traded on the floor of the exchange; the rest (as well as foreign stocks) are handled by computer.

Other Asian markets include Hong Kong, India, Indonesia, South Korea, Malaysia, Pakistan, the Philippines, Singapore, Sri Lanka, Taiwan, and Thailand. Hong Kong, Singapore, South Korea, and Taiwan tend to dominate these markets when Japan is excluded.

The big player in Asian markets now is, of course, China, a rapidly emerging economy that is having a significant impact on the rest of the world. China has been booming as an economy, offering potentially high returns, but with greater risks, because political decisions can strongly affect investments. Chinese companies trade on the Hong Kong exchange as well as on two mainland exchanges in China, the Shanghai Stock Exchange and the Shenzhen Stock Exchange. Some Chinese companies are listed on U.S. exchanges.

China has had an undeveloped domestic stock market. Mainland Chinese were restricted to investing in domestic "A" shares (yuan-denominated) on the Shanghai and Shenzhen exchanges until late 2011. It was announced that exchange traded funds based on Hong Kong stocks would be available on the two exchanges. Other changes involving Hong Kong's established capital markets are under way; nevertheless, China still has a way to go to achieve free and open two-way capital flows.

Latin America is the remaining emerging marketplace that has been of increasing interest to investors. The markets in Latin America include Argentina, Brazil, Chile, Colombia, Mexico, Peru, and Venezuela. Mexico and Brazil have large markets, with the others smaller in terms of market capitalization. As we would expect in emerging markets, profit potentials are large, but so are risks—volatile prices, liquidity problems, and political risks such as assassinations or nationalizations. Brazil has been of particular interest to investors because of the overall strong growth in its economy in recent years.

Checking Your Understanding

3. What are some important differences between the NYSE and NASDAQ?
4. Distinguish between NASDAQ and the over-the-counter market.
5. Why might a company opt to have its shares traded on NASDAQ rather than the NYSE? What about the reverse?

Stock Market Indexes

Quick! Suppose you own some common stocks and your friend tells you that the market closed down 110 points today. What exactly does this mean? Is this a really large loss for stocks? Assuming you owned some stocks, how are you affected?

The most popular financial question asked by individuals daily is probably, "What did the market do today?" To answer this question, we need a composite report on market performance, which is what stock market averages and indexes are designed to provide. Because of the large number of equity markets, both domestic and foreign, there are numerous stock market indicators. In this section, we outline some basic information on these averages and indexes, with subsequent chapters containing more analysis and discussion as needed.

It is important to note in the discussion below the difference between a stock index, measuring prices only, and a total return index. For example, the Dow Jones Industrial Average, like all major stock indexes, measures only the change in prices of a defined group of stocks over some period of time. Such indexes ignore dividend payments, which, as we shall see in Chapter 6, constitute the other part of the total return for a common stock. Dividend payments often make total returns much larger than the price change component alone.

✓ Stock market indexes generally understate the total returns to investors from owning common stocks because they do not include the cash payments received on the stocks (dividends). These indexes measure only the price change; however, this is how we describe how equity markets are performing, whether for a day, a month, or a year.

Example 4-5   In 2011 the S&P 500 Index has a 0 percent change. The index began at 1,257.6 and ended at 1,257.6. However, this index had a 2.1 percent dividend yield for the year. Therefore, although the market index was unchanged, the total return for an investor was 2.1 percent.

THE DOW JONES AVERAGES

Dow Jones Industrial Average (DJIA) A price-weighted series of 30 leading stocks, used as a measure of stock market activity

Blue-Chip Stocks Stocks with long records of earnings and dividends—well-known, stable, mature companies

The best-known average in the United States is the **Dow Jones Industrial Average (DJIA)**, probably because it has always been affiliated with Dow Jones & Company, publishers of *The Wall Street Journal*, and it is reported daily on virtually all major newscasts.[10] It is the oldest market measure, originating in 1896 and modified over the years.[11] The DJIA is computed from 30 leading stocks chosen somewhat arbitrarily by Dow Jones & Company to represent different industries. Traditionally, this average is said to be composed of **blue-chip stocks**, meaning large, well-established, and well-known companies.

A Price-Weighted Index   Because of its historical origins the DJIA is a *price-weighted series*, which is extremely unusual. Because it gives equal weight to equal dollar changes, high-priced stocks carry more weight than low-priced stocks. A 10 percent change in the price of stock A at $200 will have a much different impact on the DJIA from that of a 10 percent change in stock B at $20. This also means that as high-priced stocks split and their prices decline, they lose relative importance in the calculation of the average, whereas nonsplit stocks increase in relative importance. This bias against growth stocks, which are the most likely stocks to split, can result in a downward bias in the DJIA.

✓ The DJIA is a price-weighted stock market index, the only major market index constructed in this manner.

---

[10] There are three other Dow Jones Averages: the transportation, the public utility, and the composite. The first two encompass 20 and 15 stocks, respectively, and the composite consists of these two groups plus the DJIA (i.e., 65 stocks). Each average is calculated similarly to the DJIA, with changes made in the divisor to adjust for splits and other factors. Daily information on these averages can be found in *The Wall Street Journal* and other newspapers.

[11] The first average of U.S. stocks was created by Charles Dow in 1884 and consisted of 11 stocks, mostly railroads. The Dow Industrial Average, first published in 1896, consisted of 12 industrial companies.

The Dow Divisor   The divisor for this 30-stock index began at 30. However, stock dividends and splits presented a problem. To deal with this problem, the divisor is changed to offset the effect of the stock dividend or split. Because of the many ongoing adjustments in the divisor of the DJIA over many years, one point on the Dow is not equal to $1. At the beginning of 2012, the divisor was .132129493; therefore, if we divide 1 by the divisor we obtain a "multiplier" that shows how much the DJIA will change for a one-point change in only one stock in the index. This multiplier was 1/.132129493 or 7.568 points.[12]

Example 4-6   What if the DJIA fell 73 points on one day, which most people would consider a notable decline? With a multiplier of 7.568, a decrease in price of only one of the Dow's 30 stocks of $3.75 would produce a change of 28.38 points. Therefore, 28.38/73 = 39 percent (rounded) of the decrease in the DJIA that day was accounted for by the movements in only one of the stocks in this index.

Dow Index Points and Levels   Investors need to distinguish between point changes in the DJIA and percentage changes. When the index is at a level such as 11,000 or 12,000, a 300-point change in one day has less impact than when the index was at 5,000, years ago. Therefore, we need to be careful to put point changes in perspective.

Example 4-7   On March 18, 2000, the Dow gained approximately 500 points to close at 10,630.6. This was a percentage gain of 4.94 percent. In contrast, on October 21, 1987, the Dow gained 186.84 points to close at 2,027.85—this represented a percentage gain of 10.15 percent because the base was much lower. On July 24, 2002, the Dow gained about 489 points to close at 8,191.29, a gain of 6.35 percent. (All calculations are done using the opening level of the index that day.)

Like any index, the level of the DJIA simply reflects the decisions that have been made on which stocks to include in the index. The stocks in this index are chosen by the senior editors of *The Wall Street Journal*. Changes occur periodically, primarily because of acquisitions or the loss of importance in an index company.[13] For example, U.S. Steel was once in the DJIA, but is no longer.

The Dow did not reach the 10,000 level until 1999, and it hit its all-time high on October 09, 2007, when it closed at almost 14,164. One year later, on October 10, 2008, the Dow was at 7,774 because of the financial crisis in the United States.[14] It closed the year 2008 at 8,776, and by March 9, 2009, it was at 6,547. The Dow ended 2011 at 12,217.56.

✓   What should matter to investors is the percentage change in the DJIA, or any index, for a specified time period. The level of an index, and the point change in that level, are not important (they are, in effect, artificial numbers).

---

[12] Using the divisor, a movement of 30 points in the DJIA results in an *average* movement in each component stock of only $0.1321.

[13] In November, 1999 Chevron, Goodyear, Union Carbide and Sears were removed from the index and replaced by Intel, Microsoft, Home Depot, and SBC Communications. In 2004 other traditional American companies, AT&T, Kodak, and International Paper, were replaced by American International Group, Pfizer and Verizon Communications. In 2008, two more stocks in the index were replaced.

[14] It closed in 2004 at 10,783.01, an increase of 3.15 percent for the year. For 2003, the increase was about 25 percent. For 2008, the change was −34 percent. Clearly, yearly changes can vary widely.

In the case of the DJIA its level simply reflects the decisions made by a committee as to which stocks to include in the index, and its point change on any given day does not directly represent dollars and cents.

Criticisms of the DJIA   The DJIA has been criticized because of its use of only 30 stocks to reflect what the overall market is doing, and because it is price-weighted (rather than value-weighted). Furthermore, one can argue that it is no longer an "industrial" index because two-thirds of its weighting comes from sectors involving consumer products, financial services companies, and technology companies. Nevertheless, it is the oldest continuous measure of the stock market, and it remains the most prominent measure of market activity for most individual investors. Regardless of its problems, the DJIA remains relevant because it is so widely reported and cited in daily newspapers, broadcasts, and Internet sites, and because it is closely associated with *The Wall Street Journal*. The DJIA does fulfill its role as a measure of market activity for large stocks such as those on the New York Stock Exchange.

STANDARD & POOR'S STOCK PRICE INDEXES

Standard & Poor's Corporation makes available the widely cited **Standard & Poor's 500 Composite Index (S&P 500 Index)**.[15] This index is carried in the popular press such as *The Wall Street Journal* and on many Internet sites, and investors often refer to it as a "good" measure of what the overall market is doing, at least for large NYSE stocks. The S&P 500 is typically the measure of the market preferred by institutional investors when comparing their performance for a portfolio of large stocks to that of the market. One justification for this is that it accounts for about 75 percent of U.S. stock market value.

The S&P 500 includes most of the big companies familiar to investors. All 30 of the Dow Jones Industrials are in this index. Unlike the DJIA, the makeup of the S&P 500 changes several times a year as a result of acquisitions and mergers as well as other reasons.

Standard & Poor's 500 Composite Index (S&P 500) Market value index of stock market activity covering 500 stocks

Capitalization-Weighted Indexes   Unlike the Dow Jones Industrial Average, the S&P 500 Index is a market value index or capitalization-weighted index. It is expressed in relative numbers with a base value arbitrarily set to 10 (1941–1943). Technically what this means is that the current level of this index—for example, if it were 1,200—is some multiple of the base; in this case it is 120 times larger than the base. Of course, exactly like other indexes, what actually matters to investors is the percentage change in the index. For example, if the index goes from 1,075 to 1,190 in one year, this is an increase of (1190/1075) – 1.0, or 10.7 percent.

All stock splits and dividends are automatically accounted for in calculating the value of the index because the number of shares currently outstanding (i.e., after the split or dividend) and the new price are used in the calculation. Unlike the Dow Jones Average, each stock's importance is based on relative total market value instead of relative per share price. If two stocks in the S&P 500 have approximately equal market values, a 10 percent change in the price of one would affect the index about the same as a 10 percent change in the other. On the other hand, a 10 percent change in a larger stock in this index, as measured by total market value, would have a bigger impact on the index.

UNDERSTANDING A CAPITALIZATION-WEIGHTED INDEX

Table 4-1 illustrates how a market value, or capitalization-weighted, index is constructed. For each stock the share price is multiplied by the number of shares outstanding to obtain the

---

[15] Standard & Poor's also publishes indexes for various groupings of stocks, covering specific industries, low-priced stocks, high-grade stocks, and so on.

Table 4-1 Illustration of How a Value-Weighted Index Is Constructed and Calculated

	Stock	Price	Number of Shares	Market Value (price × shares)
Year-end				
1				
	ABD	$10	10,000,000	$ 100,000,000
	TWE	20	15,000,000	300,000,000
	CWF	40	25,000,000	1,000,000,000
				Total Market Value = $1,400,000,000

Base Value of Index = 100 (by construction)

	Stock	Price	Number of Shares	Market Value (price × shares)
Year-end				
2				
	ABD	$ 7	20,000,000*	$ 140,000,000
	TWE	14	15,000,000	210,000,000
	CWF	50	25,000,000	1,250,000,000
				Total Market Value = $1,600,000,000

New Value of Index = $1,600,000,000/$1,400,000,000 × 100 = 1.1429 × 100 = 114.29

*ABD splits 2-for-1 during year 2.

current market value of the stock. A base value has to be set by construction—in Table 4-1 the value at the end of the first year is set at 100. At the end of the second year, market value is calculated the same way. Notice in Table 4-1 that stock ABD has a two-for-one stock split in the second year, and this is automatically adjusted for because we are multiplying share price by number of shares to obtain market value. The new index value is 114.29, because the total market value of the stocks in this index has increased by that amount.

Using the S&P 500 Index   The S&P 500 is obviously a much broader measure than the Dow, and it should be more representative of the general market. In fact, although this index constitutes less than 10 percent of all stocks in the Wilshire 5000 Total Market Index, the broadest market measure, it represents about three-fourths of the value of all U.S. stocks.

✓   The S&P 500 Index comprises about three-quarters of the value of all U.S. equities, making it very useful as a benchmark of the overall stock market. Because of its widespread availability and general familiarity, it is often used by institutional investors and money managers, as well as knowledgeable individual investors.

It is important to note that the S&P 500 consists primarily of NYSE stocks, and it is clearly dominated by the largest corporations.[16] Like any index, it is affected by the performance of the individual stocks in the index. Being capitalization-weighted, the performance of the S&P 500 Index is significantly affected by a relatively small number of companies. For example, the largest 10 companies (based on total market value) in the S&P make up about one-fourth of its total value, and the largest 100 comprise over two-thirds of its total value. Therefore, if these few companies are quite cheap or quite expensive using valuation metrics,

---

[16] The S&P 500 contains some stocks from the NASDAQ Stock Market.

any conclusions about "the market" based solely on the valuation of the S&P 500 will be flawed.

What about international exposure for this index? In July 2002, the committee at Standard & Poor's that handles the S&P 500 Index decided that henceforth foreign corporations would no longer be included in the index. This resulted in dropping seven foreign-based firms, including Royal Dutch Petroleum and Unilever. They were replaced with, among others, eBay and UPS.

The S&P 500 Index hit its all-time high on October 9, 2007, when it reached 1,565.15. After suffering three consecutive years of declines in 2000, 2001, and 2002, it had positive gains each year through 2007. 2008, of course, was a different story, as stocks suffered very large losses. 2009 and 2010 showed strong positive percentage gains in the S&P 500 Index.

NASDAQ INDEXES

NASDAQ Composite Index Measures all NASDAQ domestic-and international-based common type stocks listed on the NASDAQ Stock Market

The NASDAQ indexes of most interest to investors, the Composite Index and the 100 Index, are widely available daily. The **NASDAQ Composite Index** measures all NASDAQ domestic- and international-based common type stocks listed on the NASDAQ Stock Market.[17] The NASDAQ 100 consists of 100 of the largest domestic and international nonfinancial firms listed on NASDAQ.

The NASDAQ Composite Index suffered the most horrific declines of all the major U.S. indexes during the period 2000–2002. After reaching a record level of almost 5,050 on March 10, 2000, it closed at 1,240 on July 25, 2002, falling about 4 percent on that day alone. At that point it had declined about 75 percent from its record high (it declined 36 percent in 2002 alone up to July 25). By the end of 2004 the index stood at 2,175.44, gaining 8.59 percent for the year.

The NASDAQ Composite Index is heavily dominated by the technology stocks such as Cisco, Dell, Microsoft, Oracle, and Intel. Therefore, this index is going to significantly be affected by the performance of technology stocks. In the 1990s such stocks soared, but in 2000–2002 these stocks collapsed. The index clearly reflected both events.

Concepts in Action

When Indexes Really Go South

The U.S. economy and financial markets suffered a number of significant negative events in 2008. In October 2008, the S&P Index suffered its biggest monthly decline since 1987, losing 16.9 percent. In both September and October 2008, the stock market suffered large losses. For example, the week of October 6-10 saw the DJIA decline 18 percent, the largest one-week decline in the history of this index.

OTHER INDEXES

The *Russell 1000 Index* is closely correlated with the S&P 500, because it consists primarily of "large cap" stocks. These 1,000 stocks make up about 90 percent of the total market value of the Russell 3000. The *Russell 2000* consists of the remaining 10 percent of the Russell 3000. These "small caps" have an average market capitalization of about $200 million compared

---

[17] The base period January 1971 is assigned a value of 100 for the Composite Index and the Industrial Index, and monthly data are available from January 1971.

to $4 billion for the Russell 1000. The Russell 2000 is often cited as an index of small common stocks.

The Wilshire 5000 Total Market Index claims to be the most comprehensive measure of the entire U.S. stock market. Included are the primary equity issues of all U.S. equity securities with readily available prices.[18] This index can be used to approximate dollar changes in the U.S. equity market. As usual, however, investors should be looking at percentage changes. Wilshire provides numerous indexes besides market indexes, including real estate and U.S.-style indexes.

Concepts in Action

Obtaining and Using Market Indexes

Daily information on the major market indexes is widely available at sites such as wsj.com, marketwatch. com, brokerage websites, and many others. For detailed data on domestic and foreign S&P indexes, go to www.standardandpoors.com. Information about the Wilshire indexes can be found at www.wilshire. com. Wilshire offers an index calculator for varying amounts of time. Yahoo! Finance provides daily, weekly and monthly prices for the major market indexes for starting and ending dates of your choice.

USING THE CORRECT DOMESTIC STOCK INDEXES

As the previous discussion indicates, numerous measures of the "market," ranging from the DJIA to the broadest measure of the market, the Wilshire Index, are available. It is obvious that the overall market is measured and reported on in several different ways.

Investors should use the correct index for the purpose at hand:

(a) To better measure how large stocks are doing, use the S&P 500 or the Russell 1000. Alternatively, use the DJIA but be aware of its potential problems and limitations, consisting as it does of only 30 stocks. Also be aware that since 2001 the DJIA has consistently outperformed the S&P 500 Index. Figure 4-2 shows the DJIA and the S&P 500 Index for a five-year period from early 2007 through early 2012. Note the divergence in the two over time, with the DJIA finishing in positive territory and the S&P 500 in negative territory.

(b) To measure how NASDAQ stocks are doing, use the NASDAQ Composite index to cover all NASDAQ securities, or the NASDAQ 100 to cover 100 of the largest companies. Figure 4-2 shows that the NASDAQ Composite Index outperformed the DJIA and the S&P 500 over the early 2007-early 2012 period.

(c) To measure small capitalization stocks, "small cap" stocks, use the Russell 2000 Index.

(d) To measure "mid-cap" stocks, use the S&P 400 Index.

(e) To measure the U.S. stock markets in the broadest sense, use the Wilshire 5000 Total Market Index.

---

[18] To be included, a company must be a U.S. company, and the security must have its primary market listing in the United States.

Figure 4-2

A Comparison of the Dow Jones Industrial Average, the S&P 500 Index, and the NASDAQ Index, Early 2007–Early 2012.

SOURCE: Reproduced with the Permission of YAHOO! Inc. Copyright © 2012 by YAHOO! Inc. YAHOO! and the YAHOO! Logo are Trademarks of YAHOO! Inc.

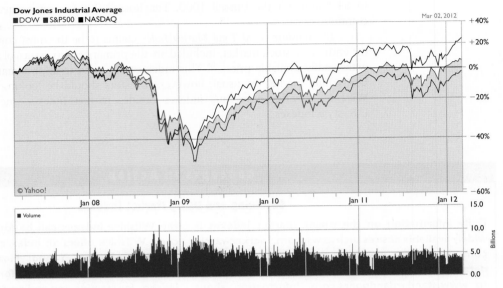

Investments Intuition

When Indexes Diverge

It is reasonable to assume that if investors use both the DJIA and the S&P 500 Index to measure market changes, the two indexes should produce similar results most of the time. However, significant differences can occur. In 2011, for example, the DJIA gained 5.53 percent for the year, while the S&P 500 Index was virtually flat (that is, the change for the year was essentially 0 percent). Therefore, you could give two completely different answers for the market change for large stocks for 2011, and both answers would be correct. Nevertheless, unless you were holding only the 30 stocks in the Dow, the 5.53 percent gain would be misleading to you as an investor when assessing your portfolio performance.

FOREIGN STOCK MARKET INDICATORS

MSCI EAFE Index The Europe, Australia, and Far East Index, a value-weighted index of the equity performance of major foreign markets

Dow Jones World Stock Index A capitalization-weighted index designed to be a comprehensive measure of worldwide stock performance

Stock market indexes are available for most foreign markets, but the composition, weighting, and computational procedures vary widely from index to index. This makes it difficult to make comparisons. To deal with these problems, some organizations have constructed their own set of indexes on a consistent basis. Certain international indexes also are regularly computed.

A well-known index of foreign stocks, and also the oldest international index, is the **MSCI EAFE Index**, or the Europe, Australia, and Far East Index. This index, compiled by Morgan Stanley Capital International, is, in effect, a non-American world index. It is often used to measure the performance of major international equity markets.[19] A limitation of this index is that it does not include rapidly growing emerging markets such as Brazil and India.

The **Dow Jones World Stock Index** covers the Pacific Region, Europe, Canada, Mexico, and the United States. It is designed to be a comprehensive measure, and represents approximately 80 percent of the world's stock markets. Unlike the DJIA, the World Stock Index is a capitalization-weighted index. *The Wall Street Journal* calculates and reports the DJ

---

[19] A number of index funds are designed to mirror the performance of the EAFE index.

World Stock Index as part of its "International Stock Indexes" carried daily in the *Journal*. Stock market indexes for all of the major foreign markets are also shown in this section.

Global Dow^{SM} **Index**
A stock market index designed to reflect the global stock market as it actually exists in terms of industries and regions

The **Global Dow**^{SM} **Index** is designed to reflect the global stock market as it actually exists in terms of industries and regions. It consists of 150 stocks representing leading companies from around the world, whether in a developed or emerging economy. This index declined about 13.5 percent in 2011.

Other foreign indexes include the STOXX® Europe 600 Index, created in 1986, which covers small, midcap and large capitalization companies in 18 countries. This index was down about 11.3 percent in 2011. The STOXX® Europe 50 Index covers "bluechip" companies in 12 Eurozone countries.

Checking Your Understanding

6. What is the major presumed deficiency of the DJIA?

7. Is the S&P 500 Index affected by the size of the companies in the index?

Bond Markets

Just as stockholders need good secondary markets to be able to trade stocks and thus preserve their flexibility, bondholders need a viable market in order to sell before maturity. Otherwise, many investors would be reluctant to tie up their funds for up to 30 years. At the very least, they would demand higher initial yields on bonds, which would hinder raising funds by those who wish to invest productively.

Investors can purchase either new bonds being issued in the primary market or existing bonds outstanding in the secondary market. Yields for the two must be in equilibrium.

The NYSE has the largest centralized bond market of any exchange. It is called NYSE Bonds. The trading platform incorporates an all-electronic trading platform, and involves corporates, agencies, and Treasury bonds. The majority of the volume is in corporate debt.

INDIVIDUAL INVESTORS AND BOND TRADING

Traditionally, the bond market has not been friendly to individual investors. Currently, individual investors can buy bonds directly only from the Federal government.[20] Moving beyond Treasuries, investors generally must use a broker to buy bonds.

Most bonds trade over the counter, which means there is no centralized marketplace or exchange. The bond market is actually a dealer to dealer market, with brokerage firms employing traders to deal in specific types of bonds. Bond brokers are generally buying bonds for their own accounts, and reselling them at a profit. Brokers typically earn a spread (the difference between the current market price and the cost to buy the bonds) and may also add a service charge to the transaction. A small number of corporate bonds are listed on the exchanges.

Better bond information has become available because of the Internet. More sites are offering pricing information. For example, Fidelity Investments allows you to access screens of all the major bond categories. Fidelity's online fixed income service, called Open Bond Market, offers an inventory of more than 15,000 fixed-income securities. Other brokerage firms also offer bonds, often charging a flat fee. Keep in mind that the fees do not tell investors the spreads between the buy and sell prices that are imbedded in the transactions.

---

[20] As noted in Chapter 2, TreasuryDirect allows investors to maintain accounts directly with the U.S. Treasury online, buying bills, notes, and bonds at auction without paying a commission.

Derivatives Markets

We discuss the details of derivatives markets in their respective chapters. At this point, however, we can note that options trade on the floor of exchanges, such as the Chicago Board Options Exchange, using a system of market makers. A bid and asked price is quoted by the market maker, and floor brokers can trade with the market maker or with other floor brokers.

Futures contracts traditionally were traded on exchanges in designated "pits," using as a trading mechanism an open-outcry process. Under this system, the pit trader offers to buy or sell contracts at an offered price and other pit traders are free to transact if they wish. Futures markets now tend to be electronic. For example, the CME Globex electronic trading platform is an electronic marketplace with a wide range of products across all asset classes. Investors can trade around the clock and around the world, with millisecond response time.

The Globalization of Markets

Instinet, mentioned earlier in the chapter, is an electronic trading mechanism allowing large investors (primarily institutions) to trade with each other electronically at any hour. Through such sources as Instinet, stock prices can change quickly although the exchanges themselves are closed. The after-hours trading is particularly important when significant news events occur, or when an institutional investor simply is anxious to trade a position. Such activity could lead to the 24-hour trading for stocks such as that which already exists for currencies.

What about bonds? In today's world, bonds increasingly are being traded at all hours around the globe, more so than stocks. The emergence of global offerings means that bonds are traded around the clock, and around the world. The U.S. Treasury securities market in particular has become a 24-hour-a-day marketplace. The result of this global trading in bonds is that bond dealers and investors are having to adapt to the new demands of the marketplace, being available to react and trade at all hours of the day and night. This includes new employees in various locales, expanded hours, and computer terminals in the home.

Investors can more easily trade on a global basis today. For example, E*Trade, a brokerage firm, offers investors the chance to trade not only in Germany, France, Canada, and the UK, but also in Japan and Hong Kong. They can also diversify in five local currencies.

Summary

▶ Financial markets include primary markets, where new securities are sold, and secondary markets, where existing securities are traded.

▶ Primary markets involve investment bankers who specialize in selling new securities. They offer the issuer several functions, including advisory, underwriting, and marketing services.

▶ Alternatives to the traditional public placements include private placements.

► We now live in a global economy, where funds can be raised around the world.

► Secondary markets consist of equity markets, bond markets, and derivative markets.

► The equity markets consist of auction markets (exchanges), negotiated markets, and electronic communication networks (ECNs) that match investor orders. Brokers act as intermediaries, representing both buyers and sellers; dealers make markets in securities, buying and selling for their own account.

► On the New York Stock Exchange (NYSE), long thought of as the premier secondary market, specialists act to provide a continuous market for NYSE stocks. Alternatively, investors can use Arca, the ECN associated with the NYSE.

► The Amex, on which fewer and generally smaller stocks trade, resembles the NYSE in its operations. It agreed to merge with the NYSE in 2008.

► The NASDAQ Stock Market is an electronic network of terminals linking together hundreds of market makers who compete for investor orders by buying and selling for their own account.

► Investors have become increasingly interested in equity markets around the world because the United States now accounts for only about one-third of the world's stock market capitalization. Many equity markets exist.

► The best-known stock market indicator in the United States is the Dow Jones Industrial Average (DJIA), computed from 30 leading industrial stocks.

► Standard & Poor's 500-stock Composite Index is carried in the popular press, and investors often refer to it as a "good" measure of what the overall market is doing, at least for large NYSE stocks. Other indexes cover various market segments.

► Although a few corporate bonds are traded on exchanges, most bond trading occurs in the over-the-counter (OTC) market involving a network of dealers.

► Treasury bonds and federal agency bonds enjoy broad markets, while the markets for municipal bonds and corporate bonds are often less liquid.

► Derivatives markets involve options and futures contracts. Puts and calls are traded on option exchanges using market makers, while futures contracts traded were traded in pits using an open-outcry system but increasingly are traded in electronic markets.

► Securities markets increasingly are linked globally. For example, we now have the NYSE Euronext, and the CME Group offers a wide range of options and futures products to serve customers around the globe.

Questions

4-1 Discuss the importance of the financial markets to the U.S. economy. Can primary markets exist without secondary markets?

4-2 Discuss the functions of an investment banker.

4-3 Outline the process for a primary offering of securities involving investment bankers.

4-4 Outline the structure of equity markets in the United States. Distinguish between auction markets and negotiated markets.

4-5 In what way is an investment banker similar to a commission broker?

4-6 Explain the role of the Designated Market Makers, the successors to specialists. Refer to the NYSE for information.

4-7 Since the NYSE features a fully automated auction, why do you think it also features a physical auction as well?

4-8 Is there any similarity between a NASDAQ market maker and a Designated Market Maker on an exchange?

4-9 Explain the difference between NASD and NASDAQ.

4-10 Explain what an ECN is.

4-11 What advantages do ECNs offer?

4-12 Why do you think the New York Stock Exchange in 2005 agreed to a merger with ArcaEx, a very different type of marketplace?

4-13 What is an OTC security? How are such securities traded?

4-14 In terms of how they are constructed, what are the two primary types of stock indexes currently being used in the United States?

4-15 What is the Dow Jones Industrial Average? How does it differ from the S&P 500 Composite Index?

4-16 What is meant by the term *blue-chip stocks*? Cite three examples.

4-17 What is the EAFE Index?

4-18 What is meant by block activity on the NYSE? How important is it on the NYSE?

4-19 Why can the NYSE now describe itself as a hybrid market, given its long history of using specialists?

4-20 Approximately how many stocks are listed on the NYSE? Does NASDAQ have more listed?

4-21 What is meant by in-house trading? Who is likely to benefit from this activity?

4-22 What is meant by the statement, "The bond market is primarily an OTC market?"

4-23 How is the DJIA biased against growth stocks?

4-24 Using *The Wall Street Journal* or a comparable source of information, determine the current divisor for the DJIA.

4-25 Which would have a greater impact on the DJIA: a 10 percent change in the price of Altria, or a 10 percent change in the price of Pfizer?

4-26 Assume that AT&T and Altria, both of which are in the DJIA and in the S&P 500, have approximately equivalent market values (price multiplied by the number of shares outstanding) but very different market prices (which in fact is the case). Would a 5 percent move in each stock have about the same effect on the S&P 500 Index?

4-27 As an investor with a portfolio of stocks, would you rather see the S&P 500 Index and DJIA performing in a similar manner over some period of time, or quite differently?

Problems

4-1 Assume that you construct a price-weighted index of 20 stocks. The sum of the prices of these stocks is $2,000. The divisor for this index is 20, and the value of this index is 100. Now assume that one of the 20 stocks, with an average price of $100, has a two-for-one stock split, while the value of the other stocks remains unchanged.

a. If you make no adjustment to the index, what will be the new value of the index?

b. What does the new divisor have to be to keep the value of the index unchanged at 100?

CFA
4-2 An analyst gathered the following data about stocks J, K, and L, which together form a value-weighted index:

| Stock | December 31, Year 1 | | December 31, Year 2 | |
	Price	Shares Outstanding	Price	Shares Outstanding
J	$30	10,000	$50	10,000
K	$30	6,000	$25	12,000*
L	$40	8,000	$60	8,000

*2 for 1 stock split.

The ending value-weighted index (base index = 100) is closest to

a. 112.50.
b. 133.33.
c. 136.17.
d. 137.28.

4-3 Assume that you have a stock currently priced at $580 that moves exactly proportional to the S&P 500 Index. Over a six-month period the index moves from 1,325.83 to 1,440.67. What should the price of your stock be?

4-4 Assume the DJIA is at 10,000. Some people are predicting that this index could lose 50 percent because of the economy's difficulties. If that were to happen, what percentage rate of return would be necessary to restore the index to its former level?

4-5 The 52-week low for the NASDAQ index occurred on 9/4/09 at 1982.05, while the 52-week high occurred on 4/26/10 at 2,535.28. For the DJIA, the dates are the same, and the comparable numbers are 9,302.28 and 11,308.95. Which market performed better during that time period?

Computational Problems

4-1 Assume that the DJIA closed at 13,327 one day recently, and the divisor was .12493117.

a. What is the sum of the prices of the 30 stocks in the index, given this information?

b. Assume that one stock in the index, Pfizer, moved $4.40 that day, while the index itself moved about 102 points (to close at 13,327). What percentage of the total movement in the DJIA that day was accounted for by the movement in Pfizer?

c. Now assume that one of the 30 stocks had a 2-for-1 stock split that day, declining from $47.50 to $23.75. What would the new divisor have to be to keep the index unchanged at 13,327?

4-2 The DJIA reached a level of 11,722.98 in January 2000, and the S&P 500 reached a level of 1,527.46 in March 2000. Prior to that, on one particular day, the DJIA was at 10,995.63 and the S&P 500 was at 1,281.91.

a. What percentage gain was necessary in each index for it to advance to the two levels indicated above, given the two lower prices stated?

b. If the S&P index declined 7.62 percent over the following year from 1,281.91, what would its new level be?

4-3 From October 2007 to March 2009 the market declined about 57 percent. It then advanced in one year about 69 percent. Determine by calculations if investors were ahead after the advance, or not?

4-4 For the 20th century, the compound annual average return on the S&P 500 was 10.35 percent. How much would $1 have grown to over these 100 years?

Spreadsheet Exercises

4-1 Assume that the spreadsheet below shows the closing prices for the S&P 500 Index for the month of November 2012. Using a column with six decimal places:

a. Calculate the daily percentage changes in the S&P 500 Index. The last daily change is for 11/1/2012, resulting in 21 daily changes.

b. Calculate the average daily change in the Index, shown to 6 decimal places.

c. State the average daily change in the S&P 500 Index for the month of November 2012 as a percentage.

d. State the *implied* monthly change in the S&P 500 Index for the month of November 2012 as a percentage. (Notice the word *implied*—this in fact is not the correct percentage change for the month, as we will learn when we discuss the difference between the arithmetic mean and the geometric mean).

Date	Closing Pr
11/30/2012	1,400.38
11/29/2012	1,398.26
11/28/2012	1,390.84
11/27/2012	1,385.35
11/23/2012	1,375.93
11/22/2012	1,394.35
11/21/2012	1,390.71
11/20/2012	1,413.4
11/19/2012	1,426.63
11/16/2012	1,425.35
11/15/2012	1,423.57
11/14/2012	1,408.66
11/13/2012	1,403.04
11/12/2012	1,403.58
11/9/2012	1,388.28
11/8/2012	1,397.68
11/7/2012	1,392.57
11/6/2012	1,418.26
11/5/2012	1,407.49
11/2/2012	1,413.9
11/1/2012	1,409.34
10/31/2012	1,385.59
Average =	

4-2   The spreadsheet below contains the total returns for the S&P 500 Index for the years 2000–2009 in decimal form. This 10-year period has been called the "Lost Decade."

a. Calculate the average annual total return (geometric mean) for this index for this 10-year period. Interpret your result.

b. What was the cumulative wealth on December 31, 2009, per dollar invested on January 1, 2000?

c. What was the cumulative wealth on December 31, 2002, per dollar invested on January 1, 2000?

d. Given a $100 investment in the S&P 500 Index on January 1, 2000, in what year did this investment finally break above $100?

2000	0.9088
2001	0.8812
2002	0.7791
2003	1.2867
2004	1.1087
2005	1.0491
2006	1.1574
2007	1.0549
2008	0.63
2009	1.2646

Checking Your Understanding

4-1 The term "underwriting" technically involves a firm commitment, meaning the investment bankers have agreed to purchase the securities outright from the issuer. This is different, for example, from a "best effort," where the risk of selling the issue is shared by the issuer and the underwriters.

4-2 The underwriters have an incentive to quickly sell an issue, thereby reducing their risk as well as enhancing their reputation as successful investment bankers.

4-3 The NYSE is the oldest stock exchange in the United States. NASDAQ only recently became an exchange. The NYSE trades many large, very well-known companies, while NASDAQ trades some smaller companies that are not well known, as well as some of the most important technology companies in the world. NASDAQ now has more companies listed than the NYSE. The NYSE is a physical location market while NASDAQ is based on dealers or market makers. The merger between the NYSE and ArcaEx marked a significant change in the way the NYSE operates.

4-4 NASDAQ is a marketplace distinguishable by its trading mechanisms and processes. The term over-the-counter market has traditionally referred to the trading of securities not listed on the organized exchanges.

4-5 Companies may have to disclose less information on NASDAQ, or may prefer having multiple market makers for their stock. On the other hand, companies may prefer to have their shares traded on the NYSE, long considered to be the premier secondary market for the trading of equities.

4-6 The DJIA is a price-weighted index, while almost all others are market-value–weighted. Also, it consists of only 30 stocks.

4-7 The S&P 500 Index is affected by the size of the companies in the index because it is a market-value–weighted index. Therefore, each stock's weight in the index is proportionate to its market value.

chapter 5

All Financial Markets Have Regulations and Trading Practices

Now that you know what investing alternatives are available to you, both direct and indirect, and where they trade, you need to consider the details of trading securities as you prepare to invest your inheritance. What type of brokerage account will best meet your needs? What type of orders can you use to buy and sell securities? How well does the securities legislation in place today protect you from the many pitfalls awaiting you as an investor? Should you take additional risk by buying stocks on margin, and if so, how do you go about trading on margin? Should you bet on security price declines by selling short, or is this technique too risky for average investors? Details, details, but investors must deal with them. Unless you master these details, you will not be able to take full advantage of the trading opportunities that financial markets offer. Furthermore, you will be at the mercy of others who may not have your best interests at heart.

In Chapter 4 we considered how securities markets are organized. In this chapter we learn the mechanics of trading securities which investors must know in order to operate successfully in the marketplace. Chapter 5 discusses various details involved in trading securities, critical information for every investor. Brokerage firms and their activities are analyzed, as are the types of orders to buy and sell securities, and the handling of these orders. The regulation of the securities markets is discussed. Finally, the various aspects of trading securities that investors often encounter are considered. Although the details of trading, like the organization of securities markets, continue to evolve, the basic procedures remain the same.

AFTER READING THIS CHAPTER YOU WILL BE ABLE TO:

▶ Explain brokers' roles and how brokerage firms operate.

▶ Understand the types of orders investors use in trading securities.

▶ Assess the role of regulation in the securities markets.

▶ Appreciate how margin trading and short selling contribute to investor opportunities.

Introduction

Could you as an investor carry out the following transactions? If so, how?

1. Buy Treasury securities directly from the Treasury, bypassing brokers.
2. Buy any stock you want directly from the company, bypassing brokers.
3. Specify an exact price or better on a stock you buy or sell if your order is executed.
4. Buy securities by only putting up half the cost.
5. Sell a stock you don't own in an attempt to make money on the transaction.

Brokerage Transactions

BROKERAGE FIRMS

In general, it is quite easy for any responsible person to open a brokerage account. An investor selects a broker or brokerage house by personal contact, referral, reputation, and so forth. Member firms of the NYSE are supposed to learn certain basic facts about potential customers, but only minimal information is normally required. Actually, personal contact between broker and customer seldom occurs in today's world, with transactions carried out by phone or by computer.

Customers can choose the type of broker they wish to use. They can be classified according to the services offered and fees charged.

Full-Service Brokers Traditionally, brokerage firms offered a variety of services to investors, particularly information and advice. Today, investors can still obtain a wide variety of information on the economy, particular industries, individual companies, and the bond market from **full-service brokers** such as Merrill Lynch, Morgan Stanley Smith Barney, Edward Jones, Raymond James, and Wells Fargo Advisors. These large retail brokerage firms execute their customers' orders, provide investment research, and offer advice and recommendations to investors.

> **Full-Service Brokers** A brokerage firm offering a full range of services, including information and advice

Today's full-service stockbrokers go by different titles, such as financial consultants or investment executives (or simply registered representatives). This change in title reflects the significant changes that have occurred in the industry. Full-service brokerage firms now derive only a small percentage of their revenues from commissions paid by individual investors, a major change from the past.[1] And the typical full-service stockbroker, whatever he or she is called, now derives much less of his or her income from customer commissions than was the case in the past. This is why firms such as Merrill Lynch encourage their brokers to become more like fee-based financial planners and less like salespeople.

✓ Full-service brokers seek to build relationships with clients by meeting all of the needs of a client, whether it be retirement planning, estate planning, taxes, financing children's education, or providing you access to such exotic assets as coffee futures and thinly traded foreign stocks.

Commissions charged by full-service brokers vary by product. For stocks, commissions vary across firms, although costs are typically higher than for discount brokers. Treasury

---

[1] Other sources of revenue for these firms include the sale of mutual funds run by the firms, the sale of new issues of securities (IPOs) (discussed in Chapter 4) and "principal transactions," which involves brokerage firms trading for their own accounts. Lastly, underwriting new issues is generally a profitable activity for large firms which have brokerage operations, and brokers may have an incentive to steer their customers into the new issues.

securities may carry a commission of less than 1 percent, whereas a complicated limited partnership may carry a commission of 8 percent or more. In some cases, the commission is "transparent" to the investor, meaning that the investor does not see an explicit commission.

Discount Broker
Brokerage firms offering execution services at prices typically significantly less than full-line brokerage firms

Discount Brokers   Investors can choose to use a **discount broker** who will provide virtually all of the same services except they may or may not offer advice and publications and will charge less for the execution of trades.[2] Smart investors choose the alternative that is best for them in terms of their own needs. Some investors need and want personal attention and detailed research publications, and are willing to pay in the form of higher brokerage commissions. Others, however, prefer to do their own research, make their own decisions, and pay only for order execution.

At the beginning of 2008, a survey by the American Association of Individual Investors (AAII) covered 52 discount brokers, 45 of which offered online trading.[3] Note that the total number includes the well-known large discount brokers such as Schwab, Fidelity, and E*Trade, as well as an array of often less-known brokerages offering a varied mix of services. Thus, with online discount brokers, investors must carefully evaluate the total package of services offered.

The AAII survey found that most of these firms offer many of the same basic services to customers. For example, all of them offered SIPC coverage, which insures the securities and cash in customer accounts, and all offered margin accounts (discussed later in the chapter). On the other hand, only three-fourths of the firms allow customers to write personal checks against cash balances in their brokerage accounts. Some discount brokerage firms offer research information and investment recommendations. More than half of the firms in this survey used an outside source for their research offerings, while a few had in-house analysts. Some charge for research information, and some do not.

International investing is available from discount brokers. For example, Scottrade offers access to foreign stocks, allowing investors to trade stocks from over 20 countries, and most of these trades cost only $7.

Some Practical Advice

Broker Responsibilities or The Lack Thereof

You may have heard the term "fiduciary" or not—surveys suggest a majority of investors do not understand what the term means. For brokers and investment advisors a fiduciary standard basically means that the client, as opposed to the interests of the broker or investment advisor comes first. However, there is a difference in the manner in which this standard is applied. Investment advisors are held to a fiduciary standard that requires them to put the client's interest first. For example, when recommending two investment products for a client that would accomplish the same objective but at different costs, they are required to recommend the cheaper of the two. Brokers, on the other hand, are not held to this standard. As long as the investment products they sell their clients are suitable, brokers have satisfied their obligations. Thus, in the previous example they are not required to recommend the cheaper alternative. Investors should be aware of this situation.

---

[2] Some discount brokers do provide research information beyond very basic information. This includes standard information supplied to the brokerage from outside sources and customized information generated in-house.

[3] See "2008 Discount Broker Guide," *AAII Journal*, February 2008, pp. 5–15. This journal is a publication of the American Association of Individual Investors, an organization serving individual investors. Their website is www.aaii.com.

Commissions Not surprisingly, commissions charged by brokers vary in both the amount and how they are calculated. According to a survey of brokers in 2011 conducted by *Smart Money* magazine, the average commission for a basic stock trade was $8.27.[4]

Ethics in Investing

Do You Have an Obligation Arising from Unsolicited Good Advice?

Investors have a choice of brokers, ranging from those providing advice and recommendations (and typically charging more), and those offering little or no advice (and typically charging less). While we generally think of an investor seeking out a broker, brokers often seek out customers. Assume that you as an investor have a brokerage account of your own choosing where you transact your investing decisions. Out of the blue, a broker you have never met, employed at a brokerage firm you are not familiar with, calls you (for obvious reasons, this is referred to in the business as "cold-calling"). He offers to send you for free some investing ideas. You accept the offer. You later decide to invest

in one of the stocks he has recommended, because after thinking about it and checking further, you decide that this stock has merit. You execute the transaction in your regular brokerage account rather than through a new account with the broker who called. Is this ethical behavior on your part?

Most observers would agree that in this situation you are under no obligation to transact with the broker who sought you out as a potential customer. Had you solicited the recommendation, you would have an obligation, but in this case you do not. Of course, you may not receive any more recommendations from this broker.

BROKERAGE ACCOUNTS

Margin Borrowing
Borrowing from a brokerage firm to finance a securities transaction

The most basic type of account is the cash account, whereby the customer pays the brokerage house the full price for any securities purchased. Many customers add **margin borrowing** to the account, which allows the customer to borrow from the brokerage firm to purchase securities. (Margin is explained in some detail later in this chapter.) To have the margin feature, investors are required by both the NYSE and NASD to deposit with their brokerage firm a minimum of $2,000 or 100 percent of the purchase price, whichever is less (this is referred to as the "minimum margin"). Some firms may require a deposit of more than $2,000.

Most brokerage accounts today are cash management accounts (also called core accounts and sweep accounts), which means they offer a variety of what are essentially banking services to the investor. For example, account holders can write checks against the account. Debit and/or credit cards may be offered. In addition, instant loans based on the marginable securities in the account can be obtained for virtually any purpose, not just securities transactions, at the current broker's call money rate plus 0.75 to 2.25 percent.

With a sweep account, the brokerage firm "sweeps" any excess cash in the account daily and invests it in some interest-earning fund. Although many of these sweep accounts are federally insured, the interest rates paid on them can be incredibly low. For example, in late 2011 one well-known discount broker was paying only 0.05 percent on its regular sweep account, which obviously is very close to zero.

---

[4]J. Alex Tarquinio, "Annual Broker Survey 2011," *Smart Money*, June 2011, p. 54. *Smart Money* conducts a survey of brokers annually and names the top full service broker and the top discount broker.

Some Practical Advice

You Snooze, You Lose

Investors with sweep accounts should pay close attention to what their brokerage firm is paying in the way of interest on their sweep account. The brokerage default account typically pays the lowest rate possible, and the brokerage firm is not going to go out of its way to tell you about alternatives. Brokerage firms can make billions on the spread between what they pay on their default sweep account and what they earn investing the cash balances. However, most firms offer alternatives that pay higher rates of interest, some of which are disclosed on their websites. Investors should be diligent about this if their cash balances are significant.

Wrap Accounts   Brokers can act as middlemen, matching clients with independent money managers. Using the broker as a consultant, the client chooses an outside money manager from a list provided by the broker. Under this **wrap account**, all costs—the cost of the broker-consultant and money manager, all transactions costs, custody fees, and the cost of detailed performance reports—are wrapped in one fee. For stocks, the fee is 1–3 percent of the assets managed.[5]

Wrap Account A new type of brokerage account where all costs are wrapped in one fee

Large brokerage houses such as Merrill Lynch pioneered wrap accounts for investors with a minimum of $100,000 to commit. Merrill Lynch now offers several different types of wrap programs ranging from the traditional consultant wrap (the placement of client funds with institutional money managers) to a program where the investor makes the buy and sell decisions and can have unlimited no-commission trading. Because of their popularity, other financial companies, such as bank trusts, have begun offering these accounts.

A newer variation of wrap programs is the *mutual fund wrap account*, involving an investment in various mutual funds. Minimum account size requirements are more modest at $10,000 to $100,000. A few mutual fund companies such as Fidelity participate in this market directly. Fees average 1.1 percent to 1.4 percent of assets. Mutual fund wrap accounts are based on an asset allocation model that is updated quarterly to account for market conditions and client needs. The advisor may decide, for example, to shift some funds from bonds to stocks.

Dividend Reinvestment Plans (DRIPs) A plan offered by a company whereby stockholders can reinvest dividends in additional shares of stock at no cost

DRIPs   Many companies now offer **Dividend Reinvestment Plans (DRIPs)**. For investors enrolled in these plans, the company uses the dividends paid on shares owned to purchase additional shares, either full or fractional. Typically, no brokerage or administrative fees are involved. The advantages of such plans include dollar cost averaging, whereby more shares are purchased when the stock price is low than when it is high.

In order to be in a company's dividend reinvestment plan, investors often buy the stock through their brokers, although some companies sell directly to individuals. On becoming stockholders, investors can join the dividend reinvestment program and invest additional cash at specified intervals.

DRIPs are starting to resemble brokerage accounts. Investors can purchase additional shares by having money withdrawn from bank accounts periodically, and shares can even be redeemed by phone at many companies.

It is possible to invest in the market without a stockbroker or a brokerage account in the traditional sense. As an outgrowth of their dividend reinvestment plans, a number of companies now offer *direct stock purchase programs* (DSPs) to first-time investors. Investors make their initial purchase of stock directly from the company for small purchase fees. The price

---

[5] Fees are lower for bond portfolios or combinations of stocks and bonds.

paid typically is based on the closing price of the stock on designated dates (no limit orders are allowed). The companies selling stock by this method view it as a way to raise capital without underwriting fees and as a way to build goodwill with investors.

Example 5-1

Exxon/Mobil permits investors to buy up to $250,000 a year worth of Exxon stock from the company itself, with no commissions. Investors can open a direct-purchase account with Exxon for as little as $250. Other companies that offer similar plans include Kroger, Sears, Procter & Gamble, and Home Depot.

Treasury bond buyers can also avoid brokers by using the *Treasury Direct Program*. Investors can buy or sell Treasuries by phone or Internet, and check account balances, reinvest Treasuries as they mature, and get the forms necessary to sell Treasuries. Investors eliminate brokerage commissions, but some fees are involved ($34 per security sold, and in some cases a $25 account fee).[6]

How Orders Work

TRADING ON TODAY'S EXCHANGES

The NYSE was traditionally thought of as an agency auction market. That is, agents represent the public at an auction where the interactions of buyers and sellers determine the price of stocks traded on the NYSE. Given the volume of shares handled by the NYSE, several billion shares a day, trading must be highly automated.

As explained in Chapter 4, NYSE EuroNext operates the NYSE and NYSE Amex markets. Designated Market Makers have the responsibility for maintaining a fair and orderly market. According to the NYSE, "DMMs serve as a buffer against market volatility, increase liquidity and are obligated to maintain a fair and orderly market. The NYSE features both a physical auction convened by DMMs and a completely automated auction that includes algorithmic quotes from DMMs and other participants."[7]

As noted in Chapter 4, the NYSE merged with ArcaEx, an Electronic Communication Network (ECN), The NYSE now describes itself as a hybrid market, offering both an auction path seeking best price and an electronic path seeking the quickest execution. In effect, NYSE EuroNext operates two exchanges in the United States—the NYSE (and NYSE Amex) and NYSE Arca—which provide differentiated trading models to meet different customer needs.

ORDERS IN THE NASDAQ STOCK MARKET

NASDAQ has been thought of as an electronic screen-based equity market. It is now a U.S. stock exchange, providing free, universal real-time stock data to individual investors.

Market makers (dealers) match the forces of supply and demand, with each market maker making a market in certain securities. They do this by standing ready to buy a particular security from a seller or to sell it to a buyer. Market makers quote bid and asked prices for each security. The dealer profits from the spread between these two prices.

---

[6] Treasury Direct can be reached at 800–943–6864 or www.publicdebt.treas.gov.
[7] NYSE website.

Assume you place an order for a NASDAQ stock. The brokerage firm will enter it into the computer system, which will find the best price. Market makers are constantly buying and selling shares and earning the spread, the compensation for acting as a middleman. In effect, they are being paid to make the market.

MODERN DAY TRADING

Individual investors should think of the financial markets for equities primarily as the processes they follow to transact on the NYSE Euronext and NASDAQ, because these are the marketplaces that will most often affect them. However, they should also be aware of some terminology and practices that affect stock trading in today's world.

Algorithmic trading (also called automated trading or algo trading) involves the use of computer programs to initiate trading orders. A computer algorithm makes decisions on such details of the order as price, quantity, and timing. The order is often carried out without human intervention. Large institutional investors frequently use algorithmic trading to break large orders into several smaller orders in order to manage the impact of the order on the market. For example, a buy order for one million shares could impact the price of a stock significantly more than five orders for the same 1 million shares.

High-frequency traders, or "HFT" firms, hold shares for less than a day, and sometimes only for minutes. Using the very latest in technology, these firms can execute trades in fractions of a second in an attempt to gain an advantage over other traders. HFT-firms now account for a large percentage of all volumes. Institutional investors often complain that such trading makes it difficult for them to transact in the large volumes they wish to transact. How are individual investors affected? Buy and hold investors will not be affected by this type of trading, except perhaps psychologically. And when they need to buy or sell, they can easily and cheaply do so.

On May 6, 2010, a flash crash occurred in the financial markets. The Dow Jones Industrial Average suddenly plunged about 1,000 points on an intraday basis, although it recovered quickly. Algorithmic trading and HFT have been cited as contributing factors to the flash crash.

As if the above is not enough in terms of rapid trading, consider this. A $300 million cable is being laid underwater between New York and London to speed up trading by six milliseconds. Can it really be worth it to hedge funds, foreign exchange firms, and other types of traders to pay for the use of this cable to gain that advantage? One estimate is that a 1-millisecond advantage can be worth $100 million to a hedge fund.

TYPES OF ORDERS

Market order An order to buy or sell at the best price when the order reaches the trading floor

Limit order An order to buy or sell at a specified (or better) price

Stop order An order specifying a certain price at which a market order takes effect

Investors use three basic types of orders: market orders, limit orders, and stop orders. Each of these orders is explained in Exhibit 5-1. Briefly,

- A **market order** ensures that the order will be executed upon receipt, but the exact price at which the transaction occurs is not guaranteed
- A **limit order** ensures that the price specified by the investor will be met or bettered, but execution of the order may be delayed or may not occur
- A **stop order** directs that when a stock reaches a specified price a market order takes effect, but the exact transaction price is not assured

Investors can enter limit orders as day orders, which are effective for only one day, or as good-until-canceled orders or open orders, which remain in effect for six months unless

---

EXHIBIT 5-1

Types of Orders Used by Investors

1. *Market orders*, the most common type of order, instruct the broker to buy or sell the securities immediately at the best price available. As a representative of the buyer or seller, it is incumbent upon the broker to obtain the best price possible. A market order ensures that the transaction will be carried out, but the exact price at which it will occur is not known until its execution and subsequent confirmation to the customer.

2. *Limit orders* specify a particular price to be met or bettered. They may result in the customer obtaining a better price than with a market order or in no purchase or sale occurring because the market price never reaches the specified limit. The purchase or sale will occur only if the broker obtains that price, or betters it (lower for a purchase, higher for a sale). Limit orders can be tried immediately or left with the broker for a specific time or indefinitely. In turn, the broker leaves the order with the specialist who enters it in the limit book.

EXAMPLE: Assume that the current market price of a stock is $50. An investor might enter a buy limit order at $47. If the stock declines in prices to $47, this limit order, which is on the specialist's book, will be executed at $47 or less. Similarly, another investor might enter a sell limit order for this stock at $55. If the price of this stock rises to $55, this investor's shares will be sold.

3. *Stop orders* specify a certain price at which a market order takes effect. For example, a stop order to sell at $50 becomes a market order to sell as soon as the market price reaches (declines to) $50. However, the order may not be filled exactly at $50 because the closest price at which the stock trades may be $49.95. The exact price specified in the stop order is therefore not guaranteed and may not be realized.

EXAMPLE 1: A sell stop order can be used to protect a profit in the case of a price decline. Assume, for example, that a stock bought at $32 currently trades at $50. The investor does not want to limit additional gains, but may wish to protect against a price decline. To lock in most of the profit, a sell stop order could be placed at $47.

EXAMPLE 2: A buy stop order could be used to protect a profit from a short sale. Assume an investor sold short at $50, and the current market price of the stock is $32. A buy stop order placed at, say, $36 would protect most of the profit from the short sale.

---

canceled or renewed.[8] There is no guarantee that all orders will be filled at a particular price limit when that price is reached because orders are filled in a sequence determined by the rules of the various exchanges.[9]

Stop orders are used to buy and sell after a stock reaches a certain price level. A buy stop order is placed above the current market price, while a sell stop order is placed below the current price. A stop limit order automatically becomes a limit order when the stop limit price is reached.

✓ Use a market order to ensure execution of the order (exact price is not assured). Use a limit order to ensure a specified price or better (execution not assured).

Some Practical Advice

As we should expect, certain types of orders can have both good and bad effects. A stop loss order calls for a stock to be automatically sold when the price drops by a specified percentage or hits a specified price. This can limit losses on short-term trades, and can be effective in locking in profits. However, the normal volatility of the market can cause investors to buy at a higher price and sell at a lower price, only to see the price rebound and continue upward. Setting the right price at which the stock is to be sold is critical, and difficult to do.

---

[8] A market order remains in effect only for the day.

[9] Limit orders for more than one share can be filled in whole or in part until completed (involving more than one trading day) unless the order is specified as *all or none* (fill the whole order or no part of it), *immediate or cancel* (fill the whole order or any part immediately, canceling the balance), or *fill or kill* (fill the entire order immediately or cancel it).

A standard order is a round lot, which is 100 shares or a multiple of 100; an odd lot is any number of shares between one and 99. Odd lots are now executed by the NYSE directly by computer, and the overall volume of such transactions is small.[10]

CLEARING PROCEDURES

Most securities are sold on a regular way basis, meaning the settlement date is three business days after the trade date. On the settlement date the customer becomes the legal owner of any securities bought, or gives them up if sold, and must settle with the brokerage firm by that time. Most customers allow their brokerage firm to keep their securities in a street name—that is, the name of the brokerage firm. The customer receives a monthly statement showing his or her position as to cash, securities held, any funds borrowed from the broker, and so on.[11]

Checking Your Understanding

1. Assume you bought a stock for $50 and it has now increased in price to $75. You think it may go higher, but you want to protect most of your current profit, realizing a minimum gain of about $23 per share. What type of order could you place to accomplish this?
2. State two reasons why an investor establishing a brokerage account might prefer a wrap account to the more traditional asset management account.

Investor Protection in The Securities Markets

Investors should be concerned that securities markets are properly regulated for their protection. Our financial system depends heavily on confidence in that system. In the late nineteenth and early twentieth centuries, significant abuses in securities trading did occur; at the same time there was a lack of information disclosure, and trading procedures were not always sound. The market crash in 1929 and the Great Depression served as catalysts for reforms, which effectively began in the 1930s.

Investor protection can be divided into government regulation, primarily federal, and self-regulation by the industry. Although states also regulate securities transactions, the primary emphasis is on federal regulation, and so we will concentrate on that.

GOVERNMENT REGULATION

Federal Legislation   Much of the legislation governing the securities markets and industry was enacted during the Great Depression. Many fraudulent and undesirable practices occurred in the 1920s, and the markets as a whole were shattered in the crash of 1929. Congress subsequently sought to improve the stability and viability of the securities markets, enacting the basis of all securities regulation in the 1930s. Additional acts have been legislated

---

[10] Some large brokerage firms now handle their own odd lots, and most investors who transact in odd lots are actually transacting with a dealer.

[11] Use of stock certificates as part of the settlement is dying out in the United States. The Depository Trust Company (DTC) has helped to eliminate stock certificates by placing these transactions on computers. Members (brokers and dealers) who own certificates (in street name) deposit them in an account and can then deliver securities to each other in the form of a bookkeeping entry. This book-entry system, as opposed to the actual physical possession of securities in either registered or "bearer" form, is essential to minimize the tremendous amount of paperwork that would otherwise occur with stock certificates.

EXHIBIT 5-2

Major Legislation Regulating the Securities Markets

1. The Securities Act of 1933 (the Securities Act) deals primarily with new issues of securities. The intent was to protect potential investors in new securities by requiring issuers to register an issue with full disclosure of information. False information is subject to criminal penalties and lawsuits by purchasers to recover lost funds.

2. The Securities Exchange Act of 1934 (SEA) extended the disclosure requirements to the secondary market and established the SEC to oversee registration and disclosure requirements. Organized exchanges are required to register with the SEC and agree to be governed by existing legislation.

3. The Maloney Act of 1936 extended SEC control to the OTC market. It provides for the self-regulation of OTC dealers through the National Association of Securities Dealers (NASD), which licenses and regulates members of OTC firms. The SEC has authority over the NASD, which must report all its rules to the SEC.

4. The Investment Company Act of 1940 requires investment companies to register with the SEC and provides a regulatory framework within which they must operate. Investment companies are required to disclose considerable information and to follow procedures designed to protect their shareholders. This industry is heavily regulated.

5. The Investment Advisors Act of 1940 requires individuals or firms who sell advice about investments to register with the SEC. Registration connotes only compliance with the law. Almost anyone can become an investment advisor because the SEC cannot deny anyone the right to sell investment advice unless it can demonstrate dishonesty or fraud.

6. The Securities Investor Protection Act of 1970 established the Securities Investor Protection Corporation (SPIC) to act as an insurance company in protecting investors form brokerage firms that fail. Assessments are made against brokerage firms to provide the funds with backup government support available.

7. The Securities Act Amendments of 1975 was a far-reaching piece of legislation, calling for the SEC to move toward the establishment of a national market. This act abolished fixed brokerage commissions.

---

over the last 50 years. Exhibit 5-2 contains a brief description of the major legislation affecting securities markets.

The Justice Department can investigate alleged abuses in the financial markets. For example, an important development occurred in late 1994 concerning bid and asked prices on NASDAQ. Two professors discovered that actively traded NASDAQ stock spreads were typically quoted in quarters rather than eighths.[12] This finding caused quite an uproar, with the Justice Department looking into the issue of alleged price fixing among brokerage firms on the NASDAQ market. Settlements of such cases vary widely.

Example 5-2   In July 1996, the Justice Department settled a civil agreement whereby the 24 firms involved did not have to admit any violations but did have to agree to obey the law in the future and establish trade-monitoring systems at a cost of $100 million. The Justice Department claims that spreads have narrowed on many of the most actively traded NASDAQ stocks.

Securities and Exchange Commission (SEC) A federal government agency established by the Securities Exchange Act of 1934 to protect investors

The Securities and Exchange Commission   In 1934, Congress created the **Securities and Exchange Commission (SEC)** as an independent, quasi-judicial agency of the U.S. government. Its mission is to administer laws in the securities field and to protect investors and the public in securities transactions. The commission consists of five members appointed by the president for five-year terms. Its staff consists of lawyers, accountants,

---

[12] Stock prices in the 1990s were quoted on the basis of eighths, whereas today they are quoted in dollars and cents.

security analysts, and others divided into divisions and offices (including nine regional offices). The SEC has approximately 200 examiners.

In general, the SEC administers all securities laws. Thus, under the Securities Act of 1933, the SEC ensures that new securities being offered for public sale are registered with the commission, and under the 1934 act it does the same for securities trading on national exchanges. The registration of securities in no way ensures that investors purchasing them will not lose money. Registration means only that the issuer has made adequate disclosure. In fact, the SEC has no power to disapprove securities for lack of merit.

Under the two acts of 1940—the Investment Company Act and the Investment Advisors Act—investment companies and investment advisors must register with the SEC and disclose certain information. The SEC ensures that these two groups will meet the requirements of the laws affecting them. One problem, however, is that the number of registered investment advisors has increased significantly over the years, as has the number of investment companies. The SEC has a relatively small staff to deal with these two groups.

Some Practical Advice

Brokers are obligated to ensure that investments are "suitable" for their clients, a relatively weak standard, and charge commissions. Registered investment advisors (RIA) have a legal requirement to put their clients' interest ahead of theirs, and charge fees instead of commissions. However, oversight is very weak. Registering with the SEC simply is a notification that an individual is doing business as an RIA. There are no educational requirements or other standards. Furthermore, RIAs do not have to disclose their performance history to clients; therefore, clients may have no idea how well a particular RIA has managed money. Disputes between an RIA and a client typically must be settled by arbitration, which can be very costly.

The SEC is required to investigate complaints or indications of violations in securities transactions. As mentioned above, the Justice Department began an antitrust investigation of the NASDAQ Stock Market. The focus was particularly on the spreads—the difference between what buyers pay for a stock and what they sell it for. The SEC launched its own investigation of this and related issues. It forced the NASD into significant reforms, such as becoming a holding company with two units, the NASDAQ market itself and a separate unit for regulation called NASD Regulation Inc.

SEC actions are designed to help investors. SEC investigations and actions cover a wide range of activities.

Example 5-3   The SEC announced in 2008 that it filed a civil action against an individual and his two wholly owned companies for violations of the antifraud and registration provisions of the federal securities laws. The SEC alleged that this individual and his companies raised about $10 million from hundreds of investors nationwide through a series of unregistered offerings of fractional interests in oil and gas projects.

The SEC and Insider Trading   A well-known illustration of SEC activity involves "insider trading," which has been a primary enforcement emphasis of the SEC. Insider trading can be defined as a breach of a fiduciary duty while in possession of material, nonpublic information about a security. "Insiders" (officers and directors of corporations) are prohibited from misusing (i.e., trading on) corporate information that is not generally available to the public and are required to file reports with the SEC showing their equity holdings.

Several major insider-trading "scandals" have been reported over the years. For example, a well-known arbitrageur, Ivan Boesky, was fined $100 million by the SEC in a highly publicized insider-trading case. In late 2011, Raj Rajaratnam, a hedge fund operator, was sentenced to 11 years in prison, the longest prison sentence ever for insider trading. The trend now is for a higher percentage of those found guilty of insider trading to serve prison terms, and for the sentences received to be longer. In the past jail sentences were often light, a few months, but now they often are for periods of two to three years.

Although questions remain about exactly what constitutes insider trading, small investors can, and are, charged with possessing "material, nonpublic information." This happens regularly as a result of mergers and takeovers where the individuals involved are charged with the use of inside information to trade the stock of a company about to be acquired. Investors are well advised to be very careful to avoid insider trading.

SELF-REGULATION

Regulation of the Stock Exchange   Stock exchanges regulate and monitor trading for the benefit of investors and the protection of the financial system. The NYSE in particular has a stringent set of self-regulations and declares that it "provides the most meaningful market regulation in the world." The NYSE regulates itself as part of a combined effort involving the SEC (already discussed), itself, and member firms (discussed below). Together, this triad enforces federal legislation and self-regulation for the benefit of the investing public.

NYSE Regulation, Inc., a subsidiary of NYSE Euronext, is a not-for-profit corporation which focuses on protecting investors and strengthening market integrity. NYSE Regulation is independent in its decision making.[13] It seeks to protect investors by enforcing federal securities laws as well as exchange rules. NYSE Regulation also ensures that companies listed on the NYSE and on NYSE Arca meet the listing standards.

During a typical trading day, the NYSE continuously monitors all market participants. It also closely monitors the performance of specialists in their responsibility for maintaining a fair and orderly market in their assigned stocks. NYSE rules and regulations are self-imposed and approved by the SEC.

The NYSE has instituted several measures to reduce market volatility and serve the investors' best interests. These safeguards are referred to as "circuit-breakers." A "Trading Halt" is an example of a circuit breaker. A trading halt—which typically lasts less than an hour but can be longer—is called during the trading day to allow a company to announce important news or where there is a significant order imbalance between buyers and sellers in a security. A trading delay (or "delayed opening") is called if either of these situations occurs at the beginning of the trading day.

The Financial Industry Regulatory Authority (FINRA), created in 2007, is now the largest regulator for all securities firms doing business in the United States.[14] Its oversight includes 5,000 brokerage firms, about 172,000 branch offices and more than 674,000 registered securities representatives.[15] FINRA's objective is to protect investors and ensure market integrity. It accomplishes this objective through both regulation and compliance measures. FINRA's impact on the securities business is widespread. For example, it examines securities

---

[13] The organization consists of three divisions: Market Surveillance, Enforcement, and Listed Company Compliance.

[14] FINRA came about from the consolidation of the National Association of Securities Dealers (NASD) and the member regulation, enforcement, and arbitration functions of the New York Stock Exchange.

[15] FINRA has approximately 3,000 employees and operates from Washington, DC, and New York City. It has 15 district offices around the country.

firms and enforces federal securities laws. FINRA also performs market regulation under contract with certain exchanges.

Some Practical Advice

Conflicts between brokers and customers are inevitable, and investors should take steps to protect themselves. Investors can go to www.finra.org (website for the Financial Industry Regulatory Authority) and click on "FINRA BrokerCheck under Investor Resources. FINRA regulates brokerage firms. State regulators can provide Central Registration Depository reports which offer more disciplinary details than provided by the NASD. Links to state regulators can be found at nasaa.org (website for the North American Securities Administrators Association).

OTHER INVESTOR PROTECTIONS

Insured Brokerage Accounts The Securities Investor Protection Corporation (SIPC) is a nonprofit, membership corporation overseen by the SEC. It insures each customer account of its member brokers against brokerage firm failure. Each account is covered for as much as $500,000. (Coverage of cash is limited to $100,000.)[16] From its creation by Congress in 1970 through December 2010, SIPC states that it has advanced $1.6 billion in order to make possible the recovery of $109 billion in assets for an estimated 739,000 investors. SIPC's figures indicate that more than 99 percent of eligible investors have been made whole in the failed brokerage firm cases that it has handled to date.[17]

Mediation and Arbitration Investors who have disputes with their brokers generally cannot seek relief in court. When they open an account, investors pledge to resolve disputes through mediation or arbitration rather than go to court. When investors have problems, there are three stages of possible resolution.

First, investors can try to solve the problem with the brokerage firm. It is important to file a written claim (not an email), providing as much documentation as possible. Also, the claim should be sent to NASDR, the regulatory arm of the National Association of Securities Dealers as well as the investor's state securities regulator (which licenses brokers in a state).

The second state, particularly where compensation or damages is being sought, is mediation, which is voluntary. NASDR maintains a list of mediators and can appoint one if requested (investors have veto power over the choice of mediator). Mediation decisions are nonbinding.

The last stage is arbitration, which is a binding process that can determine damages. Arbiters can be a person or panel which examines the evidence and makes a ruling. Arbitration is not free, and investors should probably hire a lawyer.

In general, arbitration rulings cannot be appealed. The few exceptions (such as bias by the arbitrator) must be appealed within three months. Finally, litigation is possible, but difficult because of the arbitration clause investors sign. An example of when this might occur would be cases alleging broker fraud. Suit must be filed within one year of the alleged incident.

---

[16] In addition, many brokerage firms carry additional insurance, often for several million dollars, to provide even more protection for customers.

[17] Investors should make sure they are dealing with an SIPC firm by verifying the words "Member SIPC" in the signs and ads provided by members.

Checking Your Understanding

3. The Securities Act of 1933 ensures investors that every new issue of stock has met its quality standards and is likely to be a good investment. Agree or disagree, and explain your reasoning.
4. When resolving investor disputes with brokers, what is the major difference between mediation and arbitration?

Margin

As previously noted, investors often add a margin borrowing feature to their brokerage accounts. Doing so requires some deposit of cash or marginable securities. The NYSE requires that member firms establish a minimum deposit of $2,000 or its equivalent in securities for customers opening a margin account, but individual firms may require more to simply open an account. For example, Fidelity Brokerage Services requires $2,500 to open an account, while First Discount Brokerage requires $5,000.

With a margin account, the customer can choose to pay part of the total amount due and borrow the remainder from the broker, who in turn typically borrows from a bank to finance customers. The bank charges the broker the "broker call rate," and the broker in turn charges the customer a "margin interest rate," which is the broker call rate plus a percentage added on by the brokerage firm.[18] Cash has 100 percent loan value, and most stock securities have 50 percent loan value. Other securities have differing amounts.

HOW MARGIN ACCOUNTS CAN BE USED

A margin account can be used to

1. Purchase additional securities by leveraging the value of the eligible shares to buy more
2. Borrow money from a brokerage account for personal purposes (the margin interest rate is comparable to a bank's prime rate)
3. Provide overdraft protection in amounts up to the loan value of the marginable securities for checks written (or debit card purchases)

Margin trading involves a secured loan, with securities serving as collateral.

Investments Intuition

The traditional appeal of margin trading to investors is that it magnifies the percentage gains on your equity by the reciprocal of the margin requirement (i.e., 1/margin percentage; for example, with a margin of 40 percent, the magnification is 1/0.4 = 2.50). Unfortunately, the use of margin also magnifies the percentage losses. Regardless of what happens, the margin trader must pay the interest costs on the margin account. An investor considering a margined stock purchase should remember that the stock price can go up, remain the same, or go down. In two of these three cases, the investor loses. Even if the stock rises, the breakeven point is higher by the amount of the interest charges.

---

[18] One large discount brokerage firm adds 2 percent for margin loans up to $10,000, 1.5 percent for loans up to $25,000, 1 percent for loans up to $50,000, and 0.50 percent for loans above $50,000.

MARGIN REQUIREMENTS AND OBLIGATIONS

Margin The investor's equity in a transaction

✓ **Margin** is the customer's equity in a transaction; that is, it is that part of the total value of the transaction that is *not* borrowed from the broker.

There are two separate margin requirements. The initial margin requirement must be met when the transaction is initiated, but the maintenance margin must be met on an ongoing basis. Failure to meet the latter requirements can result in a margin call. We consider each of these issues in turn.

✓ An investor must meet both the initial margin requirement (at the time of the transaction) and the maintenance (ongoing) margin requirement.

Initial Margin In dollar terms, the initial equity an investor has in a margin transaction

Initial Margin   The Board of Governors of the Federal Reserve System (Fed), using Regulation T, has the authority to specify the **initial margin**, which is used as a policy device to influence the economy. Historically, the initial margin for stocks has ranged between 40 and 100 percent, with a current level of 50 percent since 1974.[19] The initial margin can be defined as

$$\text{Initial margin} = \frac{\text{Amount investor puts up}}{\text{Value of the transaction}} \qquad \text{(5-1)}$$

Example 5-4

If the initial margin requirement is 50 percent on a $9,000 transaction (100 shares at $90 per share), an investor who wants to fully use the margin provision must put up $4,500, borrowing $4,500 from the broker.[20] The investor could put up $4,500 in cash or deposit $9,000 in marginable securities. (We abstract from brokerage costs and any other costs in these examples).

Example 5-5

To illustrate the leverage impact, assume that the stock in Example 5-4 goes up 20 percent from $90 to $108, for a gain of $18 × 100 shares, or $1,800. The investor has a $1,800/$4,500 = 40 percent gain on his or her equity, the actual cash put up by the investor (once again, ignoring any costs involved). On the other hand, if the stock goes down 6 percent to $84.60, a loss of $540, the investor has a $540/$4,500 = 12 percent loss on his or her equity.

Maintenance Margin The percentage of a transaction's value that must be on hand at all times as equity

Maintenance Margin   In addition[21] to the initial margin, all exchanges and brokers require a **maintenance margin** below which the actual margin cannot go. The maintenance margin is the absolute minimum amount of margin (equity) that an investor must have in the account at all times. Brokers usually require 30 percent or more on long positions.[21]

✓ An investor's equity is calculated as the market value of the stock minus the amount borrowed. In turn, the market value of the stock is equal to the current market price multiplied by the number of shares.

---

[19] Exchanges and brokerage houses can require more initial margin than that set by the Fed, if they choose.

[20] With a 60 percent requirement, the customer must initially put up $6,000.

[21] The NYSE requires an investor to maintain an equity of 25 percent of the market value of any securities held.

If the investor's equity exceeds the initial margin, the excess margin can be withdrawn from the account, or more stock can be purchased without additional cash. Conversely, if the investor's equity declines below the initial margin, problems can arise, depending on the amount of the decline. It is at this point that the maintenance margin must be considered.

Example 5-6

Assume that the maintenance margin is 30 percent, with a 50 percent initial margin, and that the price of the stock declines from $100 to $90 per share. Equation 5-2 is used to calculate actual margin (as a percentage).[22]

$$\text{Actual margin \%} = \frac{\text{Current value of securities} - \text{Amount borrowed}}{\text{Current value of securities}} \qquad (5\text{-}2)$$

$$44.44\% = (\$9,000 - \$5,000)/\$9,000$$

The investor's dollar equity amount is now $4,000. The actual margin percentage now is between the initial margin of 50 percent and the maintenance margin of 30 percent. This could result in a restricted account, meaning that additional margin purchases are prohibited, although the customer does not have to put additional equity (cash) into the account.

Marked to market The daily posting of all profits and losses in an investor's account

Brokerage houses calculate the actual margin in their customers' accounts daily to determine whether a margin call is required. This is known as having the brokerage accounts **marked to market**.

Margin call A demand from the broker for additional cash or securities as a result of the actual margin declining below the maintenance margin

Margin Call

A **margin call** (maintenance call or "house call") occurs when the market value of the margined securities less the debit balance (amount owed) of the margin account declines below the maintenance requirement set by the brokerage house (typically 30 percent on stocks). This type of call is payable on demand, and the brokerage house may reserve the right to take action without notice if market conditions are deteriorating badly enough.

Example 5-7

Assume in the previous example that the maintenance margin is 30 percent. If the price of the stock drops to $80, the actual margin percentage will be 37.5 percent [($8,000 − $5,000)/ $8,000]. Because this is above the 30 percent maintenance margin requirement, there is no margin call. However, if the price of the stock declines to $66.66, the actual margin percentage will be 25 percent [($6,666 − $5,000)/$6,666]. This results in a maintenance call to restore the investor's equity to the minimum maintenance margin.

The price at which a margin call will be issued can be calculated as

$$\text{Margin call price} = \frac{\text{Amount borrowed}}{\text{Number of shares}(1 - \text{Maintenance margin percentage})} \qquad (5\text{-}3)$$

where margin call price equals the price of the stock that triggers a margin call.

---

[22] The difference between the market value of the securities and the amount borrowed is the investor's equity.

Example 5-8

Using the above data, for 100 shares, $5,000 borrowed, and a maintenance margin of 30 percent, a margin call will be issued when the price is

$$\text{MC price} = \frac{\$5,000}{100(1 - .30)} = \$71.43$$

Appendix 5-A contains detailed examples of margin calculations. Included are examples of what happens when an investor is on margin as well as example of satisfying a margin call.

MARGIN REQUIREMENTS ON OTHER SECURITIES

Although the initial margin requirement for common stocks and convertible bonds is 50 percent, it is only 30 percent (or less) of market value for "acceptable" municipal and corporate bonds.[23] U.S. government securities and GNMAs require an initial margin of only 8 to 15 percent, whereas Treasury bills may require only 1 percent of market value.

SOME MISCONCEPTIONS ABOUT MARGIN

1. *The broker must contact me before selling my securities.* In fact, while most brokers will attempt to contact their customers before selling, they are not obligated to do so.
2. *I choose which securities to sell to meet my margin obligations.* In fact, the brokerage can choose which of your securities to sell in order to best protect their interests.
3. *I am entitled to an extension of time.* In fact, a customer is not entitled to an extension of time, although in certain situations an extension could be granted.
4. *My broker must notify me before increasing the firm's maintenance requirements.* In fact, a brokerage firm can do this at any time, and without notice to you.
5. *The brokerage firm must set the same margin requirements on all stocks in my account.* In fact, a brokerage firm can set different requirements on the stocks in your account.

Short Sales

The purchase of a security technically results in the investor being "long" the security or position. This is well-known Wall Street terminology.

- A normal transaction (investor is long the position)—A security is bought, and owned, because the investor believes the price is likely to rise. Eventually, the security is sold and the position is closed out. First you buy, then you sell.
- Reverse the transaction (investor is short the position)—What if the investor thinks that the price of a security will decline? If he or she owns it, you might be wise to sell. If the security is not owned, the investor wishing to profit from the expected decline in price

---

[23] This may also be stated as a percentage of principal—for example, 10 percent for nonconvertible corporates and 15 percent for municipals.

can sell the security short. You do this by borrowing the stock, selling it, buying it back later, and replacing the borrowed shares.

Short Sale The sale of a stock not owned in order to take advantage of an expected decline in the price of the stock

✓ A **short sale** involves selling a security the seller does not own because of a belief that the price will decline, and buying back the security later to close the position. First you sell, then you buy. Having sold first, and before you repurchase, you are said to be "short" the position—hence the term short sale.

How can an investor sell short, which is to say sell something he or she typically does not own? Not owning the security to begin with, the investor will have to borrow from a third party. The broker, on being instructed to sell short, will make these arrangements for the short seller by borrowing the security from another investor who does business with the firm, and in effect, lending it to the short seller. Therefore, short selling is simply borrowing a stock, selling it, and replacing it later (hopefully when the price has declined). After all, when you borrow your neighbor's lawnmower or power tools, you are expected to bring them back or replace them. The short seller has an obligation someday to replace the shorted (borrowed) stock.

The short seller's broker sells the borrowed security in the open market, exactly like any other sale, to some investor who wishes to own it. The short seller expects the price of the security to decline. Assume that it does. The short seller instructs the broker to repurchase the security at the currently lower price and cancel the short position (by replacing the borrowed security). The investor profits by the difference between the price at which the borrowed stock was sold and the price at which it was repurchased (once again we are ignoring brokerage costs). This process is illustrated graphically in Figure 5-1.

The process of short selling is spelled out in more detail in Exhibit 5-3.

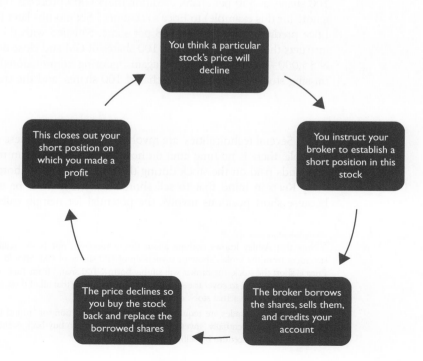

Figure 5-1

The Short Sale Process.

EXHIBIT 5-3

How Short Selling Works

1. An investor believes that IBM is overpriced at $60 a share and will decline. This investor does not own IBM stock but wishes to profit if her beliefs are correct and the price goes down.
2. You instruct your brokerage firm to short 100 share of IBM for you, a transaction valued at $6,000 (ignore brokerage costs). The brokerage firm does this by borrowing the 100 shares from another investor's account, lending them to this investor, and selling the shares at the current market price of $6,000.
3. The sale proceeds of $6,000 are credited to your margin account because you sold the stock. The investor must put up 50 percent of the borrowed amount, or $3,000, as initial margin. The investor who sold short is now responsible for paying back 100 shares of IBM stock to replace the 100 shares that were borrowed.
4. Assume that the price of IBM goes to $40 three months later. The investor is now ahead by $2,000 because she can buy back 100 shares of IBM for $4,000 on the open market and replace the 100 shares she borrowed.
5. Having closed out the short sale, the investor regains access to the $3,000 margin she had to put up.
6. Should the price of IBM rise, the investor has two choices. One, buy the stock back and close out the position, taking a loss. For example, buying back at $70 would result in a loss of $1,000. Two, continue to hold the position and hope the price eventually drops. In the case of a rising stock price for a short position, the investor may face a margin call requiring cash or equivalents equal to 25 to 30 percent of the stock's value. Exact maintenance margin requirements vary by firm.

Example 5-9 Assume an investor named Erica believes that the price of General Motors (GM) will decline over the next few months and wants to profit if her assessment is correct. She calls her broker with instructions to sell 100 shares of GM short (she does not own GM) at its current market price of $50 per share. The broker borrows 100 shares of GM from Ashley, who has a brokerage account with the firm and currently owns GM ("long"). The broker sells the borrowed 100 shares at $50 per share, crediting the $5,000 proceeds (less commissions, which we will ignore for this example) to Erica's account.[24] Six months later the price of GM has declined, as Erica predicted, and is now $38 per share. Satisfied with this drop in the price of GM, she instructs the broker to purchase 100 shares of GM and close out the short position. Her profit is $5,000–$3,800, or $1,200 (again, ignoring commissions). The broker replaces Ashley's missing stock with the just-purchased 100 shares, and the transaction is complete.[25]

Several technicalities are involved in a short sale; these are outlined in Exhibit 5-4. For example, there is no time limit on how long an investor can remain short in a stock, and any dividends paid on the stock during the time the seller is short must be covered by the seller.

Keep in mind that to sell short an investor must be approved for a margin account because short positions involve the potential for margin calls. Using our earlier example of

---

[24] Note that Ashley knows nothing about this transaction, nor is she really affected. Ashley receives a monthly statement from the broker showing ownership of 100 shares of GM. Should Ashley wish to sell the GM stock while Erica is short the stock, the broker will simply borrow 100 shares from Tara, a third investor who deals with this firm and owns GM stock, to cover the sale. It is important to note that all of these transactions are book entries and do not typically involve the actual stock certificates.

[25] Notice that two trades are required to complete a transaction, or "round trip." Investors who purchase securities plan to sell them eventually. Investors who sell short plan to buy back eventually; they have simply reversed the normal buy-sell procedure by selling and then buying.

EXHIBIT 5-4

The Details of Short Selling

1. Dividends declared on any stock sold short must be covered by the short seller. After all, the person from whom the shares were borrowed still owns the stock and expects all dividends paid on it.

2. Short sellers must have a margin account to sell short and must put up margin as if they had gone long. The margin can consist of cash or any restricted securities held long.

3. The net proceeds from a short sale, plus the required margin, are held by the broker; thus, no funds are immediately received by the short seller. The lender must be fully protected. To do this, the account is marked-to-the-market

(as mentioned earlier in connection with margin accounts). If the price of the stock, declines as expected by the short seller, he or she can withdraw the difference between the sale price and the current market price. If the price of the stock rises, however, the short seller will have to put up more funds.

4. There is no time limit on a short sale. Short sellers can remain short indefinitely. The only exception arises when the lender of the securities wants them back. In most cases the broker can borrow elsewhere, but in some situations, such as a thinly capitalized stock, this may not be possible.

Fidelity Brokerage Services, we see that the initial minimum equity to open a margin account required by Fidelity would be $2,500, the initial margin requirement would be 50 percent of the short sale, and the maintenance margin would be 30 percent of market value (the absolute minimum to open a margin account is $2,000 in cash or securities).[26] That is, the maintenance requirements for short sales are 100 percent of the current market value of the short sale plus (typically) 30 percent of the total market value of the securities in the margin account. Should the price of the security shorted rise enough, an investor will be required by the broker to put more cash in the account, or sell some securities.[27]

Example 5-10   Assume an investor shorts 100 shares of Merck at $100 per share. The investor must have $5,000 in the account (initial margin of 50 percent). The proceeds of the short sale are left in the account, making the total initial margin requirement $15,000 ($10,000 proceeds + $5,000 margin). If Merck rises to $110, the short sale value is now $11,000 and the maintenance margin is now 30 percent of that, or $3,300, for a total margin requirement of $14,300. Because the investor started with a total margin requirement of $15,000, no action is necessary. Now assume the price of Merck goes to $140. The short sale value is now $14,000, and the maintenance margin is now 30 percent of that, or $4,200. The total margin requirement is now $18,200, generating a margin call for an additional cash deposit of $3,200 (recall that the investor started with $15,000 after selling the stock short and putting up 50 percent of the value of the transaction as collateral).

---

[26] The Regulation T initial margin requirement for a short sale is 150 percent of the short sale proceeds.

[27] It is possible for investors to get caught in a "short squeeze." As a stock continues to rise in price, short sellers start buying to cover their positions, pushing the price even higher. Short sellers can actually create significant runups in the stock price, thereby causing the opposite of what they are trying to achieve. Brokers, in turn, may force the short sellers to cover their short positions if the price is rising dramatically. One way for short sellers to protect themselves against this is to use a buy stop loss order.

SELLING SHORT AS AN INVESTOR

Short sellers argue that short sales help the overall market. For example, short sales provide liquidity and can help smooth out the highs and lows in stock prices. And, of course, there have been many periods in the stock market when prices did not rise, but instead fell. During such periods, short selling might be a good strategy for some investors.

Example 5-11   The DJIA was approximately 10,100 at the beginning of March 2000. By the end of September 2002 it was approximately 7,600, a very large decline in a relatively short time. Many short sellers did well during this period.

Some investors argue that a portfolio consisting of both long and short positions can dampen volatility while still producing good returns. Some evidence suggests that a portfolio holding positions that are 65 percent long and 35 percent short is half as volatile as a portfolio that is 100 percent long.[28]

If you are interested in selling stocks short, how do you go about obtaining short-sale recommendations? Investors can do their own analysis or use investment advisory services. When you perform your own analysis, which types of companies should you look for to sell short? It makes sense to focus on companies in declining industries, companies that are in the news for possible fraudulent activity, companies with declining financial situations, and, perhaps most commonly, companies whose earnings are disappointing the market. As for advisory services, the results of those who provide recommendations vary over a wide range. And as you would expect, there are many more investment advisory services making buy recommendations than short sell recommendations.

Short Interest Ratio The ratio of total shares sold short to average daily trading volume

Short Interest Ratio   Is it possible to measure how bearish investors are about a stock? The **short interest ratio** is calculated for a stock by dividing the amount of shares sold short by the average daily trading volume. It indicates the number of days it would take for short sellers to buy back (cover) all of the shares sold short. The higher the ratio, the more bearish they are. Some studies suggest there is a strong negative relationship between short interest and subsequent stock returns, indicating that the short interest conveys negative information.

Concepts in Action

Do You Want to Be a Short Seller?

The feverish market of the late 1990s, when the market indexes were hitting new highs and technology stocks seemed greatly overpriced to many, sparked the interest of some investors in selling short. How popular is this activity, and what exactly is involved?

First of all, short selling as a percentage of total volume on the NYSE is small. Clearly, most investors are not selling short. Part of the reason is the mechanics involved. Short sellers must put up 50 percent of the short sale as collateral for the initial

---

[28] A popular recent trend has been that of active extension funds, or long-short equity funds. Also called 130/30 funds, this type of investing involves being long and short at the same time. By having 130 percent long exposure, and 30 percent short exposure, the portfolio is using the proceeds from the short sale to invest more than 100 percent on the long side.

margin requirement, and then meet ongoing margin requirements. They must also replace any dividends paid on the stock while the short position is open. Finally, there is the widely stated note of caution to investors that while potential gains from short selling are limited, potential losses are not.

The bear market of 2000–2002 was a short seller's dream for those who recognized the situation and acted accordingly. Markets declined sharply, and many stocks collapsed. A number of technology stocks went bankrupt, with the price essentially going to zero. Even the big-name technology stocks dropped like a rock. For example, Cisco, one of the great stocks to own in the 1990s, declined about 90 percent.

This was the best environment for short selling in many years, until 2008–2009, when many stocks dropped dramatically.

Some short sellers could encounter a so-called short squeeze. This can occur when there is an excess demand for a stock but a lack of supply, which will drive up the price of the stock. If a stock starts to rise rapidly, many short sellers may choose to cover their position and get out. As more short sellers buy back the stock, the stock price rises even more. Short squeezes are more likely with smaller capitalization stocks with relatively fewer shares outstanding. Finally, if you plan to sell short, remember the old Wall Street ditty: "He who sells what isn't his'n/Buys it back or goes to prison."

Checking Your Understanding

5. Why is it necessary for brokerage accounts to be marked to the market every day?
6. Why sell short instead of using puts?
7. What does it mean to say the losses from short selling are infinite while the gains are finite?

Summary

▶ Brokerage firms consist of full-service brokers and discount brokers.

▶ Full-service stockbrokers earn their incomes from a variety of sources, including individuals' trades, in-house mutual fund sales, principal transactions, new issues, and fees.

▶ With a cash brokerage account, the customer pays in full on the settlement date, whereas with a margin account money can be borrowed from the broker to finance purchases.

▶ Asset management accounts offering a variety of services are commonplace. With a wrap account, brokers, acting as middlemen, match clients with independent money managers. All costs—the cost of the broker-consultant and money manager, all transactions costs, custody fees, and the cost of detailed performance reports—are wrapped in one fee.

▶ Brokerage commissions are negotiable. Full-line brokerage houses charge more than discount brokers but

offer recommendations and research. Some Internet-only discount brokers charge the least.

▶ Investors can invest without a broker through dividend reinvestment plans. Some companies sell shares directly to investors.

▶ The stock exchanges are highly automated, allowing billions of shares to be traded.

▶ Market orders are executed at the best price available, whereas limit orders specify a particular price to be met or bettered. Stop orders specify a certain price at which a market order is to take over.

▶ Investor protection includes government regulation, primarily federal, and self-regulation by the industry. The Securities and Exchange Commission administers the securities laws.

▶ The major exchanges have a stringent set of self-regulations. The Financial Industry Regulatory Authority (FINRA), created in 2007, is now the largest regulator for all securities firms doing business in the United States.

► Margin is the equity an investor has in a transaction. The Federal Reserve sets the initial margin, but all exchanges and brokers require a maintenance (ongoing) margin. The appeal of margin to investors is that it can magnify any gains on a transaction, but it can also magnify losses.

► An investor sells short if a security's price is expected to decline. The investor borrows the securities sold short from the broker, hoping to replace them through a later purchase at a lower price.

Questions

5-1 Discuss the advantages and disadvantages of a limit order versus a market order. How does a stop order differ from a limit order?

What is a wrap account? How does it involve a change in the traditional role of the broker?

5-2 For a typical investor with a wrap account, how much attention do you think he or she receives from the designated money manager?

5-3 Why are investors interested in having margin accounts? What risk do such accounts involve?

5-4 Explain the margin process, distinguishing between initial margin and maintenance margin. Who sets these margins?

5-5 What conditions result in an account being "restricted"? What prompts a margin call?

5-6 How can an investor sell a security that is not currently owned?

5-7 What conditions must be met for an investor to sell short?

5-8 Explain the difference, relative to the current market price of a stock, between the following types of orders: sell limit, buy limit, buy stop, and sell stop.

5-9 What is the margin requirement for U.S. government securities?

5-10 Distinguish between a large discount broker such as Fidelity and an Internet-only discount broker.

5-11 How can investors invest without a broker?

5-12 Explain the role of market makers on NASDAQ.

5-13 What is the difference between a day order and an open order?

5-14 What is the role of the SEC in the regulation of securities markets?

5-15 How popular are short sales relative to all reported sales?

5-16 Explain the basis of regulation of mutual funds. How successful has this regulation been?

5-17 What assurances does the Investment Advisors Act of 1940 provide investors in dealing with people who offer investment advice?

5-18 Given the lower brokerage costs charged by discount brokers and deep-discount brokers, why might an investor choose to use a full-service broker?

5-19 What assurances as to the success of a company does the SEC provide investors when an IPO is marketed?

5-20 Contrast the specialist system traditionally used on the NYSE with the dealer system associated with the NASDAQ market.

5-21 What is meant by having margin accounts "marked to the market" daily?

5-22 Is there any link between margin accounts and short selling?

5-23 Why do people say "The losses on short selling are unlimited?"

Problems

5-1 **a.** Consider an investor who purchased a stock at $80 per share. The current market price is $105. At what price would a limit order be placed to assure a profit of $30 per share?

b. What type of stop order would be placed to ensure a profit of at least $20 per share?

5-2 Assume an investor sells short 100 shares of stock at $50 per share. At what price must the investor cover the short sale in order to realize a gross profit of $3,000? $1,000?

5-3 Assume that an investor buys 200 shares of stock at $40 per share and the stock rises to $55 per share. What is the percentage return on the investor's cash outlay, assuming an initial margin requirement of 50 percent? 40 percent? 60 percent?

5-4 Assume an initial margin requirement of 50 percent and a maintenance margin of 30 percent. An investor buys 100 shares of stock on margin at $30 per share. The price of the stock subsequently drops to $25.

   a. What is the actual margin at $25?

   b. The price now rises to $28. Is the account restricted?

   c. If the price declines to $24, is there a margin call?

   d. Assume that the price declines to $20. What is the amount of the margin call? At $18?

Computational Problems

5-1 You open a margin account at Chas Pigeon, a discount broker. You subsequently short Exciting.com at $86, believing it to be overpriced. This transaction is done on margin, which has an annual interest rate cost of 4 percent. Exactly one year later Exciting has declined to $54 a share, at which point you cover your short position. You pay brokerage costs of $7 on each transaction you make.

   a. The margin requirement is 50 percent. Calculate your dollar gain or loss on this position, taking into account both the margin interest and the transaction cost to sell.

   b. Calculate the percentage return on your investment (the amount of money you put up initially, counting the brokerage costs to buy).

5-2 Using your same brokerage account as in Problem 5-1 (same margin rate and transaction costs), assume that you buy IBM at $176 a share, on 50 percent margin. During the year IBM pays a dividend of $3.40 per share. One year later you sell the position at $212. Treat the brokerage cost to sell in calculating the gain or loss, and the brokerage cost to buy as part of your investment.

   a. Calculate the dollar gain or loss on this position.

   b. Calculate the percentage return on your investment.

5-3 An investor buys 200 shares of Altria at $62 per share on margin. The initial margin requirement is 50 percent, and the maintenance margin is 30 percent.

   a. The price of Altria drops to $51 per share. What is the actual margin now?

   b. The price of Altria declines further to $49.50. Show why a margin call is generated, or is not warranted.

   c. The price declines yet again to $42.25. Show by calculations why a margin call is generated.

   d. Using the information in (3), how much cash must be added to the account to bring it into compliance with the margin requirements?

5-4 Assume you bought 100 shares of DataPoint for $25 per share, and it is currently selling for $40 per share. Assume the stock eventually declines to $31. Ignore brokerage commissions and margin interest costs.

   a. Calculate your percentage rate of return at the $31 price assuming that you placed a sell stop order at $40 per share and the order executed at that price.

b. Calculate your percentage rate of return at the $31 price assuming you did not place the stop loss order.

c. Calculate your percentage rate of return on your equity investment assuming you bought 100 shares of this stock on 50 percent margin when it was selling for $25, and you sold the stock for $40 per share.

Spreadsheet Exercises

a. Assume that you can buy U.S. Coal for $20 per share, either paying cash or buying on margin. The initial margin requirement is 50 percent, and the maintenance margin is 30 percent. U.S. Coal pays $0.25 per share in annual dividends. The margin interest cost is 6 percent. Using the spreadsheet format illustrated, calculate the $ gain or loss on both a cash basis and on a margin basis for 100 shares assuming possible ending prices for the stock as illustrated. The projected holding period is 6 months. Also calculate the percentage gain or loss on the initial investment for both a cash basis and a margin basis. Note that the holding period is expressed as part of a year in decimal form (e. g., 3 months = .25). Dividends are assumed to be paid quarterly. Thus, if the holding period is 3 months, and the annual dividend is $40, the dividend for the holding period is $10. Ignore tax considerations.

	Ending St Prce	$ Gain (L) Cash	% Ret. On Inv	$ Gain (L) Margin	% Ret. on Inv
Purchase Price	20	5			
# of Shares Purchased	100	10			
Annual Dividend		15			
Total Investment if purchased for cash		20			
Initial Margin Requirement (decimal)	0.5	25			
Mainten. Margin Requirement (decimal)	0.3	30			
Annual Margin Interest Rate		35			
Initial Investment if Bought on Margin		40			
Amount Borrowed if Bought on Margin		45			
Holding Period as % of a Year		50			
Holding Period * Ann. Margin Int. Rate					

b. If you buy 500 shares instead of 100 shares, with all other parameters the same, would the percentage return on investment change?

Checking Your Understanding

5-1 To realize a minimum gain of approximately $23 per share, you could place a stop loss order (to sell) at $73. If the price declined below $73, your order would become a market order and be executed close to $73, thereby giving you a profit of approximately $23, since you bought the stock for $50.

5-2 A wrap account means that all costs are included in the wrap fee, which some investors prefer. Also, some investors want to have a consultant in the form of a money manager for their account, and a wrap account can provide for this.

5-3 Disagree. The Securities Act of 1933 ensures investors only that the issuer has complied with all regulations, particularly those involving disclosure of information. The company may still be a weak company without good prospects for success.

5-4 Mediation is voluntary, and mediation decisions are nonbinding.

Arbitration is a binding process that can determine damages.

5-5 Brokerage firms must calculate the actual margin in their customers' accounts daily to determine if a margin call is required.

5-6 Puts are only available on a limited number of stocks. Therefore, to profit from an expected decline in price, short selling is often the only alternative. Also, there is no time limit on short selling, while puts have a very short life of several months at most.

5-7 Because there is no theoretical limit to how high a stock price can rise, the theoretical losses from short selling are said to be infinite. In practice, of course, the majority of all stocks don't rise in price to thousands of dollars a share. In contrast, the most a stock price can drop to is zero, so the gains from short selling are finite.

chapter 6

Return and Risk: The Foundation of Investing Worldwide

As you continue to prepare yourself to put together and manage a $1 million portfolio, you realize you need to have a very clear understanding of risk and return. After all, as you recall from your introductory finance class, these are the basic parameters of all investing decisions. While you agree that the past is not a sure predictor of the future, it seems reasonable that knowing the history of the returns and risks on the major financial assets will be useful. After all, if stocks in general have never returned more than about 10 percent on average, does it make sense for you to think of earning 15 or 20 percent annually on a regular basis? And what about compounding, supposedly an important part of long-term investing? How much, realistically, can you expect your portfolio to grow over time? Finally, exactly what does it mean to talk about the risk of stocks? How can you put stock risk into perspective? If stocks are really as risky as people say, maybe they should be only a small part of your portfolio.

Although math is not your long suit, you realize that it is not unreasonable that a $1 million gift should impose a little burden on you. Therefore, you resolve to get out your financial calculator and go to work on return and risk concepts, knowing that with some basic understanding of the concepts you can take the easy way out and let your computer spreadsheet program do the hard work.

Chapter 6 analyzes the returns and risks from investing. We learn how well investors have done in the past investing in the major financial assets. Investors need a good understanding of the returns and risk that have been experienced to date before attempting to estimate returns and risk, which they must do as they build and hold portfolios for the future.

AFTER READING THIS CHAPTER YOU WILL BE ABLE TO:

► Calculate important return and risk measures for financial assets, using the formulation appropriate for the task.

► Use key terms involved with return and risk, including geometric mean, cumulative wealth index,

inflation-adjusted returns, and currency-adjusted returns.

► Understand clearly the returns and risk investors have experienced in the past, an important step in estimating future returns and risk.

An Overview

How do investors go about calculating the returns on their securities over time? What about the risk of these securities? Assume you invested an equal amount in each of three stocks over a five-year period, which has now ended. The five annual returns for stocks 1, 2, and 3 are as follows:

1	2	3
−0.1	0.04	0.4
−0.2	0.05	−0.02
0.29	0.07	−0.1
0.19	0.06	−0.15
0.12	0.09	0.17

Stock 1 started off with two negative returns but then had three good years. Stock 2's returns are all positive, but quite low. Stock 3 had a 40 percent return in one year and a 17 percent return in another year, but it also suffered three negative returns. Which stock would have produced the largest final wealth for you, and which stock had the lowest risk over this five-year period? Which stock had the lowest compound annual average return over this five-year period? How would you proceed to determine your answers?

How would investors have fared, on average, over the past by investing in each of the major asset classes such as stocks and bonds? What are the returns and risk from investing, based on the historical record? What about nominal returns versus inflation-adjusted returns? We answer important questions such as these in this chapter.

Although there is no guarantee that the future will be exactly like the past, a knowledge of historical risk-return relationships is a necessary first step for investors in making investment decisions for the future. Furthermore, there is no reason to assume that *relative* relationships will differ significantly in the future. If stocks have returned more than bonds, and Treasury bonds more than Treasury bills, over the entire financial history available, there is every reason to assume that such relationships will continue over the *long-run* future. Therefore, it is very important for investors to understand what has occurred in the past.

Return

In Chapter 1, we learned that the objective of investors is to maximize expected returns subject to constraints, primarily risk. Return is the motivating force in the investment process. It is the reward for undertaking the investment.

Returns from investing are crucial to investors; they are what the game of investments is all about. The measurement of realized (historical) returns is necessary for investors to assess how well they have done or how well investment managers have done on their behalf. Furthermore, the historical return plays a large part in estimating future, unknown returns.

THE TWO COMPONENTS OF ASSET RETURNS

Return on a typical investment consists of two components:

- ❑ **Yield**: The basic component many investors think of when discussing investing returns is the periodic cash flows (or income) on the investment, either interest (from bonds) or

Yield The income component of a security's return

Capital Gain (Loss) The change in price on a security over some period

dividends (from stocks). The distinguishing feature of these payments is that the issuer makes the payments in cash to the holder of the asset. **Yield** measures a security's cash flows relative to some price, such as the purchase price or the current market price.

■ **Capital gain (loss):** The second component is the appreciation (or depreciation) in the price of the asset, commonly called the **capital gain (loss)**. We will refer to it simply as the price change. In the case of an asset purchased (long position), it is the difference between the purchase price and the price at which the asset can be, or is, sold; for an asset sold first and then bought back (short position), it is the difference between the sale price and the subsequent price at which the short position is closed out. In either case, a gain or a loss can occur.[1]

Putting the Two Components Together

Add these two components together to form the total return:

$$\text{Total return} = \text{Yield} + \text{Price change} \qquad (6\text{-}1)$$

where the yield component can be 0 or +
the price change component can be 0, +, or −

Example 6-1

A bond purchased at par ($1,000) and held to maturity provides a yield in the form of a stream of cash flows or interest payments, but no price change. A bond purchased for $800 and held to maturity provides both a yield (the interest payments) and a price change, in this case a gain. The purchase of a nondividend-paying stock, such as Apple, that is sold six months later produces either a capital gain or a capital loss but no income. A dividend-paying stock, such as Microsoft, produces both a yield component and a price change component (a realized or unrealized capital gain or loss).

Equation 6-1 is a conceptual statement for the total return *for any security*. Investors' returns from financial assets come only from these two components—an income component (the yield) and/or a price change component, regardless of the asset. Investors sometimes mistakenly focus only on the yield component of their investments, rather than the total return, and mistakenly assume they are achieving acceptable performance when they are not.

Example 6-2

In one recent year a $500,000 portfolio was invested half in stocks and half in bonds. At the end of the year this portfolio had yielded about $19,000 in dividends and interest. However, because of the declining stock market, the value of the portfolio at the end of the year was about $475,000. Therefore, the capital loss exceeded the yield, resulting in a negative total return for that one-year period.

---

[1] This component involves only the difference between the beginning price and the ending price in the transaction. An investor can purchase or short an asset and close out the position one day, one hour, or one minute later for a capital gain or loss. Furthermore, gains can be realized or unrealized. See online Appendix 2-A for more discussion on capital gains and losses and their taxation.

Measuring Returns

TOTAL RETURN

Total Return (TR)
Percentage measure
relating all cash flows on a
security for a given time
period to its purchase
price

We now know that a correct returns measure must incorporate the two components of return, yield and price change, keeping in mind that either component could be zero. The **Total Return (TR)** for a given holding period is a decimal or percentage number relating all the cash flows received by an investor during any designated time period to the purchase price of the asset calculated as

$$TR = \frac{CF_t + (P_E - P_B)}{P_B} = \frac{CF_t + PC}{P_B} \qquad (6\text{-}2)$$

where

CF_t = cash flows during the measurement period t

P_E = price at the end of period t or sale price

P_B = purchase price of the asset or price at the beginning of the period

PC = change in price during the period, or P_E minus P_B

The periodic cash flows from a bond consists of the interest payments received, and for a stock, the dividends received. For some assets, such as a warrant or a stock that pays no dividends, there is only a price change. Part A of Exhibit 6-1 illustrates the calculation of TR for a bond, a common stock, and a warrant. Although one year is often used for convenience, the TR calculation can be applied to periods of any length.

EXHIBIT 6-1

Examples of Total Return and Price Relative Calculations

A. Total Return (TR) Calculations

I. Bond TR

$$\text{Bond TR} = \frac{I_t + (P_E - P_B)}{P_B} = \frac{I_t + PC}{P_B}$$

I_t = the interest payment(s) received during the period:

P_B and P_E = the beginning and ending prices, respectively

PC = the change in price during the period

Example: Assume the purchase of a 10-percent-coupon Treasury bond at a price of $960, held one year, and sold for $1,020. The TR is

$$\text{Bond TR} = \frac{100 + (1,020 - 960)}{960} = \frac{100 + 60}{960} = 0.1667 \text{ or } 16.67\%$$

II. Stock TR

$$\text{Stock TR} = \frac{D_t + (P_E - P_B)}{P_B} = \frac{D_t + PC}{P_B}$$

D_t = the dividend(s) paid during the period

Example: 100 shares of DataShield are purchased at $30 per share and sold one year later at $26 per share. A dividend of $2 per share is paid.

$$\text{Stock TR} = \frac{2 + (26 - 30)}{30} = \frac{2 + (-4)}{30} = -.0667 \text{ or } -6.67\%$$

III. Warrant TR

$$\text{Warrant TR} = \frac{C_t + (P_E - P_B)}{P_B} = \frac{C_t + PC}{P_B} = \frac{PC}{P_B}$$

where, C_t = any cash payment received by the warrant holder during the period. Because warrants pay no dividends, the only return to an investor from owning a warrant is the change in price during the period.

Example: Assume the purchase of warrants of DataShield at $3 per share, a holding period of six months, and the sale at $3.75 per share.

$$\text{Warrant TR} = \frac{0 + (3.75 - 3.00)}{3.00} = \frac{0.75}{3.00} = 0.25 \text{ or } 25\%$$

B. Return Relative Calculations

The return relative for the preceding bond example shown is

$$\text{Bond return relative} = \frac{100 + 1020}{960} = 1.1667$$

The return relative for the stock example is

$$\text{Stock return relative} = \frac{2 + 26}{30} = 0.9333$$

The return relative for the warrant example is

$$\text{Warrant return relative} = \frac{3.75}{3.00} = 1.25$$

To convert from a return relative to a total return, subtract 1.0 from the return relative.

Calculating Total Returns for the S&P 500 Index   Table 6-1 shows the Standard & Poor's (S&P) 500 Stock Composite Index for the years 1926 through 2011 (a total of 86 years because the data start on January 1, 1926). Included in the table are *end-of-year* values for the index, from which capital gains and losses can be computed, and dividends on the index, which constitute the income component.

Table 6-1 Historical Composite Stock Price Index, Based on Standard & Poor's 500 Index, Dividends in Index Form, and Total Returns (TRs), 1926–2011. Values are End-of-Year. (No monthly compounding.)

Year	Index Val	Div	TR%	Year	Index Val	Div	TR%
1925	10.34			1969	92.06	3.16	−8.32
1926	15.03	0.75	8.20	1970	92.15	3.14	3.51
1927	19.15	0.81	32.76	1971	102.09	3.07	14.12
1928	25.61	0.84	38.14	1972	118.05	3.15	18.72
1929	22.05	0.95	−10.18	1973	97.55	3.38	−14.50
1930	15.31	0.90	−26.48	1974	68.56	3.60	−26.03
1931	7.89	0.76	−43.49	1975	90.19	3.68	36.92
1932	6.80	0.46	−8.01	1976	107.46	4.05	23.64
1933	10.19	0.36	55.34	1977	95.10	4.67	−7.16
1934	10.10	0.40	3.00	1978	96.11	5.07	6.39
1935	13.91	0.41	41.79	1979	107.94	5.65	18.19
1936	17.60	0.68	31.38	1980	135.76	6.16	31.48
1937	11.14	0.78	32.29	1981	122.55	6.63	−4.85
1938	13.60	0.52	26.70	1982	140.64	6.87	20.37
1939	13.19	0.59	1.31	1983	164.93	7.09	22.31
1940	11.51	0.67	−7.63	1984	167.24	7.53	5.97
1941	9.59	0.75	−10.24	1985	211.28	7.90	31.06
1942	10.45	0.64	15.67	1986	242.17	8.28	18.54
1943	12.59	0.64	26.71	1987	247.08	8.81	5.67
1944	14.33	0.68	19.18	1988	277.72	9.73	16.34
1945	18.87	0.67	36.43	1989	353.40	11.05	31.23
1946	17.08	0.77	−5.44	1990	330.22	12.10	−3.14
1947	16.74	0.92	3.43	1991	417.09	12.20	30.00
1948	16.11	1.05	2.45	1992	435.71	12.38	7.43
1949	18.11	1.14	19.48	1993	466.45	12.58	9.94
1950	21.94	1.40	28.92	1994	459.27	13.18	1.29
1951	24.98	1.35	19.99	1995	615.93	13.79	37.11
1952	26.94	1.37	13.34	1996	740.74	14.90	22.68
1953	25.85	1.41	1.17	1997	970.43	15.50	33.10
1954	36.73	1.49	47.87	1998	1229.23	16.38	28.36
1955	43.89	1.68	24.06	1999	1469.25	16.48	20.87
1956	46.30	1.82	9.65	2000	1,320.28	15.97	−9.05
1957	39.99	1.87	−9.59	2001	1,148.08	15.71	−11.85
1958	55.21	1.75	42.44	2002	879.82	16.07	−22.10
1959	59.89	1.83	11.79	2003	1111.92	17.49	28.37
1960	58.11	1.95	0.28	2004	1,211.92	19.54	10.75
1961	71.55	2.02	26.60	2005	1248.29	22.22	4.83
1962	63.10	2.13	−8.83	2006	1,418.30	24.88	15.61
1963	75.02	2.28	22.50	2007	1468.36	27.73	5.48
1964	84.75	2.50	16.3	2008	903.25	28.39	−36.55
1965	92.43	2.72	12.27	2009	1115.10	22.31	25.92
1966	80.33	2.87	−9.99	2010	1,257.64	23.12	14.86
1967	96.47	2.92	23.73	2011	1257.64	26.41	2.1
1968	103.86	3.07	10.84				

Example 6-3   The TRs for each year as shown in Table 6-1 can be calculated as shown in Equation 6-2. As a demonstration of these calculations, the TR for 2010 for the S&P 500 Index was 14.86 percent, calculated as:[2]

$$TR_{2010} = [1257.64 - 1115.10 + 23.12]/1115.10 = .1486 \text{ or } 14.86\%$$

In contrast, in 2000 the TR was −9.07 percent, calculated as:

$$TR_{2000} = [1320.28 - 1469.25 + 15.69]/1469.25 = -.0907 = -9.07\%$$

Conclusions About Total Return   In summary, the TR concept is valuable as a measure of return because it is all-inclusive, measuring the total return per dollar of original investment.

✓   TR is *the* basic measure of the return earned by investors on any financial asset for any specified period of time. It can be stated on a decimal or percentage basis.

TR facilitates the comparison of asset returns over a specified period, whether the comparison is of different assets, such as stocks versus bonds, or different securities within the same type, such as several common stocks. Remember that using this concept does not mean that the securities have to be sold and the gains or losses actually realized—that is, the calculation applies to realized or unrealized gains (see Appendix 2-A).

Some Practical Advice

As you analyze and consider common stocks, never forget the important role that dividends have played historically in the TRs shown for large common stocks. For example, for the 85-year period 1926–2010, for the S&P 500 Index, the compound annual average return was 9.6 percent (rounded). Dividends averaged 4 percent, and obviously were an important component of the TR. However, in the 1990s the dividend yield on the major stock indexes continued to decline, and reached levels of about 1.5 percent in 2001 and 2002. Clearly, if all other things remained equal, TRs on the S&P 500 Index would decline relative to the past because of the significant decreases in the dividend yield. Not surprisingly, given the turmoil in the economy, more large companies cut dividends in 2008 than in any year since 2001. At the beginning of 2012, the dividend yield on the S&P 500 Index was approximately 2.1 percent.

What about the importance of dividends for individual stocks? Consider a company with an ordinary product consumed daily around the world, Coca-Cola.

What if a member of your family bought one share in 1919 for $40 when Coca-Cola had its IPO? One share would be worth $322,421 at the end of 2011.[3] Coca-Cola also paid dividends. How much impact do you think the reinvested dividends would have on the

---

[2] Note carefully that these calculations do not account for the reinvestment of dividends during the year and will differ from the total returns calculated as part of the official series of returns later in the chapter.

[3] This example is based on *"Never Underestimate the Winning Role Dividends Play," AAII Dividend Investing*, Internet mailing, February 25, 2012.

terminal wealth of this one share at the end of 2011? According to one calculation, that one share would have been worth $9.3 million at the end of 2011! Such is the impact of compounding reinvested dividends over a very long period of time.

RETURN RELATIVE

It is often necessary to measure returns on a slightly different basis than total returns. This is particularly true when calculating either a cumulative wealth index or a geometric mean, both of which are explained below, because negative returns cannot be used in the calculation.

Return Relative (RR)
The total return for an investment for a given period stated on the basis of 1.0

✓ The **Return Relative (RR)** eliminates negative numbers by adding 1.0 to the TR. It provides the same information as the TR, but in a different form.

- RR = TR in decimal form + 1.0
- TR in decimal form = RR − 1.0

Example 6-4

A TR of 0.10 for some holding period is equivalent to a return relative of 1.10, and a TR of −9.07, as calculated in Example 6-3 for the year 2000, is equivalent to a return relative of 0.9093.

Equation 6-2 can be modified to calculate return relatives directly by using the price at the end of the holding period in the numerator, rather than the change in price, as in Equation 6-3.

$$\text{Return relative} = RR = \frac{CF_t + P_E}{P_B} \tag{6-3}$$

Examples of RR calculations for the same three assets as the preceding are shown in Part B of Exhibit 6-1.

Example 6-5

The RR for 2010 for the S&P 500 calculated using Equation 6-3 is

$$(1257.64 + 23.12)/1115.10 = 1.1486$$

CUMULATIVE WEALTH INDEX

Return measures such as TRs measure the rate of change in an asset's price or return, and percentage rates of return have multiple uses. Nevertheless, we all understand dollar amounts! Therefore, it is often desirable to measure how one's wealth in dollars changes over time. In other words, we measure the cumulative effect of returns compounding over time given *some stated initial investment*, which typically is shown as $1 for convenience ($1 is the default value). Note that having calculated ending wealth (cumulative wealth) over some time period on the basis of a $1 initial investment, it is simple enough to multiply by an investor's actual beginning amount invested, such as $10,000 or $22,536 or any other beginning amount.

Cumulative Wealth Index
Cumulative wealth over time, given an initial wealth and a series of returns on some asset

The **Cumulative Wealth Index**, CWI_n, is computed as

$$CWI_n = WI_0(1 + TR_1)(1 + TR_2)\dots(1 + TR_n) \tag{6-4}$$

where

CWI_n = the cumulative wealth index as of the end of period n

WI_0 = the beginning index value; typically \$1 is used but any amount can be used

$TR_{1,n}$ = the periodic TRs in decimal form (when added to 1.0 in Equation 6-4, they become return relatives)

Example 6-6

Let's calculate cumulative wealth per \$1 invested for the 1990s, one of the two greatest decades in the 20th century in which to own common stocks. This will provide you with a perspective on common stock returns at their best. Using the S&P Total Returns in Table 6-1, and converting them to return relatives, the CWI for the decade of the 1990s (the 10-year period 1990–1999) would be

$$CWI_{90-99} = 1.00(0.969)(1.30)(1.0743)(1.0994)(1.0129)(1.3711)(1.2268)(1.331)$$
$$(1.2834)(1.2088)$$
$$= 5.23$$

Thus, \$1 (the beginning value arbitrarily chosen) invested at the beginning of 1990 would have been worth \$5.23 by the end of 1999. Obviously, any beginning wealth value can be used to calculate cumulative wealth. For example, \$10,000 invested under the same conditions would have been worth \$52,300 at the end of 1999, and \$37,500 invested under the same conditions would have been worth \$196,125.

✓ Cumulative wealth is always stated in dollars, and represents the effects of compounding returns over some period of time, given any initial investment. Typically, \$1 is used as the initial investment.

Our three returns measures are shown in Figure 6-1.

A Global Perspective

As noted in Chapter 1, international investing offers potential return opportunities and potential reduction in risk through diversification. Based on the historical record, investments in certain foreign markets would have increased investor returns during certain periods of time. For example, in the first decade of the 21st century European stocks performed much better than U.S. stocks. Dividend yields abroad were about 1 percentage point higher than U.S. dividend yields during that period.

U.S. investors need to understand how the returns on their investment in foreign securities are calculated, and the additional risk they are taking relative to domestic securities. This additional risk may pay off, or penalize them.

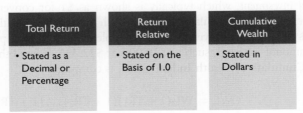

Total Return	Return Relative	Cumulative Wealth
• Stated as a Decimal or Percentage	• Stated on the Basis of 1.0	• Stated in Dollars

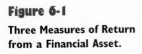

Figure 6-1

Three Measures of Return from a Financial Asset.

INTERNATIONAL RETURNS AND CURRENCY RISK

When investors buy and sell assets in other countries, they must consider exchange rate risk or currency risk. This risk can convert a gain from the asset itself into a loss on the investment or a loss from the asset itself into a gain on the investment. We need to remember that international stocks are priced in local currencies—for example, a French stock is priced in Euros, and a Japanese stock is priced in yen. For a U.S. investor who buys a foreign security, the ultimate return to him or her in spendable dollars depends on the rate of exchange between the foreign currency and the dollar, and this rate typically changes daily.

Currency Risk (Exchange Rate Risk)
The risk of an adverse impact on the return from a foreign investment as a result of movements in currencies

Currency risk (exchange rate risk) is the risk that any change in the value of the investor's home currency relative to the foreign currency involved will be unfavorable; however, like risk in general, currency risk can work in the investor's favor, enhancing the return that would otherwise be received.

How Currency Changes Affect Investors   An investment denominated in an appreciating currency relative to the investor's domestic currency will experience a gain from the currency movement, while an investment denominated in a depreciating currency relative to the investor's domestic currency will experience a decrease in the return because of the currency movement. Said differently, when you buy a foreign asset, you sell the home currency to do so, and when you sell the foreign asset, you buy back the home currency. For a U.S. investor,

✓ if the foreign currency strengthens while you hold the foreign asset, when you sell the asset you will be able to buy back more dollars using the now stronger foreign currency. Your dollar-denominated return will increase.
✓ if the dollar strengthens while you hold the foreign asset, when you sell your asset and convert back to dollars, you will be able to buy back fewer of the now more-expensive dollars, thereby decreasing your dollar-denominated return.

Example 6-7

In one recent year, the Brazilian market was up about 150 percent, but the currency adjustment for U.S. investors was negative (83 percent), leaving a U.S. dollar return for the year of approximately 67 percent instead of 150 percent. On the other hand, the Japanese market enjoyed a 47 percent return, and the currency adjustment was positive, 15 percent, resulting in a U.S. dollar return of approximately 62 percent for the year.

Calculating Currency-Adjusted Returns   To understand the logic of currency adjustments on investor returns, consider Table 6-2. It shows the actual change in the dollar relative to the Euro over the period 2002–2004, from 1 Euro = $1.05 to 1 Euro = $1.35 (in other words, the value of the dollar dropped sharply during this period). Assume one share of EurTel at the end of 2002 was €75 (75 Euros). The dollar cost at this time was

Table 6-2 Impact of Currency Changes on an Investment in EurTel Stock Denominated in Euros

December 30, 2000	December year-end, 2004	Return to Investor
Exchange Rate	1.00 = $1.05	1.00 = $1.35
Cost in Euros of 1 share of EurTel 40% (in euros)	€75	€105
Cost in Dollars of 1 share of EurTel 80% (in dollars)	$78.75	$141.75

$1.05 (75) = $78.75. At the end of 2004 the value of one share had risen to €105, an increase of 40 percent for an investor transacting only in Euros. However, the value of the dollar fell sharply during this period, and when the shares of EurTel were sold, the euro proceeds bought back more dollars. The dollar value of one share is now $1.35 (105) = $141.75. The return on this investment, in dollar terms, is $(141.75/78.75) - 1.0 = 80$ percent.

To calculate directly the return to a U.S. investor from an investment in a foreign country, we can use Equation 6-5. The foreign currency is stated in domestic terms; that is, the amount of domestic currency necessary to purchase one unit of the foreign currency.

$$\text{TR in domestic terms} = \left[\text{RR} \times \frac{\text{Ending value of foreign currency}}{\text{Beginning value of foreign currency}} \right] - 1.0 \qquad \textbf{(6-5)}$$

Example 6-8

Consider a U.S. investor who invests in WalMex at 40.25 pesos when the value of the peso stated in dollars is $0.10. One year later WalMex is at 52.35 pesos, and the stock did not pay a dividend. The peso is now at $0.093, which means that the dollar appreciated against the peso.

$$\text{RR for WalMex} = 52.35/40.25 = 1.3006$$

TR to the U.S. investor *after currency adjustment* is

$$\text{TR denominated in \$} = \left[1.3006 \times \frac{\$0.093}{\$0.10} \right] - 1.0$$
$$= [1.3006 \times 0.93] - 1.0$$
$$= 1.2096 - 1.0$$
$$= .2096 \text{ or } 20.96\%$$

In this example, using round numbers, the U.S. investor earned a 30 percent TR denominated in Mexican currency, but only 21 percent denominated in dollars because the peso declined in value against the U.S. dollar. With the strengthening of the dollar, the pesos received when the investor sells WalMex buy fewer U.S. dollars, decreasing the 30 percent return a Mexican investor would earn to only 21 percent for a U.S. investor.

The Dollar and Investors   How much difference can currency adjustments make to investors? They can make a substantial difference for selected periods of time.

Example 6-9

Let's consider the impact of the falling dollar on U.S. investors for one year, 2007. Canadian stocks earned Canadian investors 10.5 percent, but the gain for U.S. investors was 28.4 percent because of the strengthening of the Canadian dollar against the U.S. dollar. Meanwhile, French investors in a French stock index fund earned only 1.2 percent TR in 2007, while U.S. investors in the same index earned 12.1 percent (as a benchmark, the S&P 500 had a TR of 5.5 percent for 2007).

In 2000 a Euro was worth about $.82. By mid-2008 it was worth roughly $1.56, which means that the value of the dollar declined sharply over this entire period. As the dollar fell, foreign investors owning U.S. stocks suffered from the declining stock market and an unfavorable currency movement. On the other hand, U.S. investors in foreign securities benefited from currency movements. In 2011, despite Greece's sovereign debt crises and other issues about some European countries sovereign debt, as well as concerns about the viability of some financial institutions, the Euro continued to hover around $1.36. This was at least partly a reflection of problems in the United States regarding the national debt and the weak economy. However, in early 2012 the Euro was at $1.27, reflecting the ongoing European crisis.

Investments Intuition

As we now know, a declining dollar benefits U.S. investors in foreign securities, but also benefits investors holding large multinational companies like McDonald's and Apple. First, U.S. exports increase because they become more competitive around the world. Second, the foreign sales and earnings become more valuable in dollar terms.

Checking Your Understanding

1. The Cumulative Wealth Index can be calculated for nominal stock returns, but it cannot show the impact of inflation. Agree or disagree, and explain your reasoning.
2. What does it mean to say that when you buy a foreign asset, you are selling the dollar?
3. Is it correct to say that in recent years anti-dollar bets by U.S. investors paid off?

Summary Statistics for Returns

The total return, return relative, and cumulative wealth index are useful measures of return for a specified period of time. Also needed for investment analysis are statistics to describe a series of returns. For example, investing in a particular stock for 10 years or a different stock in each of 10 years could result in 10 TRs, which need to be described by summary statistics. Two such measures used with returns data are described below.

ARITHMETIC MEAN

The best-known statistic to most people is the arithmetic mean. Therefore, when someone refers to the *mean return* they usually are referring to the arithmetic mean unless otherwise specified. The arithmetic mean, customarily designated by the symbol X-bar, of a set of values is calculated as

$$\overline{X} = \frac{\sum X}{n} \tag{6-6}$$

or the sum of each of the values being considered divided by the total number of values n.

Example 6-10 Based on data from Table 6-1 for the 10 years of the 1990s ending in 1999, the arithmetic mean is calculated in Table 6-3.

$$\overline{X} = [-3.14 + 30.00 + \cdots + 20.88]/10$$
$$= 187.63/10$$
$$= .1876 \text{ or } 18.76\%$$

Table 6-3 Calculation of the Arithmetic and Geometric Mean for the Years 1990–1999 for the S&P 500 Stock Composite Index

Year	S&P 500 TRs (%)	S&P 500 RR
1990	−3.14	0.9687
1991	30.00	1.3000
1992	7.43	1.0743
1993	9.94	1.0994
1994	1.29	1.0129
1995	37.11	1.3711
1996	22.68	1.2268
1997	33.10	1.3310
1998	28.34	1.2834
1999	20.88	1.2088

Arithmetic Mean $= [-3.14 + 30.00 + \cdots + 20.88]/10$
$= 18.76\%$

Geometric Mean $= [(0.9687)(1.30001)(1.07432)(1.09942)(1.01286)$
$(1.37113)(1.22683)(1.33101)(1.28338)(1.2088)]^{1/10} - 1$
$= 1.18 - 1$
$= 0.18, \text{ or } 18\%$

GEOMETRIC MEAN

The arithmetic mean return is an appropriate measure of the central tendency of a distribution consisting of returns calculated for a particular time period, such as 10 years. However, when an ending value is the result of compounding over time, the geometric mean, is needed to describe accurately the "true" average rate of return over multiple periods.

Geometric Mean The compound rate of return over time

The **geometric mean** is defined as the *n*th root of the product resulting from multiplying a series of return relatives together, as in Equation 6-7.

$$G = [(1 + TR_1)(1 + TR_2) \ldots (1 + TR_n)]^{1/n} - 1 \qquad \textbf{(6-7)}$$

where TR is a series of total returns in decimal form. Note that adding 1.0 to each total return produces a return relative. RRs are used in calculating geometric mean returns, because TRs, which can be negative or zero, cannot be used in the calculation.[4]

[4] An alternative method of calculating the geometric mean is to find the log of each return relative, sum them, divide by *n*, and take the antilog.

The geometric mean return measures the compound rate of growth over time. It is important to note that the geometric mean assumes that all cash flows are reinvested in the asset and that those reinvested funds earn the subsequent rates of return available on that asset for some specified period. It reflects the steady *growth rate* of invested funds over some past period; that is, the uniform rate at which money actually grew over time per period, taking into account all gains and losses.

Example 6-11   Continuing the example from Table 6-3, consisting of the 10 years of data ending in 1999 for the S&P 500, the geometric mean is

$$G = [(0.969)(1.30)(1.0743)(1.0994)(1.0129)(1.3711)(1.2268)(1.331)(1.2834)(1.2088)]^{1/10} - 1$$
$$= 1.1800 - 1 = .18, \text{ or } 18\%$$

Using the Calculator

In Example 6-6, we calculated the CWI for 1990–1999 as 5.23. Knowing this number, we can calculate the geometric mean return for these years by raising 5.23 to y^x, taking the 10th root, and subtracting 1.0:

$5.23 y^x$; 10; $1/x$; =; answer is 1.1799; 1.1799 − 1.0 = .1799 or .18 or 18%

✓ Think of the annual geometric mean as the equal annual return that makes a beginning amount of money grow to a particular ending amount of money.

For example, we saw in Example 6-6 that $1 invested in the S&P 500 Composite Index on January 1, 1990 would have grown to $5.23 by December 31, 1999 (10 years). This is a result of the money compounding at the annual rate of 18 percent. At the end of year 1, the $1 would grow to $1.18; at the end of year 2, the $1.18 would grow to $1.39; at the end of year 3, the $1.39 would grow to $1.64, and so on, until at the end of year 10 the original $1 is worth $5.23. Notice that this geometric average rate of return is lower than the arithmetic average rate of return of 18.76 percent, because it reflects the variability of the returns.

✓ The geometric mean will always be less than the arithmetic mean unless the values being considered are identical, an unlikely event. The spread between the two depends on the dispersion of the distribution: the greater the dispersion, the greater the spread between the two means.

ARITHMETIC MEAN VERSUS GEOMETRIC MEAN

When should we use the arithmetic mean and when should we use the geometric mean to describe the returns from financial assets? The answer depends on the investor's objective:

◻ The arithmetic mean is a better measure of average (typical) performance over single periods. It is the best estimate of the expected return for next period.

◻ The geometric mean is a better measure of the change in wealth over the past (multiple periods). It is typically used by investors to measure the realized compound rate of return at which money grew over a specified period of time.

Example 6-12   As an illustration of how the arithmetic mean can be misleading in describing returns over multiple periods, consider the data in Table 6-4, which show the movements in price for two stocks over two successive holding periods. Both stocks have a beginning price of $10. Stock A rises to $20 in period 1 and then declines to $10 in period 2. Stock B falls to $8 in period 1 and then rises 50 percent to $12 in period 2. For stock A, the indicated annual average arithmetic rate of change in price is 25 percent [(100% − 50%)/2]. This is clearly not sensible, because the price of stock A at the end of period 2 is $10, the same as the beginning price. The geometric mean calculation gives the correct annual average rate of change in price of 0 percent per year.

For stock B, the arithmetic average of the annual percentage changes in price is 15 percent. However, if the price actually increased 15 percent each period, the ending price in period 2 would be $10 (1.15) (1.15) = $13.23. We know that this is not correct, because the price at the end of period 2 is $12. The annual geometric rate of return, 9.54 percent, produces the correct price at the end of period 2: $10 (1.0954)(1.0954) = $12.

Table 6-4 Contrasting the Arithmetic and Geometric Means

Stock	Period 1	Period 2	Annual Arithmetic Rate of Return	Annual Geometric Rate of Return
A	$20	$10	[100% + (−50%)]/2 = 25%	$[2.0(0.5)]^{1/2} - 1 = 0\%$
B	$8	$12	[−20% + (50%)]/2 = 15%	$[0.8(1.5)]^{1/2} - 1 = 9.54\%$

✓ Over multiple periods, such as years, the geometric mean shows the true average compound rate of growth that actually occurred—that is, the *annual average rate* at which an invested dollar grew, taking into account the gains and losses over time.

On the other hand, we should use the arithmetic mean to represent the likely or typical performance for a single period. Consider the TR data for the S&P Index for the years 1990−1999 as described earlier. Our best representation of any one year's performance would be the arithmetic mean of 18.76 percent because it was necessary to average this rate of return, given the variability in the yearly numbers, in order to realize an annual compound growth rate of 18 percent after the fact.

Concepts in Action

Using the Geometric Mean to Measure Market Performance

The geometric mean for the S&P 500 Index for the 20th century was 10.35 percent. Thus, $1 invested in this index compounded at an average rate of 10.35 percent every year during the period 1900−1999. What about the first decade of the 21st century (defined as 2000−2009)?

The S&P 500 Index suffered losses for the first three years of the decade, followed by positive returns during 2003−2007. 2008 was a disaster, but 2009 showed a very large return. The geometric mean for the first decade is calculated as

Return Relatives for the S&P 500 Index:

2000	.909	2004	1.107	2008	.634
2001	.881	2005	1.049	2009	1.265
2002	.779	2006	1.157		
2003	1.287	2007	1.055		

$$[(.909)(.881)(.779)(1.287)(1.107)(1.049)(1.157)(1.055)$$
$$(.634)(1.265)]^{1/10} - 1.0 = [.9127]^{1/10} - 1.0 = .9909$$
$$-1.0 = -.0091$$

This indicates that $1 invested in the S&P 500 Index at the beginning of 2000 compounded at an average annual rate of approximately minus one percent a year for the first 10 years of the 21st century. The market, as measured by the S&P 500 Index, got a very bad start for the first three years of the decade, and it is quite difficult to overcome such a bad start. The severely negative performance in 2008 sealed the fate for this decade. This poor performance has led some to name this period the "Lost Decade" for common stocks. In fact, this decade was the worst-performing decade for stocks in the history of reliable stock market data.

INFLATION-ADJUSTED RETURNS

Nominal Return Return in current dollars, with no adjustment for inflation

Real Returns Nominal (dollar) returns adjusted for inflation

All of the returns discussed above are **nominal returns**, based on dollar amounts that do not take inflation into account. Typically, the percentage rates of return we see daily on the news, being paid by financial institutions, or quoted to us by lenders, are nominal rates of return.

We need to consider the purchasing power of the dollars involved in investing. To capture this dimension, we analyze **real returns**, or inflation-adjusted returns. When nominal returns are adjusted for inflation, the result is in constant purchasing-power terms.

Why is this important to you? What really matters is the purchasing power that your dollars have. It is not simply a case of how many dollars you have, but what those dollars will buy.[5]

Since 1871, the starting point for reliable data on a broad cross-section of stocks, the United States has had a few periods of deflation, but on average it has experienced mild inflation over a long period of time. Therefore, on average, the purchasing power of the dollar has declined over the long run. We define the rate of inflation or deflation as the percentage change in the CPI.[6]

Example 6-13

Suppose one of your parents or relatives earned a salary of $35,000 in 1975, and by 2010 his or her salary had increased to $135,000. How much better off is this individual in terms of purchasing power? We can convert the $35,000 in 1975 dollars to 2010 dollars. When we do this, we find that the 1975 salary is worth $141,822 dollars in 2010 dollars. So in terms of purchasing power, this individual has suffered a lost over this long time period.

The Consumer Price Index The Consumer Price Index (CPI) typically is used as the measure of inflation. The compound annual rate of inflation over the period 1926–2010 and over 1926–2011 was 3.00 percent. This means that a basket of consumer goods purchased at the beginning of for $1 would cost approximately $12.34 at year-end 2010. This is calculated as $(1.03)^{85}$, because there are 85 years from the beginning of 1926 through the end of 2010.[7] For 1926–2011, the calculation is $(1.03)^{86}$, which is approximately $12.71.

---

[5] A handy calculator for making the conversions illustrated in Example 6-13 can be found at http://buyupside.com/calculators/purchasepowerjan08.htm.

[6] Detailed information on the CPI can be found at the Bureau of Labor Statistics (BLS) website.

[7] To determine the number of years in a series such as this, subtract the beginning year from the ending year and add 1.0. For example, 1926 − 2010 = 84, and we add 1.0 to account for the fact that we start at the beginning of 1926.

Relation Between Nominal Return and Real Return   As an approximation, the nominal return (nr) is equal to the real return (rr) plus the expected rate of inflation (expinf), or

$$nr \approx rr + expinf$$

Reversing this equation, we can approximate the real return as

$$rr \approx nr - expinf$$

To drop the approximation, we can calculate inflation-adjusted returns by dividing $1 +$ (nominal) total return by $1 +$ the inflation rate as shown in Equation 6-8.

$$TR_{IA} = \frac{(1 + TR)}{(1 + IF)} - 1 \qquad (6\text{-}8)$$

where TR_{IA} = the inflation−adjusted total return
   IF = the rate of inflation

This equation can be applied to both individual years and average TRs.

Example 6-14   The TR for the S&P 500 Composite in 2004 was 10.87 percent (assuming monthly reinvestment of dividends). The rate of inflation was 3.26 percent Therefore, the real (inflation-adjusted) total return for large common stocks in 2004, as measured by the S&P 500, was

$$1.1087/1.0326 = 1.0737$$
$$1.0737 - 1.0 = .0737 \text{ or } 7.37\%$$

Example 6-15   Consider the period 1926−2011. The geometric mean for the S&P 500 Composite for the entire period was 9.5 percent, and for the CPI, 3.00 percent. Therefore, the real (inflation-adjusted) geometric mean rate of return for large common stocks for the period 1926−2011 was

$$1.095/1.03 = 1.063$$
$$1.063 - 1.0 = .063 \text{ or } 6.3\%$$

Checking Your Understanding

4. Assume that you invest $1,000 in a stock at the beginning of year 1. The rate of return is 15 percent for year 1, followed by a loss of 15 percent for year two. Did you break even by the end of year 2? Would it matter if the sequence of returns were reversed?

5. It is well known that the inflation rate was very low in recent years. Why, then, should investors be concerned with inflation-adjusted returns?

Risk

It is not sensible to talk about investment returns without talking about risk, because investment decisions involve a tradeoff between the two. Investors must constantly be aware of the risk they are assuming, understand how their investment decisions can be impacted, and be prepared for the consequences.

✓ Return and risk are opposite sides of the same coin.

Risk was defined in Chapter 1 as the chance that the actual outcome from an investment will differ from the expected outcome. Specifically, most investors are concerned that the actual outcome will be less than the expected outcome. The more variable the possible outcomes that can occur (i.e., the broader the range of possible outcomes), the greater the risk.

Investors should be willing to purchase a particular asset if the expected return is adequate to compensate for the risk, but they must understand that their expectation about the asset's return may not materialize. If not, the realized return will differ from the expected return. In fact, realized returns on securities show considerable variability—sometimes they are larger than expected, and other times they are smaller than expected, or even negative. Although investors may receive their expected returns on risky securities on a long-run average basis, they often fail to do so on a short-run basis. It is a fact of investing life that realized returns often differ from expected returns.

Investments Intuition

It is important to remember how risk and return go together when investing. An investor cannot reasonably *expect* larger returns without being willing to assume larger risks. Consider the investor who wishes to avoid any practical risk on a nominal basis. Such an investor can deposit money in an insured savings account, thereby earning a guaranteed return of a known amount. However, this return will be fixed, and the investor cannot earn more than this rate. Although risk is effectively eliminated, the chance of earning a larger return is also removed. To have the opportunity to earn a return larger than the savings account provides, investors must be willing to assume risks—and when they do so, they may gain a larger return, but they may also lose money.

SOURCES OF RISK

What makes a financial asset risky? In this text we equate risk with variability of returns. One-period rates of return fluctuate over time. Traditionally, investors have talked about several sources of total risk, such as interest rate risk and market risk, which are explained below because these terms are used so widely.

Interest Rate Risk   The variability in a security's return resulting from changes in the level of interest rates is referred to as **interest rate risk**. Such changes generally affect securities inversely; that is, other things being equal, security prices move inversely to interest rates.[8] Interest rate risk affects bonds more directly than common stocks, but it affects both and is a very important consideration for most investors.

Market Risk   The variability in returns resulting from fluctuations in the overall market—that is, the aggregate stock market—is referred to as **market risk**. All securities are exposed to market risk, although it affects primarily common stocks.

Market risk includes a wide range of factors exogenous to securities themselves, including recessions, wars, structural changes in the economy, and changes in consumer preferences.

Inflation Risk   A factor affecting all securities is purchasing power risk, or the chance that the purchasing power of invested dollars will decline. With uncertain inflation, the real (inflation-adjusted) return involves risk even if the nominal return is safe (e.g., a Treasury bond). This risk is related to interest rate risk, since interest rates generally rise as inflation increases, because lenders demand additional inflation premiums to compensate for the loss of purchasing power.

Business Risk   The risk of doing business in a particular industry or environment is called business risk. For example, AT&T, the traditional telephone powerhouse, faces major changes today in the rapidly changing telecommunications industry.

Financial Risk   Financial risk is associated with the use of debt financing by companies. The larger the proportion of assets financed by debt (as opposed to equity), the larger the variability in the returns, other things being equal. Financial risk involves the concept of financial leverage, explained in managerial finance courses.

Liquidity Risk   Liquidity risk is the risk associated with the particular secondary market in which a security trades. An investment that can be bought or sold quickly and without significant price concession is considered liquid. The more uncertainty about the time element and the price concession, the greater the liquidity risk. A Treasury bill has little or no liquidity risk, whereas a small OTC stock may have substantial liquidity risk.

Currency Risk (Exchange Rate Risk)   All investors who invest internationally in today's increasingly global investment arena face the prospect of uncertainty in the returns after they convert the foreign gains back to their own currency. Investors today must recognize and understand exchange rate risk, which was illustrated earlier in the chapter.

As an example, a U.S. investor who buys a German stock denominated in Euros must ultimately convert the returns from this stock back to dollars. If the exchange rate has moved against the investor, losses from these exchange rate movements can partially or totally negate the original return earned.

Obviously, U.S. investors who invest only in U.S. stocks on U.S. markets do not face this risk, but in today's global environment where investors increasingly consider alternatives from other countries, currency fluctuations have become important. U.S. investors who invest in

---

[8] The reason for this movement is tied up with the valuation of securities and will be explained in later chapters.

such financial assets as international mutual funds, global mutual funds, closed-end single-country funds, foreign stocks, and foreign bonds can be affected by currency risk.

Country Risk Country risk, also referred to as political risk, is an important risk for investors today—probably more important now than in the past. With more investors investing internationally, both directly and indirectly, the political, and therefore economic, stability and viability of a country's economy need to be considered. The United States has one of the lowest country risks, and other countries can be judged on a relative basis using the United States as a benchmark. In today's world, countries that may require careful attention include Russia, Pakistan, Greece, Portugal, and Mexico.

Measuring Risk

We can easily calculate the average return on stocks over a period of time. Why, then, do we need to know anything else? The answer is that while the average return, however measured, is probably the most important piece of information to an investor, it tells us only the center of the data. It does not tell us anything about the spread of the data.

Risk is often associated with the dispersion in the likely outcomes. Dispersion refers to variability. Risk is assumed to arise out of variability, which is consistent with our definition of risk as the chance that the actual outcome of an investment will differ from the expected outcome. If an asset's return has no variability, in effect it has no risk. Thus, a one-year Treasury bill purchased to yield 10 percent and held to maturity will, in fact, yield (a nominal) 10 percent. No other outcome is possible, barring default by the U.S. government, which is typically not considered a likely possibility.

Consider an investor analyzing a series of returns (TRs) for the major types of financial assets over some period of years. Knowing the mean of this series is not enough; the investor also needs to know something about the variability, or dispersion, in the returns. Relative to the other assets, common stocks show the largest variability (dispersion) in returns, with small common stocks showing even greater variability. Corporate bonds have a much smaller variability and therefore a more compact distribution of returns. Of course, Treasury bills are the least risky. The dispersion of annual returns for bills is compact.

In order to appreciate the range of outcomes for major financial asset classes, consider Figure 6-2. It shows the range of outcomes, and the mean (given by the circle) for each of the following asset classes for the period 1926 through 2011, in order from left to right: inflation, Treasury bills, Treasury bonds, corporate bonds, large common stocks (S&P 500 Composite Index), and smaller common stocks. (Don't worry about the numbers and the means here—instead, concentrate on the visual range of outcomes for the different asset classes.)

As we can see from Figure 6-2, stocks have a considerably wider range of outcomes than do bonds and bills. Smaller common stocks have a much wider range of outcomes than do large common stocks. Given this variability, investors must be able to measure it as a proxy for risk. They often do so using the standard deviation.

Variance A statistical term measuring dispersion—the standard deviation squared

Standard Deviation A measure of the dispersion in outcomes around the expected value

VARIANCE AND STANDARD DEVIATION

In this text we equate risk with the variability of returns—how do one-period rates of return vary over time? The risk of financial assets can be measured with an absolute measure of dispersion, or variability of returns, called the **variance**. An equivalent measure of total risk is the square root of the variance, the **standard deviation**, which measures the deviation of each observation from the arithmetic mean of the observations and is a reliable measure of

Figure 6-2

Graph of Spread in Returns for Major Asset Classes for the Period 1926–2011.

SOURCE: Jack W. Wilson and Charles P. Jones.

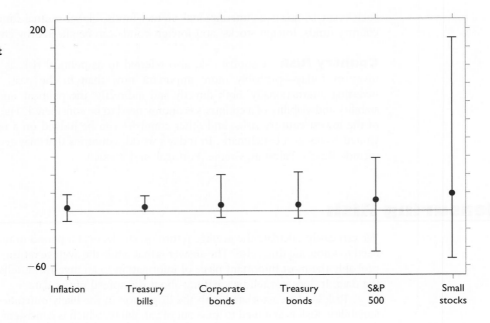

variability because all the information in a sample is used.[9] The symbol σ^2 is used to denote the variance, and σ to denote the standard deviation.

The standard deviation is a measure of the total risk of an asset or a portfolio. It captures the total variability in the asset's or portfolio's return, whatever the source(s) of that variability. The standard deviation can be calculated from the variance, which is calculated as

$$\sigma^2 = \frac{\sum\limits_{i=1}^{n} (X - \overline{X})^2}{n - 1} \tag{6-9}$$

where

$$
\begin{aligned}
\sigma^2 &= \text{the variance of a set of values} \\
X &= \text{each value in the set} \\
\overline{X} &= \text{the mean of the observations} \\
n &= \text{the number of returns in the sample} \\
\sigma &= (\sigma^2)^{1/2} = \text{standard deviation}
\end{aligned}
$$

Knowing the returns from the sample, we can calculate the standard deviation quite easily.

Example 6-16   The standard deviation of the 10 TRs for the decade of the 1970s, 1970–1979, for the Standard & Poor's 500 Index can be calculated as shown in Table 6-5.

---

[9] The variance is the standard deviation squared. The variance and the standard deviation are similar and can be used for the same purposes; specifically, in investment analysis, both are used as measures of risk. The standard deviation, however, is used more often.

Table 6-5 Calculating the Historical Standard Deviation for the Period 1970–1979

Year	TR (%), X	X−X̄	(X−X̄)²
1970	3.51	−3.87	14.98
1971	14.12	6.74	45.43
1972	18.72	11.34	128.6
1973	−14.50	−21.88	478.73
1974	−26.03	33.41	1116.23
1975	36.92	29.54	872.61
1976	23.64	16.26	264.39
1977	−7.16	−14.54	211.41
1978	6.39	−0.99	0.98
1979	18.19	10.81	116.86

$$\overline{X} = 7.38$$

$$\sum (X - \overline{X})^2 = 3250.22$$

$$\sigma^2 = \frac{3250.22}{9} = 361.14$$

$$\sigma = (361.14)^{1/2} = 19.00\%$$

In summary, the standard deviation of return measures the total risk of one security or the total risk of a portfolio of securities. The historical standard deviation can be calculated for individual securities or portfolios of securities using TRs for some specified period of time. This *ex post* value is useful in evaluating the total risk for a particular historical period and in estimating the total risk that is expected to prevail over some future period.

The standard deviation, combined with the normal distribution, can provide some useful information about the dispersion or variation in returns. For a *normal distribution*, the probability that a particular outcome will be above (or below) a specified value can be determined. With one standard deviation on either side of the arithmetic mean of the distribution, 68.3 percent of the outcomes will be encompassed; that is, there is a 68.3 percent probability that the actual outcome will be within one (plus or minus) standard deviation of the arithmetic mean. The probabilities are 95 and 99 percent that the actual outcome will be within two or three standard deviations, respectively, of the arithmetic mean.

RISK PREMIUMS

Risk Premium That part of a security's return above the risk-free rate of return

A **risk premium** is the additional return investors expect to receive, or did receive, by taking on increasing amounts of risk. It measures the payoff for taking various types of risk. Such premiums can be calculated between any two classes of securities. For example, a time premium measures the additional compensation for investing in long-term Treasuries versus Treasury bills, and a default premium measures the additional compensation for investing in risky corporate bonds versus riskless Treasury securities.

Equity Risk Premium The difference between stock returns and the risk-free rate

Defining the Equity Risk Premium An often-discussed risk premium is the **equity risk premium**, defined as the difference between the return on stocks and a risk-free rate using Treasury securities. The equity risk premium measures the additional compensation for assuming risk, since Treasury securities have little risk of default. The equity risk premium is an important concept in finance. Note that the *historical equity risk premium* measures the difference between stock returns and Treasuries over some past period of time. When we talk about the future, however, we must consider the *expected equity risk premium* which is, of course, an unknown quantity, since it involves the future.

The equity risk premium affects several important issues and has become an often-discussed topic in Investments. The size of the risk premium is controversial, with varying estimates as to the actual risk premium in the past as well as the prospective risk premium in the future.

Calculating the Equity Risk Premium   There are alternative ways to calculate the equity risk premium, involving arithmetic means, geometric means, Treasury bonds, and so forth.

It can be calculated as

1. Equities minus Treasury bills, using the arithmetic mean or the geometric mean
2. Equities minus long-term Treasury bonds, using the arithmetic mean or the geometric mean

Historically the equity risk premium (based on the S&P 500 Index) had a wide range depending upon time period and methodology, but 5—6 percent would be a reasonable average range.

The Expected Equity Risk Premium   Obviously, common stock investors care whether the expected risk premium is 5 percent, or 6 percent, because that affects what they will earn on their investment in stocks. Holding interest rates constant, a narrowing of the equity risk premium implies a decline in the rate of return on stocks because the amount earned beyond the risk-free rate is reduced. A number of prominent observers have argued that the equity risk premium in the future is likely to be very different from that of the past, specifically considerably lower.

Checking Your Understanding

6. What do we mean when we say that we need to know something about the spread of the data?
7. Why do some market observers expect the equity risk premium in the future to be much lower than it has been in the past?

Realized Returns and Risks From Investing

We can now examine the returns and risks from investing in major financial assets that have occurred in the United States. We also will see how the preceding return and risk measures are typically used in presenting realized return and risk data of interest to virtually all financial market participants.

TOTAL RETURNS AND STANDARD DEVIATIONS FOR THE MAJOR FINANCIAL ASSETS

Table 6-6 shows the average annual geometric and arithmetic returns, as well as standard deviations, for major financial assets for the period 1926—2010 (85 years). Included are both nominal returns and real returns. These data are comparable to those produced and distributed by Ibbotson Associates on a commercial basis. This is an alternative series reconstructed

Table 6-6 Summary Statistics of Annual Total Returns for Major Financial Assets for 85 Years, January 1, 1926–December 31, 2010, Nominal and Inflation-Adjusted

	Arithmetic		Geometric
	Mean	Std.Dev.	Mean
Nominal Total Returns Summary			
S&P 500 Composite	11.5%	19.9%	9.6%
Aaa Corporate Bond	6.3	8.5	5.9
US Treasury Bond	5.8	9.2	5.4
Treasury bill	3.7	3.0	3.6
Inflation	3.1	4.2	3.0
Inflation-Adjusted Total Returns Summary			
S&P 500 Composite	8.3%	19.9%	6.3%
Aaa Corporate Bond	3.3	9.7	2.8
US Treasury Bond	2.7	10.3	2.3
Treasury bill	0.7	3.9	0.6

Source: Jack W. Wilson and Charles P. Jones.

by Jack Wilson and Charles Jones that provides basically the same information (but with a more comprehensive set of S&P 500 companies for the period 1926–1957).[10]

Table 6-6 indicates that large common stocks, as measured by the well-known Standard & Poor's 500 Composite Index, had a geometric mean annual return over this 85-year period of 9.6 percent (rounded). Hence, $1 invested in this market index at the *beginning* of 1926 would have grown at an average annual compound rate of 9.6 percent over this very long period. In contrast, the arithmetic mean annual return for large stocks was 11.4 percent. The best estimate of the "average" return for stocks in any one year, using only this information, would be 11.4 percent, based on the arithmetic mean, and not the 9.6 percent based on the geometric mean return. The standard deviation for large stocks for 1926–2010 was 19.9 percent.

The difference between these two means is related to the variability of the stock return series. The linkage between the geometric mean and the arithmetic mean is approximated by Equation 6-10:

$$(1 + G)^2 \approx (1 + \text{A.M.})^2 - (\text{S.D.})^2 \tag{6-10}$$

where

G = the geometric mean of a series of asset returns

A.M. = the arithmetic mean of a series of asset returns

S.D. = the standard deviation of the arithmetic series of returns

---

[10] A primary difference in the return series shown here and that of Ibbotson Associates is the return for large common stocks (S&P 500 Index). Wilson and Jones used a larger set of stocks between 1926 and 1957, whereas Ibbotson Associates used 90 large stocks. Large stocks did better during this period than did stocks in general, resulting in a larger geometric mean for the Ibbotson Associates data. Wilson and Jones believe that the S&P series used here, which was laboriously reconstructed after the Ibbotson Associates series was put together and used, is a more complete representation of the S&P 500 Index because of this difference.

Example 6-17   Using data with more decimal places than Table 6-6 for 1926–2010 for the S&P 500 Index:

$$(1.0957)^2 \approx (1.1152)^2 - (0.1992)^2$$
$$1.201 \approx 1.2437 - 0.0397$$
$$1.201 \approx 1.204$$

✓   If we know the arithmetic mean of a series of asset returns and the standard deviation of the series, we can approximate the geometric mean for this series. As the standard deviation of the series increases, holding the arithmetic mean constant, the geometric mean decreases.

Although not shown in Table 6-6, smaller common stocks have greater returns and greater risk relative to large common stocks. "Smaller" here means the smallest stocks on the NYSE and not the really small stocks traded on the over-the-counter market. The arithmetic mean for this series is much higher than for the S&P 500 Index, typically 5 or 6 percentage points.[11] However, because of the much larger standard deviation for smaller common stocks, roughly 30 percent, the geometric mean is considerably less than that, typically around 2 percentage points more than the geometric mean for large common stocks (the framework of Equation 6-10 explains why there is a large difference between the two means). Small common stocks have by far the largest variability of any of the returns series considered in Table 6-6.

Corporate and Treasury bonds had geometric means that were roughly 50 to 60 percent of the S&P 500 Composite Index, at 5.9 and 5.4 percent, respectively, but the risk was considerably smaller. Standard deviations for the bond series were less than half as large as that for the S&P 500 Composite.[12]

Finally, as we would expect, Treasury bills had the smallest returns of any of the major assets shown in Table 6-6, 3.6 percent, as well as the smallest standard deviation by far.

The deviations for each of the major financial assets in Table 6-6 reflect the dispersion of the returns over the 85-year period covered in the data. The standard deviations clearly show the wide dispersion in the returns from common stocks compared with bonds and Treasury bills. Furthermore, smaller common stocks can logically be expected to be riskier than the S&P 500 stocks, and the standard deviation indicates a much wider dispersion.

CUMULATIVE WEALTH INDEXES

Figure 6-3 shows the CWIs for the major financial assets and the corresponding index number for inflation from the data in Table 6-6. The series starts at the beginning of 1926 and shows the cumulative results of starting with $1 in each of these series and going through the end of 2010. Note that the vertical axis of Figure 6-3 is a log scale.[13]

---

[11] The data for small common stocks is omitted because of the difficulty in getting one series that spans the entire time period, determining the yield for the series, and because of some unusual values in the 1930s exceeding 100 percent.

[12] The reason for the distribution of Treasury bonds and Treasury bills, which have no practical risk of default, is that this is a distribution of annual returns, where negative numbers are possible. Thus, a new 10-year Treasury bond purchased at $1,000 on January 1 could decline to, say, $900 by December 31, resulting in a negative TR for that year. For the full 10-year period, its return will, of course, be positive since it will be redeemed for $1,000.

[13] A logarithmic scale greatly facilitates comparisons of different series across time because the same vertical distance represents the same percentage change in a particular series return. The logarithmic scale allows the user to concentrate on rates of return and ignore the dollar amounts involved.

Figure 6-3

Cumulative Wealth for Major Asset Classes and Cumulative Inflation (Amounts are Rounded).

Source: Jack W. Wilson and Charles P. Jones.

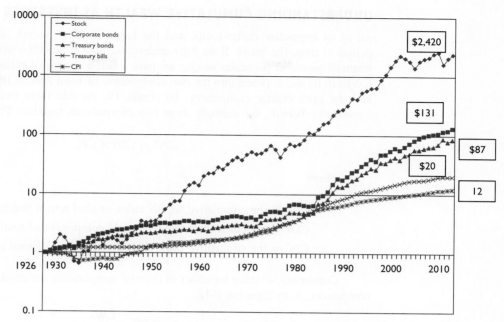

As Figure 6-3 shows, the cumulative wealth for stocks, as measured by the S&P 500 Composite Index, completely dominated the returns on corporate bonds over this period—$2,420.46 versus $130.66. Note that we use the geometric mean from Table 6-6 to calculate cumulative ending wealth for each of the series shown in Figure 6-3 by raising (1 + the geometric mean stated as a decimal) to the power represented by the number of periods, which in this case is 85.

Example 6-18

The ending wealth value of $2,420.46 for common stocks in Figure 6-3 is the result of compounding at 9.6 percent for 85 years, or

$$CWI = WI_0(1.096)^{85} = \$1.00(2,420.46) = \$2,420.46$$

The large CWI value for stocks shown in Figure 6-3 speaks for itself. Remember, however, that the variability of this series is considerably larger than that for bonds or Treasury bills, as shown by the standard deviations in Table 6-6.[14]

---

[14] On an inflation-adjusted basis, the cumulative ending wealth for any of the series can be calculated as

$$CWI_{IA} = \frac{CWI}{CI_{INF}}$$

where

CWI_{IA} = the cumulative wealth index value for any asset on inflation − adjusted basis

CWI = the cumulative wealth index value for any asset on a nominal basis

CI_{INF} = the ending index value for inflation, calculated as $(1 + \text{geometric rate of inflation})^n$, where n is the number of periods considered

UNDERSTANDING CUMULATIVE WEALTH AS INVESTORS

All of us appreciate dollar totals, and the larger the final wealth accumulated over some period of time, the better. If we fully understand how cumulative wealth comes about from financial assets, in particular stocks, we have a better chance of enhancing that wealth. The CWI can be decomposed into the two components of Total Return: the dividend component and the price change component. To obtain TR, we add these two components, but for Cumulative Wealth, we multiply these two components together. Thus,

$$CWI = CDY \times CPC \qquad \text{(6-11)}$$

where

CWI = the cumulative wealth index or total return index for a series

CDY = the cumulative dividend yield component of total return

CPC = the cumulative price change component of total return

Conversely, to solve for either of the two components, we divide the CWI by the other component, as in Equation 6-12.

$$CPC = \frac{CWI}{CDY} \qquad \text{(6-12)}$$

$$CDY = \frac{CWI}{CPC} \qquad \text{(6-13)}$$

Example 6-19   The CWI for common stocks (S&P 500) for 1926–2010 (85 years) was $2,364.78, based on a geometric mean of 9.57 percent for that period (rounded to 9.6 percent in Table 6-6). The average dividend yield for those 85 years was 3.99 percent. Raising 1.0399 to the 85th power, the cumulative dividend yield, CDY, was $27.82. Therefore, the cumulative price change index for the S&P 500 for that period was $2,364.78/$27.82, or $85.00. This is a compound annual average return of

$$(\$85.00)^{1/85} - 1.0 = .0537 \text{ or } 5.37\%$$

Note that the annual average geometric mean return relative for common stocks is the product of the corresponding geometric mean return relatives for the two components:
For 1926–2010, an 85-year period,

$$G_{DY} \times G_{PC} = G_{TR} \qquad \text{(6-14)}$$

$$1.0399 \times 1.0537 = 1.0957$$
$$1.0957 - 1.0 = .0957 \text{ or } 9.57\% \text{ (rounded to 9.6\% in Table 6-6)}$$

It is important to understand that for the S&P 500 stocks historically, which many investors hold as an index fund or EFT, dividends played an important role in the overall compound rate of return that was achieved. As we can see, almost 42 percent (3.99%/9.57%) of the TR from large stocks over that long period of time was attributable to dividends.

Dividend yields on the S&P 500 have been low for the past several years, roughly half their historical level. This means that either investors will have to earn more from the price change component of cumulative wealth, or their cumulative wealth will be lower than it was in the past because of the lower dividend yield component.

Compounding and Discounting

Of course, the single most striking feature of Figure 6-3 is the tremendous difference in ending wealth between stocks and bonds. This difference reflects the impact of compounding substantially different mean returns over long periods, which produces almost unbelievable results. The use of compounding points out the importance of this concept and of its complement, discounting. Both are important in investment analysis and are used often. *Compounding* involves future value resulting from compound interest—earning interest on interest. As we saw, the calculation of wealth indexes involves compounding at the geometric mean return over some historical period.

Present value (discounting) is the value today of a dollar to be received in the future. Such dollars are not comparable, because of the time value of money. In order to be comparable, they must be discounted back to the present. Present value concepts are used extensively in Chapters 10 and 17, and in other chapters as needed.

Summary

► Return and risk go together in investments; indeed, these two parameters are the underlying basis of the subject. Everything an investor does, or is concerned with, is tied directly or indirectly to return and risk.

► The term *return* can be used in different ways. It is important to distinguish between realized (ex post, or historical) return and expected (ex ante, or anticipated) return.

► The two components of return are yield and price change (capital gain or loss).

► The total return is a decimal or percentage return concept that can be used to correctly measure the return for any security.

► The return relative, which adds 1.0 to the total return, is used when calculating the geometric mean of a series of returns.

► The cumulative wealth index (total return index) is used to measure the cumulative wealth over time given some initial starting wealth—typically, $1—and a series of returns for some asset.

► Return relatives, along with the beginning and ending values of the foreign currency, can be used to convert the return on a foreign investment into a domestic return.

► The geometric mean measures the compound rate of return over time. The arithmetic mean, on the other hand, is simply the average return for a series and is used to measure the typical performance for a single period.

► Inflation-adjusted returns can be calculated by dividing 1 + the nominal return by 1 + the inflation rate as measured by the CPI.

► Risk is the other side of the coin: risk and expected return should always be considered together. An investor cannot reasonably expect to earn large returns without assuming greater risks.

► The primary components of risk have traditionally been categorized into interest rate, market, inflation, business, financial, and liquidity risks. Investors today must also consider exchange rate risk and country risk. Each security has its own sources of risk, which we will discuss when we discuss the security itself.

▶ Historical returns can be described in terms of a frequency distribution and their variability measured by use of the standard deviation.

▶ The standard deviation provides useful information about the distribution of returns and aids investors in assessing the possible outcomes of an investment.

▶ Common stocks over the period 1926–2010 had an annualized geometric mean total return of 9.6 percent, compared to 5.4 percent for long-term Treasury bonds.

▶ Over the period 1920–2010, common stocks had a standard deviation of returns of approximately 19.9 percent, about two and one-half times that of long-term government and corporate bonds and about six times that of Treasury bills.

Questions

6-1 Distinguish between historical return and expected return.

6-2 How long must an asset be held to calculate a TR?

6-3 Define the components of TR. Can any of these components be negative?

6-4 Distinguish between TR and holding period return.

6-5 When should the geometric mean return be used to measure returns? Why will it always be less than the arithmetic mean (unless the numbers are identical)?

6-6 When should the arithmetic mean be used in describing stock returns?

6-7 What is the mathematical linkage between the arithmetic mean and the geometric mean for a set of security returns?

6-8 What is an equity risk premium?

6-9 According to Table 6-6, common stocks have generally returned more than bonds. How, then, can they be considered more risky?

6-10 Distinguish between market risk and business risk. How is interest rate risk related to inflation risk?

6-11 Classify the traditional sources of risk as to whether they are general sources of risk or specific sources of risk.

6-12 Explain what is meant by country risk. How would you evaluate the country risk of Canada and Mexico?

6-13 Assume that you purchase a stock on a Japanese market, denominated in yen. During the period you hold the stock, the yen weakens relative to the dollar. Assume you sell at a profit on the Japanese market. How will your return, when converted to dollars, be affected?

6-14 Define risk. How does use of the standard deviation as a measure of risk relate to this definition of risk?

6-15 Explain verbally the relationship between the geometric mean and a CWI.

6-16 As Table 6-6 shows, the geometric mean return for stocks over a long period has been 9.6 percent. Thus, on average, on a compound basis, stocks have averaged a 9.6 percent TR per year over a long time period. Should investors be surprised if they hold stocks for a 10-year period, or a 15-year period, and earn an average return of only 1 or 2 percent?

6-17 Explain how the geometric mean annual average inflation rate can be used to calculate inflation-adjusted stock returns over the period 1926–2010.

6-18 Explain the two components of the CWI for common stocks. Assume we know one of these two components. How can the other be calculated?

6-19 Common stocks have returned slightly less than twice the compound annual rate of return for corporate bonds. Does this mean that common stocks are about twice as risky as corporates?

6-20 Can cumulative wealth be stated on an inflation-adjusted basis?

6-21 Over the long run, stocks have returned a lot more than bonds, given the compounding effect? Why, then, do investors buy bonds?

6-22 Given the strong performance of stocks over the last 85 years, do you think it is possible for stocks to show an average negative return over a 10-year period?

6-23 Is there a case to be made for an investor to hold only Treasury bills over a long period of time?

6-24 How can we calculate the returns from holding gold?

6-25 Don't worry too much if your retirement funds earn 5.5 percent over the next 40 years instead of 6 percent. It won't affect final wealth very much. Evaluate this claim.

6-26 Suppose someone promises to double your money in 10 years. What rate of return are they implicitly promising you?

6-27 A technical analyst claimed in the popular press to have earned 25 percent a month for 10 years using his technical analysis technique. Is this claim feasible?

6-28 Which alternative would you prefer: (a) 1 percent a month, compounded monthly, or (2) ½ percent a month, compounded semimonthly (24 periods)?

Demonstration Problems

6-1 Calculation of Arithmetic Mean and Geometric Mean: Data for Extell Corp.

Year (t)	(1) End-of-Year Price (P_t)	(2) Calendar-Year Dividends (D_t)	TR%
2007	$ 74.60	$2.88	--
2008	64.30	3.44	−9.2%
2009	67.70	3.44	10.6%
2010	56.70	3.44	−11.2%
2011	96.25	3.44	75.8%
2012	122.00	3.71	30.6%

The arithmetic mean of the TR for Extell, 2008−2012:

$$\frac{\sum (TR\%)}{n} = \frac{96.6}{5} = 19.32\%$$

To calculate the *geometric* mean in this example, convert the TRs to decimals, and add 1.0, producing return relatives, RR. The GM is the fifth root of the product of the RRs.

Year	TR%	TR decimal	RR
2008	−9.2%	−0.092	0.908
2009	10.6%	0.106	1.106
2010	−11.2%	−0.112	0.888
2011	75.8%	0.758	1.758
2012	−30.6%	0.306	1.306

The geometric mean is $GM = [(1 + RR_1)(1 + RR_2)\ldots(1 + RR_n)]^{1/n} - 1$. Therefore, take the fifth root of the product

$$(0.908)(1.106)(0.888)(1.758)(1.306) = 2.0474, \text{ and } (2.0474)^{1/5} = 1.154; 1.154 - 1.0$$
$$= .154 \text{ or } 15.4\% \text{ TR}$$

6-2   **The Effects of Reinvesting Returns:** The difference in meaning of the arithmetic and geometric mean, holding Extell stock over the period January 1, 2008 through December 31, 2012 for two different investment strategies, is as follows:

Strategy A—keep a fixed amount (say, $1,000) invested and do not reinvest returns.
Strategy B—reinvest returns and allow compounding.

First, take Extell's TRs and convert them to decimal form (r) for Strategy A, and then to $(1 + r)$ form for Strategy B.

Strategy A					Strategy B		
Jan. I Year	Amt. Inv.	×	r_t	= Return	Jan. I Year	Amt. Inv. × $(1 + r_t)$ = Terminal Amt.		
2008	$1000		−0.092	−$92.00	2008	$1000	0.908	$908.00
2009	1000		0.106	106.00	2009	908.0	1.106	1004.25
2010	1000		−0.112	−112.00	2010	1004.25	0.888	891.77
2011	1000		0.758	758.00	2011	891.77	1.758	1567.74
2012	1000		0.306	306.00	2012	1567.74	1.306	2047.46

Using Strategy A, keeping $1,000 invested at the beginning of the year, TRs for the years 2008–2012 were $966, or $193.20 per year average ($966/5), which on a $1,000 investment is $193.20/1000 = 0.1932, or 19.32 percent per year—the same value as the arithmetic mean in Demonstration Problem 6-1 earlier.

Using Strategy B, compounding gains and losses, TR was $1,047.46 (the terminal amount $2,047.46 minus the initial $1,000). The average annual rate of return in this situation can be found by taking the nth root of the terminal/initial amount:

$$[2047.46/1000]^{1/5} = (2.0474)^{1/5} = 1.1541 = (1 + r), r\% = 15.41\%$$

which is exactly the set of values we ended up with in Demonstration Problem 6-1 when calculating the geometric mean.

6-3   **Calculating the Standard Deviation:** Using the TR values for Extell for the years 2008–2012, we can illustrate the deviation of the values from the mean.

The numerator for the formula for the variance of these Y_t values is $\sum (Y_t\text{-}Y)^2$, which we will call SS_y, the sum of the squared deviations of the Y_t around the mean. Algebraically, there is a simpler alternative formula.

$$SS_y = \sum (Y_t - \bar{Y})^2 = \sum Y^2{}_t - \frac{(\sum Y_t)^2}{n}$$

Using Extell's annual total returns, we will calculate the SS_y both ways.

Year	Y_t=TR	$(Y_t - \overline{Y})$	$(Y_t - \overline{Y})^2$	Y_t^2
2008	−9.2%	28.52	813.3904	84.64
2009	10.6%	−8.72	76.0384	112.36
2010	−11.2%	−30.52	931.4704	125.44
2011	75.8%	56.48	3189.9904	5745.64
2012	30.6%	11.28	127.2384	936.36
Sum	96.6%	−0−	5138.1280	7004.44

$$\overline{Y} = 19.32\%$$

$$SS_y = \sum (Y_t - \overline{Y})^2 = 5138.128, \text{ and also}$$

$$SS_y = \sum Y^2 - \frac{(\sum Y_t)^2}{n} = 7004.44 - \frac{(96.6)^2}{5} = 5138.128$$

The variance is the "average" squared deviation from the mean:

$$\sigma^2 = \frac{SS_y}{(n-1)} = \frac{5138.128}{4} = 1284.532 \text{ "squared percent"}$$

The standard deviation is the square root of the variance:

$$\sigma = (\sigma^2)^{1/2} = (1284.532)^{1/2} = 35.84\%$$

The standard deviation is in the same units of measurement as the original observations, as is the arithmetic mean.

6-4   **Calculation of Cumulative Wealth Index and Geometric Mean:** By using the geometric mean annual average rate of return for a particular financial asset, the CWI can be found by converting the TR on a geometric mean basis to a return relative, and raising this return relative to the power representing the number of years involved. Consider the geometric mean of 12.47 percent for small common stocks for the period 1926−2007. The CWI, using a starting index value of $1, is (note the 82 periods):

$$\$1(1.1247)^{82} = \$15,311.19$$

Conversely, if we know the CWI value, we can solve for the geometric mean by taking the nth root and subtracting out 1.0.

$$(\$15,311.19)^{1/82} - 1.0 = 1.1247 - 1.0 = .1247 \text{ or } 12.47\%$$

note : number of years to use = [ending year-beginning year] + 1

6-5   **Calculation of Inflation-Adjusted Returns:** Knowing the geometric mean for inflation for some time period, we can add 1.0 and raise it to the nth power. We then divide the CWI on a nominal basis by the ending value for inflation to obtain inflation-adjusted returns. For example, given a CWI of $2,364.78 for common stocks for 1926−2010, and a geometric mean inflation rate of 3.00 percent, the inflation-adjusted cumulative wealth index for this 85-year period is calculated as

$$\$2364.78/(1.03)^{85} = \$2364.78/12.336 = \$191.70$$

6-6   **Analyzing the Components of a Cumulative Wealth Index:** Assume that we know that for the period 1926–2010 the yield component for common stocks was 3.99 percent, and that the CWI was $2,364.78. The CWI value for the yield component was

$$(1.0399)^{85} = 27.82$$

The CWI value for the price change component was

$$\$2,364.78/27.82 = 85.00$$

The geometric mean annual average rate of return for the price change component for common stocks was

$$(85.00)^{1/85} = 1.0537$$

The geometric mean for common stocks is linked to its components by the following:

$$1.0399(1.0537) = 1.0957; 1.0957 - 1.0 = .0957 \text{ or } 9.57\%$$

The CWI can be found by multiplying together the individual component CWIs:

$$\$85.00(\$27.82) = \$2,364.70^*$$

(*rounding accounts for any differences)

Problems

6-1   Calculate the TR and the RR for the following assets:

   a. A preferred stock bought for $70 per share, held one year during which $5 per share dividends are collected, and sold for $62

   b. A warrant bought for $10 and sold three months later for $13

   c. A 12 percent bond bought for $830, held two years during which interest is collected, and sold for $920

6-2   Calculate, using a calculator, the arithmetic and geometric mean rate of return for the Standard & Poor 500 Composite Index (Table 6-1) for the years 2001–2004. How does this change when 2005 is included?

6-3   Calculate the index value for the S&P 500 (Table 6-1) assuming a $1 investment at the beginning of 1990 and extending through the end of 1999. Using only these index values, calculate the geometric mean for these years.

6-4   Assume that one of your relatives, on your behalf, invested $50,000 in a trust holding S&P 500 stocks at the beginning of 1926. Using the data in Table 6-6, determine the value of this trust at the end of 2010.

6-5   Now assume that your relative had invested $50,000 in a trust holding "small stocks" at the beginning of 1926. Determine the value of this trust at the end of 2010.

6-6 What if your relative had invested $50,000 in a trust holding long-term Treasury bonds at the beginning of 1926. Determine the value of this trust at the end of 2010.

6-7 Finally, what if this relative had invested $50,000 in a trust holding Treasury bills at the beginning of 1926. Determine the value of this trust by the end of 2010.

6-8 Calculate cumulative wealth for corporate bonds for the period 1926–2010, using a geometric mean of 5.9 percent (85-year period).

6-9 Given a CWI for Treasury bills of $20.21 for the period 1926–2010, calculate the geometric mean.

6-10 Given an inflation rate of 3 percent over the period 1926–2010 (geometric mean annual average), calculate the inflation-adjusted CWI for corporate bonds as of year-end 2010.

6-11 Given a geometric mean inflation rate of 4 percent, determine how long it would take to cut the purchasing power of money in half using the rule of 72.

6-12 If a basket of consumer goods cost $1 at the beginning of 1926 and $12.34 at the end of 2010, calculate the geometric mean rate of inflation over this period.

6-13 Assume that over the period 1926–2010 the yield index component of common stocks had a geometric mean annual average of 3.99 percent. Calculate the CWI for this component as of year-end 2010. Using this value, calculate the CWI for the price change component of common stocks using information in Figure 6-3.

6-14 Assume that Treasury bonds continued to have a geometric mean as shown in Table 6-6 until 100 years have elapsed. Calculate the cumulative ending wealth per $1 invested for this 100-year period.

6-15 Assume that over the period 1926–2010 the geometric mean rate of return for Treasury bonds was 5.4 percent. The corresponding number for the rate of inflation was 3 percent. Calculate, two different ways, the CWI for government bonds for the period, on an inflation-adjusted basis.

6-16 Using the TRs for the years 1926–1931 from Table 6-1, determine the geometric mean for this period. Show how the same result can be obtained from the ending wealth index value for 1931 of 0.7405.

6-17 Using data for three periods, construct a set of TRs that will produce a geometric mean equal to the arithmetic mean.

6-18 According to Table 6-6, the standard deviation for all common stocks for the period 1926–2010 was 19.9 percent. Using data from Table 6-1, calculate the standard deviation for the years 1981–1991 and compare your results.

6-19 Someone offers you a choice between $50,000 to be received 10 years from now, or a $20,000 portfolio of stocks guaranteed to earn a compound annual average rate of return of 8 percent per year for the next 10 years. Determine the better alternative based solely on this information

Computational Problems

6-1 Assume that we know the performance of the S&P 500 Index for the first five years of the second decade of the 21st century, defined as 2010–2019. What annual geometric mean must the market average for the last five years (2015–2019) to produce an overall geometric mean for the decade of 10 percent? The TRs for the first 5 years are 2010, 15.06 percent; 2011, −9.9 percent; 2012, 16.1 percent; 2013, −19.7 percent; and 2014, 10.7 percent.

6-2   Using the five years of TRs in 6−1, assume that one of the five years during the second half of the decade, 2015−2019, shows a loss of 15 percent. What would the geometric mean of the remaining four years have to be for the decade as a whole to average the 10 percent return for the S&P 500 Index?

6-3   The geometric mean for the TR for the S&P 500 Index for the period 1926−2010 was 9.57 percent. Assume that the geometric mean for the yield component of the TR on the S&P 500 for the period 1926−2010 was 3.99 percent. What is the cumulative wealth for the other component of the CWI for the S&P 500 for the period 1926−2010?

6-4   Suppose you know that cumulative inflation for the period 1926−2010 was 12.34. You also know that the geometric mean for Treasury bills for this period was 3.6 percent. What was the real return for Treasury bills for the period 1926−2010?

6-5   Based on some calculations you have done, you know that the cumulative wealth for corporate bonds for the period 2008−2012 was $1.234. However, you have misplaced the return for 2010. The other four returns are: 9.3 percent, −6.2 percent, 12.1 percent, and 7.4 percent. What is the return for 2010, based on this information? (Use 3 decimal places.)

Spreadsheet Exercises

6-1   Warren Buffett, arguably the most famous investor in the United States, is the CEO of Berkshire Hathaway (BRK), a company that has enjoyed great success in terms of its stock price. Below are the actual year-end stock prices for BRK-A from 1965 through 2011. (Yes, these are the actual stock prices, believe it or not.)

a. Calculate the RRs for each year starting in 1966. Use two decimal places.

b. Calculate the arithmetic mean and geometric mean for these price relatives, using three decimal places.

c. Calculate the CWI for 1966−2011, assuming an initial investment of $1,000, and $10,000. State the answers without decimal places.

Year-End Price		Year-End Price	
1965	$16.25	1976	94.00
1966	17.50	1977	138.00
1967	20.25	1978	157.00
1968	37.00	1979	320.00
1969	42.00	1980	425.00
1970	39.00	1981	560.00
1971	70.00	1982	775.00
1972	80.00	1983	1,310.00
1973	71.00	1984	1,275.00
1974	40.00	1985	2,470.00
1975	38.00	1986	2,820.00

Year-End Price		Year-End Price	
1987	2,950.00	2000	71,000.00
1988	4,700.00	2001	75,600.00
1989	8,675.00	2002	72,750.00
1990	6,675.00	2003	84,250.00
1991	9,050.00	2004	87,900.00
1992	11,750.00	2005	88,620.00
1993	16,325.00	2006	109,990.00
1994	20,400.00	2007	141,600.00
1995	32,100.00	2008	96,600.00
1996	34,100.00	2009	99,200.00
1997	46,000.00	2010	120,450.00
1998	70,000.00	2011	114,755.00
1999	56,100.00		

(Continued)

6-2 **a.** Using the spreadsheet data in 6−1, and spreadsheet formulas, determine the compound annual average rate of return for Berkshire Hathaway for the last 10 years and the last five years.

b. What was the percentage rate of return on this stock in 2008?

6-3 The following data for Coca-Cola (ticker symbol = KO) are the December ending prices (adjusted for stock splits and dividends) and the annual dividend. This information can be obtained from a source such as *Yahoo! Finance*. Place these data in a spreadsheet for columns A-C. Use 3 decimal places and calculate results in decimal form (not percentages). You will need the 2000 price to calculate the 2001 return.

For each year 2001−2010:

a. Calculate as column D the RR for the price change only.

b. Calculate as column E the TR based on price change only.

c. Calculate as column F the RR based on price change and dividends.

d. Calculate as column G the TR based on price change and dividends.

e. Calculate the arithmetic and geometric means for 2001−2010 for price change only and for TR.

f. Calculate the ending wealth as of December 31, 2010, based on TRs, for $1 invested in Coca-Cola stock at the beginning of 2001.

g. Calculate the standard deviation of the TRs for the years 2001−2010. (Note: use the total returns and not the return relatives.)

Coca-Cola ending prices and dividends

2010 $64.39, $1.76; 2009 $54.10, $1.64; 2008 $41.52, $1.52; 2007 $54.70, $1.36; 2006 $41.93, $1.24

2005 $34.06, $1.12; 2004 $34.29, $1,00; 2003 $40.88, $0.88; 2002 $34.61, $0.80; 2001 $36.62, $0.72, 2000 $46.80

Checking Your Understanding

6-1 Disagree. The Cumulative Wealth Index can be calculated for nominal stock returns or inflation-adjusted (real) returns, just as Total Returns and Return Relatives can be used on either a nominal or real basis.

6-2 When an investor buys a foreign asset, he or she is, in effect, selling dollars to obtain the foreign currency needed to buy the security. When this security is sold in the foreign market by a U.S. investor, the proceeds will need to be converted back to dollars.

6-3 Yes. The dollar declined against many foreign currencies in the first few years of the 21st century. This increased the returns to U.S. investors from investing in foreign countries. Investors often viewed this approach as a bet against the dollar.

6-4 This investment showed a loss on a geometric mean basis even though the arithmetic mean is zero. It is calculated as $1000*1.15*.85 = $977.50. The sequence of returns does not matter.

6-5 The long-term financial history of the United States shows that inflation is an issue over a period of many years. While it was very low in recent years, it is expected to be higher in the future. Even at an average inflation rate of 3 percent a year, the purchasing power of money will be cut in half in approximately 24 years. Many retirees will live this long after retiring.

6-6 The spread of the data tells us something about the risk involved. How likely is the average, or mean, to be realized?

6-7 A number of market observers expect equity returns to be lower in the future because dividend yields are currently about half what they were for many years, on average. Other things equal, equity returns will be reduced (unless price appreciation makes up the difference) and, unless interest rates decline, equity risk premiums will be lower.

NOTE: Answers to the three-stock example at the beginning of the chapter using 2 decimal places:

Stock 2 has the largest geometric mean and would produce the greatest ending wealth. It also has the lowest risk by far based on calculating standard deviations. Stocks 1 and 3 have identical geometric means and would produce identical ending wealths.

−0.1	0.04	0.4	0.9	1.04	1.4
−0.2	0.05	−0.02	0.8	1.05	0.98
0.29	0.07	−0.1	1.29	1.07	0.9
0.19	0.06	−0.15	1.19	1.06	0.85
0.12	0.09	0.17	1.12	1.09	1.17
0.204	0.019	0.226 Std Dev	1.04	1.06	1.04 G.M.
0.060	0.062	0.060 A.M.			

chapter 7

Portfolio Theory is Universal

Everyone keeps telling you that with $1 million to invest, you can have a nice portfolio of securities. And then the thought occurs: what is a portfolio exactly? You begin to wonder if a portfolio has characteristics you need to consider, because you can recall someone talking about portfolio theory, and what it means to investors. You have heard people say *don't put all of your eggs in one basket*, so how does that apply to investing? If you decide to put the entire $1 million in two stocks, what will the trustee say? It is not difficult to pick up a popular press article on investing and read about the importance of diversification, or hear about how some stocks seem to react negatively to threats of rising inflation while others seem to respond positively. Therefore, it seems like a good idea to expose yourself to at least the basics of portfolio theory. Then you will not be intimidated when someone starts talking about Markowitz portfolio theory, a universal concept in today's global investing world that is widely known and discussed.

In this chapter, we outline the nature of risk and return as it applies to making investment decisions. Unlike Chapter 6, we are talking about the future—which involves *expected returns*, and not the past—which involves *realized returns*. Investors must estimate and manage the returns and risk from their investments. They reduce risk to the extent possible without affecting returns by building diversified portfolios. Therefore, we must be concerned with the investor's total portfolio and analyze investment risk accordingly. As we shall see, *diversification is the key to effective risk management*. We will consider the critically important principle of Markowitz diversification, focusing primarily on the concepts of the correlation coefficient and covariance as applied to security returns.

AFTER READING THIS CHAPTER YOU WILL BE ABLE TO:

▶ Understand the meaning and calculation of expected return and risk measures for an individual security.

▶ Recognize what it means to talk about modern portfolio theory.

▶ Calculate portfolio return and risk measures as formulated by Markowitz.

▶ Understand how diversification works.

Dealing With Uncertainty

In Chapter 6 we discussed the average returns, both arithmetic and geometric, that investors have experienced over the years from investing in the major financial assets available to them. We also considered the risk of these asset returns as measured by the standard deviation. Analysts often refer to the realized returns for a security, or class of securities, over time using these measures as well as other measures such as the cumulative wealth index.

Realized returns are important for several reasons. For example, investors need to know how their portfolios have performed relative to relevant market indexes. Realized returns are also important in helping investors to form expectations about future returns by providing a foundation upon which to make estimates of expected returns. For example, if over a long period Treasury bills have averaged less than 4 percent on a geometric mean basis, it would be unrealistic to expect long-run average compound returns of 6 or 7 percent in the future from Treasury bills unless the investing environment has changed significantly.

How do we go about estimating returns, which is what investors must actually do in managing their portfolios? First of all, note that we will use the return and risk measures developed in Chapter 6. The total return measure, TR, is applicable whether one is measuring realized returns or estimating future (expected) returns. Because it includes everything the investor can expect to receive over any specified future period, the TR is useful in conceptualizing the estimated returns from securities.

Similarly, the variance, or its square root, the standard deviation, is an accepted measure of variability for both realized returns and expected returns. We will calculate both the variance and the standard deviation below and use them interchangeably as the situation dictates. Sometimes it is preferable to use one, and sometimes the other.

To estimate the returns from various securities, investors must estimate the cash flows these securities are likely to provide. The basis for doing so for bonds and stocks will be covered in their respective chapters. For now it is sufficient to remind ourselves of the uncertainty of estimates of the future, a problem emphasized at the outset of Chapter 1.

Box 7-1 is an interesting discussion of risk, and how best to understand it. In this essay Peter Bernstein, one of the most prominent observers of the investing environment over many years, argues that risky decisions are all about three elements. His second point, "expect the unexpected," turned out to be particularly relevant given what happened to the financial system in 2008. The unexpected did occur, and very few were prepared to deal with the situation. The resulting damage has been enormous.

USING PROBABILITIES

The return an investor will earn from investing is not known; it must be estimated. Future return is an *expected* return and may or may not actually be realized. An investor may expect the TR on a particular security to be 0.10 for the coming year, but in truth this is only a "point estimate." Risk, or the chance that some unfavorable event will occur, is involved when investment decisions are made. Investors are often overly optimistic about expected returns. We can use the term *random variable* to describe the one-period rate of return from a stock (or bond)—it has an uncertain value which fluctuates randomly.

To deal with the uncertainty of returns, investors need to think explicitly about a security's distribution of probable TRs. In other words, while investors may expect a security to return 10 percent, for example, this is only a one-point estimate of the entire range of possibilities. Given that investors must deal with the uncertain future, a number of possible returns can, and will, occur.

BOX 7-1

Risk: The Whole Versus the Parts

Many years ago, in the middle of a staff meeting, a colleague passed me a scrap of paper on which he had written, "When all is said and done, more things are said than done." When I consider the plethora of books, articles, consultants, and conferences on risk in today's world, my friend's aphorism has never seemed more appropriate. Are we never going to nail risk down and bring it under control? How much more can anyone reveal to us beyond what we have already been told?

In a very real sense, this flood of material about risk is inherently risky. Sorting out the pieces and searching for main themes has become an escalating challenge. The root of the matter gets lost in the shuffle while we are analyzing all the elegant advances in risk measurement and the impressive broadening of the kinds of risks we seek to manage. More is said than is done, or what is done loses touch with what has been said.

If we go back to first principles for a moment, perhaps we can put the multifarious individual pieces into some kind of a larger framework and optimize the choices among the masses of information we are attempting to master.

Professor Elroy Dimson of the London Business School once said risk means more things can happen than will happen. Dimson's formulation is only a fancy way of saying that we do not know what is going to happen—good or bad. Even the range of possible outcomes remains indeterminate, much as we would like to nail it down. Remember always: Risk is not about uncertainty but about the unknown, the inescapable darkness of the future.

If more things can happen than will happen, and if we are denied precise knowledge of the range of possible outcomes, *some decisions we make are going to be wrong.* How many, how often, how seriously? We have no way of knowing even that. Even the most elegant model, as Leibniz reminded Jacob Bernouilli in 1703, is going to work "only for the most part." What lurks in the smaller part is hidden from us, but it could turn into a load of dynamite.

The beginning of wisdom in life is in accepting the inevitability of being wrong on occasion. Or, to turn that phrase around, the greatest risks we take are those where we are certain of the outcome—as masses of people are at classic market bottoms and tops. My investment philosophy has always been that victory in the long run accrues to the humble rather than to the bold.

This emphasis on ignorance is the necessary first step toward the larger framework we need if we hope to sort out the flood of information about risk that assails us. Now we can break down the problem of risk into what appear to me to be its three primary constituent parts.

First, what is the balance between the consequences of being wrong and the probability of being wrong? Many mistakes do not matter. Other mistakes can be fatal. No matter how small the probability you will be hit by a car when you cross against the lights, the consequences of being hit deserve the greater weight in the decision. This line of questioning is the beginning, and in some ways the end, of risk management. All decisions must pass through this sieve. It is the end if you decide not to take the risk, but it is also the end in the sense that distinguishing between consequences and probabilities is what risk management is all about.

Second, expect the unexpected. That sounds like an empty cliché, but it has profound meaning for risk management. It is easy to prepare for the risks you know—earnings fail to meet expectations, clients depart, bonds go sour, a valued associate goes to a competitor. Insurance and hedging strategies cover other kinds of risks lying in wait out there, from price volatility to premature death.

But preparation for the unexpected is a matter of the decision-making structure, *and nothing else.* Who is in charge here? That is the critical question in any organization. And if it is just you there when the unexpected strikes, then you should prepare in advance for where you will turn for help when matters seem to be running out of control.

Finally, note that word "control." With an exit strategy—when decisions are easily reversible—control over outcomes can be a secondary matter. But with decisions such as launching a new product or getting married, the costs of reversibility are so high that you should not enter into them unless you have some control over the outcome if things turn out differently from what you expect. Gambling is fun because your bet is irreversible and you have no control over the outcome. But real life is not a gambling casino.

These three elements are what risky decisions are all about—consequences versus probabilities, preparation for dealing with unexpected outcomes, and the distinction between reversibility and control. These are where things get done, not said.

Source: Peter Bernstein, "Risk:The Whole Versus the Parts," *CFA Magazine,* March/ April 2004, p. 5. Reprinted by permission.

In the case of a Treasury bond paying a fixed rate of interest, the interest payment will be made with 100 percent certainty barring a financial collapse of the economy. The probability of occurrence is 1.0, because no other outcome is possible.

With the possibility of two or more outcomes, which is the norm for common stocks, each possible likely outcome must be considered and a probability of its occurrence assessed. The probability for a particular outcome is simply the chance that the specified outcome will occur and is typically expressed as a decimal or fraction.

PROBABILITY DISTRIBUTIONS

A *probability distribution* for a security brings together the likely outcomes that may occur for that security for a specified time period along with the probabilities associated with these likely outcomes. The set of probabilities in a probability distribution must sum to 1.0, or 100 percent, because they must completely describe all the (perceived) likely occurrences.

How are these probabilities and associated outcomes obtained? In the final analysis, investing for some future period involves uncertainty, and therefore subjective estimates. Although past occurrences (frequencies) may be relied on heavily to estimate the probabilities, the past must be modified for any changes expected in the future.

Probability distributions can be either discrete or continuous. With a discrete probability distribution, a probability is assigned to each possible outcome. In Figure 7-1a, five possible TRs are assumed for General Foods for next year. Each of these five possible outcomes— .01, .07, .08, .10, and .15—has an associated probability; these probabilities sum to 1.0, indicating that the possible outcomes that an investor foresees for General Foods for next year have been accounted for.

With a continuous probability distribution, as shown in Figure 7-1b, an infinite number of possible outcomes exist. Because probability is now measured as the area under the curve in Figure 7-1b, the emphasis is on the probability that a particular outcome is within some range of values.

Figure 7-1

(a) A Discrete Probability Distribution.
(b) A Continuous Probability Distribution.

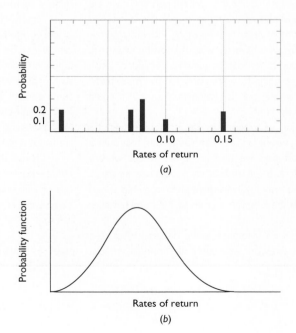

The most familiar continuous distribution is the normal distribution depicted in Figure 7-1*b*. This is the well-known bell-shaped curve often used in statistics. It is a two-parameter distribution in that the mean and the variance fully describe it.

CALCULATING EXPECTED RETURN FOR A SECURITY

To describe the single most likely outcome from a particular probability distribution, it is necessary to calculate its *expected value*. The expected value of a probability distribution is the weighted average of all possible outcomes, where each outcome is weighted by its respective probability of occurrence. Since investors are interested in returns, we will call this expected value the *expected rate of return*, or simply **expected return**, and for any security, it is calculated as

Expected Return The ex ante return expected by investors over some future holding period

$$E(R) = \sum_{i=1}^{m} R_i pr_i \qquad (7\text{-}1)$$

where

$$
\begin{aligned}
E(R) &= \text{the expected rate of return on a security} \\
R_i &= \text{the } i\text{th possible return} \\
pr_i &= \text{the probability of the } i\text{th return } R_i \\
m &= \text{the number of possible returns}
\end{aligned}
$$

Example 7-1   Based on your analysis, you think that General Foods will have a positive return for next period, ranging from 1 percent to 5 percent as described above. The expected value of the probability distribution for General Foods is calculated in the first three columns of Table 7-1. We will call this expected value the expected rate of return, or simply expected return, for General Foods.

CALCULATING RISK FOR A SECURITY

Investors must be able to quantify and measure risk. To calculate the total (standalone) risk associated with the expected return, the variance or standard deviation is used. As we know from Chapter 6, the variance and its square root, standard deviation, are measures of the spread or dispersion in the probability distribution; that is, they measure the dispersion of a random variable around its mean. The larger this dispersion, the larger the variance or standard deviation.

✓   The tighter the probability distribution of expected returns, the smaller the standard deviation, and the smaller the risk.

To calculate the variance or standard deviation from the probability distribution, first calculate the expected return of the distribution using Equation 7-1. Essentially, the same procedure used in Chapter 6 to measure risk applies here, but now the probabilities associated with the outcomes must be included, as in Equation 7-2.

$$\text{the variance of returns} = \sigma^2 = \sum_{i=1}^{m} [R_i - E(R)]^2 pr_i \qquad (7\text{-}2)$$

and

$$\text{the standard deviation of returns} = \sigma = (\sigma^2)^{1/2} \qquad \textbf{(7-3)}$$

where all terms are as defined previously.

Note that the standard deviation is simply a weighted average of the deviations from the expected value. As such, it provides some measure of how far the actual value may be from the expected value, either above or below. With a normal probability distribution, the actual return on a security will be within ± 1 standard deviation of the expected return approximately 68 percent of the time, and within ± 2 standard deviations approximately 95 percent of the time.

Example 7-2 The variance and standard deviation for General Foods, using the information above, is calculated in Table 7-1.

Calculating a standard deviation using probability distributions involves making subjective estimates of the probabilities and the likely returns. However, we cannot avoid such estimates because future returns are uncertain. The prices of securities are based on investors' expectations about the future. The relevant standard deviation in this situation is the *ex ante* standard deviation and not the *ex post* based on realized returns.

Although standard deviations based on realized returns are often used as proxies for *ex ante* standard deviations, investors should be careful to remember that the past cannot always be extrapolated into the future without modifications.

✓ Standard deviations calculated using historical data may be convenient, but they are subject to errors when used as estimates of the future.

Checking Your Understanding

1. The expected return for a security is typically different from any of the possible outcomes (returns) used to calculate it. How, then, can we say that it is the security's expected return?
2. Having calculated a security's standard deviation using a probability distribution, how confident can we be in this number?

Table 7-1 Calculating the Standard Deviation Using Expected Data

(1) Possible Return	(2) Probability	(3) (1)×(2)	(4) $R_i - E(R)$	(5) $(R_i - E(R))^2$	(6) $(R_i - E(R))^2 pr_i$
0.01	0.2	0.002	−0.070	0.0049	0.00098
0.07	0.2	0.014	−0.010	0.0001	0.00002
0.08	0.3	0.024	0.000	0.0000	0.00000
0.10	0.1	0.010	0.020	0.0004	0.00004
0.15	0.2	0.030	0.070	0.0049	0.00098
	1.0	0.080 = E(R)			0.00202

$\sigma = (0.00202)^{1/2} = 0.0449 = 4.49\%$

Introduction to Modern Portfolio Theory

In the 1950s, Harry Markowitz, considered the father of Modern Portfolio Theory (MPT), developed the basic portfolio principles that underlie modern portfolio theory. His original contribution was published in 1952, making portfolio theory about 60 years old. Over time, these principles have been widely adopted by the financial community in a variety of ways, with the result that his legacy of MPT is very broad today.[1]

The primary impact of MPT is on portfolio management, because it provides a framework for the systematic selection of portfolios based on expected return and risk principles. Most portfolio managers today are aware of, and to varying degrees use, the basic principles of MPT. Major mutual fund families employ the implications of MPT in managing their funds, financial advisors use the principles of MPT in advising their individual investor clients, many financial commentators use MPT terms in discussing the current investing environment, and so forth.

Before Markowitz, investors dealt loosely with the concepts of return and risk. Investors have known intuitively for many years that it is smart to diversify, that is, not to "put all of your eggs in one basket." Markowitz, however, was the first to develop the concept of portfolio diversification in a formal way—he quantified the concept of diversification. He showed quantitatively why, and how, portfolio diversification works to reduce the risk of a portfolio to an investor when individual risks are correlated.

Markowitz sought to organize the existing thoughts and practices into a more formal framework and to answer a basic question: Is the risk of a portfolio equal to the sum of the risks of the individual securities comprising it? The answer is no! Markowitz was the first to show that we must account for the interrelationships among security returns in order to calculate portfolio risk, and in order to reduce portfolio risk to its minimum level for any given level of return.

Investments Intuition

Clearly, investors thought about diversifying a portfolio before Markowitz's landmark work. But they did so in general terms. And it is true that not everyone uses his analysis today. However, the tenets of portfolio theory are widely used today, by themselves or in conjunction with other techniques, and by both institutional investors and individual investors.

Portfolio Return and Risk

When we analyze investment returns and risks, we must be concerned with the total portfolio held by an investor. Individual security returns and risks are important, but it is the return and risk to the investor's total portfolio that ultimately matters. Optimal portfolios can be constructed if portfolios are diversified correctly. As we learned in Chapter 1, an investor's portfolio is his or her combination of assets.

As we will see, portfolio risk is a unique characteristic and not simply the sum of individual security risks. A security may have a large risk if it is held by itself but much less risk when held in a portfolio of securities. Since the investor is concerned primarily with the risk to

---

[1] See Frank J. Fabozzi, Francis Gupta, and Harry M. Markowitz, "The Legacy of Modern Portfolio Theory," *The Journal of Investing*, Fall 2002, pp. 7–22.

his or her total wealth, as represented by his or her portfolio, individual stocks are risky only to the extent that they add risk to the total portfolio.

✓ Investors should always diversify to reduce their risk. Because they should not hold only one security, that security's risk, taken by itself, is not the relevant issue for investors.

PORTFOLIO EXPECTED RETURN

Portfolio Weights   The percentages of a portfolio's total value that are invested in each portfolio asset are referred to as **portfolio weights**, which we will denote by w. The combined portfolio weights are assumed to sum to 100 percent of total investable funds, or 1.0, indicating that all portfolio funds are invested. That is,

Portfolio Weights
Percentages of portfolio funds invested in each security, summing to 1.0.

$$w_1 + w_2 + \cdots + w_n = \sum_{i=1}^{n} w_i = 1.0 \qquad \text{(7-4)}$$

Example 7-3   With equal dollar amounts in three securities, the portfolio weights are 0.333, 0.333, and 0.333. Under the same conditions with a portfolio of five securities, each security would have a portfolio weight of 0.20. Of course, dollar amounts do not have to be equal. A five-stock portfolio could have weights of .40, .10, .15, .25, and .10, or .18, .33, .11, .22, and .16.

Calculating the Expected Return on a Portfolio   The expected return on any portfolio p can be calculated as a weighted average of the individual securities expected returns.

$$E(R_p) = \sum_{i=1}^{n} w_i E(R_i) \qquad \text{(7-5)}$$

where

$$
\begin{aligned}
E(R_p) &= \text{the expected return on the portfolio} \\
w_i &= \text{the portfolio weight for the ith security} \\
\sum w_i &= 1.0 \\
E(R_i) &= \text{the expected return on the ith security} \\
n &= \text{the number of different securities in the portfolio}
\end{aligned}
$$

Example 7-4   Consider a three-stock portfolio consisting of stocks G, H, and I with expected returns of 12 percent, 20 percent, and 17 percent, respectively. Assume that 50 percent of investable funds is invested in security G, 30 percent in H, and 20 percent in I. The expected return on this portfolio is:

$$E(R_p) = 0.5(12\%) + 0.3(20\%) + 0.2(17\%) = 15.4\%$$

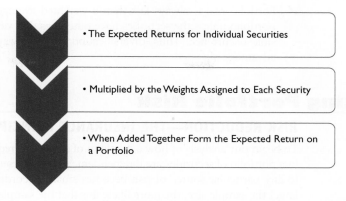

- The Expected Returns for Individual Securities

- Multiplied by the Weights Assigned to Each Security

- When Added Together Form the Expected Return on a Portfolio

✓ Regardless of the number of assets held in a portfolio, or the proportion of total investable funds placed in each asset, *the expected return on the portfolio is always a weighted average of the expected returns for individual assets in the portfolio.*

PORTFOLIO RISK

We know that return and risk are the basis of all investing decisions. Therefore, in addition to calculating the expected return for a portfolio, we must also measure the risk of the portfolio. Risk is measured by the variance (or standard deviation) of the portfolio's return, exactly as in the case of each individual security. Typically, portfolio risk is stated in terms of standard deviation.

It is at this point that the basis of modern portfolio theory emerges, which can be stated as follows: Although the expected return of a portfolio is a weighted average of its expected returns, portfolio risk (as measured by the variance or standard deviation) is typically *not* a weighted average of the risk of the individual securities in the portfolio. Symbolically,

$$E(R_p) = \sum_{i=1}^{n} w_i E(R_i) \tag{7-6}$$

But

$$\sigma_p^2 \neq \sum_{i=1}^{n} w_i \sigma_i^2 \tag{7-7}$$

Precisely because Equation 7-7 is an inequality, investors can reduce the risk of a portfolio beyond what it would be if risk were, in fact, simply a weighted average of the individual securities' risk. In order to see how this risk reduction can be accomplished, we will analyze portfolio risk in detail.

✓ Portfolio risk is always less than a weighted average of the risks of the securities in the portfolio unless the securities have outcomes that vary together exactly, an almost impossible occurrence. Thus, diversification almost always lowers risk, and should be taken advantage of.

Analyzing Portfolio Risk

RISK REDUCTION—THE INSURANCE PRINCIPLE

To begin our analysis of how a portfolio of assets can reduce risk, assume that all risk sources in a portfolio of securities are independent. As we add securities to this portfolio, the exposure to any particular source of risk becomes small. According to the *Law of Large Numbers*, the larger the sample size, the more likely it is that the sample mean will be close to the population expected value. Risk reduction in the case of independent risk sources can be thought of as the *insurance principle*, named for the idea that an insurance company reduces its risk by writing many policies against many independent sources of risk.

Note that in the case of the insurance principle, we are assuming that rates of return on individual securities are *statistically independent* such that any one security's rate of return is unaffected by another's rate of return. In this situation, and only in this situation, the standard deviation of the portfolio is given by

$$\sigma_p = \frac{\sigma_i}{n^{1/2}} \qquad (7\text{-}8)$$

As Figure 7-2 shows, the risk of the portfolio will quickly decline as more securities are added. Notice that no decision is to be made about which security to add because all have identical properties. The only issue is how many securities are added.

Figure 7-2

Risk Reduction When Returns are Independent.

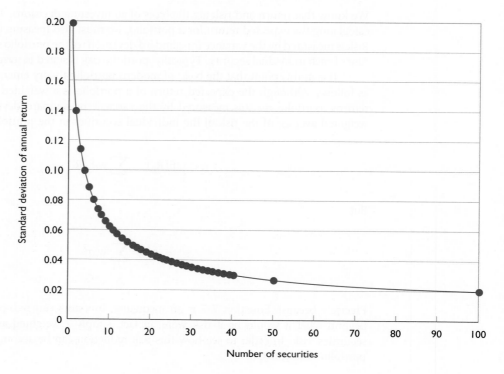

Number of securities

Example 7-5

Figure 7-2 shows how risk declines given that the risk of each security is 0.20. The risk of the portfolio will quickly decline as more and more of these securities are added. Equation 7-8 indicates that for the case of 100 securities the risk of the portfolio is reduced to 0.02:

$$\sigma_p = \frac{0.20}{100^{1/2}}$$

$$= 0.02$$

Figure 7-2 illustrates the case of independent risk sources. As applied to investing, all risk in this situation is firm-specific. Therefore, the total risk *in this situation* can continue to be reduced. Unfortunately, when it comes to investing in financial assets the assumption of statistically independent returns is unrealistic.

Going back to the definition of market risk in Chapter 6, we find that most stocks are positively correlated with each other; that is, the movements in their returns are related. We can call this market risk. While total risk can be reduced, it cannot be eliminated because market risk cannot be eliminated. Unlike firm-specific risk, common sources of risk affect all firms and cannot be diversified away. For example, a rise in interest rates will affect most firms adversely, because most firms borrow funds to finance part of their operations.

DIVERSIFICATION

The insurance principle illustrates the concept of risk reduction when the sources of risk are independent. This situation does not apply to stocks because of market risk. Therefore, we must consider how to reduce risk when the sources of risk are not independent. We do this by diversifying our portfolio of stocks, taking into account how the stocks interact with each other.

✓   Diversification is the key to the management of portfolio risk because it allows investors to significantly lower portfolio risk without adversely affecting return.

Therefore, we focus on portfolio diversification, beginning with random diversification and moving to efficient portfolio diversification based on modern portfolio theory principles.

Random Diversification   *Random or naive diversification* refers to the act of randomly diversifying without regard to how security returns are related to each other. An investor simply selects a relatively large number of securities randomly—the proverbial "throwing a dart at *The Wall Street Journal* page showing stock quotes." For simplicity, we assume equal dollar amounts are invested in each stock. As we add securities to a portfolio, the total risk associated with the portfolio of stocks declines rapidly. The first few stocks cause a large decrease in portfolio risk.

The benefits of diversification kick in immediately—two stocks are better than one, three stocks are better than two, and so on. However, diversification cannot eliminate the risk in a portfolio. As additional stocks are added, risk is reduced but the marginal risk reduction is small. Furthermore, and very important to note, recent studies suggest that it takes far more securities to diversify properly than has traditionally been believed to be the case (this point is discussed in detail in Chapter 8).

Although random diversification is clearly beneficial, it is generally not optimal. To take full advantage of the benefits of diversification, we need to understand efficient diversification; that is, we need to understand portfolio risk within a modern portfolio theory context.

Checking Your Understanding

3. What does it mean to an investor that the benefits of diversification kick in immediately, but are limited?

The Components of Portfolio Risk

In order to remove the inequality sign from Equation 7-7 and develop an equation that will calculate the risk of a portfolio as measured by the variance, we must account for two factors:

1. Weighted individual security risks (i.e., the variance of each individual security, weighted by the percentage of investable funds placed in each individual security).
2. Weighted co-movements between securities' returns (i.e., the covariance between the securities' returns, again weighted by the percentage of investable funds placed in each security).

As explained below, covariance is an absolute measure of the co-movements between security returns used in the calculation of portfolio risk. We need the actual covariance between securities in a portfolio in order to calculate portfolio variance or standard deviation. Before considering covariance, however, we can easily illustrate how security returns move together by considering the correlation coefficient, a relative measure of association learned in statistics.

THE CORRELATION COEFFICIENT

Correlation Coefficient
A statistical measure of the extent to which two variables are associated

As used in portfolio theory, the **correlation coefficient** ρ_{ij} (pronounced "rho") is a statistical measure of the *relative* co-movements between security returns. It measures the extent to which the returns on any two securities move together; however, it denotes only association, not causation. It is a relative measure of association that is bounded by $+1.0$ and -1.0, with

$$\rho_{ij} = +1.0$$
$$= \text{perfect positive correlation}$$
$$\rho_{ij} = -1.0$$
$$= \text{perfect negative (inverse) correlation}$$
$$\rho_{ij} = 0.0$$
$$= \text{zero correlation}$$

Perfect Positive Correlation   With perfect positive correlation, the returns have a perfect direct linear relationship. Knowing what the return on one security will do allows an investor to forecast perfectly what the other will do. In Figure 7-3, stocks A and B have identical return patterns over the six-year period 2007–2012. When stock A's return goes up, stock B's does also. When stock A's return goes down, stock B's does also.

Consider the return and standard deviation information in Figure 7-3. Notice that a portfolio combining stocks A and B, with 50 percent invested in each, has exactly the same return

Figure 7-3

Returns for the Years 2007-2012 on Two Stocks, A and B, and a Portfolio Consisting of 50 Percent A and 50 Percent of B, When the Correction Coefficient is +1.0.

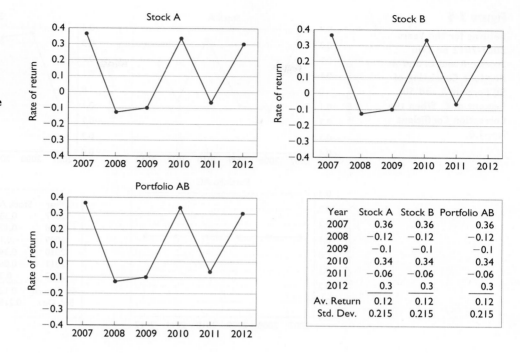

Year	Stock A	Stock B	Portfolio AB
2007	0.36	0.36	0.36
2008	−0.12	−0.12	−0.12
2009	−0.1	−0.1	−0.1
2010	0.34	0.34	0.34
2011	−0.06	−0.06	−0.06
2012	0.3	0.3	0.3
Av. Return	0.12	0.12	0.12
Std. Dev.	0.215	0.215	0.215

as does either stock by itself, since the returns are identical. The risk of the portfolio, as measured by the standard deviation, is identical to the standard deviation of either stock by itself.

✓ When returns are perfectly positively correlated, the risk of a portfolio is simply a weighted average of the individual risks of the securities. This is the one case where diversification does not lead to a reduction in risk.

Perfect Negative Correlation   On the other hand, with perfect negative correlation, the securities' returns have a perfect inverse linear relationship to each other. Therefore, knowing the return on one security provides full knowledge about the return on the second security. When one security's return is high, the other is low.

In Figure 7-4, stocks A and C are perfectly negatively correlated with each other. Notice that the information given for these two stocks states that each stock has exactly the same return and standard deviation. When combined, however, the deviations in the returns on these stocks around their average return of 12 percent cancel out, resulting in a portfolio return of 12 percent. This portfolio has no risk. It will earn 12 percent each year over the period measured, and the average return will be 12 percent.

Notice carefully what perfect negative correlation does for an investor. By offsetting all the variations around the expected return for the portfolio, the investor is assured of earning the expected return. At first glance it might appear that offsetting a negative return with an exactly equal positive return produces a zero return, but that is not the case. The expected return for the portfolio is a positive number (otherwise, we would not invest). What is being offset in this case are any variations around that expected return.

Zero Correlation   With zero correlation, there is no *linear* relationship between the returns on the two securities. Combining two securities with zero correlation with each other

Figure 7-4

Returns for the Years 2007-2012 on Two Stocks, A and C, and a Portfolio Consisting of 50 Percent A and 50 Percent of C, When the Correction Coefficient is −1.0.

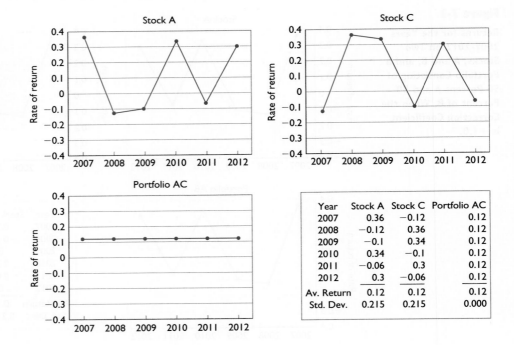

Year	Stock A	Stock C	Portfolio AC
2007	0.36	−0.12	0.12
2008	−0.12	0.36	0.12
2009	−0.1	0.34	0.12
2010	0.34	−0.1	0.12
2011	−0.06	0.3	0.12
2012	0.3	−0.06	0.12
Av. Return	0.12	0.12	0.12
Std. Dev.	0.215	0.215	0.000

reduces the risk of the portfolio. If more securities with uncorrelated returns are added to the portfolio, significant risk reduction can be achieved. However, portfolio risk cannot be eliminated in the case of zero correlation. While a zero correlation between two security returns is better than a positive correlation, it does not produce the risk reduction benefits of a negative correlation coefficient.

Less Than Perfect Positive Correlation   Figure 7-5 illustrates a case where stocks A and D are positively correlated with each other at a level of $\rho = +0.55$. Investors may encounter situations such as this and feel there is not much benefit to be gained from diversifying. Note that the standard deviation of each security is still .215, with an average return of .12, but when combined with equal weights of .50 into the portfolio the risk is somewhat reduced, to a level of .18. Any reduction in risk that does not adversely affect return has to be considered beneficial.

With positive correlation risk can be reduced but it cannot be eliminated. Other things being equal, investors wish to find securities with the least positive correlation possible.

✓   Ideally, investors would like securities with negative correlation or low positive correlation, but they generally will be faced with positively correlated security returns.

Over the decade ending in 2011, the average correlation between the stocks in the S&P 500 and the Index itself was about .55, so our example above reflects the actual situation, on average, that has existed. Of course, the correlation fluctuates. For example, in 2011 it rose as high as .86 before dropping back some.

Checking Your Understanding

4. Why is negative correlation between two securities in a portfolio better than no (zero) correlation?

Figure 7-5

Returns for the Years
2007-2012 on Two
Stocks, A and D, and a
Portfolio Consisting
of 50 Percent A and
50 Percent of D, When
the Correction Coefficient
is +0.55.

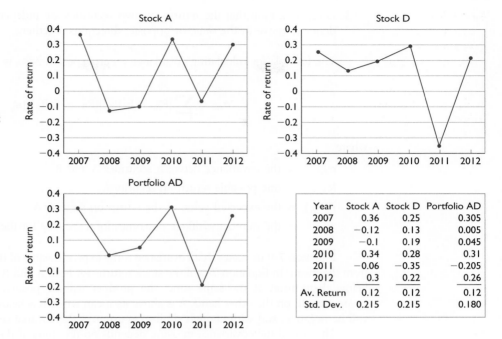

Year	Stock A	Stock D	Portfolio AD
2007	0.36	0.25	0.305
2008	−0.12	0.13	0.005
2009	−0.1	0.19	0.045
2010	0.34	0.28	0.31
2011	−0.06	−0.35	−0.205
2012	0.3	0.22	0.26
Av. Return	0.12	0.12	0.12
Std. Dev.	0.215	0.215	0.180

COVARIANCE

The previous discussion of the correlation coefficient shows us that the variability in security returns may offset each other to some extent. This is why, to calculate a portfolio's risk (variance), we must take account not only of each security's own risk but also the interactions among the returns of the securities in the portfolio based on the correlation coefficients. However, we must measure the actual amount of co-movement among security returns and incorporate it into the calculation of portfolio risk because the size of the co-movements affect the portfolio's variance (or standard deviation). The covariance measure does this.

✓ Whereas the correlation coefficient measures the relative association between the returns for a pair of securities, the covariance is an absolute measure of the degree of association between the returns for a pair of securities.

Covariance An absolute measure of the extent to which two variables tend to covary, or move together

Covariance is defined as the extent to which two random variables covary (move together) over time. As is true throughout our discussion, the variables in question are the returns (TRs) on two securities. Similar to the correlation coefficient, the covariance can be

1. Positive, indicating that the returns on the two securities tend to move in the same direction at the same time; when one increases (decreases), the other tends to do the same.[2] When the covariance is positive, the correlation coefficient will also be positive.
2. Negative, indicating that the returns on the two securities tend to move inversely; when one increases (decreases), the other tends to decrease (increase). When the covariance is negative, the correlation coefficient will also be negative.

---

[2] Another way to say this is that *higher* than average values of one random variable tend to be paired with *higher*-than-average values of the other random variable.

3. Zero, indicating that the returns on two securities are independent and have no tendency to move in the same or opposite directions together.

The formula for calculating covariance on an expected basis is

$$\sigma_{AB} = \sum_{i=1}^{m} [R_{A,i} - E(R_A)][R_{B,i} - E(R_B)]pr_i \tag{7-9}$$

where

σ_{AB} = the covariance between securities A and B[3]
$R_{A,i}$ = one possible return on security A
$E(R_A)$ = the expected value of the return on security A
m = the number of likely outcomes for a security for the period

Equation 7-9 indicates that covariance is the expected value of the product of deviations from the mean. In Equation 7-9, if the stock returns for both A and B are above their mean or below their mean at the same time, the product will be positive, leading to a positive covariance. If, on the other hand, A is above its mean when B is below its mean, the product will be negative, and with enough similar occurrences the covariance will be negative.

The size of the covariance measure depends on the units of the variables involved and usually changes when these units are changed. Therefore, the covariance primarily provides information to investors about whether the association between asset returns is positive, negative, or zero because simply observing the number itself, without any context with which to assess the number, is not very useful.

RELATING THE CORRELATION COEFFICIENT AND THE COVARIANCE

The covariance and the correlation coefficient can be related in the following manner:

$$\rho_{AB} = \frac{\sigma_{AB}}{\sigma_A \sigma_B} \tag{7-10}$$

This equation shows that the correlation coefficient is simply the covariance standardized by dividing by the product of the two standard deviations of returns.

Given this definition of the correlation coefficient, the covariance can be written as

$$\sigma_{AB} = \rho_{AB}\sigma_A\sigma_B \tag{7-11}$$

Therefore, knowing the correlation coefficient, we can calculate the covariance because the standard deviations of the assets' rates of return will already be available. Knowing the covariance, we can easily calculate the correlation coefficient.

When analyzing how security returns move together, it is always convenient to talk about the correlation coefficients because we can immediately assess the degree of association (the boundaries are +1 and −1). However, our final objective is to calculate portfolio risk, and to do that we must understand and calculate the covariances.

---

[3] The order does not matter, because $\sigma_{AB} = \sigma_{BA}$.

Calculating Portfolio Risk

Now that we understand that covariances quantitatively account for the co-movements in security returns, we are ready to calculate portfolio risk. First, we will consider the simplest possible case, two securities, in order to see what is happening in the portfolio risk equation. We will then consider the case of many securities, where the calculations soon become too large and complex to analyze with any means other than a computer.

THE TWO-SECURITY CASE

The risk of a portfolio, as measured by the standard deviation of returns, for the case of two securities, 1 and 2, is

$$\sigma_P = [w_1^2 \sigma_1^2 + w_2^2 \sigma_2^2 + 2(w_1)(w_2)(\rho_{1,2}) \sigma_1 \sigma_2]^{1/2} \qquad \text{(7-12)}$$

Equation 7-12 shows us that the risk for a portfolio encompasses not only the individual security risks but also the covariance between these two securities and that *three factors, not two, determine portfolio risk:*

❏ The variance of each security, as shown by σ_1^2 and σ_2^2 in Equation 7-12
❏ The covariance between securities, as shown by $\rho_{1,2}\sigma_1\sigma_2$ in Equation 7-12
❏ The portfolio weights for each security, as shown by the w_i's in Equation 7-12

Note the following about Equation 7-12:

❏ The covariance term contains two covariances—the (weighted) covariance between stock 1 and stock 2, and between stock 2 and stock 1. Since each covariance is identical, we simply multiply the first covariance by two. Otherwise, there would be four terms in Equation 7-12, rather than three.
❏ We first solve for the variance of the portfolio, and then take the square root to obtain the standard deviation of the portfolio.

Example 7-6

Consider the Total Returns between Southeast Utilities and Precision Instruments for the period 2003–2012. The summary statistics for these two stocks are as follows:

	Southeast	Precision
Return (%)	10.1	15.4
Standard Deviation (%)	16.8	27.5
Correlation Coeff.	.29	

Assume, for expositional purposes, we place equal amounts in each stock; therefore, the weights are 0.5 and 0.5.

$$
\begin{aligned}
\sigma_P &= [w_1^2 \sigma_1^2 + w_2^2 \sigma_2^2 + 2(w_1)(w_2)(\rho_{1,2}) \sigma_1 \sigma_2]^{1/2} \\
&= [(.5)^2(16.8)^2 + (.5)^2(27.5)^2 + 2(.5)(.5)(.29)(16.8)(27.5)]^{1/2} \\
&= [70.56 + 189.06 + 66.99]^{1/2} \\
&= 18.1\%
\end{aligned}
$$

Alternatively,

$$\sigma_P = [w_1^2\sigma_1^2 + w_2^2\sigma_2^2 + (w_1)(w_2)(\rho_{1,2})\sigma_1\sigma_2 + (w_2)(w_1)(\rho_{2,1})\sigma_2\sigma_1]^{1/2}$$
$$= [(.5)^2(16.8)^2 + (.5)^2(27.5)^2 + (.5)(.5)(.29)(16.8)(27.5)$$
$$+ (.5)(.5)(.29)(27.3)(16.8)]^{1/2}$$
$$= [70.56 + 189.06 + 33.5 + 33.5]^{1/2}$$
$$= 18.1\%$$

The Impact of the Correlation Coefficient   The standard deviation of the portfolio is directly affected by the correlation between the two stocks. Portfolio risk will be reduced as the correlation coefficient moves from $+1.0$ downward, everything else constant.

Example 7-7   Let's continue with the data in Example 7-6. The correlation coefficient between Southeast Utilities and Precision Instruments returns is $+0.29$. In order to focus on the effects of a changing correlation coefficient, we continue to assume weights of 0.5 each—50 percent of investable funds is to be placed in each security. Summarizing the data in this example,

$$\sigma_{SU} = 16.8$$
$$\sigma_{PI} = 27.5$$
$$w_{SU} = 0.5$$
$$w_{PI} = 0.5$$

With these data, the standard deviation, or risk, for this portfolio, σ_ρ, is

$$\sigma_P = [(0.5)^2(16.8)^2 + (0.5)^2(27.5)^2 + 2(0.5)(0.5)(16.8)(27.5)\rho]^{1/2}$$
$$= [70.56 + 189.06 + 229.32\rho]^{1/2}$$

since $2(0.5)(0.5)(16.8)(27.5) = 229.32$.

The risk of this portfolio clearly depends heavily on the value of the third term, which in turn depends on the correlation coefficient between the returns for SEUT and PI. To assess the potential impact of the correlation, consider the following cases: a ρ of $+1$, $+0.5$, $+0.29$, 0, -0.5, and -1.0. Calculating portfolio risk under each of these scenarios produces the following portfolio risks:

If $\rho = +1.0$: $\sigma_p = 22.2\%$
If $\rho = +0.5$: $\sigma_p = 19.4\%$
If $\rho = +0.29$: $\sigma_p = 18.1\%$
If $\rho = 0.0$: $\sigma_p = 16.1\%$
If $\rho = -0.5$: $\sigma_p = 12.0\%$
If $\rho = -1.0$: $\sigma_p = 5.4\%$

These calculations clearly show the impact that combining securities with less than perfect positive correlation will have on portfolio risk. The risk of the portfolio steadily decreases from 22.2 percent to 5.4 percent as the correlation coefficient declines from $+1.0$ to -1.0. Note, however, that the risk has declined from 22.2 percent to only 16.1 percent as the correlation coefficient drops from $+1$ to 0, and it has only been cut in half (approximately) by the time ρ drops to -0.5.

Investments Intuition

Correlations are a key variable when considering how diversification can reduce risk. However, a little reflection indicates they are not the complete story.

As Equation 7-12 shows, the benefits also depend on the standard deviations of the asset returns and the portfolio weights.

The Impact of Portfolio Weights   We saw earlier (Figure 7-4) that with a two-stock portfolio and perfect negative correlation, the risk can be reduced to zero. Notice that this did not happen in Example 7-8 (the risk when $\rho = -1.0$ was 5.4 percent). The reason for this is that the weights for each stock were selected to be 0.50 for illustration purposes. To reduce the risk to zero in the two-security case, and to minimize risk in general, it is necessary to select optimal weights, which can be calculated.

Let's consider the impact of the portfolio weights in the calculation of portfolio risk. The size of the portfolio weights assigned to each security has an effect on portfolio risk, holding the correlation coefficient constant.

Example 7-8

Using the same data as Example 7-7, let's consider the portfolio risk for these two securities. Recall that the correlation coefficient between Southeast Utilities and Precision Instruments is $+0.29$. For illustration purposes, we will examine five different sets of weights, each of which must sum to 1.0.

Southeast	Precision	σ_p
0.1	0.9	25.3%
0.3	0.7	21.3%
0.5	0.5	18.1%
0.7	0.3	16.2%
0.9	0.1	16.1%

As we can see, in this two-stock portfolio example, holding the correlation coefficient constant at $+0.29$, the risk of the portfolio varies as the weights for each of the assets changes. Because Southeast has a substantially lower standard deviation than does Precision, portfolio risk decreases as the weight assigned to Southeast increases. However, with a positive correlation coefficient, portfolio risk can decrease only so much.

✓   Portfolio risk is affected both by the correlation between assets and by the percentages of funds invested in each asset.

THE *n*-SECURITY CASE

The two-security case can be generalized to the *n*-security case. Portfolio risk can be reduced by combining assets with less than perfect positive correlation. Furthermore, the smaller the positive correlation, the better.

Portfolio risk is a function of each individual security's risk and the covariances between the returns on the individual securities. Stated in terms of variance, portfolio risk is

$$\sigma_p^2 = \sum_{i=1}^{n} w_i^2 \sigma_i^2 + \sum_{i=1}^{n} \sum_{\substack{j=1 \\ i \neq j}}^{n} w_i w_j \sigma_{ij} \tag{7-13}$$

where

σ_p^2 = the variance of the return on the portfolio

σ_i^2 = the variance of return for security *i*

σ_{ij} = the covariance between the returns for securities *i* and *j*

w_i = the portfolio weights or percentage of investable funds invested in security *i*

$\displaystyle\sum_{i=1}^{n}\sum_{j=1}^{n}$ = a double summation sign indicating that n^2 numbers are to be added together (*i.e.*, all possible pairs of values for *i* and *j*)

Although Equation 7-13 appears formidable, it states exactly the same message as Equation 7-12 for the two-stock portfolio:

Portfolio risk is a function of

❏ The weighted risk of each individual security (as measured by its variance)
❏ The weighted covariances among all pairs of securities

We can rewrite Equation 7-13 into a shorter format:

$$\sigma_p^2 = \sum_{i=1}^{n} \sum_{j=1}^{n} w_i w_j \sigma_{ij} \tag{7-14}$$

or

$$\sigma_p^2 = \sum_{i=1}^{n} \sum_{j=1}^{n} w_i w_j \rho_{ij} \sigma_i \sigma_j$$

These equations account for both the variance and the covariances, because when $i = j$, the variance is calculated; when $i \neq j$, the covariance is calculated.

✓ As noted previously, three variables determine portfolio risk: variances, covariances, and weights.

Because of its importance, we emphasize the components of portfolio risk in Figure 7-6.

Checking Your Understanding

5. Given the use of the correlation coefficient, which is clear and easy to understand, why do we need to consider covariances?
6. Suppose we add a very risky stock to a well-diversified portfolio. Could such an action lower the portfolio's risk?

Figure 7-6

The Components of Portfolio Risk.

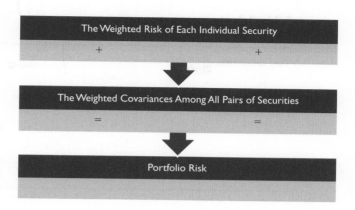

The Weighted Risk of Each Individual Security

+   +

The Weighted Covariances Among All Pairs of Securities

=   =

Portfolio Risk

The Importance of Covariance   One of Markowitz's important contributions to portfolio theory is his insight about the relative importance of the variances and covariances. When we add a new security to a large portfolio of securities, there are two impacts.

1. The asset's own risk, as measured by its variance, is added to the portfolio's risk.
2. A covariance between the new security and every other security already in the portfolio is also added.

✓ As the number of securities held in a portfolio increases, the importance of each individual security's risk (variance) decreases, while the importance of the covariance relationships increases.

For example, in a portfolio of 150 securities, the contribution of each security's own risk to the total portfolio risk will be extremely small. When a new security is added to a large portfolio of securities, what matters most is its average covariance with the other securities in the portfolio.

Portfolio risk will consist almost entirely of the covariance risk between securities. Thus, individual security risks can be diversified away in a large portfolio, but the covariance terms cannot be diversified away and therefore contribute to the risk of the portfolio.

Obtaining the Data

To calculate portfolio risk using Equation 7-13, we need estimates of the variance for each security and estimates of the correlation coefficients or covariances. Both variances and correlation coefficients can be (and are) calculated using either *ex post* or *ex ante* data. If an analyst uses *ex post* data to calculate the correlation coefficient or the covariance and then uses these estimates in the Markowitz model, the implicit assumption is that the relationship that existed in the past will continue into the future. The same is true of the variances for individual securities. If the historical variance is thought to be the best estimate of the expected variance, it should be used. However, it must be remembered that an individual security's variance and the correlation coefficient between securities can change over time (and does), as can the expected return.

Table 7-2 The Variance-Covariance Matrix Involved in Calculating the Standard Deviation of a Portfolio

Two securities:

$\sigma_{1,1}$	$\sigma_{1,2}$
$\sigma_{2,1}$	$\sigma_{2,2}$

Four securities:

$\sigma_{1,1}$	$\sigma_{1,2}$	$\sigma_{1,3}$	$\sigma_{1,4}$
$\sigma_{2,1}$	$\sigma_{2,2}$	$\sigma_{2,3}$	$\sigma_{2,4}$
$\sigma_{3,1}$	$\sigma_{3,2}$	$\sigma_{3,3}$	$\sigma_{3,4}$
$\sigma_{4,1}$	$\sigma_{4,2}$	$\sigma_{4,3}$	$\sigma_{4,4}$

SIMPLIFYING THE MARKOWITZ CALCULATIONS

Equation 7-13 illustrates the problem associated with the calculation of portfolio risk using the Markowitz mean-variance analysis. In the case of two securities, there are two covariances, and we multiply the weighted covariance term in Equation 7-12 by two since the covariance of A with B is the same as the covariance of B with A. In the case of three securities, there are six covariances; with four securities, 12 covariances; and so forth, based on the fact that the total number of covariances in the Markowitz model is calculated as $n\,(n-1)$, where n is the number of securities.

Table 7-2 shows the variance-covariance matrix associated with these calculations. For the case of two securities, there are n^2, or four, total terms in the matrix—two variances and two covariances. For the case of four securities, there are n^2, or 16 total terms in the matrix—four variances and 12 covariances. The variance terms are on the diagonal of the matrix and, in effect, represent the covariance of a security with itself. Note that the covariance terms above the diagonal are a mirror image of the covariance terms below the diagonal—that is, each covariance is repeated twice since COV_{AB} is the same as COV_{BA}.

✓ The number of covariances in the Markowitz model is based on the calculation $n(n-1)$, where n is the number of securities involved. Because the covariance of A with B is the same as the covariance of B with A, there are $[n(n-1)]/2$ unique covariances.

Example 7-9

An analyst considering 100 securities must estimate $[100(99)]/2 = 4{,}950$ unique covariances. For 250 securities, the number is $[250(249)]/2 = 31{,}125$ unique covariances.

Obviously, estimating large numbers of covariances quickly becomes a major problem for model users. Since many institutional investors follow as many as 250 or 300 securities, the number of inputs required may become an impossibility. In fact, until the basic Markowitz model was simplified in terms of the covariance inputs, it remained primarily of academic interest.

On a practical basis, analysts are unlikely to be able to directly estimate the large number of correlations necessary for a complete Markowitz analysis. In his original work, Markowitz suggested using an index to which securities are related as a means of generating covariances.

Summary

▶ The expected return from a security must be estimated. Since this is done under conditions of uncertainty, it may not be realized. Risk (or uncertainty) is always present in the estimation of expected returns for risky assets.

▶ Probability distributions are involved in the calculation of a security's expected return.

▶ The standard deviation or variance of expected return for a security is a measure of the risk involved in the expected return; therefore, it also incorporates the probabilities used in calculating the expected return.

▶ The expected return for a portfolio is always a weighted average of the individual security expected returns.

▶ Portfolio weights, designated w_i, are the percentages of a portfolio's total funds that are invested in each security, where the weights sum to 1.0.

▶ Portfolio risk is not a weighted average of the individual security risks. To calculate portfolio risk, we must take account of the relationships between the securities' returns.

▶ The correlation coefficient is a relative measure of the association between security returns. It is bounded by +1.0 and −1.0, with 0 representing no association.

▶ The covariance is an absolute measure of association between security returns and is used in the calculation of portfolio risk.

▶ Portfolio risk is a function of security variances, covariances, and portfolio weights.

▶ The covariance term captures the correlations between security returns and determines how much portfolio risk can be reduced through diversification.

▶ The risk of a well-diversified portfolio is largely attributable to the impact of the covariances. When a new security is added to a large portfolio of securities, what matters most is its average covariance with the other securities in the portfolio.

▶ As the number of securities held in a portfolio increases, the importance of each individual security's risk (variance) decreases, while the importance of the covariance relationships increases.

▶ The major problem with the Markowitz model is that it requires a full set of covariances between the returns of all securities being considered in order to calculate portfolio variance.

▶ The number of covariances in the Markowitz model is $n(n-1)$; the number of unique covariances is $[n(n-1)]/2$.

Questions

7-1 Distinguish between historical return and expected return.

7-2 How is expected return for one security determined? For a portfolio?

7-3 The Markowitz approach is often referred to as a mean-variance approach. Why?

7-4 How would the expected return for a portfolio of 500 securities be calculated?

7-5 What does it mean to say that portfolio weights sum to 1.0 or 100 percent?

7-6 What are the boundaries for the expected return of a portfolio?

7-7 Many investors have known for years that they should not "put all of their eggs in one basket." How does the Markowitz analysis shed light on this old principle?

7-8 Evaluate this statement: With regard to portfolio risk, the whole is not equal to the sum of the parts.

7-9 How many, and which, factors determine portfolio risk?

7-10 What is the relationship between the correlation coefficient and the covariance, both qualitatively and quantitatively?

7-11 How many covariance terms would exist for a portfolio of 10 securities using the Markowitz analysis? How many unique covariances?

7-12 How many total terms (variances and covariances) would exist in the variance-covariance matrix for a portfolio of 30 securities using the Markowitz analysis? How many of these are variances, and how many covariances?

7-13 When, if ever, would a stock with a large risk (standard deviation) be desirable in building a portfolio?

7-14 Evaluate the following statement: As the number of securities held in a portfolio increases, the importance of each individual security's risk decreases.

7-15 Should investors generally expect positive correlations between stocks and bonds? Bonds and bills? Stocks and real estate? Stocks and gold?

7-16 What are the inputs for a set of securities using the Markowitz model?

7-17 Evaluate this statement: For any two-stock portfolio, a correlation coefficient of −1.0 guarantees a portfolio risk of zero.

7-18 Agree or disagree with this statement: The variance of a portfolio is the expected value of the squared deviations of the returns for the portfolio from its mean return.

7-19 Evaluate this statement: Portfolio risk is the key issue in portfolio theory. It is not a weighted average of individual security risks.

7-20 Agree or disagree with these statements: There are n^2 terms in the variance covariance matrix, where n is the number of securities.

There are $n(n-1)$ total covariances for any set of n securities. Divide by two to obtain the number of unique covariances.

7-21 Holding a large number of stocks ensures an optimal portfolio. Agree or disagree and explain your reasoning.

CFA
7-22 The variance of a stock portfolio depends on the variances of each individual stock in the portfolio and also the covariances among the stocks in the portfolio. If you have five stocks, how many unique covariances (excluding variance) must you use in order to compute the variance of return on your portfolio? (Recall that the covariance of a stock with itself is the stock's variance.)

CFA
7-23 Given the large-cap stock index and the government bond index data in the following table, calculate the expected mean return and standard deviation of return for a portfolio 75 percent invested in the stock index and 25 percent invested in the bond index.

Assumed Returns, Variances, and Correlations

	Large-Cap Stock Index	Government Bond Index
Expected return	15%	5%
Variance	225	100
Standard Deviation	15%	10%
Correlation	0.5	

CFA
7-24 Suppose a risk-free asset has a 5 percent return and a second asset has an expected return of 13 percent with a standard deviation of 23 percent. Calculate the expected portfolio return and standard deviation of a portfolio consisting of 10 percent of the risk-free asset and 90 percent of the second asset.

7-25 Consider the following information for Exxon and Merck:
- Expected return for each stock is 15 percent.
- Standard deviation for each stock is 22 percent.
- Covariances with other securities vary.

Everything else being equal, would the prices of these two stocks be expected to be the same? Why or why not?

7-26 Select the **CORRECT** statement from among the following:
a. The risk for a portfolio is a weighted average of individual security risks.
b. Two factors determine portfolio risk.
c. Having established the portfolio weights, the calculation of the expected return on the portfolio is independent of the calculation of portfolio risk.
d. When adding a security to a portfolio, the average covariance between it and the other securities in the portfolio is less important than the security's own risk.

7-27 Select the **CORRECT** statement from among the following:

a. The risk of a portfolio of two securities, as measured by the standard deviation, would consist of two terms.

b. The expected return on a portfolio is usually a weighted average of the expected returns of the individual assets in the portfolio.

c. The risk of a portfolio of four securities, as measured by the standard deviation, would consist of 16 covariances and four variances.

d. Combining two securities with perfect negative correlation could eliminate risk altogether.

7-28 Select the **INCORRECT** statement from among the following:

a. Under the Markowitz formulation, a portfolio of 30 securities would have 870 covariances.

b. Under the Markowitz formulation, a portfolio of 30 securities would have 30 variances in the variance-covariance matrix.

c. Under the Markowitz formulation, a portfolio of 30 securities would have 870 terms in the variance-covariance matrix.

d. Under the Markowitz formulation, a portfolio of 30 securities would require 435 unique covariances to calculate portfolio risk.

7-29 Concerning the riskiness of a portfolio of two securities using the Markowitz model, select the **CORRECT** statements from among the following set:

a. The riskiness depends on the variability of the securities in the portfolio.

b. The riskiness depends on the percentage of portfolio assets invested in each security.

c. The riskiness depends on the expected return of each security.

d. The riskiness depends on the amount of correlation among the security returns.

e. The riskiness depends on the beta of each security.

7-30 Select the **CORRECT** statement from the following statements regarding the Markowitz model:

a. As the number of securities held in a portfolio increases, the importance of each individual security's risk also increases.

b. As the number of securities held in a portfolio increases, the importance of the covariance relationships increases.

c. In a large portfolio, portfolio risk will consist almost entirely of each security's own risk contribution to the total portfolio risk.

d. In a large portfolio, the covariance term can be driven almost to zero.

Problems

7-1 Calculate the expected return and risk (standard deviation) for General Foods for 2012, given the following information:

Probabilities:	0.10	0.20	0.40	0.15	0.15
Expected returns:	0.20	0.16	0.12	0.05	−0.05

7-2 Four securities have the following expected returns:

$$A = 12\%, B = 15\%, C = 22\%, \text{ and } D = 30\%$$

Calculate the expected returns for a portfolio consisting of all four securities under the following conditions:

a. The portfolio weights are 25 percent each.

b. The portfolio weights are 10 percent in A, with the remainder equally divided among the other three stocks.

c. The portfolio weights are 20 percent each in A and B, and 30 percent each in C and D.

7-3   Assume the additional information provided below for the four stocks in Problem 7-2.

		Correlations With			
	σ(%)	A	B	C	D
A	10	1.0			
B	8	0.6	1.0		
C	20	0.2	−1.0	1.0	
D	16	0.5	0.3	0.8	1.0

a. Assuming equal weights for each stock, what are the standard deviations for the following portfolios?
   A, B, and C
   B and C
   B and D
   C and D

b. Calculate the standard deviation for a portfolio consisting of stocks B and C, assuming the following weights: (1) 30 percent in B and 70 percent in C; (2) 70 percent in C and 30 percent in B.

c. In part a, which portfolio(s) would an investor prefer?

Computational Problems

The following data apply to Problems 7-1 through 7—4.
Assume expected returns and standard deviations as follows:

	EG&G	GF
Return (%)	25	23
Standard deviation (%)	30	25
Covariance (%)	112.5	

The correlation coefficient, ρ, is +.15.

Proportion In		(1)	(2)	(3)
EG&G w_i	GF $w_j = (1 - w_i)$	Portfolio Expected Returns (%)	Variance (%)	Standard Deviation (%)
1.0	0.0	25.0	900	30.0
0.8	0.2	24.6	637	25.2
0.6	0.4	24.2	478	21.9
0.2	0.8	23.4	472	21.7
0.0	1.0	23.0	625	25.0

7-1   Confirm the expected portfolio returns in column 1.

7-2   Confirm the expected portfolio variances in column 2.

7-3   Confirm the expected standard deviations in column 3.

7-4   On the basis of these data, determine the lowest risk portfolio.

7-5   Assume that RF is 4 percent, the estimated return on the market is 15 percent, and the standard deviation of the market's expected return is 20 percent. Calculate the expected return and risk (standard deviation) for the following portfolios:

    a. 60 percent of investable wealth in riskless assets, 40 percent in the market portfolio

    b. 150 percent of investable wealth in the market portfolio

    c. 100 percent of investable wealth in the market portfolio

Spreadsheet Exercises

7-1   Given two stocks and returns for five or six periods, construct combinations of returns in Excel for these two stocks that will produce the following four different correlation coefficients: -1, 0, $+.20$, $-.20$. Use the CORREL function to show that your returns achieve the indicated correlation coefficient. The following example shows returns for two stocks, A and B, that produce a correlation coefficient of 1.0. You can use either five periods or six periods. Note that numerous combinations are possible in each case, so there is no one correct answer.

A	B
-2	-2
9	9
6	6
8	8
3	3
20	20

CORREL $= +1.0$

7-2   The data below are annual total returns for General Foods (GF) and Sigma Technology (ST) for the period 1997–2011. Sigma Technology is highly regarded by many investors for its innovative products. It had returns more than twice as large as that of General Foods. What would have been the results if an investor had placed half her funds in General Foods and half in Sigma Technology during this 15-year period in order to try to earn a larger return than that available in General Foods alone? Would the risk have been too large?

    a. Calculate the arithmetic mean returns for each stock.

    b. Calculate the standard deviation for each stock using the STDEV function in the spreadsheet.

    c. Calculate the correlation coefficient using the CORREL function in the spreadsheet.

    d. Calculate the covariance using the COVAR function in the spreadsheet.

    e. Calculate the portfolio return assuming equal weights for each stock.

f. Set up a calculation for the standard deviation of the portfolio that will allow you to substitute different values for the correlation coefficient or the standard deviations of the stocks. Using equal weights for the two stocks, calculate the standard deviation of the portfolio consisting of equal parts of the two stocks.

g. How does the portfolio return compare to the return on General Foods alone? How does the risk of the portfolio compare to the risk of having held General Foods alone?

h. Assume that the correlation between the two stocks had been −0.20. How much would portfolio risk have changed relative to the result calculated in f?

	GF	ST
2011	−0.141	0.222
2010	0.203	0.079
2009	−0.036	−0.220
2008	−0.204	0.527
2007	0.073	−0.628
2006	−0.111	0.684
2005	0.023	1.146
2004	0.291	0.564
2003	0.448	0.885
2002	0.482	0.433
2001	0.196	0.516
2000	0.103	−0.056
1999	0.075	0.153
1998	0.780	1.207
1997	0.254	0.736

7-3 Fill in the spreadsheet below to calculate the portfolio return and risk between Zenon and Dynamics, given the 10 years of annual returns for each stock, and portfolio weights of 50/50.

a. How would your answer change if the weights were 40 percent for Zenon and 60 percent for Dynamics?

b. How would your answer change if the weights were 30 percent for Zenon and 70 percent for Dynamics?

	Zenon	Dynamics
Expected Return		
Variance		
Standard Deviation		
Covariance		
Weight for Zenon	50%	
Weight for Dynamics	50%	
Expected Portfolio Return		
Portfolio Variance		
Portfolio Standard Deviation		

Zenon	Dynamics	
Zenon Ret	Dynam Ret	
9.89%	−47.67%	2011
−12.34%	30.79%	2010
13.56%	24.78%	2009
34.56%	7.89%	2008
−15.23%	24.42%	2007
20.09%	34.56%	2006
7.56%	67.56%	2005
16.47%	44.67%	2004
18.34%	78.56%	2003
15.56%	51.00%	2002

Checking Your Understanding

7-1 The expected return for a security is a weighted average of the possible outcomes that could occur. It is the best one-point estimate of the return. If this opportunity were to be repeated for a large number of trials, the average return realized would be the expected return.

7-2 Assuming a normal probability distribution, we can be quite confident.

7-3 The benefits of diversification do kick in immediately. Therefore, two securities provide better risk reduction than one, three are better than two, and so forth. However, at some point there is very little benefit to be gained by adding securities (the gains are so small as to be insignificant), and, therefore, the benefits of diversification are limited.

7-4 Negative correlation means that security returns move inversely to each other. This provides better risk reduction because the negative movement of one security can be offset by the positive movement of another security.

7-5 Covariances are needed to calculate portfolio risk since it consists of weighted variances and weighted covariances. The correlation coefficient is a component of the covariance, given by $COV_{AB} = \rho_{AB}\sigma_A\sigma_B$.

7-6 When adding a security to a well-diversified portfolio, what matters is its relationship to the other securities and not its own individual risk. If this security is negatively correlated with the other securities in the portfolio, having a large risk will work to reduce the overall risk of the portfolio.

chapter 8

Portfolio Selection for All Investors

Having learned about the importance of diversification, it seems logical that there are limits to its use. How many stocks are enough? How can you know if you have chosen the right portfolio?

We know that return and risk are the key parameters to consider, but how do we balance them against each other? It seems prudent at this point to learn about optimal portfolios, and in fact the basic principles about optimal portfolios can now be readily understood, given what we have learned so far. Going further, what about an overall plan to ensure that you have evaluated all of your investing opportunities? It is time to consider asset allocation, one of the most important decisions when it comes to investing. After all, many of the websites devoted to investing refer to asset allocation when discussing what investors should be doing. With a good asset allocation plan in place for your $1,000,000, you can sleep better at night.

Suppose someone whose opinions you respect suggest that you invest a sizeable portion of your $1 million in gold bullion, given the rise in gold prices. How would you respond?

Calculation of portfolio risk is a key issue in portfolio management. Risk reduction through diversification is a very important concept. Closely related to the principle of diversification is the concept of asset allocation. This involves the choices the investor makes among asset classes, such as stocks, bonds, and cash equivalents. The asset allocation decision is the most important single decision made by investors in terms of the impact on the performance of their portfolios.

AFTER READING THIS CHAPTER YOU WILL BE ABLE TO:

► Appreciate the significance of the efficient frontier and understand how an optimal portfolio of risky assets is determined.

► Understand the importance of the asset allocation decision.

► Apply the Markowitz optimization procedure to asset classes and understand the practical implications of doing so.

► Recognize how the total risk of a portfolio can be broken into two components.

Building a Portfolio using Markowitz Principles

To select an optimal portfolio of financial assets using the Markowitz analysis, investors should:

1. Identify optimal risk-return combinations (the efficient set) available from the set of risky assets being considered by using the Markowitz efficient frontier analysis. This step uses the inputs from Chapter 7, the expected returns, variances and covariances for a set of securities.
2. Select the optimal portfolio from among those in the efficient set based on an investor's preferences.

In Chapter 9 we examine how investors can invest in both risky assets and riskless assets, and buy assets on margin or with borrowed funds. As we shall see, the use of a risk-free asset changes the investor's ultimate portfolio position from that derived under the Markowitz analysis.

IDENTIFY OPTIMAL RISK-RETURN COMBINATIONS

As we saw in Chapter 7, even if portfolios are selected arbitrarily, some diversification benefits are gained. This results in a reduction of portfolio risk. However, to take the full information set into account, we use portfolio theory as developed by Markowitz. Portfolio theory is normative, meaning that it tells investors how they should act to diversify optimally. It is based on a small set of assumptions, including

1. A single investment period; for example, one year.
2. Liquidity of positions; for example, there are no transaction costs.
3. Investor preferences based only on a portfolio's expected return and risk, as measured by variance or standard deviation.

THE ATTAINABLE SET OF PORTFOLIOS

Markowitz's approach to portfolio selection is that an investor should evaluate portfolios on the basis of their expected returns and risk as measured by the standard deviation. Therefore, we must first determine the risk-return opportunities available to an investor from a given set of securities. Figure 8-1 illustrates the opportunities available from a given set of securities. A large number of possible portfolios exist when we realize that varying percentages of an investor's wealth can be invested in each of the assets under consideration.

The assets in Figure 8-1 constitute the *attainable set* of portfolios, or the opportunity set. The attainable set is the entire set of all portfolios that could be found from a group of *n* securities. However, risk-averse investors should be interested only in those portfolios with the lowest possible risk for any given level of return. All other portfolios in the attainable set are *dominated*.

Efficient Portfolios   Markowitz was the first to derive the concept of an **efficient portfolio**, defined as one that has the smallest portfolio risk for a given level of expected return or the largest expected return for a given level of risk. Investors can identify efficient portfolios by specifying an expected portfolio return and minimizing the portfolio risk at this level of return. Alternatively, they can specify a portfolio risk level they are willing to assume and maximize the expected return on the portfolio for this level of risk. Rational investors will seek efficient portfolios, because these portfolios are optimized on the basis of the two dimensions of most importance to investors, expected return and risk.

Efficient Portfolio A portfolio with the highest level of expected return for a given level of risk or a portfolio with the lowest risk for a given level of expected return

Figure 8-1

The Attainable Set and the Efficient Set of Portfolios.

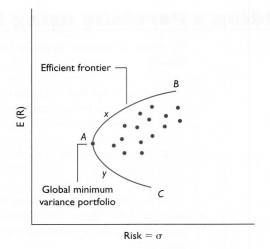

Using the inputs described earlier—expected returns, variances, and covariances—we can calculate the portfolio with the smallest variance, or risk, for a given level of expected return based on these inputs. Given the minimum-variance portfolios, we can plot the *minimum-variance frontier* as shown in Figure 8-1. Point A represents the *global minimum-variance portfolio* because no other minimum-variance portfolio has a smaller risk. The bottom segment of the minimum-variance frontier, AC, is dominated by portfolios on the upper segment, AB. For example, since portfolio X has a larger return than portfolio Y for the same level of risk, investors would not want to own portfolio Y.

The Efficient Set (Frontier)   The segment of the minimum-variance frontier above the global minimum-variance portfolio, AB, offers the best risk-return combinations available to investors from this particular set of inputs. This segment is referred to as the **efficient set** or **efficient frontier** of portfolios. The efficient set is determined by the principle of dominance— portfolio X dominates portfolio Y if it has the same level of risk but a larger expected return, or the same expected return but a lower risk.

Efficient Set The set of portfolios generated by the Markowitz portfolio model

Efficient Frontier The Markowitz tradeoff between expected portfolio return and portfolio risk (standard deviation) showing all efficient portfolios given some set of securities

✓   An efficient portfolio has the smallest portfolio risk for a given level of expected return or the largest expected return for a given level of risk. All efficient portfolios for a specified group of securities are referred to as the efficient set of portfolios.

The arc AB in Figure 8-1 is the Markowitz efficient frontier. Note again that expected return is on the vertical axis while risk, as measured by the standard deviation, is on the horizontal axis. There are many efficient portfolios on the arc AB in Figure 8-1.

Understanding the Markowitz Solution   The solution to the Markowitz model revolves around the portfolio weights, or percentages of investable funds to be invested in each security. Because the expected returns, standard deviations, and correlation coefficients for the securities being considered are inputs in the Markowitz analysis, the portfolio weights are the only variable that can be manipulated to solve the portfolio problem of determining efficient portfolios.

✓   A computer program varies the portfolio weights to determine the set of efficient portfolios.

Think of efficient portfolios as being derived in the following manner. The inputs are obtained and a level of desired expected return for a portfolio is specified, for example, 10 percent. Then all combinations of securities that can be combined to form a portfolio with an expected return of 10 percent are determined, and the one with the smallest variance of return is selected as the efficient portfolio. Next, a new level of portfolio expected return is specified—for example, 11 percent—and the process is repeated. This continues until the feasible range of expected returns is processed. Of course, the problem could be solved by specifying levels of portfolio risk and choosing that portfolio with the largest expected return for the specified level of risk.

SELECTING AN OPTIMAL PORTFOLIO OF RISKY ASSETS

Once the efficient set of portfolios is determined using the Markowitz model, investors must select from this set the portfolio most appropriate for them.

✓   The Markowitz model does not specify one optimum portfolio.

Rather, it generates the efficient set of portfolios, all of which, by definition, are optimal portfolios (for a given level of expected return or risk). From this efficient set an investor chooses the portfolio that is optimal for him or her.

Indifference Curves   We assume investors are risk-averse.[1] To illustrate the expected return-risk combination that will satisfy such an investor's personal preferences, Markowitz used **indifference curves** (which are assumed to be known for an investor). These curves, shown in Figure 8-2 for a risk-averse investor, describe investor preferences for risk and return.[2] Each indifference curve represents the combinations of risk and expected return that are equally desirable to a particular investor (that is, they provide the same level of utility).[3]

Indifference Curves
Curves describing investor preferences for risk and return

Selecting the Optimal Portfolio   The optimal portfolio for a risk-averse investor is the one on the efficient frontier tangent to the investor's highest indifference curve. In Figure 8-3 this occurs at point 0. This portfolio maximizes investor utility because the indifference curves reflect *investor preferences,* while the efficient set represents *portfolio possibilities.*

✓   In selecting one portfolio from the efficient frontier, we are matching investor preferences (as given by his or her indifference curves) with portfolio possibilities (as given by the efficient frontier).

Notice that curves U2 and U1 are unattainable, and that U3 is the highest indifference curve for this investor that is tangent to the efficient frontier. On the other hand, U4, though

---

[1] This means that investors, if given a choice, will not take a "fair gamble," defined as one with an expected payoff of zero and equal probabilities of a gain or a loss. In effect, with a fair gamble, the disutility from the potential loss is greater than the utility from the potential gain. The greater the risk-aversion, the greater the disutility from the potential loss.

[2] Although not shown, investors could also be risk-neutral (the risk is unimportant in evaluating portfolios) or risk-seekers. A risk-seeking investor, given a fair gamble, will want to take the fair gamble, and larger gambles are preferable to smaller gambles.

[3] A few important points about indifference curves should be noted. Indifference curves cannot intersect since they represent different levels of desirability. Investors have an infinite number of indifference curves. The curves for all risk-averse investors will be upward-sloping, but the shapes of the curves can vary depending on risk preferences. Higher indifference curves are more desirable than lower indifference curves. The greater the slope of the indifference curves, the greater the risk-aversion of investors. Finally, the farther an indifference curve is from the horizontal axis, the greater the utility.

Figure 8-2

Indifference Curves.

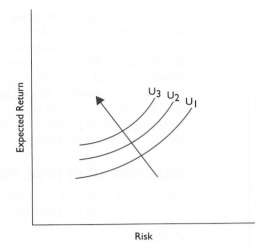

Figure 8-3

Selecting a Portfolio on the Efficient Frontier.

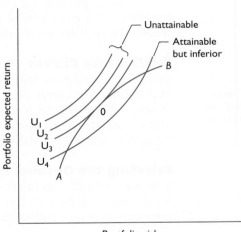

attainable, is inferior to U3, which offers a higher expected return for the same risk (and therefore more utility). If an investor had a different preference for expected return and risk, he or she would have different indifference curves, and another portfolio on the efficient frontier would be optimal.

Investments Intuition

Stated on a practical basis, conservative investors would select portfolios on the left end of the efficient set AB in Figure 8-3 because these portfolios have less risk (and, of course, less expected return). Conversely, aggressive investors would choose portfolios toward point B because these portfolios offer higher expected returns (along with higher levels of risk). Investors typically select their optimal efficient portfolio based on their risk tolerance, which can change depending on conditions. For example, given two really bad stock markets in the first decade of the 21st century (2000−2002 and 2008), along with the natural aging of the population, we would expect risk tolerance to decrease. And surveys of U.S. households show that the willingness to take risk when investing has dropped sharply since 2008.

The Global Perspective—International Diversification

Our discussion has implicitly assumed diversification in domestic securities such as stocks traded on the NYSE and on NASDAQ. However, we now know the importance of taking a global approach to investing. The United States may be the world's largest financial market, but it still accounts for less than half of the total market value of the world's stocks.

What effect would the addition of international stocks have on our diversification analysis? Considering only the potential for risk reduction and ignoring the additional risks of foreign investing, such as currency risk, we could reasonably conclude that if domestic diversification is good, international diversification must be better. And empirical studies have confirmed that at least historically, adding foreign stocks to a well-diversified portfolio reduced the overall volatility.

Bruno Solnik, a leading authority on international investing, has noted that *in the past* country factors dominated stock prices and the correlation of country factors was weak.[4] This means equity markets around the world were in fact different, and because of the low correlations investors could reduce the total variance of their portfolio by diversifying across countries. However, conditions changed dramatically in recent years as financial markets became more and more integrated. There is enormous growth in what is called cross-border mergers and acquisitions, which means, for example, that a British company wishing to grow will buy the same type of business in another country rather than buying another type of British company.

When correlations among country returns increased significantly starting around 1995, the immediate benefits of risk reduction through combining assets with low correlations was reduced. By 2008 global equity correlations were historically high and the MSCI-EAFE index, an international equity index, moved in unison with the S&P 500 index about 90 percent of the time. Even the MSCI Emerging Markets index was correlated with the S&P 500 index at the 80 percent level.[5]

Some Important Conclusions about the Markowitz Model

Five important points must be noted about the Markowitz portfolio selection model:

1. Markowitz portfolio theory is referred to as a two-parameter model because investors are assumed to make decisions on the basis of two parameters, expected return and risk. Thus, it is sometimes referred to as the mean-variance model.
2. The Markowitz analysis generates an entire set, or frontier, of efficient portfolios, all of which are equally "good." No portfolio on the efficient frontier, as generated, dominates any other portfolio on the efficient frontier.
3. The Markowitz model does not address the issue of investors using borrowed money along with their own portfolio funds to purchase a portfolio of risky assets; that is, investors are not allowed to use leverage. As we shall see in Chapter 9, allowing investors to purchase a risk-free asset increases investor utility and leads to a different efficient set on what is called the capital market line.

---

[4] These comments are based on Bruno Solnik, "Global Considerations for Portfolio Construction," in *AIMR Conference Proceedings: Equity Portfolio Construction,* Association for Investment Management and Research, Charlottesville, VA, 2002, pp. 29–35.

[5] Based on Alec Young, "Dwindling Diversification," Standard & Poor's *The Outlook,* Vol. 80, No. 43, November 12, 2008, p. 5.

4. In practice, different investors, or portfolio managers, will estimate the inputs to the Markowitz model differently. This will produce different efficient frontiers. This results from the uncertainty inherent in the security analysis part of investments as described in Chapter 1.

5. The Markowitz model remains cumbersome to work with because of the large variance-covariance matrix needed for a set of stocks. For example, using only 100 stocks the variance-covariance matrix has 10,000 terms in it (although each covariance is repeated twice).

   This raises two issues, which we will deal with in turn below:

   (a) Are there simpler methods for computing the efficient frontier?

   (b) Can the Markowitz analysis be used to optimize asset classes rather than individual assets?

Checking Your Understanding

1. Given the large number of portfolios in the attainable set, why are there so relatively few portfolios in the efficient set?

2. On an intuitive level, what is the value of talking about indifference curves when discussing the efficient frontier?

3. How should evidence of high correlations between domestic and foreign stock indexes influence investor behavior with regard to international investing?

Alternative Methods of Obtaining the Efficient Frontier

Single-Index Model A model that relates returns on each security to the returns on a market index

The **single-index model** provides an alternative expression for portfolio variance, which is easier to calculate than in the case of the Markowitz analysis. This alternative approach can be used to solve the portfolio problem as formulated by Markowitz—determining the efficient set of portfolios. It requires considerably fewer calculations. Multi-index models have also been examined and evaluated. Both are discussed in Appendix 8-A.

Selecting Optimal Asset Classes—The Asset Allocation Decision

The Markowitz model is typically thought of in terms of selecting portfolios of individual stocks; indeed, that is how Markowitz expected his model to be used. As we know, however, it is a cumbersome model to employ because of the number of covariance estimates needed when dealing with a large number of individual securities.

An alternative way to use the Markowitz model as a selection technique is to think in terms of asset classes, such as domestic stocks, foreign stocks of industrialized countries, the stocks of emerging markets, bonds, and so forth. Using the model in this manner, investors decide what asset classes to own and what proportions of the asset classes to hold.

Asset Allocation Decision The allocation of a portfolio's funds to classes of assets, such as cash equivalents, bonds, and equities

✓ The **asset allocation decision** refers to the allocation of portfolio assets to broad asset markets; in other words, how much of the portfolio's funds is to be invested in stocks, how much in bonds, money market assets, and so forth. Each weight can range from 0 to 100 percent.

Not only is asset allocation one of the most widely used applications of MPT, it is likely the most important single decision an investor makes when holding a portfolio of securities. Examining the asset allocation decision globally leads us to ask the following questions:

1. What percentage of portfolio funds is to be invested in each of the countries for which financial markets are available to investors?
2. Within each country, what percentage of portfolio funds is to be invested in stocks, bonds, bills, and other assets?
3. Within each of the major asset classes, what percentage of portfolio funds is to be invested in various individual securities?

Some Practical Advice

Investors making asset allocation decisions may wish to separate short-term accounts from long-term accounts. For example, we know from Chapter 6 that stocks historically have outperformed other asset classes over very long periods of time. Therefore, a young investor should seriously consider a heavy allocation of funds to stocks in an account that is considered as a long-term holding. On the other hand, when saving for a short-term objective, such as the down payment on a house purchase within a few years, investors need to seriously weigh the risk of common stocks. Consider what happened in 2000–2002 when the S&P 500 Index declined a cumulative 20 percent in two years, and a cumulative 38 percent in three years—measured exactly, the S&P 500 Index declined almost 50 percent from March 24, 2000 (the peak) to October 9, 2002 (the trough), a period of 929 days.

Many knowledgeable market observers agree that the asset allocation decision is the most important decision made by an investor. For example, a widely circulated study found that the asset allocation decision accounts for more than 90 percent of the variance in quarterly returns for a typical large pension fund.[6] A followup study by Ibbotson and Kaplan confirmed these results, finding that approximately 90 percent of the variability in a fund's return across time is explained by the variability in the asset allocation decision.[7] Furthermore, this study concluded that "On average, the pension funds and balanced mutual funds are not adding value above their policy benchmarks because of a combination of timing, security selection, management fees, and expenses."[8]

✓   Asset allocation largely determines an investor's success or lack thereof.

Example 8-1   Consider the 25-month bear market that occurred during 2000–2002. A 100 percent stock portfolio (Wilshire 5000 Index) would have lost about 44 percent of its value, while an investor who chose a 60 percent stock/40 percent bond combination would have lost only about 17 percent. On the other hand, a 100 percent bond portfolio (Lehman Bond Index) would have gained about 23 percent in value.

---

[6] Gary P. Brinson, L. Randolph Hood, and Gilbert L. Beebower, "Determinants of Portfolio Performance," *Financial Analysts Review* (July/August 1986).

[7] Roger D. Ibbotson and Paul D. Kaplan, "Does Asset Allocation Policy Explain 40, 90, or 100 Percent of Performance?" *Financial Analysts Journal,* January/February 2000, Vol. 56, No. 1, pp. 26–33.

[8] Ibbotson and Kaplan, op. cit., p. 33.

Of course, if we knew stocks were going to go up strongly during some period of time, such as this year, or the next two years, we would like to be 100 percent invested in stocks to take full advantage of this. We know in such a market stocks are very likely to outperform bonds. But the point is no one can be sure what financial markets are going to do over some future period of time. And if, in fact, stocks decline sharply, as they invariably will, asset allocation becomes critical to wealth preservation.

Example 8-2

Consider a shorter period of recent history. The stock market hit a record high on October 9, 2007, and officially entered a declining phase by June 30, 2008. The typical U.S. stock index fund lost about 16 percent over this roughly nine-month period. On the other hand, a 60 percent stock/40 percent bond portfolio lost only half that amount.

Different asset classes offer various potential returns and various levels of risk, and the correlation coefficients between some of these asset classes may be quite low, thereby providing beneficial diversification effects. As with the Markowitz analysis applied to individual securities, inputs remain a problem because they must be estimated. However, this will always be a problem in investing because we are selecting assets to be held over the uncertain future.

ASSET ALLOCATION AND DIVERSIFICATION

The emphasis in Chapter 7 was on diversification of a stock portfolio. Here we have been discussing asset allocation. How do these two concepts connect?

Choosing an asset allocation model does not assure you of a diversified portfolio. For example, choosing to put 90 percent of your funds in an equity mutual fund concentrating on technology stocks and 10 percent in cash is not a diversified portfolio. And if you hold only a diversified stock portfolio, you are making a one-dimensional bet on asset classes.

✓ For many investors a diversified portfolio consists of two elements: diversifying between asset categories and diversifying within asset categories. Such an action can provide a truly diversified portfolio.

SOME MAJOR ASSET CLASSES

Let's consider some of the major asset classes, in addition to U.S. stocks, that investors can use in building a portfolio. It should be noted that investors have more money in Treasury bills, bonds, accounts at banks and real estate than they do in stocks. This is a non-exhaustive list, although it does encompass asset classes that many investors either consider or use.

1. International Investing Investment counselors have regularly recommended that investors diversify internationally by holding foreign securities. The rationale for this has been that such investing reduces the risk of the portfolio because domestic and foreign markets may not move together and potential opportunities in other markets may be greater than those available in the United States.

U.S. investors have taken this rationale to heart. Whereas the average allocation for international equities was about 15 percent in 2001, it was twice that by 2011. Despite the amount of U.S. investor money flowing into international funds, there are limits. A study by the Vanguard Group found that investing more than 40 percent of one's equity allocation in foreign equities did not provide any additional diversification benefits.

Historically, international diversification clearly provided some risk-reducing benefits because of some low positive correlations between asset returns in various countries. Numerous studies confirmed these lower correlations and led many in the investing business to recommend foreign holdings as an asset class. Regardless of the previous studies showing how international diversification can lower portfolio risk, it appears that the benefits of international diversification have decreased recently as the correlation between U.S. stocks and international stocks increased.

The world is changing rapidly. It is clear that many economies have become more integrated as a result of global mergers, rapid money flows around the world, a more-integrated European community, and so forth. Therefore, we might reasonably expect that the correlation between U.S. stocks and some index of foreign stocks has increased over time, and this is exactly the case as noted earlier. Whereas the correlation between the S&P 500 Index and MSCI-EAFE Index was only 58 percent in 1992, by 2008 it was about 90 percent. Furthermore, the new, higher correlation between markets can stay high when markets decline, thereby failing investors when they most need it.

Should investors give up on international diversification? In short, NO! Good opportunities are going to exist in different countries and regions at different times, and a diversified portfolio can capture some of these opportunities. For example, for the decade ending in 2011, European and Pacific index funds produced average returns that were higher than those available on broad U.S. indexes. Other strong economies are emerging, and will emerge in the future. Also, as we know from Chapter 6, a weakening dollar increases dollar-denominated foreign returns to U.S. investors, and if a weakening dollar is anticipated it might be a good time to invest internationally.

How easy is it to choose foreign markets to add to a domestic portfolio? History teaches us that the best-performing markets differ from year to year. Emerging markets may produce good returns for certain periods, and very bad returns during other periods. The same is true of developed countries. Japan had great equity returns in the 1980s and disastrous returns in the 1990s and into the 21st century. History also teaches us that past returns are not necessarily accurate predictors of future returns. For the 10 years ending in 1994, the EAFE Index showed higher returns than did the broadest measure of U.S. stock returns. However, the five years starting in 1995 and ending in 1999 were the greatest consecutive five years in U.S. market history, and clearly where U.S. investors would have liked to be invested during that time period.

2. Bonds are an obvious choice as one of the asset classes to hold in a diversified portfolio. Traditionally, asset allocation was described as dividing one's funds between stocks, bonds, and Treasury bills. The average correlation between the returns on the S&P 500 Index and 15-year Treasury bonds over a very long period was about 0.20. In some time periods, such as 1989–2010, the correlation between these two asset classes was negative.[9]

3. Treasury Inflation-Indexed Securities (TIPS) Inflation-indexed bonds are a relatively new asset class of growing importance because they are the only asset class to provide systematic protection against inflation risk. They are now regarded as a major asset class because these securities often do not follow the movements of other types of securities, including conventional bonds.

TIPS pay a base interest rate that is fixed at the time the bonds are auctioned.[10] However, the principal value of the bonds is adjusted for inflation. Therefore, the fixed rate of interest is applied semiannually to the inflation-adjusted principal of the bonds rather than their par value.

---

[9] See Burton Malkiel, "How Much Diversification Is Enough?" in *AIMR Conference Proceedings: Equity Portfolio Construction*, Association for Investment Management and Research, Charlottesville, VA, 2002, p. 23.

[10] Details as well as buying instructions for TIPS can be found at http://www.treasurydirect.gov/indiv/products/prod_tips_glance.htm.

Malkiel estimated that the correlation between the S&P 500 Index and TIPS has fluc-tuated around zero but would actually have often been negative during the 1980s and 1990s.[11] During the period 1999–2004 TIPS had a negative correlation with both stocks (S&P 500) and bonds (U.S. Aggregate Bond Index). As we know, negative correlations provide significant risk-reducing possibilities. Furthermore, while TIPS prices will fluctuate as inflation expec-tations change, they are about one third less volatile than regular Treasury bonds of similar maturity.

TIPS performed well in 2010, with an average 6.1 percent return. For 2011, the average return was 13.5 percent.

4. Real Estate   Real estate is another obvious choice for portfolio diversification. Investors can easily hold real estate by buying Real Estate Investment Trusts (REITs). In recent years REITs have been positively correlated with U.S. stocks, but over a wide range. Based on the FTSE EPRA/NAREIT Global Real Estate Index Series, U.S. equity REITS had an average annual compound rate of return of 11.9 percent for the 30 years ending in 2010.

5. Gold   In 2011 gold reached prices of $1,900+ an ounce, although it typically traded for somewhat less. Given that investors can own gold through mutual funds, ETFs, coins, gold mining stocks, and the commodity itself, gold may appeal to a range of portfolio builders. The correlation between gold and the S&P 500 index varies, although it has generally been positive for 12-month periods since 2003. In 2011, however, it was negative.

6. Commodities   As most of us know, commodities enjoyed a great rise in some recent years, with steel, cooper, oil, cement, agricultural products, and so forth showing large increases in price. Many investors rushed to cash in on this booming alternative investment. By 2012, there were roughly 200 commodity funds available to investors, a very large change from a few years prior. Commodities often have had low positive correlation with U.S. stocks. Many commodity prices declined sharply in 2012.

COMBINING ASSET CLASSES

As an indication of what can be accomplished using asset classes for an investment program, consider a simple analysis whereby investors diversify across mutual funds representing dif-ferent asset classes. For example, portfolio funds are spread across asset classes such as blue-chip stocks, small-cap stocks, international equities, domestic bonds, international bonds, gold, and money markets. Tests of such portfolios indicate that they have outperformed the S&P 500 Index over long periods, and with less risk. And this analysis does not employ the Markowitz efficient frontier technique, because it simply uses equal portfolio weights for each of the asset classes. Presumably, the Markowitz optimization procedure could improve the results obtained from this simple strategy.

Programs exist to calculate efficient frontiers using asset classes. These programs allow for a variety of constraints, such as minimum yield and no short selling.

Table 8-1 shows an example of calculating efficient portfolios using the Markowitz optimization technique. It contains return and risk data for "traditional" asset allocation portfolios consisting of stocks (S&P 500 Index), Treasury bonds, and Treasury bills, as well as "nontraditional" portfolios which could also include real estate and TIPS. Notice that three different portfolios are shown: (1) a low-risk portfolio, with a standard deviation of 5 percent, (2) a moderate-risk portfolio, with a standard deviation of 10 percent, (3) and a high-risk portfolio with a standard deviation of 15 percent.

The nontraditional portfolios can include all five assets, as opposed to three for the traditional. As we can see in Table 8-1, the standard deviations for both portfolios are the same

---

[11] Ibid., p. 22.

Table 8-1 Comparison of Traditional Portfolio and Nontraditional Portfolio,
March 1991—September 2001

Characteristic	Low Risk	Moderate Risk	High Risk
Traditional			
Expected return (%)	9.13	12.98	14.51
Standard deviation (%)	5.00	10.00	15.00
Sharpe ratio	0.88	0.83	0.65
Efficient asset allocation			
S&P 500 Index (%)	22.80	56.54	92.34
U.S. long-term government bonds (%)	36.28	43.46	7.66
U.S. T-bills (%)	40.92	0.00	0.00
Nontraditional			
Expected return (%)	10.11	13.57	14.80
Standard deviation (%)	5.00	10.00	15.00
Sharpe ratio	1.08	0.89	0.67
Efficient asset allocation			
S&P 500 Index (%)	18.65	39.23	88.20
U.S. long-term government bonds (%)	26.47	26.93	0.00
U.S. T-bills (%)	0.00	0.00	0.00
TIPS (%)	41.53	0.00	0.00
NAREIT Equity Index (%)	13.08	33.85	11.80

Note: The average risk-free rate during the period was 4.71 percent.

for each of three risk levels: 5, 10, and 15 percent. But note that the expected returns are higher in each case for the nontraditional portfolios as compared to the traditional portfolios.

For the traditional portfolios, an investor seeking low risk (5 percent standard deviation) would place funds in each of the three major asset classes, ranging from 22.8 percent in stocks to 40.92 percent in Treasury bills. With a nontraditional portfolio, four of the five asset classes would be held for a low-risk position, with no funds in Treasury bills. In contrast, for the high-risk portfolio, funds are allocated only to stocks and bonds with the traditional portfolio and only to stocks and real estate for the nontraditional.

Figure 8-4 shows a plot of the efficient frontiers for the traditional and nontraditional portfolios. Note that the boundaries are Treasury bills on the low end and stocks on the high end. As we would expect, the nontraditional efficient frontier plots above the traditional efficient frontier. Thus, using the Markowitz analysis investors can determine efficient portfolios by calculating the optimal allocations to each asset class being considered.

Whether we use the Markowitz analysis for asset classes or individual securities, the end result is an efficient frontier of risky portfolios and the choice of an optimal risky portfolio based on investor preferences.

ASSET CLASSES AND CORRELATION COEFFICIENTS

The correlation between asset classes is obviously a key factor in building an optimal portfolio. Investors would like to have asset classes that are negatively correlated with each other, or at least not highly positively correlated with each other.

Figure 8-4

Efficient Frontiers of a Traditional and a Nontraditional Portfolio, March 1991–September 2001.

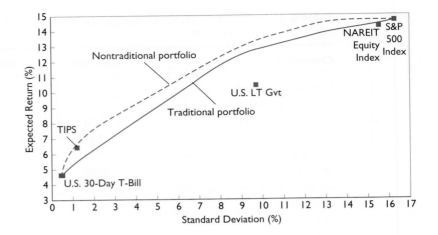

For many years, up until about 2000, the correlation between stocks and bonds ranged from +.3 to +.6. More recently, this relationship seems to have broken down, and been negative at times. Nor is the change surprising. We should expect changes in the correlations among asset classes over time. Correlations between U.S. stocks and REITS have been rising quite sharply since 2002. While the correlation between U.S. stocks and international stocks has risen in recent years from about .60 to .70, the correlation between U.S. stocks and foreign government bonds in developed markets has fallen sharply in recent years. Gold is often considered to have low or negative correlation with U.S. stocks, but there are yearly periods recently when this was not true.

It is obvious that correlation coefficients change over time. It is also clear that the historical correlation between two asset classes will vary somewhat depending on the time period chosen to do the calculation; the frequency of the data (monthly, yearly, etc.); and the exact asset class used (S&P 500, DJIA, Wilshire 5000, etc.). Of course, what really matters when building a portfolio are the future correlation coefficients, which may well be different from the historical.

Asset Allocation and the Individual Investor

Individual investors must confront the asset allocation issue if they are to be successful over time. Having a diversified portfolio of stocks is often not enough. Of course, owning only a portfolio of stocks and not properly diversifying is a prescription for poor, if not disastrous, investment performance. All investors should diversify, simply because we live in an uncertain world, and proper diversification does eliminate some of the risk of owning stocks.

Chapter 7 should convince you that Markowitz diversification pays; that is, portfolio risk can be reduced depending on the covariance relationships. Figure 8-5 makes a strong case for asset allocation by demonstrating that the traditional efficient frontier using stocks, bonds, and risk-free assets can be improved with the addition of other asset classes which have low or negative correlation with the traditional asset classes. For additional evidence on the importance of asset allocation for individual investors, see Box 8-1.

For individual investors, the asset allocation decision depends heavily upon their time horizon and their risk tolerance. Investors tend to be more comfortable with equities when they have long time horizons, given the year to year volatility of stocks. Investors with a low tolerance for risk may only be able to tolerate a relatively modest allocation to stocks.

Asset Allocation Using Stocks and Bonds
Let's first consider owning the two major asset classes that a majority of investors are familiar with, and own, in addition to cash assets such as a money market fund. Most investors own portfolios of stocks or bonds or a

BOX 8-1

Spread It Around

DIVERSIFYING MAY HELP REDUCE RISK IN YOUR PORTFOLIO

Over the last few years, investors have learned a hard lesson in market volatility. One small example: The S&P 500, which ended 2002 with a total return of -23.37 percent, finished 2003 with a flourish, up 26.38 percent. This dramatic one-year change in performance demonstrates how much the financial markets can fluctuate. Alas, performance ups and downs—whether over the short or long term—are a given in the world of investing. And in a sharp market downturn, this volatility can significantly shrink your holdings.

Certainly, last year's rise in equity values came as a great relief to investors after three years of steep stock market declines. But with stock returns flat so far this year and interest rates beginning to go back up, you may wonder whether you want (or need) to adjust your investment strategy.

When reviewing your portfolio, first realize that you cannot predict how the markets will perform. As a result, trying to "time" the market—attempting to guess which way the markets will move, and basing your investment decisions on these predictions—is bound to fail, at least most of the time.

Since market timing is not the answer, you need a better approach for building your portfolio. A tried and true method, based on substantial research, is to diversify your money across different types of investments. "Given the uncertainty of the markets, *asset allocation*, or dividing holdings among different asset classes like stocks, bonds and real estate, provides a good way to manage risk and to build a portfolio for the long term," says Leonard Govia, participant advice manager, TIAA-CREF. (However, diversification doesn't guarantee against loss.)

THE BIRTH OF A THEORY

The concept of asset allocation is based on modern portfolio theory, which was developed in the 1950s by the economist Harry M. Markowitz, who later shared a Nobel Prize for his work. Markowitz measured the risk inherent in various types of securities and developed methods for combining investments to maximize the tradeoff between risk and return.

Basically, the theory says that investors shouldn't view the prospects of a particular security in isolation, but instead look at each investment and how it fits into an overall portfolio. By combining securities that have a low (or, better yet, negative) *correlation* with each other—that is, securities that don't perform in the same way under similar market conditions—investors will create a less risky portfolio than if they invested only in securities that perform similarly (i.e., have a high correlation).

"The advantage of diversifying investments is that each type of security won't react to the ups and downs of the market in the same way," says Govia. "So by diversifying, you spread the risk in your portfolio around. The result is a more balanced portfolio that can help you withstand drops in the market."

Other studies demonstrate the impact asset allocation has on volatility. For example, in a notable 10-year study of large pension funds, Gary P. Brinson, L. Randolph Hood, and Gilbert Beebower found that, over time, more than 90 percent of the variability of a portfolio's performance is due to allocation among specific asset classes, while less than 5 percent of the variability of performance results from investment selection.

CREATE A PORTFOLIO FOR YOU

If diversification works, your next question may be "How do I ensure that my portfolio is right for my needs?" Many investment companies give you a simple way to develop an appropriate strategy: model portfolios, diversified among asset classes like stocks, bonds and money markets, that are based on different risk tolerances, investment preferences and "time horizons" (the number of years you have to invest before needing to use the money, and how many years you'll need that money to last).

At TIAA-CREF, we've developed model portfolios diversified among five asset classes—stocks, fixed income, real estate, guaranteed and money market—for a variety of investor types. To ensure appropriate diversification for retirement, our portfolios are diversified among at least three asset classes, with one being stocks; virtually all our after-tax mutual fund portfolios are diversified among at least two asset classes, including stocks.

SOURCE: "Spread It Around," *Balance*, Quarterly News and Tools From TIAA-CREF, Summer 2004, pp. 10–11. Reprinted by permission.

Table 8-2 Annual Average Compound Returns and Risks for Portfolio Combinations of Stocks and Bonds for Two 20-Year Periods

Stocks	Bonds	1963–1982		1983–2002	
		Return	SD	Return	SD
1.00	.00	8.3154	17.6383	12.6902	16.9656
.95	.05	8.1115	16.7606	12.6115	16.1947
.90	.10	7.9080	15.9057	12.5327	15.4504
.85	.15	7.7048	15.0760	12.4541	14.7353
.80	.20	7.5021	14.2739	12.3754	14.0525
.75	.25	7.2997	13.5025	12.2969	13.4052
.70	.30	7.0977	12.7655	12.2184	12.7975
.65	.35	6.8961	12.0673	12.1399	12.2336
.60	.40	6.6949	11.4130	12.0615	11.7184
.55	.45	6.4941	10.8086	11.9832	11.2572
.50	.50	6.2936	10.2611	11.9049	10.8556
.45	.55	6.0935	9.7781	11.8266	10.5192
.40	.60	5.8938	9.3679	11.7484	10.2532
.35	.65	5.6941	9.0389	11.6703	10.0626
.30	.70	5.4955	8.7987	11.5922	9.9508
.25	.75	5.2969	8.6540	11.5142	9.9203
.20	.80	5.0987	8.6087	11.4363	9.9716
.15	.85	4.9009	8.6644	11.3584	10.1038
.10	.90	4.7034	8.8193	11.2805	10.3140
.05	.95	4.5063	9.0690	11.2027	10.5984
00	1.00	4.3666	9.5131	11.0475	11.1496

combination of the two. It stands to reason that bonds are the safer of the two assets, and this in fact is why many investors allocate at least part of their portfolio to bonds. Bonds historically have provided a lower return than stocks, but with a considerably lower risk. We saw in Table 6-6 that the standard deviation for bonds has been roughly 40 percent of the standard deviation for stocks. A severe stock market decline such as that of 2000–2002 convinced a number of investors that they should be holding bonds, thereby lessening or avoiding the really sharp losses in stocks that occurred during that period. An important question remains: What is the best approach for an investor given what we can learn from asset allocation strategies and the history of asset returns?

Table 8-2 shows the geometric mean return and risk combinations for bonds and stocks for two recent 20-year periods.[12] Shown are the returns and standard deviations of portfolio combinations of stocks and bonds in 5 percent increments. Clearly, in general, return and risk go together. A portfolio consisting only of stocks (the first row) has a higher return than does a portfolio consisting only of bonds, or a portfolio consisting of 50 percent stocks and 50 percent bonds. However, the risk of such a portfolio is also higher than the alternatives.

---

[12] These data come from Charles P. Jones and Jack W. Wilson, "The Changing Nature of Stock and Bond Volatility," unpublished manuscript.

Now consider the situation for an investor who because of his or her risk tolerance really wishes to own a portfolio of bonds. This investor understands that the return on such a portfolio is expected to be lower than that of a stock portfolio, but also knows that the risk will be lower, and the investor's risk tolerance drives the decision. Let us assume the investor owned a 100 percent bond portfolio over the second 20-year period.

This investor earned an annual compound rate of return of 11.05 percent with a risk level of 11.15 percent. However, Table 8-2 shows us that a portfolio of 50 percent stocks and 50 percent bonds had a lower standard deviation, 10.85 percent, and a higher annual return of 11.90 percent. The same is true for the prior period. A portfolio of 65 percent bonds and 35 percent stocks had a slightly lower risk than a portfolio of 100 percent bonds, but a return that was almost 1.2 percentage points higher on a compound annual basis.

Clearly, for the 40-year period shown here, asset allocation between stocks and bonds paid off for investors. Unless one expects the future to be quite different from the past, it is difficult to justify holding a portfolio consisting only of bonds.

Some Limitations on Asset Allocation   Individual investors, in choosing asset classes, should be aware that the benefits of asset allocation are not always present. We noted above that gold was typically negatively correlated with U.S. stocks in 2011. This would seem to make gold a good candidate for at least some percentage of an investor's portfolio. A recent study over the period 1975–2005 found, not unexpectedly, that gold as a standalone investment performed poorly relative to stocks over the long run. What about a 5 percent buy-and-hold gold investment added to an optimized global portfolio? This study found that over this long period, there was no real benefit to investing in gold. Over certain time periods, of course, gold performed well, but on balance it did not.[13] Given the hype about gold in 2011 when it reached very high price levels, this is good information to keep in mind as a long-run investor.

Investors should also note that asset allocation does not guarantee that an investor will not lose money during some time period. During the financial crisis of 2008 almost all asset classes declined. This has led some observers to argue that asset allocation/diversification is overrated and can be ignored. Such an argument is wrong. 2008 was a true financial crisis in the same sense that the Great Depression was a true financial crisis. Such an event happens only rarely, fortunately. For all other bad times in the U.S. economy, asset allocation/diversification pays off, reducing the investor's risk and losses. Investors would be ill advised to go against the entire history of diversification because of one catastrophic event in recent history.

Some Practical Advice

Despite investor interest in, and use of, several different asset classes such as gold or commodities, it is still true today that the three major categories for asset allocation for many investors are stocks, bonds and cash equivalents. U.S. investment-grade bonds tend to have low correlations with stocks over long time periods, and provide investors the opportunity to have a balanced portfolio that cushions against market shocks.

For investors who feel that three asset classes are not sufficient, consider the following. Considerable research suggests that an investor needs no more than seven asset classes to achieve optimal asset allocation: blue-chip U.S. stocks, blue-chip foreign stocks, small company stocks, value stocks, high quality bonds, inflation-protected bonds, and cash equivalents. Furthermore, almost all of these asset classes can be built using index funds, which as we know from Chapter 3 have minimal costs and good diversification.

[13] See Mitchell Ratner and Steven Klein, "The Portfolio Implications of Gold Investment," *The Journal of Investing*, 17, Spring 2008, pp. 77–87.

ASSET ALLOCATION AND INDEX MUTUAL FUNDS

Investors can build a sound portfolio using index mutual funds or ETFs. Starting with equities, funds would be needed to cover domestic large cap stocks and small cap stocks. An intermediate cap stock fund might be added. Because we live in a global economy, we would add an international large stock fund and an emerging markets fund. An intermediate U.S. government bond fund could add stability and income. Individuals in high tax brackets might opt for a municipal bond fund.

This asset allocation plan, using only stock and bond funds, both domestic and international, should be sufficient for many investors. Adding additional asset classes may add value, but they also increase the overall portfolio risk. For example, gold, with no cash flow, could easily decline in price following a big runup.

LIFE CYCLE ANALYSIS

Traditionally, recommended asset allocations for investors have focused on the stage of the life cycle they are in. For example, young investors with a 30-year working horizon ahead of them were assumed to be able to invest in risky common stocks, while investors nearing retirement were assumed to favor mostly bonds in their portfolio. However, as investors have become more familiar with what inflation can do to the value of a fixed portfolio over a long period, and as they realize that a retiree may well have a life expectancy of 25 years or more, some have changed their views of asset allocation.

Life-Cycle Fund Funds that automatically become more conservative as your retirement date approaches

A simple approach for some individual investors in managing their retirement funds is to buy a **life-cycle fund** (also called a **target-date fund**). Life-cycle funds are balanced funds (holding both equity and fixed income investments) with an asset allocation that automatically adjusts to a more conservative posture as your retirement date approaches. They are available in many 401(k) plans.

Fidelity and Vanguard are the two largest providers of life-cycle funds. Fidelity uses 18 underlying mutual funds in an active management approach while Vanguard uses only a few funds in a passive management approach. For example, the Vanguard Target Retirement 2050 Fund is for people in their 20s with approximately 40 years to retirement. The fund starts out mostly invested in stocks, but by approximately 2026 the fund starts to annually reduce stocks and increase bonds.

OTHER APPROACHES

There is no "one" answer to the question, what is an ideal asset allocation for a particular investor? There are a number of suggested allocations readily available, with differences that might well be justified depending on the circumstances.

Concepts in Action

Making Asset Allocation Recommendations for Investors

As noted in the chapter, studies suggest that the asset allocation decision can account for more than 90 percent of the variance in returns for large pension fund portfolios. Many investors now regard the asset allocation decision as the most important one to be made in determining the success of their portfolio over time.

How does asset allocation get implemented in practice? Consider the model portfolios of TIAA-CREF, one of the largest financial service providers in the world. This organization provides retirement planning and investment services for a very large clientele.

TIAA-CREF illustrates several model portfolios that accommodate a range of investor risk tolerances. For example, for a conservative investor who emphasizes safety and stability, the following asset allocation is recommended.

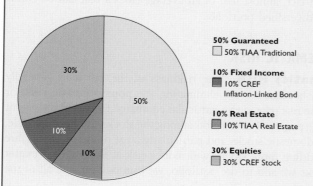

Notice that 50 percent of the portfolio is allocated to a guaranteed fund. Even so, 30 percent is allocated to equities to provide some growth opportunities over time.

What about a moderately aggressive investor who seeks more growth possibilities while still emphasizing stability? TIAA-CREF recommends the following asset allocation:

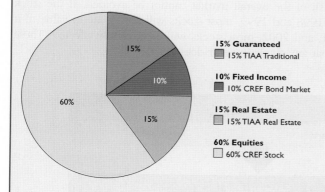

Finally, what about the "aggressive" investor building a retirement portfolio (as opposed to a speculator). This approach offers investors both growth and income stocks, and both domestic and international opportunities. Note that even at this stage only 75 percent of funds are invested in equities, because the investor still needs diversification and some stability.

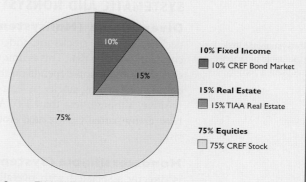

SOURCE: TIAA-CREF website.

Other asset allocation examples are readily available. AAII, the American Association of Individual Investors, has a website with a section on asset allocation models. Suggested allocation breakdowns are shown for conservative, moderate, and aggressive investors using seven asset classes.

Asset allocation calculators are also readily available. By supplying your data, a suggested asset allocation model tailored to you can be generated. As one example, see http://www.ipers.org/calcs/AssetAllocator.html.

Checking Your Understanding

4. Relative to Figure 8-5, what does it mean to say that an efficient frontier is pushed out?
5. Explain why, using the bear markets of 2000–2002 or 2008, one can argue that the Asset Allocation decision is the most important decision made by an investor.

The Impact of Diversification on Risk

The Markowitz analysis demonstrates that the standard deviation of a portfolio is typically less than the weighted average of the standard deviations of the securities in the portfolio. Thus, diversification typically reduces the risk of a portfolio—as the number of portfolio holdings increases, portfolio risk declines. In fact, almost half of an average stock's risk can be eliminated if the stock is held in a well-diversified portfolio.

SYSTEMATIC AND NONSYSTEMATIC RISK

Nonsystematic Risk Risk attributable to factors unique to a security

Diversifiable (Nonsystematic) Risk   The riskiness of the portfolio generally declines as more stocks are added because we are eliminating the **nonsystematic risk**, or company-specific risk. This is unique risk related to a particular company. However, the extent of the risk reduction depends on the degree of correlation among the stocks. As a general rule, correlations among stocks, at least domestic stocks and particularly large domestic stocks, are positive, although less than 1.0. Adding more stocks will reduce risk at first, but no matter how many partially correlated stocks we add to the portfolio, we cannot eliminate all of the risk.

Systematic Risk Risk attributable to broad macro factors affecting all securities

Nondiversifiable (Systematic) Risk   Variability in a security's total returns that is directly associated with overall movements in the general market or economy is called **systematic risk**, or market risk, or nondiversifiable risk. Virtually all securities have some systematic risk, whether bonds or stocks, because systematic risk directly encompasses interest rate risk, recession, inflation, and so on. Most stocks are negatively impacted by such factors; therefore, diversification cannot eliminate market risk.

After the nonsystematic risk is eliminated, what is left is the nondiversifiable portion, or the market risk (systematic part). This part of the risk is inescapable, because no matter how well an investor diversifies, the risk of the overall market cannot be avoided. If the stock market rises strongly, as it did in 1998 and 1999, most stocks will appreciate in value; if it declines sharply, as in 2000, 2001, and 2002, most stocks will be adversely affected. These movements occur regardless of what any single investor does.

Remember:

Risk and the Number of Securities   Investors can construct a diversified portfolio and eliminate part of the total risk, the diversifiable or nonmarket part. Figure 8-5

Figure 8-5

Systematic and Non-systematic Risk.

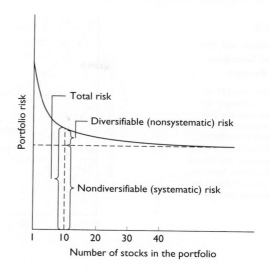

illustrates this concept of declining nonsystematic risk in a portfolio of securities. As more securities are added, the nonsystematic risk becomes smaller and smaller, and the total risk for the portfolio approaches its systematic risk. Since diversification cannot reduce systematic risk, total portfolio risk can be reduced no lower than the total risk of the market portfolio.

Diversification can substantially reduce the unique risk of a portfolio. However, Figure 8-5 indicates that no matter how much we diversify, we cannot eliminate systematic risk. The declining total risk curve in that figure levels off and at most becomes asymptotic to the systematic risk. Clearly, market risk is critical to all investors. It plays a central role in asset pricing because it is the risk that investors can expect to be rewarded for taking.

HOW MANY SECURITIES ARE NEEDED TO FULLY DIVERSIFY?

A study done by Evans and Archer in 1968 is often cited in answering the question of how many securities are needed to have a well-diversified portfolio.[14] Their analysis suggested as few as 15 stocks could be adequate. Thus, based on studies done in the 1960s, 1970s, and 1980s it had become commonplace for investors to believe that 15 or so stocks provides adequate diversification, and investors will often find reference to this belief today. This belief is now being revised.

According to a recent study by Campbell, Lettau, Malkiel, and Xu, between 1962 and 1997 the market's overall volatility did not change while the volatility of individual stocks increased sharply.[15] Market volatility was found to be essentially trendless, while the volatility of individual stocks has risen. This study suggests that investors need more stocks in today's environment to adequately diversify.

In a separate article, Malkiel illustrates how today's situation differs from the past in terms of idiosyncratic (nonsystematic) risk and risk reduction.[16] Figure 8-6 shows how total risk declines based on the 1960s and the 1990s. Using the 1960s, which is the typical diagram traditionally shown to illustrate this, total risk declines rapidly as the idiosyncratic (labeled

---

[14] See John Evans and Stephen Archer, "Diversification and the Reduction of Dispersion: An Empirical Analysis," *Journal of Finance,* 23, 1968, pp. 761–767.

[15] See John Campbell, Martin Lettau, Burton Malkiel, and Yexiao Xu, "Have Individual Stocks Become More Volatile? An Empirical Exploration of Idiosyncratic Risk," *Journal of Finance,* 56, (February 2001), pp. 1–43.

[16] Malkiel, op. cit., p. 19.

Figure 8-6

Diversification and the Number of Securities Past and Present.

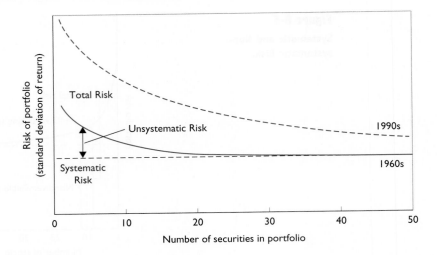

unsystematic in Figure 8-6) risk is eliminated. Twenty stocks diversified by sector could effectively eliminate the company-specific risk. In contrast, for the 1990s even a 50-stock portfolio contains a significant amount of idiosyncratic risk. Malkiel goes on to say that in "today's market, a portfolio must hold many more stocks than the 20 stocks that in the 1960s achieved sufficient diversification."[17] Malkiel has suggested that it could take as many as 200 stocks to provide the level of diversification in the earlier studies.

So how many securities are needed to adequately diversify a portfolio? Some research suggests 40 stocks are needed. Campbell et al. suggest that for recent periods at least 50 randomly selected stocks are needed. Another study by Boscaljon et al. focused on portfolios of about 60 stocks chosen from different industries.[18] Based on the recent research done on diversification, it seems reasonable to state that at least 40 securities, and perhaps 50 or 60, are needed to ensure adequate diversification.

The Implications of Reducing Risk by Holding Portfolios

The construction of optimal portfolios and the selection of the best portfolio for an investor have implications for the pricing of financial assets. As we saw in the previous discussion, part of the riskiness of the average stock can be eliminated by holding a well-diversified portfolio. This means that part of the risk of the average stock can be eliminated and part cannot. Investors need to focus on that part of the risk that cannot be eliminated by diversification because this is the risk that should be priced in the financial markets.

The relevant risk of an individual stock is its contribution to the riskiness of a well-diversified portfolio. The return that should be expected on the basis of this contribution can be estimated by the capital asset pricing model. We consider these topics in Chapter 9.

---

[17] Malkiel, op. cit., p. 19.

[18] See Brian Boscaljon, Greg Filback, and Chia-Cheng Ho, "How Many Stocks Are Required for a Well-Diversified Portfolio?" *Advances in Financial Education*, 3, Fall 2005, pp. 60–71.

Summary

▶ Markowitz portfolio theory provides the way to select optimal portfolios based on using the full information set about securities.

▶ Having calculated the expected returns and standard deviations for a set of portfolios, the efficient set (or efficient frontier) can be determined.

▶ The expected returns, standard deviations, and correlation coefficients for the securities being considered are inputs in the Markowitz analysis. Therefore, the portfolio weights are the variable manipulated to determine efficient portfolios.

▶ An efficient portfolio has the highest expected return for a given level of risk, or the lowest level of risk for a given level of expected return.

▶ The Markowitz analysis determines the efficient set of portfolios, all of which are equally desirable. The efficient set is an arc in expected return—standard deviation space.

▶ The efficient frontier captures the possibilities that exist from a given set of securities. Indifference curves express investor preferences.

▶ The optimal portfolio for a risk-averse investor occurs at the point of tangency between the investor's highest indifference curve and the efficient set of portfolios.

▶ The single-index model provides an alternative expression for portfolio variance, which is easier to calculate than in the case of the Markowitz analysis. This alternative approach can be used to solve the portfolio problem as formulated by Markowitz.

▶ The asset allocation decision refers to the allocation of portfolio assets to broad asset markets; in other words, how much of the portfolio's funds is to be invested in stocks, how much in bonds, money market assets, and so forth. Each weight can range from 0 to 100 percent. Asset allocation is one of the most widely used applications of MPT.

▶ The Markowitz analysis can be applied to asset classes to determine optimal portfolios to hold. Efficient frontiers involving asset classes can be generated.

▶ Diversification can substantially reduce the unique risk of a portfolio. However, no matter how much we diversify, we cannot eliminate systematic risk. Therefore, systematic (market) risk is critical to all investors.

▶ New research indicates that it takes substantially more stocks to diversify adequately than has previously been thought. This number appears to be at least 40, and could be more.

▶ The relevant risk of an individual stock is its contribution to the riskiness of a well-diversified portfolio.

Questions

8-1 Consider a diagram of the efficient frontier. The vertical axis is _____. The horizontal axis is _____, as measured by the _____.

8-2 How many portfolios are on an efficient frontier? What is the Markowitz efficient set?

8-3 Why do rational investors seek efficient portfolios?

8-4 Using the Markowitz analysis, how does an investor select an optimal portfolio?

8-5 How is an investor's risk-aversion indicated in an indifference curve? Are all indifference curves upward-sloping?

8-6 What does it mean to say that the efficient frontier with indifference curves matches possibilities with preferences?

8-7 With regard to international investing, how has the situation changed in recent years with regard to correlations among the stocks of different countries?

8-8 If the correlations among country returns have increased in recent years, should U.S. investors give up, or decrease significantly, their positions in foreign securities?

8-9 What is meant by the asset allocation decision? How important is this decision?

8-10 When efficient frontiers are calculated using asset classes, what types of results are generally found?

8-11 As we add securities to a portfolio, what happens to the total risk of the portfolio?

8-12 How well does diversification work in reducing the risk of a portfolio? Are there limits to diversification? Do the effects kick in immediately?

8-13 Assume that you have an investment portfolio worth $100,000 invested in bonds because you are a conservative investor. Based on the discussion in this chapter, is this a sound decision?

8-14 Now assume that you inherit $25,000 and decide to invest this amount in bonds also, adding the new bonds to your existing bond portfolio. Is such a decision consistent with the lessons of modern portfolio theory?

8-15 What is the difference between traditional beliefs (starting in the 1960s) as to the number of securities needed to properly diversify, and the very recent evidence that has been presented by Malkiel and others?

8-16 Can gold be used as part of an asset allocation plan? If so, how can this be accomplished?

8-17 Suppose you are considering a stock fund and a bond fund and determine that the covariance between the two is −179. Does this indicate a strong negative relationship?

8-18 Can a single asset portfolio be efficient?

8-19 Can the original Markowitz efficient frontier ever be a straight line?

Problems

8-1 Given the following information:

Standard deviation for stock X = 12%
Standard deviation for stock Y = 20%
Expected return for stock X = 18%
Expected return for stock Y = 25%
Correlation coefficient between X and Y = 0.60

The covariance between stock X and Y is
  a. .048
  b. 144.00
  c. 3.60
  d. 105.6

8-2 Given the information in Problem 8-1 regarding risk, the expected return for a portfolio consisting of 50 percent invested in X and 50 percent invested in Y can be seen to be
  a. 21.5%
  b. 18%
  c. Less than 18%
  d. More than 25%

8-3 Given the information in Problem 8-1, assume now that the correlation coefficient between stocks X and Y is −1.0. Choose the investment below that represents the minimum-risk portfolio.
  a. 100% investment in stock X
  b. 100% investment in stock Y

c. 50% investment in stock X and 50% investment in stock Y

d. 80% investment in stock X and 20% investment in stock Y

8-4 Assume a family member is approaching retirement. Her retirement assets include her house and Social Security payments. She also has a 401(k) plan representing one-third of her assets. If she wants to own some foreign securities and decides to invest 15 percent of her 401(k) assets accordingly, what percentage of her total assets will this constitute?

Spreadsheet Exercises

8-1 Closing prices for SilTech and New Mines for the years 1997–2012 are shown below.

a. Calculate the total returns for each stock for the years 2012–1998 to 3 decimal places. Note that the price for 1997 is used to calculate the total return for 1998.

b. Assume that similar returns will continue in the future (i.e., average returns = expected returns). Calculate the expected return, variance and standard deviation for both stocks and insert these values in the spreadsheet. Use Average, Var, and Stdev functions.

c. Calculate the covariance between these two stocks based on the 15 years of returns.

d. Using the 11 different proportions that SilTech could constitute of the portfolio ranging from 0 percent to 100 percent in 10 percent increments, calculate the portfolio variance, standard deviation, and expected return.

e. Plot the tradeoff between return and risk for these two stocks based on the calculation in (d). Use the XY scatter diagram in Excel.

	SILTECH	NEWMINES
2012	198.08	21.634
2011	84.84	34.867
2010	71.89	44.67
2009	32.2	49.8
2008	10.69	49.55
2007	7.16	46.86
2006	10.95	53.11
2005	7.44	48.75
2004	25.7	63.12
2003	10.23	37.04
2002	3.28	31.67
2001	5.22	21.78
2000	7.97	14.45
1999	9.64	9.39
1998	7.13	14.99
1997	14.39	10.72

8-2 You are trying to decide whether to buy Banguard's Large Stock Equity Fund and/or its Treasury Bond Fund. You believe that next year involves several possible scenarios to which you have assigned probabilities. You have also estimated expected returns for each of the two funds for each scenario. Your spreadsheet looks like the following.

Next Year's Possibilities	Probability	Stock Fund Rate of Return	Column D	Bond Fund Rate of Return	Column F
Recession	0.2	−13		15	
Weak Econ	0.15	5		3	
Average Econ	0.6	10		7	
Strong Econ	0.05	24		−9	
		Exp Value =		Exp Value =	

a. Fill in columns D and F and calculate the expected return for each fund, given the probabilities for the four possible economic conditions and their associated rates of return.

b. Given the expected value for each fund for next year, fill out the following spreadsheet to calculate the standard deviation of each fund. Note that you need to fill in columns D, E, and F for the stock fund, and columns H, I, and J for the bond fund. The first two columns in each set are labeled; you need to determine what goes in columns F and J, respectively, which will lead to the variance, and then the standard deviation.

c.

		Stock Fund				Bond Fund			
Scenario	Probability	Forecast Return	Column D Deviation from Exp.	Column E Squared Deviation	Column F	Forecast Return	Column H Deviation from Exp.	Column I Squared Deviation	Column J
Recession	0.2	−13				15			
Weak Econ	0.15	5				3			
Moderate Econ	0.6	10				7			
Strong Econ	0.05	24				−9			
Exp. Ret.		9.1		Variance =				Variance =	
				Std Dev =				Std Dev =	

d. Now calculate the covariance between the two funds, and the correlation coefficient, using the following format.

Scenario	Column B Probability	Deviation from Exp. Return for Stock fund	Deviation from Exp. Return for Bond fund	Product of Deviations	Col B × Col E
Recession	0.2				
Weak Econ	0.15				
Moderate Econ	0.6				
Strong Econ	0.05				
				Covariance =	Corr Coeff =

e. Using the formulas for the expected return and risk of a portfolio, calculate these values for each of the following portfolio weights.

w1 = stock fd % of funds in	w2 = bond fd % of funds in	Portfolio Expected Ret	Std Dev
0.1	0.9		
0.2	0.8		
0.3	0.7		
0.4	0.6		
0.5	0.5		
0.6	0.4		
0.7	0.3		
0.8	0.2		
0.9	0.1		

f. Which of the portfolios in (d) is the minimum variance portfolio?

g. Based on your analysis, should investors hold a portfolio of 100 percent bonds?

Answer to Question at the Beginning of the Chapter The price of gold can be very volatile, going down as well as up. Gold bullion has no current return (no income component) and has a carrying cost (interest cost if borrowed money is used to buy it, storage costs, and opportunity costs—an income-producing asset could have been bought instead).

Checking Your Understanding

8-1 Most portfolios are dominated by another portfolio that has either a higher return for the same level of risk or a lower risk for the same level of return.

8-2 Indifference curves allow us to talk about preferences with regard to the return-risk tradeoff.

8-3 International investing may not be as beneficial today as it was several years ago, but it is still beneficial, and investors should diversify internationally.

8-4 An efficient frontier that is pushed out has a higher level of return for a given level of risk than does the frontier below it.

8-5 Having made an asset allocation decision in 2001 to own common stocks, and stick with them, an investor's performance was essentially determined. Since the market performed badly during that period, this investor's portfolio would almost assuredly perform badly also. Conversely, another investor who decided to invest in Treasury bills in 2001 would have a positive performance.

chapter 9

Asset Pricing Principles

Although you have postponed dealing with the issue, in the back of your mind you remember from your finance course a well-known model called the CAPM. It occurs to you that this model, which was said to be so important in finance, probably has a role to play in your investing decisions. And in fact it does because it captures the concept of a required rate of return for a stock, which is important to consider when you are trying to decide which stocks to buy. So the time has come to bite the bullet and review some theory regarding asset prices and markets, and consider the CAPM once again. Knowing about the required rate of return will be important when you start trying to value common stocks, a topic that you are almost ready to tackle. Furthermore, understanding how risk is priced in financial markets can be very valuable to an investor.

In the last chapter we discussed portfolio theory, which is normative, describing how investors should act in selecting an optimal portfolio of risky securities. In this chapter we consider theories about asset pricing. What happens if all investors seek portfolios of risky securities using the Markowitz framework under idealized conditions? How will this affect equilibrium security prices and returns? In other words, how does optimal diversification affect the market prices of securities? Under these idealized conditions, what is the risk-return tradeoff that investors face? In general, we wish to examine models that explain security prices under conditions of market equilibrium. These are asset pricing models, or models for the valuation of risky assets.

We devote most of our attention to capital market theory (CMT), which begins where portfolio theory ends. CMT provides a model for pricing risky assets.[1] While CMT has its shortcomings, and arbitrage pricing theory provides an alternative, it remains the case that most investors are much more likely to encounter, and use, CMT in the form of the CAPM.

---

[1] Much of this analysis is attributable to the work of Sharpe. See W. Sharpe, "Capital Asset Prices: A Theory of Market Equilibrium under Conditions of Risk," *The Journal of Finance*, 19 (September 1964): pp. 425–442. Lintner and Mossin developed a similar analysis.

AFTER READING THIS CHAPTER YOU WILL BE ABLE TO:

▶ Understand capital market theory as an extension of portfolio theory.

▶ Recognize the capital market line, which applies to efficient portfolios, and the security market line, which applies to all portfolios as well as individual securities.

▶ Understand and use the capital asset pricing model (CAPM) equation to calculate the required rate of return for a security.

▶ Recognize an alternative theory of how assets are priced, arbitrage pricing theory.

Capital Market Theory

Capital market theory is a positive theory in that it hypothesizes how investors do behave rather than how investors should behave, as in the case of modern portfolio theory (MPT). It is reasonable to view capital market theory as an extension of portfolio theory, but it is important to understand that MPT is not based on the validity, or lack thereof, of capital market theory.

The specific equilibrium model of interest to many investors is known as the capital asset pricing model, typically referred to as the CAPM. It allows us to assess the relevant risk of an individual security as well as to assess the relationship between risk and the returns expected from investing. The CAPM is attractive as an equilibrium model because of its simplicity and its implications. As a result of serious challenges to the model over time, however, alternatives have been developed. The primary alternative to the CAPM is arbitrage pricing theory, or APT, which allows for multiple sources of risk.

CAPITAL MARKET THEORY ASSUMPTIONS

Capital market theory involves a set of predictions concerning equilibrium expected returns on risky assets. It typically is derived by making some simplifying assumptions in order to facilitate the analysis and help us to more easily understand the arguments without fundamentally changing the predictions of asset pricing theory.

Capital market theory builds on Markowitz portfolio theory. Each investor is assumed to diversify his or her portfolio according to the Markowitz model, choosing a location on the efficient frontier that matches his or her return-risk references. Because of the complexity of the real world, additional assumptions are made to make individuals more alike:

1. All investors can borrow or lend money at the risk-free rate of return (designated RF in this text).

2. All investors have identical probability distributions for future rates of return; they have **homogeneous expectations** with respect to the three inputs of the portfolio model explained in Chapter 7: expected returns, the variance of returns, and the correlation matrix. Therefore, given a set of security prices and a risk-free rate, all investors use the same information to generate an efficient frontier.

Homogeneous Expectations Investors have the same expectations regarding the expected return and risk of securities

3. All investors have the same one-period time horizon.

4. There are no transaction costs.

5. There are no personal income taxes—investors are indifferent between capital gains and dividends.

6. There is no inflation.

7. There are many investors, and no single investor can affect the price of a stock through his or her buying and selling decisions. Investors are price-takers and act as if prices are unaffected by their own trades.
8. Capital markets are in equilibrium.

Realism of the Assumptions   These assumptions appear unrealistic and often disturb investors encountering capital market theory for the first time. However, the important issue is how well the theory predicts or describes reality, and not the realism of its assumptions. If capital market theory does a good job of explaining the returns on risky assets, it is very useful and the assumptions made in deriving the theory are of less importance.

Most of these assumptions can be relaxed without significant effects on the capital asset pricing model (CAPM) or its implications; in other words, the CAPM is robust.[2] Although the results from such a relaxation of the assumptions may be less clear-cut and precise, no significant damage is done. Many conclusions of the basic model still hold.

Finally, most investors recognize that all of the assumptions of capital market theory are not unrealistic. For example, some institutional investors such as pension funds are tax-exempt, and brokerage costs today, as a percentage of the transaction, are very, very small. Nor is it too unreasonable to assume that for the one-period horizon of the model, inflation may be fully (or mostly) anticipated and, therefore, not a major factor.

INTRODUCTION OF THE RISK-FREE ASSET

The first assumption of capital market theory listed above is that investors can borrow and lend at the risk-free rate. Although the introduction of a risk-free asset appears to be a simple step to take in the evolution of portfolio and capital market theory, it is a very significant step. In fact, it is the introduction of a risk-free asset that allows us to develop capital market theory from portfolio theory.

With the introduction of a risk-free asset, investors can now invest part of their wealth in this asset and the remainder in any of the risky portfolios in the Markowitz efficient set. This allows Markowitz portfolio theory to be extended in such a way that the efficient frontier is completely changed, which in turn leads to a general theory for pricing assets under uncertainty.

Defining a Risk-Free Asset   A risk-free asset can be defined as one with a certain-to-be-earned expected return and a variance of return of zero. (Note, however, that this is a nominal return and not a real return, which is uncertain because inflation is uncertain.) Since variance = 0, the nominal risk-free rate in each period will be equal to its expected value. Furthermore, the covariance between the risk-free asset and any risky asset i will be zero.

The true risk-free asset is best thought of as a Treasury security, which has little or no practical risk of default, with a maturity matching the holding period of the investor. In this case, the amount of money to be received at the end of the holding period is known with certainty at the beginning of the period. The Treasury bill (discussed in Chapter 2) typically is taken to be the risk-free asset, and its rate of return is referred to here as RF.

RISK-FREE BORROWING AND LENDING

Assume that the efficient frontier, as shown by the arc AB in Figure 9-1, has been derived by an investor. The arc AB delineates the efficient set of portfolios of *risky* assets as explained in

---

[2] For a discussion of changing these assumptions, see E. Elton, M. Gruber, S. Brown, and W. Goetzmann, *Modern Portfolio Theory and Investment Analysis*, 8th edition (New York: John Wiley & Sons, 2010), Chapter 14.

Figure 9-1

The Markowitz Efficient Frontier and the Possibilities Resulting from Introducing a Risk-Free Asset.

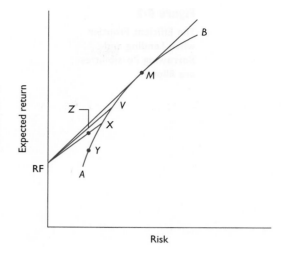

Chapter 8. (For simplicity, assume these are portfolios of common stocks.) We now introduce a risk-free asset with return RF and $\sigma = 0$.

As shown in Figure 9-1, the return on the risk-free asset (RF) will plot on the vertical axis because the risk is zero. Investors can combine this riskless asset with the efficient set of portfolios on the efficient frontier. By drawing a line between RF and various risky portfolios on the efficient frontier, we can examine combinations of risk-return possibilities that did not exist previously.

Lending Possibilities   In Figure 9-1 a new line could be drawn between RF and the Markowitz efficient frontier above point X, for example, connecting RF to point V. Each successively higher line will dominate the preceding set of portfolios. This process ends when a line is drawn tangent to the efficient set of risky portfolios, given a vertical intercept of RF. In Figure 9-1, we call this tangency point M. The set of portfolio opportunities on this line (RF to M) dominates all portfolios below it.

The straight line from RF to the efficient frontier at point M, RF-M, dominates all straight lines below it and contains the superior *lending portfolios* given the Markowitz efficient set depicted in Figure 9-1. Lending refers to the purchase of a riskless asset such as Treasury bills, because by making such a purchase, the investor is lending money to the issuer of the securities, the U.S. government. We can think of this risk-free lending simply as *risk-free investing*.

Borrowing Possibilities   What if we extend this analysis to allow investors to borrow money? The investor is no longer restricted to his or her wealth when investing in risky assets. Technically, we are short-selling the riskless asset. One way to accomplish this borrowing is to buy stocks on margin, which has a current initial margin requirement of 50 percent. We will assume that investors can also borrow at the risk-free rate RF.[3] This assumption can be removed without changing the basic arguments.

Borrowing additional investable funds and investing them together with the investor's own wealth allows investors to seek higher expected returns while assuming greater risk. These

---

[3] Keep in mind that with lending the investor earns a rate RF, whereas with borrowing the investor pays the rate RF on the borrowed funds.

Figure 9-2

The Efficient Frontier when Lending and Borrowing Possibilities are Allowed.

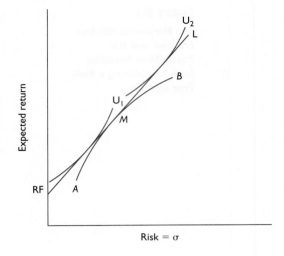

borrowed funds can be used to leverage the portfolio position beyond point M, the point of tangency between the straight line emanating from RF and the efficient frontier AB. As in the lending discussion, point M represents 100 percent of an investor's wealth in the risky asset portfolio M. The straight line RF-M is now extended upward, as shown in Figure 9-2, and can be designated RF-M-L.

Checking Your Understanding

1. Why is the introduction of risk-free borrowing and lending such an important change relative to where the Markowitz analysis left off?

The Equilibrium Return-Risk Tradeoff

Given the previous analysis, we can now derive some predictions concerning equilibrium expected returns and risk. On an overall basis, we need an equilibrium model that encompasses two important relationships.

- ❑ The capital market line specifies the equilibrium relationship between expected return and risk for efficient portfolios.
- ❑ The security market line specifies the equilibrium relationship between expected return and systematic risk. It applies to individual securities as well as portfolios.

THE CAPITAL MARKET LINE

The straight line shown in Figure 9-2, which traces out the risk-return tradeoff for efficient portfolios, is tangent to the Markowitz efficient frontier at point M and has a vertical intercept RF. We now know that portfolio M is the tangency point to a straight line drawn from RF to the efficient frontier, and that this straight line is the best obtainable efficient-set line. All investors will hold portfolio M as their optimal risky portfolio, and all investors will be somewhere on this steepest tradeoff line between expected return and risk, because it represents those combinations of risk-free investing/borrowing and portfolio M that yield the highest return obtainable for a given level of risk.

Let's summarize what we have learned so far:

1. A risk-averse investor makes investment decisions based on Markowitz principles. Such investors select efficient portfolios of risky assets.
2. Investors can borrow and lend freely at the risk-free rate.
3. Each investor should construct an optimal portfolio that matches his or her preferred risk-return combination. Conservative investors lend, and aggressive investors borrow.
4. All investors can construct an optimal portfolio by combining an efficient portfolio, M, with a risk-free asset (fund). The result is a straight line in expected return, standard deviation of return space.

Defining the Capital Market Line   This straight line, usually referred to as the **Capital Market Line (CML)**, depicts the equilibrium conditions that prevail in the market for *efficient portfolios* consisting of the optimal portfolio of risky assets and the risk-free asset. All combinations of the risk-free asset and the risky portfolio M are on the CML, and, in equilibrium, all investors will end up with a portfolio somewhere on the CML based on their risk tolerance.

Capital Market Line (CML) The tradeoff between expected return and risk for efficient portfolios

Understanding the CML   The CML is shown as a straight line in Figure 9-3 without the now-dominated Markowitz frontier. We know that this line has an intercept of RF. If investors are to invest in risky assets, they must be compensated for this additional risk with a risk premium. The vertical distance between the risk-free rate and the CML at point M in Figure 9-3 is the amount of return expected for bearing the risk of owning a portfolio of stocks, that is, the excess return above the risk-free rate. At that point, the amount of risk for the risky portfolio of stocks is given by the horizontal dotted line between RF and σ_M.

Therefore,

$$\frac{E(R_M) - RF}{\sigma_M} = \text{Slope of the CML}$$

$$= \text{Expected return-risk tradeoff for efficient portfolios}$$

Figure 9-3

The Capital Market Line and the Components of its Slope.

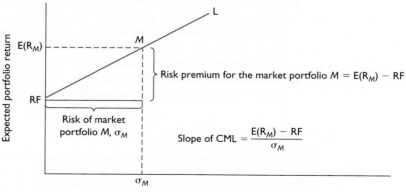

The slope of the CML is the *market price of risk* for efficient portfolios. It is also called the equilibrium market price of risk.[4] It indicates the additional return that the market demands for each percentage increase in a portfolio's risk, that is, in its standard deviation of return.

Example 9-1   Assume that the expected return on portfolio M is 13 percent, with a standard deviation of 20 percent, and that RF is 5 percent. The slope of the CML is

$$(0.13 - 0.05)/0.20 = 0.40$$

In our example a risk premium of 0.40 indicates that the market demands this amount of return for each percentage increase in a portfolio's risk.

The Equation for the CML   We now know the intercept and slope of the CML. Since the CML is the tradeoff between expected return and risk for efficient portfolios, and risk is being measured by the standard deviation, the equation for the CML is shown as Equation 9-1:

$$E(R_p) = RF + \frac{E(R_M) - RF}{\sigma_M} \sigma p \qquad (9\text{-}1)$$

where

$$\begin{aligned}
E(R_p) &= \text{the expected return on any efficient portfolio on the CML} \\
RF &= \text{the rate of return on the risk-free asset} \\
E(R_M) &= \text{the expected return on the market portfolio M} \\
\sigma_M &= \text{the standard deviation of the returns on the market portfolio} \\
\sigma_p &= \text{the standard deviation of the efficient portfolio being considered}
\end{aligned}$$

In words, the expected return for any portfolio on the CML is equal to the risk-free rate plus a risk premium. The risk premium is the product of the market price of risk and the amount of risk for the portfolio under consideration.

Important Points About the CML   The following points should be noted about the CML:

1. Only efficient portfolios consisting of the risk-free asset and portfolio M lie on the CML. Portfolio M, the market portfolio of risky securities, contains all securities weighted by their respective market values—it is the optimum combination of risky securities and is, by definition, an efficient portfolio. The risk-free asset has no risk. Therefore, all combinations of these two assets on the CML are efficient portfolios.
2. As a statement of equilibrium, the CML must always be upward-sloping, because the price of risk must always be positive. Remember that the CML is formulated in a world

---

[4] The assumption throughout this discussion is that $E(R_M)$ is greater than RF. This is the only reasonable assumption to make, because the CAPM is concerned with expected returns (i.e., ex ante returns). After the fact, this assumption may not hold for particular periods—that is, over historical periods such as a year, RF has exceeded the return on the market, which is sometimes negative.

of expected return, and risk-averse investors will not invest unless they expect to be compensated for the risk. The greater the risk, the greater the expected return.

3. On a historical basis, for some particular period of time such as a year or two, or four consecutive quarters, the CML can be downward-sloping; that is, the return on RF exceeds the return on the market portfolio. This does not negate the validity of the CML; it merely indicates that returns actually realized differ from those that were expected. Obviously, investor expectations are not always realized. (If they were, there would be no risk.) Thus, although the CML must be upward-sloping ex ante (before the fact), it can be, and sometimes is, downward-sloping ex post (after the fact).

4. The CML can be used to determine the optimal expected returns associated with different portfolio risk levels. Therefore, the CML indicates the required return for each portfolio risk level.

Market Portfolio The portfolio of all risky assets, with each asset weighted by the ratio of its market value to the market value of all risky assets

The Market Portfolio   Portfolio M in Figure 9-2 is called the **market portfolio** of risky securities. It is the highest point of tangency between RF and the efficient frontier and is *the* optimal risky portfolio. All investors would want to be on the optimal line RF-M-L, and, unless they invested 100 percent of their wealth in the risk-free asset, they would own portfolio M with some portion of their investable wealth, or they would invest their own wealth plus borrowed funds in portfolio M.

✓   Portfolio M is the optimal portfolio of risky assets.[5]

Why do all investors hold identical risky portfolios? Based on our assumptions above, all investors use the same Markowitz analysis on the same set of securities, have the same expected returns and covariances, and have an identical time horizon. Therefore, they will arrive at the same optimal risky portfolio, and it will be the market portfolio, designated M.

It is critical to note that although investors take different positions on the straight-line efficient set in Figure 9-2, all investors are investing in portfolio M, the same portfolio of risky assets. This portfolio will always consist of all risky assets in existence. The emergence of the market portfolio as the optimal efficient portfolio is the most important implication of the CAPM.

In equilibrium, all risky assets must be in portfolio M because all investors are assumed to arrive at, and hold, the same risky portfolio. If the optimal portfolio did not include a particular asset, the price of this asset would decline dramatically until it became an attractive investment opportunity. At some point investors will purchase it, and it will be included in the market portfolio. Because the market portfolio includes all risky assets, *portfolio M is completely diversified*. Portfolio M contains only market (systematic) risk, which, even with perfect diversification, cannot be eliminated because it is the result of macroeconomic factors that affect the value of all securities.

---

[5] All assets are included in portfolio M in proportion to their market value. For example, if the market value of IBM constitutes 2 percent of the market value of all risky assets, IBM will constitute 2 percent of the market value of portfolio M, and, therefore, 2 percent of the market value of each investor's portfolio of risky assets. Therefore, we can state that security *i*'s percentage in the risky portfolio M is equal to the total market value of security *i* relative to the total market value of all securities.

In theory, the market portfolio should include all risky assets worldwide, both financial (bonds, options, futures, etc.) and real (gold, real estate, etc.), in their proper proportions. The global aspects of such a portfolio are important to note. By one estimate, the value of non-U.S. assets exceeds 60 percent of the world total. U.S. equities make up only about 10 percent of total world assets. Therefore, international diversification is clearly important. A worldwide portfolio, if it could be constructed, would be completely diversified. Of course, the market portfolio is unobservable.

The market portfolio is often proxied by the portfolio of all common stocks, which, in turn, is proxied by a market index such as the Standard & Poor's 500 Composite Index, which has been used throughout the text. Therefore, to facilitate this discussion, think of portfolio M as a broad market index such as the S&P 500 Index. The market portfolio is, of course, a risky portfolio, because it consists of risky common stocks, and its risk will be designated σ_M.

The Separation Theorem   We have established that each investor will hold combinations of the risk-free asset (either lending or borrowing) and the tangency portfolio from the efficient frontier, which we now know is the market portfolio M. Because we are assuming homogeneous expectations, in equilibrium all investors will determine the same tangency portfolio. Further, under the assumptions of CMT all investors agree on the risk-free rate. Therefore, the linear efficient set shown in Figure 9-2 now applies to all investors.

Borrowing and lending possibilities, combined with one portfolio of risky assets, M, offer an investor whatever risk-expected return combination he or she seeks; that is, investors can be anywhere they choose on this line, depending on their risk-return preferences. An investor could

(a) Invest 100 percent of investable funds in the risk-free asset, providing an expected return of RF and zero risk
(b) Invest 100 percent of investable funds in risky-asset portfolio M, offering $E(R_M)$, with its risk σ_M
(c) Invest in any combination of return and risk between these two points, obtained by varying the proportion w_{RF} invested in the risk-free asset
(d) Invest more than 100 percent of investable funds in the risky-asset portfolio M by borrowing money at the rate RF, thereby increasing both the expected return and the risk beyond that offered by portfolio M

Different investors will choose different portfolios because of their risk preferences (they have different indifference curves), but they will choose the same combination of risky securities as denoted by the tangency point in Figure 9-2, M. Investors will then borrow or lend to achieve various positions on the linear tradeoff between expected return and risk.

Unlike the Markowitz analysis, it is not necessary to match each client's indifference curves with a particular efficient portfolio, because only one efficient portfolio is held by all investors. Rather, each client will use his or her indifference curves to determine where along the new efficient frontier RF-M-L he or she should be. In effect, each client must determine how much of investable funds should be lent or borrowed at RF and how much should be invested in portfolio M. This result is referred to as a separation property.

Separation Theorem
The idea that the decision of which portfolio of risky assets to hold is separate from the decision of how to allocate investable funds between the risk-free asset and the risky asset

The **separation theorem** states that the investment decision (which portfolio of risky assets to hold) is separate from the financing decision (how to allocate investable funds between the risk-free asset and the risky asset).

▪ The investment decision is a technical decision not involving the investor. The risky portfolio M is optimal for every investor regardless of that investor's utility function.
▪ The financing decision depends on an investor's preferences and is the decision of the investor.

All investors, by investing in the same portfolio of risky assets (M) and either borrowing or lending at the rate RF, can achieve any point on the straight line RF-M-L in Figure 9-2. Each point on that line represents a different expected return-risk tradeoff. An investor with utility curve U1 will be at the lower end of the line, representing a combination of lending and investment in M. On the other hand, utility curve U2 represents an investor borrowing at the rate RF to invest in risky assets—specifically, portfolio M.

The capital market line depicts the risk-return tradeoff in the financial markets in equilibrium. However, it applies only to efficient portfolios and cannot be used to assess the equilibrium expected return on a single security.

What about individual securities or inefficient portfolios? To relate expected return and risk for any asset or portfolio, efficient or inefficient, we need the expected return–beta form of the capital asset pricing model.

Checking Your Understanding

2. Explain why the CML applies only to efficient portfolios.

3. Why, under capital market theory, do investors not have to make the investment decision?

THE SECURITY MARKET LINE

The capital market line depicts the risk-return tradeoff in the financial markets in equilibrium. However, it applies only to efficient portfolios and cannot be used to assess the equilibrium expected return for a single security. What about individual securities or inefficient portfolios?

Under the CAPM all investors will hold the market portfolio, which is the benchmark portfolio against which other portfolios are measured. How does an individual security contribute to the risk of the market portfolio?

Investors should expect a risk premium for buying a risky asset such as a stock. The greater the riskiness of that stock, the higher the risk premium should be. If investors hold well-diversified portfolios, they should be interested in portfolio risk rather than individual security risk. Different stocks will affect a well-diversified portfolio differently. The relevant risk for an individual stock is its contribution to the riskiness of a well-diversified portfolio. And the risk of a well-diversified portfolio is market risk, or systematic risk, which is non-diversifiable (see Chapter 8).

We now know that investors should hold diversified portfolios to reduce the portfolio risk. When an investor adds a security to a large portfolio, what matters is the security's average covariance with the other securities in the portfolio. We also now know that under CMT all investors will hold the same portfolio of risky assets, the market portfolio. Therefore, the risk that matters when we consider any security is its covariance with the market portfolio.

✓ The major conclusion of the CAPM is: The relevant risk of any security is the amount of risk that security contributes to a well-diversified portfolio.

We could relate the expected return on a stock to its covariance with the market portfolio. This would result in an equation similar to Equation 9-1, except now it applies to any single asset i.

$$E(R_i) = RF + \frac{E(R_M) - RF}{\sigma_M^2} Cov_{i,M} \qquad (9\text{-}2)$$

where

$E(R_i)$ = the expected return on any individual security i

RF = the rate of return on the risk-free asset

$E(R_M)$ = the expected return on the market portfolio M

σ_M^2 = the variance of the returns on the market portfolio

$Cov_{i,M}$ = the covariance of the stock with the market

Equation 9-2 states that the expected return for any security is the sum of the risk-free rate and a risk premium. This risk premium reflects the asset's covariance with the market portfolio.

Beta   We know that the relevant risk measure for any asset i is its covariance with the market portfolio. However, it is more convenient to use a standardized measure of the systematic risk that cannot be avoided through diversification. **Beta** relates the covariance of an asset with the market portfolio to the variance of the market portfolio, and is defined as

Beta A measure of volatility, or relative systematic risk, for a stock or a portfolio

$$\beta_i = COV_{i,M}/\sigma_M^2$$

✓   Beta is a *relative measure* of risk—the risk of an individual stock relative to the market portfolio of all stocks.

If the security's returns move more (less) than the market's returns as the latter changes, the security's returns have more (less) volatility (fluctuations in price) than those of the market. For example, a security whose returns rise or fall on average 15 percent when the market return rises or falls 10 percent is said to be an aggressive, or volatile, security.

Securities with different slopes have different sensitivities to the returns of the market index. If the slope of this relationship for a particular security is a 45-degree angle, as shown for security B in Figure 9-4, the beta is 1.0. This means that for every 1 percent change in the market's return, *on average* this security's returns change 1 percent. The market portfolio has a beta of 1.0.

Example 9-2

In Figure 9-4 Security A's beta of 1.5 indicates that, *on average*, security returns are 1.5 times as volatile as market returns, both up and down. A security whose returns rise or fall on average 15 percent when the market return rises or falls 10 percent is said to be an aggressive, or volatile, security. If the line is less steep than the 45-degree line, beta is less than 1.0; this indicates that on average, a stock's returns have less volatility than the market as a whole. For example, security C's beta of 0.6 indicates that stock returns move up or down, on average, only 60 percent as much as the market as a whole.

Figure 9-4

Illustrative Betas of 1.5 (A), 1.0 (B), and 0.6 (C).

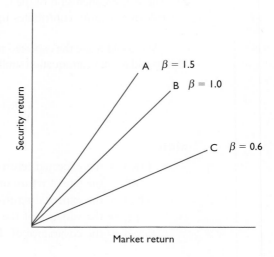

In summary, the aggregate market has a beta of 1.0. More volatile (risky) stocks have betas larger than 1.0, and less volatile (risky) stocks have betas smaller than 1.0. As a relative measure of risk, beta is very convenient. Beta is useful for comparing the relative systematic risk of different stocks and, in practice, is used by investors to judge a stock's riskiness. Stocks can be ranked by their betas. Because the variance of the market is a constant across all securities for a particular period, ranking stocks by beta is the same as ranking them by their absolute systematic risk. Stocks with high (low) betas are said to be high- (low-) risk securities.

Investments Intuition

Investors first exposed to the concepts of beta and **CAPM** may hear someone say that a high-beta stock or group of stocks held last year produced a lower return than did low-beta stocks, and therefore something is wrong with this concept. This is a fallacy, however, because the **CAPM** relationship is an equilibrium relationship expected to prevail. High-beta stocks are more risky than low-beta stocks and are expected to produce higher returns. However, they will not typically produce higher returns every period and over all intervals of time. If they did, they would be less risky than low-beta stocks, not more risky. The correct statement is that over long periods of time, high-beta stocks should produce higher average returns.

Security Market Line (SML) The graphical depiction of the CAPM

The CAPM's Expected Return–Beta Relationship   The **Security Market Line (SML)** is the CAPM specification of how risk and expected rate of return for any asset, security or portfolio, are related. This theory posits a linear relationship between an asset's risk and its expected rate of return. This linear relationship, called the security market line (SML), is shown in Figure 9-5. Required rate of return is on the vertical axis and beta, the measure of risk, is on the horizontal return.[6] The slope of the line is the difference between the required rate of return on the market index and RF, the risk-free rate.

Investments Intuition

As we could (and should) expect, Figure 9-5 again demonstrates that if investors are to seek higher expected returns, they must assume a larger risk as measured by beta, the relative measure of systematic risk. The tradeoff between expected return and risk must always be positive. In Figure 9-5 the vertical axis can be thought of as the expected return for an asset. In equilibrium, investors require a minimum expected return before they will invest in a particular security. That is, given its risk, a security must offer some minimum expected return before a given investor can be persuaded to purchase it. Thus, in discussing the SML concept, we are simultaneously talking about the required and expected rate of return.

Capital Asset Pricing Model (CAPM) Relates the required rate of return for any security with the risk for that security as measured by beta

The **Capital Asset Pricing Model (CAPM)** formally relates the expected rate of return for any security or portfolio with the relevant risk measure. The CAPM's expected return–beta relationship is the most-often cited form of the relationship. Beta is the relevant measure of risk that cannot be diversified away in a portfolio of securities and, as such, is the measure that investors should consider in their portfolio management decision process.

---

[6] We use required rate of return in the figure to point out that in equilibrium the expected and required rates of return are the same for a security.

Figure 9-5

**The Security Market
Line (SML).**

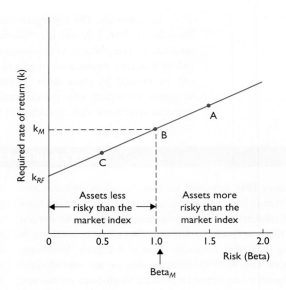

The CAPM in its expected return–beta relationship form is a simple but elegant statement. It says that the expected rate of return on an asset is a function of the two components of the required rate of return—the risk-free rate and the risk premium. Thus,

$$k_i = \text{Risk-free rate} + \text{Risk premium}$$
$$= \text{RF} + \beta_i[E(R_M) - \text{RF}]$$

(9-3)

where

$$k_i = \text{the required rate of return on asset } i$$
$$E(R_M) = \text{the expected rate of return on the market portfolio}$$
$$\beta_i = \text{the beta coefficient for asset } i$$

The risk premium should reflect all the uncertainty involved in the asset. Thinking of risk in terms of its traditional sources, such components as the business risk and the financial risk of a corporation would certainly contribute to the risk premium demanded by investors for purchasing the common stock of the corporation. After all, the risk to the investor is that the expected return will not be realized because of unforeseen events.

The particular business that a company is in will significantly affect the risk to the investor. One has only to look at the textile and steel industries in the last few years to appreciate business risk [which leads to an understanding of why industry analysis (Chapter 14) is important]. And the financial decisions that a firm makes (or fails to make) will also affect the riskiness of the stock.

The CAPM relationship described in Equation 9-3 provides an explicit measure of the risk premium. It is the product of the beta for a particular security i and the **market risk premium**, $E(R_M) - \text{RF}$. Thus,

Market Risk Premium
The difference between
the expected return for the
equities market and the
risk-free rate of return

$$\text{Risk premium for security } i = \beta_i(\text{market risk premium})$$
$$= \beta_i[E(R_M) - \text{RF}]$$

Investments Intuition

Equation 9-3 indicates that securities with betas greater than the market beta of 1.0 should have larger risk premiums than that of the average stock and therefore, when added to RF, larger required rates of return. This is exactly what investors should expect, since beta is a measure of risk, and greater risk should be accompanied by greater return. Conversely, securities with betas less than that of the market are less risky and should have required rates of return lower than that for the market as a whole. This will be the indicated result from the CAPM, because the risk premium for the security will be less than the market risk premium and, when added to RF, will produce a lower required rate of return for the security.

The CAPM's expected return–beta relationship is a simple but elegant statement about expected (required) return and risk for any security or portfolio. It formalizes the basis of investments, which is that the greater the risk assumed, the greater the expected (required) return should be. This relationship states that an investor requires (expects) a return on a risky asset equal to the return on a risk-free asset plus a risk premium, and the greater the risk assumed, the greater the risk premium.

Example 9-3

Assume that the beta for IBM is 1.15. Also assume that RF is 0.05 and that the expected return on the market is 0.12. The required return for IBM can be calculated as

$$k_{IBM} = 0.05 + 1.15(0.12 - 0.05)$$
$$= 13.05\%$$

The required (or expected) return for IBM is, as it should be, larger than that of the market because IBM's beta is larger—once again, the greater the risk assumed, the larger the required return.

Over-and-Undervalued Securities   The SML has important implications for security prices. In equilibrium, each security should lie on the SML because the expected return on the security should be that needed to compensate investors for the systematic risk.

What happens if investors determine that a security does not lie on the SML? To make this determination, they must employ a separate methodology to estimate the expected returns for securities. In other words, a SML can be fitted to a sample of securities to determine the required return-risk tradeoff that exists. Knowing the beta for any stock, we can determine the required return from the SML. Then, independently estimating the expected return from, say, fundamental analysis, an investor can assess a security in relation to the SML and determine whether it is under- or overvalued.

Example 9-4

In Figure 9-6, two securities are plotted around the SML. Security X has a high expected return derived from fundamental analysis and plots above the SML; security Y has a low expected return and plots below the SML. Which is undervalued?

Security X, plotting above the SML, is undervalued because it offers more expected return than investors require, given its level of systematic risk. Investors require a minimum expected return of $E(R_X)$, but security X, according to fundamental analysis, is offering $E(R_X')$. If investors recognize this, they will do the following:

> Purchase security X, because it offers more return than required. This demand will drive up the price of X, as more of it is purchased. The return will be driven down, until it is at the level indicated by the SML.

Now consider security Y. This security, according to investors' fundamental analysis, does not offer enough expected return given its level of systematic risk. Investors require $E(R_Y)$ for security Y, based on the SML, but Y offers only $E(R_Y')$. As investors recognize this, they will do the following:

> Sell security Y (or perhaps sell Y short), because it offers less than the required return. This increase in the supply of Y will drive down its price. The return will be driven up for new buyers because any dividends paid are now relative to a lower price, as is any expected price appreciation. The price will fall until the expected return rises enough to reach the SML and the security is once again in equilibrium.

Alpha The difference between an independently determined expected rate of return on a stock and the required rate of return on that stock.

Alpha is the expected return for a stock above or below the expected return predicted for the stock by the CAPM. We can see this clearly in Figure 9-6. Alpha will be zero for stocks that are fairly priced; that is, on the SML. According to the CAPM, the expected value for alpha is zero for all securities.

Checking Your Understanding

4. We can relate the expected return on a security to its covariance with the market portfolio. Why, then, is the CAPM equation written using beta instead of covariance?
5. Why do overvalued securities plot below the SML?

Figure 9-6

Overvalued and Under-valued Securities Using the SML.

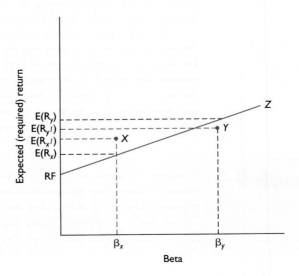

Estimating the SML

To implement the SML approach described here, an investor needs estimates of the return on the risk-free asset, the expected return on the market index, and the beta for an individual security. How difficult are these to obtain?

The return on a risk-free asset, RF, should be the easiest of the three variables to obtain. In estimating RF, the investor can use the return on Treasury bills for the coming period (e.g., a year).

Estimating the market return is more difficult, because the expected return for the market index is not observable. Furthermore, several different market indexes could be used. Estimates of the market return could be derived from a study of previous market returns (such as the Standard & Poor's data in Table 6-1). Alternatively, probability estimates of market returns could be made, and the expected value calculated. This would provide an estimate of both the expected return and the standard deviation for the market.

Finally, it is necessary to estimate the betas for individual securities. This is a crucial part of the CAPM estimation process. The estimates of RF and the expected return on the market are the same for each security being evaluated. Only beta is unique, bringing together the investor's expectations of returns for the stock with those for the market. Beta is the only company-specific factor in the CAPM; therefore, risk is the only asset-specific forecast that must be made in the CAPM.

ESTIMATING BETA

Market Model Relates the return on each stock to the return on the market, using a linear relationship with intercept and slope

A less restrictive form of the single index model referred to in Chapter 8 is known as the **market model**. This model is identical to the single index model except that the assumption of the error terms for different securities being uncorrelated is not made.

The market model equation can be expressed as

$$R_i = \alpha_i + \beta_i R_M + e_i \tag{9-4}$$

where

R_i = the return (TR) on security i
R_M = the return (TR) on the market index
α_i = the intercept term
β_i = the slope term
e_i = the random residual error

The market model produces an estimate of return for any stock.

To estimate the market model, the TRs for stock i can be regressed on the corresponding TRs for the market index. Estimates will be obtained of α_i (the constant return on security i that is earned regardless of the level of market returns) and β_i (the slope coefficient that indicates the expected increase in a security's return for a 1 percent increase in market return). This is how the estimate of a stock's beta is often derived.

Example 9-5

To illustrate the calculation of the Market Model, we use Total Return (TR) data for the Coca-Cola company (ticker symbol "KO"). Fitting a regression equation to 60 months of return data along with corresponding TRs for the S&P 500, the estimated equation is

$$R_{KO} = 1.06 + 1.149 R_{S\&P500}$$

Figure 9-7

The Characteristic Line for Coca-Cola, Monthly Data.

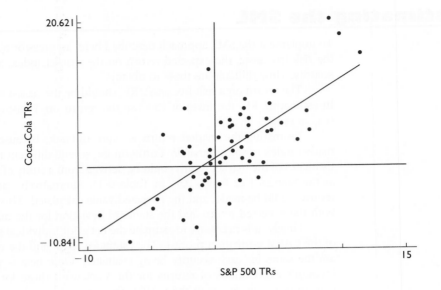

When the TRs for a stock are plotted against the market index TRs, the regression line fitted to these points is referred to as the **characteristic line**. Coca-Cola's characteristic line is shown in Figure 9-7.

The characteristic line is often fitted using *excess returns*. The excess return is calculated by subtracting out the risk-free rate, RF, from both the return on the stock and the return on the market.

In excess return form, the same analysis as before applies. The alpha is the intercept of the characteristic line on the vertical axis and, in theory, should be zero for any stock. It measures the excess return for a stock when the excess return for the market portfolio is zero. In excess return form, the beta coefficient remains the slope of the characteristic line. It measures the sensitivity of a stock's excess return to that of the market portfolio.

The variance of the error term measures the variability of a stock's excess return not associated with movements in the market's excess return. Diversification can reduce this variability.

Many brokerage houses and investment advisory services report betas as part of the total information given for individual stocks. For example, *The Value Line Investment Survey* reports the beta for each stock covered, as do such brokerage firms as Merrill Lynch. Both measures of risk discussed above, standard deviation and beta, are widely known and discussed by investors.

Whether we use the single index model or the market model, beta can be estimated using regression analysis. However, the values of α_i and β_i obtained in this manner are estimates of the true parameters and are subject to error. Furthermore, beta can shift over time as a company's situation changes. A legitimate question, therefore, is how accurate are the estimates of beta?

As noted, beta is usually estimated by fitting a characteristic line to the data. However, this is an estimate of the beta called for in the CAPM. The market proxy used in the equations for estimating beta may not fully reflect the market portfolio specified in the CAPM. Furthermore, several points should be kept in mind:

1. We are trying to estimate the future beta for a security, which may differ from the historical beta.
2. In theory, the independent variable R_M represents the total of all marketable assets in the economy. This is typically approximated with a stock market index, which, in turn, is an approximation of the return on all common stocks.

Characteristic Line A regression equation used to estimate beta by regressing stock returns on market returns

3. The characteristic line can be fitted over varying numbers of observations and time periods. There is no one correct period or number of observations for calculating beta. As a result, estimates of beta will vary. For example, *The Value Line Investment Survey* calculates betas from weekly rates of return for five years, whereas other analysts often use monthly rates of return over a comparable period.
4. The regression estimates of α and β from the characteristic line are only estimates of the true α and β, and are subject to error. Thus, these estimates may not be equal to the true α and β.
5. As the fundamental variables (e.g., earnings, cash flow) of a company change, beta should change; that is, the beta is not perfectly stationary over time. This issue is important enough to be considered separately.

Blume found that in comparing nonoverlapping seven-year periods for 1, 2, 4, 7, 10, 21, etc., stocks in a portfolio, the following observations could be made:[7]

1. Betas estimated for individual securities are unstable; that is, they contain relatively little information about future betas.
2. Betas estimated for large portfolios are stable; that is, they contain much information about future betas.

In effect, a large portfolio (e.g., 50 stocks) provides stability because of the averaging effect. Although the betas of some stocks in the portfolio go up from period to period, others go down, and these two movements tend to cancel each other. Furthermore, the errors involved in estimating betas tend to cancel out in a portfolio. Therefore, estimates of portfolio betas show less change from period to period and are much more reliable than are the estimates for individual securities.

Researchers have found that betas in the forecast period are, on average, closer to 1.0 than the estimate obtained using historical data. This would imply that we can improve the estimates of beta by measuring the adjustment in one period and using it as an estimate of the adjustment in the next period. For example, we could adjust each beta toward the average beta by taking half the historical beta and adding it to half of the average beta. Merrill Lynch, the largest brokerage firm, reports adjusted betas based on a technique such as this. Other methods have also been proposed, including a Bayesian estimation technique.

Concepts in Action

Beta Management

Beta has emerged as a key concept in Investments. A measure of relative systematic risk, it relates stock or portfolio returns to the overall market. A portfolio with a beta of 1.0 should perform like the overall market, which by definition has a beta of 1.0. A portfolio with a beta greater than 1.0 would be expected to be more volatile than the market, while a portfolio with a beta less than one would be expected to be less volatile.

Beta management involves adjusting the beta of the portfolio to take account of expected market conditions. If the market is expected to go up (down), the portfolio manager would increase (decrease) the beta of the portfolio. During the 1980s and 1990s the market performed, on average, very strongly, and investors in stocks typically enjoyed good performance across the board. However, a beta management approach could show even better results by

[7] See M. Blume, "Betas and Their Regression Tendencies," *The Journal of Finance*, 10 (June 1975): pp. 785–795; and R. Levy, "On the Short-Term Stationarity of Beta Coefficients," *Financial Analysts Journal*, 27 (December 1971): pp. 55–62.

increasing the beta of the portfolio, leading to returns even better than the market.

With the market declines in 2000–2002, good returns were difficult to come by. Those who had to maintain stock portfolios regardless during these years (such as equity fund managers) but lowered the beta of the portfolio significantly were able to avoid the steep losses suffered by many. Of course, owning Treasury securities and avoiding stocks altogether in 2000–2002 was an even better strategy, in hindsight.

Simple beta management strategies continue to be in play. With low costs, a disciplined approach to managing the beta of the portfolio, along with well-defined goals, should continue to be rewarding. Nevertheless, in today's institutional investing world, merely providing some beta exposure while charging active-management fees is no longer considered appropriate by some overseers, such as pension fund executives. In today's world of lower stock returns and flattened yield curves, the pressures are intense for managers to produce some results beyond what could be attained by a passive approach such as owning a market index.

How has beta management changed over time? In the latter part of the twentieth century, based on the development of the CAPM and beta, investing centered on being in cash or in the market (risky assets), depending upon one's expectations. In today's global environment, the emphasis may be more on examining and shifting assets from one market to another. Some argue that global markets weaken the case for beta management, because the emphasis is more on getting out of one market and into another at the right time.

Tests of the CAPM

The conclusions of the CAPM are entirely sensible:

1. Return and risk are positively related—greater risk should carry greater return.
2. The relevant risk for a security is a measure of its effect on portfolio risk.

The question, therefore, is how well the theory works. After all, the assumptions on which capital market theory rest are, for the most part, unrealistic. To assess the validity of this or any other theory, empirical tests must be performed. If the CAPM is valid, and the market tends to balance out so that realized security returns average out to equal expected returns, equations of the following type can be estimated:

$$R_i = a_1 + a_2 \beta i \tag{9-5}$$

where

R_i = the average return on security i over some number of periods

β_i = the estimated beta for security i

When Equation 9-5 is estimated, a_1 should approximate the average risk-free rate during the periods studied, and a_2 should approximate the average market risk premium during the periods studied.

An extensive literature exists involving tests of capital market theory, in particular, the CAPM. Although it is not possible to summarize the scope of this literature entirely and to reconcile findings from different studies that seem to be in disagreement, the following points represent a reasonable consensus of the empirical results:[8]

1. The SML appears to be linear; that is, the tradeoff between expected (required) return and risk is an upward-sloping straight line.

---

[8] For a discussion of empirical tests of the CAPM, see Elton, Gruber, Brown and Goetzmann, *Modern Portfolio Theory and Investment Analysis*, 8th edition, John Wiley & Sons, Inc,. 2010.

2. The intercept term, a_1, is generally found to be higher than RF.
3. The slope of the CAPM, a_2, is generally found to be less steep than posited by the theory.
4. Although the evidence is mixed, no persuasive case has been made that unsystematic risk commands a risk premium. In other words, investors are rewarded only for assuming systematic risk.

The major problem in testing capital market theory is that it is formulated on an ex ante basis but can be tested only on an ex post basis. We can never know investor expectations with certainty. Therefore, it should come as no surprise that tests of the model have produced conflicting results in some cases, and that the empirical results diverge from the predictions of the model. In fact, it is amazing that the empirical results support the basic CAPM as well as they do. Based on studies of many years of data, it appears that the stock market prices securities on the basis of a linear relationship between systematic risk and return, with diversifiable (unsystematic) risk playing little or no part in the pricing mechanism.

The CAPM has not been proved empirically, nor will it be. In fact, Roll has argued that the CAPM is untestable because the market portfolio, which consists of all risky assets, is unobservable.[9] In effect, Roll argues that tests of the CAPM are actually tests of the mean-variance efficiency of the market portfolio. Nevertheless, the CAPM remains a logical way to view the expected return-risk tradeoff as well as a frequently used model in finance.

Arbitrage Pricing Theory

Arbitrage Pricing Theory (APT) An equilibrium theory of expected returns for securities involving few assumptions about investor preferences

The CAPM is not the only model of security pricing. Another model that has received attention is based on **Arbitrage Pricing Theory (APT)** as developed by Ross and enhanced by others. In recent years APT has emerged as an alternative theory of asset pricing to the CAPM. Its appeal is that it is more general than the CAPM, with less restrictive assumptions. However, like the CAPM, it has limitations, and like the CAPM, it is not the final word in asset pricing.

Similar to the CAPM, or any other asset pricing model, APT posits a relationship between expected return and risk. It does so, however, using different assumptions and procedures. Very importantly, APT is not critically dependent on an underlying market portfolio as is the CAPM, which predicts that only market risk influences expected returns. Instead, APT recognizes that several types of risk may affect security returns.

THE LAW OF ONE PRICE

APT is based on the *law of one price*, which states that two otherwise identical assets cannot sell at different prices. APT assumes that asset returns are linearly related to a set of indexes, where each index represents a factor that influences the return on an asset. Market participants develop expectations about the sensitivities of assets to the factors. They buy and sell securities so that, given the law of one price, securities affected equally by the same factors will have equal expected returns. This buying and selling is the arbitrage process, which determines the prices of securities.

APT states that equilibrium market prices will adjust to eliminate any arbitrage opportunities, which refer to situations where a *zero investment portfolio* can be constructed that will yield a risk-free profit. If arbitrage opportunities arise, a relatively few investors can act to restore equilibrium.

---

[9] R. Roll, "A Critique of the Asset Pricing Theory's Tests; Part I: On Past and Potential Testability of the Theory," *Journal of Financial Economics*, 4 (March 1977): pp. 129–176.

ASSUMPTIONS OF APT

Unlike the CAPM, APT does not assume

1. A single-period investment horizon
2. The absence of taxes
3. Borrowing and lending at the rate RF
4. Investors select portfolios on the basis of expected return and variance

APT, like the CAPM, does assume that

1. Investors have homogeneous beliefs
2. Investors are risk-averse utility maximizers
3. Markets are perfect
4. Returns are generated by a factor model

FACTOR MODELS

Factor Model Used to depict the behavior of security prices by identifying major factors in the economy that affect large numbers of securities

A **factor model** is based on the view that there are underlying *risk factors* that affect realized and expected security returns. These risk factors represent broad economic forces and not company-specific characteristics and, by definition, they represent the element of surprise in the risk factor—the difference between the actual value for the factor and its expected value.

The factors must possess three characteristics:[10]

1. Each risk factor must have a pervasive influence on stock returns. Firm-specific events are not APT risk factors.
2. These risk factors must influence expected return, which means they must have non-zero prices. This issue must be determined empirically, by statistically analyzing stock returns to see which factors pervasively affect returns.
3. At the beginning of each period, the risk factors must be unpredictable to the market as a whole. This raises an important point. In our example above, we used inflation and the economy's output as the two factors affecting portfolio returns. The rate of inflation is **not** an APT risk factor, because it is at least partially predictable. In an economy with reasonable growth where the quarterly rate of inflation has averaged 3 percent on an annual basis, we can reasonably assume that next quarter's inflation rate is not going to be 10 percent. On the other hand, unexpected inflation—the difference between actual inflation and expected inflation—is an APT risk factor. By definition, it cannot be predicted since it is unexpected.

What really matters are the *deviations* of the factors from their expected values. For example, if the expected value of inflation is 5 percent and the actual rate of inflation for a period is only 4 percent, this 1 percent deviation will affect the actual return for the period.

---

[10] See Michael A. Berry, Edwin Burmeister, and Marjorie B. McElroy, "Sorting Out Risks Using Known APT Factors," *Financial Analysts Journal* (March–April 1988): pp. 29–42.

Example 9-6 An investor holds a portfolio of stocks that she thinks is influenced by only two basic economic factors, inflation and the economy's output. Diversification once again plays a role, because the portfolio's sensitivity to all other factors can be eliminated by diversification.

Portfolio return varies directly with output, and inversely with inflation. Each of these factors has an expected value, and the portfolio has an expected return when the factors are at their expected values. If either or both of the factors deviates from expected value, the portfolio return will be affected.

We must measure the sensitivity of each stock in our investor's portfolio to changes in each of the two factors. Each stock will have its own sensitivity to each of the factors. For example, stock #1 (a mortgage company) may be particularly sensitive to inflation and have a sensitivity of 2.0, while stock #2 (a food manufacturer) may have a sensitivity to inflation of only 1.0.

UNDERSTANDING THE APT MODEL

Based on this analysis, we can now understand the APT model. It assumes that investors believe that asset returns are randomly generated according to a n-factor model, which, for security i, can be formally stated as

$$R_i = E(R_i) + \beta_{i1}f_1 + \beta_{i2}f_2 + \cdots + \beta_{in}f_n + e_i \tag{9-6}$$

where

$$
\begin{aligned}
R_i &= \text{the actual (random) rate of return on security } i \text{ in any given period } t \\
E(R_i) &= \text{the expected return on security } i \\
f &= \text{the deviation of a systematic factor F from its expected value} \\
\beta_i &= \text{sensitivity of security } i \text{ to a factor} \\
e_i &= \text{random error term, unique to security } i^{[11]}
\end{aligned}
$$

It is important to note that the expected value of each factor, F, is zero. Therefore, the *f*s in Equation 9-6 are measuring the deviation of each factor from its expected value. Notice in Equation 9-6 that the actual return for a security in a given period will be at the expected or required rate of return if the factors are at expected levels [e.g., $F_1 - E(F_1) = 0$, $F_2 - E(F_2) = 0$, and so forth] and if the chance element represented by the error term is at zero.

A factor model makes no statement about equilibrium. If we transform Equation 9-10 into an equilibrium model, we are saying something about *expected* returns across securities. APT is an equilibrium theory of expected returns that requires a factor model such as Equation 9-6. The equation for expected return on a security is given by Equation 9-7:

$$E(R_i) = a_0 + b_{i1}\overline{F}_1 + b_{i2}\overline{F}_2 + \cdots + b_{in}\overline{F}_n \tag{9-7}$$

where

$$
\begin{aligned}
E(R_i) &= \text{the expected return on security } i \\
a_0 &= \text{the expected return on a security with zero systematic risk} \\
\overline{F} &= \text{the risk premium for a factor (for example, the risk premium} \\
&\quad\ \text{for } F_1 \text{ is equal to } E(F_1) - a_0)
\end{aligned}
$$

---

[11] It is assumed that all covariances between returns on securities are attributable to the effects of the factors; therefore, the error terms are uncorrelated.

With APT, risk is defined in terms of a stock's sensitivity to basic economic factors, while expected return is directly related to sensitivity. As always, expected return increases with risk.

The expected return-risk relationship for the CAPM is

$$E(R_i) = RF + \beta_i[\text{market risk premium}]$$

The CAPM assumes that the only required measure of risk is the sensitivity to the market. The risk premium for a stock depends on this sensitivity and the market risk premium (the difference between the expected return on the market and the risk-free rate).

The expected return-risk relationship for the APT can be described as

$$\begin{aligned} E(R_i) = RF &+ b_{i1}(\text{risk premium for factor 1}) \\ &+ b_{i2}(\text{risk premium for factor 2}) + \cdots \\ &+ b_{in}(\text{risk premium for factor } n) \end{aligned}$$

Note that the sensitivity measures (β_i and b_i) have similar interpretations. They are measures of the relative sensitivity of a security's return to a particular risk premium. Also notice that we are dealing with risk premiums in both cases. Finally, notice that the CAPM relationship is the same as would be provided by APT if there were only one pervasive factor influencing returns. APT is more general than CAPM.

IDENTIFYING THE FACTORS

The problem with APT is that the factors are not well specified, at least ex ante. To implement the APT model, we need to know the factors that account for the differences among security returns. The APT makes no statements about the size or the sign of the F_i's. Both the factor model and these values must be identified empirically. In contrast, with the CAPM the factor that matters is the market portfolio, a concept that is well understood conceptually; however, as noted earlier, Roll has argued that the market portfolio is unobservable.

Early empirical work by Roll and Ross suggested that three to five factors influence security returns and are priced in the market.[12] Typically, systematic factors such as the following have been identified:

1. Changes in expected inflation
2. Unanticipated changes in inflation
3. Unanticipated changes in industrial production
4. Unanticipated changes in the default-risk premium
5. Unanticipated changes in the term structure of interest rates

These factors are related to the components of a valuation model. The first three affect the cash flows of a company while the last two affect the discount rate.

According to APT models, different securities have different sensitivities to these systematic factors, and investor risk preferences are characterized by these dimensions. Each

---

[12] R. Roll and S. Ross, "An Empirical Investigation of the Arbitrage Pricing Theory," *The Journal of Finance*, 35 (December 1980), pp. 1073–1103.

investor has different risk attitudes. Investors could construct a portfolio depending upon desired risk exposure to each of these factors. Knowing the market prices of these risk factors and the sensitivities of securities to changes in the factors, the expected returns for various stocks could be estimated.

Another study has suggested that an APT model that incorporates unanticipated changes in five macroeconomic variables is superior to the CAPM. These five variables are[13]

1. Default risk
2. The term structure of interest rates
3. Inflation or deflation
4. The long-run expected growth rate of profits for the economy
5. Residual market risk

USING APT IN INVESTMENT DECISIONS

Roll and Ross have argued that APT offers an approach to strategic portfolio planning. The idea is to recognize that a few systematic factors affect long-term average returns. Investors should seek to identify the few factors affecting most assets in order to appreciate their influence on portfolio returns. Based on this knowledge, they should seek to structure the portfolio in such a way as to improve its design and performance.

Some researchers have identified and measured, for both economic sectors and industries, the risk exposures associated with APT risk factors such as the five identified above as changes in five macroeconomic variables. These "risk exposure profiles" vary widely. For example, the financial, growth, and transportation sectors were found to be particularly sensitive to default risk, while the utility sector was relatively insensitive to both unexpected inflation and the unexpected change in the growth rate of profits.

An analysis of 82 different industry classifications showed the same result—exposure to different types of risk varies widely. For example, some industries were particularly sensitive to unexpected inflation risk, such as the mobile home building industry, retailers, hotels and motels, toys, and eating places. The industries least sensitive to this risk factor included foods, tire and rubber goods, shoes, and breweries. Several industries showed no significant sensitivity to unexpected inflation risk, such as corn and soybean refiners and sugar refiners.

A portfolio manager could design strategies that would expose them to one or more types of these risk factors, or "sterilize" a portfolio such that its exposure to the unexpected change in the growth rate of profits matched that of the market as a whole. Taking an active approach, a portfolio manager who believes that he or she can forecast a factor realization can build a portfolio that emphasizes or deemphasizes that factor. In doing this, the manager would select stocks that have exposures to the remaining risk factors that are exactly proportional to the market. If the manager is accurate with the forecast—and remember that such a manager must forecast the unexpected component of the risk factor—he or she can outperform the market for that period.

Checking Your Understanding

6. Can the CAPM be considered simply a special case of APT?

---

[13] These factors are based on Berry et al.

Some Conclusions about Asset Pricing

The question of how security prices and equilibrium returns are established—whether as described by the CAPM or APT or some other model—remains open. Some researchers are convinced that the APT model is superior to the CAPM. For example, based on their research using the five factors discussed above, the authors concluded that "[t]he APT model with these five risk factors is vastly superior to both the market model and the CAPM for explaining stock returns." The CAPM relies on the observation of the market portfolio, which, in actuality, cannot be observed. On the other hand, APT offers no clues as to the identity of the factors that are priced in the factor structure.

In the final analysis, neither model has been proven superior. Both rely on expectations which are not directly observable. Additional testing is needed.

Summary

▶ Capital market theory, based on the concept of efficient diversification, describes the pricing of capital assets in the marketplace.

▶ Capital market theory is derived from several assumptions that appear unrealistic; however, the important issue is the ability of the theory to predict. Relaxation of most of the assumptions does not change the major implications of capital market theory.

▶ Risk-free borrowing and lending changes the efficient set to a straight line.

▶ Borrowing and lending possibilities, combined with one portfolio of risky assets, offer an investor whatever risk-expected return combination he or she seeks; that is, investors can be anywhere they choose on this line, depending on their risk-return preferences.

▶ Given risk-free borrowing and lending, the new efficient frontier has a vertical intercept of RF and is tangent to the old efficient frontier at point M, the market portfolio. The new efficient set is no longer a curve, or arc, as in the Markowitz analysis. It is now linear.

▶ All investors can achieve an optimal point on the new efficient frontier by investing in portfolio M and either borrowing or lending at the risk-free rate RF.

▶ The new efficient frontier is called the capital market line, and its slope indicates the equilibrium price of risk in the market. In effect, it is the expected return-risk tradeoff for efficient portfolios.

▶ Ex ante, the CML must always be upward-sloping, although ex post it may be downward-sloping for certain periods.

▶ In theory, the market-value-weighted market portfolio, M, should include all risky assets, although in practice it is typically proxied by a stock market index such as the Standard & Poor's 500.

▶ The separation theorem states that the investment decision (what portfolio of risky assets to buy) can be separated from the financing decision (how much of investable funds should be put in risky assets and how much in the risk-free asset).

▶ Under the separation theorem, all investors should hold the same portfolio of risky assets and achieve their own position on the return-risk tradeoff through borrowing and lending.

▶ Investors need to focus on that part of portfolio risk that cannot be eliminated by diversification because this is the risk that should be priced in financial markets.

▶ Total risk can be divided into systematic risk and nonsystematic risk. Nonsystematic risk, also called diversifiable risk, can be eliminated by diversification.

▶ Market risk cannot be eliminated by diversification and is the relevant risk for the pricing of financial assets in the market.

▶ Based on the separation of risk into its systematic and nonsystematic components, the security market line can be constructed for individual securities (and portfolios). What is important is each security's contribution to the total risk of the portfolio, as measured by beta.

▶ Using beta as the measure of risk, the SML depicts the tradeoff between required return and risk for all securities and all portfolios.

▶ The market model can be used to estimate the alpha and beta for a security by regressing total returns for a security against total returns for a market index.

▶ The characteristic line is a graph of the regression involved in the market model.

▶ Beta, the slope of the characteristic line, is a relative measure of risk. It indicates the volatility of a stock.

▶ Betas for individual stocks are unstable while betas for large portfolios are quite stable.

▶ If the expected returns for securities can be estimated from security analysis, and plotted against the SML, undervalued and overvalued securities can be identified.

▶ Problems exist in estimating the SML, in particular, estimating the betas for securities. The stability of beta is a concern, especially for individual securities; however, portfolio betas tend to be more stable across time.

▶ Tests of the CAPM are inconclusive. An ex ante model is being tested with ex post data. It has not been proved empirically, nor is it likely to be, but its basic implications seem to be supported.

▶ Alternative theories of asset pricing, such as the arbitrage pricing theory, also exist but are unproved.

▶ APT is not critically dependent on an underlying market portfolio as is the CAPM, which predicts that only market risk influences expected returns. Instead, APT recognizes that several types of risk may affect security returns.

▶ A factor model recognizes risk factors that affect realized and expected security returns. These risk factors represent broad economic forces and not company-specific characteristics and, by definition, they represent the element of surprise in the risk factor.

▶ APT is more general than the CAPM. If only one factor exists, the two models can be shown to be identical.

▶ The problem with APT is that the factors are not well specified, at least ex ante.

▶ Most empirical work suggests that three to five factors influence security returns and are priced in the market.

Questions

9-1 How do lending possibilities change the Markowitz model? borrowing possibilities?

9-2 Why, under the CAPM, do all investors hold identical risky portfolios?

9-3 In terms of their appearance as a graph, what is the difference between the CML and the SML?

9-4 What is the market portfolio?

9-5 What is the slope of the CML? What does it measure?

9-6 Why does the CML contain only efficient portfolios?

9-7 How can we measure a security's contribution to the risk of the market portfolio?

9-8 How can the SML be used to identify over- and undervalued securities?

9-9 What happens to the price and return of a security when investors recognize it as undervalued?

9-10 What are the difficulties involved in estimating a security's beta?

9-11 What is the major problem in testing capital market theory?

9-12 How can the CAPM be tested empirically? What are the expected results of regressing average returns on betas?

9-13 What is "the law of one price"?

9-14 Why does Roll argue that the CAPM is untestable?

9-15 The CAPM provides required returns for individual securities or portfolios. What uses can you see for such a model?

9-16 What is the relationship between the CML and the Markowitz efficient frontier?

9-17 How does an investor decide where to be on the new efficient frontier represented by the CML?

9-18 The CML can be described as representing a tradeoff. What is this tradeoff? Be specific.

9-19 Draw a diagram of the SML. Label the axes and the intercept.

    a. Assume the risk-free rate shifts upward. Draw the new SML.

    b. Assume that the risk-free rate remains the same as before the change in (a), but that investors become more pessimistic about the stock market. Draw the new SML.

9-20 What common assumptions do the CAPM and APT share? How do they differ in assumptions?

9-21 What is a factor model?

9-22 What characteristics must the factors in a factor model possess?

9-23 Based on empirical work, how many factors are thought to influence security returns? Name some of these likely factors.

9-24 What does a factor model say about equilibrium in the marketplace?

9-25 How can APT be used in investment decisions?

9-26 What role does the market portfolio play in the APT model?

9-27 What is meant by an "arbitrage profit"? What ensures that investors could act quickly to take advantage of such opportunities?

9-28 Why is the standard deviation of a security's returns an inadequate measure of the contribution of that security to the risk of a portfolio that is well diversified?

9-29 Explain the separation theorem.

9-30 What does the separation theorem imply about the "tailored" approach to portfolio selection?

CFA
9-31 Suppose that the risk-free rate of 6 percent and the expected return on the investor's tangency portfolio is 14 percent, with a standard deviation of 24 percent.

    a. Calculate the investor's expected risk premium per unit of risk.

    b. Calculate the portfolio's expected return if the portfolio's standard deviation of return is 20 percent.

CFA
9-32 Suppose that the risk-free rate is 5 percent and the expected return on the market portfolio of risky assets is 13 percent. An investor with $1 million to invest wants to achieve a 17 percent rate of return on a portfolio combining a risk-free asset and the market portfolio of risky assets. Calculate how much this investor would need to borrow at the risk-free rate in order to establish this target expected return.

CFA
9-33 Eduardo Martinez is evaluating the following investments:

Portfolio A: $E(RA) = 12$ percent, $\sigma(RA) = 15$
Portfolio B: $E(RB) = 10$ percent, $\sigma(RB) = 8$
Portfolio C: $E(RC) = 10$ percent, $\sigma(RC) = 9$

Explain the choice among Portfolios A, B, and C, assuming that borrowing and lending at a risk-free rate of RF = 2 percent is possible.

CFA
9-34 Suppose that the best predictor for a stock's future beta is determined to be Expected beta = 0.33 + 0.67 (historical beta). The historical beta is calculated as 1.2. The risk-free rate is 5 percent, and the market risk premium is 8.5 percent. Calculate the expected return on the stock using expected (adjusted) beta in the CAPM.

CFA
9-35 Suppose that the expected return on the stock in the following table is 11 percent. Using a two-factor model, calculate the stock's return if the company-specific surprise for the year is 3 percent.

Variable	Actual Value	Expected Value	Stock's Factor Sensitivity
Change in interest rate	0%	.0%	−1.5
Growth in GDP	1.0%	4.0%	2.0

Demonstration Problems

9-1   **CALCULATION OF THE CHARACTERISTIC LINE:** Calculate the characteristic line for EG&G by letting Y be the annual TRs for EG&G and X be the TRs for the S&P 500 Index. The summary statistics are as follows:

$$n = 10; \quad \Sigma Y = 264.5; \quad \Sigma Y^2 = 19,503.65; \quad \Sigma X = 84.5; \quad \Sigma X^2 = 4,660.31;$$

$$\Sigma XY = 6,995.76$$

$$SS_y = \Sigma(Y - \overline{Y})^2 = \Sigma Y^2 - \frac{(\Sigma Y)^2}{n} = 12,507.625$$

$$SS_x = \Sigma(X - \overline{X})^2 = \Sigma X^2 - \frac{(\Sigma X)^2}{n} = 3,946.285$$

$$SS_{xy} = \Sigma(X - \overline{X})^2(Y - \overline{Y})^2 = \Sigma XY - \frac{(\Sigma X)(\Sigma Y)}{n} = 4,760.735$$

$$\hat{\beta} = \frac{SS_{xy}}{SS_x} = 1.206384$$

$$\hat{\alpha} = \overline{Y} - \hat{\beta}\overline{X} = 16.256$$

$$\hat{Y} = 16.256 + 1.206X$$

Analysis of Variance Source (Risk)		Sum of Squares	No. of Observations	Variance
Total SS$_y$	=	12,507.625	$n - 1 = 9$	1,389.736 = Total Var.
Systematic $\beta^2 SS_x$	=	5,743.275	$n - 1 = 9$	638.142 = Systematic Var.
Nonsystematic	=	6,764.350	$n - 1 = 9$	751.594 = Nonsystematic Var.

Problems

9-1   The market has an expected return of 12 percent, and the risk-free rate is 5 percent. Pfizer has a beta of 0.73. What is the required rate of return for Pfizer?

9-2   The market has an expected return of 14 percent, and the risk-free rate is 4 percent. Activalue Corp. is 80 percent as risky as the market as a whole. What is the required rate of return for this company?

9-3   Electron Corporation is 30 percent more volatile than the market as a whole. The market risk premium is 8 percent. The risk-free rate is 5 percent. What is the required rate of return for Electron?

9-4   The expected return for the market is 12 percent, and the risk-free rate is 4 percent. The following information is available for each of five stocks.

Stock	Beta	$E(R_i)$
1	0.9	12
2	1.3	13
3	0.5	11
4	1.1	12.5
5	1.0	12

a. Calculate the required return for each stock.

b. Assume that an investor, using fundamental analysis, develops the estimates of expected return labeled $E(R_i)$ for these stocks. Determine which stocks are undervalued and which are overvalued.

c. What is the market's risk premium?

9-5   Assume that the risk-free rate is 7 percent and the expected market return is 13 percent. Show that the security market line is

$$E(R_i) = 7.0 + 6.0\beta$$

Assume that an investor has estimated the following values for six different corporations:

Corporation	β_i	$R_i(\%)$
GF	0.8	12
PepsiCo	0.9	13
IBM	1.0	14
NCNB	1.2	11
EG&G	1.3	18
EAL	1.5	10

Calculate the ER_i for each corporation using the SML, and evaluate which securities are overvalued and which are undervalued.

Computational Problems

9-1   Given the following, show that the characteristic line for this company is $\hat{Y} = 5.055 + 0.776X$:

$\Sigma X = 264.5$; $\Sigma X^2 = 4,660.31$; $\Sigma Y = 116.1$; $\Sigma Y^2 = 6,217.13$; $\Sigma XY = 4,042.23$;
$SS_x = 3,946.285$; $SS_y = 4,869.209$; $SS_{xy} = 3,061.185$

9-2   Assume that Exxon is priced in equilibrium. Its expected return next year is 14 percent, and its beta is 0.41. The risk-free rate is 6 percent.

a. Calculate the slope of the SML.

b. Calculate the expected return on the market.

9-3   Given the following information:
Expected return for the market, 12 percent; Standard deviation of market return, 21 percent; Risk-free rate, 4 percent; Correlation coefficient between Stock A and the market, 0.8; Stock B

and the market, 0.6; Standard deviation for stock A, 25 percent; Standard deviation for stock B, 30 percent.

a. Calculate the beta for stock A and stock B.

b. Calculate the required return for each stock.

9-4 The expected return for the market is 12 percent, with a standard deviation of 21 percent. The expected risk-free rate is 4 percent. Information is available for five mutual funds, all assumed to be efficient:

Mutual Funds	SD(%)
Affiliated	14
Omega	16
Ivy	21
Value Line Fund	25
New Horizons	30

a. Calculate the slope of the CML.

b. Calculate the expected return for each portfolio.

c. Rank the portfolios in increasing order of expected return.

d. Do any of the portfolios have the same expected return as the market? Why?

Spreadsheet Problems

9-1 Assume the annual price data below is for General Foods and the S&P 500, covering the period 1997–2012. Calculate the beta for General Foods. Use the ESTLIN function or the SLOPE function in the spreadsheet.

Year	GF	S&P
2012	45.08	1,211.92
2011	48.38	1,111.92
2010	40.96	879.82
2009	48.23	1,148.08
2008	50.17	1,320.28
2007	52.26	1,469.25
2006	59.49	1,229.23
2005	57.24	970.43
2004	45.93	740.74
2003	32.06	615.93
2002	21.93	459.27
2001	20.35	466.45
2000	17.24	435.71
1999	16.3	417.09
1998	9.29	330.22
1997	7.57	353.4

9-2   Given the spreadsheet below, calculate the portfolio beta and the expected return on this two stock portfolio using the CAPM.

a. If the weights were 50/50, would this increase or decrease the portfolio return?

b. If the market's expected return had been 8 percent with the 60/40 weights, would this increase or decreased the portfolio return?

The Market's Expected Return	10%
The Risk Free Rate	1.25%
Beta for Bateman Industires	0.64
Beta for Advanced Solar Arrays	1.78
Weight for Bateman	60%
Weigh for Solar Arrays	40%
Portfolio Beta	
Expected Return on the Portfolio	

Checking Your Understanding

9-1   The introduction of risk-free borrowing and lending is an important change relative to the original Markowitz analysis, because it changes the nature of the efficient frontier. Under the Markowitz analysis, the frontier is always a curve in expected return—risk space. With the introduction of borrowing and lending, the efficient frontier becomes a straight line.

9-2   The CML is tangent to the Markowitz efficient frontier. The point of tangency is an efficient portfolio, since only efficient portfolios are on the efficient frontier. All points on the CML are combinations of this efficient portfolio and borrowing and lending.

9-3   Under capital market theory, the Separation Theorem states that the investment decision (what assets to hold) is separate from the financing decision (how much of one's funds are invested in the risky portfolio vs the risk-free asset). Since all investors should hold the market portfolio as the risky asset, the investment decision is made for them.

9-4   Beta is a relative measure of systematic risk. Beta is easily understandable since the beta for the market as a whole is 1.0 and the betas for individual stocks cluster around 1.0.

9-5   Overvalued securities plot below the SML because they do not offer a large enough return given their risk. Thus investors would prefer a security on the SML. As investors sell these securities, their price will be driven down and their return will go up until they converge on the SML.

9-6   APT is more general than the CAPM. The CAPM is a special case of APT when there is only one factor.

chapter 10

Common Stock Valuation Lessons for All Investors

The moment you have been waiting for is almost at hand. Having prepared yourself to manage your inheritance by dealing with the numerous issues you have now reviewed, whether it be mutual funds, or selling short, or basic portfolio theory, or the capital asset pricing model (CAPM), what you really want to do is what most people are dying to do—get out there and buy some stocks. After all, you know someone who bought Cisco in the 1990s at $20 and it went to $90, and you know for sure this person is not the brightest bulb in the chandelier. On the other hand, you have read all the horror stories about the folks who bought the technology stocks which subsequently collapsed, if indeed they even survived—and some of these people were surely smart. So there must be more to it than meets the eye.

Once again you decide you have to bite the bullet, this time learning the principles of stock valuation. The bad news, as you are about to learn, is that valuation is an art and not a science—it requires judgment as well as skill. The good news is that learning the basic principles of valuation, while not a guarantee of success, will in fact give you an advantage over many investors who simply act on tips or jump in without doing adequate analysis.

How do investors typically go about analyzing stocks to buy and sell? Chapter 10 concentrates on the valuation of common stocks, while Chapter 11 concentrates on how investors should analyze and manage their equity holdings. Here we consider the major approaches used by investors in the valuation of stocks: discounted cash flow techniques, target prices and relative valuation techniques. Every serious investor should be comfortable with the basic principles of common stock valuation represented by these approaches.

AFTER READING THIS CHAPTER YOU WILL BE ABLE TO:

► Understand the foundation of valuation for common stocks, discounted cash flow techniques, and the concept of intrinsic value.

► Use the dividend discount model to estimate the intrinsic value of a stock.

► Estimate target prices for stocks using the P/E ratio and EPS.

► Recognize the role of relative valuation metrics in the valuation process.

Overview

Major approaches to valuing common stocks using fundamental security analysis include

1. Discounted cash flow techniques
2. Earnings multiplier approach
3. Relative valuation metrics

Discounted Cash Flow (DCF) techniques attempt to estimate the value of a stock today (its intrinsic value) using a present value analysis. For example, using the Dividend Discount Model (DDM), the future stream of dividends to be received from a common stock is discounted back to the present at an appropriate discount rate [that is, the investor's required rate of return (RR) discussed in Chapter 9] and summed. Alternative discounted cash flow versions discount such variables as free cash flow. The end result is an estimate of the current "fair value" or intrinsic value of the stock.

The earnings multiplier approach attempts to estimate intrinsic value based on estimated earnings and a multiplier, the P/E ratio. To implement this approach:

- Estimate the earnings per share (EPS) for the next period, typically the next 12 months.
- Determine an appropriate P/E ratio. Part of this process may involve comparing the company being valued with its peers in order to derive the appropriate P/E ratio.
- Multiply the estimated EPS by the P/E ratio that has been determined.

Once again, the end result is an estimate of the intrinsic value of the stock, or the estimated value of the stock today.

Relative valuation metrics typically involve the P/E ratio, the Price/Book Value ratio, and the Sales/Price ratio, although others could be used. With this approach, the emphasis is on selecting stocks for possible purchase rather than estimating their value.

Exhibit 10-1 summarizes these approaches to common stock valuation. We will discuss these approaches in order in the chapter. Before doing so, however, let's briefly consider the difference between the common "textbook" approach to valuation and what we might call the typical practitioner's approach.

Finance textbooks traditionally have emphasized the DDM as the foundation of stock valuation because, conceptually, it is widely agreed to be correct. However, a 2006 study found that practitioners and investment advisory services often do not use DCF models.[1] Instead, they use techniques such as a multiplier (P/E ratio) and expected earnings, relative valuation metrics, and the estimation of expected returns.

We recognize at the outset of this discussion that many practitioners use a multiplier approach, and we will use it extensively here and in Chapter 15. Nevertheless, it is important in understanding stock valuation to appreciate DCF models for at least two reasons. First, virtually all informed students of valuation agree that a model such as the DDM is conceptually correct. It may have its limitations (as do all other valuation models), but we can learn from it. Secondly, some of the most popular investment advisory services, in particular *Morningstar* and Standard & Poor's *Outlook*, use a DCF model based on free cash flows. A basic understanding of DCF techniques is very useful in an overall understanding of the valuation of common stocks.

---

[1] William P. Dukes, Zhuoming Peng, and Philip C. English II, "How do Practitioners Value Common Stock?" *The Journal of Investing*, Vol. 15, No. 3, Fall 2006, pp. 90–104.

Valuation Techniques, Variables Used, and the End Result Sought

Valuation Technique	Variables Used	End Product Produced
1. Discounted Cash Flow techniques		
a. Dividend Discount Model	Expected Future Dividends, Stockholders Required Rate of Return	Intrinsic Value
b. Free Cash Flow to Equity	Free Cash Flow to Equity, Cost of Equity Capital	Intrinsic Value
c. Free Cash Flow to Firm	Free Cash Flow to the Firm, Firm's Cost of Capital	Intrinsic Value
2. Earnings Multiplier Approach	Estimated EPS for next year, P/E ratio thought to be appropriate	Estimated Price
3. Relative Valuation Metrics	Based on Relative Judgments	Stock Selection
i. P/E ratio (price/earnings ratio)		
ii. P/B ratio (price to book ratio)		
iii. P/S ratio (price to sales ratio)		

Discounted Cash Flow Models

The classic method of calculating the estimated value of any security is the DCF model, which involves a present value analysis.

✓ The DCF model estimates the value of a security by discounting its expected future cash flows back to the present and adding them together.

The estimated value of a security is equal to the discounted (present) value of the future stream of cash flows that an investor expects to receive from the security, as shown in Equation 10-1:

$$\text{Estimated value } V_0 = \sum_{t=1}^{n} \frac{\text{Expected cash flows}}{(1+k)^t} \tag{10-1}$$

where

$k =$ the appropriate discount rate

To use such a model, an investor must

1. Estimate the amount and timing of the future cash flows
2. Estimate an appropriate discount rate
3. Use these two components in a present value model to estimate the **intrinsic value** of the security, which we denote as V_0, and then compare V_0 to the current market price of the security

Intrinsic Value The estimated value of a security

Figure 10-1

The Present Value Approach to Valuation.

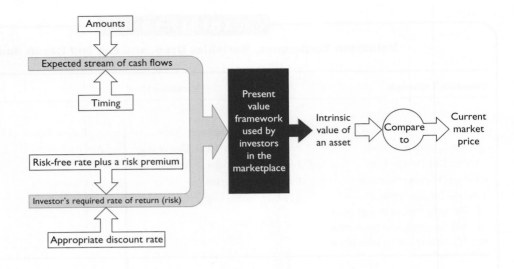

✓ The intrinsic value for a stock is simply its estimated value—what the investor believes the stock is worth

TWO DCF APPROACHES

There are two different approaches to the cash flows and discount rates used in the valuation of stocks.

1. Value the equity of the firm, using the required rate of return to shareholders (the cost of equity capital).
2. Value the entire firm, using the weighted average cost of capital.

Figure 10-1 summarizes the DCF process used in fundamental analysis. It emphasizes the factors that go into valuing common stocks. The exact nature of the present value process used by investors in the marketplace depends upon which cash flows are used to value the asset.

Because we emphasize the stockholder's required rate of return, this discussion of DCF techniques concentrates on valuing the equity of the firm.

✓ The Dividend Discount Model (DDM) is simply a special case of valuing the equity to the firm. It is prominently featured in virtually all discussions of valuation, and indeed can be regarded as the basis for common stock valuation using DCF techniques.

Following a discussion of the DDM, we will consider other models for valuing the equity of the firm. The alternative approach, valuing the firm as a whole, is also considered.

The Dividend Discount Model

To understand the basis of the Dividend Discount Model (DDM), ask yourself the following question: If I buy a particular common stock and place it in a special trust fund for the perpetual benefit of myself and my heirs, what benefits will I and my heirs receive from doing this? The answer is a stream of cash dividends, because this is the only cash distribution that a corporation actually makes to its stockholders. Although a firm's EPS in any year belong to the

Figure 10-2

The Process Involved with the Dividend Discount Model.

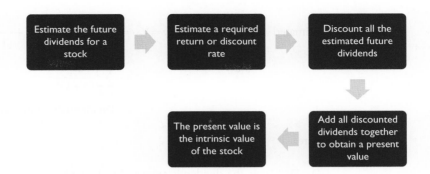

stockholders, corporations generally do not pay out all their earnings to their stockholders; furthermore, EPS is an accounting concept, whereas dividends represent cash payments. Investors can't spend EPS, but they can spend dividends received.

Stockholders may plan to sell their shares sometime in the future, resulting in a cash flow from the sale price. As shown later, however, even if investors think of the stream of cash flows from a common stock as a combination of dividends and a future price at which the stock can be sold, this is equivalent to evaluating the stream of all dividends to be received on the stock. Therefore, we can concentrate on a company's estimated future dividends and an appropriate required rate of return.

APPLYING THE DDM

Adapting Equation 10-1 specifically to value common stocks, the cash flows are the dividends expected to be paid in each future period. An investor or analyst using this approach carefully studies the future prospects for a company and estimates the likely dividends to be paid. In addition, the analyst estimates an appropriate required rate of return or discount rate based on the risk foreseen in the dividends and given the alternatives available. Finally, he or she discounts the entire stream of estimated future dividends, properly identified as to amount and timing, and adds them together. The derived present value is the intrinsic value of the stock. This process is illustrated in Figure 10-2.

Required Rate of Return The minimum expected rate of return necessary to induce an investor to purchase a security

The **required rate of return (RR)** is the *minimum* expected rate of return necessary to induce an investor to buy a particular stock, given its risk. Note that it is an expected rate of return, and that it is the *minimum* rate necessary to induce purchase.

✓   The required rate of return, capitalization rate, and discount rate are interchangeable terms in valuation analysis. Regardless of the terminology, it is challenging to determine the precise numerical value to use for a particular stock. In the final analysis, it is, at best, an intelligent estimate.

Because in practice it is not easy to determine a precise discount rate, we will assume for purposes of this discussion that we know the discount rate and concentrate on the other issues involved in valuation, which are difficult enough. The CAPM model discussed in Chapter 9 serves as a basis for thinking about, and calculating, a required rate of return.

THE DDM EQUATION

The DDM states that the estimated value (per share) of a stock today is the discounted value of all future dividends:

$$\text{Estimated value of a stock today} = V_0 = \frac{D_1}{(1+k)} + \frac{D_2}{(1+k)^2} + \frac{D_3}{(1+k)^3} + \cdots + \frac{D_\infty}{(1+k)^\infty}$$

$$= \sum_{t=1}^{\infty} \frac{D_t}{(1+k)^t}$$

$$= \text{Dividend discount model} \qquad \textbf{(10-2)}$$

where

$D_1, D_2, \ldots$ = the dividends expected to be received in each future period

k = the required rate of return for this stock, which is the discount rate applicable for an investment with this degree of riskiness (the opportunity cost of a comparable risk alternative)

IMPLEMENTING THE DDM

Two immediate issues with Equation 10-2 are the following:

1. The last term in Equation 10-2 indicates that investors are dealing with infinity. They must value a stream of dividends that may be paid forever, since common stock has no maturity date.
2. The dividend stream is uncertain:
   (a) There is no specified number of dividends, if in fact any are paid at all. Dividends must be declared periodically by the firm's board of directors. (Technically, they are typically declared quarterly, but conventional valuation analysis uses annual dividends.)
   (b) The dividends for most firms are expected to grow over time; therefore, investors usually cannot simplify Equation 10-2 to a perpetuity as in the case of a preferred stock.[2]

Who's Afraid of Infinity? The first issue, that Equation 10-2 involves an infinite number of periods and dividends, will be resolved when we deal with the second issue, specifying the expected stream of dividends. However, from a practical standpoint the infinity problem is not as troublesome as it first appears. At reasonably high discount rates, such as 12 percent, 14 percent, or 16 percent, dividends received 40 or 50 years in the future are worth very little today, so that investors need not worry about them. For example, the present value of $1 to be received 50 years from now, if the discount rate is 15 percent, is only $0.0009, which is zero for practical purposes.

ESTIMATING FUTURE DIVIDENDS

The conventional solution to the second issue, that the dollar amount of the dividend is expected to grow over time, is to make some assumptions about the expected growth rate of dividends. That is, given some starting dividend amount, the investor or analyst estimates or models the expected percentage rate of growth in the future stream of dividends, accounting

---

[2] Refer to Appendix 10-A for the valuation of preferred stock.

for all dividends from now to infinity. To do this, he or she classifies each stock to be valued into one of three categories based on the expected growth rate in dividends.

✓ The DDM is operationalized by estimating the expected growth rate(s) in the dividend stream.

Checking Your Understanding

1. Why is the required rate of return for a stock also an expected rate of return?
2. What does it mean to say that the estimated value of a stock today is the discounted value of all future dividends?

GROWTH RATE CASES FOR THE DDM

There are three growth rate cases:

Zero Growth Rate Case One of three growth rate cases of the dividend discount model, when the dollar dividend being paid is not expected to change

1. **The zero growth rate case**: A dividend stream with a zero growth rate resulting from a fixed dollar dividend equal to the current dividend, D_0, being paid every year from now to infinity.

$$\frac{D_0 \quad D_0 \quad D_0 \quad D_0 + \cdots + D_0}{0 \quad 1 \quad 2 \quad 3 \quad + \cdots + \infty} \quad \begin{array}{l} \text{Dividend stream} \\ \text{Time period} \end{array}$$

Constant (Normal) Growth Rate Case A well-known scenario in valuation in which dividends are expected to grow at a constant growth rate over time

2. **The constant (normal) growth rate case**: A dividend stream that is growing at a constant rate g, starting with D_0.

$$\frac{D_0 \quad D_0(1+g)^1 \quad D_0(1+g)^2 \quad D_0(1+g)^3 + \cdots + (1+g)^\infty}{0 \quad 1 \quad 2 \quad 3 \quad + \cdots + \quad \infty} \quad \begin{array}{l} \text{Dividend stream} \\ \text{Time period} \end{array}$$

Multiple Growth Rate Case One of three possible forms of the dividend discount model, involving two or more expected growth rates for dividends.

3. **The multiple growth rate case**: A dividend stream that is growing at variable rates, for example, g_1 for the first four years and g_2 thereafter.

$$\frac{D_0 \quad D_1 = D_0(1+g_1) \quad D_2 = D_1(1+g_1) \quad D_3 = D_2(1+g_1) \quad D_4 = D_3(1+g_1)}{0 \quad 1 \quad 2 \quad 3 \quad 4}$$

$$\frac{D_5 = D_4(1+g_2) + \cdots + D_\infty = D_{\infty-1}(1+g_2)}{5 \quad + \cdots + \quad \infty} \quad \begin{array}{l} \text{Dividend stream} \\ \text{Time period} \end{array}$$

THE ZERO GROWTH RATE MODEL

A zero growth rate equates to a fixed dollar dividend that does not change over time. For example, a firm pays a dividend of $1.00 a share annually, and has no plans to change this dollar amount. The zero growth rate dividend case reduces to a perpetuity. Assuming a constant dollar dividend, which implies a zero growth rate, Equation 10-2 simplifies to the zero growth rate model shown as Equation 10-3.

$$V_0 = \frac{D_0}{k} = \text{Zero growth rate version of the dividend discount model} \qquad \textbf{(10-3)}$$

where D_0 is the constant dollar dividend expected for all future time periods and k is the opportunity cost or required rate of return for this particular common stock.[3]

A Present Value Process   The discounting process is not apparent when the perpetuity formula associated with the zero growth rate case is used. Nevertheless, we are accounting for all dividends from now to infinity in this case, as with the other DDM cases. It is simply a mathematical fact—not to mention a great calculation convenience—that dividing a constant dollar amount by the discount rate, k, produces a result equivalent to discounting each dividend from now to infinity separately and summing all of the present values.

✓   It is extremely important in understanding the valuation of common stocks using the DDM to recognize that in all cases considered an investor is discounting the future stream of dividends from now to infinity. This fact tends to be overlooked.

THE CONSTANT GROWTH RATE MODEL

The other two versions of the DDM indicate that to establish the cash flow stream of expected dividends, which is to be subsequently discounted, it is first necessary to compound some beginning dividend into the future. Most companies paying a dividend expect that dividend to grow over time. Obviously, the higher the growth rate used, the greater the *future dollar* amounts of dividends will be.

The Constant Growth Rate Equation   A well-known scenario in valuation is the case in which dividends are expected to grow at a constant growth rate over time. This constant growth rate model is shown as Equation 10-4.

$$V_0 = \frac{D_0(1+g)}{(1+k_{cs})} + \frac{D_0(1+g)^2}{(1+k_{cs})^2} + \frac{D_0(1+g)^3}{(1+k_{cs})^3} + \cdots + \frac{D_0(1+g)^\infty}{(1+k_{cs})^\infty} \qquad \textbf{(10-4)}$$

where D_0 is the current dividend being paid and growing at the constant growth rate g, and k is the appropriate discount rate.

Equation 10-4 can be simplified to the following equation:[4]

$$V_0 = \frac{D_1}{k-g} = \text{Constant growth rate version of the dividend discount model} \qquad \textbf{(10-5)}$$

where D_1 is the dividend expected to be received at the end of Year 1.

Equation 10-5 is used whenever the growth rate of future dividends is expected to be more or less a constant. In actual practice, it is used quite often because of its simplicity, and because it is the best description of the expected dividend stream for a large number of companies, in particular large, stable companies and, in many instances, the market as a whole.

---

[3] The no-growth rate case is equivalent to the valuation process for a preferred stock because, exactly like a preferred stock, the dividend (numerator of Equation 10-3 remains unchanged. Equation 10-3 applies to all perpetuities.

[4] Note that k must be greater than g, or nonsensical results are produced. Equation 10-4 collapses to Equation 10-5 as the number of periods involved approaches infinity.

Example 10-1

Assume Summa Corporation is currently paying $1 per share in dividends and investors expect dividends to grow at the rate of 7 percent a year for the foreseeable future. For investments at this risk level, investors require a return of 15 percent a year. The estimated value of Summa today, which we call time period 0, V_0, is

$$V_0 = \frac{D_1}{k - g}$$

$$V_0 = \frac{\$1.00\,(1.07)}{0.15 - 0.07} = \$13.38$$

D_0 vs. D_1 Note that the current dividend of $1.00, ($D_0$), must be compounded one period because the constant growth version of the DDM specifies the numerator as the dividend expected to be received one period from now, which is D_1. In valuation terminology, D_0 represents the dividend currently being paid, and D_1 represents the dividend expected to be paid in the next period.

Given D_0, which is known and observable, D_1 can always be determined:[5]

$$D_0 = \text{Current dividend}$$
$$D_1 = D_0(1 + g)$$

where g is the expected growth rate of dividends.

Understanding the Constant Growth Rate Model

To completely understand the constant growth model, which is widely used in valuation analysis, it is instructive to think about the process that occurs under constant growth.[6]

We must recognize that the constant growth version of the DDM (Equation 10-5) takes account of all future cash flows from now to infinity although this is not apparent when we look at the equation itself. Nevertheless, the mathematics of the process involving a constant growth rate to infinity reduces to a very simple expression, masking the fact that all dividends from now to infinity are being accounted for and discounted.

Growth in Stock Price

The constant growth rate version of the DDM implies that the stock price for any one period is estimated to grow at the same rate as the dividends, which is g. In fact, holding the payout ratio (the ratio of dividends to earnings) constant, the constant growth model implies that dividends, earnings, and stock price are all expected to grow at the expected constant growth rate, g.

---

[5] D_2 can be determined in the constant growth model as $D_0(1 + g)^2$ or $D_1(1 + g)$.

[6] Appendix 10A illustrates in more detail the process involved with the constant growth version of the DDM.

Example 10-2 For Summa, the estimated value today, V_0, is $13.38, and for the end of Period 1, using D_2 in the numerator of Equation 10-5, it is:

$$V_1 = \frac{(\$1.07)(1.07)}{0.15 - 0.07} = \$14.31$$

This estimated value at the end of Period 1 is 7 percent higher than the estimated value today of $13.38. Thus, the stock price has changed by the amount of the growth rate, g.[7]

HOW *k* AND *g* AFFECT VALUE

An examination of Equation 10-5 quickly demonstrates the factors affecting the estimated value of a common stock, assuming the constant growth version of the dividend discount model to be the applicable valuation approach:

1. If the market lowers the required rate of return for a stock, estimated value will rise (other things being equal).
2. If investors decide that the expected growth in dividends will be higher as the result of some favorable development for the firm, estimated value will also rise (other things being equal). Of course, the converse for these two situations also holds—a rise in the discount rate or a reduction in the expected growth rate of dividends will lower estimated value.

Limitations of the Constant Growth Rate Model   One of the limitations of the DDM is that the model is not *robust*—that is, the estimated value is very sensitive to the exact inputs used. The present value calculated from Equation 10-5 is quite sensitive to the estimates used by the investor.

Example 10-3 For Summa, assume the discount rate used, k, is 16 percent instead of 15 percent, with other variables held constant:

$$V_0 = \frac{\$1(1.07)}{0.16 - 0.07} = \$11.89$$

In this example, a 1-percentage-point rise in k results in an 11.14 percent decrease in estimated value, from $13.38 to $11.89.

Example 10-4 Assume that for Summa the growth rate, g, is 8 percent instead of 7 percent, with other variables held constant:

$$V_0 = \frac{\$1(1.08)}{0.15 - 0.08} = \$15.43$$

In this example, a 1-percentage-point increase in g results in a 15.3 percent increase in estimated value, from $13.38 to $15.43.

---

[7] $\text{Change in estimated value} = \dfrac{\text{Ending value} - \text{Beginning value}}{\text{Beginning value}}$

$= (\$14.31 - \$13.38)/\$13.38 = 7\%$

Example 10-5   Assume that for Summa the discount rate increases to 16 percent, and the growth rate declines to 4 percent:

$$V_0 = \frac{\$1(1.04)}{0.16 - 0.04} = \$8.67$$

In this example, the estimated value declines from \$13.38 to \$8.67, a 35 percent change.

✓ Relatively small variations in the inputs to the constant growth model can change the estimated value of the stock by large percentage amounts.

Why Stock Prices Fluctuate   The differences in estimated stock values illustrated in the previous section suggest why stock prices constantly fluctuate as investors make their buy and sell decisions. Even if all investors use the constant growth version of the dividend discount model to value a particular common stock, many different estimates of value will be obtained because of the following:

1. Each investor has his or her own required rate of return, resulting in a relatively wide range of values of k.
2. Each investor has his or her own estimate of the expected growth rate in dividends. Although this range will be reasonably narrow in many valuation situations, small differences in g can produce significant differences in price, everything else held constant.

Thus, at any point in time for a particular stock, some investors are willing to buy, whereas others wish to sell, depending on their estimate of the intrinsic value of the stock. This helps to make markets active and liquid.

THE MULTIPLE GROWTH RATE MODEL

Many companies grow at a rapid rate (or rates) for a number of years and then slow down to an "average" growth rate. Other companies pay no dividends for a period of years, often during their early growth period. The constant growth model discussed earlier is unable to deal with these situations; therefore, a model is needed that can. Such a variation of the DDM is the multiple growth rate model.

Definition   Multiple growth is defined as a situation in which a company's expected future growth in dividends needs to be described using two or more growth rates (one of which could be zero). Although any number of growth rates is possible, most stocks can be described using two or possibly three different growth rates.

✓ The distinguishing characteristic of multiple growth situations is that at least two different growth rates are involved, one of which could be zero.

A number of companies have experienced rapid growth that could not be sustained forever. During part of their lives the growth rate exceeded that of the average company in the economy, but later the growth rate slowed. Examples from the late 1990s when stocks were booming include Cisco and Dell. More recent examples of a slowdown in growth include Yahoo! and Google.

The Two-Stage Growth Rate Model   A well-known multiple growth rate model is the two-stage model. This model assumes near-term growth at a rapid rate for some period (typically, 2 to 10 years) followed by a steady long-term growth rate that is sustainable (i.e., a constant growth rate as discussed earlier). This can be described in equation form as: (we again use V_0 to represent the estimated value of a stock):

$$V_0 = \sum_{t=1}^{n} \frac{D_0(1+g_s)^t}{(1+k)^t} + \frac{D_n(1+g_c)}{k-g_c} + \frac{1}{(1+k)^n} \qquad (10\text{-}6)$$

where

$V_0 =$ the estimated value of the stock today

$D_0 =$ the current dividend

$g_s =$ the supernormal (or subnormal) growth rate for dividends

$g_c =$ the constant growth rate for dividends

$k =$ required rate of return

$n =$ the number of periods of supernormal (or subnormal) growth

$D_n =$ the dividend at the end of the abnormal growth period

Understanding the Equation   Notice in Equation 10-6 that the first term on the right side defines a dividend stream covering n periods, growing at a high (or low) growth rate of g_s and discounted at the required rate of return, k. This term covers the period of supernormal (or subnormal) growth, at which time the dividend is expected to grow at a constant rate forever. In effect, we must identify each of the dividends during this abnormal growth period, and then discount them back to the present using the required rate of return.

The second term on the right-hand side is the constant growth version discussed earlier, which takes the dividend expected for the next period, $n+1$, and divides by the difference between k and g_c.[8] Notice, however, that the value obtained from this calculation is the value of the stock at the beginning of period $n+1$ (or the end of period n), which we shall call P_n. This value must be discounted back to time period zero by multiplying by the appropriate discount (present value) factor, which is accomplished in Equation 10-6 by multiplying by $1/(1+k)^n$.

The valuation process outlined here is as stated above:

$V_0 =$ PV of the dividends during the period of unusual growth based on the growth rate g_s

$\quad$ + PV of the terminal price (which is a function of all dividends at the

$\qquad$ constant growth rate g_c)

Think about the second term in Equation 10-6 as representing the estimated value of the stock derived from the constant growth model as of the beginning of period $n+1$. The constant growth version of the dividend discount model is used to solve for estimated value at the beginning of period $n+1$, which is the same as the end of period n. Therefore,

$$V_n = \frac{D_{n+1}}{k-g_c}$$

[8] The dividend at period $n+1$ is equal to the dividend paid in period n compounded up by the new growth rate, g_c. The designation $n+1$ refers to the first period after the years of abnormal growth.

Because V_n is the estimated value of the stock at the end of period n (the beginning of period $n + 1$) it must be discounted back to the present.[9] When it is added to the value of the discounted dividends from the first term, we have the estimated value of the stock today.

Example 10-6   Figure 10-3 illustrates the concept of valuing a multiple growth rate company. In this example, the current dividend is $1 and is expected to grow at the higher rate (g_s) of 12 percent a year for five years, at the end of which time the new growth rate (g_c) is expected to be a constant 6 percent a year. The required rate of return is 10 percent.

The first step in the valuation process illustrated in Figure 10-2 is to determine the dollar dividends in each year of supernormal growth. This is done by compounding the beginning dividend, $1, at 12 percent for each of the first five years:

$$D_0 = \$1.00$$
$$D_1 = \$1.00(1.12) \quad = \$1.12$$
$$D_2 = \$1.00(1.12)^2 = \$1.25$$
$$D_3 = \$1.00(1.12)^3 = \$1.40$$
$$D_4 = \$1.00(1.12)^4 = \$1.57$$
$$D_5 = \$1.00(1.12)^5 = \$1.76$$

Once the stream of dividends over the supergrowth period has been determined, they must be discounted to the present using the required rate of return of 10 percent. Thus,

$$\$1.12(0.909) = \$1.02$$
$$\$1.25(0.826) = \$1.03$$
$$\$1.40(0.751) = \$1.05$$
$$\$1.57(0.683) = \$1.07$$
$$\$1.76(0.621) = \underline{\$1.09}$$
$$\$5.26$$

Summing the five discounted dividends produces the value of the stock for its first five years only, which is $5.26. To evaluate Years 6 on, when constant growth is expected, the constant growth model is used.

$$P_n = \frac{D_{n+1}}{(k - g_c)}$$
$$= \frac{D_6}{(k - g_c)}$$
$$= \frac{D_5(1.06)}{(k - g_c)}$$
$$= \frac{1.76(1.06)}{0.10 - 0.06}$$
$$= \$46.64$$

---

[9] For valuation purposes, think of the end of period n as December 31 and the beginning of period $n + 1$ as January 1. These are, effectively, the same date.

Thus, $46.64 is the expected price of the stock at the beginning of Year 6 (end of Year 5). It must be discounted back to the present, using the present value factor for five years and 10 percent, 0.621. Therefore,

$$P_n \text{ discounted to today} = P_n(\text{PV factor for five years}, 10\%)$$
$$= \$46.64(0.621)$$
$$= \$28.96$$

The last step is to add the two present values together:

5.26 = present value of the first five years of dividends

$+ 28.96$ = present value of the price at the end of Year 5, representing the discounted
value of dividends from Year 6 to ∞

$= \$34.22 = P_0$, the value today of this multiple growth rate stock

Figure 10-3

Valuing a Multiple Growth Rate Company.

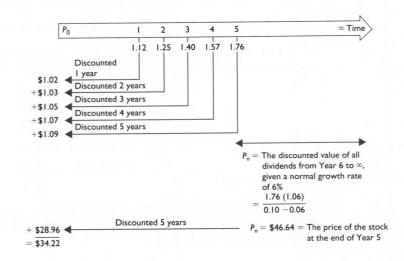

Limitations of the Multiple Growth Rate Case   As mentioned previously, the DDM is subject to limitations, and these clearly apply to multiple growth rate models.

(a) As before, this model is very sensitive to the inputs. Since a large part of the model involves a constant growth rate calculation, changing one of the parameters will obviously impact the final estimate of value.

(b) Determining the length of the abnormal growth period is quite difficult to do in practice. Will it last five years, or 12 years?

(c) The model as described above assumes an immediate transition from unusual growth to constant growth, while in reality the transition may not take place that quickly.

DIVIDENDS, DIVIDENDS—WHAT ABOUT CAPITAL GAINS?

In their initial study of valuation concepts, investors often are bothered by the fact that the dividend discount model contains only dividends, and an infinite stream of dividends at that. Although this is the correct formulation, many investors are sure that (1) they will not be here forever and (2) they really want capital gains. Dividends may be nice, but buying low and selling high is wonderful! Since so many investors are interested in capital gains, which by definition involves the difference between the price paid for a security and the price at which this security is later sold, a valuation model should seemingly contain a stock price somewhere. Thus, in computing present value for a stock, investors are interested in the present value of the estimated price two years from now, or six months from now, or whatever the expected, and finite, holding period is. How can price be incorporated into the valuation—or should it be?

How Capital Gains are Accounted For Because of the construction of the DDM, investors need only be concerned with dividends. Expected price in the future is built into the dividend discount model in Equation 10-2—it is simply not visible. To see this, ask yourself at what price you can expect to sell your stock at some point in the future. Assume, for example, that you purchase the stock today and plan to hold it for three years. The price you receive three years from now will reflect the buyer's expectations of dividends from that point forward (at the end of Years 4, 5, etc.). The estimated price today of the stock, V_0, is equal to

$$V_0 = \frac{D_1}{(1+k)} + \frac{D_2}{(1+k)^2} + \frac{D_3}{(1+k)^3} + \frac{P_3}{(1+k)^3} \qquad \textbf{(10-7)}$$

But P_3 (the estimated price of the stock at the end of Year 3), is, in turn, equal to the discounted value of all future dividends from Year 4 to infinity. That is,

$$P_3 = \frac{D_4}{(1+k)^4} + \frac{D_5}{(1+k)^5} + \cdots + \frac{D_\infty}{(1+k)^\infty} \qquad \textbf{(10-8)}$$

Substituting Equation 10-8 into Equation 10-7 produces Equation 10-2, the basic DDM. Thus, in principle, investors obtain the same estimate of value today whether they discount

(a) Only the stream of dividends expected to be paid on the stock, or

(b) A combination of dividends for some period and an expected terminal price.

Since expected price at any point in the future is a function of the dividends to be received after that time, the estimated value today for a common stock is best thought of as the discounted value of all future dividends.

THE DIVIDEND DISCOUNT MODEL IN PRACTICE

Many money managers and investment services firms, including a number of large Wall Street firms, use the DDM in various ways to estimate the intrinsic values of stocks. Regardless of who uses the model, and how it is used, estimates will always be involved. Investors should always remember this in using, or evaluating, output from these models. However, this also applies to any other valuation model that is used.

✓ All valuation models involve judgments and estimates because all valuation models are dealing with the uncertain future.

In practice, investors may use the Dividend Discount Model in other ways to select stocks. This results from rearranging Equation 10-5 to solve for k, which we can think of in this context as the expected rate of return on a stock (we will use the current price, P_0, instead of V_0).

$$k = D_1/P_0 + g \qquad (10\text{-}9)$$

Equation 10-9 says that the expected rate of a return on a constant growth stock is equal to the dividend yield plus the expected growth rate in dividends and price, g. The latter term can be thought of as the price change component or capital gains component. Therefore, an investor's expected rate of return from a stock is the sum of the income component and the price change component, which together constitute the total return from a stock as discussed in Chapter 6.

Investors can use Equation 10-9 to estimate the expected rate of return on a constant growth stock, E(R), and then compare that estimate to their required rate of return (RR). Recall that the required rate of return for a common stock, or any security, is defined as the minimum *expected* rate of return needed to induce an investor to purchase it. That is, given its risk, a security must offer some minimum expected return before a particular investor can be persuaded to buy it.

The CAPM, as discussed in Chapter 9, provides investors with a method of calculating a required rate of return for a stock, an industry, or the market as a whole. If the expected return on a stock is greater than the required return for that stock, the stock would be a buy candidate because it would be considered undervalued. Specifically,

If E(R) > RR, buy because the expected return > the required return

RR > E(R), do not buy because the required return > expected return

Checking Your Understanding

3. Neither the zero growth rate case nor the constant growth rate case show any signs of a present value process in their equations. How, then, can the DDM be said to involve a present value process?
4. Assume a group of investors uses the constant growth version of the DDM to value GE. Are they likely to come up with different estimates of value?

Other Discounted Cash Flow Approaches

The DDM is certainly not the only DCF model used by investors and analysts. Others are being used and promoted. Regardless, all involve the same basic concepts—an estimation of future cash flows, discounted back to today using a discount rate to reflect the time value of money and the risk involved. As noted at the outset of this discussion, the primary differences are the cash flows (to equity or to the firm) to be discounted and the discount rate to be used (the required rate of return or the average weighted cost of capital). We consider each of these in turn.

Free Cash Flow to Equity (FCFE) Model It differs from the DDM in that FCFE measures what a firm *could* pay out as dividends, rather than what they actually do pay out

FREE CASH FLOW TO EQUITY

The DCF model involving cash flows to equity is referred to as the **Free Cash Flow to Equity (FCFE) model**. It differs from the DDM discussed above in that FCFE measures what a firm *could* pay out as dividends, rather than what they actually do pay out. Dividends are at times higher than FCFE, and at other times lower. Note that the FCFE variable is placed on a per share basis.[10]

Definition of Free Cash Flow to Equity FCFE, is defined as the cash flow remaining after interest and principal repayments on debt have been made and capital expenditures provided for (both to maintain existing assets and provide for new assets needed for growth). It can be calculated as

$$FCFE = \text{Net income} + \text{Depreciation} - \text{Debt repayments} - \text{Capital expenditures}$$
$$- \text{Change in working capital} + \text{New debt issues}[11]$$

Implementing the Model To implement this model for a firm whose cash flows are growing at a stable rate, an analyst or investor could apply the constant growth format discussed with the DDM. This results in the following equation:

$$V_0 = \frac{\text{Expected FCFE}}{k - g} \qquad\qquad \textbf{(10-10)}$$

where g is the expected constant growth rate in FCFE for a company, and k is the cost of equity capital for the company.[12]

This free cash flow model is an alternative to the DDM. It may provide an estimated value similar to that produced by the DDM, or it may provide a different estimate. One example of when a difference could occur is if the firm is paying dividends in amounts greater than the free cash flows. The firm will have to finance these dividends out of external capital, which could have significant consequences for the valuation of the stock.

FREE CASH FLOW TO THE FIRM

Free cash flow to the firm (FCFF) is similar to the definition of FCFE. The major differences arise from the use of debt financing, including both the repayment of existing debt, and the interest thereon, and the sale of new debt. Preferred dividends may also need to be accounted for.

Definition of Free Cash Flow to the Firm FCFF starts with FCFE and can be defined as follows:[13]

$$FCFF = FCFE + \text{Interest expense} (1 - \text{Tax rate}) + \text{Principal repayments}$$
$$- \text{New debt Issues} - \text{Preferred dividends} \qquad\qquad \textbf{(10-11)}$$

---

[10] Chapter 15 discusses the cash flow statement as a part of the financial statements a firm prepares. For our purposes in discussing valuation, we will concentrate on the definitions of cash flow as they are used in valuation analysis.

[11] An alternative format is FCFE = Net income − (Capital expenditures − Depreciation) − (Change in non-cash working capital) + (New debt issued − Debt repayments).

[12] In a similar manner, this model can be applied to firms with multiple growth rates, again using the methodology outlined in the DDM discussion. Once again, the standard assumption is that after some period of rapid growth, free cash flows slow down and grow at a normal growth rate for the indefinite future.

[13] An alternative formulation uses EBIT (Earnings Before Interest and Taxes) as follows: FCFF = EBIT (1 − Tax rate) + Depreciation − Capital expenditures − Change in working capital.

As noted, DCF models using FCFF employ the weighted average cost of capital as the discount rate. Therefore, for a constant growth firm, use FCFF in the numerator, the weighted cost of capital as the discount rate, and the expected growth rate in FCFF as *g*.

Implementing the Model   The details of this model can be tedious. Rather than expand on them, let's consider an example of this model in practice. As noted in Chapter 3, *Morningstar* is a well-known provider of information on mutual funds. However, *Morningstar* also provides analyses of individual stocks using a valuation approach based on DCF techniques. Their methodology is as follows:

1. Project expected cash flows, taking into account several factors such as the company's relative position compared to competitors, growth prospects, management, and the attractiveness of the company's industry.
2. Discount these estimated cash flows back to the present using an estimate of the company's weighted cost of capital (and taking into account such factors as the risk of the company and how much debt and equity it has).
3. Adjust the present value of the expected cash flows to account for the debt, cash, and off-balance sheet assets and liabilities of the company.
4. Divide the result by the number of diluted shares outstanding, which results in a per-share estimate of fair value.

Recognizing that any estimation process such as this is subject to errors, *Morningstar* recommends a stock as a buy only if the current market price is below the fair value estimate by a certain percentage (often 20 percent) in order to account for the uncertainty.

Other well-known advisory services also use a DCF method, often as a complement to other models. For example, Standard & Poor's *Outlook* sometimes uses a discounted free cash flow model as part of its valuation of individual companies.

INTRINSIC VALUE AND MARKET PRICE

The end objective of a DCF technique is an estimate of intrinsic value. What does intrinsic value imply? Again, it is simply the estimated value of the stock today, derived from estimating and discounting the future cash flows for a stock. How is it used? Investors and analysts specify a relationship between the intrinsic value (which we shall call V_0) of an asset and its current market price, CMP.

Specifically,

If $V_0 > $ CMP, the asset is undervalued and should be purchased or held if already owned.

If $V_0 < $ CMP, the asset is overvalued and should be avoided, sold if held, or possibly sold short.

If $V_0 = $ CMP, this implies an equilibrium in that the asset is correctly valued.

Security analysis has traditionally been thought of as the search for undervalued or overvalued stocks. To do this, one can calculate the estimated or intrinsic value of the stock and compare this value to the current market price of the stock. Most investors believe that stocks are not always priced at their intrinsic values, thereby leading to buy and sell opportunities.

Using Intrinsic Value   Always remember that the valuation process is an art and not a science—it can never be an exact process because it involves estimates of the future.

✓ When an investor calculates an intrinsic value, it is an estimate, no more and no less. It is always subject to error.

The intelligent way to make investment decisions using intrinsic value is to base them on significant differences in current price versus estimated (calculated) value. If you estimate the value of Cisco at $20 per share and it is selling for $19 or $21.50, then it really doesn't matter too much. But if you do careful analysis and you estimate an intrinsic value for Cisco of $20 when it is selling for $10, then you should buy because the stock is substantially undervalued. In a similar vein, if your careful analysis indicates an intrinsic value for Cisco of $14 when it is currently selling for $22, you should avoid the stock at all costs, or perhaps sell it short.

In actual daily practice, some analysts use a 15 percent rule in recognition of the fact that the estimation of a security's value is an inexact process. Thus, if the CMP is not 15 percent or more on either side of the estimated value, no action is warranted.[14]

As discussed in Chapter 1, uncertainty will always be the dominant feature of the environment in which investment decisions are made. Furthermore, other factors are at play, including the psychology of the market. And with the rise of the Internet, and investors interacting with each other there, information, including false or misleading information, can be spread quickly, and prices affected accordingly.

Checking Your Understanding

5. Does the use of models involving free cash flows make an investor's job when estimating stock values any easier?
6. Is the intrinsic value of a stock a formula value or an estimated value?

The Earnings Multiplier Approach

Most analysts and knowledgeable investors recognize the underlying foundation and intuitive nature of the DCF techniques, but they also recognize the difficulties of using these models in practice. Small differences in inputs result in large differences in estimates of intrinsic value, which in turn can easily lead to errors in determining if a stock is undervalued or overvalued. This has led many investors and analysts to alternative approaches to the valuation of stocks such as earnings multiplier models and relative valuations.

Analysts are most comfortable talking about such variables as earnings per share (EPS) and P/E ratios, and this is how their reports are often worded. Without question the P/E ratio is one of the most widely mentioned and discussed variables pertaining to a common stock, and will typically appear in some form in any report from an analyst or an investment advisory service.

As a definition, the P/E ratio is simply the number of times investors value earnings as expressed in the stock price. As one example, a stock priced at $100, with most recent 12-month earnings of $5, is said to be selling for a multiple of 20 times trailing 12-month (TTM) earnings. In contrast, if another stock had earnings of $2.50 and was selling for $100, investors would be valuing the stock at 40 times TTM earnings.

✓ The P/E ratio as *typically reported daily* is simply an identity (it is true by definition) calculated by dividing the current market price of the stock by the latest 12-month

---

[14] Obviously, some number other than 15 percent can be used.

earnings. As such, it only tells investors the price currently being paid for each $1 of most recent 12-month earnings.

It is true by definition that

$$P_0 = \text{Current stock price} = E_0(P_0/E_0) \tag{10-12}$$

where

P_0 = the current stock price

E_0 = the most recent 12-month earnings per share

It is worth emphasizing:

Stock price is the product of two variables when using this type of approach.

1. EPS
2. The P/E multiple

Equation 10-12 tells us what is true by definition, but it is not very useful for valuing a stock. However, we can make a forecast of next year's EPS and apply an appropriate P/E ratio to this earnings number to obtain an estimate of intrinsic value. Assume that we are talking about a stock that has a constant growth rate. Expected earnings per share, E_1, can be found by taking this year's earnings, E_0, and compounding them up one period by the expected growth rate, g.

$$E_1 = E_0(1 + g)$$

Alternatively, investors can obtain estimates of next year's EPS from security analysts and investment advisory services such as *The Value Line Investment Survey* or Standard & Poor's *Outlook*.

Multiply the EPS estimate by what is thought to be an appropriate P/E ratio to obtain an estimated price, which we will call P_E:

Example 10-7   In early 2012, Standard & Poor's was estimating 2012 earnings for Cliff's Natural Resources of $12.18. S&P estimated an appropriate P/E to be 7.8. Multiplying these two numbers together produced a target price of $95.[15]

$$P_E = E_1 \times P_E/E_1$$

An appealing aspect of this approach is its apparent simplicity—multiply two variables together to derive an estimate of intrinsic value. However, the problem is that both variables used, next period's EPS and what is thought to be an appropriate P/E ratio, are both estimates, and therefore are subject to misestimation.

✓ Once again, we must always remember that all valuation techniques are subject to error, and mistakes will be made.

---

[15] Based on S&P's Focus Stock of the Week, *AAII Weekly Features*, February 13, 2012, Internet edition.

Relative Valuation Metrics

Rather than try to estimate the current or future value of a stock, investors may do a comparative analysis of stocks as a guide to stock selection. This relative valuation involves analyzing a company's peers as a guide to trying to determine stocks that may be undervalued without having to say what the stock is worth or how much it is undervalued.

Information on relative valuation ratios can be easily found at sites such as *Yahoo! Finance* (look under "Key Statistics" for any stock you call up by its ticker symbol). On the *Morningstar* website, look under the "Valuation" section.

THE PRICE/EARNINGS RATIO

Most investors intuitively realize that the P/E ratio should be higher for companies whose earnings are expected to grow rapidly. However, how much higher is not an easy question to answer. Furthermore, the high growth rate may be attributable to several different factors, some of which are more desirable than others. For example, rapid growth in unit sales owing to strong demand for a firm's products is preferable to favorable tax situations, which may change, or liberal accounting procedures, which one day may cause a reversal in the firm's situation.

Typically, the P/E ratio metric is used to compare companies in the same industry, or the company to the overall market, or the company's current P/E ratio to its past P/E ratios. Note that while the P/E ratios for comparable companies can be evaluated, companies in different industries are expected to have different average P/E ratios, sometimes dramatically different.

As an example, if several companies in the same industry are selling for an average P/E of 15, another company in this group might be given a P/E of 15; however, if the company is thought to be superior in terms of expected growth, a P/E of 16 or 18 might be applied. This means that a relative valuation judgment, or comparative judgment, is being made.

As a general proposition, the higher the P/E ratio, the greater the market's expectations about future earnings growth. However, the market will assess the degree of risk involved in the expected future growth of earnings. The average long-term P/E for the S&P 500 stocks is around 16. Stocks that have very high P/E ratios, such as 50, 60, and 70, are very vulnerable to a market disappointment about earnings. If investors lose confidence in their expectations about the strong future earnings growth expected for a stock, the price can decline very quickly.

PRICE/BOOK VALUE

Price to book value is calculated as the ratio of price to stockholders' equity as measured on the balance sheet (and explained in Chapter 15). Book value, the accounting value of the firm's equity as reflected in its financial statements, measures the actual values recorded under accounting conventions (typically on a historical cost basis). As such, book values have the advantages and disadvantages of accounting numbers. If the value of this ratio is 1.0, the market price is equal to the accounting (book) value. If the ratio is less than 1.0, price is less than book value.

Example 10-8   In February 2012, Ford Motors, with a large amount of plant and equipment, had a price to book value ratio of 8.1. Coca-Cola, on the other hand, had a price to book value ratio of 4.7, while the same ratio for the S&P 500 was 2.1 Banks, on the other hand, tend to have investments that are easily valued and closer to book value, so their ratios tend to be closer to one. J. P. Morgan Chase had a ratio of 0.8.

The price to book value ratio has received support in empirical tests. For example, a study by Rosenberg et al. found that stocks with low price to book values significantly outperformed the average stock.[16] This variable got a major boost in 1992 with the publication of an article by Eugene Fama and Kenneth French. They found that two basic variables, size (market value of equity, or ME) and book to market equity (BV/ME), effectively combined to capture the cross-sectional variation in average stock returns during the period 1963−1990.[17] Furthermore, the book to market equity ratio had a consistently stronger role in average returns.[18]

Several analysts recommend as a decision rule stocks with low price to book value ratios.[19] To use this measure of relative value, comparisons should be made to the firm's own ratio over time as well as to its industry ratio and that of the market as a whole.

Investors obviously need to be careful when interpreting this ratio, like all valuation ratios. For example, how relevant is book value to the business? This ratio works best for companies with hard assets, such as plant and equipment. However, for firms with significant "intellectual property" like research and development, it tends to have problems. And what about service companies with famous brand names like Microsoft and Google?

PRICE/SALES RATIO (PSR)

A valuation technique that has received increased attention in recent years is the price/sales ratio (PSR). P/E ratios can be a problem because a company can have erratic earnings, or, in some cases, no earnings. Also, earnings can be defined different ways (for example, with or without writeoffs). In contrast, the PSR ratio can be used to value any public company, including companies with no earnings. It tends to be stable, particularly compared to earnings or cash flows. Furthermore, many believe that sales are much less likely to be "managed" by the company as opposed to earnings; that is, sales should be much less subject to manipulation than are earnings.

This ratio is calculated by dividing a company's current stock price by its revenues per share over the four most recent quarters (typically it may be easier to divide a company's total

---

[16] See Barr Rosenberg, Kenneth Reid, and Ronald Lanstein, "Persuasive Evidence of Market Inefficiency," *The Journal of Portfolio Management* 11 (Spring 1985): pp. 9−17.

[17] Note that in this study the P/B ratio is being stated differently.

[18] See Eugene Fama and Kenneth French, "The Cross-Section of Expected Stock Returns," *The Journal of Finance* 47 (June 1992): pp. 427−465.

[19] An obvious issue is what constitutes "low"?

market value (price times number of shares) by its annual sales. In effect, it indicates what the market is willing to pay for a firm's revenues.

Example 10-9   In February 2012, Coca-Cola had a P/S ratio of 3.5, based on trailing 12 months data. In contrast, Walmart had a P/S of 0.5 at the same point in time.

One rule of thumb for the PSR is to say that a PSR of 1.0 is average for all companies, and therefore those with a PSR considerably less than 1.0, such as 0.5, are bargains. Obviously, such a simplistic approach is not always reliable. It is important to interpret the ratio within industry bounds. For example, retailers tend to have low price/sales ratios because of their low margins, while biotechnology companies tend to have high price/sales ratios.[20] Furthermore, a company's PSR ratio should be compared to that of its competitors as well as its own history.[21]

In *What Works on Wall Street*, James O'Shaughnessy, gave new emphasis to the price/sales ratio, finding that stocks with low PSRs outperformed other selection measures, such as the P/E ratio.[22] He rejects stocks with a P/S ratio greater than 1.5. It should be noted that the portfolios evaluated in his study were rebalanced annually, and that O'Shaughnessy found that portfolios selected on multiple criteria outperform portfolios selected on only a single criteria (such as low PSR).

ECONOMIC VALUE ADDED ANALYSIS

A newer technique for evaluating stocks is to calculate the economic value added, or EVA™.[23] In effect, this variable is the difference between operating profits and a company's true cost of capital for both debt and equity and reflects an emphasis on return on capital. If this difference is positive, the company has added value. Its creator calls this variable "the measure of a company's true profitability."

Some mutual funds are now using EVA™ analysis as the primary tool for selecting stocks for the fund to hold. One recommendation for investors interested in this approach is to search for companies with a return on capital in excess of 20 percent, because this will in all likelihood exceed the cost of capital and, therefore the company is adding value.

ETHICS IN INVESTING

Truth in the Financial Markets

Investors seeking to value stocks using valuation principles have a difficult enough job without having to worry about who is telling the truth, and who is not, when it comes to corporate disclosures of important financial information. Recently, a number of corporate scandals have been uncovered involving

---

[20] In addition, a firm's financing can play an important role in interpreting this ratio. Quite a few companies that sell at PSRs of less than 1.0 have a large amount of debt and are not profitable; some could go bankrupt.

[21] Some recent research suggests investors should focus on stocks with both earnings surprises and revenue surprises. The logic here is that earnings surprises based on revenue gains are more significant than those based on lower expenses.

[22] See James O'Shaughnessy, *What Works on Wall Street: A Guide to the Best-Performing Investment Strategies of All Time.* McGraw-Hill, 2011.

[23] This term has been trademarked by Stern Stewart, a consulting firm that pioneered the use of this concept.

manipulation to make corporate earnings appear more favorable. We need only think of Enron, WorldCom, HealthSouth, ImClone, and so forth. Lying appears to have been a prominent feature in multiple corporations of late, and that has serious implications for financial markets.

Hopefully, the trials and convictions of a number of corporate executives will send the message that lying about issues that affect the valuation of a company's shares will not be tolerated. It is unrealistic, of course, to think that the recent publicized trials and headlines will stop all false statements that are issued by corporate executives, because the potential payoffs are often large. However, investors need to be able to rely on the integrity of public disclosures by companies if they are to have faith in the financial markets. Otherwise, they may conclude that trying to value companies in a reasonable, intelligent manner is simply a shot in the dark, akin to gambling at a roulette wheel or slot machine.

Bottom line? Ethical behavior, and the perception of ethical behavior, is critical to the orderly functioning of the stock market.

Which Approach To Use?

We have described the most often used approaches in fundamental analysis—discounted cash flow techniques, earnings multiples, and relative valuation techniques. Which should be used?

In theory, the DCF approach is a correct, logical, and sound position. Conceptually, the best estimate of the current value of a company's common stock is the present value of the (estimated) cash flows to be generated by that company. However, some analysts and investors feel that this model is unrealistic. After all, they argue, with regard to the DDM no one can forecast dividends into the distant future with very much accuracy. Technically, the model calls for an estimate of all dividends from now to infinity, which is an impossible task. However, as we have learned, infinity is not a problem and future dividends can be modeled based on expected growth rates.

Possibly because of the objections to the dividend discount model cited here, or possibly because it is easier to use, valuation techniques such as the earnings multiplier remain a popular approach to valuation. Relative or comparative valuation metrics, while less sophisticated and less formal, can also be helpful as stock selection models. The P/E ratio can serve in a dual role. It can help investors estimate a stock's intrinsic value as part of the earnings multiplier model as well as serve as a relative valuation technique.

Regardless of which approach is used, it is important to remember that valuation employing fundamental analysis, or any other approach, is always subject to error. This is because we are dealing with the uncertain future. No matter who does the analysis, or how it is done, mistakes will be made.

✓ Every valuation model and approach, properly done, requires estimates of the uncertain future and/or judgments about current values. Anyone who argues differently is grossly ignorant when it comes to valuing stocks.

Concepts in Action

How Some Investment Advisory Services Recommend Stocks

There are of course a large number of investment advisory services as well as brokerage firms that make stock recommendations. They use a variety of valuation techniques. We will review some of these from well-known services that investors can subscribe to or read in a public library, or access on the Internet (where a premium service with a cost may be required).

Consider first *Morningstar*, which provides information on mutual funds as well as individual stocks. *Morningstar* calculates and reports the "fair value" for stocks based on a discounted cash flow analysis (think of it as an intrinsic value). Meanwhile, Standard & Poor's, in its *Outlook*, recommends stocks using discounted cash flow analysis, target prices involving relative valuation metrics, and often a combination of these two.

The Value Line Investment Survey, perhaps the best-known investment service because of its long history and wide availability in libraries, uses a proprietary ranking system to recommend stocks, with "1" being the highest recommendation and "5" the lowest. An investor can refer to the writeups for each of these stocks and obtain earnings estimates for the following year, earnings growth rates, a safety rating, some information on P/E ratios, and so forth.

Bursting the Bubble on New Economy Stocks—A Lesson in Valuation

At the end of the 1990s and into 2000, investors were caught up in a speculative bubble involving "New Economy" stocks, such as eToys and Dr.Koop.com. These new companies, involving the Internet, were thought to represent the wave of the future and to be more desirable than "Old Economy" stocks such as 3M or Procter & Gamble. There seemed to be no upper limit as the prices of these stocks were bid higher and higher. Tremendous fortunes, mostly on paper, were being made.

Example 10-10   From the beginning of 1998, the Amex Interactive Week Internet Index rose to 689 in late March 2000 from a starting point of about 87 (split adjusted). Therefore, in just over two years this index showed a gain of almost 700 percent.

Because these companies involved revolutionary new technology, many investors argued that they should be valued using revolutionary techniques because the old methods no longer applied. As one of the leading Internet gurus at Merrill Lynch proclaimed in early 2000, "Valuation is often not a helpful tool in determining when to sell hyper growth stocks." Other star analysts were talking about "usage metrics" when discussing these stocks, which basically means nonfinancial metrics such as customer loyalty, site hits, and "engaged shoppers." Many analysts and investors did not want to talk about EPS, cash flows, P/E ratios, etc., and of course for many of these companies these variables did not exist. They had no profitability, and in many cases little hope of profitability for the foreseeable future.

As we now know, the bubble started to burst in March 2000 and continued, with horrific declines in 2001 and 2002. Many of the hot New Economy stocks dropped 80 percent or more, and hundreds of Internet companies went out of business. The aggregate dollar loss in the value of investor portfolios was staggering—roughly $4 trillion from March 2000 to March 2001 alone. The Index mentioned in Example 10-10 declined to about 280 by the end of 2000, a 60 percent loss, and declined even further in early 2001.

By early 2001 it became apparent again to all but the most obtuse that the old metrics of valuation really do apply. To survive and succeed, companies sooner or later have to generate cash flows, and be profitable. Investors no longer believe statements such as that of a major brokerage firm report which argued that cash burned by dot-com companies is "primarily an investor sentiment issue" and not a long-term risk for the sector.[24]

---

[24] This statement and some of the thoughts in this section are based on Gretchen Morgenson, "How Did They Value Stocks? Count the Absurd Ways," *The New York Times*, March 18, 2001.

The bottom line here is that valuation standards apply, at least in part, to New Economy stocks, and stocks must be valued on a rational basis. Revenues and profits do matter, and so do P/E ratios when they get too far out of line.

Example 10-11   At the peak of the NASDAQ market rise, which occurred on March 10, 2000, Cisco had a P/E ratio of about 150, Yahoo about 650, and JDS Uniphase about 640. One year later, the same companies had P/E ratios of 31, 35, and 41.

Checking Your Understanding

7. Why is the definition of the P/E ratio often a problem when using this relative valuation technique?
8. What did the extraordinary rise in stock valuations in the late 1990s, ending in March 2000, demonstrate about the valuation of common stock?

Some Final Thoughts on Valuation

Valuing stocks is difficult under the best of circumstances. Judgments must be made, and variables estimated. No one knows with precision which valuation model should be used for any particular stock. It is almost impossible to prove that an investor's calculations for a valuation model are correct, or incorrect (although many calculations could be judged by most people to be "reasonable" or not "reasonable)." Valuation of stocks always has been, is, and will continue to be an art, and not a science. Errors are to be expected.

In the final analysis, stocks are worth what investors pay for them. Valuations may appear out of line, but market prices prevail.

Example 10-12   Google went public in August 2004 at $85, a price regarded by many at the time as ridiculous. By May of 2005, the price had tripled. By late 2007, the price was over $700 a share, but fell below $500 in early 2008. In late 2011, it ranged from $500 to $600. What is Google really worth? Who knows?

Summary

▶ Two primary approaches for analyzing and selecting common stocks are fundamental analysis and technical analysis. Efficient market considerations should be taken into account.

▶ Fundamental analysis seeks to estimate the intrinsic value of a stock, which is a function of its expected returns and risk.

▶ Major approaches to valuing common stocks using fundamental analysis include discounted cash flow

techniques and the earnings multiplier approach as well as relative valuation techniques.

▶ Discounted cash flow techniques attempt to estimate the value of a stock today (its intrinsic value) using a present value analysis. The intrinsic value of a stock is its estimated value, or formula value.

▶ The dividend discount model (DDM) is the best-known DCF model and is widely considered a foundation of stock valuation. It states that the value of a stock today is the discounted value of all future dividends.

▶ The future stream of dividends to be received from a common stock is discounted back to the present at an appropriate discount rate (that is, the investor's required rate of return discussed in Chapter 9).

▶ To account for an infinite stream of dividends, stocks to be valued are classified by their expected growth rate in dividends.

▶ If no growth is expected, the dividend discount model reduces to a perpetuity. If two or more growth rates are expected, a multiple growth model must be used in which the future stream of dividends is identified before being discounted.

▶ The constant growth version of the dividend discount model is used most often. Using this version of the DDM, the dividend expected next period is divided by the difference between the required rate of return and the expected growth rate in dividends.

▶ The multiple growth rate case involves stocks where the expected future growth in dividends must be described using two or more growth rates.

▶ The dividend discount model is sensitive to the estimates of the variables used in it; therefore, investors will calculate different prices for the same stock while using an identical model. This model implicitly accounts for the terminal price of a stock.

▶ Other discounted cash flow approaches involve free cash flow, both to equity and to the firm.

▶ The end objective of a discounted cash flow technique is an estimate of intrinsic value. Intrinsic value is compared to current market price to make a buy or sell decision.

▶ A P/E ratio can be calculated by dividing the current price by the most recent 12-month earnings per share.

▶ The earnings multiplier approach is based on the identity that a stock's current price is the product of its most recent 12-month earnings per share and the P/E ratio.

▶ The earnings multiplier approach attempts to estimate intrinsic value based on estimated earnings for the next year and an appropriate multiplier, or P/E ratio.

▶ The relative value concept is based on making comparisons in order to determine value. By calculating measures such as the P/E ratio, and making comparisons to some benchmark(s), analysts can avoid having to estimate the g and k parameters of the DDM as well as one-point estimates of the value of a stock in the form of intrinsic values.

▶ Relative valuation techniques include, among others, the P/E ratio, P/B, and P/S. Like all valuation techniques, each has its strengths and weaknesses.

Questions

10-1 What is meant by "intrinsic value"? How is it determined?

10-2 Why is the required rate of return for a stock the discount rate to be used in valuation analysis?

10-3 Why can earnings not be used as readily as dividends in the present value approach?

10-4 What is the dividend discount model? Write this model in equation form.

10-5 What problems are encountered in using the dividend discount model?

10-6 Describe the three possibilities for dividend growth. Which is the most likely to apply to the typical company?

10-7 Since dividends are paid to infinity, how is this problem handled in the present value analysis?

10-8 Demonstrate how the dividend discount model is the same as a method that includes a specified number of dividends and a terminal price.

10-9 Assume that two investors are valuing General Foods Company and have agreed to use the constant growth version of the dividend valuation model. Both use $3 a share as the expected dividend for the coming year. Are these two investors likely to derive different prices? Why or why not?

10-10   Once an investor calculates intrinsic value for a particular stock, how does he or she decide whether or not to buy it?

10-11   How valuable are the trailing 12-month P/E ratios typically shown for stocks?

10-12   The P/E ratio can be used in valuation analysis in two completely different ways. Explain.

10-13   Many investors prefer the earnings multiplier model to the present value analysis on the grounds that the latter is more difficult to use. State these alleged difficulties and respond to them.

10-14   Is it always correct to say that the valuation of common stocks is an art and not a science?

10-15   Assume you are trying to value a company using relative valuation techniques but the company has no earnings. Which techniques could you use?

10-16   List two advantages of using the Price/Sales ratio as a valuation technique. How is this ratio calculated without using per share numbers?

10-17   Do you think cash flow could be used in the valuation of stocks?

10-18   Is it possible to derive the "true" value of a common stock?

10-19   Agree or disagree. Given the three growth rate cases of the DDM, not all of them involve a present value process.

10-20   Agree or disagree. Two investors have the same required rate of return. They also have identical expectations about Gritta Corp with regard to its expected dividend and growth rate, and both agree it is a constant growth company. However, investor A plans to hold the stock for only one year, while investor B plans to hold it for 10 years. Both investors should derive the same value for this stock when they value it.

10-21   Agree or disagree. One of the strong points in favor of using the DDM is that estimates of intrinsic value are not very sensitive to estimates of the expected growth rate in dividends.

10-22   Agree or disagree. Using the equation $g = br$ ensures that the correct growth rate in dividends is calculated.

10-23   Having estimated the expected rate of return on a constant growth stock, how can an investor decide whether to buy that stock?

10-24   Agree or disagree. Some hedge funds, earning very large returns, must be using models that correctly determine intrinsic values much of the time.

Demonstration Problems

10-1   Cole Pharmaceuticals is currently paying a dividend of $2 per share, which is not expected to change. Investors require a rate of return of 20 percent to invest in a stock with the riskiness of Cole. Calculate the intrinsic value of the stock.

Solution:

The first step to solving a common stock valuation problem is to identify the type of growth involved in the dividend stream. The second step is to determine whether the dividend given in the problem is D_0 or D_1.

In this problem it is clear that the growth rate is zero and that we must solve a zero growth valuation problem (Equation 10-3). The second step is not relevant here because all of the dividends are the same.

$$P_0 = \frac{D_0}{k}$$

$$= \frac{\$2.00}{0.20}$$

$$= \$10.00$$

10-2 Baddour Legal Services is currently paying a dividend of $2 per share, which is expected to grow at a constant rate of 7 percent per year. Investors require a rate of return of 16 percent. Phil Baddour, CEO, has asked you to calculate the estimated value of his company.

Solution:

Since dividends are expected to grow at a constant rate, we use the constant growth version of the dividend discount model (Equation 10-5). Note carefully that this equation calls for D_1 in the numerator and that the dividend given in this problem is the current dividend being paid, D_0. Therefore, we must compound this dividend up one period to obtain D_1 before solving the problem. The expected dividend for Baddour Legal Services is:

$$D_1 = D_0(1 + g)$$
$$= \$2.00(1.07)$$
$$= \$2.14$$

and the estimated value is:

$$V_0 = D_1/(k - g)$$
$$= \frac{\$2.14}{16 - .07}$$
$$= \$23.78$$

10-3 Bibbins Software Company is currently selling for $60 per share and is expected to pay a dividend of $3. The expected growth rate in dividends is 8 percent for the foreseeable future. Calculate the expected rate of return for this stock.

Solution:

To solve this problem, note first that this is a constant growth model problem. Second, note that the dividend given in the problem is D_1 because it is stated as the dividend to be paid in the next period. To solve this problem for k, the expected rate of return, we simply rearrange Equation 10-5 substituting P_0 for V_0 because we know the current price:

$$k = \frac{D_1}{P_0} + g$$
$$= \frac{\$3.00}{\$60} + 0.08$$
$$= .13$$

Note that we could also solve for g by rearranging Equation 10-5 to solve for g rather than k.

10-4 Grieb Electronics has been undergoing rapid growth for the last few years. The current dividend of $2 per share is expected to continue to grow at the rapid rate of 20 percent a year for the next three years. After that time Grieb is expected to slow down, with the dividend growing at a more normal rate of 7 percent a year for the indefinite future. Because of the risk involved in such rapid growth, the required rate of return on this stock is 22 percent. Calculate the implied price for Grieb Electronics.

Solution:

We can recognize at once that this is a multiple growth case of valuation because more than one growth rate is given. To solve for the value of this stock, it is necessary to identify the entire stream of future dividends from Year 1 to infinity, and discount the entire stream back to time period zero. After the third year a constant growth model can be used which accounts for all dividends from the beginning of Year 4 to infinity.

We first calculate the dividends for each individual year of the abnormal growth period, and we discount each of these dividends at the required rate of return.

$$D_1 = \$2.00(1+0.20) = \$2.40$$
$$D_2 = \$2.00(1+0.20)^2 = \$2.88$$
$$D_3 = \$2.00(1+0.20)^3 = \$3.46$$
$$\$2.40(0.820) = \text{present value of } D_1 = \$1.97$$
$$\$2.88(0.672) = \text{present value of } D_2 = \$1.94$$
$$\$3.46(0.551) = \text{present value of } D_3 = \$1.91$$

Present value of the first three years of dividends = \$5.82

$$P_3 = \frac{\$3.46(1.07)}{0.22 - 0.07} = \$24.68,$$

which is the present value of the stock at the end of Year 3 (the beginning of Year 4)

$$P_0 = \$24.68(0.551) = \$13.60,$$

which is the present value of P_3 at time period zero

$$V_0 = \$5.82 + \$13.60 = \$19.42,$$

which is the present value of the stock at time period zero—the intrinsic value.

Note that the price derived from the constant model is the price of the stock at the end of Year 3, which is equivalent to the price of the stock at the beginning of Year 4. Therefore, we discount it back three periods to time period zero. Adding this value to the present value of all dividends to be received during the abnormal growth period produces the intrinsic value of this multiple growth period stock.

Problems

10-1   Assume that Ritchey Industries is expected by investors to have a dividend growth rate over the foreseeable future of 8 percent a year, and that the required rate of return for this stock is 14 percent. The current dividend being paid is \$1.25. What is the estimated value of the stock?

10-2   Jay Technology is currently selling for \$60 a share with an expected dividend in the coming year of \$2 per share. If the growth rate in dividends expected by investors is 5 percent, what is the required rate of return for Jay?

10-3   Dukes Longhorn Steaks is currently selling for \$40 per share and pays \$1.80 in dividends. Investors require 12 percent return on this stock. What is the expected growth rate of dividends?

10-4   Zhou Technology pays \$1.50 a year in dividends, which is expected to remain unchanged. Investors require a 12 percent rate of return on this stock. What is the estimated price?

10-5   **a.** Given a preferred stock with an annual dividend of $3.5 per share and a price of $40, what is the required rate of return?

　　　　b. Assume now that interest rates rise, leading investors to demand a required rate of return of 10 percent. What will the new price of this preferred stock be?

10-6   An investor purchases the common stock of a well-known company, Toma Inc., for $30 per share. The expected dividend for the next year is $4 per share, and the investor is confident that the stock can be sold one year from now for $35. What is the implied rate of return?

10-7   **a.** The current risk-free rate (RF) is 4 percent, and the expected return on the market for the coming year is 15 percent. Calculate the required rate of return for (1) stock A, with a beta of 1.0, (2) stock B, with a beta of 1.6, and (3) stock C, with a beta of 0.7.

　　　　b. How would your answers change if RF in part (a) were to increase to 8 percent, with the other variables unchanged?

　　　　c. How would your answers change if the expected return on the market changed to 20 percent, with the other variables unchanged?

10-8   The John G. Getsinger Fishing Tours Company is currently selling for $60 and is paying a $2 dividend.

　　　　a. If investors expect dividends to double in 10 years, what is the required rate of return for this stock?

　　　　b. John G. Getsinger, CEO, expects dividends to approximately triple in eight years. In this event, what would the required rate of return be?

10-9   Kendall Consulting Company is currently selling for $30, paying $1.20 in dividends, and investors expect dividends to grow at a constant rate of 5 percent a year.

　　　　a. If an investor requires a rate of return of 14 percent for a stock with the riskiness of Kendall Company, is it a good buy for this investor?

　　　　b. What is the maximum an investor with a 14 percent required return should pay for Kendall Company? What is the maximum if the required return is 15 percent?

10-10   The Parker Dental Supply Company sells at $36 per share, and Ray Parker, the CEO of this well-known Research Triangle firm, estimates the latest 12-month earnings are $3 per share with a dividend payout of 50 percent. Dr. Parker's earnings estimates are very accurate.

　　　　a. What is Parker's current P/E ratio?

　　　　b. If an investor expects earnings to grow by 10 percent a year, what is the projected price for next year if the P/E ratio remains unchanged?

　　　　c. Dr. Parker analyzes the data and estimates that the payout ratio will remain the same. Assume the expected growth rate of dividends is 10 percent, and an investor has a required rate of return of 16 percent, would this stock be a good buy? Why or why not?

　　　　d. If interest rates are expected to decline, what is the likely effect on Parker's P/E ratio?

10-11   The required rate of return for Ola Industries is 15.75 percent. The stock pays a current dividend of $2.30, and the expected growth rate is 12 percent. Calculate the estimated price.

10-12   In Problem 10-11, assume that the growth rate is 16 percent. Calculate the estimated price for this stock.

10-13   Hernandez Products is a rapidly growing firm. Dividends are expected to grow at the rate of 18 percent annually for the next 10 years. The growth rate after the first 10 years is expected to be 7 percent annually. The current dividend is $1.48. Investors require a rate of return of 20 percent on this stock. Calculate the intrinsic value of this stock.

10-14   Wansley Corporation is currently paying a dividend of $1.60 per year, and this dividend is expected to grow at a constant rate of 8 percent a year. Investors require a 14 percent rate of return on Wansley. What is its estimated price?

10-15   Johnson and Johnson Pharmaceuticals is expected to earn $5.46 per share next year. Johnson has a payout ratio of 74 percent. Earnings and dividends have been growing at a constant rate of 10 percent per year, but analysts are estimating that the growth rate will be 7.9 percent a year for the indefinite future. Investors require a 15 percent rate of return on Johnson and Johnson. What is its estimated price?

10-16   Puckett Foundries is expected to pay a dividend of $0.80 next year, $1.25 the following year, and $1.40 each year thereafter. The required rate of return on this stock is 10 percent. How much should investors be willing to pay for this stock?

10-17   McCalla Food Distributors is currently paying a dividend of $1.80. This dividend is expected to grow at a rate of 6 percent in the future. McCalla is 10 percent less risky than the market as a whole. The market risk premium is 7 percent, and the risk-free rate is 5 percent. What is the estimated price of this stock?

10-18   Mansur Industries is currently paying a dividend of $5 per share, which is not expected to change in the future. The current price of this stock is $60. What is the expected rate of return on this stock?

10-19   You expect a stock to increase by a compound factor of 1.7835 over eight years (compound growth). The current price is $45. The expected dividend is $2.00. The expected return on this stock is?

10-20   McMillan Company is not expected to pay a dividend until five years have elapsed. At the beginning of Year 6, investors expect the dividend to be $3 per share and to remain that amount forever. If an investor has a 20 percent required rate of return for this stock, what should he or she be willing to pay for McMillan?

10-21   Majadillas is currently selling for $50. It is expected to pay a dividend of $2 next period. If the required rate of return is 10 percent, what is the expected growth rate?

10-22   Batler Corp is currently selling for $50 and currently paying a $2 dividend. Dividends are expected to double in eight years. What is the expected rate of return for this stock?

10-23   Wislow Corp. is currently selling for $40, currently paying $1.20 in dividends, and investors expect dividends to grow at a constant rate of 5 percent a year. If an investor has an 8 percent required rate of return, is the stock a good buy for that investor?

10-24   Naidu Corporation makes advanced computer components. It pays no dividends currently, but it expects to begin paying $5 a share 10 years from now. The expected dividends in subsequent years are also $5 a share. The required rate of return is 18 percent. What is the estimated price for Naidu?

Computational Problems

10-1   Boni Software Products is currently paying a dividend of $1.20. This dividend is expected to grow at the rate of 30 percent a year for the next five years, followed by a growth rate of 20 percent a year for the following five years. After 10 years the dividend is expected to grow at the rate of 6 percent a year. The required rate of return for this stock is 25 percent. What is its intrinsic value?

10-2 In Problem 10-1, assume that the growth rate for the first five years is 28 percent rather than 30 percent. How would you expect the value calculated in Problem 10-1 to change? Confirm your answer by calculating the new intrinsic value.

10-3 Runyon Industries is expected to enjoy a very rapid growth rate in dividends of 30 percent a year for the next four years. This growth rate is then expected to slow to 20 percent a year for the next five years. After that time, the growth rate is expected to be 5 percent a year. D_0 is $2. The beta for this stock is 1.2. The expected return on the market is 14 percent, and the risk-free rate is 5 percent. The required rate of return is 15.8 percent. What is the estimated price of the stock?

10-4 Shakoori Corp. is expected to pay a dividend of $2.25, and the dividend is expected to grow at a constant rate of 6 percent. This stock is 25 percent more risky than the market as a whole. The risk-free rate is 6 percent, and the equity risk premium for the market is 8 percent. The estimated price of the stock is?

10-5 You can buy Anoruo Inc. today for $85. Over the next year it is expected to pay a dividend of $2. You think the price one year from now will be $90.50. Based on this information, what is your implied rate of return from Anoruo, stated as a percentage? Show two ways to calculate your answer that produce identical results.

10-6 Thiewes Corp is valued as a constant growth model. It has an expected dividend of $1.75, a $k = .13$, and a $g = .07$. What is the expected price of this stock at the end of four years?

10-7 Ammermann Components recently paid a dividend of $1 per share. This dividend is expected to grow at a rate of 25 percent a year for the next five years, after which it is expected to grow at a rate of 7 percent a year. The required rate of return for this stock is 18 percent. What is the estimated price of the stock?

10-8 Swanton Industries is expected to pay a dividend of $10 per year for 10 years and then increase the dividend to $15 per share for every year thereafter. The required rate of return on this stock is 20 percent. What is the estimated stock price for Swanton?

Spreadsheet Exercises

10-1 The Richter Company, a technology company, has been growing rapidly. After examining the company's operations very carefully, analysts at Meril Link have estimated that dividends and earnings will grow at a rate of 22 percent a year for the next eight years, followed by 16 percent growth for another six years. After 14 years, the expected growth rate is 5 percent The risk-free rate appropriate for this analysis is 5.5 percent, and the expected return on the market is 10.5 percent. The beta for Richter is 1.1. It currently pays a dividend of $1.10. As major stockholders, the Richter family has asked you to estimate the intrinsic value of this stock today. Note the following:

1 Calculate the required rate of return in cell H2 using the CAPM.

2 Calculate the dollar amount of each dividend for the first 14 years in cells B5 through B18, and the present value of these amounts in cells C5 through C18. Be sure to allow for the change in growth rates in Year 9.

3 In cell G19, calculate the price of the stock at the beginning of Year 15, using the then-constant growth rate of 5 percent.

4 In cell G20, discount the price found in 3) back to today using the proper number of periods for discounting.

5 Sum the present value of the dividends in cell C21. Add to this the present value of the price found in 4) by putting this value in C22.

6 In cell C23, add the values found in 5) in cell C24.

Curr Divid	1st gr Rate	2nd gr Rate	Normal gr	RF	Exp Mk Rt	Beta	k
$1.1	0.22 8 yrs	0.16 6 yrs	0.05	5.5	10.5	1.1	0.11
Year	Dividend	PV of Div					
1							
2							
3							
4							
5							
6							
7							
8							
9							
10							
11							
12							
13							
14							

Price at beginning of Year 15 =

PV of Price today =

Sum of PV of dividends for first 14 years

+ PV of Price at Beginning of Year 15

Sum of PV of dividends and PV of price

Checking Your Understanding

10-1 The required rate of return for a stock is the minimum expected rate of return an investor needs to induce him or her to purchase a stock. As such, it takes into account the amount of risk involved.

10-2 Dividends are the only cash payment a common stock owner will receive from the corporation. If all future dividends are discounted back to today at a proper rate of return, that is the most (on a present value basis) the stockholder will receive by owning the stock, and therefore that is the estimated value of the stock.

10-3 Although neither the zero growth rate case nor the constant growth rate case show a present value process in their equations, a present value process is involved in both cases. It just happens that the model reduces to the indicated forms while still involving a present value process.

10-4   Yes. Different investors will have different required rates of return, and they may estimate the expected growth rate in dividends differently.

10-5   No. Free cash flows are difficult to estimate, as are other variables used in a valuation model.

10-6   Both. The intrinsic value of a stock is an estimated value, and is often estimated using a formula.

10-7   There are various ways to measure and state P/E ratios.

10-8   The late 1990s demonstrated that valuations can rise at a rapid rate for several years in a row. Many observers feel there was a bubble in the market for technology stocks, related to investors overvaluing stocks based on their fundamentals.

chapter 11

Managing a Stock Portfolio: A Worldwide Issue

G iven your new $1 million portfolio, you will need to manage it. You recognize that the market has a substantial impact on individual stocks and portfolios, and therefore you realize you need to better understand the impact of the overall market on individual stocks and on portfolios. You must manage your portfolio on an ongoing basis, and that requires that you think about what approaches and strategies you may wish to follow.

One of the most important decisions each investor must make is whether to take an active approach or a passive approach to investing. Can it be true, as some argue, that a passive approach will reduce investor costs and produce as good or better results as an active approach most of the time? Such an approach will relieve you of a lot of the work of managing a portfolio, but it could also leave you with average results and little hope of doing better. Or, if you choose an active approach, should you try to select stocks or try to time the market? These issues will be covered here.

Chapter 10 discussed the valuation of stocks based on procedures used by investors. Chapter 11 covers the analysis and strategy for selecting and managing common stocks. Common stock investors need to carefully consider whether they will follow an active approach, a passive approach, or a combination of the two. Using a passive approach, investors can follow a buy-and-hold strategy, or buy index funds that mimic some market index. For the active approach, we analyze the primary alternatives of stock selection, sector rotation, and market timing. The implications of the efficient market hypothesis should be considered when deciding upon a strategy. We will do so in Chapter 12.

AFTER READING THIS CHAPTER YOU WILL BE ABLE TO:

- ▶ Recognize the overall impact of the market on stocks and portfolios.
- ▶ Analyze the pros and cons of a passive approach to building a stock portfolio.
- ▶ Evaluate critically the well-known active strategies for stocks used by investors.

A Global Perspective

In today's investing world, investors cross borders more and more when they invest. And the investing is more sophisticated. Rather than start with a portfolio of U.S.-listed stocks and add selected foreign equities, investors today search for the truly "good" companies wherever they are—the industry giants, the innovative leaders, those with proven track records, and so forth. What matters today is being a world-class firm, whether that is Petrobras in Brazil or Nestle in Switzerland. When it comes to important sectors such as oil and telecommunications, globalization is the name of the game.

American investors have traditionally been myopic, focusing only on companies they are familiar with, such as Walmart or Apple. Now that we truly are in an age of globalization, investors increasingly recognize that they should take a global perspective. Consider, for example, that for the five years ending in January 2008, foreign equities were up more than 125 percent. Is it surprising that many financial advisors regularly recommend to clients that some percentage of their overall portfolio be devoted to international investing?

How much of a U.S. investor's portfolio should be allocated to foreign securities? A general consensus among market observers years ago was that a typical U.S. investor should have at least 10 to 20 percent of his or her portfolio in international markets over the long run. U.S. investors in recent years have allocated 30 percent to foreign securities. Of course, all foreign markets are not the same—emerging markets are generally much more risky than developed economies and investors may wish to limit a commitment in emerging markets to a small percentage of portfolio assets. And, of course, unexpected changes occur, such as the European debt crisis.

The Impact of the Overall Market on Stocks

Aggregate market movements remain the largest single factor explaining fluctuations in both individual stock prices and portfolios of stocks. The impact of the market on every investor in common stocks is pervasive and dominant, and must be fully appreciated by investors if they are to be successful.

When the market is going up strongly, as it did in the five-year period 1995–1999, most stocks appreciate significantly. It would be unlikely for an investor with a diversified portfolio not to have earned very handsome returns during that period of time. Similarly, when the market declines sharply, as it did in 2000–2002, or in 2008, most stocks react accordingly. Few, if any, investors who owned stocks during this period, and whose positions were unhedged (which was true for most investors), escaped some degree of losses on their portfolios—the real question is how much did they lose?

Some Practical Advice

Bad things can, and do, happen to investors. A bear market is typically defined as a stock market decline of 20 percent or more. Since the 1960s, nine stock market declines of 20 percent or more have occurred. One-third of these declines involved losses of more than 30 percent. If you are going to be a stock investor, you should accept the likelihood of these declines occurring, sooner or later. That said, as we know from Chapter 6 the long-run compound annual average rate of return on stocks is approximately 9.5 percent through 2011. Even if, as many believe, average returns will be somewhat lower over the next few years, they are still likely to exceed bond returns. Furthermore, stocks typically recover from bear markets quite quickly.

The impact of the market is particularly important for a diversified portfolio of stocks. As we now know, the basic tenet of portfolio theory is to diversify into a number of securities

Figure 11-1

Performance of T. Rowe Price Mutual Fund vs. S&P 500 Total Returns, 2002–2010.

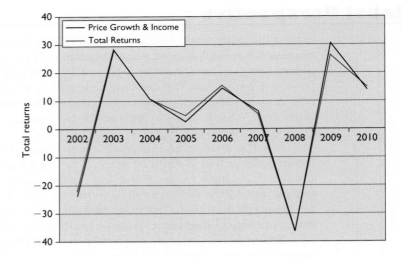

(properly chosen). For a well-diversified portfolio, which each investor should hold, the market is the dominant factor affecting the variability of its return. Although any given portfolio may outperform the market, almost all typical stock portfolios are significantly influenced by what happens to the market as a whole.

✓ Market risk is the single most important risk affecting the price movements of common stocks. For very well diversified portfolios, market effects can account for 90 percent and more of the variability in the portfolio's return.

Example 11-1

Consider the performance of the T. Rowe Price Growth and Income Fund for a recent multiyear period, as shown in Figure 11-1. Notice how this fund's total returns and the total returns for the S&P 500 Index track very closely over this period, based on an initial investment of $10,000. The market's performance explains most of the fund's performance for this time period.

Market Risk Abroad U.S. investors buying foreign stocks face the same issues when it comes to market risk. Some of these markets have performed very well, and some have performed poorly over specified periods of time. For example, in 2006 and 2007 European stocks increased at an annual rate of 23 percent, so U.S. investors buying many of the stocks in these markets enjoyed strong stock performance as well as a favorable currency movement during that time period. Of course, the opposite also happens.

Example 11-2

Perhaps the best foreign example of the impact of the overall market on investors is Japan, an economic superpower in recent years. In the 1980s, Japan seemed invincible in its economic performance, and its stock market, as measured by the Nikkei stock index, reflected Japan's success with seemingly unending rises in stock prices. The Nikkei stock index peaked at the end of 1989 at a level of almost 39,000. By mid-1992, the index had declined below the 15,000 level, representing a staggering decline of some 60 percent. As one well-known magazine put it at the time, this was the "biggest erasure of wealth in history." Such is the impact of the overall market on investor wealth. From its peak in 1989 through November 2008, the Nikkei stock index had lost almost 80 percent of its value. Regardless of an investor's prowess, virtually no portfolio invested in Japanese stocks over that period could have performed well.

Building Stock Portfolios

We now consider how investors go about selecting stocks to be held in portfolios. Individual investors often consider the investment decision—based on objectives, constraints, and preferences—as consisting of two steps:

1. Asset allocation
2. Security selection

Asset allocation, discussed in Chapter 8, refers to allocating total portfolio wealth to various asset classes, such as stocks, bonds, and cash equivalents. The percentages invested in each asset class add up to 100 percent, indicating that all portfolio funds have been allocated. A common asset allocation for a number of institutional investors using only two asset classes is 60 percent equities and 40 percent bonds. Of course, many investors use several asset classes, including foreign stocks, foreign bonds, real estate, and small capitalization stocks. And some of these categories can be further divided—foreign stocks can be allocated by region, type of economy (developed vs. developing), and so forth.

✓ In many respects, asset allocation is the most important decision an investor makes.

Having made the portfolio allocation decision, the largest part of an investor's success or failure is locked in.

Example 11-3 Think of one investor allocating her portfolio as 90 percent NASDAQ stocks and 10 percent cash equivalents, and another investor doing the opposite, 90 percent cash equivalents and 10 percent NASDAQ stocks. Now imagine the NASDAQ market declining about 75 percent, as it did in 2000–2002. Clearly, the results of these two portfolios will be vastly different regardless of the exact securities selected. Such is the importance of asset allocation.

We will assume that the asset allocation decision—what percentage of portfolio funds to allocate to each asset class such as stocks, bonds, and bills—has been made so that our focus is only on common stocks. The common stock portion could constitute 100 percent of the total portfolio or any other percentage an investor chooses.

In discussing strategies we will consider the passive and active approaches separately, allowing us to focus on each. These approaches are applicable to investors as they select and manage common stock portfolios, or select investment company managers who will manage such portfolios on their behalf. Which of these to pursue will depend on a number of factors, including the investor's expertise, time, and temperament, and, importantly, what an investor believes about the efficiency of the market, as discussed in Chapter 12. While we consider each of these two strategies in turn, it is important to realize that investors can, and often do, employ some combination of these strategies in their approach to investing.

Checking Your Understanding

1. Suppose you knew with certainty that the stock market would rise sharply over the next three years. Assuming you are willing to hold common stocks, would you be comfortable letting someone choose for you a broadly diversified subsample of the S&P 500 Index?
2. If you expect a severe gasoline shortage in the United States for a period of a few months, what would you predict will happen to the required rate of return for stocks?

The Passive Strategy

A natural outcome of a belief in efficient markets is to employ some type of passive strategy in owning and managing common stocks. If the market is highly efficient, impounding information into prices quickly and on balance accurately, no active strategy should be able to outperform the market on a risk-adjusted basis over a reasonable period of time. The efficient market hypothesis (EMH), discussed in Chapter 12, has implications for fundamental analysis and technical analysis, both of which are active strategies for selecting common stocks.

Passive Management Strategy A strategy whereby investors do not actively seek out trading possibilities in an attempt to outperform the market

A **passive management strategy** means that the investor does not actively seek out trading possibilities in an attempt to outperform the market. Passive strategies simply aim to do as well as the market. The emphasis is on minimizing transaction costs and time spent in managing the portfolio because any expected benefits from active trading or analysis are likely to be less than the costs. Passive investors act as if the market is efficient and accept the consensus estimates of return and risk, recognizing current market price as the best estimate of a security's value.

✓ Passive investment management does not try to find undervalued stocks, nor does it try to time the market. Instead, passive investing is concerned with achieving the returns available in various market sectors at minimum costs.

An investor can simply follow a buy-and-hold strategy for whatever portfolio of stocks is owned. Alternatively, a very effective way to employ a passive strategy with common stocks is to invest in an indexed portfolio. We will consider each of these strategies in turn.

Investments Intuition

It is important to understand the logic of why passive investing is likely to be a superior strategy for most investors. Consider a capitalization-weighted index portfolio that holds virtually all of the stocks in the market. Each year this portfolio will generate a return— in effect, the market return. Now consider the average dollar invested in the market and the return it earns. Are the two equal? No, not if the active management costs attached to the average dollar exceeds the cost of the index portfolio, which is almost always the case.

BUY-AND-HOLD STRATEGY

A buy-and-hold strategy means exactly that—an investor buys stocks and basically holds them until some future time in order to meet some objective. The emphasis is on avoiding transaction costs, frequent taxable transactions, additional search costs, the investment in time necessary to actively manage a portfolio, and so forth. The investor believes that such a strategy will, over some period of time, produce results as good as alternatives that require active management. These alternatives incur search and transaction costs, and inevitably involve mistakes.

Evidence to support this view comes from a study by Odean and Barber, who examined 60,000 investors. They found the average investor earned 15.3 percent over a five-year period while the most active traders (turning over about 10 percent of their holdings each month) averaged only 10 percent.[1]

---

[1] Terrance Odean and Brad Barber, "Trading Is Hazardous to Your Wealth: The Common Stock Investment Performance of Individual Investors", *Journal of Finance*, Vol. LV, No. 2, April 2000, pp. 773–806.

Notice that a buy-and-hold strategy is applicable to the investor's portfolio, whatever its composition. It may be large or small, and it may emphasize various types of stocks. Also note that an initial selection must be made to implement the strategy. The investor must decide to buy stocks A, B, and C, and not X, Y, and Z.

It is also important to recognize that the investor will, in fact, have to perform certain functions while the buy-and-hold strategy is in existence. For example, any income generated by the portfolio may be reinvested in other securities. Alternatively, a few stocks may do so well that they dominate the total market value of the portfolio and reduce its diversification. If the portfolio changes in such a way that it is no longer compatible with the investor's risk tolerance, adjustments may be required. The point is simply that even under such a strategy investors must still take certain actions.

INDEX FUNDS

An increasing amount of mutual fund and pension fund assets can be described as passive equity investments. These asset pools are designed to duplicate as precisely as possible the performance of some market index. Recall from Chapter 3 that an index fund is an unmanaged fund designed to replicate as closely as possible (or practical) the performance of a specified index of market activity. Index funds arose in response to the large body of evidence concerning the efficiency of the market, and they have grown as evidence of the inability of mutual funds to consistently, or even very often, outperform the market continues to accumulate.

Index Funds Illustrated   A stock-index fund may consist of all the stocks in a well-known market average such as the S&P 500 Composite Stock Index. No attempt is made to forecast market movements and act accordingly, or to select under- or overvalued securities. Expenses are kept to a minimum, including research costs (security analysis), portfolio managers' fees, and brokerage commissions. Index funds can be run efficiently by a small staff.

Example 11-4   Vanguard offers a large selection of index funds, which allows investors to duplicate various market segments at a very low cost. Some examples:

1. The *500 Index Portfolio* consists of stocks selected to duplicate the S&P 500 and emphasizes large-capitalization stocks.
2. The *Extended Market Portfolio* consists of a statistically selected sample of the Wilshire 4500 Index, and of medium- and small-capitalization stocks.
3. The *Total Stock Market Portfolio* seeks to match the performance of all (approximately 7,000) publicly traded U.S. stocks.
4. The *Small Capitalization Stock Portfolio* seeks to match the performance of the Russell 2000 Small Stock Index, consisting of 2,000 small-capitalization stocks.
5. The *U.S. Value Portfolio* seeks to match the investment performance of the S&P/BARRA Value Index, which consists of stocks selected from the S&P 500 Index with lower than average ratios of market price to book value.
6. The *U.S. Growth Portfolio* seeks to match the investment performance of the S&P 500/BARRA Growth Index, which consists of stocks selected from the S&P 500 Index with higher than average ratios of market price to book value.
7. The *Total International Portfolio* covers multiple countries across Europe, the Pacific, and emerging markets, and holds over 1,500 stocks. The European Portfolio invests in

Europe's 14 largest markets, while the Pacific Portfolio invests in the six most developed countries in the Pacific region. The Emerging Markets Portfolio invests in 14 of the most accessible markets in the less developed countries.

There are no sales charges or exit charges of any kind. Total operating expenses for several of these funds is about 0.20 percent annually, which is extremely low.

Importance of Equity Index Funds   How important are equity index funds in today's investing world? Vanguard's 500 Index fund had approximately $100 billion in assets by the beginning of 2012, making it one of the largest mutual funds in terms of assets in the United States. And Vanguard Group is one of the largest fund families (along with Fidelity) in the United States, based primarily on the amount of money in its index funds. Fidelity Investments, also one of the largest fund families based on assets under management, traditionally emphasized the performance of its actively managed equity funds. However, Fidelity has increased its index offerings and has cut the total expense ratio on some of its equity index funds to a very low rate. In 2010, equity index funds comprised about 15 percent of all equity mutual funds.

ETFs   Vanguard also offers a number of ETFs which can accomplish the same objectives as an index fund. Expenses are typically even lower than those for an index fund, and shares can be bought and sold when the market is open.

Tax Efficiency of Index Funds   A significant advantage of index funds is their tax efficiency. Index funds basically buy and hold, selling shares only when necessary. Actively managed funds, on the other hand, do more frequent trading and generate larger tax bills, some of which may be short-term gains taxable at ordinary income tax rates. The tax issue really hit investors in 2001 when they paid their taxes for 2000—many funds made large, taxable distributions based on prior years of good returns, but the value of the fund shares themselves declined in 2000, many quite sharply. Thus, these investors were watching the value of their funds decline significantly while paying taxes on prior gains. The same thing happened again in 2008, for the tax year 2007—many mutual funds made large distributions.

Example 11-5   Although an extreme example, the Boston Company International Small Cap fund had a 2007 distribution equal to $23.17 per share. If earlier that year you had invested $100,000 in the fund, your tax bill on this distribution would have exceeded $14,000. Vanguard's S&P 500 Index fund, on the other hand, paid no capital gains distribution for the seventh consecutive year.

Enhanced Index Funds   Investors can also purchase so-called "enhanced" index funds, which are index funds that are tweaked by their managers to be a little different. For example, an enhanced fund tracking the S&P 500 Index could have the same sector weighting in, say, technology stocks as the S&P 500 but hold somewhat different stocks, perhaps with lower P/E ratios. Or an enhanced fund can use futures and options to hold the S&P 500 Index and invest the remainder of the funds in bonds or other securities. The theory is that the manager can, by tweaking the fund slightly, outperform the index. The reality is, according to a study of 40 of these funds since their start dates, that about half of the funds outperformed their benchmark, and half did not.

Table 11-1 Percentage of Actively Managed Funds Underperforming Their Benchmarks for the 15-Year Period Ending in 2010

	Small	Medium	Large
Value	82%	96%	63%
Blend	93	94	84
Growth	83	97	79

Adapted from Christopher B. Philips, "The Case for Indexing," Vanguard research, February 2011, p. 15, Figure 10.

The Case for Index Funds   One of the strongest cases for index funds has been made by Burton Malkiel, an economics professor at Princeton and author of the new book *Earn More, Sleep Better: The Index Fund Solution.* According to Malkiel, "On average, the typical actively managed fund underperforms the index by about two percentage points a year. And that calculation ignores the sales charges that are imposed by some actively managed funds and the extra taxes an investor pays on funds that turn over their portfolios rapidly."[2]

According to Malkiel, there are four reasons why indexing works:

1. Securities markets are extremely efficient in digesting information.
2. Indexing is cost-efficient, with expenses much lower than actively managed funds.
3. Funds incur heavy trading expenses. Trading costs can amount to 0.5 percent to 1.0 percent per year.
4. Indexing has a tax advantage, deferring the realization of capital gains while earlier realization of capital gains reduces net returns significantly.

Performance of Index Funds   As for actual performance of equity index funds, consider the following. *Morningstar*, the mutual fund tracking company, studied the "success ratio" for active and passive funds taken together within each asset class, adjusting for survivorship bias, for the five years ending in 2010.[3] Overall, passive funds outperformed active funds. Balanced funds showed the biggest win for passive investing, while active funds did better on the international side. As for taxable bond funds, the passive funds did better.

According to John Bogle, founder of the Vanguard Group and a leading proponent of index funds, the S&P Index will outperform 70 percent of all actively managed equity funds over time. According to Standard & Poor's, over a recent five-year period 75 percent of actively managed mutual funds failed to outperform the market.

Table 11-1 shows the percentage of actively managed funds that underperformed their benchmark for the 15-year period ending in 2010. These results are adjusted for survivorship bias (explained in Chapter 3). As Table 11-1 shows, for large cap actively managed growth funds, 79 percent underperformed their benchmark. Notice the astounding results for medium capitalization funds—96 percent, 94 percent, and 97 percent for the value, blend, and growth categories respectively underperformed their benchmarks. The excess returns (not shown) for eight of the nine categories were negative, meaning they underperformed their benchmark returns. The one positive excess return was only .02 percent.

---

[2] Burton Malkiel, "The Case for Index Funds," *Mutual Funds Magazine*, February 1999, p. 72. This entire discussion involving Malkiel is based on this article, pp. 72–75.

[3] Russel Kinnel, "Index vs. Active: What the Data Say," *Morningstar* online, September 12, 2011.

Checking Your Understanding

3. Your financial advisor urges you to adopt a passive investing strategy. You decide to hold a broadly diversified portfolio of stocks. Your advisor argues that you are now protected from the collateral damage to a portfolio that occurs when an overvalued sector of the market declines. Agree or disagree, and explain your reasoning.

The Active Strategy

Most of the techniques discussed in this text involve an active approach to investing. In the area of common stocks the use of valuation models to value and select stocks indicates that investors are analyzing and valuing stocks in an attempt to improve their performance relative to some benchmark such as a market index. They assume or expect the benefits to be greater than the costs.

Active Management Strategy A strategy designed to provide additional returns by trading activities

An **active management strategy** assumes (implicitly or explicitly) that investors possess some advantage relative to other market participants. Such advantages could include superior analytical or judgment skills, superior information, or the ability or willingness to do what other investors, particularly institutions, are unable to do. For example, many large institutional investors cannot take positions in very small companies, leaving this field for individual investors. Furthermore, individuals are not required to own diversified portfolios and are typically not prohibited from short sales or margin trading as are some institutions.

Most investors still favor an active approach to common stock selection and management, despite the accumulating evidence from efficient market studies and the published performance results of institutional investors. The reason for this is obvious—the potential rewards are very large, and many investors feel confident that they can achieve such rewards even if other investors cannot. We discuss three components of the active approach to stock selection and management.

Active Approach	• Security Selection
	• Sector Analysis
	• Market Timing

SECURITY SELECTION

✓ The most traditional and popular form of active stock strategies is the selection of individual stocks believed to offer superior return-risk characteristics.

Stocks typically are selected using fundamental security analysis, but technical analysis is also used, and sometimes a combination of the two.[4] Many investors have always believed, and continue to believe despite evidence to the contrary from the market efficiency literature, that they possess the requisite skill, patience, and ability to identify undervalued stocks.

We know from Chapter 1 that a key feature of the investments environment is the uncertainty that always surrounds investing decisions. Most stock pickers recognize the pervasiveness of this uncertainty and protect themselves accordingly by diversifying. Therefore, the standard assumption of rational, intelligent investors who select stocks to buy and sell is that such selections will be part of a diversified portfolio.

---

[4] Technical analysis is discussed in Chapter 16.

The Justification for Stock Selection To gain some appreciation of the importance of stock selection, consider the cross-sectional variation in common stock returns. Latane, Tuttle, and Jones were the first to point out the widely differing performances of stocks in a given year using the interquartile range.[5] They found a remarkable constancy from year to year in the spread between the performance of stocks in the upper quartile and the performance of stocks in the lower quartile.

A subsequent study by McEnally and Todd for the period 1946–1989 found that investors who successfully confined stock selection to the stocks in the highest quartile would have largely avoided losing years, and even the bad years showed only modest losses.[6] Conversely, for the bottom quarter, results were negative about 55 percent of the time, and about 25 percent of the time even the best stocks would have lost money despite generally favorable market conditions. The implication of these results is that "For those who do attempt to pick stocks, the rewards can be very high, but the risk and negative consequences of poor selection are substantial."[7]

The Importance of Stock Selection How important is stock selection in the overall investment process? As Peter Lynch, one of the most celebrated portfolio managers of recent years as former head of Fidelity's Magellan Fund, states: "If it's a choice between investing in a good company in a great industry, or a great company in a lousy industry, I'll take the great company in the lousy industry any day." Most active investors, individuals or institutions, are, to various degrees, stock selectors. The majority of investment advice and investment advisory services are geared to the selection of stocks thought to be attractive candidates at the time.

The Importance of Earnings per Share (EPS) in Stock Selection Investors should carefully study a company's earnings, and estimates of earnings, before investing. One of the most important components of stock selection is the forecast of earnings per share for particular companies because of the widely perceived linkage between expected EPS and stock returns (explained in Chapter 15). Earnings are critical in determining stock prices, and what really matters is a company's *expected* earnings (what is referred to on Wall Street as earnings estimates).

✓ The primary emphasis in fundamental security analysis is on expected EPS.

Considerable effort is devoted by investors and investment advisory services to the forecast of EPS.

Value Stocks Stocks whose prices are considered "cheap" relative to earnings, book value, and other measures thought indicative of value
Growth Stocks Stocks that emphasize expectations about future growth in earnings

Growth Stocks and Value Stocks **Value stocks** are stocks whose prices are considered "cheap" relative to earnings, book value, and other measures thought indicative of value. **Growth stocks**, on the other hand, emphasize expectations about future growth in earnings.[8]

---

[5] H. Latane, D. Tuttle, and C. Jones, *Security Analysis and Portfolio Management*, 2nd ed. (New York: Ronald Press, 1975), pp. 192–193. In an ordered set of numbers, the interquartile range is the difference between the value that cuts off the top quarter of these numbers and the value that cuts off the bottom quarter of these numbers. The interquartile range is an alternative measure of dispersion.

[6] Richard McEnally and Rebecca Todd, "Cross-Sectional Variation in Common Stock Returns," *Financial Analysts Journal* (May/June 1992): pp. 59–63. The quote is on p. 61 of this article.

[7] An additional finding of this study is that cross-sectional variation of returns increased steadily over the decades, making stock selection even more important.

[8] Following up from Chapter 10 on the mention of Fama and French in connection with the book to market value ratio, they define value stocks as those with high ratios of book value to market value and growth stocks as those that have low ratios of book value to market value. "The intuition is that value stocks have low prices relative to their book value, so the market feels they're relatively distressed," says Fama. "The intuition is the opposite for growth stocks."

A growth stock that has performed well may be priced to continue to perform well, but bad news can cause a sharp decline in price. It is generally assumed that growth stocks have high P/E ratios while value stocks have low P/E ratios.

Through 2006, value stocks outperformed in the market by wide margins for seven years. However, the year to year variation can be startling. For example, for the one-year period through mid-2000, growth stocks outperformed value stocks by 34 percentage points. One year later, value stocks outperformed growth stocks by 47 percentage points. For the years 2009–2011, growth stocks outperformed value stocks. What about 2012?

Overall, over a long period such as the last 40 years, value stocks have outperformed growth stocks, on average, by about 2 percentage points for large stocks (geometric mean). For smaller stocks, the difference is even greater in favor of value stocks. Needless to say, such differences may not hold in the future.

✓ Value investing is based on taking a long-term approach, and often involves a contrary approach, going against the consensus. Value investing emphasizes downside protection while attempting to earn a return on the upside.

Some Practical Advice

An index of value stocks is significantly affected by the financial sector, which can make up one-fourth of a value index based on market value. Therefore, if you think the financial sector will perform poorly for a certain time period, you may wish to avoid a value index. Conversely, if you expect a rally in the financial sector, investing in a value index could be a smart move. Furthermore, portfolio managers employing a growth strategy typically avoid high dividend paying stocks because dividend yield is related to value investing. In 2011 high-dividend sectors did well, which hurt the performance of growth stock portfolio managers.[9]

Security Analysts and Stock Selection Stocks are, of course, selected by both individual investors and institutional investors. Rather than do their own security analysis, including earnings forecasts, individual investors may choose to rely on the recommendations of the professionals. An important part of the institutional side of stock selection and recommendation is the role of the security analyst (also called equity analyst, or, simply, analyst) in the investment process. When considering stock selection investors must understand the role of the analyst, and why there has been so much controversy concerning analysts.

"Wall Street" analysts, called **sell-side analysts**, cover, to various degrees, the actively traded stocks in the United States (some stocks are heavily covered, while others are covered by only one or two analysts, and some stocks are not covered at all). Their research reports are used to "sell" an idea to investors, both individuals and institutions. Some of these analysts work for firms such as Value Line and Standard and Poor's which provide "independent" research and recommendations to investors; that is, these companies do not have brokerage operations to support. On the other hand, **buy-side analysts** are employed by money management firms (such as pension funds, mutual funds, and investment advisors). These analysts search for equities for their firms to buy and hopefully profit from, and their research is typically available only to their employers.[10]

Sell-Side Analysts "Wall Street" analysts who cover stocks and make recommendation on them to investors

Buy-Side Analysts Analysts employed by money management firms to search for equities for their firms to buy as investing opportunities

[9] This analysis is based on Ben Levisohn, "Growth Stocks or Value? Yes!," *The Wall Street Journal*, January 7–8, 2012, p. B9.

[10] Buy-side analysts follow more stocks than do sell-side analysts and write very brief reports compared to the typical sell-side analyst report.

Figure 11-2

Average Percentage
Amount a Stock Moved
in a Single Day Following
a Change in Analysts'
Recommendations,
1994–2002 (a) Following
an Upgrade; (b) Following
a Downgrade.

<small>Source: Copyright © StarMine
Corporation, 2002–2006.
Reprinted by Permission.</small>

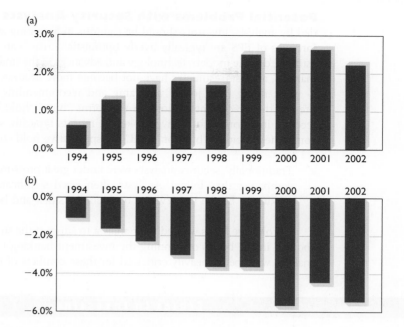

A typical analyst report contains a description of the company's business, how the analyst expects the company to perform, earnings estimates, price estimates or price targets for the year ahead, and recommendations as to buy, hold, or sell. The central focus of the analysts' job is to attempt to forecast a specific company's price, growth rate, or return. Alternatively, it can involve the inputs to a valuation model such as those we considered in the previous chapter. The most important part of what the analyst produces in this regard is the estimate of a company's earnings.

What sources of information do analysts use in evaluating common stocks for possible selection or selling? The major sources of information are presentations from the top management of the companies being considered, annual reports, and Form 10-K reports that must be filed by the companies with the SEC. According to surveys of analysts, they consistently emphasize the long term over the short term. Variables of major importance in their analysis include expected changes in earnings per share, expected return on equity (ROE), and industry outlook.[11]

Analysts spend much of their time forecasting earnings. StarMine did an analysis that measures the impact that analysts have on stock prices when they change their recommendations. Figure 11-2 shows the results of the StarMine analysis.[12] On the day of an upgrade by security analysts, stocks rose an average of 2.1 percent; following a downgrade, stocks declined an average of 5.4 percent. Downgrades are more prominent because investors who trade stocks are more concerned with bad news. StarMine also reported a continued drift in stock prices for several months following a change in recommendation. This suggests that investors can benefit by buying those stocks that are upgraded and shorting those that are downgraded.

---

[11] The security analysis process used by financial analysts—in terms of information sources and processes—is the same one that we will learn in Part IV.

[12] Based on information on the Starmine website, October 2002. Starmine newsletters have moved to the website Apha Now.

Potential Problems with Security Analysts   Regardless of the effort expended by analysts, investors should be cautious in accepting analysts' forecasts of EPS. Analysts forecasts of EPS are typically overly optimistic. Errors can be large, and occur often. Interestingly, despite modern technology and advances in the understanding of stocks and financial markets, analysts' estimates have not become more accurate.

In doing their job of analyzing and recommending companies, analysts supposedly present their recommendations in the forms "buy," "hold," and "sell." However, until very recently investors who receive brokerage reports typically saw recommendations for specific companies as either "buy" or "hold" or "speculative hold" or other words such as these.

✓   Traditionally, security analysts were under great pressure to avoid the word "sell" from the companies they follow. Analysts often faced significant pressure from their own firms seeking to be the underwriter on lucrative stock and bond underwritings.

Brokerage firms wanted their analyst to support the stock by making positive statements about it in the hopes of winning the investment banking business. By 2000–2001, security analysts were being heavily criticized for these conflicts of interest, and rightly so.

Ethics In Investing

Should Brokers and Analysts Be Fined for Rumors?

In early 2005, the **NASD** announced it had fined a stock analyst $75,000 for spreading a rumor about a small semiconductor manufacturer. It was said to be a "sensational negative rumor," and the stock fell that day although the company publicly denied the rumor the same day. The company complained to the **NASD**, which, after investigation, levied the fine.

The **NASD** alleged that the broker/analyst in this situation did not adequately investigate to determine if there was a reasonable basis for the rumor. Obviously, the question arises as to what is "adequate." If the rumor had simply been fabricated, or the analyst

spread it knowing it was false, there would be clear grounds for a fine. In this case, however, the charge was that the analyst simply circulated it. Analysts and brokers are not fined for passing on rumors thought to come from a reliable source, or if the rumor is qualified by saying that the accuracy of the rumor could be in serious doubt. Furthermore, rumors are a daily part of trading stocks, happening regularly. Many investors sometimes invest on the basis of rumors or limited information, only later obtaining the actual facts. What is ethical in situations like this, and who determines when an analyst crosses the line?

As of 2008, only about 6 percent of analyst recommendations were sell recommendations. In general, the larger investment firms had more sell ratings. In 2008, Merrill Lynch began requiring its analysts to assign at least 20 percent of the stocks they follow the lowest rating used by Merrill Lynch (the name for this recommendation category was changed from "sell" to "underperform").[13]

---

[13] In 2002, Merrill Lynch agreed to a $100 million fine to settle charges that its analysts were overly optimistic in their research recommendations in order to win investment banking business. Some other large firms followed suit in changing their practices, primarily because of this action.

Following the Merrill Lynch settlement, a so-called "global settlement" occurred at the end of 2002. Negotiated by the SEC, the NYSE, NASD, and others, the global settlement was intended to put a stop to fraudulent research growing out of the investment banking conflicts. Ten large firms settled for $1.3 billion, and agreed to separate investment banking from analyst research in every way, such as, for example, operationally and financially.

Figure 11-3

Number of Analyst Recommendations by Type for the S&P 500 Stocks.

SOURCE: Jack Hough, "How to Profit from Analysts' Stock Recommendations," *The Wall Street Journal*, January 14–15, p. B7.

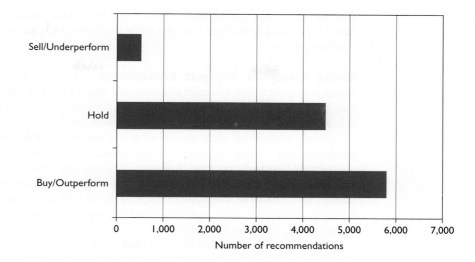

Figure 11-3 shows the number of analyst recommendations by type of recommendation—buy, hold, or sell—for the S&P 500 stocks as of a recent point in time. Out of a total of almost 11,000 recommendations, only 530 were sell/underperform.

Some Practical Advice

Can You Believe Security Analysts?

As the stock market peaked in 2000, prior to three years of large declines, only 1 percent of analysts' recommendations were "sell." The collapse of Enron in 2001 was a major scandal on Wall Street. The company was reporting fraudulent earnings to investors while appearing to be making large amounts of money, and attracting more investors. It finally collapsed in a spectacular bankruptcy. Almost up to the collapse, analysts were recommending Enron to investors to buy, or at least hold. And they virtually never issued a sell recommendation on any stock.

The years following the Enron scandal supposedly saw analysts' recommendations become more objective. But how much really changed? At the peak of the housing boom (2005–2006), analysts were very positive about the house building industry. According to one study of Wall Street analyst ratings based on 1,500 companies, only .08 percent of the recommendations were "sell" recommendations, and only 4.2 percent were "weak hold" recommendations. Clearly, out of so many companies, it is impossible to believe there were almost no sell candidates. Instead, it appears analysts are doing what they have always done, being optimistic in their recommendations and going out of their way not to find sell candidates. Investors should be extremely cautious when reviewing sell-side analyst recommendations. Instead, they should rely on independent sources for recommendations.

So far we have been discussing security analysts in the United States covering primarily U.S. stocks. What about Chinese stocks, given the emphasis in today's world on China and its growing impact? According to a recent analysis, analysts employed by investment banks around the world rated almost every Chinese stock they covered a "buy" by a ratio of 19 buy recommendations for every one sell recommendation.[14] Reasons given for this by sell-side

---

[14] This information is based on Kate O'Keefe, "Seldom Heard on China: Sell," *The Wall Street Journal*, November 28, 2011, p. C1.

analysts are strong pressures to believe in the "China cannot fail" story, the desire for investment banking business, and the desire to obtain better access to Chinese companies and their executives.

Using Analysts' Output Effectively   Investors should still be wary of analysts forecasts and their buy recommendations, but should not disregard some of the information they produce. Despite all the negative criticism leveled at analysts recently, most of which is richly deserved, investors can use analysts reports and information intelligently.

Many analysts are quite good at analyzing industries, trends in the economy and various industries, and companies. They compile useful information, and often have good insights as to future prospects because they have followed the industries and companies for years. Investors should use this information in conjunction with their own analysis. On the other hand, they should be skeptical of such items as earnings estimates, because analysts are typically overly optimistic, and they should be greatly skeptical about price targets and estimates of price one year from now.

It is important to note that investors need not rely on Wall Street analysts for their recommendations and analysis. Some firms employ independent analysts to study companies, and the information from these firms is available to investors, either by paid subscription, free in a library, or even free on a website. Three outstanding sources of independent information are

- *The Value Line Investment Survey* (discussed in Chapter 15) is one of the most famous sources of stock information for investors. Value Line has ranked stocks into five categories since 1965. It is available in printed and electronic format by subscription, and widely available in libraries.
- Standard and Poor's *Outlook* is available by subscription and at libraries. A very informative weekly source of information.
- Morningstar, although best known for mutual funds, now analyzes and recommends individual stocks.

SECTOR ROTATION

An active strategy that is similar to stock selection is group or sector rotation. This strategy involves shifting sector weights in the portfolio in order to take advantage of those sectors that are expected to do relatively better, and avoid or deemphasize those sectors that are expected to do relatively worse. Investors employing this strategy are betting that particular sectors will repeat their price performance relative to the current phase of the business and credit cycle.

An investor could think of larger groups as the relevant sectors, shifting between cyclicals, growth stocks, and value stocks. Growth stocks and value stocks are found in a wide range of industries. Cyclicals can cover multiple industry groupings, such as energy, industrials, materials, and information technology.

One standard approach in sector analysis is to divide common stocks into four broad sectors: interest-sensitive stocks, consumer durable stocks, capital goods stocks, and defensive stocks. Each of these sectors is expected to perform differently during the various phases of the business and credit cycles. For example, interest-sensitive stocks would be expected to be adversely impacted during periods of high interest rates, and such periods tend to occur at the latter stages of the business cycle. As interest rates decline, the earnings of the companies in this sector—banks, finance companies, savings and loans, utilities, and residential construction firms—should improve.

Defensive stocks deserve some explanation. Included here are companies in such businesses as food production, soft drinks, beer, pharmaceuticals, and so forth that often are not hurt as badly during the downside of the business cycle as are other companies, because people will still purchase bread, milk, soft drinks, and so forth. As the economy worsens and more problems are foreseen, investors may move into these stocks for investment protection. These stocks often do well during the late phases of a business cycle.

Using Sector Analysis   Investors may view industries as sectors and act accordingly. For example, if interest rates are expected to drop significantly, increased emphasis could be placed on the interest-sensitive industries such as housing and banking. The defense industry is a good example of an industry in recent years that has experienced wide swings in performance over multiyear periods.

It is clear that effective strategies involving sector rotation depend heavily on an accurate assessment of current economic conditions. A knowledge and understanding of the phases of the business cycle are important, as is an understanding of political environments, international linkages among economies, and credit conditions both domestic and international. Investors are searching for indicators that successfully identify when to shift a portfolio to a more aggressive or defensive position. A recent study strongly suggests that changes in Federal Reserve monetary policy can act as one such indicator.[15]

Sector bets are, relative to investing in a market index, narrow bets. They can result in big gains, or big losses. Investors should not expect year-to-year continuity in results. Nevertheless, a 2008 study using 33 years of equity returns strongly suggests that a simple sector rotation strategy "could have been used to significantly improve risk-adjusted portfolio performance."[16]

✓   Sector investing is subject to greater risks than investing in the overall market.

As for information, Standard & Poor's *Industry Surveys* is published weekly, and contains detailed data on more than 50 industry groups. *Investor's Business Daily*, published five days a week, ranks almost 200 industry groups with each issue. Each weekly issue of Bloomberg *Business Week* reports best and worst performing sectors for the last month and the last 12 months, as well as information on sector mutual funds.

Indirect Investing in Sectors   Investors can pursue the sector investing approach using what are called sector mutual funds, or simply sector funds. Several hundred sector funds are available. Real estate, utilities, and health care are three prominent sectors for funds. Morningstar, a provider of mutual fund information, has increased its coverage of sector listings. Sector funds are often at both the bottom and the top of the rankings for some period. The dramatic increase in the number and types of ETFs also make sector/industry rotation strategies much easier to implement and manage.

It is also possible to construct a balanced portfolio consisting solely of sector funds or ETFs. For example, an investor could include blue-chips, technology stocks, real estate stocks, financial stocks, natural resources, and utilities with six sector funds or ETFs.

Industry Momentum and Sector Investing   Sector funds are particularly popular with momentum traders. **Momentum** in stock returns refers to the tendency of stocks that have performed well (poorly) to continue to perform well (poorly). Academic research has uncovered an intermediate (3- to 12-month) momentum in U.S. stock returns and attributed it

Momentum Investing on the basis of recent movements in the price of a stock

---

[15] See Mitchell Conover, Gerald Jensen, Robert Johnson and Jeffrey Mercer, "Is Fed Policy Still Relevant for Investors?" *Financial Analysts Journal*, 61, January/February 2005, pp. 70–79.

[16] See Mitchell Conover, Gerald Jensen, Robert Johnson and Jeffrey Mercer, "Sector Rotation and Monetary Conditions" *The Journal of Investing*, 171, Spring 2008, pp. 34–46.

to an industry effect. This suggests that strong (weak) industry performance is followed by strong (weak) industry performance over periods of months.

O'Neal has considered exploiting this momentum in stock prices by using actively traded sector mutual funds.[17] He used Fidelity SelectPortfolios sector funds and found strong evidence of industry momentum. The difference between high and low portfolios averaged across 12 portfolio strategies was 8.6 percentage points on an annualized basis, and momentum appeared to be particularly strong for 12-month holding periods. These annualized differences in return support the evidence that industry momentum does exist.

MARKET TIMING

Market timers attempt to earn excess returns by varying the percentage of portfolio assets in equity securities. One has only to observe a chart of stock prices over time to appreciate the profit potential of being in the stock market at the right times and being out of the stock market at the bad times. For example, if you could have recognized a market peak in Spring 2008 and sold your equities, you would have avoided a disaster. Similarly, if you could have recognized the market bottom in March 2009, and bought equities, you could have realized a 60 percent return on your money. If, if, if—If you could see all your college tests and exams before you take them, you undoubtedly would do much better on them.

When equities are expected to do well, timers shift from cash equivalents such as money market funds to common stocks. When equities are expected to do poorly, the opposite occurs. Alternatively, timers could increase the betas of their portfolios when the market is expected to rise and carry most stocks up, or decrease the betas of their portfolio when the market is expected to go down. One important factor affecting the success of a market timing strategy is the amount of brokerage commissions and taxes paid with such a strategy as opposed to those paid with a buy-and-hold strategy.

Some believe that the popularity of market timing follows a cycle of its own. If the market is strongly up, market timing falls into disrepute, and buying and holding is the popular strategy. Following a severe market decline, however, market timing comes into vogue, and the buy-and-hold strategy is not popular.

The Controversy Surrounding Market Timing
Like many issues in the investing arena, the subject of market timing is controversial. Can some investors regularly time the market effectively enough to provide excess returns on a risk-adjusted basis? The only way to attempt to answer this question is to consider the available evidence on the subject, keeping in mind that market timing is a broad topic and that it is difficult to summarize all viewpoints.

Much of the empirical evidence on market timing comes from studies of mutual funds. A basic issue is whether fund managers increase the beta of their portfolios when they anticipate a rising market and reduce the beta when they anticipate a declining market. Several studies found no evidence that funds were able to time market changes and change their risk levels in response.

Chang and Lewellen examined the performance of mutual funds and found little evidence of any market timing ability. Furthermore, the average estimated down-market beta turned out to be slightly higher than the average estimated up-market beta. Overall, this study supported the conclusion that mutual funds do not outperform a passive investment strategy. Henriksson found that mutual fund managers are not able to successfully employ strategies

---

[17] Edward S. O'Neal, "Industry Momentum and Sector Mutual Funds," *Financial Analysts Journal*, 58, no. 4, July/August 2000, pp. 37−49.

Figure 11-4

Growth of $1.00 in the S&P 500 Index Over the Period 1980–2000 Assuming Investment During the Entire Period versus Leaving Out the Best 15 Months of Performance.

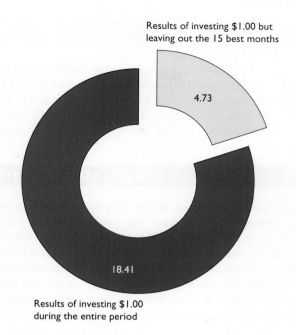

Results of investing $1.00 but leaving out the 15 best months

4.73

18.41

Results of investing $1.00 during the entire period

involving market timing. Moreover, these managers were not successful with market timing involving only large changes in the market.[18]

A recent study of the entire time period 1926–1999 concluded that for monthly market timing involving large-cap stocks or T-bills, "the investor would need to have a predictive accuracy, or average, of greater than 66 percent to outperform choices made from simply flipping a coin. As the holding period increases, the needed accuracy also increases."[19] *The Hulbert Financial Digest* tracks many market timing newsletters, and consistently finds that approximately 80 of them underperform the market indexes. Mark Hulbert is quoted as saying, "It's such a constant it's like, end of story, might as well go home."[20]

Why Market Timing Is Risky   Investors who miss only a few key months of being invested in the market may suffer significantly. For example, over a recent 40-year period, investors who missed the 34 best months for stocks would have seen an initial $1,000 investment grow to only $4,492 instead of $86,650. Even Treasury bills would have been a better alternative in this situation. According to another estimate, as Figure 11-4 shows, for the period 1980–2000 the value of $1.00 invested in the S&P 500 would have grown to $18.41. However, taking out the best 15 months of S&P performance, $1.00 would have grown to only $4.73, which would have been about the same return one could have earned from bonds yielding 8 percent a year. As one magazine summed up these statistics, "You gotta be in it to win it."[21]

[18] Eric Chang and Wilbur Lewellen, "Market Timing and Mutual Fund Investment Performance," *Journal of Business*, 57, no. 1, part 1 (January 1984): 57–72. Roy D. Henriksson, "Market Timing and Mutual Fund Performance: An Empirical Investigation," *Journal of Business*, 57, no. 1, part 1 (January 1984): pp. 73–96.

[19] Richard J. Bauer, Jr., and Julie R. Dahlquist, "Market Timing and Roulette Wheels," *Financial Analysts Journal*, 57, no. 1, (January/February 2001): 28–40. See also William F. Sharpe, "Likely Gains from Market Timing," *Financial Analysts Review*, 31, no. 2 (March/April 1975): pp. 60–69.

[20] Jeff Schlegel, "Time to Reappraise Market Timing," *Financial Advisor Magazine*, as quoted on the SmartMoney website at http://www.smartmoney.com/fp/index.cfm?story=0904market.

[21] Statistics and quote are from John Curran, "The Money Fund Trap," *Mutual Funds*, April 2001, p. 14.

✓ Considerable research now suggests that the biggest risk of market timing is that investors will not be in the market at critical times, thereby significantly reducing their overall returns.

Ibbotson Associates, who distributes returns data for stocks and other major asset classes, reported that the hypothetical value of $1 invested in the S&P 500 from year-end 1983 through 2003 earned $11.50. This compared to $2.71 for the S&P 500, leaving out the best 17 months during that same time period. For the period 1926–2003, $1 would grow to $2,285, compared to $17.42 leaving out the best 37 months during that period.[22]

Some Practical Advice

Available evidence today, as shown above, clearly suggests market timing will not work for most investors. Not only must you decide when to get out of stocks, you must also decide when to get back in stocks. And, as shown earlier, being out of the market for relatively short periods can dramatically lower average returns. Charles Ellis, in his well-known book about why investors are not likely to outperform the market, summed it up well: "Market timing is a wicked idea. Don't try it—ever"[23] Finally, consider this quote from Warren Buffett, arguably the most successful investor in the world: "Investors need to avoid the negatives of buying fads, crummy companies, and timing the market."[24]

Checking Your Understanding

4. What causes the conflicts of interest that security analysts have been accused of having?
5. How can investors be confident that really good security analysis would be profitable year after year?
6. State two reasons why market timing will likely not be a successful strategy for investors.

Rational Markets and Active Strategies

One of the most significant developments in recent years is the proposition that securities markets are efficient and that rational-asset-pricing models predominate. Under this scenario investors are assumed to make rational, informed decisions on the basis of the best information available at the time. In a rational market, security prices accurately reflect investor expectations about future cash flows. This idea has generated considerable controversy concerning the analysis and valuation of securities because of its significant implications for investors. Regardless of how much (or how little) an investor learns about investments, and regardless of whether an investor ends up being convinced by the efficient markets literature, it is prudent to learn something about this idea early in one's study of investments.

Much evidence exists to support the basic concepts of market efficiency and rational asset pricing, and it cannot be ignored simply because one is uncomfortable with the idea or because it sounds too improbable. It is appropriate to consider this concept with any discussion of active strategies designed to produce excess returns—that is, returns in excess of those commensurate with the risk being taken. After all, if the evidence suggests that active strategies are unlikely to be successful over time after all costs have been assessed, the case for a passive strategy becomes much more important.

---

[22] Schlegel, op. cit.

[23] Charles Ellis, *Winning the Loser's Game*, McGraw-Hill, 4th Edition, 2002, p. 10.

[24] Andy Serwer, "The Oracle of Everything," *Fortune*, November 11, 2002, p. 71.

As explained in the next chapter, the efficient market hypothesis is concerned with the assessment of information by investors. Security prices are determined by expectations about the future. Investors use the information available to them in forming their expectations. If security prices fully reflect all the relevant information that is available and usable, a securities market is said to be efficient. In the same vein, rational-asset-pricing models use changes in valuation parameters to explain changes in equity valuations.

If the stock market is efficient, prices reflect their fair economic value as estimated by investors. Even if this is not strictly true, prices may reflect their approximate fair value after transaction costs are taken into account, a condition known as economic efficiency. In such a market, where prices of stocks depart only slightly from their fair economic value, investors should not employ trading strategies designed to "beat the market" by identifying undervalued stocks. Nor should they attempt to time the market in the belief that an advantage can be gained. Sector rotation also will be unsuccessful on average in a highly efficient market.

The implications of a rational market are extremely important for investors. They include one's beliefs about how to value securities. Other implications include the management of a portfolio of securities. Efficient market proponents often argue that less time should be devoted to the analysis of securities for possible inclusion in a portfolio, and more to such considerations as reducing taxes and transaction costs and maintaining the chosen risk level of a portfolio over time. Because a person's beliefs about market efficiency will have a significant impact on the type of stock strategy implemented, we consider the issue of market efficiency in the next chapter.

A Simple Strategy—The Coffeehouse Portfolio

An appropriate way to conclude our discussion of common stock strategies, given the evidence on efficient markets and the difficulties involved in selecting stocks or timing the market, is to consider one of the simplest of strategies an investor can follow. Short of simply investing 100 percent of one's money in one fund, one of the simplest strategies for investors to follow is the "Coffeehouse Portfolio," created by an ex-Smith Barney broker named Bill Schultheis.[25] It involves no trading, no rebalancing, no security analysis, and no strategizing.

Forty percent of the portfolio is allocated to bonds, and 60 percent to equity. This can be accomplished with index funds or ETFs. For example, for the 60 percent equity portion, put 10 percent in the S&P 500, 10 percent in large cap value stocks, 10 percent in small cap stocks, 10 percent in small cap value stocks, 10 percent in international stocks, and 10 percent in REITs. Over the five-year period starting with the bear market of 2000–2002, this portfolio outperformed the indexes with no additional costs or effort. Over the 10-year period ending in 2011, according to the Coffeehouse website, the annualized rate of return was 6.47 percent. Although not a direct comparison because the coffeehouse portfolio holds bonds, small stocks, etc., the S&P 500 compound annual rate of return for these 10 years was 2.9 percent.

Such a portfolio would typically not outperform the market when it is booming, which is why it was laughed at in 1999 at the height of the dotcom frenzy. Nevertheless, over time things have a way of evening out, as the performance of the coffeehouse portfolio demonstrates. Once again, it illustrates the importance of good asset allocation.

---

[25] There is a book by Schultheis with the same title, copyright 2005 by the author. A new book by him was published in 2009 titled *The New Coffeehouse Investor: How to Build Wealth, Ignore Wall Street, and Get on With Your Life.*

Summary

▶ Market risk is the single most important risk affecting the price movements of common stocks.

▶ For well-diversified portfolios, market effects account for 90 percent and more of the variability in the portfolio's return.

▶ The required rate of return for a common stock, or any security, is defined as the minimum expected rate of return needed to induce an investor to purchase the stock.

▶ The required rate of return for any investment opportunity can be expressed as the sum of the risk-free rate of return and a risk premium.

▶ The tradeoff between the required rate of return and risk is viewed as linear and upward-sloping, which means that the required rate of return increases as the risk, measured by beta, increases.

▶ If the market is totally efficient, no active strategy should be able to beat the market on a risk-adjusted basis, and, therefore, a passive strategy may be superior.

▶ Passive strategies include buy-and-hold and the use of index funds.

▶ Pursuit of an active strategy assumes that investors possess some advantage relative to other market participants.

▶ Active strategies include stock selection, sector rotation, and market timing.

▶ The most important active strategy is stock selection. Sector rotation is a variation of this activity.

▶ Security analysts play a large role in providing information relevant to stock valuation and selection. Some of their output has been heavily criticized because of conflicts of interest. Other parts of their output can be of real value to investors doing security analysis.

▶ Market timing is not a likely success story for investors. Missing a relatively few days or months in the market may lower average returns dramatically.

▶ The efficient market hypothesis, which states that current stock prices reflect information quickly and without bias, has implications for all stock investors.

Questions

11-1 What impact does the market have on well-diversified portfolios? What does this suggest about the performance of mutual funds?

11-2 How does an investor in common stocks reconcile the large variability in stock returns, and the big drops that have occurred, with taking a prudent position in owning a portfolio of financial assets?

11-3 Given the drastic—some would say unprecedented—drop in the prices of Japanese stocks in the past, how can U.S. investors justify owning foreign stocks?

11-4 Outline the rationale for passive strategies.

11-5 What is the relation between passive investing and the efficient markets concept?

11-6 From an investor's standpoint, why are actively managed mutual funds likely to be tax inefficient?

11-7 Can a standard index mutual fund outperform its index?

11-8 Describe three active strategies involving common stocks.

11-9 What are the major sources of information used by security analysts in evaluating common stocks?

11-10 How does the cross-sectional variation in common stock returns relate to the issue of stock selection?

11-11 What is meant by sector rotation? What is the key input in implementing effective strategies in sector rotation?

11-12 What does the evidence cited on market timing suggest about the likelihood of success in this area?

11-13 What does it mean to say that investors at large brokerage firms now have access to independent research when buying securities?

11-14 Name three independent sources of information investors can use in doing their own research on stocks?

11-15 What is the basic idea behind the efficient market hypothesis?

11-16 What are the implications of the efficient market hypothesis to both stock selectors and market timers?

11-17 If more investors became passive investors, how would that affect investment companies?

11-18 How should active investors determine if their efforts are worth the cost relative to passive investing?

11-19 Vanguard's S&P 500 Index fund consistently outperforms Morgan Stanley's S&P 500 Index fund, although both hold the same portfolio of stocks. Ignoring sales charges, what is the obvious reason for the underperformance of the Morgan Stanley fund?

11-20 Vanguard's Health Care Fund (VGHCX) outperformed Vanguard's S&P 500 Index fund during the period 2000–2005, although it had a higher operating expense ratio. What is the reason for this outperformance?

Problems

11-1 The average equity mutual fund charges about 1.5 percent annually as an operating expense ratio. Assuming that the average fund earns 13 percent on a gross basis over a 20-year period, determine how much $10,000 invested in a fund would grow to on a net basis after 20 years (after deducting the annual expense ratio).

11-2 Go to www.morningstar.com and look at Morgan Stanley's S&P 500 "A" shares (symbol = SPIAX). Assuming you invest $20,000 in these shares, how much would your account be worth on the first day after deduction of the load charge?

11-3 Suppose you had bought Putnam's Multi Cap Growth "A" shares (symbol = PNOPX) and owned it for the years 2007–2011. Calculate the geometric mean annual average return for this five-year period. Use *Morningstar* to determine the average annual total returns for these five years.

Computational Problems

11-1 You can buy Vanguard's S&P 500 fund with an annual operating expense of 0.15 percent, or you can buy Morgan Stanley's S&P 500 fund with an annual operating expense of 1.80 percent. Given S&P 500 total returns for 2007–2011 of 5.49, 36.6, 26.46, 15.06, and 2.1 respectively, determine how much $10,000 invested in each fund on January 1, 2007, would be worth on December 31, 2011.

Spreadsheet Exercises

11-1 Using the spreadsheet information below,

a. Determine how much a passive investor would have on December 31, 2011 if she invested $50,000 on January 1, 2002 in the passive portfolio

b. Determine how much a passive investor would have on December 31, 2011 if she invested $50,000 on January 1, 2002 in the active portfolio

c. Which portfolio was more risky?

d. Calculate the correlation between the returns for these two portfolios.

e. How do you explain the close association in returns?

	Vanguard 500 Index Fund	Vanguard Growth & Income Fund
2011	2.08%	2.42%
2010	15.05%	14.62%
2009	26.62%	22.42%
2008	−36.97%	−37.72%
2007	5.47%	2.62%
2006	15.75%	14.01%
2005	4.87%	5.82%
2004	10.82%	11.11%
2003	28.59%	30.15%
2002	−22.10%	−21.92%

Checking Your Understanding

11-1   Yes. Stocks would be expected to go up, and a diversified portfolio is always important. This portfolio would be expected to perform well.

11-2   The required rate of return would be expected to rise because of investor pessimism. This happened in the United States in the 1970s during a gasoline shortage.

11-3   Diversification cannot protect your portfolio from the collateral damage that occurs when an overvalued sector declines. After all, this sector will be in your portfolio if it is truly diversified, and therefore your portfolio will be adversely affected. However, diversification will limit the damage of this sector decline, because you will also be exposed to those sectors that perform the best.

11-4   Security analysts have been accused of conflicts of interest because of their ties to the investment banking side of their firm's activities. Brokerage firms wanted to please their investment banking clients, both actual and prospective, in order to retain/acquire their business in selling securities, and to do so they did not want their analysts issuing negative reports about the companies.

11-5   Historically, some firms have always performed well in any given year regardless of what the market does. Therefore, if these firms can be identified, investors could profit. Another way to say this is that there is always wide cross-sectional variation in stock returns, ranging from very good performance to very poor performance.

11-6   There are two significant issues with regard to market timing. First, while some investors may be able to identify approximate times to get out of the stock market because it is going to decline, it is extremely difficult to determine when to get back in the market. That is, periodically deciding when to get out can be much easier than deciding when to get back in. Related to this is the second issue. Studies have shown that much of the market's good performance over a relatively long period occurs during a few days. Thus, being out of the market greatly increases the chances that one will miss some of these few days when the market enjoys very strong performance, thereby diminishing their overall performance substantially.

chapter *12*

What Happens If Markets Are Efficient—Or Not?

Having considered the issue of market equilibrium, it occurs to you that while it is relatively easy to discuss, it may be simply that—talk! What matters is how quickly markets digest information, and how well and quickly stock prices reflect information. You have heard some people say investors can beat the market with the right techniques because there are market inefficiencies, while others say the market is efficient and most investors cannot beat the market. You even recall someone telling you about the January effect. So who is right?

With a little reflection, you realize you could end up wasting a lot of time if you employ techniques to pick stocks that have been shown to be of little or no value—and people are always selling a wide variety of services which claim to aid investors in picking stocks. On the other hand, if there really are some apparent exceptions to market efficiency, it could pay to know about them. Also, you have now heard some talk about behavioral finance, which suggests psychology plays a role in investor actions, which would seem to imply that investors may not always be acting "rationally." Therefore, it seems logical to you to consider this whole issue of market efficiency.

Chapter 12 considers the question of how quickly and accurately information about securities is disseminated in financial markets; that is, how effectively are investor expectations translated into security prices? In a perfectly efficient market all securities are priced correctly. In such a market, investors earn a return on their investment that is directly commensurate with the amount of risk they assume, which is in agreement with the CAPM model discussed in Chapter 9.

AFTER READING THIS CHAPTER YOU WILL BE ABLE TO:

- ▶ Analyze the efficient market hypothesis (EMH) and recognize its significance to investors.
- ▶ Evaluate how the EMH is tested, and what the evidence has shown.
- ▶ Recognize the anomalies (exceptions to market efficiency) that have been put forward
- ▶ Understand the behavioral finance arguments being made today.

Overview

"**If the markets aren't completely efficient, they're close to it!!!**" (a quote in 2002 from a long-time, well-known developer of stock selection techniques—exclamation points added for emphasis)[1]

Because of its significant impact and implications, the idea that markets are informational efficient deserves careful thought and study. Beginning investors should approach it with an open mind. The fact that some well-known market observers and participants reject or disparage this idea does not reduce its validity. Much evidence exists to support the market efficiency argument, regardless of the counter-arguments and the rise in prominence of behavioral finance. The intelligent approach for investors, therefore, is to learn about it and from it, understand the basics of behavioral finance, and make up your own mind.

The Concept of an Efficient Market

WHAT IS AN EFFICIENT MARKET?

Investors determine stock prices on the basis of the expected cash flows to be received from a stock and the risk involved. Rational investors should use all the information they have available or can reasonably obtain. This information set consists of both known information and beliefs about the future (i.e., information that can reasonably be inferred).

✓   *Information is the key to the determination of stock prices and therefore is the central issue of the efficient markets concept.*

Efficient Market (EM) A market in which prices of securities quickly and fully reflect all available information

An **Efficient Market (EM)** is defined as one in which the prices of all securities quickly and fully reflect all available relevant information.

- In an efficient market, the current market price of a security incorporates all relevant information.
- In an efficient market, securities prices reflect available information so as to offer an expected return consistent with the level of risk.

This concept postulates that investors will assimilate all relevant information into prices in making their buy-and-sell decisions. Therefore, the current price of a stock reflects

1. All known information, including
   - Past information (e.g., last year's or last quarter's earnings)
   - Current information as well as events that have been announced but are still forthcoming (such as a stock split)
2. Information that can reasonably be inferred; for example, if many investors believe that the Fed will cut interest rates at its meeting next week, prices will reflect (to a large degree) this belief before the actual event occurs.

To summarize, a market is efficient relative to any information set if investors are unable to earn abnormal profits (returns beyond those warranted by the amount of risk assumed) by using that information set in their investing decisions. In an efficient market, competition between investors seeking abnormal profits drives stock prices to their equilibrium ("correct") values.

---

[1] Quote is from Samuel Eisenstadt, the major player in the development of Value Line's famed stock ranking system which is decades old. See Steven T. Goldberg, "Civil Warriors," *Kiplinger's Personal Finance*, August 2002, p. 39.

Figure 12-1

The adjustment of Stock Prices to Information: **(a)** if the Market is Efficient; **(b)** One Possibility if the Market is Inefficient.

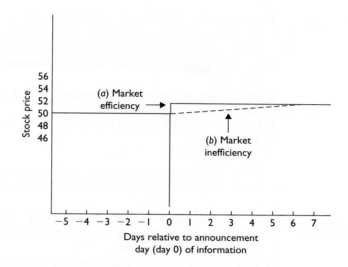

Market efficiency requires that the adjustment to new information occurs very quickly as the information becomes known. Given the extremely rapid dissemination of information in the United States, with the Internet widely accessible to most investors, information is spread very quickly, almost instantaneously, to market participants with access to these sources. Numerous websites offer updated information during the day about the economy, the financial markets, and individual companies. Clearly, the Internet has made the market more efficient in the sense of how widely and quickly information is disseminated.

The concept that markets are efficient does not claim, or require, a perfect adjustment in price following the new information. Rather, the correct statement involved here is that the adjustment in prices resulting from information is "unbiased" (this means that the adjustment is sometimes too large and at other times too small, but on average, over many observations, it balances out). The new price does not have to be the new equilibrium price, but only an unbiased estimate of the final equilibrium price that will be established after investors have fully assessed the impact of the information.

Figure 12-1 illustrates the concept of market efficiency for one company for which a significant event occurs that has an effect on its expected profitability. The stock is trading at $50 on the announcement date of the significant event—Date 0 in Figure 12-1 is the announcement date for the event. If the market is efficient, the price of a stock quickly reflects the available information. Investors will very quickly adjust a stock's price toward its intrinsic (fair) value. Assume that the new fair value estimate for the stock is $52. In an efficient market, an immediate increase in the price of the stock to $52 will occur, as represented by the solid line in Figure 12-1. Since, in our example, no additional new information occurs at this time, the price of the stock continues at $52.

If the market adjustment process occurs in an inefficient market, a lag in the adjustment of the stock prices to the new information can occur and is represented by the dotted line. The price eventually adjusts to the new fair value estimate of $52 as brokerage houses disseminate the new information and investors revise their estimates of the stock's fair value. Note that the time it would take for the price to adjust is not known ahead of time—the dotted line is only illustrative.

WHY THE U.S. STOCK MARKET CAN BE EXPECTED TO BE EFFICIENT

If the type of market adjustment described above seems too much to expect, consider the situation from the following standpoint. It can be shown that an efficient market can exist if the following conditions come about:

1. A large number of rational, profit-maximizing investors exist who actively participate in the market by analyzing, valuing, and trading stocks. These investors are price takers; that is, one participant alone cannot affect the price of a security.
2. Information is costless and widely available to market participants at approximately the same time.
3. Information is generated in a random fashion such that announcements are basically independent of one another.
4. Investors react quickly and fully to the new information, causing stock prices to adjust accordingly.

These conditions may seem strict, and in some sense they are. Nevertheless, consider how closely they parallel the actual investment environment.

- A large number of investors are constantly "playing the game." Both individuals and institutions follow the market closely on a daily basis, standing ready to buy or sell when they think it is appropriate.
- Although the production of information is not costless, for institutions in the investment business generating various types of information is a necessary cost of business, and many participants receive it "free" (investors may pay indirectly for such items in their brokerage costs and other fees).
- Information is largely generated in a random fashion, in the sense that most investors cannot predict when companies will announce significant new developments, when oil disruptions will occur, when major weather events will affect economies, when currencies will be devalued, when important leaders will suddenly suffer a heart attack, and so forth. Although there is some dependence in information events over time, by and large announcements are independent and occur more or less randomly.
- The efficient market concept does not say that all investors are rational and react quickly to new information, only that markets in the aggregate are rational. Many investors with substantial resources, and arbitrageurs, are generally rational and ready to act on information.

The result of these conditions that exist is that markets efficiently reflect available information about securities. Although mistakes are made, and some irrational behavior does occur, by and large the market does a good job when it comes to pricing securities.

Concepts in Action

In mid-2008, it was revealed that Warren Buffett, arguably the most famous investor in the United States, had entered into a wager on January 1 of that year that would extend for 10 years. Buffett bet Protégé Funds, a money management firm which seeks to place client money in the best hedge funds, that the collection of hedge funds chosen by this firm would not outperform the S&P 500 (using a Vanguard index fund) over the next 10 years, net of all expenses incurred by either alternative. Buffett has been a big critic of the fees charged by hedge funds. Each party put up roughly $320,000 each, and a zero coupon bond with a payoff of $1 million was purchased, with the proceeds going to charity. The money management firm hoped to show that expert selection of five hedge funds could outperform the index fund, while Buffett's argument was that this would be unlikely after deducting fees.

Although not explicitly discussed, it is clear that Buffett is relying on the notion of efficient markets to win this bet. The market should perform at least as well as actively managed equity funds net of fees.

THE INTERNATIONAL PERSPECTIVE

A strong case can be made for U.S. financial markets being efficient, based on the arguments above. After all, U.S. markets have thousands of analysts, and millions of investors buying and selling stocks regularly. What about foreign markets? Are the securities in foreign markets analyzed less closely? Of course, the large developed countries provide much information and tend to have companies that are well known and scrutinized. The less developed countries have less well developed flows of information, and the emerging markets may have significant gaps in information.

If there is less efficiency in the financial markets of other countries than in the United States, there should be some evidence of more success involving international investing. During the 1990s, only 10 percent of U.S. mutual fund managers outperformed the S&P 500 Index, while 31 percent outperformed a European index. While the international money managers clearly did better, both groups make an argument for market efficiency and passive investing.

Some recent time periods show that international money managers are still not turning in great performance. For the three-year period ending mid-2011, 57 percent of global funds and 65 percent of international funds underperformed their benchmarks. As for emerging markets, where logically more inefficiencies should occur, 81 percent of emerging market funds underperformed their benchmarks.

FORMS OF MARKET EFFICIENCY

We have defined an efficient market as one in which all relevant information is reflected in stock prices quickly and fully. Thus, the key to assessing market efficiency is to determine how well information is reflected in stock prices. In a perfectly efficient market, security prices quickly reflect all available relevant information, and investors are not able to use available information to earn excess returns because it is already impounded in prices. In such a market, every security's price is equal to its intrinsic (investment) value, which reflects all information about that security's prospects.

Efficient Market Hypothesis (EMH) The proposition that securities markets are efficient, with the prices of securities reflecting their economic value

We define the major concept involved with efficient markets as the **Efficient Market Hypothesis (EMH)**, which is simply the formal statement of market efficiency concerned with the extent to which security prices quickly and fully reflect available information. In 1970, Fama proposed dividing the hypothesis into three categories, and these have typically been used since that time in discussions of the EMH. These three classifications are illustrated in Figure 12-2.[2]

For purposes of our discussion, we will continue to follow these widely referred-to classifications because of their popularity. However, it should be noted that in a subsequent article some 20 years later Fama refers to a "weaker and economically more sensible version of the efficiency hypothesis" which deals with prices reflecting information to the extent that it is not financially worthwhile to act on any information.[3] In this article he changed the weak-form (described below) tests to be more general tests of return predictability, and he changed semi-strong efficiency (described below) to studies of announcements, which is associated with what is often called event studies. Therefore, we will consider what an event study is, and how it relates to this discussion.

Market Data Price and volume information for stocks or indexes

Weak Form That part of the Efficient Market Hypothesis stating that prices reflect all price and volume data

1. Weak Form: One of the most traditional types of information used in assessing security values are **market data**, which refers primarily to all past price information (volume data also included). If security prices are determined in a market that is **weak-form** efficient,

---

[2] E. Fama, "Efficient Capital Markets: A Review of Theory and Empirical Work," *The Journal of Finance*, 25, No. 2 (May 1970): pp. 383–417.

[3] Eugene F. Fama, "Efficient Capital Markets: II," *The Journal of Finance*, 46 (December 1991): pp. 1575–1617.

Figure 12-2

Cumulative Levels of Market Efficiency and the Information Associated with Each.

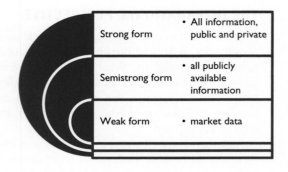

Strong form	• All information, public and private
Semistrong form	• all publicly available information
Weak form	• market data

historical price data should already be reflected in current prices and should be of no value in predicting future price changes. Since price data are the basis of technical analysis (discussed in Chapter 16), technical analysis that relies on the past history of price information is of little or no value.

Example 12-1

As explained in Chapter 16, technical analysts look for patterns in stock prices that can be exploited. Figure 12-3 shows 30 days of price changes for Botox Company. Notice that in every case but one, whenever the price change is less than 20 cents, the next price change is strongly positive. Furthermore, whenever the price change is above 80 cents, the next price change is almost always lower. Is this a successful example of using past price information to predict future price changes?

The answer is NO! The changes in Figure 12-3 were generated by the random number generator function in Excel. This illustrates the danger of trying to find useful patterns in stock prices where none exists.

Figure 12-3

Price Changes for 30 Days for Botox Company.

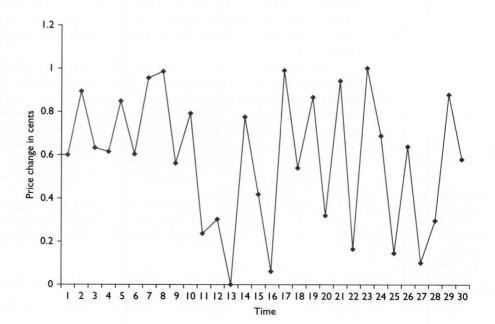

Tests of the usefulness of price data are called weak-form tests of the EMH. If the weak form of the EMH is correct, past price changes should be unrelated to future price changes in an economic sense. In other words, a market can be said to be weakly efficient if the current price reflects all past market data. The correct implication of a weak-form efficient market is that the past history of price information is of no value in assessing future changes in price.[4]

2. Semistrong Form: A more comprehensive level of market efficiency involves not only known and publicly available market data, but also all publicly known and available data, such as earnings, dividends, stock split announcements, new product developments, financing difficulties, and accounting changes. A market that quickly incorporates all such information into prices is said to show **semistrong-form** efficiency. Note that a semistrong-efficient market encompasses the weak form of the hypothesis, because market data are part of the larger set of all publicly available information.

A semistrong-efficient market implies that investors cannot act on new *public* information after its announcement and expect to earn above-average risk-adjusted returns. If lags exist in the adjustment of stock prices to certain announcements, and investors can exploit these lags and earn abnormal returns, then the market is not fully efficient in the semistrong sense.

3. Strong Form: The most stringent form of market efficiency is the **strong form**, which asserts that stock prices fully reflect all information, public and nonpublic. The strong form goes beyond the semistrong form in considering the value of the information contained in announcements, while the semistrong form focuses on the speed with which information is impounded into stock prices. If the market is strong-form efficient, no group of investors should be able to earn, over a reasonable period of time, abnormal rates of return by using information in a superior manner.

A second aspect of the strong form has to do with private information—that is, information not publicly available because it is restricted to certain groups such as corporate insiders and specialists on the exchanges. At the extreme, the strong form holds that no one with private information can make money using this information. Needless to say, such an extreme belief is not held by many people.

As noted earlier, if one believes in semistrong-form efficiency, the weak form is also encompassed. Strong-form efficiency encompasses the weak and semistrong forms and represents the highest level of market efficiency. An investor who believes in the strong form of the EMH should be a passive investor. On the other hand, an investor who accepts the weak form but rejects the other two could be an aggressive investor, trading actively in pursuit of investing gains.

Semistrong Form That part of the efficient market hypothesis stating that prices reflect all publicly available information

Strong Form That part of the Efficient Market Hypothesis stating that prices reflect all information, public and private

Checking Your Understanding

1. Should investors expect stock prices to reflect all available information?
2. Suppose stock price movements are predictable. Would this be evidence of market efficiency or market inefficiency? Explain.

How to Test for Market Efficiency

Because of the significance of the efficient markets hypothesis to all investors, and because of the controversy that surrounds the EMH, we will consider some empirical evidence on market

---

[4] It is incorrect to state, as is sometimes done, that the best estimate of price at time $t + 1$ is the current (time t) price, because this implies an expected return of zero. The efficient market in no way implies that the expected return on any security is zero.

efficiency. A very large number of studies have been done over the years. Our purpose here is simply to present an idea of how these tests are done, and some generalized notion of results.

✓　The key to testing the validity of any of the three forms of market efficiency is the consistency with which investors can earn returns in excess of those commensurate with the risk involved, conditional upon the information set involved.

Short-lived inefficiencies appearing on a random basis do not constitute evidence of market inefficiencies, at least in an economic (as opposed to a statistical) sense. Therefore, it makes sense to talk about an *economically efficient* market, where assets are priced in such a manner that investors cannot exploit any discrepancies and earn excess risk-adjusted returns after consideration of all transaction costs. In such a market, some securities could be priced slightly above their true values and some slightly below, and lags can exist in the processing of information, but, again, not in such a way that the differences can be profitably exploited by the average investor.

Example 12-2　In one study of how capital markets are linked, the authors examined a trading rule for one of the most significant lags found between international markets, Hong Kong versus the United States. Although much of the earnings adjustment occurred overnight, they found a statistically significant spread of up to 11.5 basis points that could be earned over and above a buy-and-hold strategy. They concluded that arbitrage might be possible if trading costs are lower than 11.5 basis points, but that this was not likely except for a trading house (and even that is not assured). Thus, these results suggest that while statistically significant differences may exist, the markets are probably economically efficient.

What about the time period involved? In the short run, investors may earn unusual returns even if the market is efficient. After all, you could buy a stock today, and tomorrow a major discovery could be announced that would cause its stock price to increase significantly. Does this mean the market is inefficient? Obviously not; it means you are either very skillful or, more likely, very lucky. The question is, can you, and enough other investors, do this a sufficient number of times in the long run to earn abnormal profits? Even in the long run, some people will be lucky, given the total number of investors.

WEAK-FORM TESTS

As noted, weak-form efficiency means that price data are incorporated into current stock prices. If prices follow nonrandom trends, stock-price changes are dependent; otherwise, they are independent. Therefore, weak-form tests involve the question of whether all information contained in the sequence of past prices is fully reflected in the current price.

Random Walk A theory from the 1960s stating that stock prices wander randomly across time

The weak-form EMH is related to, but not identical with, an idea popular in the 1960s stating that stock price changes should follow a **random walk.** If prices follow a random walk, price changes over time are random (independent).[5] The price change for today is unrelated to the price change yesterday, or the day before, or any other day. This is a result of the scenario described at the outset of the chapter. If new information arrives randomly in the market and investors react to it immediately, changes in prices will also be random.

---

[5] Technically, the random walk hypothesis is more restrictive than the weak-form EMH. Stock prices can conform to weak-form efficiency without meeting the conditions of a random walk. The random walk model specifies that successive returns are independent and are identically distributed over time.

There are two primary ways to test for weak-form efficiency:

1. Statistically test the independence of stock-price changes. If the statistical tests suggest that price changes are independent, the implication is that knowing and using the past sequence of price information is of no value to an investor. In other words, trends in price changes, to the extent they exist, cannot be profitably exploited.
2. Test specific trading rules that attempt to use past price data. If such tests legitimately produce risk-adjusted returns beyond that available from simply buying a portfolio of stocks and holding it until a common liquidation date, after deducting all costs, it would suggest that the market is not weak-form efficient.

✓ When considering weak-form tests of market efficiency, it is important to distinguish between *statistical dependence* and *economic dependence* in stock-price changes.

The statistical tests discussed earlier detected some small amount of dependence in price changes. Not all of the series could be said to be completely independent statistically. However, they were economically independent in that one could not exploit the small statistical dependence that existed. After brokerage costs, excess returns disappear.[6]

Weak-form tests, of both the statistical and the trading rule types, are numerous and almost unanimous in their findings (after necessary corrections and adjustments have been made). These tests support the notion that the market is weak-form efficient.

SEMISTRONG-FORM TESTS

Semistrong-form tests are largely tests of the speed of price adjustments to publicly available information. The question is whether investors can use publicly available information to earn excess returns, after proper adjustments. As noted earlier, Fama has changed the traditional notion of semistrong-form efficiencies to studies of announcements of various types, which involves event studies.

Event Studies   The empirical research into semistrong-form efficiency often involves an **event study**, which means that a company's stock returns are examined to determine the impact of a particular event on the stock price.[7]

Event Study An empirical analysis of stock price behavior surrounding a particular event

✓ Event studies allow us to control aggregate market returns while firm-unique events are examined.

Example 12-3   Suppose an analyst wants to study the relationship between earnings surprises and stock prices. An event study would quantify the relationship between quarterly earnings announcements (which contain the surprises) and stock prices around the announcement dates for the earnings.

---

[6] Some studies have indicated that trading rules can produce profits after making the necessary adjustments. For a study that argues that trading rules may not be so readily implemented under actual conditions, see Ray Ball, S. P. Kothari. and Charles Wasley, "Can We Implement Research on Stock Trading Rules?" *The Journal of Portfolio Management* (Winter 1995): pp. 54–63.

[7] See Fama, "Efficient Capital Markets."

This methodology typically uses an index model of stock returns to calculate an expected return for a stock. An index model states that security returns are determined by a market factor (index) and a unique company factor. The single-index model mentioned in Chapter 8 is an example.

Company-unique returns are the residual error terms representing the difference between the security's actual return and that given by the index model. In other words, after adjusting for what the company's return should have been, given the index model, any remaining portion of the actual return is an **abnormal return** representing the impact of a particular event.

Abnormal Return Return on a security beyond that expected on the basis of its risk

$$\text{Abnormal return} = AR_{it} = R_{it} - E(R_{it})$$

where

$$AR_{it} = \text{the abnormal rate of return for security } i \text{ during period } t$$
$$R_{it} = \text{the actual rate of return on security } i \text{ during period } t$$
$$E(R_{it}) = \text{the expected rate of return for security } i \text{ during period } t,$$
$$\text{based on an index model relationship}$$

Thus, the abnormal return is the stock's return over and above what the stock should earn as predicted by the index model used. When studying a particular event, such as earnings surprises, we want to be sure the abnormal return measures the event and not some other economic factor occurring at the same time. To do this, studies include multiple firms with the same event from different dates in order that other economic factors cancel each other. This allows us to calculate an average AR for any time period under consideration by averaging the abnormal firms across companies. We will call this average AR_t, whereas for each individual company the abnormal return is AR_{it}.

Cumulative Abnormal Return (CAR) The sum of the individual abnormal returns over the time period under examination

The **cumulative abnormal return (CAR)** is the sum of the average abnormal returns over the period of time under examination and is calculated as

$$CAR = \sum_{t=1}^{n} AR_t$$

where

$$CAR = \text{the cumulative abnormal return}$$

The CAR captures the average firm-specific stock movements over some period of time during which the event being studied is expected to affect stock returns.

Consider Figure 12-4 (a), which shows a situation where the announcement is unanticipated in an efficient market. The CARs move around zero prior to the announcement date. On the announcement date there is an immediate upward adjustment to new, and positive, information. After this adjustment takes place, stocks are once again fairly valued, and the CARs fluctuate along a horizontal path.

Now consider Figure 12-4 (b), the case of an anticipated favorable event in an efficient market. Investors anticipate the event before the announcement, and the CAR rises as investors bid up the stock price. By the announcement date the event is reflected in stock prices, and there is no adjustment upward. Instead returns continue along their horizontal path.

Figure 12-4

Cumulative Abnormal Returns.

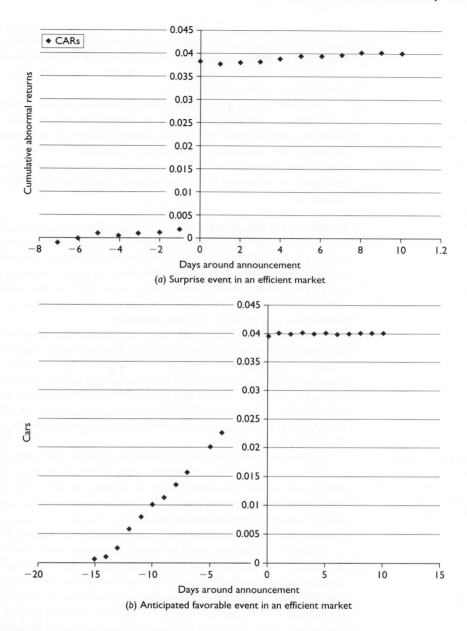

(a) Surprise event in an efficient market

(b) Anticipated favorable event in an efficient market

STRONG-FORM EVIDENCE

The strong form of the EMH states that stock prices quickly adjust to reflect all information, including private information.[8] Thus, no group of investors has information that allows them to earn abnormal profits consistently, even those investors with monopolistic access to information. Note that investors are prohibited not from possessing monopolistic information, but from profiting from the use of such information. This is an important point in light of the studies of insider trading reported below.

---

[8] Fama, in his 1991 paper, refers to these tests as "tests for private information" instead of strong-form tests. See Fama, "Efficient Capital Markets."

One way to test for strong-form efficiency is to examine the performance of groups presumed to have access to "true" nonpublic information. If such groups can consistently earn above-average risk-adjusted returns, this version of the strong form will not be supported. We will consider corporate insiders, a group that presumably falls into the category of having monopolistic access to information.

Another aspect of the strong form is the ability of any investor to earn excess returns as a result of using information in a superior manner. In other words, can an investor, or group of investors, use the value of the information contained in an announcement to earn excess returns? If not, the market is strong-form efficient. This aspect of the strong form has been examined in several ways, including analyzing the returns of the professional money managers such as those of mutual funds and pension funds, and examining the value of what security analysts do.

Corporate Insiders   We considered insider trading in Chapter 5. A corporate insider is an officer, director, or major stockholder of a corporation who might be expected to have valuable inside information. The Securities and Exchange Commission (SEC) requires insiders (officers, directors, and owners of more than 10 percent of a company's stock) to report their monthly purchase or sale transactions to the SEC by the tenth of the next month. This information is made public in the SEC's monthly publication, *Official Summary of Security Transactions and Holdings (Official Summary)*.

Insiders have access to privileged information and are able to act on it and profit before the information is made public. Therefore, it is not surprising that several studies of corporate insiders found they consistently earned abnormal returns on their stock transactions.[9] A study covering the period 1975–1995 by Lakonishok and Lee found that companies with a high incidence of insider buying outperform those where insiders have done a large amount of selling.[10] The margin was almost 8 percentage points for the subsequent 12-month period. Interestingly, the largest differences occurred in companies with a market capitalization of less than $1 billion.

Profitable insider trading is a violation of strong-form efficiency, which requires a market in which no investor can consistently earn abnormal profits. Investors without access to this private information can observe what the insiders are doing by studying the publicly available reports that appear in the *Official Summary* mentioned above. Several investment information services compile this information and sell it to the public. Successful use of this information by outsiders (the general public) would be a violation of semistrong efficiency.

Rozeff and Zaman used the typical abnormal return methodology of previous studies and found that outsiders can earn profits by acting on the publicly available information concerning insider transactions.[11] However, when they used an abnormal returns measure that takes into account size and earnings/price ratio effects, these profits decreased substantially—and disappeared altogether, when transactions cost of 2 percent are included. Furthermore, imposition of the 2 percent transactions cost on corporate insiders reduces their abnormal returns to an average of 3 to 3.5 percent per year. Therefore, this study reaffirms semistrong market efficiency with respect to insider trading and also suggests that corporate insiders do

---

[9] See, for example, J. Jaffe, "Special Information and Insider Trading," *Journal of Business*, 47 (July 1974): pp. 410–428, and Ken Nunn, G. P. Madden, and Michael Gombola, "Are Some Investors More 'Inside' Than Others?" *Journal of Portfolio Management*, 9 (Spring 1983): pp. 18–22.

[10] Josef Lakonishok and Inmoon Lee, "Are Insider Trades Informative?" *Review of Financial Studies*, 14 (Spring 2001).

[11] Michael S. Rozeff and Mir A. Zaman, "Market Efficiency and Insider Trading: New Evidence," *Journal of Business* (January 1988): pp. 25–45.

not earn substantial profits from directly using inside information, which in effect supports strong-form efficiency.

There are several reasons why insider transactions can be very misleading, or simply of no value as an indicator of where the stock price is likely to go. Selling shares acquired by option grants to key executives has become commonplace—they need the cash, and they sell shares acquired as part of their compensation. Similarly, acquiring shares through the exercise of options can simply represent an investment decision by the executive.

Checking Your Understanding

3. Assume stock prices truly follow a random walk. Is this evidence of market irrationality?
4. Given the overall evidence supporting market efficiency, how might an institutional investor, such as a mutual fund or endowment fund, justify spending relatively large amounts on stock selection techniques?

Market Anomalies

Market Anomalies Techniques or strategies that appear to be contrary to an efficient market

Market anomalies are in contrast to what would be expected in a totally efficient market. To date, most of them have not been explained away and until that happens, they remain anomalies or exceptions to market efficiency.

✓ Market anomalies constitute exceptions to market efficiency.

We will examine several anomalies that have generated much attention and have yet to be satisfactorily explained. However, investors must be cautious in viewing any of these anomalies as a stock selection device guaranteed to outperform the market. There is no such guarantee because empirical tests of these anomalies may not approximate actual trading strategies that could be followed by investors. Furthermore, even if anomalies exist and can be identified, investors should still hold a portfolio of stocks rather than concentrating on a few stocks identified by one of these methods. As we saw in Chapter 7, diversification is crucial for all investors—indeed, diversification is the number one rule of all portfolio management.

EARNINGS ANNOUNCEMENTS

The adjustment of stock prices to earnings announcements has been studied in several papers, opening up some interesting questions and possibilities. The information found in such announcements should, and does, affect stock prices. The questions that need to be answered are as follows:

1. How much of the earnings announcement is new information and how much has been anticipated by the market. In other words, how much of the announcement is a "surprise"?
2. How quickly is the "surprise" portion of the announcement reflected in the price of the stock? Is it immediate, as would be expected in an efficient market, or is there a lag in the adjustment process? If a lag occurs, investors have a chance to realize excess returns by quickly acting on the publicly available earnings announcements.

To assess the earnings announcement issue properly, we must separate a particular earnings announcement into an expected and an unexpected part. The expected part is that portion anticipated by investors by the time of announcement and that requires no adjustment in stock prices, whereas the unexpected part is unanticipated by investors and requires an adjustment in price.

Latane, Tuttle, and Jones studied quarterly earnings reports in 1968 and found them to be positively correlated with subsequent short-term price movements.[12] This finding indicated a lag in the adjustment of stock prices to the information in these reports. Following several papers that examined the value of quarterly earnings in stock selection, Latane, Jones, and Rieke in 1974 developed the concept of **standardized unexpected earnings (SUE)** as a means of investigating the earnings surprises in quarterly data. SUE is defined as

$$SUE = \frac{\text{Actual quarterly earnings} - \text{Predicted quarterly earnings}}{\text{Standardization factor to adjust for size differences}}$$

$$= \text{Unexpected earnings/Standard error of the estimate}$$

The actual quarterly earnings are the earnings reported by the company and available to investors soon after reported. Predicted earnings for a particular company are estimated from historical earnings data before the earnings are reported. As each company's earnings are announced, the SUE can be calculated and acted on. Companies with high (low) unexpected earnings are expected to have a positive (negative) price response.[13]

Figure 12-5 shows a similar analysis for an updated period involving a sample size ranging from about 1,700 companies per quarter to almost 2,000 companies. SUEs are separated into 10 categories based on the size and sign of the unexpected earnings. Category 10 contains all SUEs larger than 4.0, and category 1 contains all SUEs smaller than −4.0; categories 5 and 6 contain the smallest unexpected earnings.

As Figure 12-5 shows, the SUE categories follow a monotonic discrimination, with category 10 performing the best and category 1 the worst. Categories 5 and 6 show virtually no excess returns after the announcement date of earnings, as would be expected from the smallest unexpected earnings.[14] The substantial adjustment that occurs with a lag after the day of earnings announcement is the unexplained part of the SUE puzzle. In an efficient market, prices should adjust quickly to earnings, rather than with a lag.

By the mid-1980s, considerable evidence had been presented about the relationship between unexpected earnings and subsequent stock returns. Although such evidence is not in any way conclusive, neither can it be easily dismissed. Different researchers, using different samples and different techniques, have examined the unexpected earnings issue and have found similar results. It must be emphasized, however, that techniques such as SUE are not a guarantee of major success for investors. The relationships discussed are averages and do not necessarily reflect what any single investor would experience.

[12] H. A. Latane, Donald L. Tuttle, and Charles P. Jones, "E/P Ratios vs. Changes in Earnings in Forecasting Future Price Changes," *Financial Analysts Journal* (January–February 1969): pp. 117–120, p. 123.

[13] Latane and Jones documented the performance of SUE in a series of papers. SUE was shown to have a definite relationship with subsequent excess holding-period returns. In one paper the authors documented the precise response of stock prices to earnings announcements using a large sample of stocks (over 1,400) for the 36 quarters covering mid-1971 to mid-1980. Daily returns were used, allowing the exact response of stock prices to quarterly earnings announcements to be analyzed before, on, and after the day the earnings were announced. See Charles P. Jones, Richard J. Rendleman, and Henry A. Latane, "Stock Returns and SUEs during the 1970s," *Journal of Portfolio Management* (Winter 1984): pp. 18–22.

[14] Excess returns are calculated for each security as the difference between a security's return for each day and the market's return for that day. These excess returns are cumulated for the period beginning 63 days before the announcement date of earnings through 63 days following the announcement date. (There are approximately 63 trading days in a quarter.)

Standardized Unexpected Earnings (SUE) A variable used in the selection of common stocks, calculated as the ratio of unexpected earnings to a standardization factor

Figure 12-5

Cumulative Excess
Returns Surrounding the
Announcement Date of
Quarterly Earnings for
10 SUE Categories.

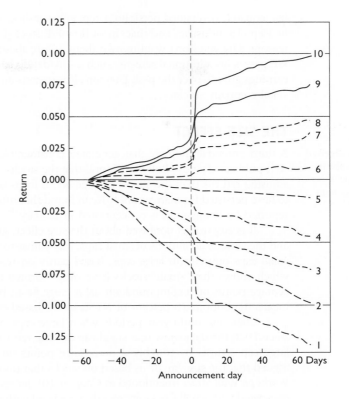

LOW P/E RATIOS

One of the more enduring concepts in investments concerns the price/earnings (P/E) ratio
discussed earlier in the valuation chapters. A number of investors believe that low P/E stocks,
on average, outperform high P/E stocks. The rationale for this concept is not explicit, but the
belief persists.[15,16]

The P/E ratio anomaly appears to offer investors a potential strategy for investing that
could produce returns superior to many alternatives they may be using. Some well-known
commentators continue to advocate investing in low P/E stocks. For example, David Dreman,
a money manager and financial columnist, recommends that investors ignore professional
investment advice and select stocks with low P/E ratios. His hypothesis is that low P/E stocks
may currently be unwanted, but if they have strong finances, high yields, and good earnings
records, they almost always do well eventually.

Investors need to be careful when following the low P/E strategy. Although a diversified
portfolio, as always, is critical, rigid adherence to a low P/E strategy could result in an

---

[15] Basu studied this issue by ranking stocks by their P/E ratios and comparing the results of the high P/E ratio group
with those of the low P/E ratio group 12 months following purchase. The results of Basu's study indicated that the low
P/E ratio stocks outperformed the high P/E ratio stocks. Furthermore, risk was not an explanatory factor. See S. Basu,
"Investment Performance of Common Stocks in Relation to Their Price-Earnings Ratios: A Test of the Efficient Market
Hypothesis," *The Journal of Finance*, 32, No. 2 (June 1977): pp. 663–682.

[16] In response to questions raised about these findings, Basu conducted a study to reexamine the relationship between
the P/E ratio, the size effect, and returns on NYSE stocks for the period 1963–1980. He found that the stocks of low
P/E firms generally had higher risk-adjusted returns than firms with high P/E ratios. Furthermore, this P/E ratio effect
was significant even after adjustments were made for differences in firm size. See S. Basu, "The Relationship Between
Earnings' Yield, Market Value and Return for NYSE Common Stocks: Further Evidence," *Journal of Financial Economics*,
12 (June 1983): pp. 129–156.

inadequately diversified portfolio. Dreman has indicated that he takes a minimum of 25 stocks in 15 to 18 industries and that "most [low-P/E stocks] have significant problems or very good reasons why you don't want to own them." Only about 1 in 10 candidates on the basis of low P/E passes his additional screens, such as dividend yields higher than average and accelerating earnings growth over the past. Dreman also suggests an emphasis on large stocks as opposed to small-company stocks.

THE SIZE EFFECT

Size Effect The observed tendency for smaller firms to have higher stock returns than large firms

A third potential anomaly that generated considerable attention is the firm **size effect**. In a well-publicized study, Rolf Banz found that the stocks of small NYSE firms earned higher risk-adjusted returns than the stocks of large NYSE firms (on average).[17] This size effect appeared to have persisted for many years.[18] Keim found that roughly 50 percent of the return difference reported by Reinganum is concentrated in January.[19]

It is easy to get confused about the size effect, given some conflicting research findings and the various definitions of small caps. Many investors today generally accept the notion that small caps outperform large caps, based partly on results from the Ibbotson Associates data which shows that "small" stocks have outperformed the S&P 500 Index by roughly 2 percentage points on a compound annual average basis; however, "small" as used in this context means the bottom 20 percent of NYSE stocks based on market value.

There are multi-year periods when large caps outperformed small caps. Nevertheless, since 1926 the data show that small cap average returns over the entire period have exceeded large cap returns by roughly 2 percentage points on a geometric mean basis. Dreman has argued that the size "myth" is based on stocks that trade thinly or not at all. In his book *What Works on Wall Street* (mentioned in Chapter 10), James O'Shaughnessy argues that the returns associated with small stocks are mostly associated with micro-cap stocks which have very small capitalizations and are not easily bought by individuals or even institutions because of large spreads and commissions.[20]

THE JANUARY EFFECT

Several studies in the past suggested that seasonality exists in the stock market. Evidence of stock return seasonality grew out of studies of the size anomaly explained in the previous section. The strong performance in January by small-company stocks became known as the **January effect**.[21]

January Effect The observed tendency for small-company stock returns to be higher in January than in other months

---

[17] R. Banz, "The Relationship Between Returns and Market Value of Common Stocks," *Journal of Financial Economics*, 9 (March 1981): pp. 3–18.

[18] Mark Reinganum, using a sample of both NYSE and AMEX firms, also found abnormally large risk-adjusted returns for small firms. Both Banz and Reinganum attributed the results to a misspecification of the CAPM rather than to a market inefficiency. See M. Reinganum, "Misspecification of Capital Asset Pricing: Empirical Anomalies Based on Earnings Yield and Market Values," *Journal of Financial Economics*, 9 (March 1981): pp. 19–46.

[19] These results, as well as a discussion of most of the anomalies, can be found in Donald B. Keim, "The CAPM and Equity Return Regularities," *Financial Analysts Journal* (May–June 1986): pp. 19–34.

[20] A more detailed discussion of this issue can be found in Marc R. Reinganum, "The Size Effect: Evidence and Potential Explanations," in *Investing in Small-Cap and Microcap Securities*, "Association for Investment Management and Research, 1997.

[21] Richard Roll, "Vas ist das? The Turn of the Year Effect and the Return Premium of Small Firms," *The Journal of Portfolio Management* (Winter 1983): pp. 18–28. Roll also found a turn-of-the-year effect with abnormal returns for small firms on the last trading day in December.

Another paper by Keim further documented the abnormal returns for small firms in January. Keim also found a yield effect—the largest abnormal returns tended to accrue to firms either paying no dividends or having high dividend yields.[22]

The information about a possible January effect has been available for years and has been widely discussed in the press. A logical question, therefore, is whether a January effect could continue to persist in the face of widespread knowledge of this anomaly.[23]

The January effect has become controversial. While substantial evidence documents its existence in the past, a number of researchers claim that its impact has diminished over time. On the other hand, Mark Hirschey, a researcher who has studied the January effect, has been quoted as recently as 2008 saying: "On average, the first few trading days of the year is a wonderful period for returns on small-cap, beaten-down stocks."[24] In October 2011, a *Wall Street Journal* article referred to a "reliable post-Christmas rally known as the 'Santa Claus rally,' traditionally the last five trading days of December and the first two of January."[25]

✓ The January effect does not appear to exist for the large-cap stocks such as those found in the DJIA and the S&P 500 Index. There is evidence it exists for the smallest-cap stocks, those with an average market capitalization of about $100 million.

The problem with the smallest-cap stocks is their lack of liquidity. Bid-ask spreads can be very wide, and can eliminate any likely gains from trying to capture a January effect with these stocks.

THE VALUE LINE RANKING SYSTEM

The Value Line Investment Survey is the largest, and perhaps best-known, investment service in the country.[26] *Value Line* ranks each of the roughly 1,700 stocks it covers from 1 (best) to 5 (worst) as to its "timeliness"—probable relative price performance within the next 12 months. These timeliness ranks, updated weekly, have been available since 1965.

The performance of the five rankings categories has been very strong, based on *Value Line*'s calculations. For example, consider the complete record (at the time) of *Value Line* rankings for timeliness from 1965 through 2011. The ranking system clearly showed monotonic discrimination ability. That is, Group 1 stocks performed best, Group 2 stocks performed second best, and so on down to Group 5 stocks which performed the worst. Figure 12-6 shows the record for the Value Line ranks allowing for annual changes in rank.

The Value Line Investment Survey now regularly reports a comparison of the relative price performance of its Group 1 stocks with four other strategies: low P/E, low cap (small size), low

---

[22] See Donald B. Keim, "Dividend Yields and the January Effect," *The Journal of Portfolio Management* (Winter 1986): pp. 54–60.

[23] A 1992 study of the January anomaly indicates that the previous studies of abnormal returns for small firms may be biased by incomplete consideration of a price effect and transaction costs. This study argues, on the basis of the years 1967–1986, that the January effect is a low-price phenomenon rather than a small-firm effect. Further tests indicated that, after adjusting for differential transaction costs, portfolios of lower price stocks almost always underperformed the market portfolio. Therefore, the large before-transaction-costs excess January returns observed on low-price stocks may be explainable by higher transaction costs and a bid-ask bias. The implication of this study is that the reported January anomaly is not persistent and is not likely to be exploitable by most investors. See Ravinder K. Bhardaj and Leroy D. Brooks, "The January Anomaly: Effects of Low Share Price, Transaction Costs, and Bid-Ask Bias," *The Journal of Finance*, 47 (June 1992): pp. 553–575.

[24] Jeremy Gaunt, "January effect on financial markets bodes ill, so far, for 2008," *International Herald Tribune*, January 7, 2008, Internet edition.

[25] Jonathan Cheng, "Stocks Going By the Book," *The Wall Street Journal*, October 31, 2011, p. c1.

[26] This investment service is discussed in more detail in Chapter 15.

Figure 12-6

Record of Value Line Ranks for Timeliness, Allowing for Annual Changes in Rank, 1965–2011.

SOURCE: "Value Line Selection and Opinion," *The Value Line Investment Survey*, January 27, 2012, p. 1779. Reprinted by Permission.

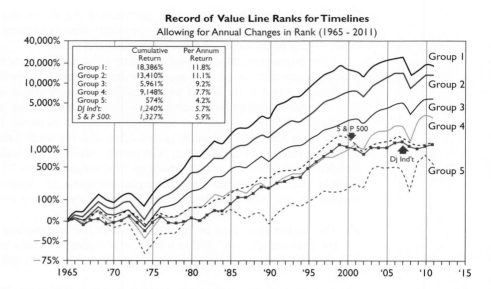

Record of Value Line Ranks for Timelines
Allowing for Annual Changes in Rank (1965 - 2011)

	Cumulative Return	Per Annum Return
Group 1:	18,386%	11.8%
Group 2:	13,410%	11.1%
Group 3:	5,961%	9.2%
Group 4:	9,148%	7.7%
Group 5:	574%	4.2%
DJ Ind't:	1,240%	5.7%
S & P 500:	1,327%	5.9%

price/book value, and low price/sales. These results provide some information on two of the strategies discussed earlier, low P/E and the size effect, as well as two valuation techniques that are discussed in Chapter 10, price/book value and price/sales. These results are shown in Figure 12-7 for the period 1966 through mid-2008.

Figure 12-7 suggests that Value Line's Group 1 stocks outperformed the other four strategies by a significant amount. Interestingly, by this comparison the small cap stocks did better than the other strategies (other than Value Line's Group 1), with the low P/E ratio strategy the next best. The low P/Sales and low Price/Book did poorly in this comparison. It is easy to see from Figure 12-7 why Value Line has stated, "The lesson is clear—stay with the Group 1s." Several studies of the success of *Value Line*'s rankings have been made. Not surprisingly, results vary somewhat depending on the exact study one examines. It appears that the rankings, and changes in the rankings, do contain useful information. For example, Mark Hulbert, who monitors the performance of investing newsletters, has noted that the *Value Line Investment Survey* has been at or near the top in his rankings for long-term risk adjusted performance for 28 years as of mid-2008 (when his publication completed 28 full years of tracking performance).

Figure 12-7

Value Line Group 1 Stocks vs. Other Strategies, 1966–2011.

SOURCE: "Value Line Selection and Opinion," *The Value Line Investment Survey*, February 10, 2012, p. 1758. Reprinted by Permission.

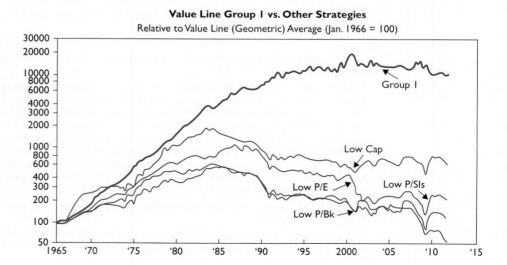

Value Line Group 1 vs. Other Strategies
Relative to Value Line (Geometric) Average (Jan. 1966 = 100)

However, there is evidence that the market adjusts quickly to this information (one or two trading days following the Friday release) and that true transaction costs can negate much of the price changes that occur as a result of adjustments to this information.[27]

    The Value Line Investment Survey is an important source of information for investors and is one of the most used investment services available. We will refer to it again in Chapter 15.

OTHER ANOMALIES

The above list of anomalies is not exhaustive. Others have been reported and discussed, including in particular several calendar anomalies such as the day of the week, turn-of-the-month, day preceding a holiday, and so forth. One anomaly of interest, because it is consistent with the commonsense notion that market efficiency is most likely applied to the larger, well-known stocks as opposed to all stocks, is the neglected firm effect. Neglect in this case means that few analysts follow the stock or that few institutions own the stock. The area of neglected stocks would appear to be a good opportunity for small investors interested in security analysis and stock selection.

DATA MINING

Data Mining The search for apparent patterns in stock returns by intensively analyzing data

In judging whether a market inefficiency has been uncovered that could be exploited, investors must guard against **data mining**. This term refers to the search for patterns in security returns by examining various techniques applied to a set of data. With enough effort, patterns will be uncovered and investing rules and techniques can be found that appear to work in the sense of providing abnormal returns. In most cases, they do not stand up to independent scrutiny or application to a different set of data or time period. The rules and selection techniques resulting from data mining often have no theoretical basis, or rationale, for existing—they simply result from mining the data.

Example 12-4

The *Motley Fool* is a popular and well-known source of investment information and ideas for individual investors. Operating a website and also producing some books and other publications, this source has advocated that small investors can often do well in the market by applying simple principles. One technique advocated by the *Motley Fool* was the "Foolish Four," a system that involved taking the 30 Dow-Jones Industrial Average stocks and calculating the ratio of the dividend yield to the square root of the share price. The stock with the highest ratio was ignored, and the next four highest became the Foolish Four. The founders of the *Motley Fool* claimed that the Foolish Four strategy, which would take only 15 minutes a year to implement, was so effective it would "crush your mutual funds." A *Money Magazine* columnist who criticized this technique was severely criticized by *Motley Fool* followers. Eventually, the founders had to admit that this technique did not work, saying it was a result of faulty analysis of historical data resulting from "finding random correlations and considering them valid and repeatable."[28]

---

[27] A study by Choi examined *Value Line's* timeliness rankings from 1965 to 1996 based on both a statistical analysis and a comparison to benchmark portfolios that corresponded to the evaluated stocks' characteristics. Choi found some evidence of performance of these stocks beyond that expected on the basis of models of expected return. However, he also found that after transaction costs, it is doubtful that investors could have earned profitable abnormal returns. See James J. Choi, "The Value Line Enigma: The Sum of Known Parts?" *Journal of Financial and Quantitative Analysis*, 35 (September 2000).

[28] This discussion is based on "Investing: Word on the Street," *Money Magazine*, February 2001, and on the Motley Fool website.

The earnings surprise evidence is particularly strong, and this technique is widely used. However, Eugene Fama, a long-time proponent of market efficiency, argues that the evidence on anomalies does not refute the EM proposition.[29] He believes that many of the studies showing anomalies contain statistical problems. He also believes that overreaction and underreaction are about equally likely to be found, which suggests that markets are efficient because this behavior can be attributable to chance. For example, the post-announcement earnings drift observed in the SUE studies and similar work suggest underreaction to information. The poor performance of IPOs over five years is evidence of overreaction.

Interestingly, even Fama, in making these arguments, recognizes the validity of the work that has been done documenting the post-announcement drift that occurs following quarterly earnings announcements. The SUE results, and similar analyses showing a delayed reaction to earnings announcements, have never been satisfactorily refuted and stand today as a documented anomaly. Thus, while Fama may be correct in general, some exceptions do seem to exist. And others, such as Dreman, continue to make a strong case for other anomalies such as low P/E ratio stocks.

Checking Your Understanding

5. Does the existence of market anomalies disprove the EMH?
6. Do you think it is easier, or more difficult, for someone to engage in data mining today?

Behavioral Finance

Much of economics and finance is grounded on the proposition that individuals act rationally and consider all available information in the decision-making process. However, markets consist of human beings who have limited information-processing capabilities, who can and do make mistakes, and who often rely on the opinions of brokers, financial advisors, and the financial press. In short, people are subject to irrationality in the form of emotional biases that alter their decisions.

In a well-known book titled Against the Gods, Bernstein notes that one finds "repeated patterns of irrationality, inconsistency, and incompetence in the ways human beings arrive at decisions and choices when faced with uncertainty."[30] His conclusion is consistent with the argument that a basis in psychology could help to explain stock market behavior.

**Behavioral Finance
(BF)** The study of
investment behavior,
based on the belief that
investors do not always act
rationally

Behavioral Finance (BF) integrates cognitive (how people think) psychology with finance. It holds that investors' emotions and biases affect stock prices and markets.

✓ Behavioral finance says investors often make systematic mistakes when processing information about the stock market. Markets overreact, both up and down. Investors are motivated by numerous "irrational" forces; other investors, recognizing these mistakes in judgment, may be able to profitably exploit them.

Behavioral finance analyzes behavioral biases and the effects these biases have on financial markets. The behavioral finance view of markets and market efficiency is based on the following propositions:[31]

---

[29] See Eugene Fama, "Market Efficiency, Long-Term Returns, and Behavioral Finance," *Journal of Financial Economics* (September 1998).

[30] Peter L. Bernstein, *Against the Gods: The Remarkable Story of Risk*, John Wiley & Sons, Inc., 1998, p. 12.

[31] These propositions and their discussion are based on Terrence Odean, "Effect of Behavioral Biases on Market Efficiency and Investors' Welfare, *Conference Proceedings Quarterly*, CFA Institute, Vol. 24, No. 1, March, 2007, pp. 6—16.

1. Informed traders face risk-aversion constraints in seeking to always keep prices efficient. With the efficient markets argument, well-informed, risk-tolerant investors keep prices at their "fair values." When prices get sufficiently out of line to warrant action by these investors, they act to move them back. However, there are limits to arbitrage, such as constraints when selling short.

2. The trading decisions of individual investors are biased because of biases associated with individual investors and human behavior. A number of biases that may affect investing decisions have been identified, including:

   (a) *Loss Aversion,* This relates to the so-called *disposition effect.* Studies of the actual trading records of investors shows that investors are nearly 50 percent more likely to sell winners than losers. Because investors are subject to loss aversion, they feel the pain of a loss more than the pleasure of a gain—therefore, they are reluctant to sell their losers despite the fact that losses are tax deductible. Furthermore, recent evidence suggests that this applies to fund managers as well as individual investors. These "sophisticated" investors are eager to sell winners and reluctant to sell losers. Poorly performing managers (based on recent 12-month performance) sell winners nearly twice as often as losers.

   ✓ Loss aversion refers to the tendency for investors to strongly prefer avoiding losses as opposed to achieving an equivalent amount of gains.

   (b) *Overconfidence*—a majority of money managers, and probably investors, tend to think their ability is above average. They think they have more skill than they actually possess. A well-known study has shown that this leads overconfident individual investors to trade more than other investors, with resulting investment performance that is below the performance of the average investor. Using a large dataset from a discount brokerage firm, Barber and Odean found that buy-and-hold investors outperformed the most active investors, on average, by about 6 percentage points a year.[32]

   (c) The *framing concept*—the way a problem is presented (framing) significantly affects the decision that is made.

   (d) The *herding effect*—this occurs when money managers in proximity to each other, such as being in the same city, tend to invest similarly, which creates a self-reinforcing herding effect. It also occurs as individual investors tend to act in a similar manner, leading to the third proposition.

3. The purchases and sales of individual investors are highly correlated. Thus, individual investors tend to buy and sell the same stocks at the same time. This herding effect by individual investors can push the prices of stocks in one direction in a significant manner.

4. Individual investors, who are considered to be the uninformed investors, generate buy/sell imbalances that drive prices away from fundamental value.

5. Over time, informed investors will drive prices back to fundamental value.

An important step in the development of behavioral finance is the work of DeBondt and Thaler. They tested an "overreaction hypothesis," which states that people overreact to unexpected and dramatic news events.[33] As applied to stock prices, the hypothesis states that,

[32] Brad Barber and Terrance Odean, "Trading is Hazardous to Your Wealth: The Common Stock Investment Performance of Individual Investors," *Journal of Finance*, Vol. 55, No. 2 (April 2000), pp. 773–806.

[33] Werner F. M. DeBondt and Richard Thaler, "Does the Stock Market Overreact?" *The Journal of Finance* (July 1985): pp. 793–805.

as a result of overreactions, "loser" portfolios outperform the market after their formation. DeBondt and Thaler interpreted this evidence as indicative of irrational behavior by investors, or "overreaction."

DeBondt and Thaler's long-term return reversals found with stock losers and winners are said to be a result of investor overreaction. For example, investors overreact to information about companies and drive stock prices to unsustainable highs or lows. When investors realize later that they overreacted to the news, prices return to their correct levels.

Similar research indicates that investors may underreact to new information, not driving stock prices high enough in response to good news. As they gradually realize the impact of the good news, stock prices will go up. Some money managers believe that this underreaction is one of the most predictable market occurrences and is a part of growth-style investing.

EFFICIENT MARKETS VS. BEHAVIORAL FINANCE

The EMH assumes that markets are rational even if all investors are not rational. Competition among investors seeking abnormal returns drives stock prices to their fundamental values. Behavioral finance, on the other hand, says investors may make systematic errors in the way they think.

✓   According to the EMH, markets are informationally efficient. According to behavioral finance, in some circumstances markets may be informationally inefficient.

A basic misunderstanding of behavioral finance is that it says people can beat the market. It does not. What it says is that market prices and fundamental values can diverge for long periods of time because of psychology. While opportunities may be present as a result of this divergence, they won't necessarily be eliminated. Why? The informed investors are not willing to take the risk involved to try to exploit these opportunities, or constraints exist that prevent them from doing so.

BEHAVIORAL FINANCE IMPLICATIONS FOR INVESTORS

David Dreman, a money manager and columnist for *Forbes*, has been a leading proponent of behavioral finance. He particularly espouses the "investor overreaction hypothesis," which states that investors overreact to events in a predictable manner, overvaluing the best alternatives and undervaluing the worst. Premiums and discounts are the result, and eventually these situations reverse as assets regress toward the mean, or average valuation.

Contrarian Investing The theory that it pays to trade contrary to most investors

This behavior has led Dreman to his **"contrarian investing"** philosophy, which involves taking positions that are currently out of favor. For example, in 1998 growth investing was much more profitable than value investing, but Dreman continued to recommend stocks that looked promising on a value basis on the assumption that value stocks would once again excel.[34] And Dreman is famous for recommending that investors buy the low P/E ratio stocks (which are often out of favor) rather than the often-currently-popular high P/E ratio stocks.

BEHAVIORAL FINANCE TODAY

Behavioral Finance can perhaps be traced back to 1979 when Tversky and Kahneman offered the first significant alternative to the expected utility theory underlying traditional rational

---

[34] Dreman has published a book called *Contrarian Investment Strategies: The Next Generation*, by Simon and Schuster. He also started a new journal, *The Journal of Psychology and Financial Markets*.

financial decision making. Clear recognition of the impact of behavioral finance came in 2002 with the awarding of the Nobel prize in economics to Daniel Kahneman, a Princeton psychologist, and to Vernon Smith of George Mason University, whose economic experiments are at odds with the efficient market hypothesis. Even Burton Malkiel, a leading proponent of market efficiency and the use of index funds, includes a chapter in the 9th edition of his well-known book, *A Random Walk Down Wall Street*, on the good lessons to be learned from Behavioral Finance.[35]

Needless to say, behavioral finance has not gone unchallenged. Eugene Fama, a leading proponent of efficient markets, has presented an argument against the behaviorists and their claims that anomalies have been found in historical asset prices.[36] He argues that data mining techniques allow researchers to discover apparent patterns, but that their significance is questionable at best.

Checking Your Understanding

7. How does the concept of investor under reaction or over reaction to news and information fit in with the concept of behavioral finance?

Some Conclusions About Market Efficiency

Given all of the evidence about market efficiency discussed previously—the studies supporting it as well as the anomalies evidence—what conclusions can be drawn? Perhaps John Maynard Keynes, one of the most famous economists of the twentieth century, was right when he noted that the stock market is a "casino" guided by "animal spirit."

The evidence in support of market efficiency has convinced many market observers because of the large amount of research done over the years by numerous investigators. And almost certainly the widespread availability of information and data on the Internet, along with the investment tools offered there, has made the market even more efficient. Consider the paragraph by Samuel Eisenstadt quoted early in the chapter. Eisenstadt was the primary force in the development of Value Line's famed ranking system for stocks, one of the best-known and most successful systems ever developed for general investor use. Eisenstadt noted that "beating the market is difficult and becoming even more so."[37]

Nevertheless, many investors are convinced that they can outperform the market, or at least provide more benefits than cost. Paradoxically, this belief helps to make the market efficient. Consider another quote, this one from Charles Ellis, a well-known investment consultant and author who has studied the results of professional managers over many years:

"The problem is not that professional managers lack skill or diligence. Quite the opposite. The problem with trying to beat the market is that professional investors are so talented, so numerous, and so dedicated to their work that as a group they make it very difficult for any one of their number to do significantly better than the others, particularly in the long run."[38]

[35] Burton G. Malkiel, *A Random Walk Down Wall Street: The Time Tested Strategy for Successful Investing,* 9th edition, W. W. Norton & Company, New York, 2007.

[36] Eugene Fama, "Market Efficiency, Long-Term Returns, and Behavioral Finance," *Journal of Financial Economics,* Vol. 49, No. 3, September 1998, pp. 283–306.

[37] Steven T. Goldberg, "Civil Warriors," *Kiplinger's Personal Finance,* August 2002, p. 39.

[38] See Charles Ellis, *Winning the Loser's Game,* McGraw Hill, 2009.

Investments Intuition

A paradox of efficient markets and active investors is that investors, in an attempt to uncover and use important information about security prices, help to make the market efficient. In other words, in the course of searching out undervalued and overvalued stocks, investors discover information and act on it as quickly as possible. If the information is favorable, the discoverers will buy immediately, and if unfavorable, they will sell immediately. As investors scramble for information and attempt to be the first to act, they make the market more efficient. If enough of this activity occurs, all information will be reflected in prices. Thus, the fact that a number of investors do not believe in the EMH results in actions that help to make the market efficient.

Perhaps the most telling evidence in favor of market efficiency is the performance of professional investors such as mutual funds, for whom we have detailed performance data. Consider some statistics on their performance:[39]

1. Approximately 70 percent of mutual fund managers underperform over a 10-year period and 80 percent underperform over a 20-year period.[40]
2. Over a very recent five-year period, only 6 percent of all U.S. stock funds achieved a ranking in the top half for five consecutive 12-month periods.
3. Over a 30+-year period, of the mutual funds in existence for the entire period, 139, there were only 20 winners by 2 percentage points or more.
4. Consider the consistency of performance of mutual funds over a recent 10-year period. Take the top 25 percent of large capitalization funds during the period 2001–2006. Over the subsequent five years, 2007–2011, only 12 percent of the earlier top performers were in the top 25 percent, an uninspiring performance.
5. As for institutional portfolios as a group, new research shows that after adjusting for risk well under 1 percent achieve superior results after all adjustments for costs.[41]

Investments Intuition

What Can Hedge Fund Portfolios Tell Us About Market Efficiency?

We know from Chapter 3 that hedge funds are supposed to represent sophisticated investment funds run by top portfolio managers who have great flexibility with the portfolio, charge substantial fees, and are expected to produce outstanding results. There are even firms that advise investors on which hedge funds to own.

Consider the performance of funds that hold hedge funds expected to perform well. According to a recent study with data through 2009 for 1,300 funds that hold hedge funds, after deducting fees only about 5 percent of the funds actually added value above the underlying hedge-fund indices.[42] Almost half of the funds did not perform as well as the hedge-fund indices. This is strong evidence for market efficiency, because the presumed best talent in the money management business, with advantages that most investors are not presumed to have, could not perform very well.

---

[39] See Burton Malkiel, "Reflections on the Efficient Market Hypothesis: 30 Years Later," *The Financial Review*, 40, 2005, pp. 1–9.

[40] Charles D. Ellis, " Murder on the Orient Express: The Mystery of Underperformance," *Financial Analysts Journal*, Vol. 68, No. 4, July/August 2012, p. 13.

[41] Laurent Barras, Olivier Scaillet, and Russ Wermers, "False Discoveries in Mutual Fund Performance: Measuring Luck in Estimated Alphas," *Journal of Finance*, Vol. 65, No. 1, February 2010, pp. 179–216.

[42] Benoît Dewaele, Hugues Pirotte, N. Tuchschmid, E. Wallerstein, "Assessing the Performance of Funds of Hedge Funds," Universite Libre de Bruxelles in its series Working Papers CEB with number 11–041, 2011.

For some additional strong evidence about the efficiency of the market, consider the 28-year results of the *Hulbert Financial Digest*. The *Digest*, which tracks the performance of investment newsletters, completed 28 years in business as of mid-2008. Over that 28-year period, 41 percent of the newsletters did not survive. Only four of the 17 (24 percent) newsletters that existed for the entire time period beat the market on a risk-adjusted basis. As of June 30, 2000, with two decades of data available, only 8 percent of the newsletters in existence the entire time beat the market on a risk-adjusted basis. Mark Hulbert, editor of the *Digest*, concluded from these results that:

"Though not impossible, it is incredibly difficult to beat the stock market over the long term."[43]

Some anomalies appear to exist, and may offer opportunities to astute investors. However, the anomalies that have been reported are *not* conclusive proof of market inefficiencies. It may be that better testing procedures and/or better data may explain some of these anomalies away.

One difficult problem for those who believe in efficient markets is the crash of October 1987. The S&P 500 Index lost over 20 percent in one day. Is it really reasonable to argue that investors, efficiently discounting information, decided in one day that the market should be valued some 20 percent less? Not many people, including efficient market proponents, are comfortable making this argument.

Another recent example is the Internet market bubble that burst in 2000, with the stock market declining sharply over the next two years. Most observers today accept the proposition that a bubble did occur, that it was not based on rational behavior, and that this is not in agreement with the efficient markets view. This fits in with the behavioral finance view, and its current ascendancy in finance thinking. Even Burton Malkiel, a well-known economics professor who is a leading proponent of efficient markets, recently stated: "No one understands better than I do that sometimes markets go crazy. . . . sometimes, markets just get it wrong."[44]

The controversy about market efficiency and behavioral finance remains. Every investor is still faced with the choice between pursuing an active investment strategy or a passive investment strategy, or some combination thereof. Making this choice depends heavily upon what the investor believes about efficient markets. Investors who plan, or wish, to pursue some type of active strategy should consider a quote attributed to Warren Buffett, arguably the most famous U.S. investor of our time:

"Most investors, both institutional and individual, will find that the best way to own common stocks (shares) is through an index fund that charges minimal fees. Those following this path are sure to beat the net results (after fees and expenses) of the great majority of investment professionals."

Ethics in Investing

What Obligations Do Financial Advisors Have to Clients?

Given the evidence cited earlier on the mediocre performance of most professional money managers, should financial advisors explain this information to their clients? These advisors often earn their living by the commissions they receive when investors trade, or the fees they earn when clients buy load

---

[43] This quote, and the related statistics cited here, come from Mark Hulbert, "Long-Term Newsletter Performance: It's Not Easy to Beat the Market," *AAII Journal,* American Association of Individual Investors, Vol. 30, No. 6, July 2008, pp. 27–29.

[44] Burton G. Malkiel, "In Defense of Indexing," *Conference Proceedings Quarterly,* CFA Institute, December 2007, p. 9.

funds. What would happen if more and more clients opted for no-load funds, index funds, ETFs, and so forth?

Would most investors not be better off with an index fund such as Vanguard's S&P 500 fund, which has very low costs and has outperformed most actively managed funds over long periods of time?

How can someone justify to a client interested in buying an index equity fund the purchase of Morgan Stanley's S&P 500 fund, with a 5.25 percent sales charge and an annual operating fee that is several times higher than the fee of Vanguard's fund? Most financial advisors face ethical issues such as these many times.

Summary

▶ An efficient market is defined as one in which the prices of securities fully reflect all known information quickly and accurately.

▶ The conditions that guarantee an efficient market can be shown to hold to a large extent: many investors are competing, information is widely available and generated more or less randomly, and investors react quickly to this information.

▶ To assess market efficiency, three cumulative forms (or degrees) of efficiency are discussed: the weak form, the semistrong form, and the strong form. The weak form involves market data, whereas the semistrong and strong form involve the assimilation of all public and private information, respectively.

▶ The weak-form evidence, whether statistical tests or trading rules, strongly supports the hypothesis.

▶ Many tests of semistrong efficiency have been conducted, including, among others, stock splits, money supply changes, accounting changes, dividend announcements, and reactions to other announcements. Although all the studies do not agree, the majority support semistrong efficiency.

▶ Event studies are used to make semistrong-form tests. Abnormal returns are calculated for each company for which a specific event is being examined. Cumulative abnormal returns show what happens before and after the event.

▶ Strong-form evidence takes the form of tests of the performance of groups presumed to have "private" information and of the ability of professional managers to outperform the market. Insiders apparently are able to do well, although the decisions of the managers of mutual funds have not been found to add value.

▶ Most knowledgeable observers accept weak-form efficiency, reject strong-form efficiency, and feel that the market is, to a large degree, semistrong efficient.

This casts doubt on the value of both technical analysis and conventional fundamental analysis.

▶ Although the EMH does not preclude investors from outperforming the market, it does suggest that this is quite difficult to accomplish and that the investor must do more than the norm.

▶ Several major "anomalies" that have appeared over the last several years have yet to be satisfactorily explained. These anomalies, which would not be expected in a totally efficient market, include the following:

1. Unexpected earnings, as represented by SUE: The market appears to adjust with a lag to the earnings surprises contained in quarterly earnings. SUE has been shown to be a monotonic discriminator of subsequent short-term (e.g., three-month) stock returns.

2. P/E ratios: Low P/E stocks appear to outperform high P/E stocks over annual periods, even after adjustment for risk and size.

3. The size effect: Evidence suggests that small firms outperformed large firms, on a risk-adjusted basis, for a number of years. However, substantial evidence today suggests the "small cap" premium has disappeared.

4. The January effect: Much of the abnormal return for small firms occurs in the month of January, possibly because tax-induced sales in December temporarily depress prices, which then recover in January. The January effect is controversial today, with some claiming that its impact has diminished over time, while others argue the effect is still present.

5. *Value Line*'s performance: The *Value Line* rankings for timeliness appear to have performed well over time, on average, and therefore may offer the average investor a chance to outperform the averages.

▶ Data mining refers to the search for patterns in security returns by examining various techniques applied to a set of data. With enough effort, patterns will be uncovered and investing rules and techniques can be found that *appear* to work in the sense of providing abnormal returns.

▶ Behavioral finance integrates psychology with finance. It argues that investors often make systematic mistakes when processing information about the stock market.

▶ According to behavioral finance, in some circumstances markets may be informationally inefficient. The EMH, in contrast, holds that markets are informationally efficient.

▶ In the final analysis the market is very efficient (although not perfectly efficient). Most investors should accept the efficiency of the market unless they can add value to the process.

Questions

12-1 What is meant by an efficient market?

12-2 What are the conditions for an efficient market? How closely are they met in reality?

12-3 Describe the three forms of market efficiency.

12-4 Why is a market that is weak-form efficient in direct opposition to technical analysis?

12-5 What do semistrong market efficiency tests attempt to test for?

12-6 Describe two different ways to test for weak-form efficiency.

12-7 Distinguish between economic significance and statistical significance.

12-8 If the EMH is true, what are the implications for investors?

12-9 Could the performance of mutual fund managers also be a test of semistrong efficiency?

12-10 Describe the money management activities of a portfolio manager who believes that the market is efficient.

12-11 What are market anomalies? Describe four.

12-12 If all investors believe that the market is efficient, could that eventually lead to less efficiency in the market?

12-13 What is the relationship between SUE and fundamental analysis?

12-14 What other types of events or information could be used in semistrong-form tests?

12-15 What are the benefits to society of an efficient market?

12-16 If the market moves in an upward trend over a period of years, would this be inconsistent with weak-form efficiency?

12-17 Do security analysts have a role in an efficient market?

12-18 Evaluate the following statement: "My mutual fund has outperformed the market for the last four years. How can the market be efficient?"

12-19 What are the necessary conditions for a scientific test of a trading rule?

12-20 Are filter rules related to timing strategies or stock selection strategies? What alternative should a filter rule be compared with?

12-21 Assume that you analyze the activities of insiders and find that they are able to realize consistently above-average rates of return. What form of the EMH are you testing?

12-22 What are some possible explanations for the size anomaly?

12-23 How can data on corporate insiders be used to test both the semistrong and the strong forms of the EMH?

12-24 How can data on the performance of mutual funds be used to test both the semistrong and the strong forms of the EMH?

12-25 Assume that the price of a stock remains constant from time period 0 to time period 1, at which time a significant piece of information about the stock becomes available. Draw a diagram that depicts the situation if (a) the market is semistrong efficient and (b) there is a lag in the adjustment of the price to this information.

12-26 How is the SUE concept related to technical analysis?

12-27 What is meant by an operationally efficient market?

Problems

12-1   Calculate the SUE for a stock with actual quarterly earnings of $0.30 per share and expected quarterly earnings of $0.18 per share. The standard error of estimate is 0.04. Is this a good buy?

12-2   Consider a portfolio manager whose portfolio has $2 billion in assets. If this manager could increase the return on the portfolio an additional two-tenths of 1 percent, how much would that add to the value of the portfolio?

Checking Your Understanding

12-1   In an efficient market, stock prices should reflect available information. This includes past information, current information, and information that can reasonably be inferred today. Since markets have been shown to be highly efficient, although not perfectly, investors should expect, on average, for prices to reflect available information.

12-2   If stock price movements are predictable, they certainly cannot be following a random walk process. The Random Walk theory is related to, although not identical with, weak-form efficiency.

12-3   No. Information comes into the market randomly, which, with the other specified conditions, leads to market efficiency. Market efficiency and rationality are related. An irrational market would be one where investors do not react to information quickly and, on balance, accurately.

12-4   An institutional investor, like any investor, can justify spending money on stock selection techniques if it can be shown that the benefits outweigh the costs. In most cases this cannot be shown, but in some cases it can. Perhaps the institutional investor has a disciplined technique that has been worked out over time, or perhaps this investor has analysts with true skill and ability.

12-5   The existence of market anomalies does not disprove the EMH. First, there are only a relatively few anomalies that have received wide support over time. Second, some of these anomalies, such as the size effect, have less support today than they had previously. In other words, there is more doubt about the validity of some, such as the size effect. And finally, it may be the case that the anomalies come about as a result of inadequate means of testing them correctly. It may be the case that researchers have not been clever enough to unravel the true story behind these apparent inefficiencies, with the result that they may not be inefficiencies at all.

12-6   In general, it should be easier to engage in data mining today because of the widespread availability of both personal computers and financial data. Investors can now search through thousands of companies for long periods, using multiple selection criteria.

12-7   Behavioral finance says investors often make systematic mistakes when processing information about the stock market. Markets overreact, both up and down. Investors are motivated by numerous "irrational" forces, such as overconfidence, regrets about decisions, aversion to losses, and so forth. Other investors, recognizing these mistakes in judgment, may be able to profitably exploit them.

The long-term return reversals that have been found with stock losers and winners is said to be a result of investor overreaction. For example, investors overreact to information about companies and drive stock prices to unsustainable highs or lows. When investors realize later that they overreacted to the news, prices return to their correct levels. Similar research indicates that investors may underreact to financial news, not driving stock prices high enough in response to good news. As they gradually realize the impact of the good news, stock prices will go up.

chapter *13*

Economy/ Market Analysis Must Be Considered By All Investors

Based on your knowledge of how stocks are valued (Chapter 10), and the impact of the market on stocks in general (Chapter 11), you realize that part of your investments education should be to consider the economy/market in more detail. After all, a poorly performing economy does not bode well for stocks. You have read enough about the recession that started in 2001, and the severe stock market decline that occurred during 2000–2002, as well as the December 2007–June 2009 recession and the dramatic market decline in 2008, to understand that if possible, such events are to be avoided, or at least the impact minimized. Clearly, it is worthwhile to know something about the overall tone of the economy and market, and at least be able to intelligently consider likely outcomes in the future.

Chapter 13 begins our discussion of fundamental security analysis by considering the economy and the market. This is the first step in the top-down approach because of the overall importance of the economy/market in impacting stock returns. A key issue here is the relationship between the economy and the stock market since they do not move in lockstep. Exhibit 13–1 illustrates the top-down approach to fundamental security analysis, which is covered in Chapters 13–15.

AFTER READING THIS CHAPTER YOU WILL BE ABLE TO:

▶ Understand the relationship between the stock market and the economy.
▶ Analyze conceptually the determinants of the stock market.

▶ Make some basic forecasts of possible changes in the level of the market.

Introduction

Many investors want to make intelligent judgments about the current state of the financial markets as well as changes that have a high probability of occurring in the future. Are specific markets at unusually high or low levels, and what are they likely to do in the next year or next

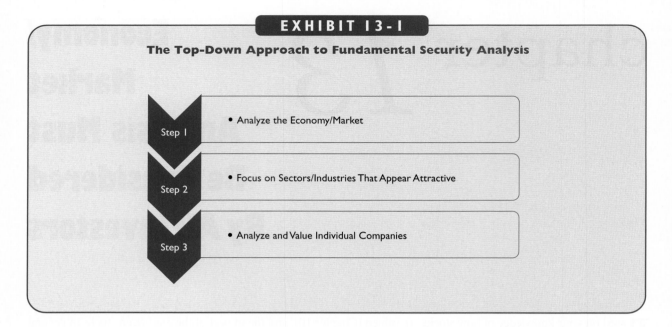

EXHIBIT 13-1

The Top-Down Approach to Fundamental Security Analysis

Step 1
- Analyze the Economy/Market

Step 2
- Focus on Sectors/Industries That Appear Attractive

Step 3
- Analyze and Value Individual Companies

few years? Understanding the current and future condition of the economy is the first step in understanding what is happening and what is likely to happen to the financial markets.

Based on a knowledge of the U.S. economy–stock market relationship, we apply our knowledge of valuation concepts discussed in Chapter 10 to understanding the stock market. We also consider forecasts of changes in the stock market. Although *investors cannot possibly hope to be consistently correct in their forecasts of the stock market*, they can reasonably expect to make some intelligent inferences about *major* trends in the market. Because of the market's impact on investor success, all but the really long-term investor should consider, at least to some extent, the market's likely direction over some future period. On the other hand, the true long-term investor following a buy-and-hold strategy (discussed in Chapter 11) need not be directly concerned with the market's direction most of the time, because this investor will be making few changes in his or her portfolio.

Taking a Global Perspective

As noted throughout this text, investors must now think globally. U.S. investors can choose equities from numerous countries, and these equities comprise considerably more than half of the world's market capitalization and two-thirds of the world's GDP. Therefore, they should think about economies in other countries and parts of the world. For example, how is the Euro currency performing, and how will expected movements in the Euro affect returns to U.S. investors?

Multinational corporations have often followed the U.S. lead in restructuring traditional processes and embracing new technologies. Therefore, as a general rule, the analysis we consider in this chapter of the U.S. market and economy applies to other countries as well. Foreign equity markets are going to be driven by earnings growth and interest rate changes, just as U.S. markets are. By understanding the U.S. equity markets, investors are in a better position to understand foreign equity markets despite the cultural, economic, and political differences.

Another reason why investors must consider the global perspective is currency changes. In 2000 the Euro was worth about $.82. In 2008 the Euro hit a record $1.69, although it subsequently declined quite sharply by the Fall of 2008. As late as November 2011, despite the European crisis, the Euro was at $1.36. This means that the dollar remained weak against the Euro for several years. A falling dollar boosts the returns from foreign securities for U.S. investors, and helps the earnings of U.S. corporations that have significant international operations, such as Coca-Cola. Thus, U.S. investors benefited from the dollar's decline and the Euro's appreciation.

Assessing the Economy

Gross Domestic Product (GDP) The basic measure of a country's output used in National Income accounts

A basic measure of the economy is **Gross Domestic Product (GDP)**, defined as the market value of final goods and services produced by an economy for some time period (typically a year). It consists of the sum of consumption spending, investment spending, government spending, and net exports. Consumption now comprises 70 percent or more of GDP.

GDP numbers are prepared quarterly and released a few weeks following the end of the quarter. These numbers constitute a basic measure of the economic health and strength of the economy. GDP can be measured on both a nominal and real (inflation-adjusted) basis. Figure 13-1 shows the percent change from a year ago for real GDP since 1994. Note the ups and downs since 1994, and the upward movement from 1994 into 2000, and the much smaller changes since 2000. The impact of the recessions of 2001 and 2008–2009 are clearly visible in the figure.

✓   Real GDP is the single best measure of overall economic activity.

GDP is revised twice in the first three months after its initial release.[1] The Bureau of Economic Analysis releases an advance estimate of quarterly GDP in the first month following quarter end. In the second month it provides a preliminary estimate, and in the third month it provides a final estimate (however, even this estimate is subject to annual revisions). The cycle then starts over again. Over the last 30 odd years, the average revision of GDP growth from the advance to the final estimate has been about 2/3 of a percentage point. It should be noted that almost 90 percent of the time the advance estimate correctly predicts the direction of quarterly change in real GDP growth.

Of more immediate interest to investors, GDP ups and downs directly affect companies. The mechanism is relatively straightforward—if growth in GDP slows, as it did by the end of 2000, corporate revenues will slow, and profits will slow. The stock market reacts negatively to the prospect of diminished economic activity.

For discussion purposes, think of the economy in terms of the activity that occurs over time. Investors are very concerned about whether the economy is experiencing an expansion or a contraction because stock prices, interest rates, and inflation will clearly be affected.

Business Cycle The recurring patterns of expansion, boom, contraction, and recession in the economy

✓   The recurring pattern of expansion and contraction in economic activity is referred to as the **business cycle.**

THE BUSINESS CYCLE

The business cycle reflects movements in economic activity as a whole, which is comprised of many diverse parts. The diversity of the parts ensures that business cycles are virtually unique,

---

[1] This discussion is based on Abbigail J. Chiodo and Michael T. Owyang, "Subject to Revision," *National Economic Trends*, The Federal Reserve Bank of St. Louis, June 2002, p. 1.

Figure 13-1

Percent Change in Real Gross Domestic Product (GDP), 1994–2011.

SOURCE: *Monetary Trends*, The Federal Reserve Bank of St. Louis, February 2012, p. 13.

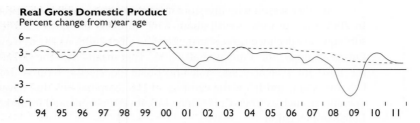

Real Gross Domestic Product
Percent change from year age

with no two parts identical. However, cycles do have a common framework, with a beginning (they start from a trough), a peak, and an ending (a new trough). Thus, economic activity starts in depressed conditions, builds up in the expansionary phase, and ends in a downturn, only to start again (perhaps because of government stimulus). The word "*trough*" is used to indicate when the economy has hit bottom.

- The period from a peak to a trough is a recession.
- The period from a trough to a peak is an expansion.

The typical business cycle in the United States since the end of World War II seems to consist of an expansion averaging about 57 months. Contractions since the war average about 10 months in duration. Obviously, however, these are only averages, and we cannot rely on them exclusively to interpret current or future situations. For example, the March 1991 expansion became the longest peacetime expansion, ending in March 2001. Business cycles cannot be neatly categorized as to length and turning points at the time they are occurring; only in hindsight can such precise distinctions be made. The National Bureau of Economic Research (NBER), a private nonprofit organization, measures business cycles and officially decides on the economic "turning points," the dates at which the economy goes from an expansion mode to a contraction mode, and vice versa.[2]

✓ The turning points of the business cycle typically are determined well after the fact, so that observers do not know on a current basis, at least officially, when a peak or trough has been reached.

Some Practical Advice

What exactly is the definition of a recession, and how do we know when we are in one? This was a hotly debated topic in early 2008 as the economy appeared to be weakening rapidly. A commonly accepted definition of a recession among the general public is two consecutive quarters in which real GDP declines. However, the NBER defines a recession as "a significant decline in economic activity spread across the economy, lasting more than a few months." The

official declaration that a recession has occurred comes from the NBER's dating committee. Unfortunately, in either case you won't know about it until after it has started. With the GDP definition, you must wait until the data for the two consecutive quarters have been released. In the NBER case, the committee usually declares that a recession has started some six to 18 months after economic activity has peaked (it took 12 months in the case of the 2008 recession).

---

[2] The NBER's Business Cycle Dating Committee determines the turning points of the business cycle.

It is possible to identify those components of economic activity that move at different times from each other. Such variables can serve as indicators of the economy in general. The Conference Board now provides these data.[3]

Composite Economic Indexes Leading, coincident, and lagging indicators of economic activity

Standard practice is to identify leading, coincident, and lagging **composite economic indexes**. The leading indicators consist of variables such as stock prices, an index of consumer expectations, money supply, and interest rate spread. The coincident indicators consist of four variables, such as industrial production and manufacturing and trade sales, and the lagging indicators consist of seven variables such as duration of unemployment and commercial and industrial loans outstanding.

The composite indexes are used to indicate peaks and troughs in the business cycle. The intent of using all three is to better summarize and reveal turning point patterns in economic data. Note that a change in direction in a composite index does not automatically indicate a cyclical turning point. The movement must be of sufficient size, duration, and scope.[4]

Example 13-1 In March 2001, following the stock market plunge and weakening of the economy, it was reported that the index of leading economic indicators declined in February for the fourth time in five months. In November 2001, the NBER declared that a recession began in March 2001. In 2007 there were widespread weaknesses among the leading indicators. We now know that the latest recession officially started in December 2007.

Some Practical Advice

In the last half of 2011 many people were worried that the United States would suffer another recession—a double dip, given the previous one. However, the leading economic indicator index was at a high level and had been rising for five months. The United States has not suffered a recession under these conditions. While this is not in any way a guarantee, it is about as good an assurance as we can get about the economy from any single piece of information.

The Global Perspective The most recent downturn in economic activity in the United States occurred as other countries were experiencing the same thing. Thus, there was a synchronized global downturn, which has been the case for most recent recessions. As we noted in Chapter 1, economies around the world are now more integrated and linked to each other because of increased trade and capital flows among countries. However, the most important reason for synchronized recessions among many countries is a common shock that is felt around the world. For example, in the 1970s there was an oil price shock, and it affected numerous countries. The collapse of the technology sector, and with it the technology stocks, was the common shock that occurred in several countries in 2000–2001. In 2008, the

---

[3] The Conference Board, a business membership and research network founded in 1916, assumed the responsibility for computing the composite indexes from the Department of Commerce.

[4] All of this information is available at the Conference Board website, http://www.conference-board.org/data/bciarchive.cfm?cid=1.

subprime mortgage fiasco and the related liquidity problems with financial institutions constituted a common shock to a number of countries.

Keep in mind the potential importance of foreign trade to GDP. While the growth rate of real GDP may be positive, the growth rate of gross domestic spending (which excludes net foreign trade) can be negative. In the same manner, an increase in overseas corporate profits for U.S. companies can offset (partially or totally) a decrease in domestic corporate profits.

Has the Business Cycle Been Tamed?   From the end of World War II (WWII) through the end of the twentieth century, there were nine recessions. A record-long expansion began in 1991 and peaked in March 2001, when the tenth recession since WWII started. Some observers were asking, prior to the peak in 2001, if the business cycle is dead. As one CEO noted, "We are in a global economy . . ." which "has changed the paradigm. . . . We don't see the cyclical events that characterized the past."[5] As it turns out, this was an unfortunate observation, given the financial crisis that would stagger the United States.

The other side of the coin is that as the expansion continued, people tend to forget the lessons learned from prior recessions. As one researcher on business cycles noted, "Who can eliminate herding?"—referring to the tendency of people getting collectively carried away. Expansions typically end for one of the following reasons: an overheating economy with rising inflation, forcing the Fed to raise interest rates; an external shock, such as a sharp rise in oil prices; or a financial crash following a break in a speculative **bubble** (when speculation pushes asset prices to unsustainable highs). For example, the Japanese economic expansion of the 1980s was a speculative bubble that drove stock prices and land values to record levels, and the bubble burst at the end of the 1980s—the Japanese economy and market have yet to fully recover.

Bubble When speculation pushes asset prices to unsustainable highs

One can argue that a bubble occurred in U.S. stock markets in the late 1990s, peaking in March 2001.[6] Regardless of whether a "true" bubble occurred or not, and whether such a bubble caused a recession, the tenth recession since WWII officially began in March 2001, demonstrating once again that the business cycle is not dead. This recession was short and ended eight months later, in November 2001.

While business cycles may be different from what they used to be, they will continue to exist. This was made clear by the start of the eleventh recession since WWII in December 2007. And 2008 brought new shocks to the U.S. economy not seen since the Great Depression. Unprecedented events happened in the form of government bailouts, government involvement in banks and other companies, severe changes on Wall Street, and turbulence in the stock market that truly frightened many people. Anyone who previously believed that the business cycle had been tamed, given the short recession in 2001, was surely cured of that belief in 2008 as unemployment reached levels not seen in 30 years, at least two automakers were on the brink of bankruptcy, the financial sector suffered incredible turmoil, and so on.

FORECASTS OF THE ECONOMY

Good economic forecasts are of obvious significant value to investors. How good are such forecasts, which are widely available? Some research suggests that forecasts made by the prominent forecasters are very similar and that differences in accuracy are very small, suggesting that investors can use any of a number of such forecasts. Obviously, not all forecasters are equally accurate, and all forecasters make errors. The only good news is that forecast accuracy apparently has increased over time.

---

[5] This quote and discussion are based on Jacob M. Schlesinger, "The Business Cycle Is Tamed, Many Say, Alarming Some Others," *The Wall Street Journal*, November 15, 1996, pp. A1, A16.

[6] For a discussion of whether the U.S. markets underwent a speculative bubble, see Robert J. Shiller, "Bubbles, Human Judgment, and Expert Opinion," *Financial Analysts Journal*, May/June 2002, pp. 18–26.

Investors can find forecasts of the economy from various sources. Some of these are what are referred to as "consensus" forecasts, in the same way that we talk about consensus earnings forecasts for stocks (Chapter 15). For example, *Blue Chip Economic Indicators* is a publication that compiles consensus forecasts from well-known economic forecasters of such important economic variables as real GDP, consumer prices, and interest rates. Thus, investors can find reputable, consistently done (but not necessarily accurate) forecasts of the economy for at least the year ahead.

Because of its vital role in the economy, monetary policy traditionally has been assumed to have an important effect on the economy, stock prices, and interest rates. Almost all theories of the macroeconomy postulate a relationship between money and future economic activity, with the relationship depending on whether changes in money stock can be attributed to shifts in money supply or money demand. For example, increases in money supply tend to increase economic activity, whereas increases in money demand tend to reduce economic activity.

The Impact of the Fed Many investors keep an eye on the actions of the Federal Reserve because of its role in monetary policy and its impact on interest rates. When the chairman of the Federal Reserve testifies before Congress or otherwise makes a public statement, the financial markets scrutinize every word for clues as to the future of the economy and financial markets. During normal economic times (as opposed to the financial crisis starting in 2008), the Fed carries out monetary policy through the federal funds rate. However, because of the crisis, this rate was close to zero starting in late 2008. Furthermore, departing from tradition, the Fed announced it would keep the rate at about that level past 2014. The Fed is undertaking a new approach to make its deliberations and plans more transparent.

Not surprisingly, relationships between macro variables are imprecise. Controversies still exist about the impact of changes in some policy variables on the economy. For example, most economists agree that monetary policy tightening can slow an overheating economy, but there is substantial disagreement about the power of monetary policy to stimulate a weak economy. While certainly not conclusive, some estimates suggest that in the short run the response to increases in the federal funds rate (associated with monetary policy tightening) is more than twice the response to decreases in the federal funds rate (associated with monetary policy stimulus).[7]

Insights from the Yield Curve The yield curve depicts the relationship between bond yields and time, holding the issuer (typically, the U.S. government) constant, and in effect shows how interest rates vary across time on any given day.[8] It should contain valuable information, because it reflects bond traders' views about the future of the economy. Several studies suggest that the yield curve is very useful in making economic forecasts. Professional traders and money managers use the yield curve as an indicator of how the Fed is managing the economy.

It has long been recognized that the shape of the yield curve is related to the stage of the business cycle. In the early stages of an expansion yield curves tend to be low and upward-sloping, and as the peak of the cycle approaches yield curves tend to be high and downwardsloping. More specifically,

- ❑ A steepening yield curve suggests that the economy is accelerating in terms of activity as monetary policy stimulates the economy

---

[7] Jeremy Piger, "Pushing On a String," *Monetary Trends*, The Federal Reserve Bank of St. Louis, March 2003, p. 1.

[8] In Chapter 17 we will consider the yield curve and its role in understanding interest rates.

■ When the yield curve becomes more flat, it suggests that economic activity is slowing down

■ An inverted yield curve carries an ominous message, however—expectations of an economic slowdown (every recession since World War II has been preceded by a downward-sloping yield curve)

The top panel of Figure 13-2 shows some Treasury yield curves for 2011 and 2012 as the economy struggled to grow. They were upward-sloping, which is the normal shape of the yield curve. The middle panel of Figure 13-2 shows an upward-sloping yield curve in January 2005 which had become basically flat by January 2006. The bottom panel shows yield curves in

Figure 13-2

Treasury Yield Curves.

SOURCE: *Monetary Trends*, Federal Reserve Bank of St. Louis, September 2012, p. 3; *National Economic Trends*, Federal Reserve Bank of St. Louis, February 2006 p. 7; Federal Reserve Bank of Cleveland.

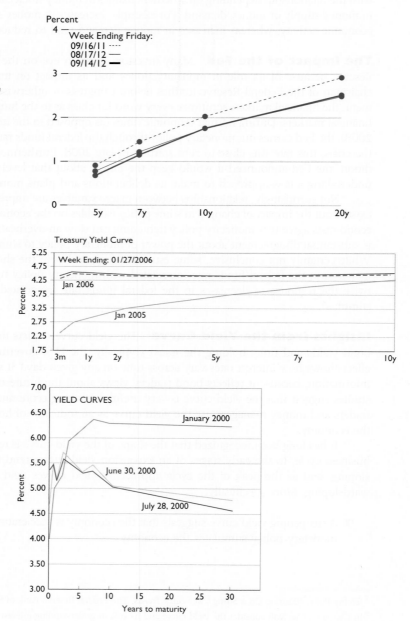

2000, which went from flat in January to clearly downward-sloping in June and July. As we now know, a recession officially began in March 2001.

Some researchers have developed a model to predict if the economy is going into a recession that uses as a prominent variable the yield spread between the 10-year Treasury security and the 3-month Treasury bill. According to the authors, this model was quite successful in predicting a recession four quarters in advance.[9]

Checking Your Understanding

1. Assume that you observe a downward-sloping yield curve. As an investor, what significance would this have to you? How much confidence would you have in the conclusions you draw from this?

The Stock Market and the Economy

The stock market is, of course, a significant and vital part of the overall economy. Clearly, a strong relationship exists between the two. If the economy is doing badly, most companies will also be performing poorly, as will the stock market. Conversely, if the economy is prospering, most companies will also be doing well, and the stock market will reflect this economic strength.

The relationship between the economy and the stock market is interesting—stock prices generally lead the economy. Historically, it is the most sensitive indicator of the business cycle (as we saw, it is one of the leading indicators). Therefore, we must take into account this leading relationship when we are using the economy's condition to evaluate the market.

✓   The market and the economy are closely related, but stock prices typically turn before the economy.

Investments Intuition

Why is the market a leading indicator of the economy? Basically, investors are discounting the future, because, as the valuation analysis in Chapter 10 showed, stocks are worth today the discounted value of all future cash flows. Current stock prices reflect investor expectations of the future. Stock prices adjust quickly if investor expectations of corporate profits change. Of course, the market can misjudge corporate profits, resulting in a false signal about future movements in the economy.

An alternative explanation for stock prices leading the economy involves an investor change in the required rate of return, which again would result in an immediate change in stock prices. Valuation models allow for a change in confidence (psychological elements), because a change in investor confidence changes the required rate of return (in the opposite direction). Psychological elements are sometimes used in explaining market movements.

How reliable is this relationship between the stock market and the business cycle? While it is generally considered reliable, it is widely known that the market has given false signals

---

[9] See Arturo Estrella and Frederic S. Mishkin, "The Yield Curve as a Predictor of U.S. Recessions," *Current Issues in Economics and Finance*, Vol. 2, June, 1996, pp. 1–6; and Estrella and Mishkin, "Predicting U.S. Recessions: Financial Variables as Leading Indicators," *Review of Economics and Statistics*, Vol. 80, February, 1998, pp. 45–61.

about future economic activity, particularly with regard to recessions. The old joke goes something like this—"The market has predicted nine out of the last five recessions."[10]

Recognizing that the market does not always lead the economy in the predicted manner, consider what an examination of the historical record shows:

◻ Stock prices often peak roughly one year before the start of a recession.

Example 13-2   The business cycle-stock-price relationship is illustrated by what happened in 2000–2001. Following a strong runup in the late 1990s, the stock markets in the United States peaked in March 2000, and the longest economic expansion in U.S. history—the 10-year expansion of the 1990s—is considered to have ended in March 2001.

◻ The typical contraction in stock prices is 25 percent from the peak. With recent recessions, however, it has been 40 percent or more. For example, in 2000–2002 the S&P 500 Index declined some 45 percent from its peak.
◻ The ability of the market to predict recoveries has been remarkably good.
◻ Stock prices almost always turn up three to five months before a recovery, with four months being very typical.

Following World War II, and preceding the recession of 2001, there were nine periods of recovery. In each of these, the market (the S&P 500) rose before the recession's trough, and continued to rise as the expansion entered its early stages. Six months into recovery, stock prices were, on average, more than 25 percent higher than they had been a year earlier.

In summary, although the leading relationship between the stock market and the economy is far from perfect, investors must take it into account.

✓ Typically, by the time investors clearly recognize what the economy is doing, such as going into recession or coming out of recession, the stock market has already anticipated the event and reacted.

The Economy and Stock Market Booms

It should come as no surprise that in a complex economy such as the U.S. economy, exact relationships cannot always be specified. Nevertheless, based on an analysis of the past, some clear guidelines have emerged. For example, most stock market booms have occurred during periods of relatively rapid economic growth.[11] Productivity growth also seems to be associated with booms.

There is little evidence to support the idea that stock market booms were caused by excessive growth in money or credit. In the past they have occurred in periods of deflation, price stability, and inflation.

In summary, stock market booms do not occur unless there are increases in real economic growth, and perhaps productivity growth. These appear to be the key indicators for investors to monitor.

---

[10] The NBER defines a recession as a "significant decline in activity spread across the economy, lasting more than a few months, visible in industrial production, real income and wholesale-retail sales."

[11] This discussion is based on Michael D. Bordo and David C. Wheelock, "Monetary Policy and Asset Prices: A Look Back at Past U.S. Stock Market Booms", *Review*, Federal Reserve Bank of St. Louis, Vol. 86, No. 6, November/December 2004, pp. 19–44.

ECONOMIC SLOWDOWNS AND BEAR MARKETS

Bear Market A downward trend in the stock market

What happens to the stock market when economic activity slows down, possibly resulting in a recession? Common sense suggests a negative impact on the market, and that is what has happened historically. By mid-July 2008, the major market indices had all declined at least 20 percent, the classic definition of a **bear market**. And, of course, the economy was in great turmoil from the subprime debacle, record oil prices, bank failures, and so forth.

According to Standard & Poor's, since World War II, eleven bear markets have occurred through 2009. These bear markets lasted an average of 16 months. It took an average of nine months for the decline to breach the −20 percent mark that defines a bear market.

A reasonable hypothesis to explain the stock market's decline when the economy slows down is that investors become more risk-averse and demand a higher return for holding stocks. Campbell and Cochrane formalized this idea in a model.[12] With an economy going into, or in, a recession, investors are less willing to bear financial risk. To induce investors to hold stocks rather than Treasury bills, for a given level of market risk, the equity risk premium (Chapter 10) must increase. This results in dividends being discounted at a higher discount rate because of the increase in the equity risk premium. Thus, stock prices fall during recessions.

RELATING THE BOND MARKET AND INTEREST RATES TO THE STOCK MARKET

What is the relationship between the bond market and the stock market? Bond prices and interest rates are opposite sides of the coin—if bond prices move up (down), interest rates move down (up).

Stock investors pay attention to the bond market because interest rates are available daily as an indicator of what is happening in the economy. The bond market can provide daily signals of what bond traders and investors think about the economy, and the stock market reacts to the state of the economy. Bond traders react to news of unemployment, or rising sales, or changes in the money supply, thereby affecting interest rates and bond prices on a daily basis.

Interest rates are a very important consideration in the valuation process. As we shall see later in the chapter, interest rates are one of the key variables involved in understanding the stock market. And, as explained earlier, yield curves from the bond market are useful in forecasting the economy.

Monetary policy actions have an impact on the stock market. Some studies have found evidence that such actions affect stock prices in the short run. A study by Bernanke before he became Chairman of the Fed found that an unanticipated 25 basis point increase in the Federal Reserve's target for the federal funds rate led to a 1 percent decline in equity prices.[13]

Checking Your Understanding

2. Assume you determine this month that the economy has reached a peak and is headed downward. What conclusions would you draw about stock prices?

---

[12] John Y. Campbell and John H. Cochrane, "By Force of Habit: A Consumption-Based Explanation of Aggregate Stock Market Behavior," *Journal of Political Economy*, Vol. 107, 1999, pp. 205–251.

[13] Ben Bernanke and Kenneth Kuttner, "What Explains the Stock Market's Reaction to Federal Reserve Policy?" *Journal of Finance*, Vol. 60, No. 3, June 2005, pp. 1221–1257.

Understanding the Stock Market

WHAT DETERMINANTS AGGREGATE STOCK PRICES?

In Chapter 10, we examined the variables that are used to estimate the intrinsic value of stocks with the dividend discount model—dividends and the required rate of return—and with the P/E ratio model—earnings and the P/E ratio. The same models apply to the aggregate stock market as represented by a market index such as the S&P 500 Index.

To value the stock market using the fundamental analysis approach explained in Chapter 10, we use as our foundation the P/E ratio or multiplier approach because a majority of investors focus on earnings and P/E ratios. Estimates of index earnings and the earnings multiplier are used in Equation 13-1. As explained in Chapter 10, this model uses an appropriate P/E ratio which we call P_0/E_1. We will use the S&P 500 Index as our measure of the stock market:

$$P_0 = P_0/E_1 \times E_1 \qquad (13\text{-}1)$$

where

$$E_1 = \text{expected earnings on the S\&P 500 Index}$$
$$P_0/E_1 = \text{the price-earnings ratio or multiplier}$$

We consider each of these variables in turn.

The Earnings Stream Estimating earnings for purposes of valuing the market is not easy. The item of interest is the earnings per share for a market index or, in general, corporate profits after taxes.

Corporate profits are derived from corporate sales, which in turn is related to GDP. A detailed, top-down fundamental analysis of the economy/market would involve estimating each of these variables, starting with GDP, then corporate sales, working down to corporate earnings before taxes, and finally to corporate earnings after taxes. Each of these steps can involve various levels of difficulty. Suffice it to say that real (inflation-adjusted) earnings growth has correlated well with real GDP growth over the long run.

✓ When estimating real earnings growth for the future, the best guide may be expected real GDP growth.

It is reasonable to expect corporate earnings to grow, on average, at about the rate of the economy as a whole. However, for the last years of the 20th century, operating earnings per share for the S&P 500 grew an average of 10.2 percent a year, versus a rate of 5.56 percent for economic growth. This simply illustrates how difficult it is to accurately forecast earnings. Extenuating factors can cause some divergences. For example, share repurchases by firms may increase the rate of earnings growth relative to historical rates. Since earnings have to be allocated over fewer shares as firms repurchase shares, earnings per share increases. Estimates are that this could add anywhere from one-half to one and one-half percentage points to the growth rate of real earnings.

Which Earnings Should We Use? Note that an annual EPS for the S&P 500 Index can be constructed in various ways. For example, assume we are 10 days away from the end of 2012. The fourth-quarter earnings for 2012 are still an estimate, and even the third quarter has a small element of uncertainty in it. All four quarters for 2013 are estimates. This is further complicated by the fact that for the S&P 500, Standard & Poor's provides both top-down and bottom-up estimates, and both "as reported" estimates and operating estimates. Furthermore, S&P is now providing its "core earnings" for the S&P 500 Index, which focuses on companies' after-tax earnings generated from their principal businesses. S&P has determined that the primary reasons that core earnings and as-reported earnings differ are pension income and stock option grant expenses, with the treatment of pension gains having a very significant impact. The differences between these two earnings numbers can be substantial.

The Multiplier or P/E Ratio   The multiplier to be applied to the earnings estimate is the other half of the valuation framework. Investors sometimes mistakenly ignore the multiplier and concentrate only on the earnings estimate. But earnings growth is not always the leading factor in significant price changes in the market. Instead, low interest rates may lead to high P/E ratios, which in turn may account for much of the market's price change over some periods of time.

Example 13-3   The S&P 500 Index increased about 150 percent between the end of 1994 and December 1998. Stock prices are a function of both corporate earnings and the P/E ratio. At the end of 1994, the P/E based on current earnings was 15. At the end of 1998, it was 32.6. Over the period 1994–1998, corporate earnings rose about 25 percent and the P/E ratio more than doubled, thereby accounting for much of the sharp rise in the S&P 500 during that period.

Figure 13-3 shows the P/E ratio for the Standard & Poor's 500 Index since 1980. The figure shows that since 1980 there has been a general upward movement of P/E ratios across time. At various times (for example, the late 1970s and early 1980s, and the late 1980s and early 1990s), P/Es tended to cluster together.

Investors cannot simply extrapolate P/E ratios because dramatic changes occur over time. While average P/E ratios over long periods are reasonably steady, the variation over shorter periods is large. For the S&P 500 Composite Index, the average P/E for 100 years or more was about 15.6. Since 1926, the average was about 16.5. Therefore, S&P 500 P/Es are typically in the range of 15.6 to 16.5 on average, However, individual years can be very different. The P/E ratio was 7.3 in 1979, 32.6 in 1998, and 46.5 in 2001. By the end of 2005, the P/E had decreased below 18. By the end of 2007, it had recovered to 22, but at the end of 2010 it was about 15.[14]

P/E ratios are generally depressed when interest rates and the rate of inflation are high, such as around 1980–1981. P/E ratios tend to be high when inflation and interest rates are low, such as the period of the mid-to-late 1990s, when P/E ratios were at quite high levels by historical standards. When earnings are growing and the upward profit trend appears sustainable, investors are willing to pay more for today's earnings. Investors must be careful, when using P/E ratios, to place them in the proper context.

✓   P/E ratios can refer to historical data, an average for the year, or a prospective period such as the year ahead.

Obviously, a significant difference can exist between P/E ratios calculated using these different definitions. Furthermore, as noted earlier, various definitions of earnings for an index such as the S&P 500 are available.

---

[14] These P/E ratios are based on reported EPS, and not operating earnings.

Figure 13-3

S&P P/E Ratios.

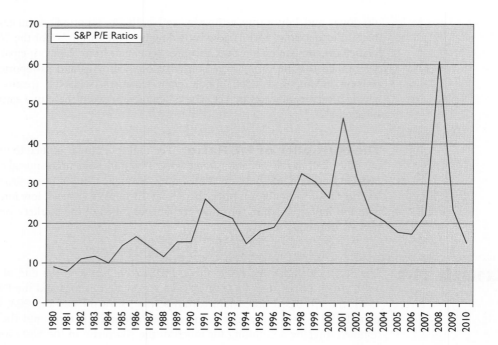

Putting the Two Together   Valuing the aggregate market is not easy, because the market is presumably always looking ahead, and current stock prices reflect this. No one knows for sure how far the market is looking ahead, and no one knows for sure what the market is willing to pay for a dollar of earnings. Furthermore, industry analysts are notoriously optimistic when forecasting market earnings, such as the earnings for next year for the S&P 500.

Regardless of the difficulties, the bottom line is this—to value the level of the market, an investor must analyze both factors that determine stock prices: corporate earnings and multipliers.

Concepts in Action

How Analysts Go About Valuing the Market

2008 was a year of great turmoil in the U.S. economy, given the subprime debacle, record high oil prices, and the stress on banks and brokerage firms. In mid-June 2008, analysts were trying to figure out where the S&P 500 Index, then at 1,360, would go. As a *Wall Street Journal* article noted, "Where the market ends up depends on how much companies earn during the rest of the year and what price, or multiple, investors put on those earnings." This illustrates the discussion above—two variables determine stock prices: earnings and multipliers.

Many analysts were already doubting the median earnings forecast of about 8 percent for the year, and were particularly dubious about forecasts of strong earnings growth for 2009. As for the P/E ratio, which was slightly less than 17 based on the previous 12 months of earnings, there were fears that higher inflation would lead to lower multipliers. Holding earnings constant, this would lead to a lower value for the S&P Index.

Quote from Tom Lauricella, "Skeptics See Stocks Mired in the Muck," *The Wall Street Journal*, June 16, 2008, p. C1.

Checking Your Understanding

3. Assume you are convinced that you accurately know what corporate earnings will be for the next year, including the definition of earnings that most investors will use. Can you then reliably predict the direction of the market?

Making Market Forecasts

✓ Accurate forecasts of the stock market, particularly short-term forecasts, are impossible for anyone to do *consistently*.

As discussed in Chapter 12, there is strong evidence that the market is efficient; this implies that changes in the market cannot be predicted on the basis of information about previous changes. Another implication is that even professional money managers cannot consistently forecast the market using available information, and the available evidence on the performance success of professional investors supports this proposition.

Nevertheless, most investors ultimately seek to estimate likely changes in the stock market. Not only do they want to try to understand what the market is doing currently and why, but they also want some reasonable estimates of the future. Part of this process, as discussed earlier, involves analyzing the overall economy. Ideally, investors need earnings estimates and the P/E ratio for next year for the market. As we have seen, however, accurate estimates are difficult to obtain, given the various constructs that are available. What, then, can investors do in trying to assess future movements in the market?

FOCUS ON THE IMPORTANT VARIABLES

It has long been known that stock prices are closely related to corporate earnings, and that interest rates play a major role in affecting both bond and stock prices. Consider an interview with Warren Buffett, arguably the best-known investor in the United States.[15] Buffett was asked to comment on the likely scenario for the market. Buffett argued that long-term movements in stock prices in the past, and likely in the future, are caused by significant changes in "two critical economic variables":

1. interest rates
2. expected corporate profits

If investors wish to understand the stock market and make reasonable judgments about future movements in stock prices, they must carefully analyze interest rates and expected corporate profits.

Corporate Earnings, Interest Rates, and Stock Prices   Interest rates and P/E ratios are generally inversely related. When fixed-income securities are paying less return, investors are willing to pay more for stocks; therefore, P/E ratios are higher. Stocks rise strongly as earnings climb and interest rates stay low. Investors should pay close attention to earnings and interest rates as they assess the outlook for stocks.

Figure 13-4 shows the three series together—interest rates, the percent change in corporate profits after taxes annually, and the percent change in total returns annually for the S&P 500 Index for the period 1987–2011. The shaded areas indicate recessions, as determined by

---

[15] See "Warren Buffett on the Stock Market," *Fortune*, December 10, 2001, p. 82.

Figure 13-4

Interest Rates, Corporate Profits, and S&P 500 Index Total Returns, 1986–2011.

Source: *National Economic Trends*, Federal Reserve Bank of St. Louis, March 2012, pp. 7, 21.

Interest Rates

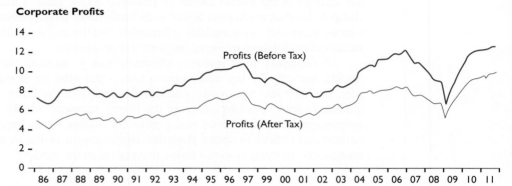

Corporate Profits

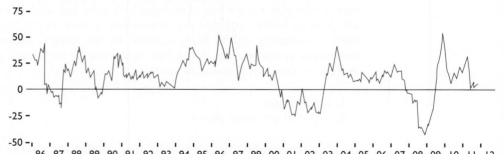

Standard and Poor's 500 Index with Reinvested Dividends

the National Bureau of Economic Research. In general, in the recessionary periods, interest rates trended upward before the recession, corporate profit changes were downward, and stock return changes were downward. Also notice the similarities in profit changes and stock return changes in terms of highs and lows, and how rising (falling) interest rates are generally associated with falling (rising) stock returns.

It is logical to expect a relationship between corporate profits and stock prices. If the economy is prospering, investors will expect corporate earnings and dividends to rise and, other things being equal, stock prices to rise. To a large extent, corporate earnings growth is thought of by most market observers as the basis for share price growth. In fact, holding the P/E ratio constant, growth in price should match growth in earnings.

Interest rates are a basic component of discount rates, with the two usually moving together. As Figure 13-4 shows, there is a relationship between interest rate movements and stock prices, just as there is with corporate profits. In this case, however, the relationship is inverse.

✔ As interest rates rise (fall), stock prices fall (rise), other things equal.

     If interest rates rise, the riskless rate of return, RF, rises, because it is tied to interest rates, and other things being equal, the required rate of return (discount rate) rises because the riskless rate is one of its two components.

     Investors must take into account the role of changes in interest rates in affecting investor expectations. Investors pay close attention to announcements by the Federal Reserve that could possibly affect interest rates, as well as to any other factors that may play a role. In turn, the popular press reports possible changes in interest rates as they might affect the stock market.

Example 13-4   Consider the following headlines from *The Wall Street Journal* within a six-week period:

    "Markets Fall on Absence of Rate Cut"
    "Recent Rise in Long-Term Interest Rates May Mean Trouble for the Stock Market"
    "As Interest Rates Rise, Will Stocks Fall?"
    "Benchmark Treasury Yield Tops 8%; Stocks Fall"

     Like most relationships involving investing, the relationship between interest rates and stock prices is not perfect. Nor do interest rates have a linear effect on stock prices. What we are seeking here are general clues as to the economy and the market's direction and the duration of a likely change. For example, to say that we are confident the market will go to 13,000 or 6,000 (as measured by the Dow Jones Industrial Average) one year from now is foolish. Similarly, a strong prediction that corporate earnings will rise next year by 10 percent, or that interest rates are sure to rise (or fall) X percent, is a virtually certain prescription for embarrassment.

✔ In truth, most individual investors—indeed, most professional investors—cannot time the market consistently.

     What, then, should they do? The best approach for most investors is to recognize the futility of attempting to consistently forecast successfully the direction of the market, but also to recognize that periodically situations will develop that suggest strong action. An example is 1982, when interest rates reached record peaks. Either rates were going to decline, or the U.S. economy would face a crisis situation. Interest rates did decline, launching one of the greatest bull markets in U.S. history.

     Investors may simply choose to hold their positions, or even buy, when the market appears to be ready to decline—or many people are claiming that it is. Why? According to available evidence, investors lose more by missing a bull market than by dodging a bear market. This is consistent with the evidence presented in Chapter 11 on market timing—investors who miss a relatively few months in the market may lose much of the gains during that period—and the period can be quite long (such as 10 years). As we know, the impact of the overall market on an investor's portfolio is enormous.

Checking Your Understanding

4. Given that earnings and the P/E ratio determine stock prices, what is the logic for arguing that interest rates are one of the two critical variables in forecasting the direction of the market?

USING THE BUSINESS CYCLE TO MAKE MARKET FORECASTS

Earlier we established the idea that certain composite indexes can be helpful in forecasting or ascertaining the position of the business cycle. However, stock prices are one of the leading indicators, tending to lead the economy's turning points, both peaks and troughs. This leading relationship between stock prices and the economy must be taken into account in forecasting likely changes in stock prices.

Stock prices generally decline in recessions, and the steeper the recession, the steeper the decline. However, investors need to think about the business cycle's turning points months before they occur in order to have a handle on the turning points in the stock market. If a business cycle downturn appears likely in the future, the market will also be likely to turn down some months ahead of the economic downturn.

We can be somewhat more precise about the leading role of stock prices. Because of this tendency to lead the economy, the total return on stocks (on an annual basis) could be negative (positive) in years in which the business cycle peaks (bottoms). Stock prices have almost always risen as the business cycle is approaching a trough. These increases have been large, so that investors do well during these periods. Furthermore, stock prices often remain steady or even decline suddenly as the business cycle enters into the initial phase of recovery. After the previous sharp rise as the bottom is approached, a period of steady prices or even a decline typically occurs. The economy, of course, is still moving ahead.

Based on the above analysis,

1. If the investor can recognize the bottoming out of the economy before it occurs, a market rise can be predicted, at least based on past experience, before the bottom is hit. In previous recessions since World War II, the market started to rise about halfway between GDP starting to decline and starting to grow again.
2. The market's average gain over the 12 months following its bottom point is about 36 percent.
3. As the economy recovers, stock prices may level off or even decline. Therefore, a second significant movement in the market may be predictable, again based on past experience.
4. Based on the most recent nine economic slumps in the twentieth century, the market P/E usually rises just before the end of the slump. It then remains roughly unchanged over the next year.

Some Practical Advice

Forecasting market movements is a humbling experience, and will cause anyone doing this on a regular basis to look foolish sooner or later—in all likelihood, sooner. The points mentioned above are based on past experience, but the past does not always repeat itself. In the spring and summer of 2002, many market observers expected a rise in the market based on an apparent ending to the economic slump. Although a profit recovery had not occurred, it appeared to many that it was time to get back in the market in anticipation of the market rising before the absolute bottom. The anticipated market rise did not occur as early as expected.

THE E/P RATIO AND THE TREASURY BOND YIELD

Practitioners on Wall Street sometimes use a valuation model that compares the earnings yield with the nominal yield on a long-term Treasury bond.[16] This model, often referred to as the "Fed Model'" has a simple premise—because investors can and do easily switch between stocks and bonds, based on the asset with the higher yield, stock returns will tend to restore an equilibrium relationship between the two assets.[17]

To measure bond yields, one can use the yield on 10-year Treasuries. Of course, this number can be observed on an updated basis every day. The earnings yield is calculated as earnings divided by stock price, using the S&P 500 Index. The earnings figure used is a forward 12-month earnings estimate, based on operating earnings.[18]

The virtues of this model are its simplicity, and the fact that variables can be obtained with relative ease. Of course, the forward 12-month earnings for the S&P 500 Index is an estimate, and is subject to error.

This model can be used to formulate decision rules in the following ways:

- When the earnings yield on the S&P 500 is greater than the 10-year Treasury yield, stocks are relatively attractive.
- When the earnings yield is less than the 10-year Treasury yield, stocks are relatively unattractive.

An alternative way to use this model is to estimate the "fair value" level of the S&P 500 Index and compare it to the actual current index value.[19] To do this, divide the estimated earnings for the S&P Index by the current 10-year Treasury bond yield (expressed as a decimal) to obtain the estimated fair value:

- If the estimated fair value of the market is greater than the current level of the market, stocks are undervalued.
- If the estimated fair value of the market is less than the current level of the market, stocks are overvalued.

This model worked quite well on average over a 30-year period or so, but it has not always performed well. Furthermore, when interest rates are very low, it does not work as

---

[16] The earnings yield is defined as the E/P ratio, which is the inverse of the P/E ratio.

[17] This model has been widely referred to as the "Fed Model" because it was discovered that the Fed had referred to such a model in its deliberations; however, the Fed neither endorses this model nor necessarily uses it on any ongoing basis.

[18] Thus, on January 1, 2013, we would use an estimate of operating earnings for the S&P 500 Index for the next 12 months, through the end of the year. In a similar manner, on April 1, 2013, we would use an estimate of the next 12-month earnings through April 1, 2014.

[19] Also note that the model implies that the reciprocal of the yield on 10-year Treasuries is an esimate of the S&P 500's equilibrium P/E ratio. That is,

$$\text{An equilibrium estimate of the S\&P 500 P/E ratio} = 1/\text{10-year Treasury yield}$$

Using this formulation, we can use P/E ratios in a relative valuation format as explained in Chapter 10.

- If the S&P 500's actual P/E ratio is less than the estimated equilibrium P/E ratio, equities are relatively attractive.
- If the S&P 500's actual P/E ratio is greater than the estimated equilibrium P/E ratio, equities are relatively unattractive.

well as when rates are in a more normal range.[20] In fact, it may break down completely as far as sensible answers. While the E/P model has the great virtue of simplicity, and has given some useful signals, it is not without its problems and limitations, which are important to note.[21]

OTHER APPROACHES TO ASSESSING THE MARKET'S LIKELY DIRECTION

A number of market indicators and macro variables have been touted as potential predictors of future movements in the economy and/or the market. We will consider several here.

The Market's P/E Ratio   Perhaps the best-known market indicator, and one watched by many investors, is the price/earnings ratio. Over the last 30-plus years the P/E ratio for the S&P 500 Index has typically ranged from roughly 7 to 47 on a reported earnings basis.[22] The market P/E was 7.25 at the beginning of 1980, and the 1980s and 1990s were two of the greatest decades in our history for common stock returns. Many market observers are extremely nervous when the P/E reaches levels in the high 20s and low 30s, as it did in the late 1990s. They were ultimately proven right, as the market declined sharply in 2000, 2001, and 2002.

Consider the following analysis of annualized total returns over rolling 10-year periods covering 1900–2010, a total of 102 periods.[23] Thirty-five percent of the time, the annualized returns exceeded 12 percent. In every case, the price-earnings ratio started at less than 15. Now consider the 43 percent of the periods when the annualized returns were less than 8 percent. The starting price-earnings ratio was usually above 15. While this is not conclusive proof of the importance of the starting price-earnings ratio in affecting future market returns, it is certainly suggestive that investors should pay close attention to the price-earnings ratio.

Interest Rates   Investors attempting to forecast the market's direction should pay attention to certain important variables. Interest rates are an obvious variable to watch, and a good benchmark is the Treasury's 10-year maturity bond. Studies have shown that since 1970 every inverted yield curve was followed by negative earnings growth for the S&P 500 Index. Furthermore, this information typically comes about a year in advance of the decline, providing adequate warning. The yield curve inverted in 2000, and the stock market performed badly during 2000–2002.

The direction of commodity prices, as opposed to levels, is also important. Finally, unit labor costs are considered by many to be an important economic indicator, with anything above 3 percent signaling a potential problem.

Monetary Policy   How much impact does the Fed have on stock prices, given its impact on short-term interest rates? One study has examined market returns during a 38-year

---

[20] It is highly probable that the model is not as reliable when interest rates are unusually low because the implied linear relationship overstates the estimated equilibrium P/E ratio.

[21] The model relies on the estimated earnings for the S&P 500 Index for the next 12 months. There are different estimates of this number, involving top-down, bottom-up, and S&P's core earnings, and they are revised often. Therefore, it is difficult to determine exactly which number to use at any given time.

[22] The market P/E in 2008 was 60 on a reported earnings basis because the financial crisis caused earnings to be abnormally low.

[23] These numbers are from Ed Easterling, "Historical Performance and Future Stock Market Return Uncertainties, *AAII Journal*, September 2011, p. 24.

period starting in mid-1963.[24] The discount rate was used to define monetary policy, with decreases in the discount rate defining expansive policy periods and discount rate increases defining restrictive policy periods. During this time period the Fed changed the direction in monetary policy 21 times.

The results of this study indicated that during periods of restrictive monetary policy the stock market performed poorly, with stock returns averaging less than 3 percent, and risk at higher-than-average levels. Conversely, during periods of expansive monetary policy, returns were higher than average and risk was lower, with stock returns averaging almost 22 percent. Thus, it is not surprising that one of the author's stated that "The Federal Reserve's management of U.S. monetary policy has a strong bearing on the stock market."

Volatility   The Chicago Board Options Exchange has a volatility index (VIX). It is often referred to as a "fear" index, but it is actually an index of expected market volatility. There is historical evidence that volatile days tend to cluster together rather than occur randomly. Investors who wish to avoid these volatile days can possibly use the VIX. Mark Hulbert has suggested a value for the VIX of about 20, which is close to its median. Below 20, investors could buy stocks. As the VIX rises above 20, investors may wish to be in cash. Hulbert's analysis suggests that over the last 20 years or so average market returns have been higher if the VIX is below its median value than if it is above this value.[25] Using this approach, investors could often be in cash for several months at a time.

January Market Performance   From 1950 through 2007, there was almost a 90 percent correlation between the market's positive performance in January and the performance for the entire year, as measured by the S&P 500 Index. As for January declines, the record for predictions is not very good. Since 1945, the market was down for the year as a whole, after a January decline, only slightly more than half the time.

January 2008 showed a decline for the month, and the market suffered a drastic loss for the year. However, 2009, 2010, and 2011 did not follow this pattern. In January 2009, the S&P 500 Index declined, but the market performed very well. What about 2010? While the S&P 500 showed a loss for January, the index for the entire year showed a sizeable gain. For 2011, the S&P 500 Index started and ended the year at the exact same level, 1,257.6, although it was up about 2.3 percent in January. This shows once again the dangers of relying solely on the past when predicting the future—it does not always work out.

It is interesting to note that since 1950 the first five days in January had predictive value when the market went up. Out of the 38 times this occurred, the market was up for the year 33 times. Once again, negative performance in the first five days did not predict full year performance, with an almost equal split between gains and losses.

Finally, as you consider the state of the market and whether you should invest now, you might ask if any particular month is riskier than others. Some believe that October is, and the historical evidence seems to support this idea: Six of the 10 biggest down days since 1926 have occurred in October. As Mark Twain said, "October is one of the peculiarly dangerous months to speculate in stocks." However, the rest of his quote goes as follows: "The others are: July, January, September, April, November, May, March, June, December, August, and February."

---

[24] See Robert Johnson, Scott Beyer and Gerald Jensen, "Don't Worry About the Election, Just Watch the Fed," *The Journal of Portfolio Management*, Summer 2004, and C. Mitchell Conover, Gerald Jensen, and Robert Johnson, "*Is Fed Policy Still Relevant for Investors,*" unpublished paper.

[25] Mark Hulbert, "Cash is Still King, at Least for Now," MarketWatch.com, January 10, 2012.

Summary

▶ The recurring pattern of expansion and contraction in the economy is referred to as the business cycle. Stock prices are related to the phases of the business cycle.

▶ Leading, lagging, and coincident indicators are used to monitor the economy in terms of business cycle turning dates.

▶ It is important to remember that stock prices are a well-known leading indicator. Therefore, although the market and the economy are clearly related, stock prices usually turn before the economy.

▶ Macroeconomic forecasts have become more accurate, but there is much room for improvement.

▶ Although money's effectiveness in forecasting the economy is controversial, investors should monitor the actions of the Federal Reserve.

▶ The "market" is the aggregate of all security prices and is conveniently measured by some average or, most commonly, by some index of stock prices.

▶ To understand the market (i.e., what determines stock prices), it is desirable to think in terms of a valuation model.

▶ To value the market, investors should think in terms of expected corporate earnings and the P/E ratio. (Alternatively, the dividend valuation model could be used.)

▶ Corporate earnings are related to the growth rate of the economy as measured by GDP.

▶ Forecasting market changes is difficult. Precise forecasts are generally out of the question. Instead, we are seeking the direction of stock prices and the duration of any trend that may be occurring.

▶ Some intelligent estimates of possible changes in the market can be made by considering what is likely to happen to corporate profits and P/E ratios (or interest rates) over some future period, such as a year.

▶ The business cycle can be of help in understanding the status of the economy, and investors then need to relate the market, which typically leads, to the economy.

▶ An alternative approach to forecasting likely changes in the market is to apply a model such as the E/P model (often called the Fed model), which involves a comparison of bond yields to earnings yields.

▶ Other approaches to assessing the market's likely direction include assessing the market's current P/E ratio relative to the past, an analysis of interest rates as seen in the yield curve, the status of monetary policy, the impact of volatility using the VIX index, and using January as an indicator.

Questions

13-1 Why is market analysis so important?

13-2 How did the performance of the Euro during 2002–2004 affect U.S. investors in foreign securities?

13-3 Why should investors be concerned with GDP growth?

13-4 On average, how long are business cycle expansions and contractions since WWII?

13-5 What is the historical relationship between stock prices, corporate profits, and interest rates?

13-6 How can investors go about valuing the market?

13-7 What was the primary cause of the rise in stock prices starting in 1982?

13-8 What is the "typical" business cycle-stock-price relationship?

13-9 If an investor can determine when the bottoming out of the economy will occur, when should stocks be purchased—before, during, or after such a bottom? Would stock prices be expected to continue to rise as the economy recovers (based on historical experience)?

13-10 Can money supply changes forecast stock-price changes?

13-11 What is the historical relationship between the market's P/E ratio and recessions?

13-12 What is the likely explanation for the stock market's negative performance in 2000–2002?

13-13 Suppose that you know with certainty that corporate earnings next year will rise 15 percent above this year's level of corporate earnings. Based on this information, should you buy stocks?

13-14 What does a steepening yield curve suggest about the economy? What about an inverted yield curve?

13-15 In general, what should be the relationship between corporate earnings growth and the growth rate for the economy as a whole?

13-16 Using the so-called "Fed Model" relating the earnings yield on the S&P 500 Index to Treasury

bond yields, when would stocks be considered an attractive investment?

13-17 Why is so much day-to-day news coverage devoted to consumer spending?

13-18 Suppose you could correctly predict that the business cycle was approaching a trough. What should your investment strategy for stocks be?

13-19 What are the implications of a negative yield curve for earnings growth and for the economy as a whole?

13-20 The P/E ratio on the S&P 500 Index for 1998 and 1999 was 30 or higher. Other things equal, would this indicate a good time to buy stocks for a multi-year holding period, or not?

Problems

13-1 During one week the NASDAQ Composite went from 1,564.32 to 1,530.24, while the NASDAQ 100 Index went from 1,217.19 to 1,185.44. Which index showed the greater loss?

13-2 The NASDAQ index lost more than 75 percent of its value in the early years of the 21st century. Assuming an 80 percent loss, what return is needed on this index to make up for the 80 percent loss?

Computational Problems

13-1 The following annual data are available for a stock market index:

Year	End-of-Year Price (P)	Earnings (E)	Dividends (D)	P/E	(D/E) (%)	(D/P) (%)
2008	107.21	13.12	5.35	8.17	40.78	4.99
2009	121.02	16.08	6.04	7.53	37.56	4.99
2010	154.45	16.13	6.55	9.58	40.61	4.24
2011	137.12	16.70	7.00	8.21	41.92	5.11
2012	157.62	13.21	7.18	11.93	54.35	4.56
2013	186.24	15.24	6.97			

The 2013 values in italics are estimates.

a. Calculate the 2013 values for those columns left blank.

b. On the assumption that $g = 0.055$, calculate k for 2013 using the formula $k = (D/P) + g$ and show that $k = 0.092425$.

c. Using the 2013 values, show that P/E = 12.22.

d. Assuming a projection that 2014 earnings will be 15 percent greater than the 2013 value, show that projected earnings are expected to be 17.53.

e. Assuming further that the dividend-payout ratio will be 0.40, show that projected dividends for 2014 will be 7.01.

f. Using the projected earnings and dividends for 2014, and the same k and g used in part b, show that the expected P/E for 2014 is 10.69.

g. Using these expected values for 2014, show that the expected price is 187.31.

h. Recalculate the values for 2014 P/E and P, using the same $g = 0.055$, but with (1) $k = 0.11$, (2) $k = 0.10$, and (3) $k = 0.09$.

Spreadsheet Exercises

13-1   Using the spreadsheet below, calculate

a. Total returns for the S&P 500 for each year from 1991 through 2010.

b. Cumulative wealth for the first 10 years (1991–2000) and for the second 10 years (2001–2010).

c. The P/E ratio for all 20 years.

d. The dividend yield for each year, using the dividend in the current year and the price at the end of the previous year (for example, 2011 would be calculated as the 2011 dividend divided by the ending price for 2010).

	Price	Dividends	Earnings	Total Ret	P/E	Div Yield
1990	330.22					
1991	417.09	12.2	15.91			
1992	435.71	12.38	19.09			
1993	466.45	12.58	21.88			
1994	459.27	13.18	30.6			
1995	615.93	13.79	33.96			
1996	740.74	14.9	38.73			
1997	970.43	15.49	39.72			
1998	1229.23	16.2	37.71			
1999	1469.25	16.69	48.17			
2000	1320.28	16.27	50			
2001	1148.08	15.74	24.69			
2002	879.82	16.08	27.59			
2003	1111.92	17.39	48.74			
2004	1211.92	19.44	58.55			
2005	1248.29	22.22	69.93			
2006	1418.3	24.88	81.51			
2007	1468.36	27.73	66.18			
2008	903.25	28.39	14.88			
2009	1115.1	22.31	50.97			
2010	1257.64	23.12	76.97			

Checking Your Understanding

13-1 Assuming that you are correct in your analysis that the economy has reached a peak this month, it is likely that the stock market has already turned sometime before now. Stock prices typically lead the economy. Therefore, the market likely would have anticipated a forthcoming peak in economic activity.

13-2 Since World War II a downward-sloping yield curve has almost always preceded a recession. While there are never guarantees about the future, this is one indicator that has been remarkably reliable in its predictions, so investors should pay close attention to it.

13-3 It takes two variables to determine stock price, whether for one stock or the market. While you may have a reliable estimate of future earnings, you do not know what the P/E ratio will be. Thus, even if you knew corporate earnings would be higher next year, the P/E ratio could decline enough to offset this increase and leave stock prices lower.

13-4 Interest rates are an important part of the required rate of return for stocks, and therefore affect stock prices. Generally, interest rates and stock prices move in opposite directions.

chapter 14

Sector/Industry Analysis

A s you prepare to invest your inheritance, you are reminded that you have read about the telecom boom and bust of the late 1990s, the strong performance of the energy sector in 2007–2008 (and possibly for years to come), the outstanding performance of stocks such as Apple, Amazon, and Google in recent years, and so forth. Therefore, it seems obvious to you that you should consider some basic information about sectors and industries that are likely to be important in future years. You already understand you must think ahead when you invest. Yesterday's performers may very well not be tomorrow's performers. You will quickly realize that you cannot become proficient in understanding how to analyze sectors and industries unless you devote a lot of time to the task, but it does seem reasonable that a small effort in this area will pay off. And indeed, it will!

Suppose in late 2011 you were ready to invest some of your money for the year ahead. Two sectors, railroads and biotechnology, have been suggested to you by different people as possibilities for good performance over the next year. Which do you think is likely to perform better? This does not seem like a difficult choice because railroads are so 19th- and 20th-century, and biotechnology is important in the 21st century.

According to an issue of *The Value Line Investment Survey* at that time, which ranks industries as to likely performance over the next year, railroads ranked close to the top and biotechnology close to the bottom in a set of almost 100 industry groups. Assuming Value Line is even reasonably accurate in this analysis, it is clear that knowing something about the major sectors of the economy is crucial to overall investing success. Over long periods some sectors/industries have greatly outperformed others, and over shorter periods of time the differences in one sector's performance can be dramatic.

AFTER READING THIS CHAPTER YOU WILL BE ABLE TO:

▶ Assess the significance of sector/industry analysis in the top-down approach to security analysis.

▶ Recognize how industries are classified and the stages that industries go through over time.

▶ Understand how to go about using sector/industry analysis as an investor.

Introduction

The second step in the fundamental analysis of common stocks is sector/industry analysis. Several recent studies suggest the industry factor is stronger than ever.[1] For example, the strongest trading patterns in institutional trading appear to be based on a sector dimension.

Investors sometimes speak about industries and sometimes about sectors. In general, a sector is a broader definition, and can include several different industries. An industry, in turn, can include several different sub-industries.

✓ For organizational purposes, think of going from sectors to industries to sub-industries.

An investor who is convinced that the economy and the market offer favorable conditions for investing should proceed to consider those sectors that promise the most opportunities in the coming years. In the next few years of the 21st century, for example, investors will not view some U.S. industries with the same enthusiasm they would have even five years earlier—desktop and laptop computers being a good example. On the other hand, it is highly likely that some industries such as the medical services and telecom services industries have, and will continue to have, an impact on many Americans.

Example 14-1 Consider the Medical Appliances and Equipment Industry. Intuitive Surgical, Inc. (ISRG) has pioneered a robotic surgery machine that has revolutionized certain surgical procedures by making possible only minor incisions in the patient and therefore very rapid recovery from surgery. The price of the stock soared, and in July 2012, reached $550 per share. This company still has plenty of opportunities for growth, both in the United States and abroad.

The actual security analysis of industries as performed by professional security analysts is typically quite tedious. Numerous factors are involved, including multiple demand and supply factors, a detailed analysis of price factors, labor issues, government regulation, and so forth. To do such analysis successfully requires experience, access to information, and hard work. Such analysis is not practical for us to consider here. Instead, we will concentrate on the justification for sector/industry analysis and on the conceptual issues involved.

The basic concepts of industry analysis are closely related to our previous discussion of valuation principles. Investors can apply these concepts in several ways, depending on the degree of rigor sought, the amount of information available, and the end objective. What we seek to accomplish here is to learn to think analytically about industries and sectors. Investors can in fact benefit from a reasonable and thoughtful approach to sector/industry analysis without getting involved in myriad details.

What Is An Industry?

At first glance, the term industry may seem self-explanatory. At its most basic, an industry consists of a group of companies primarily engaged in producing or handling the same products or in rendering the same services. Everyone is familiar with the auto industry, the pharmaceutical industry, and the electric utility industry. But are these classifications as

---

[1] See, for example, Stefano Cavaglia, Jeffrey Diermeier, Vadim Moroz, and Sonia de Zordo, "Investing in Global Equities," *Journal of Portfolio Management*, Vol. 30, Spring 2004, pp. 88–94.

clear-cut as they seem? Apparently not, because while we have had industry classification schemes for many years, the classification system for industries continues to evolve, as shown below. Furthermore, investment advisory services and popular press sources use different classification systems.

Example 14-2   Consider General Electric, a classic industrial company in business for more than 100 years. Today it is well known for making CT scanners, jet engines, locomotives, gas turbines, and, historically, appliances and light bulbs. However, it also has GE Capital, a 100 percent affiliate which traditionally provided a significant percentage of GE's profits but which is now being reduced at GE.

CLASSIFYING INDUSTRIES

Standard Industrial Classification (SIC) System A classification of firms on the basis of what they produce using census data

The **Standard Industrial Classification (SIC) System** was the basis for the collection and analysis of the U.S. economy for more than 60 years and was used to put together a comprehensive statistical analysis of an industry.[2]

SIC codes aided significantly in bringing order to the industry classification problem by providing a consistent basis for describing industries and companies in as broad, or as specific, a manner as desired. Nevertheless, the SIC system was criticized for not being able to handle rapid changes in the U.S. economy. This led to the development of the **North American Industry Classification System (NAICS)**, which replaced the SIC codes in 1997.

North American Industry Classification System (NAICS) A company classification system that uses a production-oriented conceptual framework

THE NAICS CLASSIFICATION SYSTEM

The North American Industry Classification System (NAICS) is a significant change for analyzing economic activities. It was developed using a production-oriented conceptual framework; therefore, companies are classified into industries based on the activity in which they are primarily engaged. Basically, companies that do similar things in similar ways are classified together.

NAICS uses a six-digit hierarchical coding system to classify all economic activity into 20 industry sectors, which provides greater flexibility relative to SIC codes. Fifteen of these sectors are devoted to services-producing sectors compared to five sectors that are mainly goods-producing sectors. NAICS allows for the identification of 1,170 industries.

Nine new service sectors and 250 new service industries are recognized. NAICS is now the standard used by federal statistical agencies to classify businesses.

Example 14-3   Using NAICS codes, the Plastics Product Manufacturing industry is coded 3261. Within this code number are several breakdowns, including among others, Plastic Pipe and Pipe Fitting Manufacturing (326122), and Plastics Bottle Manufacturing (326160).

OTHER INDUSTRY CLASSIFICATIONS

The SIC system of industry classification has probably been the best-known system available to users. As noted, NAICS is a new classification system providing more detail. However, in the money management field several well-known investment advisory companies have developed

---

[2] Developed in the 1930s when manufacturing dominated the U.S. economy, this system was revised many times because of rapid changes in our economy, particularly the expansion of services.

their own industry groupings. For example, Standard & Poor's Corporation provided weekly stock indexes on 11 sectors and approximately 115 industry groups for a long time. These weekly indexes have often been used to assess an industry's performance over time.

Global Industry Classification Standard (GICS) Provides a complete, continuous set of global sector and industry definitions using 10 economic sectors

As of March 2002, S&P is using a new system known as the **Global Industry Classification Standard (GICS)** in order to provide "one complete, continuous set of global sector and industry definitions." This system divides everything into 10 "economic sectors": Consumer Discretionary, Consumer Staples, Energy, Financials, Health Care, Industrials, Information Technology, Materials, Telecommunications Services, and Utilities. Within this framework there are 24 industry groupings, 68 industries, and 154 sub-industries (as of late 2011). This system is intended to classify companies around the world, and already includes more than 25,000 companies. Peer groups are defined tightly.

S&P's GICS system, developed jointly with Morgan Stanley Capital International (MSCI), provides considerably more detail than S&P's previous classification system. This in turn will permit users to more readily customize portfolios and indexes.

The Value Line Investment Survey covers roughly 1,700 companies, divided into approximately 98 industries, with a discussion of industry prospects preceding the company analysis.[3] *Value Line's* industry classifications can be quite useful to investors because *Value Line* ranks their expected performance (relatively) for the year ahead.

Other providers of information use different numbers of industries in presenting data. The important point to remember is that multiple industry classification systems are used.

The Importance Of Sector/Industry Analysis

WHY SECTOR/INDUSTRY ANALYSIS IS IMPORTANT OVER THE LONG RUN

Sector and industry analysis is important to investor success because, over the long run, very significant differences occur in the performance of industries and major economic sectors of the economy. To see this, we will examine the performance of industry groups over long periods of time using price indexes for industries.

Standard & Poor's calculated weekly and monthly stock price indexes for a variety of industries, with data available for a 50-year-plus period. Since the data are reported as index numbers, long-term comparisons of price performance can be made for any industry covered. Note that the base number for these S&P data is $1941 - 1943 = 10$; therefore, dividing the index number for any industry for a particular year by 10 indicates the number of times the index has increased over that period.

Let's measure long-term stock price performance up to March 2000 because that is when the stock market peaked after five consecutive years of strong performance, and therefore we can examine the historical record of some industries during some really strong time periods and before the sharp market declines of 2000−2002 and 2008. Recall that the first decade of the 21st century has been called the "Lost Decade" for stocks. The S&P 500 Index closed in 1999 at 1,469.25, while in late October 2008, this index closed one day below 850.

The top part of Table 14-1 shows the long-term price performance of randomly selected industries for the years 1973, 1983, and 1995 and March 2000. The S&P 500 Composite Index in 1973 was almost 10 times (98/10) its 1941−1943 level, a continuously compounded average in excess of 8 percent annually over this 31-year period. By March 2000, the index was about 150 times its base. However, this average growth rate for the index as a

---

[3] *The Value Line Investment Survey* is discussed in more detail in Chapter 15.

Table 14-1 Standard & Poor's Weekly Stock Price Indexes for Selected Industries Using Data for Various Years, All with a Base of 1941 − 1943 = 10

| | 1941 − 43 = 10 | | | |
	1973	1983	1995	2000*
Automobiles	61	100	234	508
Aluminum	90	185	393	703
Beverages (Alcoholic)	133	84	463	717
Beverages (Soft Drinks)	145	157	2343	2899
Electrical Equipment	280	522	1798	6485
Entertainment	34	264	2431	7073
Foods	59	134	1037	1222
Health Care (Drugs)	218	259	2223	5263
S&P 500 Index	98	165	616	1499

| | 1941 − 43 = 10 | | | | |
	1982	1986	1989	1995	2000*
Broadcast Media	889	2309	4980	9437	30946
Entertainment	307	577	1383	2431	7073
Health Care (Drugs)	248	540	949	2223	5264
Money Center Banks	65	66	111	233	419
Retail Stores Composite	104	159	375	321	901
S&P 500 Index	141	242	353	616	1499

*= end of March
SOURCE: Standard & Poor's *Statistical Service: Security Price Index Record*, various issues. Reprinted by permission.

whole consisted of widely varying performance over the various industries covered by Standard & Poor's.

Over the 31-year period of 1943−1973, the electrical equipment industry did well, rising to 28 times the base number, while the entertainment industry was only 3.4 times the base. By 1983, the alcoholic beverages industry was only eight times its original base, while electrical equipment was 52 times higher.

An examination of the entire time period, 1941−43 through March 2000, shows that the entertainment industry increased more than 700-fold while the electrical equipment industry did almost as well at about 650 times the base. Meanwhile, the auto industry was only about 50 times the base. Notice the dramatic difference in the alcoholic beverages industry and the soft drink beverages industry over the period ending in both 1995 and March 2000.

The lower half of Table 14-1 shows selected and matched Standard & Poor's Industry Stock Price indexes for the years 1982, 1986, 1989, and 1995 and March 2000 (based on 1941 − 1943 = 10). Therefore, Table 14-1 provides both a 58-year-plus picture of industry performance (from 1941−43), which approximates the maximum investing lifetime of many individuals, and a look at how much change can occur in shorter periods of time such as three (1986−1989), four (1982−1986), seven (1982−1989), 13 (1982−1995), and roughly 18 (1982−2000) years.

Tremendous differences existed for industries in the 1980s, and between periods in the 1980s and 2000. Notice how money center banks did nothing between 1982 and 1986, but then almost doubled and redoubled through 1995, and almost redoubled again by March 2000. Broadcast media performed in an incredibly strong manner over the entire period from 1982 to 1995, but the change from 1995 to March 2000 is astounding. Retail stores, having declined from 1989 to 1995, almost tripled from 1995 to March 2000.

The lesson to be learned from Table 14-1 is simple.

✓ Industry analysis pays because industries perform very differently over longer periods of time and portfolio performance will be significantly affected by the particular industries represented in investor portfolios, particularly for buy-and-hold investors.

Finally, let's note that Warren Buffett, arguably the best-known investor in the United States, seeks to identify "excellent" businesses based in part on the prospects for that industry.

Checking Your Understanding

1. How important is industry analysis to investors?
2. What has been the major change in the U.S. economy in the last 30 or 40 years as far as industries are concerned?

INDUSTRY PERFORMANCE OVER SHORTER PERIODS

What about shorter periods of time, and recent data? Does the same principle hold true—that industries perform very differently?

Let's consider S&P's GICS classification system, and analyze a recent five-year period that includes the recession of 2001 and the market declines during 2000–2002. As noted previously, there are 10 broad sectors in this new classification system, and these are shown in Table 14-2 along with two industries in the Information Technology sector. The base for these new S&P industry classifications is December 30, 1994 = 100. Table 14-2 shows annual rates of change over this five-year period.

Table 14-2 Performance of Sectors and Industries Using S&P 's GSIC Classification System. Data end November 2005.

	Annual Rate of Change
Consumer Discretionary	2.61%
Consumer Staples	0.97
Energy	10.25
Financials	3.17
Health Care	−3.79
Industrials	0.52
Information Technology	−8.63
Communications Equipment	−22.58
Internet Software and Services	20.77
Materials	9.64
Telecommunication Services	−10.43
Utilities	−4.36

SOURCE: S&P Sector Scoreboard, Industry Performance, *The Outlook*, December 7, 2005, p. 12. Reprinted by permission of Standard & Poor's, a division of the McGraw-Hill Co., copyright © 2005.

As we can see, these sectors performed quite differently over this five-year period, with the Energy sector performing approximately 20 times better than the Industrial sector in terms of annual rate of change. Meanwhile, the Health Care, Information Technology, Telecommunications Services and Utilities sectors had negative annual rates of price change.

Now consider the two industries shown within the information technology sector, and notice how differently they performed over this five-year period. While communications equipment experienced a −22.6 percent annual rate of change, Internet software and services was growing at almost a +21 percent annual rate. For the year 2004, communications equipment has a positive annual rate of change, 2.77 percent, but Internet software and services experienced an incredible 66.8 percent annual rate of change.

✓ Over shorter periods of time, such as a year or a few years, sectors and industries within sectors exhibit widely varying performance.

HOW ONE INDUSTRY CAN HAVE A MAJOR IMPACT ON INVESTORS—THE TELECOM INDUSTRY

Let's consider an example of an industry moving into and out of favor with investors in a very dramatic manner. The telecommunications sector was one of the great growth stories of the late 1990s. Telecom was deregulated in 1996. Predictions of how quickly Internet traffic would grow proliferated. One of the major contributing factors to what happened to the telecom industry is the huge amount of money that poured into the industry after it took off. When stock prices were rising so rapidly in the late 1990s with the tech stock boom, it was easy for the industry to raise large amounts of capital by borrowing.

Figure 14-1 shows the rise of the telecom index in 1998 and 1999, which was very strong. Many of the companies in this industry were market favorites, such as Global Crossing, WorldCom, Qwest, and so forth.

Amazingly, after only a couple of years of the telecom industry being regarded as a superstar industry, investors realized that the need for communications and bandwidth services could not grow at the rates that had been predicted. Meanwhile, the crushing debt loads

Figure 14-1

DJ Telecommunications Index, 1998 Through Mid-2002.

Source: BigCharts, Inc.

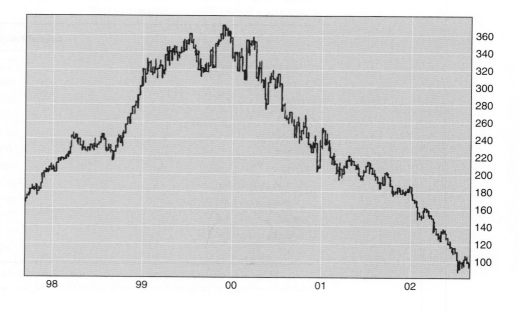

these companies had assumed were catching up with them, as was the recession in the economy that started in 2001. Telecom collapsed, and in all likelihood, was the greatest bursting of a bubble in one sector in history in terms of total dollars lost. One estimate is that investors in the telecommunications industry had lost $2 trillion by mid-2002.

Figure 14-1 tells the rest of the story, and it was ugly. The downward spiral of telecom companies seemed to be nonstop, and there were plenty of bankruptcies and accounting scandals by 2002.

CROSS-SECTIONAL VOLATILITY HAS INCREASED

Finally, consider another indication that paying attention to the relative performance of industries and sectors is important. A study by the Frank Russell Company measures "cross-sectional volatility," or the variation in returns across various sectors of the market. Sectors here refer to such groups of companies as utilities, retail companies, financial companies, and so forth. By examining the variations in returns among the different sectors on a month by month basis, some judgment about cross-sectional volatility can be made.

The Russell study found that cross-sectional volatility began to rise in the mid-1990s, and even after some decline in 2000 and 2001, it was twice what it was in 1995. Obviously, what happened in the technology sector contributed to this volatility. But the study found that even ignoring the tech sector, cross-sectional volatility has increased significantly.

✓ An increase in cross-sectional volatility across sectors enhances the importance of sector/industry analysis. Any ability to distinguish between the top and bottom performers should pay off.

Analyzing Sectors/Industries

Sectors and industries, as well as the market and companies, are analyzed through the study of a wide range of data, including sales, earnings, dividends, capital structure, product lines, regulations, innovations, and so on. Such analysis requires considerable expertise and is usually performed by industry analysts employed by brokerage firms and other institutional investors.

A useful first step is to analyze industries in terms of their stage in the life cycle. The idea is to assess the general health and current position of the industry. A second step involves a qualitative analysis of industry characteristics designed to assist investors in assessing the future prospects for an industry. Each of these steps is examined in turn.

THE INDUSTRY LIFE CYCLE

Many observers believe that industries evolve through at least four stages: the pioneering stage, the expansion stage, the stabilization stage, and the deceleration in growth and/or decline stage. There is an obvious parallel in this idea to human development. The concept of an **industry life cycle** could apply to industries or product lines within industries. The industry life cycle concept is depicted in Figure 14-2, and each stage is discussed in the following section.

Industry Life Cycle The stages of an industry's evolution from pioneering to stabilization and decline

Pioneering Stage In the pioneering stage, rapid growth in demand occurs. Although a number of companies within a growing industry will fail at this stage because they will not survive the competitive pressures, most experience rapid growth in sales and earnings, possibly at an increasing rate. The opportunities available may attract a number of companies, as well as venture capital. Considerable jockeying for position occurs as the companies battle each other for survival, with the weaker firms failing and dropping out.

Figure 14-2

The Industry Life Cycle.

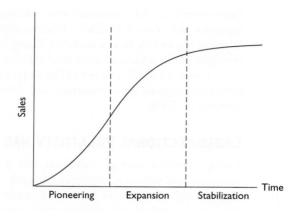

Investor risk in an unproven company is high, but so are expected returns if the company succeeds. Profit margins and profits are often small or negative. At the pioneering stage of an industry, it can be difficult for security analysts to identify the likely survivors, just when the ability to identify the future strong performers is most valuable. By the time it becomes apparent who the real winners are, their prices may have been bid up considerably beyond what they were in the earlier stages of development.

In the early 1980s, the microcomputer business—both hardware and software—offered a good example of companies in the pioneering stage. Given the explosion in expected demand for these products, many new firms entered the business, hoping to capture some share of the total market. By 1983, there were an estimated 150 manufacturers of home computers, a clearly unsustainable number over the longer run.

Expansion Stage   In the second stage of an industry's life cycle, the expansion stage, the survivors from the pioneering stage are identifiable. They continue to grow and to prosper, but the rate of growth is more moderate than before.

At the expansion stage of the cycle, industries are improving their products and perhaps lowering their prices. They are more stable and solid, and at this stage they often attract considerable investment funds. Investors are more willing to invest in these industries now that their potential has been demonstrated and the risk of failure has decreased.

Financial policies become firmly established at this stage. The capital base is widened and strengthened. Profit margins are very high. Dividends often become payable, further enhancing the attractiveness of these companies to a number of investors.

Stabilization Stage   Industries eventually evolve into the stabilization stage (sometimes referred to as the maturity stage), at which point the growth begins to moderate. This is probably the longest part of the industry life cycle. Products become more standardized and less innovative, the marketplace is full of competitors, and costs are stable rather than decreasing through efficiency moves, for example. Management's ability to control costs and produce operating efficiencies becomes very important in terms of affecting individual company profit margins.

Industries at this stage continue to move along but typically the industry growth rate matches the growth rate for the economy as a whole.

Declining Stage   An industry's sales growth can decline as new products are developed and shifts in demand occur. Think of the industry for home radios and black-and-white televisions. Some firms in an industry experiencing decline face significantly lower profits or even losses. Rates of return on invested capital will tend to be low.

Assessing the Industry Life Cycle   The industry life cycle classification of industry evolvement helps investors to assess the growth potential of different companies in an industry. Based on the stage of the industry, they can better assess the potential of different companies within an industry. This helps in estimating the return potential, and the risk, of companies.

There are limitations to this type of analysis. First, it is only a generalization, and investors must be careful not to attempt to categorize every industry, or all companies within a particular industry, into neat categories that may not apply. Second, even the general framework may not apply to some industries that are not categorized by many small companies struggling for survival. Finally, the bottom line in security analysis is stock prices, a function of the expected stream of benefits and the risk involved.

The industry life cycle tends to focus on sales and share of the market and investment in the industry. Although all of these factors are important to investors, they are not the final items of interest. Given these qualifications to industry life cycle analysis, what are the implications for investors?

The pioneering stage may offer the highest potential returns, but it also poses the greatest risk. Several companies in a particular industry will fail or do poorly. Such risk may be appropriate for some investors, but many will wish to avoid the risk inherent in this stage.

Investors interested primarily in capital gains should avoid the maturity stage. Companies at this stage may have relatively high dividend payouts because they have fewer growth prospects. These companies often offer continuing stability in earnings and dividend growth.

Clearly, companies in the fourth stage of the industrial life cycle, decline, are usually to be avoided. Investors should seek to spot industries in this stage and avoid them.

✔   It is the second stage, expansion, that is probably of most interest to investors. Industries that have survived the pioneering stage often offer good opportunities. Growth is rapid but orderly, an appealing characteristic to investors.

Checking Your Understanding

3. What does an increase in the cross-sectional volatility of various sectors mean to investors in general?

QUALITATIVE ASPECTS OF INDUSTRY ANALYSIS

The analyst or investor should consider several important qualitative factors that can characterize an industry. Knowing about these factors will help investors to analyze a particular industry and will aid in assessing its future prospects.

The Historical Performance   As we have learned, some industries perform well and others poorly over long periods of time. Although performance is not always consistent and predictable on the basis of the past, an industry's track record should not be ignored. In Table 14-1 we saw that the lead and zinc industry performed poorly in both 1950 and 1960 (in relation to the base of 1941–1943). It continued to do badly in 1973 and afterward. The broadcast media industry on the other hand, showed strength at each of the checkpoints since 1982.

Investors should consider the historical record of sales, earnings growth, and price performance. Although the past cannot simply be extrapolated into the future, it does provide some useful information.

Competition The nature of the competitive conditions existing in an industry can provide useful information in assessing its future. Is the industry protected from the entrance of new competitors as a result of control of raw materials, prohibitive cost of building plants, the level of production needed to operate profitably, and so forth?

Michael Porter has written extensively on the issue of competitive strategy, which involves the search for a competitive position in an industry.[4] The intensity of competition in an industry determines that industry's ability to sustain above-average returns. This intensity is not a matter of luck, but a reflection of underlying factors that determine the strength of five basic competitive factors:

1. Threat of new entrants
2. Bargaining power of buyers
3. Rivalry between existing competitors
4. Threat of substitute products or services
5. Bargaining power of suppliers

Because the strength of these five factors varies across industries (and can change over time), industries vary from the standpoint of inherent profitability.

The five competitive forces determine industry profitability because these influence the components of return on investment. The strength of each of these factors is a function of industry structure. Investors must analyze industry structure to assess the strength of the five competitive forces, which in turn determine industry profitability.

✓ The important point of the Porter analysis is that industry profitability is a function of industry structure.

Government Effects Government regulations and actions can have significant effects on industries. The investor must attempt to assess the results of these effects or, at the very least, be well aware that they exist and may continue.

Consider the breakup of AT&T as of January 1, 1984. This one action has changed the telecommunications industry permanently, and perhaps others as well. As a second example, the deregulating of the financial services industries resulted in banks and savings and loans competing more directly with each other, offering consumers many of the same services. Such an action has to affect the relative performance of these two industries as well as some of their other competitors, such as the brokerage industry (which can now also offer similar services in many respects).

Structural Changes A fourth factor to consider is the structural changes that occur in the economy. As the United States continues to move from an industrial society to an information-communications society, major industries will be affected. New industries with tremendous potential are, and will be, emerging, whereas some traditional industries, such as steel, may never recover to their former positions.

Structural shifts can occur even within relatively new industries. For example, in the early 1980s the microcomputer industry was a young, dynamic industry with numerous competitors, some of whom enjoyed phenomenal success in a short time. The introduction of microcomputers by IBM in 1982, however, forever changed that industry. Other hardware

---

[4] See Michael E. Porter, "Industry Structure and Competitive Strategy: Keys to Profitability," *Financial Analysts Journal* (July–August 1980), pp. 30–41. See also Michael Porter, *Competitive Advantage: Creating and Sustaining Superior Performance* (New York: Free Press, 1985).

manufacturers sought to be compatible with IBM's personal computer, and suppliers rushed to supply items such as software, printers, and additional memory boards. IBM's decision to enter this market significantly affected virtually every part of the industry.

Using Sector/Industry Analysis As An Investor

ASSESS THE BUSINESS CYCLE

A useful procedure for investors to assess industry prospects is to analyze industries by their operating ability in relation to the economy as a whole. That is, some industries perform poorly during a recession, whereas others are able to weather it reasonably well. Some industries move closely with the business cycle, outperforming the average industry in good times and under-performing it in bad times. Investors, in analyzing industries, should be aware of these relationships.

Growth Industries Industries with expected earnings growth significantly above the average of all industries

Most investors have heard of, and are usually seeking, growth companies. With **growth industries**, earnings are expected to be significantly above the average of all industries, and such growth may occur regardless of setbacks in the economy. Clearly, one of the primary goals of fundamental security analysis is to identify the growth industries of the near and far future.

Cyclical Industries Industries most affected, both up and down, by the business cycle

Cyclical industries are most volatile—they do unusually well when the economy prospers and are likely to be hurt more when the economy falters. Durable goods are a good example of the products involved in cyclical industries. Autos, refrigerators, and heavy equipment, for example, may be avidly sought when times are good, but such purchases may be postponed during a recession, because consumers can often make do with the old units.[5]

Cyclicals are said to be "bought to be sold." Investors low, relative to the historical record, and P/Es are high. This seems counterintuitive to many investors, but the rationale is that earnings are severely depressed in a recession and therefore the P/E is high, and this may occur shortly before earnings turn around.

Defensive Industries Industries least affected by recessions and economic adversity

At the opposite end of the scale are the **defensive industries**, which are least affected by recessions and economic adversity. Food has long been considered such an industry. People must eat, and they continue to drink beer, eat frozen yogurt, and so on, regardless of the economy. Public utilities might also be considered a defensive industry.

Interest-sensitive industries are particularly sensitive to expectations about changes in interest rates. The financial services, banking, and real estate industries are obvious examples of interest-sensitive industries. Another is the building industry.

If the economy is heading into a recession, cyclical industries are likely to be affected more than other industries, whereas defensive industries are the least likely to be affected.

Investments Intuition

Clearly, business cycle analysis for industries is a logical and worthwhile part of fundamental security analysis. Industries have varying sensitivities to the business conditions and interest rate expectations at any given time, and the smart investor will think carefully about these factors.

---

[5] Countercyclical industries also exist, actually moving opposite to the prevailing economic trend. The gold mining industry is said to follow this pattern.

REVIEW INVESTMENT ADVISORY SERVICES ABOUT INDUSTRIES

It is important for the investor to know what the current thinking is about sector and industry prospects. The quickest and easiest way to do this is to consult independent, trusted advisory services that have the resources to analyze industry prospects on an ongoing basis.

One of the most convenient and useful sources of information about industries is *The Value Line Investment Survey*, which ranks approximately 98 industry groupings based on its own classifications. Investors can quickly see which industries are expected to perform well over the year ahead, and which are not.

Example 14-4 Would it surprise you to learn that in early 2012 the homebuilding industry was ranked next to last out of all industries ranked by *The Value Line Investment Survey*? Probably not, given what everyone knows about the real estate market and the large inventory of empty houses. However, you probably would have been surprised to learn that railroads ranked fifth, and automotive eleventh.

SECTOR ROTATION

Numerous investors use sector analysis in their investing strategy. The premise here is simple—companies within the same industry group are generally affected by the same market and economic conditions. Therefore, if an investor can spot important developments in the sector or industry quickly enough, appropriate portfolio changes can be made to attempt to profit from these insights.

Institutional investors such as mutual funds analyze industry groupings carefully in order to determine which are losing momentum, and which are gaining. When a sector trend is spotted, these investors rotate into the favorable sector and out of a sector losing favor with investors. The strategy at the beginning of these events is to invest in the likely best-performing companies in the sector. When these companies rise in price and appear to be fully valued, secondary companies are identified and invested in. Ultimately, the entire sector becomes fairly valued or overvalued, or economic conditions for the sector become less favorable, and money rotates out of this sector and into a new one.

Individual investors can utilize sector rotation for industries and avoid analyzing individual companies. If, for example, the technology industry is ranked highly for one-year ahead performance, an investor can buy a sector fund offered by one of the mutual fund companies. For example, Fidelity Investments offers a large number of sector funds. It has six different funds in the Information Technology sector. Or an investor can buy an ETF. For example, the well-known SPDRs offers nine different sector ETFs covering such sectors as energy, health care, and technology.

EVALUATING FUTURE INDUSTRY PROSPECTS

Picking Industries for Next Year   To determine industry performance for shorter periods of time (e.g., one year), investors should ask themselves the following question: Given the current and prospective economic situation, which industries are likely to show improving earnings? In many respects, this is the key question for industry security analysis. Investors can turn to I/B/E/S, which compiles institutional brokerage earnings estimates, for security analyst estimates of earnings for various industries, which are revised during the year.

Given the importance of earnings, and the availability of earnings estimates for industries and companies, are investors able to make relatively easy investment choices? The answer is no, because earnings estimates are notoriously inaccurate. Of course, investors must also consider the likely P/E ratios for industries. Which industries are likely to show improving P/E ratios?

Other questions to consider are the likely direction of interest rates and which industries would be most affected by a significant change in interest rates? A change in interest rates, other things being equal, leads to a change in the discount rate (and a change in the multiplier). Which industries are likely to be most affected by possible future political events, such as a new administration, renewed inflation, new technology, an increase in defense spending, and so on?

As with all security analysis, we can use several procedures in analyzing industries. Much of this process is common sense. For example, if you can reasonably forecast a declining number of competitors in an industry, it stands to reason that, other things being equal, the remaining firms will be more profitable.

Assessing Longer-Term Prospects To forecast industry performance over the longer run, investors should ask the following questions:

1. Which sectors and industries are likely candidates for growth and prosperity over, say, the next decade?
2. Which sectors and industries appear likely to have difficulties as the United States continues to change to an information-collecting-and-processing economy with a significant service component?

Concepts in Action

One Way Investors Can Use Published Information Involving Industries

Standard & Poor's *Outlook*, a weekly publication available by subscription and in many libraries, periodically reports on the performance of an "Industry Momentum Portfolio." A buy recommendation results when an industry has been in the top 10 percent of all industry changes monitored (index value) over the preceding 12 months. (Note that this procedure involves relative strength, a technique discussed in Chapter 16.) The company in that industry with the highest S&P STARS rating (up to 5 stars) is selected to represent that industry. An industry can be removed when its relative 12-month performance is below the top 30 percent of all industries covered. This portfolio is updated on the last trading day of each month. According to Standard & Poor's, this portfolio has substantially outperformed the S&P 500 Index.

Summary

- Sector/industry analysis is the second of three steps in a top-down framework of fundamental security analysis, following economy/market analysis but preceding individual company analysis. The objective is to identify those sectors/industries that will perform best in the future in terms of returns to stockholders.

- Is sector/industry analysis valuable? Yes, because over the long run some sectors and industries perform much better than others.

- Industry performance is not consistent; past price performance does not always predict future price performance. Particularly over shorter periods such as one or two years, industry performance rankings may completely reverse themselves.

- Although the term industry at first seems self-explanatory, industry definitions and classifications are not straightforward, and the trend toward diversification of activities over the years has blurred the lines even more.

- North American Industry Classification System (NAICS) uses a production-oriented conceptual framework; therefore, companies are classified into industries based on the activity in which they are primarily engaged. Basically, companies that do similar things in similar ways are classified together.

▶ A number of investment information services, such as Standard & Poor's and Value Line, use their own industry classifications.

▶ To analyze industries, a useful first step is to examine their stage in the life cycle, which in its simplest form consists of the pioneering, expansion, maturity, and decline stages. Most investors will usually be interested in the expansion stage, in which growth is rapid and risk is tolerable.

▶ One industry analysis approach is business cycle analysis. Industries perform differently at various stages in the business cycle.

▶ Another approach involves a qualitative analysis of important factors affecting industries.

▶ A third approach that investors can use is sector rotation. By identifying sectors that are expected to perform well, individual company analysis can be avoided. ETFs and specialized mutual funds called sector funds can be used to implement this approach.

▶ Investors interested in evaluating future industry prospects have a wide range of data available for their use. These data can be used for a detailed, in-depth analysis of industries using standard security analysis techniques for examining recent ratings of industry performance or for ranking likely industry performance.

Questions

14-1 Why is it difficult to classify industries?

14-2 Why is the NAICS coding system said to be superior to the SIC codes?

14-3 Is sector/industry analysis valuable?

14-4 Name some industries that you would expect to perform well in the next five years and in the next 10 to 15 years.

14-5 What are the stages in the life cycle for an industry? Can you think of other stages to add?

14-6 Name an industry that currently is in each of the three life cycle stages.

14-7 In which stage of the life cycle do investors face the highest risk of losing a substantial part of the investment?

14-8 Which types of industries are the most sensitive to the business cycle? the least sensitive?

14-9 Explain how aggregate market analysis can be important in analyzing industries in relation to the business cycle.

14-10 Name the five competitive forces identified by Porter.

14-11 The important point of the Porter analysis is that industry structure is a function of industry profitability. Agree or disagree with this statement.

14-12 Explain the concept used in valuing industries.

14-13 What sources of information would be useful to an investor doing a detailed industry analysis?

14-14 Explain how Figure 14-1 might be useful to an investor doing industry analysis.

Checking Your Understanding

14-1 Being in the "right" industries over long periods of time has clearly paid off for investors. Substantial differences exist in the performance of sectors/industries over time. That said, predicting which industries will perform well in the future remains a difficult task.

14-2   Perhaps the biggest change in the economy in terms of industries is the trend toward globalization. For example, the auto industry is now a worldwide industry, with Toyota as important a manufacturer as GM or Ford. Consumers don't have to rely on a Nokia cell phone when they can just as easily purchase a Samsung or Motorola.

14-3   An increase in the cross-sectional variability of sectors/industries increases the value of sector/industry analysis because the differences between the good performers and the poor performers will widen.

chapter 15

Company Analysis

The last step in your bid to understand how investors go about doing fundamental security analysis is to consider individual companies. You knew from the outset of your quest to gain some investing knowledge that you will want to own some individual stocks regardless of whether you also plan to hold index funds and ETFs. After all, you have heard several stories about individuals who owned stocks that doubled, tripled, or did even better. And what little you have heard when investors or the media discuss stocks has often involved earnings, so you figure this must be important. Finally, you wish to be able to understand what all the fuss is about when it comes to earnings guidance, earnings surprises, and earnings disappointments. While this is a little more challenging, you can easily become comfortable with these concepts.

As we learned in Chapter 11, most investors following an active approach to investing are stock selectors. Everyone wants to hold stocks that will perform well over time, and many investors are searching for the next Apple, Google, Amazon.

Once economy/market analysis has indicated a favorable time to invest in common stocks and sector/industry analysis has been performed to find those sectors and industries that are expected to perform well in the future, it remains for the investor to choose promising companies within those sectors and industries. The last step in *top-down* fundamental analysis, therefore, is to analyze individual companies. Investors need to have a good understanding of those factors that affect security returns.

AFTER READING THIS CHAPTER YOU WILL BE ABLE TO:

▶ Understand the role of accounting data in financial analysis.

▶ Use a company's financial statements for security analysis purposes.

▶ Recognize the impact of earnings announcements and surprises on stock prices.

▶ Better understand how P/E ratios fit into security analysis.

Fundamental Analysis

Fundamental analysis at the company level involves analyzing basic financial variables in order to estimate the company's intrinsic value. These variables include sales, profit margins, depreciation, the tax rate, sources of financing, asset utilization, and other factors. Additional analysis could involve the firm's competitive position in its industry, labor relations, technological changes, management, foreign competition, and so on.

✓ One end result of fundamental analysis at the company level is a good understanding of a company's financial variables and its potential, culminating in a calculation of its intrinsic value.

As discussed in Chapter 10, investors could use the dividend discount model to estimate intrinsic value. Alternatively, they can use an earnings multiplier model, based on a forecast of next year's EPS and what is thought to be an appropriate P/E ratio.

We concentrate on earnings and P/E ratios because this is what investors typically use, and what most investment advisory services typically discuss when analyzing stocks.[1] Despite the uproar about accounting scandals several years ago, EPS is still the major variable of interest to a majority of investors. Furthermore, the close correlation between earnings changes and stock-price changes is well documented. As Jeremy Siegel states in his book, *Stocks for the Long Run*, "stock values are based on corporate earnings."[2]

✓ Future profitability is the most fundamental factor affecting stock prices; therefore, EPS and stock prices are closely related.

The Accounting Aspects of Earnings

If investors are to focus on a company's earnings per share (EPS), a critical variable in security analysis, they should understand the various uses of the word "earnings," how EPS is determined, and what it represents. For investors, an EPS figure is typically the bottom line—the item of major interest—in a company's financial statements. Furthermore, they must understand the components of EPS before they can attempt to forecast it—and earnings forecasts remain a major building-block of stock valuation.

THE FINANCIAL STATEMENTS

Financial Statements The principal published financial data about a company, primarily the balance sheet and income statement

Investors rely heavily on the **financial statements** of a corporation, which provide the major financial data about companies. To illustrate the use of financial statements in doing company analysis, we examine the financial statements for the Coca-Cola Company, a famous company with a brand name known worldwide and a company that epitomizes the global nature of business in today's world. Coca-Cola, the soft drink, is available in more than 200 countries.

---

[1] As noted in Chapter 10, many investors use relative valuation techniques, comparing a company's P/E ratio, P/B ratio, and/or P/S to various benchmarks in order to assess the relative value of the company. Using these techniques, it is not necessary to make a point estimate of intrinsic value. Instead, investors are simply trying to determine if a stock is reasonably valued, overvalued or undervalued without being too precise about the absolute amount. For many investors, this is an effective method of analysis.

[2] Siegel's book is a well-known discussion of how common stocks have performed in the past. See Jeremy Siegel, *Stocks for the Long Run*, McGraw-Hill, 5th edition, 2012.

Balance Sheet A summary of a company's assets, liabilities, and owner's equity at a specific point in time

The Balance Sheet

The **balance sheet** shows the portfolio of assets for a corporation, as well as its liabilities and owner's equity, at one point in time. The amounts at which items are carried on the balance sheet are dictated by accounting conventions. Cash is the actual dollar amount, whereas marketable securities could be at cost or market value. Stockholders' equity and the fixed assets are on a book value basis.

The balance sheet for Coca-Cola, shown in Exhibit 15-1, is for the year 2010. The asset side is divided into *Current Assets, Investments,* and *Other Assets,* as well as Property, Plant, and Equipment, *Trademarks, Goodwill* and *Other Intangible Assets.* Coca-Cola's net property, plant, and equipment are approximately two-thirds of its current assets, whereas in the case of General Motors, for example, the fixed assets exceed the current assets. Coca-Cola is also unusual in the large amount of investments and other long-term assets carried.

The right-hand side of the balance sheet is divided between *Current Liabilities* (payable within one year), *Long-Term Debt, Other Liabilities, Deferred Income Taxes,* and *Shareholders' Equity.* For 2010 Coca-Cola had $18.5 billion of current liabilities, $14 billion in long-term debt, and $31 billion in shareholders' equity, plus approximately $9.1 billion in *Other Liabilities and Deferred Income Taxes.*

The shareholders' equity includes 2.308 billion weighted average shares of stock outstanding as of year-end 2010 (out of 5.6 billion authorized), with a par value of $0.25, $10 billion of additional paid-in capital, and a substantial amount of retained earnings, $49 billion. The retained earnings item does not represent "spendable" funds for a company; rather, it designates that part of previous earnings not paid out as dividends. Note the large amount of *treasury stock* held, representing shares of Coca-Cola being held by the company itself. This amount reduces the original stockholders' equity substantially, an unusually large event compared to most companies.

It is important for investors to carefully analyze a company's balance sheet.[3] Investors wish to know which companies are undergoing true growth, as opposed to companies that are enhancing their performance by using a lot of debt they may be unable to service. In the latter years of the 1990s, numerous companies used large amounts of debt to improve their performance. Following the severe stock market downturn in 2000–2002, investors became much more concerned about both the amount of debt shown on the balance sheet as well as the amount of cash available to survive difficult periods. These issues became critical in the financial crisis of 2008.

The Income Statement

Income Statement An accounting of a company's income and expenses over a specified period of time

This statement is used more frequently by investors, not only to assess current management performance but also as a guide to the company's future profitability. The **income statement** represents a company's financial flows for a particular period, usually one year. Exhibit 15-2 shows the Consolidated Statements of Income for Coca-Cola for 2010.

The key item for investors on the income statement is the after-tax net income, which, divided by the number of common shares outstanding, produces earnings per share. Earnings from continuing operations typically are used to judge the company's success and are almost always the earnings reported in the financial press. Nonrecurring earnings, such as net extraordinary items that arise from unusual and infrequently occurring transactions, are separated from income from continuing operations.

---

[3] Several financial ratios that can be calculated from balance sheet data are useful in assessing the company's financial strength (e.g., the current ratio, a measure of liquidity, or the debt-to-total-assets ratio, a measure of leverage). These ratios are part of the standard ratio analysis which is often performed by managers, creditors, stockholders, and other interested groups, and are covered in most financial management texts and courses. Some of these ratios are demonstrated later in the analysis.

EXHIBIT 15-1

The Balance Sheet for Coca-Cola, 2010

Assets

Cash and Short Term Investments	11,337.0
Total Receivables, Net	4,430.0
Total Inventory	2,650.0
Prepaid Expenses	3,162.0
Other Current Assets, Total	0.0
Total Current Assets	**21,579.0**
Property/Plant/Equipment, Total — Net	14,727.0
Goodwill, Net	11,665.0
Intangibles, Net	15,244.0
Long Term Investments	7,585.0
Note Receivable — Long Term	0.0
Other Long Term Assets, Total	2,121.0
Other Assets, Total	0.0
Total Assets	**72,921.0**
Liabilities and Shareholders' Equity	
Accounts Payable	1,887.0
Payable/Accrued	0.0
Accrued Expenses	6,972.0
Notes Payable/Short Term Debt	8,100.0
Current Port. of LT Debt/Capital Leases	1,276.0
Other Current Liabilities, Total	273.0
Total Current Liabilities	**18,508.0**
Total Long Term Debt	14,041.0
Deferred Income Tax	4,261.0
Minority Interest	314.0
Other Liabilities, Total	4,794.0
Total Liabilities	**41,918.0**
Redeemable Preferred Stock	0.0
Preferred Stock — Non Redeemable, Net	0.0
Common Stock	880.0
Additional Paid-In Capital	10,057.0
Retained Earnings (Accumulated Deficit)	49,278.0
Treasury Stock — Common	-27,762.0
ESOP Debt Guarantee	0.0
Unrealized Gain (Loss)	0.0
Other Equity, Total	-1,450.0
Total Equity	**31,003.0**
Total Liabilities & Shareholders' Equity	**72,921.0**

EXHIBIT 15-2

The Income Statement for Coca-Cola, 2010

Total Revenue	**35,119.0**
Cost of Revenue	12,693.0
Gross Profit	**22,426.0**
Selling, General, Administrative Expenses, Total	7,199.0
Research & Development	0.0
Depreciation/Amortization	0.0
Interest Expense (Income), Net Operating	0.0
Unusual Expense (Income)	559.0
Other Operating Expenses, Total	6,219.0
Operating Income	**8,449.0**
Interest Income (Expense), Net Non-Operating	0.0
Gain (Loss) on Sale of Assets	0.0
Other, Net	5,185.0
Income Before Tax	**14,243.0**
Income Tax — Total	2,384.0
Income After Tax	**11,859.0**
Minority Interest	-50.0
Equity In Affiliates	0.0
U.S. GAAP Adjustment	0.0
Net Income Before Extra. Items	**11,809.0**
Total Extraordinary Items	0.0
Net Income	**11,809.0**

Exhibit 15-2 clearly illustrates the "flow" in an income statement. Starting with revenues (total net sales), the cost of goods sold is deducted to obtain Gross Profit. Subtraction of selling, administrative, and general expenses results in "Operating Income," which for Coca-Cola in 2010 was $8.449 billion. Operating income is then typically adjusted by subtracting the interest expense, which generally is an important item for large companies because interest is tax-deductible. It is zero for Coke for 2010. In addition, in Coca-Cola's case, other income must be added to Operating Income.

These adjustments to operating income produce "income before tax." Subtracting out income taxes results in "income after tax." After a small adjustment, we arrive at net income before extraordinary items. This is the same as net income, since there are no extraordinary items.

Dividing net income by the *average* shares outstanding produces EPS for 2010 of $5.12. Dividends per share were $1.76; therefore, the payout ratio was 34 percent in 2010.

Any charge to earnings because of an accounting change is important to investors in trying to understand earnings. Investors seek to determine the "true" earning power of a company because ultimately they attempt to forecast future earnings. The difference caused by accounting adjustments (often called nonrecurring gains or losses and extraordinary items) can be quite large for some companies in some years. In general, investors should rely on income before adjustments in trying to gauge true earning power.

The Cash-Flow Statement   The third financial statement of a company is the **cash-flow statement,** which incorporates elements of both the balance sheet and income statement as well as other items. It is designed to track the flow of cash through the firm. It consists of three parts:

- ◻ Cash from operating activities
- ◻ Cash from investing activities
- ◻ Cash from financing activities

The cash flow statement can help investors examine the quality of the earnings. For example, if inventories are rising more quickly than sales, this can be a sign of trouble—demand may be softening. If a company is cutting back on its capital expenditures, this could signal problems down the road. If accounts receivable are rising at a rate greater than sales are increasing, a company may be having trouble collecting money owed to it. If accounts payable are rising too quickly, a company may be conserving cash by delaying payments to suppliers, a potential sign of trouble for the company.

Example 15-1

Motorola's financial statements showed that net cash used for inventories went from $678 million to $2.3 billion in one year, clearly a warning sign that investors should investigate.

Earnings that are not accompanied by increases in cash flows are referred to as accruals. Investors should be wary of companies with high or increasing accruals, because these are companies whose earnings are not accompanied by cash.

One item of potential importance that investors should examine in the Statement of Cash Flows is the writeoff, supposedly a one-time charge. These writeoffs may be labeled as such items as "charges for reorganization of businesses" or "one-time charge for strategic actions." Some firms make multiple writeoffs over a period of years. Investors should determine what these writeoffs are for, and if they signal operating problems for the company.

Example 15-2

K-Mart wrote off about three-quarters of a billion dollars over a five-year period, primarily for store closings and inventory write-downs.

Exhibit 15-3 shows the Consolidated Statement of Cash Flows for Coca-Cola. Coke's cash flow appears to be quite healthy for 2010. The company started with a strong "cash and cash equivalents" balance at the beginning of the period, and generated substantial "net cash provided by operating activities" for the year. Therefore, after investing activities and financing activities Coke ended the year with a sizeable cash balance.

Because of the accounting problems with earnings, investors have increasingly been looking to cash flow from operations. However, companies are aware of this trend, and they now are massaging the cash flow data more and more. By using the prevailing GAAP procedures, cash can be made to look better than it actually is. By focusing more efforts on cash to make it look good for investors, companies may underinvest in plant and equipment.

EXHIBIT 15-3

Consolidated Statement of Cash Flows

Net Income/Starting Line	11,859.0
Depreciation/Depletion	1,443.0
Amortization	0.0
Deferred Taxes	617.0
Non-Cash Items	−4,757.0
Changes in Working Capital	370.0
Cash from Operating Activities	**9,532.0**
Capital Expenditures	−2,215.0
Other Investing Cash Flow Items, Total	−2,190.0
Cash from Investing Activities	**−4,405.0**
Financing Cash Flow Items	50.0
Total Cash Dividends Paid	−4,068.0
Issuance (Retirement) of Stock, Net	−1,295.0
Issuance (Retirement) of Debt, Net	1,848.0
Cash from Financing Activities	**−3,465.0**
Foreign Exchange Effects	−166.0
Net Change in Cash	**1,496.0**
Net Cash — Beginning Balance	7,021.0
Net Cash — Ending Balance	8,517.0

Some Practical Advice

Given the accounting problems in today's world, many investors have concluded that cash flows should assume primary importance, because they cannot easily be manipulated. While cash flows are increasingly important to investors, they need to be aware that companies can and do manipulate cash flows. WorldCom, in their summer 2002 announcement that rocked the investment community, admitted that it inflated not only earnings but cash flows as well for several quarters. Investors should pay careful attention to the first part of the Cash Flow Statement, "Cash Flows From Operations." For example, did the company sell their accounts receivable, which will immediately pump up operating cash flows? Are some expenses being capitalized, thereby creating an asset to be written off gradually (this is what WorldCom allegedly did)? Are the proceeds from securities trading being counted as part of operating cash? Investors need to look for issues such as these if they are to avoid being fooled on the cash flow statement.[4]

Certifying the Statements   The earnings shown on an income statement are derived on the basis of **Generally Accepted Accounting Principles (GAAP)**. The company adheres to a standard set of rules developed by the accounting profession on the basis of

Generally Accepted Accounting Principles (GAAP) Financial reporting requirements establishing the rules for producing financial statements

---

[4] This discussion is based on Ann Tergesen, "Cash-Flow Hocus-Pocus," *Business Week*, July 15, 2002, pp. 130, 132.

historical costs, which can be measured objectively. An auditor from an independent accounting firm certifies that the earnings have been derived according to accounting standards in a statement labeled the "auditor's report."

Example 15-3   In certifying Coca-Cola's financial statements, the accounting firm preparing the statements makes a statement such as, "In our opinion, the financial statements referred to above present fairly, in all material respects, the consolidated financial position of the Coca-Cola Company and subsidiaries."

The Financial Accounting Standards Board (FASB), which succeeded the Accounting Principles Board of the American Institute of Certified Public Accountants in 1972, currently formulates accounting and reporting standards.

✓ The auditor's report does *not* guarantee the accuracy or the quality of the earnings in an absolute sense; rather, it only attests that the statements are a *fair presentation* of the company's financial position for a particular period.

Investments Intuition

Does Repetition Lead to Complacency?

Public firms are required by law to have an independent audit each year. A survey found that 30 percent of the 1,000 leading U.S. companies have used the same auditor for the last 25 years, and 11 percent have used the same audit firm every year for 50 years.[5] This raises the question of whether the audit firms can become too complacent or intertwined with the company being audited. After all, they have a vested interest in maintaining an established relationship, and they may look less critically at their own work from previous years. Some are now calling for public companies to rotate their accounting firms every few years.

Reading the Footnotes   Regardless of how closely a company adheres to good accounting practices, and how carefully the auditors do their job, investors still need to examine the "Notes to the Financial Statements," or footnotes, if they are to really understand the company's financial situation. The footnotes are located after the consolidated financial statements, and can be found in 10-K and 10-Q Reports. They often provide important information about the accounting methods being used, any ongoing litigation, how revenue is recognized, and so forth.

✓ The footnotes can help an investor better understand the quality of the reported earnings.

[5] This information is based on Jason Zweig, "One Cure for Accounting Shenanigans," *The Wall Street Journal*, January 14–15, 2012, p. B1.

Ethics in Investing

Accounting for Options

As of fiscal 2006, U.S. companies must deduct the cost of options from their earnings. Technology companies argued for years that such an action would hit them particularly hard.

Some companies sought to lower the costs of options expenses even as the rules changed. This is possible because the cost of options must be estimated, leaving room for interpretation. Companies that charged off more in options expenses before the new rule took effect could experience lower option costs in the future, thereby boosting earnings.[6]

One way to lower costs is to change the formula used to assign a value to the options. For example, options on stocks with greater volatility are worth more. Therefore, if a company lowers the volatility estimate, they lower the cost of the option. According to one estimate, in 2004 some 200 companies cut the estimate of volatility by an average of 17 percent.

Hundreds of companies resorted to accelerated vesting, forcing options to vest in 2005 rather than in future years. Through 2005, companies could disclose option expenses in much less obvious ways than would be true starting in 2006 (for example, disclosing the information in footnotes to the financial statements).

While actions by companies such as those outlined are legal, are they really ethical? After all, a primary argument for the existence of options is that giving employees options that vest in the future is conducive to retaining valuable employees who will work hard to realize those future values. Accelerated vesting would appear to be at odds with that argument.

Checking Your Understanding

1. Given that the financial statements of a company are certified by its auditors, why should investors be concerned about the information contained therein?
2. Assume a company has completed its financial statements for the year and that the income statement shows a large loss. Does this mean the company will not have adequate cash to pay its bills?

THE PROBLEMS WITH EPS

Reported
Earnings GAAP earnings, the "official" earnings of a company as reported to stockholders and the SEC

Reported Earnings   Earnings derived under GAAP and reported on the income statement are known as **reported earnings**. Although the financial statements are derived on the basis of GAAP and are certified in an auditor's report, problems exist with reported earnings. The basic problem, simply stated, is that reported EPS for a company (i.e., accounting EPS) is the product of a set of complex GAAP principles, which are subject to subjective judgment.

✓   EPS is not a precise figure that is readily comparable over time, and the EPS figures for different companies often are not comparable to each other. Alternative accounting principles can be, and are, used to prepare the financial statements.

Many of the items in the balance sheet and income statement can be accounted for in more than one way. Given the number of items that constitutes the financial statements, the possible number of acceptable (i.e., that conform to GAAPs) combinations that could be used

---

[6] This discussion is based on Jane Sasseen, "Stock Options: Old Game, New Tricks," *Business Week*, pp. 34, 36, December 19, 2005.

is large. A company could produce several legal and permissible EPS figures, depending solely on the accounting principles used. The question that investors must try to answer is, "Which EPS best represents the 'true' position of a company?"

Because reported EPS is a function of the many alternative GAAPs in use, it is extremely difficult, if not impossible, for the "true" performance of a company to be reflected consistently in one figure. Since each company is different, is it reasonable to expect one accounting system to capture the true performance of all companies? With the business world so complex, one can make a case for the necessity of alternative treatments of the same item or process, such as inventories or depreciation.

Investments Intuition

Given the difficulties involved, and the alternative accounting treatments, investors must remember that reported EPS is not the precise figure that it first appears to be. Unless adjustments are made, the EPS of different companies may not be comparable on either a time series or a cross-sectional basis.

Accountants are caught in the middle—between investors, who want a clean, clear-cut EPS figure, and company management, which wants to present the financial statements in the most favorable light. After all, management hires the accounting firm, and, subject to certain guidelines, management can change accounting firms. As long as the company follows GAAPs, the accounting firm may find it difficult to resist management pressure to use particular principles. At some point, an accounting firm may resign as a company's auditor as a result of the problems and pressures that can arise.

The FASB faces conflicting demands when it formulates or changes accounting principles because various interest groups want items accounted for in specific ways. The end result has been that the "standards" issued by the FASB were often compromises that did not fully resolve the particular issue; in some cases, they created additional complications.

Example 15-4   FAS 133, which is concerned with financial derivatives and hedging, was issued in June 1998. The standard and its supporting documents now total more than 800 pages. There have been over 200 restatements related to derivatives accounting.

Should the FASB falter in its job, or investors actively demand more action in the way of "tighter" accounting rules, as they did in 2002 in the face of several company accounting scandals, the government can intervene and issue its own rulings. The Securities and Exchange Commission has the authority to do so because corporations must file detailed financial data with it. The SEC has issued some definitions of acceptable accounting practices over the years, thereby acting as a prod to the accounting groups to continue their progress.

The Sarbanes–Oxley Act (SOX) passed by Congress in 2002 was largely in response to the accounting scandals involving Enron, WorldCom, Global Crossing, and other companies that blew up financially in spectacular fashion. It represented a very significant change in federal securities laws and demonstrates that such changes do occur from time to time. Concisely stated, this act mandated that companies (starting in 2004) must submit an annual report to the SEC outlining the effectiveness of their internal accounting controls and provide increased financial disclosures. Substantial civil and criminal penalties can be imposed for noncompliance.

HAS THE SITUATION IMPROVED?

Given the accounting controversies in 2002—the collapse of Enron, the charges against the accounting firm of Arthur Anderson, the questioning of numerous companies as to their accounting practices—and the passage of the Sarbanes–Oxley Act, one might logically assume that the accounting situation has improved. And indeed companies are spending much more on accounting compliance as a result of Sarbanes–Oxley (SOX).

In general, SOX has had a significant impact in improving the corporate situation. CEOs no longer handpick the Board of Directors for the company. Boards have real power, and directors have significant responsibilities. Many boards have separate committees for important functions such as audit and compensation. Although more remains to be done, the corporate governance situation is better today than it was in the past.

Financial reports today remain difficult to understand. Estimates by companies are rampant, and the assumptions and rationales behind these estimates may be difficult to uncover.

The Quality of Earnings   Some EPS figures are said to be "better" than others in the sense that they have been derived using more conservative principles. In other words, they are of higher quality. Smart investors recognize that earnings numbers are often the result of subjective judgments, compromises, and changes in accounting practices.

Quality assessments are typically difficult to make and require considerable expertise in accounting and financial analysis. When it is difficult to assess the quality of a company's earnings, one alternative is to look at the first item on the Income Statement, which is Sales, or Revenues. Is revenue growth slowing or increasing? Unless (legitimate) revenues are growing over time, earnings will suffer, and the quality may be suspect. Because of the importance of

Example 15-5   For a take on earnings quality, consider J.P. Morgan Chase's 2011 third quarter earnings report. This company raised its quarterly earnings by almost $2 billion by using a debit valuation adjustment, allowed under accounting rules. Essentially, the market value of J. P. Morgan's debt declined, which allowed the company to report this "gain" as a profit. Some investors view such gains as poor earnings quality, and Moody's Investors Services removes it when evaluating a bank's earnings.

earnings quality today, more and more information sources are focusing on it.

One of the primary reasons that earnings quality has been called into doubt in recent years is the proliferation of various EPS numbers. We examine this issue next.

What About Operating Earnings?   As if the problems with reported earnings and confusing GAAPs are not bad enough, companies may use another measure of EPS, with varying levels of subjectivity. Let's examine the differences in earnings numbers in today's world.[7]

---

[7] A third form of earnings is EBITDA, or Earnings before interest, taxes, depreciation and amortization, which is sometimes called operating profit. This number essentially is revenue minus operating expenses, and leaves out interest expense and depreciation and amortization.

■ Net Income is also called Reported Earnings. It is the "official" audited number on the income statement derived under GAAP, and filed with the SEC. It is earnings from continuing operations before extraordinary items.

Operating Earnings Net income adjusted for nonrecurring or unusual items

■ **Operating Earnings** (also referred to as "Pro Forma Earnings" and "Street earnings") takes net income and adjusts it by leaving out non-recurring or unusual items (sometimes called special items). Examples include restructuring charges and gains on the sale of assets. Operating Earnings are not audited, and there are no rules on how to calculate it, leaving companies free to do as they choose.[8]

Example 15-6 Varian, Inc. reported that "Adjusted operating earnings decreased 6.0 percent to $25.9 million in the third quarter of fiscal year 2008. Adjusted operating profit margin was 10.6 percent for the same quarter. On a GAAP basis, operating earnings were $17.4 million and operating profit margin was 7.1 percent in the third quarter of fiscal year 2008."

While the concept of (operating) pro forma earnings has been around for a number of years, its use really became muddled with the explosion of dotcom companies in the late 1990s. Since many of them had no earnings in the conventional sense, they tried to report to shareholders in the most favorable light by omitting various expenses.

✓ The problem with operating (pro forma) earnings is that each company can choose its own method of calculation.

Therefore, comparisons between companies are difficult. Remember, a key issue for investors is what did the company earn? If companies can decide for themselves what numbers to report, how will investors determine what the earnings really are? *Business Week* concluded in one article: "There are almost as many measures of earnings today as there are companies. Pro forma has destroyed any serious means of measuring performance across industries and the broad economy."[9]

Some observers believe that companies often try to manipulate investor perceptions about their performance. Management may attempt to soften the blow from bad reported earnings numbers through the use of Street earnings. Companies reporting Street earnings tend to have a greater incidence of losses. Interestingly, some research indicates that investors react more to Street earnings and that such earnings are the highest quality in terms of predictive ability and information content.

A recent study of GAAP earnings vs. Street earnings, involving 29,000 annual observations and 100,000 quarterly observations for a 10-year period, found the following.[10]

1. For firms with GAAP profits, there is little difference between the two numbers.
2. Firms with GAAP losses report significantly higher Street earnings.

---

[8] It is important to distinguish Operating Earnings from the Operating Income discussed earlier. The latter number is a part of the income statement.

[9] See "A Good Idea About Earnings," *Business Week*, May 27, 2002, p. 114.

[10] Stephen J. Ciccone, "GAAP vs. Street Earnings: Making Earnings Look Higher and Smoother," Working Paper Series, University of New Hampshire.

What Investors Can Do Investors face difficult problems with accounting issues, and as a popular press article has stated, "Numbers Do Lie."[11] In 2001 and 2002 the accounting issue really came home to investors with the collapse of Enron and other companies, and the questioning of the accounting procedures of numerous other well-known companies.

The best advice for most investors is to go ahead and use the reported EPS, because it is all that is normally available, and the majority of investors will also have to rely on this figure. Investors should, however, be aware of the potential problems involved in EPS and should constantly keep in mind its nature and derivation.

Example 15-7 As the economy approaches a recession, many analysts believe that companies use aggressive accounting techniques in order to report larger earnings. Such techniques include recognizing revenues before they are actually received or delaying the recording of expenses.

Investors can take a few precautions and additional steps to help themselves when trying to interpret financial statements and earnings reports, including:[12]

- Examine the 10-K statement for additional information. This report must be filed with the SEC and is available online.
- Read the footnotes to the financial statements. Information not disclosed in the body of the discussion of the financial statements is often contained in the footnotes because the company must disclose the information somewhere.
- Obtain other opinions, found in sources such as *The Value Line Investment Survey*, which has its own independent analysts.
- Study the cash flow statement. Firms need cash to operate, and it is more difficult to disguise problems where cash is concerned. Investors should calculate free cash flow, defined as the money left after all bills are paid and dividend payments are made.[13] Starting with cash from operating activities on the statement of cash flows, subtract capital expenditures and cash dividends. Fast-growing companies may have negative cash flows for several years and still be okay, but mature companies with negative cash flows are often a sign of problems.

Investors who find U.S. accounting comparisons difficult have often had additional problems when analyzing foreign companies because of different accounting practices. In general, the United States generally was considered to have the strictest standards, based on a set of detailed rules. Foreign companies wanting to list securities on U.S. exchanges had to adopt U.S. standards up until 2007, when the SEC allowed foreign companies to file U.S. financial statements using the international standards.

The International Accounting Standards Board has formulated International Financial Reporting Standards (IFRS) that are now used by most companies worldwide. GAAP is based on a set of detailed rules while IFRS seeks to apply guiding principles of accounting, allowing more flexibility and judgment.

In August 2008 the SEC proposed a plan whereby all U.S. companies would switch to IFRS by 2014, essentially replacing U.S. Generally Accepted Accounting Principles. As of March 2012, the SEC had not made a final recommendation on the changeover. However, the belief was that IFRS would be incorporated into U.S. accounting rules.

---

[11] See Steven T. Goldberg, "Numbers Do Lie," *Kiplinger's Personal Finance*, April 2002, p. 54.

[12] Goldberg, p. 54.

[13] Free cash flow is discussed in more detail in Chapter 10.

Checking Your Understanding

3. The Sarbanes–Oxley Act has ended most of the fraudulent accounting practices recently publicized, and ensures that investors can fully understand the financial statements and their implications. Agree or disagree, and explain your reasoning.
4. In reporting their results, companies may choose to emphasize operating earnings. Why would they do this?

Using the Financial Statements to Analyze a Company's ROE and EPS

We can use a company's financial statements to analyze a company's Return on Equity and EPS, as illustrated below. This process involves standard ratio analysis and is based on what is called the Du Pont analysis, or Du Pont identity. It is important to note that different definitions of EPS are available, such as Basic EPS Excluding Extraordinary Items, Basic EPS Including Extraordinary Items, Diluted EPS Excluding Extraordinary Items, Diluted EPS Including Extraordinary Items, Comparable EPS, and so on. This analysis focuses on Basic EPS Excluding Extraordinary Items.

ANALYZING RETURN ON ASSETS (ROA)

ROA is an important measure of a company's profitability. It is a product of two factors.

$$\text{Net income margin} = \text{Net income}/\text{Sales}$$
$$\text{Turnover} = \text{Sales}/\text{Total assets}$$

The first ratio affecting ROA, the net income margin, measures the company's earning power on its sales (revenues). How much net return is realized from sales, given all costs? Obviously, the more a company earns per dollar of sales, the better.

Asset turnover is a measure of efficiency. Given some amount of total assets, how much in sales can be generated? The more sales per dollar of assets, where each dollar of assets has to be financed with a source of funds bearing a cost, the better. A company may have some assets that are unproductive, thereby adversely affecting its efficiency.

ROA can be expressed as the product of these two components:

$$\text{ROA} = \frac{\text{Net income}}{\text{Sales}} \times \frac{\text{Sales}}{\text{Total assets}}$$

$$\text{ROA} = \text{net income margin} \times \text{turnover}$$

(15-1)

Example 15-8   Using the data for Coca-Cola for 2010 from Exhibits 15-1 and 15-2 (all numbers in millions):[14]

$$\text{Net income}/\text{Sales} = \$11{,}809/\$35{,}119 = 0.336$$
$$\text{Sales}/\text{Total assets} = \$35{,}119/\$72{,}921 = .482$$
$$\text{ROA} = 0.336 \times 0.482 = 0.1381 = 16.20\%$$

---

[14] This analysis is based on Coca-Cola's 10K filing with the SEC.

Return on Assets (ROA) The accounting rate of return on a firm's assets

Return On Assets (ROA) is a fundamental measure of company profitability, reflecting how effectively and efficiently its assets are used. Obviously, the higher the net income for a given amount of assets, the better the return. For Coca-Cola, the return on assets is 16.20 percent. The ROA can be improved by increasing the net income more than the assets (in percentage terms) or by using the existing assets even more efficiently.

One of the determinants of ROA may be able to offset poor performance in the other. The net income margin may be low, but the company may be able to generate more sales per dollar of assets than comparable companies. Conversely, poor turnover may be partially offset by high net profitability. In either case, analysts and investors are trying to understand how these factors are impacting Coke, and how they are likely to do so in the future.

ROA is an important measure of a company's profitability. Ultimately, however, investors want to know what the accounting rate of return to shareholders is. ROA plays an important role in this calculation. We now focus on the return to shareholders by examining the return on equity.

ANALYZING RETURN ON EQUITY (ROE)

Return on Equity (ROE) The accounting rate of return on stockholders equity

An important variable in security analysis is the **Return On Equity (ROE)** because it is a key component in determining earnings growth and dividend growth. Analysts and investors seek to decompose the ROE into its critical components in order both to identify adverse impacts on ROE and to help predict future trends in ROE. There are several ways to show this analysis involving more detail or less detail, but the end result is a breakdown of the components that make up the ROE.

In order to understand and calculate ROE, the effects of leverage must be considered. The leverage ratio measures how the firm finances its assets.[15] Basically, firms can finance with either debt or equity. Debt, though a cheaper source of financing, is a riskier method, because of the fixed interest payments that must be systematically repaid on time to avoid bankruptcy. Leverage can magnify the returns to the stockholders (favorable leverage) or diminish them (unfavorable leverage). Thus, any given ROA can be magnified into a higher ROE by the judicious use of debt financing. The converse, however, applies; injudicious use of debt can lower the ROE below the ROA.

✓   For a typical profitable company using debt to finance part of its assets, ROE will be larger than ROA.

Investments Intuition

What this analysis does not show is the impact of leverage on a company's risk. Remember that in this analysis we are examining only the determinants of EPS. However, as we know from our discussion of valuation, two factors, EPS and a P/E ratio, are required to determine value. An increase in leverage may increase the riskiness of the company more than enough to offset the increased EPS, thereby lowering the company's value. *Investors must always consider both dimensions of the value of a stock, the return side and the risk side—in other words, EPS alone does not determine stock price.*

---

[15] Leverage can be measured in several ways, such as the ratio of total debt to total assets or the ratio of debt to equity.

To more easily capture the effects of leverage we use an equity multiplier rather than a debt percentage. This measure reflects the amount of assets financed per dollar of stockholders' equity. For example, a ratio of two would indicate that $2 in assets is being financed by $1 in stockholders' equity.

$$\text{Leverage} = \text{Total assets/Stockholders'equity}$$

Example 15-9   In 2010, for Coca-Cola, dividing total assets by equity produces an equity multiplier of 2.35, which is used as the measure of leverage. In effect, $1 of stockholders' equity was financing $2.35 of assets.

To calculate ROE, we relate ROA and leverage as shown in Equation 15-2:

$$\text{ROE} = \text{ROA} \times \text{Leverage} \tag{15-2}$$

Example 15-10   Combining these two factors, ROA and leverage, for Coca-Cola produces the following ROE:

$$\text{ROE} = 16.20\% \times 2.35 = 38.07\%$$

For Coca-Cola at the end of 2010, the use of leverage more than doubled the return on assets (ROA) to produce a return on equity of approximately 38.1 percent.

THE ACCOUNTING DETERMINANTS OF EPS

On a company level, EPS is the culmination of several important factors going on within the company. Accounting variables can be used to examine these determining factors by analyzing key financial ratios. Analysts examine the components of EPS in order to try to determine whether a company's profitability is increasing or decreasing, and why.

The following accounting identity establishes the relationship between EPS and ROE:

$$\text{EPS} = \text{ROE} \times \text{Book value per share} \tag{15-3}$$

where ROE is the return on equity and book value per share is the accounting value of the stockholders' equity on a per share basis.

Using Coca-Cola's data from Exhibits 15-1 and 15-2, we would calculate ROE and book value per share for 2010 as follows (numbers in millions):

$$\text{ROE} = \frac{\text{Net income after taxes}}{\text{Stockholder's equity}} = \frac{\$11,809}{\$31,003} = .381$$

$$\text{Book value per share} = \frac{\text{Stockholders' equity}}{\text{Shares outstanding}} = \frac{\$31,003}{2,308} = \$13.43$$

Example 15-11   In Coca-Cola's case the ROE was .381, and the book value was $13.43 per share. Therefore:

$$\text{EPS} = .381 \times \$13.43 = \$5.12$$

For 2010, using basic net income per share, there were 2,308 million shares outstanding. Dividing net income of $11,809 million by that number, we get $5.12 as the basic net income per share (EPS).

ESTIMATING THE INTERNAL (SUSTAINABLE) GROWTH RATE

Sustainable Growth Rate A firm's expected growth rate in earnings and dividends, often calculated as the product of ROE and the retention rate of earnings

An important part of company analysis is the determination of a **sustainable growth rate** in earnings and dividends. This rate represents the rate at which a company can grow from internal sources, without the issuance of additional securities. It provides a benchmark for assessing a company's actual or target growth rate. A company growing faster than the sustainable growth rate will have to issue additional securities which could dilute the existing equity (in the case of stock issues) or increase the financial risk (in the case of debt issues).

How is the sustainable growth rate calculated? The internal or sustainable growth rate, typically designated as g, is the product of the retention rate—which is calculated as 1.0 minus the dividend payout ratio—and ROE, as shown in Equation 15-4:

$$g = br = (1 - \text{Payout ratio}) \times \text{ROE} \qquad \text{(15-4)}$$

Equation 15-4 is one of the primary calculations in fundamental security analysis and is often used by security analysts.

Example 15-12

For 2010 Coca-Cola's dividend payout ratio is .343 percent . The retention rate is [1.0 − .343] = .657. ROE = .381. The internal growth rate estimate using this equation based on 2010 data as reported in the 10K statement is, therefore, .657 × .381 = .250 or 25 percent.

A problem associated with using a particular year to estimate the sustainable growth rate is that the year used may not be a "normal" year. Basing a projection on one year's results can result in a faulty estimate; this is particularly true for companies in cyclical industries. While analysts may calculate g by using data for a particular year, longer-term relationships are more meaningful. Therefore, average data are probably more appropriate.[16]

A good example of this issue is the calculation for Coca-Cola above based on 2010 10K data. The company had a very large gain because of restructuring that could not be expected to reoccur. This gain increased EPS, lowered the payout ratio, and raised the retention rate. The end result was an estimate of g of 25 percent, which is not realistic and should not be used. Average data would be more appropriate. For example, *The Value Line Investment Survey* calculates a five- and 10-year growth rate in past dividends of about 10 percent, and this would be a better choice to use as a g in this case.

The internal growth rate estimate produced by Equation 15-6 is reliable only if a company's profitability as measured by ROE remains in balance. If, for example, the ROE for a company grows significantly in the future or declines significantly, the actual growth rate will turn out to be quite different than the sustainable growth rate estimate produced by Equation 15-5.

---

[16] Technically, g is defined as the expected growth rate in dividends. However, the dividend growth rate is clearly influenced by the earnings growth rate. Although dividend and earnings growth rates can diverge in the short run, such differences would not be expected to continue for long periods of time. The standard assumption in security analysis is that g represents the growth rate for both dividends and earnings.

What matters is the future expected growth rate, not the actual historical growth rate. If investors expect the growth rate to be different in the future, they should use the expected growth rate and not simply the calculation based on current data. Payout ratios for most companies vary over time, but reasonable estimates can often be obtained for a particular company using an average of recent years. Estimating future ROE is more challenging.

Concepts in Action

Estimating Growth Rates

Many investors get carried away when estimating the expected growth rate in EPS for companies they find attractive. The natural tendency of most investors is to rely on historical rates because that is the only objective evidence available. An immediate problem when one does this is deciding what recent period of time might be relevant in forecasting the future, particularly when significant differences exist. For example, if a company had a 15 percent annual growth rate in EPS for the last 10 years, but a 25 percent annual growth rate for the last five years, which (if either) is more likely to be indicative of the future?

When we think about it logically, there must be limits to how fast a company can continue to grow, whether in price or EPS. Clearly, some can grow extremely fast for a few years. But an analysis of companies shows that the outer limit for truly long-term growth is about 20 percent. And most companies do not achieve this growth rate over long periods of time.

Consider this—Cisco, one of the great growth stocks of modern times, grew almost 100 percent a year for a 10-year period through March 2000.[17] Fantastic growth, and it produced great performance for Cisco's stockholders. However, had Cisco grown at that rate for the next 10 years, it would have had a total market value of $520 trillion in 2010. This would have far exceeded the combined value of every stock in the world in 2000. Simply put, very rapid growth cannot last indefinitely. It is not possible for a wide variety of reasons—competition, regulation, changes in technology, poor management decisions, and so forth.

Or take a well-known and highly successful company like McDonald's. As of 2011, it's stock price was up 250 percent from 2004. The price doubled from 2007. As great a stock as McDonald's has been—and it has been a magnificent blue-chip company paying a nice dividend—can such growth rates continue? Only time will tell.

Checking Your Understanding

5. Assume a company uses no debt to finance its operations. What is the relationship between its ROA and its ROE?

6. Assume that a company's EPS is $3.00, and that it pays $1.00 in dividends. Its ROE is 18 percent. Calculate an estimate of the internal growth rate.

Earnings Estimates

Stock valuation is forward looking. The EPS that investors use to value stocks is the future (expected) EPS. In doing fundamental security analysis using EPS, an investor needs to (1) know how to obtain an earnings estimate, (2) consider the accuracy of any earnings estimate obtained, and (3) understand the role of earnings surprises in impacting stock prices. We consider each of these topics in turn.

---

[17] This example is based on Jason Zweig, "Murphy was an Investor," *Money*, July 2002, p. 62.

A FORECAST OF EPS

Security Analysts' Estimates of Earnings   As discussed in Chapter 11, among the most obvious sources of earnings estimates are security analysts, who make such forecasts as a part of their job. The consensus forecast is likely to be superior to the forecasts of individual analysts. Thus, security analysts' consensus estimates are a practical and useful proxy for the market's expectations about EPS. This number reflects the average EPS estimate. The number of analysts covering a particular company can vary widely, from one to 40 or more.

Earnings estimates for companies are available to individual investors.[18] Examples include the following:

- ❏ *The Value Line Investment Survey* forecasts quarterly earnings for several quarters ahead for each company covered.
- ❏ *Yahoo! Finance* provides analyst estimates for a company under the section titled "Analyst Coverage." The average, low and high estimates are shown, along with the number of analysts making estimates. Current and next quarter estimates are provided, along with current and next year.

Consensus Forecast Most likely EPS value expected by analysts

Several studies suggest that individual analysts are by and large undistinguishable in their ability to predict EPS. The practical implication of these findings is that, in general, investors should pay more attention to the **consensus forecast** or the average of several forecasts of EPS unless they have good reason to rely on a particular analyst (such as proven performance for a particular company).

THE ACCURACY OF EARNINGS FORECASTS

Even if investors accept the relative superiority of analysts' estimates, the fact remains that analysts often over- or underestimate the earnings that are actually realized. According to one study of almost 400 companies, analysts' estimates averaged 57 percent too high in the first month of a fiscal year, and the error was still an average 12 percent by year's end.

A study by Dreman and Berry covered approximately 500,000 brokerage analysts' forecasts for an 18-year period. Analysts were given every advantage in the study—for example, forecasts could be made in the same quarter as earnings were reported, and the forecasts could be changed up to two weeks before the end of the quarter. Nevertheless, the average annual error was 44 percent, and only 25 percent of consensus estimates came within plus or minus 5 percent of reported earnings. Furthermore, the error rate actually worsened over time.

Inaccurate earnings estimates can provide opportunities for investors. Analysts are frequently wrong, and if investors can make better estimates of earnings for particular companies, they can expect to profit from their astuteness.

EARNINGS SURPRISES

We have established that changes in earnings and stock prices are highly correlated. We have also discussed the necessity of estimating EPS and how such estimates can be obtained. What remains is to examine the role of expectations about earnings in selecting common stocks.

---

[18] The Institutional Brokers Estimate System (I/B/E/S) provides earnings estimates for institutional investors. The I/B/E/S database covers over 18,000 companies in 60 countries. It provides data to a discriminating client base of 2,000 of the world's top institutional money managers. Earnings estimates are available on a consensus basis and on an individual analyst basis.

The association between earnings and stock prices is more complicated than simply demonstrating a correlation (association) between earnings growth and stock-price changes. Elton, Gruber, and Gultekin found that investors could not earn excess returns by buying and selling stocks on the basis of the consensus estimate of earnings growth.[19] They also found that analysts tended to overestimate earnings for companies they expected would perform well and to underestimate for companies they expected would perform poorly.

Investors must form expectations about EPS, and these expectations will be incorporated into stock prices if markets are efficient. Although these expectations are often inaccurate, they play an important role in affecting stock prices. Malkiel and Cragg concluded years ago that in making accurate one-year predictions, "It is far more important to know what the market will think the growth rate of earnings will be next year rather than to know the (actual) realized long-term growth rate."[20]

As Latane and Jones pointed out, new information about a stock is unexpected information.[21] The important point about EPS in terms of stock prices is the difference between what the market (i.e., investors in general) was expecting the EPS to be and what the company actually reported. Unexpected information about earnings calls for a revision in investor probability beliefs about the future and therefore an adjustment in the price of the stock.

Earnings Surprises The difference between a firm's actual earnings and its expected earnings

To assess the impact of the surprise factor in EPS, Latane and Jones developed a model to express and use the **earnings surprise** factor in the quarterly EPS of companies. This standardized unexpected earnings (SUE) model was discussed in Chapter 12 as part of the market anomalies associated with the evidence concerning market efficiency.[22] Repeating from Chapter 12,

$$SUE = \frac{\text{Actual quarterly EPS} - \text{Forecast quarterly EPS}}{\text{Standardization variable}} \qquad (15\text{-}5)$$

The SUE concept is designed to capture the surprise element in the earnings just mentioned—in other words, the difference between what the market expects the company to earn and what it actually does earn. A favorable earnings surprise, in which the actual earnings exceed the market's expectation, should bring about an upward adjustment to the price of the stock as investors revise their probability beliefs about the company's earnings. Conversely, an unfavorable earnings surprise should lead to a downward adjustment in price; in effect, the market has been disappointed in its expectations.[23]

In conclusion, stock prices are affected not only by the level of and growth in earnings, but also by the market's expectations of earnings. Investors should be concerned with both the forecast for earnings and the difference between the actual earnings and the forecast—that is, the surprise. Therefore, fundamental analysis of earnings should include more than a forecast,

---

[19] See fn. 4.

[20] Malkiel and Cragg, "Expectations and the Structure of Share Prices," p. 616.

[21] H. Latane and C. Jones, "Standardized Unexpected Earnings—A Progress Report," *Journal of Finance*, Vol. 32 December 1977, pp. 1457–1465.

[22] This model is explained in Latane and Jones, "Standardized Unexpected Earnings," p. 1457. The standardization variable is the standard error of estimate for the estimating regression equation.

[23] Stocks can be categorized by SUEs that are divided into increments of 1.0. Thus, SUE classifications can range from all stocks with a SUE ; < −4.0 (category 1), all between −4.0 and −3.0 (category 2), and so on, up to the most positive category, all stocks with SUEs > 4.0 (category 10). The larger the SUE (either positive or negative), the greater the unexpected earnings, and, therefore, other things being equal, the larger the adjustment in the stock's return should be. Stocks with small SUEs (between +1.0 and −1.0) have little or no unexpected earnings and, therefore, should show little or no subsequent adjustment in stock return.

which is difficult enough; it should involve the role of the market's expectations about earnings.

What happens when the quarterly earnings are reported and the figures are below analysts' estimates? Obviously, the price is likely to drop quickly, and in some cases sharply. In a number of cases, the stock market is very unforgiving about negative earnings surprises.

Example 15-13   Lucent Technologies announced on two different occasions that earnings would be less than expected for a particular quarter. It also expressed doubt about the next fiscal year. Following the second announcement, the price declined more than 30 percent, and this was after the price had suffered earlier declines.

If the price does drop sharply following such an announcement, should an investor interested in owning the stock react quickly to take advantage of the price drop? Some studies suggest no. The initial shock is often followed by additional shocks.

Some Practical Advice

Earnings Surprises Don't Always Tell the Entire Story

As noted, investors react to the quarterly earnings reports of companies. However, they may also react to the revenue number as well as the EPS. Thus, EPS could be up for a quarter and meet analysts' expectations, but if revenues fall short of what was expected, the stock price may decline. This is particularly true if revenues have been in a decline for a few quarters.

EARNINGS GUIDANCE

Many companies have developed the practice of providing "guidance" on their forthcoming quarterly earnings announcements. Such guidance often comes to be expected by the market.

Example 15-14   In late 2011, Green Mountain Coffee Roasters announced that its revenues increased only "91 percent." The stock dropped almost 40 percent immediately. Why? The market's expectation was for revenues to increase approximately 100 percent, and the market had come to believe that Green Mountain would always deliver on its expectations.

A trend has started among some companies that may have a major impact on how information about earnings is formulated and distributed. Warren Buffet, among others, has argued that companies should not provide guidance. In December 2002, Coca-Cola announced that it will not provide quarterly or annual EPS guidance. The company stated that it would "continue to provide investors with perspectives on its value drivers, its strategic initiatives and those factors critical to understanding [Coca-Cola's] business and operating environment."

Some companies have refused over a long period to provide earnings guidance. Others have recently dropped the practice.

THE EARNINGS GAME

Investors need to realize that the process of estimating earnings, announcing earnings, and determining earnings surprises has become much more of a game, or managed process, over time. Furthermore, this game has changed over time. The way the "game" is now being played by many companies and analysts is as follows:

1. Analysts attempt to estimate what a particular company will earn each quarter.
2. A company may provide "guidance" as to what it thinks earnings will be. Companies may subsequently revise their guidance numbers lower in a series of steps and the analysts follow by lowering their estimates.
3. This "talking the forecast down" by the company ends with the analysts' prediction, the consensus forecast, slightly below where the actual number is likely to come out. The company now is likely to beat the forecast. This provides a positive earnings surprise.
4. In the past, a positive earnings surprise typically lead to a rise in the stock price. Now, however, positive earnings surprises have become too commonplace. Through the first quarter of 2011, almost 70 percent of the companies in the S&P 500 Index had shown positive earnings surprises for nine quarters in a row. This means that there is less impact in an earnings surprise than in the past. Investors who understand this game take this into account.
5. Investors sometimes have to contend with "whisper forecasts," which are unofficial earnings estimates that circulate among professional investors and traders before earnings are announced. Think of these whisper numbers as the analysts' true expectation as opposed to the published consensus number. Some studies suggest that these estimates are more accurate than are the consensus estimates which have been guided by the companies.

Obviously, investors must try to understand the current earnings game and the likely impact it will have on stock prices as a result of earnings surprises. Suffice it to say that it has become more complicated as investors try to figure out which forecast the actual earnings are expected to beat and which companies are reporting true earning surprises as opposed to managed earnings surprises.

Regulation FD (discussed in Chapter 1), which became effective in October 2000, requires companies to make public disclosure of important information to all investors at the same time. Numerous companies are now releasing corporate information to all investors simultaneously through Internet broadcasts.

USEFUL INFORMATION FOR INVESTORS ABOUT EARNINGS ESTIMATES

Summarizing our discussion about earnings forecasts, we can note the following useful information about the role, and use, of earnings forecasts in selecting common stocks:

1. Reported earnings are a key factor affecting stock prices; however, it is the surprise element in the reports that often moves stock prices. Surprises typically involve the difference between the consensus analyst forecast and the actual earnings.
2. There appears to be a lag in the adjustment of stock prices to earnings surprises. This has been documented in numerous studies.
3. Surprises may occur because analyst estimates are often off target. Alternatively, companies may guide analysts to a slightly lower number than actually expected, resulting in an earnings "surprise."
4. In recent years, positive earnings surprises have outnumbered negative earnings surprises by a ratio of three to one.
5. Since the early 1990s, on average a little over 60 percent of the companies in the S&P 500 Index report positive earnings surprises, many because of the "guidance game."
6. The size of the surprise appears to be important information, with large surprises leading to larger returns.

7. The best guidelines to surprises may be revisions in analyst estimates. If estimates are steadily being adjusted upward, a buy signal is indicated, and if the adjustments are downward, a sell signal is indicated.

8. Investors interested in buying stocks which report bad news and suffer a sharp decline may benefit by waiting a month or two. Chances are the stock will be cheaper after the initial sharp decline.

9. Investors have to take into account both the reported earnings, and any surprises arising from that, as well as forecasts of the next quarter (or year), which can result in a stock behaving differently from what one might expect.

Example 15-15 Apple Computer reported record first-quarter earnings in mid-January for one recent year. Apple earned 68 cents a share, up from 37 cents a share in the same period a year earlier. Nevertheless, its shares dropped 3.4 percent in after-hours trading. Why? Apple announced at the same time that its current quarter earnings would be less than Wall Street expectations.

SALES GROWTH—AN ALTERNATIVE TO EARNINGS

Given the accounting problems with earnings, and the difficulty in forecasting earnings, it is not surprising that investors look at other fundamental data when selecting stocks. This is particularly true with newer companies that may not have current EPS, or the expectation thereof for several years. Amazon.com is a clear example of this—given its lack of profitability, investors must evaluate other dimensions.

A key variable is obviously revenues, or sales. After all, a company cannot have earnings without reasonable revenues. Revenues not only lead to the accounting EPS for a company but also make possible the firm's cash which it uses to pay its bills and operate. Some of the major providers of earnings estimates also offer revenue estimates.

The P/E Ratio

The other half of the valuation framework in fundamental analysis is the price/earnings (P/E) ratio, or multiplier, as discussed in Chapter 10. In effect, the P/E ratio is a measure of the relative price of a stock. In a typical year, for example, investors may be willing to pay 40 or 50 times earnings for some companies but only six or seven times earnings for other companies. Why such a large difference? We will consider this question below after we clarify the various P/E ratios an investor may encounter.

WHICH P/E RATIO IS BEING USED?

When discussing the P/E ratio, it is important to remember that different P/E ratios can be calculated for the same stock at one point in time, including

- ❑ P/E based on last year's reported earnings
- ❑ P/E based on trailing 12-month earnings
- ❑ P/E based on this year's expected earnings
- ❑ P/E based on next year's expected earnings

Furthermore, the EPS could be reported EPS (based on GAAP), operating EPS, or the new core EPS being reported by Standard & Poor's Corporation. Assuming we limit ourselves to GAAP EPS, the differences in P/E ratios that investors encounter can still be substantial.

Example 15-16   In early 2012, Coke was trading at $69.

- Based on TTM (trailing 12-month earnings), the P/E was 18.7
- Based on expected earnings for 2012 (average estimate of analysts), the P/E was 16.9
- Based on expected earnings for 2012 (Value Line estimates), the P/E was 16.4

DETERMINANTS OF THE P/E RATIO

The P/E ratio is conceptually a function of three factors[24]:

$$P/E = \frac{D_1/E_1}{k - g} \qquad (15\text{-}6)$$

where

D_1/E_1 = the expected dividend payout ratio

k = the required rate of return for the stock

g = expected growth rate in dividends

Investors attempting to determine an appropriate P/E ratio for a particular stock should think in terms of these three factors and their likely changes.

- The higher the expected payout ratio, other things being equal, the higher the P/E ratio. However, "other things" are seldom equal. If the payout rises, the expected growth rate in earnings and dividends, *g*, will probably decline, thereby adversely affecting the P/E ratio. This decline occurs because less funds will be available for reinvestment in the business, thereby leading to a decline in the expected growth rate, *g*.
- The relationship between *k* and the P/E ratio is inverse: Other things being equal, as *k* rises, the P/E ratio declines; as *k* declines, the P/E ratio rises. Because the required rate of return is a discount rate, P/E ratios and discount rates move inversely to each other.
- P/E and *g* are directly related; the higher the *g*, other things being equal, the higher the P/E ratio.[25]

---

[24] In analyzing a particular P/E ratio, we first ask what model describes the expected growth rate for that company. Recent rapid growth and published estimates of strong expected future growth would lead investors not to use the constant-growth version of the dividend valuation model. Instead, we should evaluate the company by using a multiple-growth model. At some point, however, this growth can be expected to slow down to a more normal rate.

$$\frac{P}{E_{n+1}} = \frac{D_{n+1}/E_{n+1}}{k - g}$$

where *n* is the year that the abnormal growth ends.

[25] Harris suggests that a consensus forecast of earnings growth by analysts can be used successfully as a proxy for the dividend growth rate. Robert S. Harris, "Using Analysts' Growth Forecasts to Estimate Shareholder Required Rates of Return," *Financial Management* (Spring 1986), pp. 58–67.

WHY P/E RATIOS VARY AMONG COMPANIES

Stock prices reflect market expectations about earnings. Companies that the market believes will achieve higher earnings growth rates will tend to be priced higher on a P/E ratio basis than companies that are expected to show low earnings growth rates. When problems arise, however, the P/E ratio can change quickly. Consider this quote from *The Wall Street Journal*: "High-growth companies are complex machines. At the first sign of problems, investors begin prodding areas they had never looked into."[26]

✓ A primary factor in explaining P/E ratio differences among companies is investor expectations about the future growth of earnings. Variations in the rate of earnings growth will also influence the P/E.

It is important to remember the role of interest rates, which are inversely related to P/E ratios. When interest rates are declining, the largest impact is on the P/E ratios of reliable growth stocks. This is because most of their earnings will occur far out in the future, and can now be discounted at lower rates.

An analysis of P/E ratios at any observation point will show the wide variation that exists in this variable as some companies have high ratios while others have low ratios. For example, The *Value Line Investment Survey* presents a weekly ranking of the lowest and highest P/E stocks out of the more than 1,700 companies covered.

✓ At any point in time, the spread between the lowest P/Es and the highest P/Es for a large set of companies is typically large. Of course, P/Es for the same company change over time.

The forward P/E ratio has been linked to expected earnings growth and risk. Higher forward P/E ratios imply higher investors' expectations about the growth of future earnings. A problem here is that investors often overestimate the future growth in earnings. A recent study examines whether the initial valuation in the form of the forward P/E ratio is justified by the subsequent realization in earnings growth. The results from this study demonstrate that the highest of five forward P/E portfolios does have larger earnings growth rates than the lowest forward P/E portfolio over the next 10 years. However, additional analysis shows that the realized growth rate of the highest forward P/E portfolio falls short of investor expectations. The result of this is that the highest forward P/E portfolio actually underperforms the lowest forward P/E portfolio in the three years following the formation of the portfolios.[27]

Relative to the discussion above on the earnings game, investors must be increasingly concerned with the impact of managing earnings expectations on the P/E ratio. If a fast growing company is being conservative in guiding the estimates of its earnings, and it regularly reports earnings higher than the consensus, then the forward P/E ratio is actually lower than it appears to be based on the current consensus estimate of earnings. In other words, a company may appear to sell for 50 times next year's earnings, but this is based on an underestimate of next year's earnings because the consensus estimate has been guided to be below what actually occurs. For much of the 1990s, Dell fit this model, regularly reporting significantly larger earnings than the consensus estimate.

---

[26] John Jannarone, "Green Mountain's Landslide," *The Wall Street Journal*, November 11, 2011, p. C10.

[27] See Wan-Ting Wu, "The Forward P/E Ratio and Earnings Growth," (September 2007). AAA 2008 Financial Accounting and Reporting Section (FARS). Paper available at SSRN: http://ssrn.com/abstract=1014177.

THE PEG RATIO

PEG Ratio The P/E ratio divided by the short-term earnings growth rate.

Some investors divide the P/E ratio by the short-term earnings growth rate to obtain the **PEG ratio.**

$$\text{PEG ratio} = (P/E)/g \tag{15-7}$$

✓ The advantage of the PEG ratio is that it relates the P/E ratio to earnings growth rather than relying on the P/E ratio by itself.

According to Peter Lynch, a famous manager of the Magellan Fund when it enjoyed great success, the P/E ratio of a company that is fairly valued will equal its expected growth rate. Therefore, an indication of undervaluation could be a stock with a P/E less than its earning growth rate. However, a recent analysis suggests that for correctly valued firms, the PEG ratio should frequently exceed 1.0 (particularly when the cost of capital is low).[28] In mid-2008, the S&P's PEG was 1.3. Like most calculations of this type, the PEG ratio is only a rule of thumb. There are no assurances that one is paying too much or too little.

One problem with this calculation is that it relates a ratio to a percentage number. Another is that different earnings growth rates can be used to calculate it. For example, Standard & Poor's *Outlook* uses a three-year compound annual growth rate. Some use recent earnings growth rates while others use estimated earnings.

Fundamental Security Analysis in Practice

We have analyzed several important aspects of fundamental analysis as it is applied to individual companies. Obviously, such a process can be quite detailed, involving an analysis of a company's sales potential, competition, tax situation, cost projections, accounting practices, and so on. Nevertheless, regardless of detail and complexity, the underlying process is as described. Analysts and investors are seeking to estimate a company's earnings and P/E ratio and to determine whether the stock is undervalued (a buy) or overvalued (a sell).

In doing fundamental security analysis, investors need to use published and computerized data sources both to gather information and to provide calculations and estimates of future variables such as EPS. Exhibit 15-4 shows an excerpt from *The Value Line Investment Survey* for Coca-Cola.

---

[28] See Mark A. Trombley, "Understanding the PEG Ratio," *The Journal of Investing*, Vol. 17, No. 1, Spring 2008, pp. 22–26.

EXHIBIT 15-4

A Page from a Weekly Issue of "Ratings and Reports," *The Value Line Investment Survey*

COCA-COLA NYSE-KO	RECENT PRICE **46.03**	P/E RATIO **15.0** (Trailing: 15.4 / Median: 26.0)	RELATIVE P/E RATIO **1.28**	DIV'D YLD **3.4%**	VALUE LINE **1540**

TIMELINESS **2** Raised 10/31/08
SAFETY **1** New 7/27/90
TECHNICAL **4** Lowered 10/31/08
BETA .60 (1.00 = Market)

2011-13 PROJECTIONS

	Price	Gain	Ann'l Total Return
High	90	(+95%)	20%
Low	75	(+65%)	15%

BUSINESS: The Coca-Cola Company is the world's largest beverage company. It distributes major brands (Coca-Cola, diet Coke, Sprite, Barq's, Mr. PiBB, Fanta, Fresca, Dasani, Evian, Danone, Powerade, Minute Maid, and others) through bottlers around the world. Business outside North America accounted for 74% of net sales and 77% of operating profits in 2007. Coca-Cola Enterprises (CCE) is a 36%-owned soft drink bottler. Advertising expenses, 10% of revenues. Has approximately 90,500 employees; Berkshire Hathaway owns 8.6% of stock (3/08 Proxy). Chairman and Chief Executive Officer: E. Neville Isdell. Incorporated: Delaware. Address: One Coca-Cola Plaza, Atlanta, Georgia 30313. Telephone: 404-676-2121. Internet: www.coca-cola.com.

The Coca-Cola Company continues to show strength in an increasingly challenging domestic economy. It posted third quarter top- and bottom-line gains of 9% and 14%, respectively, in comparison to the same period last year. Although the company faces near-term headwinds, like many of its competitors, it seems poised to achieve full-year sales and share-net advances of about 13% and 19%, a strong showing given the current harsh domestic operating landscape. Even so, **International markets are aiding the beverage titan at this time.** In fact, it derived about 74% of its revenues from foreign sources last year, and this trend seems likely to continue for the balance of 2008. During the third quarter, growth regions such as China and India fueled unit case volume growth in the double-digit range, which softened the blow from the 2% volume decline experienced in the U.S. **Synergistic efforts will likely generate profits.** Coca-Cola and Coca-Cola Enterprises (a large bottler for KO), recently signed an agreement with Hansen Natural, maker of the popular *Monster* energy drink, to distribute Hansen's goods, initially in certain countries in Western Europe, the U.S., and Canada. Hansen is also free to negotiate distribution rights with other Coca-Cola bottlers. We believe this is a positive move for KO, as Hansen's *Monster* energy drink has outpaced its competitors in this beverage category and will complement KO's diverse drinks portfolio. It is also eyeing a Chinese juice company as an acquisition target that, if the deal goes through, can further enhance KO's profit potential.

Still, KO will have some short term issues, mainly from its bottlers. Because of rising input costs and escalating fuel prices, many bottlers have had to increase prices of their finished goods, an action that does not sit well with current cash-strapped consumers. **This timely stock has below-average appreciation potential for the 2011-2013 haul.** KO's strong product mix and vast consumer base augur well for growth, and our conservative estimates may well prove too modest for a company that has had a fair handle on the current domestic malaise.

Nira Maharaj   *October 31, 2008*

Company's Financial Strength	A++
Stock's Price Stability	100
Price Growth Persistence	15
Earnings Predictability	100

SOURCE: *The Value Line Investment Survey*, Summary of Advice and Index, February 7, 2012, p. 1423. Reproduced with the permission of Value Line Publishing, Inc.

The Value Line Investment Survey is the largest investment advisory service in the United States and is available in many libraries. As shown in Exhibit 15-4, a significant amount of information about a particular company can be reported on one page. This information can be very helpful in terms of estimates for EPS and in terms of a prediction (by *Value Line*) as to the timeliness of each stock for the coming year.

In modern investment analysis, the risk for a stock is related to its beta coefficient, as explained in Chapter 7. Beta reflects the relative systematic risk for a stock, or the risk that cannot be diversified away. The higher the beta coefficient, the higher the risk for an individual stock, and the higher the required rate of return. Beta measures the volatility of a stock's returns—its fluctuations in relation to the market.

Example 15-17

Assume that the beta for Coca-Cola is 1.10. Therefore, we know that Coca-Cola has slightly more relative systematic risk than the market as a whole. That is, on average, its price fluctuates more than the market. If, for example, the market is expected to rise 10 percent over the next year, investors could, on average, expect Coca-Cola to rise 11 percent based on its beta of 1.10. In a market decline, Coca-Cola would be expected to decline more, on average, than the market. If the market declined 10 percent, for example, Coca-Cola would be expected, on average, to decline in price by 11 percent.

Investments Intuition

It is extremely important in analyses such as these to remember that beta is a measure of volatility, indicating what can be expected to happen, on average, to a stock when the overall market rises or falls. In fact, Coca-Cola, or any other stock, will not perform in the predicted way every time. If it did, the risk would disappear. Investors can always find examples of stocks that, over some specific period of time, did not move as their beta indicated they would. This is not an indictment of the usefulness of beta as a measure of volatility; rather, it suggests that the beta relationship can only be expected to hold on the average.

In trying to understand and predict a company's return and risk, we need to remember that both are a function of two components. The systematic component is related to the return on the overall market. The other component is the unique part attributable to the company itself and not to the overall market. It is a function of the specific positive or negative factors that affect a company independent of the market.

It should come as no surprise that because security analysis always involves the uncertain future, mistakes will be made, and analysts will differ in their outlooks for a particular company. At any particular time some investors may think it is time to sell while others see a buying opportunity.

Concepts in Action

Sooner or Later, One or More Zombies Will Get You

Investors interested in selecting stocks should do the best company analysis they can. It is not easy, and it takes time. Regardless of one's diligence, however, the analysis will not always work out. Stocks will not perform as expected. In Wall Street terms, you will have some "dead money." Your investment will be "alive" and in play, but as far as helping your portfolio it will be dead—a zombie. In mid-2011, 30 percent of the S&P 100 Index, which focuses on large cap stocks, had a stock price that was less than it was 10 years earlier. This included some of the best-known stocks in the United States, such as Microsoft, Pfizer, and General Electric.

As we might expect, security analysis in the 21st century is often done differently from how it was done in the past. The reason for this change is not so much that we have a better understanding of the basis of security analysis because the models we have discussed earlier—value as a function of expected return and risk—remain the basis of security analysis today. Rather, the differences now have to do with the increasingly sophisticated use of personal computers to perform many calculations quickly and objectively. For example, a "neural network" is a computer program that attempts to imitate the brain in doing security analysis and choosing stocks. One such program examines 11 different variables for 2,000 companies, searching for patterns that might be profitable to exploit and that are too subtle for humans to detect.

Summary

▶ The analysis of individual companies, the last of three steps in fundamental security analysis, encompasses all the basic financial variables of the company, such as sales, management, and competition. It involves applying the valuation procedures explained in earlier chapters.

▶ Intrinsic value (a company's justified price) can be estimated using either a dividend valuation model or an earnings multiplier model. It is then compared to the current market price in order to determine whether the stock is undervalued or overvalued.

▶ An important first step in fundamental analysis is to understand the earnings per share (EPS) of companies. The financial statements can be used to understand the accounting basis of EPS.

▶ The balance sheet shows the assets and liabilities of a specific date, whereas the income statement shows the flows during a period for the items that determine net income. The cash flow statement shows the sources and uses of cash by a company.

▶ Although these statements are certified by the accounting profession, alternative accounting principles result in EPS figures that are not precise, readily comparable figures. EPS is the result of the interaction of several variables.

▶ Changes in earnings are directly related to changes in stock prices. To assess expected earnings, investors often consider the earnings growth rate, which is the product of ROE and the earnings retention rate.

▶ The lack of persistence in these growth rates may lead investors to consider EPS forecasts, which are available from analysts. Such forecasts are very much subject to error.

▶ The difference between actual and forecast EPS, or unexpected earnings, is important because of the role of the market's expectations about earnings. Standardized unexpected earnings (SUE) attempts to evaluate the unexpected portion of quarterly earnings.

▶ The price/earnings (P/E) ratio is the other half of the earnings multiplier model, indicating the amount per dollar of earnings investors are willing to pay for a stock. It represents the relative price of a stock, with some companies carrying high P/E ratios and others having low ones.

▶ The P/E ratio is influenced directly by investors' expectations of the future growth of earnings and the payout ratio, and inversely by the required rate of return.

▶ There are different P/E ratios in use at any time. Typical is the P/E based on the most recent 12-month earnings. A forward P/E involves estimated earnings for the next year.

▶ P/E ratios vary among companies primarily because of investors' expectations about the future growth of earnings. If investors lower their expectations, the price of the stock may drop while earnings remain constant or even rise.

▶ The PEG ratio relates the P/E for a company to its expected growth rate in earnings. Some consider a company to be fairly valued if its P/E ratio is equal to its expected growth in earnings.

Questions

15-1 What is meant by the intrinsic value of a stock?

15-2 How can a stock's intrinsic value be determined?

15-3 What are the limitations of using Equation 15-2 to determine intrinsic value?

15-4 What is meant by GAAP?

15-5 What problems do estimating accounting earnings present?

15-6 What does the auditor's report signify about the financial statements?

15-7 How do auditors and management relate to each other in determining the financial statements?

15-8 Explain the concept of earnings quality?

15-9 Outline, in words, the determination process for EPS.

15-10 Explain the role of financing in a company's EPS.

15-11 Assuming that a firm's return on assets exceeds its interest costs, why would it not boost ROE to the maximum through the use of debt financing since higher ROE leads to higher EPS?

15-12 How can the earnings growth rate be determined?

15-13 How well do earnings growth rates for individual companies persist across time?

15-14 How can investors obtain EPS forecasts? Which source is better?

15-15 What role do earnings expectations play in selecting stocks?

15-16 How can the unexpected component of EPS be used to select stocks?

15-17 Explain the relationship between SUE and fundamental security analysis.

15-18 Describe at least two variations in calculating a P/E ratio.

15-19 Using *The Value Line Investment Survey*, list the average annual P/E ratio for the following companies for the last five years: Apple Computer, Coca-Cola, Caterpillar, and Amazon. What conclusions can you draw from this analysis?

15-20 What are the variables that affect the P/E ratio? Is the effect direct or inverse for each component?

15-21 Holding everything else constant, what effect would the following have on a company's P/E ratio?
(a) An increase in the expected growth rate of earnings
(b) A decrease in the expected dividend payout
(c) An increase in the risk-free rate of return
(d) An increase in the risk premium
(e) A decrease in the required rate of return

15-22 Why would an investor want to know the beta coefficient for a particular company? How could this information be used?

15-23 Is beta the only determinant of a company's return?

15-24 Assume that Intel announces a 40 percent increase in EPS for its most recent quarter, and the stock price immediately declines 15 percent while the market as a whole is unchanged. How would you explain this?

15-25 What is the PEG ratio? Identify one information source where this ratio can be found for individual stocks.

Problems

15-1 Shao Electronics has net assets of $550 million and stockholder's equity of $330 million. It has total debt of $225 million. ROA is 13.1 percent. What is the ROE for this company?

15-2 Hemley Corporation has estimated its ROE at .16, and it will maintain a payout ratio of 0.40. EPS_1 is estimated to be $2.50. Investors require a .12 rate of return. At what price and P/E ratio would you expect the firm to sell?

15-3 Jansken Co. has an ROE = .12 and a beta of 1.10. It plans to maintain indefinitely its traditional retention ratio of .65. This year's earnings were $2.50 per share. This year's dividend was just paid. The consensus estimate of the coming year's market return is .10, and T-bills currently offer a .05 return. Find the price at which Jansken should sell using the DDM.

15-4 Brozik Corp. expects to earn $4.96 next year. It has a payout ratio of 40 percent. The expected growth for this stock is 10 percent per year indefinitely. The leverage factor for this company is 1.9. What is the ROE?

15-5 Gritta Industries expects to earn $2.50 next year, and pay $1.75 in dividends. The expected growth rate, g, is 7 percent. Your required rate of return is 15 percent. Determine the P/E ratio for this company.

15-6 The Porras Corporation has sales of $20,000,000, total assets of $48,000,000, stockholders equity of $32,500,000, book value per share of $18.53, and net income of $4,980,000. What is the EPS for this company?

Computational Problems

15-1 PGJ is a large producer of food products. In 2012, the percentage breakdown of revenues and profits was as follows:

	Revenues (%)	Profits (%)
Packaged foods	41	62
Coffee	28	19
Processed meat	19	13
Food service-other	12	6
	100	100

International operations account for about 22 percent of sales and 17 percent of operating profit. For the 2008–2012 fiscal years, the number of shares outstanding (in millions) and selected income statement data were (in millions of dollars) as follows:

Shares Outst.	Year	Revenues	Oper. Inc.	Cap. Exp.	Deprec.	Int. Exp.	Net Income Before Tax	Net Income After Tax
49.93	2008	$5,472	$524	$121	$77	$31	$452	$232
49.97	2009	5,960	534	262	78	39	470	256
49.43	2010	6,601	565	187	89	50	473	255
49.45	2011	8,351	694	283	131	152	418	221
51.92	2012	8,256	721	266	133	139	535	289

a. For each year calculate operating income as a percentage of revenues.

b. Net profits after tax as a percentage of revenues.

c. After-tax profits per share outstanding (EPS). The balance sheet data for the same fiscal years (in millions of dollars) were as follows:

Year	Cash	Current Assets	Current Liabilities	Total Assets	Long-Term Debt	Common Equity
2008	$291	$1,736	$845	$2,565	$251	$1,321
2009	178	1,951	1,047	2,978	255	1,480
2010	309	2,019	929	3,103	391	1,610
2011	163	2,254	1,215	3,861	731	1,626
2012	285	2,315	1,342	4,310	736	1,872

d. Calculate the ratio of current assets to current liabilities for each year.

e. Calculate the long-term debt as a percentage of common equity.

f. For each year calculate the book value per share as the common equity divided by the number of shares outstanding.

g. Calculate ROE.

h. Calculate ROA.

i. Calculate leverage.

j. Calculate the net income margin.

k. Calculate turnover.

l. Calculate the EBIT.

m. Calculate the income ratio.

n. Calculate operating efficiency.

o. On the basis of these calculations, evaluate the current status of the health of PGJ and the changes over the period.

15-2 Combining information from the S&P reports and some estimated data for 2013, the following calendar-year data, on a per-share basis, are provided:

Year	Low High	Earnings	Dividends	Book Value	(D/E) 100 (%)	Annual Avg. P/E	ROE	TR%
2007	$26.5–$35.3	$4.56	$1.72	$25.98	37.7	7.0	17.6%	
2008	28.3–37.0	5.02	1.95	29.15	38.8	6.2	17.3	
2009	23.5–34.3	5.14	2.20	32.11	42.8	5.8	16.0	
2010	27.8–35.0	4.47	2.20	30.86		7.7		
2011	29.0–47.8	5.73	2.30	30.30		6.8		
2012	36.6–53.5	6.75	2.40	39.85				
2013		7.05	2.60	44.00				

a. Calculate the D/E, ROE, and TR for 2010, 2011, and 2012. (Use the average of the low and high prices to calculate TRs.)

b. Show that from 2007 through 2012 the per annum growth rate in dividends was 6.9 percent and for earnings was 8.2 percent (both rounded).

c. Using the current price of $52, with estimated earnings for 2013 of $7.05, show that the P/E would be evaluated as 7.38.

d. On the basis of the annual average P/E ratios shown above and your estimate in c), assume an expected P/E of 7. If an investor expected the earnings of PGJ for 2013 to be $8, show that the intrinsic value would be $56.

e. What factors are important in explaining the difference in the P/E ratios of Coca-Cola and PGJ?

f. From your calculation of the growth rate of dividends in b), assume that the annual rate is 7 percent. If the required rate of return for the stock is 12 percent and the expected dividend payout ratio is 0.37, show that P/E = 7.4.

g. If the dividend payout ratio is 0.37 and the return on equity is 15 percent, show that $g = 0.0945$.

h. Using $k = 0.12$ and $g = 0.0945$, with expected 2013 dividends of $2.60, show that the intrinsic value is $101.96.

i. Assume the "beta" for PGJ is 0.8 relative to Coke's beta of 1.1. Is this information of any help in explaining the different P/E ratios of these two companies?

Spreadsheet Exercises

15-1 Fill in the spreadsheet below and answer the following questions. Calculate answers to three decimal places.

a. Calculate Total Returns (TRs) and Return Relatives (RRs) for McDonald's for the 10 years 2001–2010 using the data provided below. Place TRs in Column E and RRs in Column F. Also, calculate the dividend yield for each year using dividend for a given year divided by price for the previous year.

b. What was the dividend yield on McDonald's for 2010, based on the closing price for 2009?

c. What was the arithmetic average dividend yield for this 10-year period? (NOTE: calculate the dividend yield for each year using the closing price for the previous year (2001 dividend and 2000 price, 2002 dividend and 2001 price, etc.) and then determine the 10-year arithmetic average).

d. Calculate the arithmetic mean and geometric mean TR for McDonald's for this 10-year period using Excel functions. State answers as a percentage.

e. Calculate the cumulative wealth for McDonald's for this 10-year period, assuming:
   i. $1,000 invested at the beginning of the 10 years
  ii. $10,000 invested at the beginning of the 10 years

f. The geometric mean for the S&P 500 TR for this 10-year period was 1.014 percent. Calculate the cumulative wealth for the S&P 500 for this 10-year period, assuming $1 invested at the beginning.

g. **i.** Calculate the standard deviation of these 10 years of returns for McDonald's using the **Excel function STDEV**. Note: for this calculation, you can use either TRs or RRs.

ii. Based on the information in Table 6-6, and assuming the risk information in this table applies to the 10-year period being considered here, is McDonald's more risky than the S&P 500, or less risky?

h. What is the biggest single factor in explaining McDonald's returns for 2001 and 2002?

i. For an investor who bought McDonald's stock on January 1, 2005 and held it to December 31, 2010, at what compound annual average rate of return did this investment in the stock grow? State your answer as a compound annual average percentage rate of return.

j. Assume an investor invested $5,000 in McDonald's stock on January 1, 2001, and held it for 20 years. Also assume that the geometric mean for these 20 years is the same as the geometric mean for the 10 years 2001–2010. Including the initial investment, how much money would the investor have at the end of the 20 years? In other words, what is the cumulative wealth from this investment given an initial investment of $5,000?

k. Calculate the compound annual average rate of return on McDonald's stock for the years 2001–2003. State your answer as a compound annual average percent rate of return.

l. Assume you purchased 100 shares of McDonald's stock on January 1, 2007, the year before the great financial crisis of 2008. Calculate the cumulative wealth of this position (which includes the starting amount) at the close of business on December 31, 2010. Ignore any brokerage costs.

m. Assume that over the next five years the returns on the S&P 500 index are 6 percent, −2.5 percent, −4 percent, 5.2 percent, and 3.1 percent.
(a) What will be the cumulative wealth per dollar invested in this index?
(b) At what compound annual rate of return did your money grow if you invested in this index at the start of the five years?

n. Assume that the information generated above is all the information you have about McDonald's rate of return. What would be the best estimate of the TR for McDonald's for 2011? What was the actual return?

	Clos Price	Div	TR	RR	Div Yield
2010	76.76	2.26			
2009	62.44	2.05			
2008	62.19	1.63			
2007	57.27	1.5			
2006	44.33	1			
2005	33.72	0.67			
2004	32.06	0.55			
2003	24.83	0.4			
2002	15.75	0.24			
2001	26.6	0.23			
2000	34				

Checking Your Understanding

15-1 Auditors certify that a company's financial statements are in compliance with generally accepted accounting principles. Such certification does not ensure the fiscal soundness of the company, the quality of its earnings, a lack of impending problems, and so forth.

15-2 If a company reports a large loss for the year on its income statement, this does not necessarily have anything to do with its cash position on the balance sheet. It may still have more than adequate cash with which to operate.

15-3 The Sarbanes–Oxley Act requires corporate officers to assume more responsibility for the financial statements of a company. However, this does not solve the investor's problem of trying to fully understand the financial statements and derive an accurate assessment of the operating performance of a company.

15-4 Companies may choose to report an earnings-related number that places the company in the most favorable light.

15-5 If a company uses no debt, its ROE will equal its ROA. ROE will not be boosted by the use of debt.

15-6 The payout ratio is .33; therefore the retention rate is approximately .67, or two-thirds. Therefore, the estimated growth rate would be two-thirds of 18 percent, or 12 percent.

chapter *16*

Technical Analysis

A s you complete your study of how to select and analyze common stocks, you decide you should take a look at technical analysis, because some of your friends have mentioned it, and you have read about charting in the popular press. Technical analysis sounds intriguing—study the price patterns of stocks across time and use these patterns to predict future price changes. After all, when you look at a chart of stock prices some patterns seem to clearly stand out. Alternatively, you could use some so-called technical indicators to aid you in your buy/sell decisions. However, having considered the Efficient Market Hypothesis, you suspect it might not be as easy and rewarding as it sounds. After all, if it easy to do, and it works, would not many investors be using it successfully on a regular basis?

Chapter 16 outlines technical analysis, an alternative to fundamental security analysis. This approach is very different from fundamental analysis and is directly affected by the Efficient Market Hypothesis discussed in Chapter 12.

AFTER READING THIS CHAPTER YOU WILL BE ABLE TO:

▶ Understand how technical analysis differs from fundamental analysis.
▶ Critically evaluate most of the techniques used in technical analysis as well as the claims made for these techniques.

▶ Decide what role, if any, technical analysis might play in your own investing program.

Introduction

Traditionally, stocks have been selected using two major approaches:

❑ Fundamental analysis
❑ Technical analysis

Technical analysis is entirely different from the fundamental approach to security analysis discussed in the last three chapters. How different? Consider the following quotes from popular press articles on technical analysis:

> Engage a technical analysis in a conversation about his art, and you soon feel like you're in the shadowy saloon from *Star Wars*, where freakish aliens lounge about speaking strange languages.[1]
>
> Spend some time with a technical analyst and you almost need a Technical-to-English translation guide. Conversations are full of references to support and resistance levels, Fibonacci retracements, double bottoms, and moving averages.[2]

Although the technical approach to common stock selection is the oldest approach (dating back to the late 1800s), it remains controversial. The techniques discussed in this chapter appear at first glance to have considerable merit, because they seem intuitive and plausible, but they have been severely challenged in the last three decades by evidence supporting the efficient market hypothesis discussed in Chapter 12. Despite Burton Malkiel's (a well-known proponent of efficient markets) admission that "the market is not a perfect random walk," the extensive evidence concerning the efficiency of the market has challenged the validity of technical analysis and the likelihood of its success.

Those learning about investments will in all likelihood be exposed to technical analysis, because numerous investors, investment advisory firms, and the popular press talk about it and use it. Furthermore, it may produce some insights into the psychological dimension of the market. In fact, technical analysis is becoming increasingly interrelated with behavioral finance (discussed in Chapter 11), a popular field of study today. In effect, technical indicators are being used to measure investor emotions.

Even if this approach is not effective, many investors act as if it is productive. Therefore, the prudent course of action is to study this topic, or indeed any other recommended approach to making investing decisions, and try to make an objective evaluation of its validity and usefulness. At the very least, an informed investor will be in a better position to understand what is being said, or claimed, and better able to judge the validity of the claims. Although technical analysis can be applied to bonds, currencies, and commodities as well as to common stocks, technical analysis typically involves the aggregate stock market, industry sectors, or individual common stocks. Therefore, we restrict our discussion in this chapter to common stocks.

What is Technical Analysis?

Martin J. Pring, in his book *Technical Analysis*, states: "The technical approach to investing is essentially a reflection of the idea that prices move in trends which are determined by the changing attitudes of investors toward a variety of economic, monetary, political and psychological forces. The art of technical analysis—*for it is an art* [emphasis added]—is to identify trend changes at an early stage and to maintain an investment posture until the weight of the evidence indicates that the trend is reversed."[3]

Technical Analysis The use of specific market data for the analysis of both aggregate stock prices and individual stock prices

✓ **Technical analysis** can be defined as the use of specific market-generated data for the analysis of both aggregate stock prices (market indices or industry averages) and individual stocks.

---

[1] See Michael Hirson, "Reading the Tea Leaves," *Individual Investor*, January 2001, p. 96.

[2] See Karen Talley, "Some Technical Analysts Fall off the Charts," *The Wall Street Journal*, February 20, 2002, p. B5.

[3] See Martin J. Pring, *Technical Analysis Explained* (New York: McGraw-Hill Publishers), 1991.

Technical analysis is sometimes called market or internal analysis, because it utilizes the record of the market itself to attempt to assess the demand for, and supply of, shares of a stock or the entire market. Thus, technical analysts believe that the market itself is its own best source of data—as they say, "let the market tell its own story." The theory of technical analysis is that the price movement of a security captures all the information about that security.

Economics teaches us that prices are determined by the interaction of demand and supply. Technicians do not disagree, but argue that it is extremely difficult to assess all the factors that influence demand and supply. Since not all investors are in agreement on price, the determining factor at any point in time is the net demand (or lack thereof) for a stock based on how many investors are optimistic or pessimistic. Furthermore, once the balance of investors becomes optimistic (pessimistic), this mood is likely to continue for the near term and can be detected by various technical indicators. As the chief market technician of one New York firm says, "All I care about is how people feel about those particular stocks as shown by their putting money in and taking their money out."[4]

✓ Technical analysis is based on published market data as opposed to fundamental data, such as earnings, sales, growth rates, or government regulations.

Market data Price and volume information for stocks or indexes

Market data primarily include the price of a stock or a market index and volume data (number of shares traded). Many technical analysts believe that only such market data, as opposed to fundamental data, are relevant. For example, they argue that accounting data are subject to all types of limitations and ambiguities, an argument that was strengthened by the Enron debacle and other accounting flaps in 2002.

Recall that in fundamental analysis the dividend discount model and the multiplier model produce an estimate of a stock's intrinsic value, which is then compared to the market price. Fundamentalists believe that their data, properly evaluated, can be used to estimate the intrinsic value (see Chapter 10) of a stock. Technicians, on the other hand, believe that it is extremely difficult to estimate intrinsic value and virtually impossible to obtain and analyze good information consistently. In particular, they are dubious about the value to be derived from an analysis of published financial statements. Instead, they focus on market data as an indication of the forces of supply and demand for a stock or the market.

Technicians believe that the process by which prices adjust to new information is one of a gradual adjustment toward a new (equilibrium) price. As the stock adjusts from its old equilibrium level to its new level, the price tends to move in a trend. The central concern is not why the change is taking place, but rather the very fact that it is taking place at all. Technical analysts believe that stock prices show identifiable trends that can be exploited by investors. They seek to identify changes in the direction of a stock and take a position in the stock to take advantage of the trend.

The following points summarize technical analysis:

1. Technical analysis is based on published market data and focuses on internal factors by analyzing movements in the aggregate market, industry average, or stock. In contrast, fundamental analysis focuses on economic and political factors, which are external to the market itself.
2. The focus of technical analysis is identifying changes in the direction of stock prices which tend to move in trends as the stock price adjusts to a new equilibrium level. These

---

[4] See Jonathan Butler, "Technical Analysis: A Primer," *Worth*, October 1995, p. 128.

trends can be analyzed, and changes in trends detected, by studying the action of price movements and trading volume across time. The emphasis is on likely price changes.

3. Technicians attempt to assess the overall situation concerning stocks by analyzing technical indicators, such as breadth-of-market data, market sentiment, momentum, and other indicators.

✓ The bottom line for technical analysis: Stock prices tend to move in trends, and these trends take time to unfold. Such trends can be spotted by careful analysis, and acted upon by buying and selling.

Investments Insight

Technicians believe that prices move in trends that are determined by changes in investor attitudes toward various factors, including psychological factors. They believe that investor emotions influence stock prices. Therefore, it is reasonable to think there is a connection between technical analysis and behavioral finance (discussed in Chapter 12). As one senior portfolio manager put it, "Prices do not move only in a random walk but show trends that can be exploited. Behavioral finance does not tell you what to do to exploit these trends, but it can explain why certain strategies or tools may work."[5]

A FRAMEWORK FOR TECHNICAL ANALYSIS

Technical analysis can be applied to both an aggregate of prices (the market as a whole or industry averages) and individual stocks. Technical analysis includes the use of graphs (charts) and technical indicators. Figure 16-1 depicts the technical analysis approach to investing.

Price and volume are the primary tools of the pure technical analyst, and the chart is the most important mechanism for displaying this information. Technicians believe that the forces of supply and demand result in particular patterns of price behavior, the most important of which is the trend or overall direction in price. Using a chart, the technician hopes to identify trends and patterns in stock prices that provide trading signals.

Volume data are used to gauge the general condition in the market and to help assess its trend. The evidence seems to suggest that rising (falling) stock prices are usually associated with rising (falling) volume. If stock prices rose but volume activity did not keep pace, technicians would be skeptical about the upward trend. An upward surge on contracting volume would be particularly suspect. A downside movement from some pattern or holding point, accompanied by heavy volume, would be taken as a bearish sign.

We first consider stock price and volume techniques, often referred to as charting. However, technical analysis has evolved over time, so that today it is much more than the charting of individual stocks or the market. In particular, technical indicators are used to assess market conditions (breadth) and investor sentiment. It also includes "contrary analysis," which is an intellectual process more than a technique. The idea behind contrary analysis is to go against the crowd when the crowd starts thinking alike.

---

[5] Stephen Brown, "The Behavioral Connection," *CFA Magazine*, March/April 2006, p. 45.

Figure 16-1

The Technical Analysis Approach to Common Stock Selection.

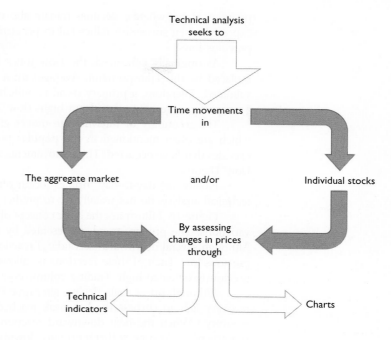

Technical analysis seeks to

Time movements in

The aggregate market   and/or   Individual stocks

By assessing changes in prices through

Technical indicators   Charts

Checking Your Understanding

1. Some technical analysts have said they do not need to know the name of the stock they are analyzing in order to make recommendations about it? Explain.
2. How useful is a stock's intrinsic value to a technical analyst?

Stock Price and Volume Techniques

THE DOW THEORY

Dow Theory A technique for detecting long-term trends in the aggregate stock market

The oldest and best-known theory of technical analysis is the **Dow Theory**, originally developed in the late 1800s by the editor of *The Wall Street Journal*, Charles H. Dow, who many regard as the father of technical analysis. Although Dow developed the theory to describe past price movements, William Hamilton followed up by using it to predict movements in the market. (It is not concerned with individual securities.) The Dow Theory was very popular in the 1920s and 1930s, and articles offering support for it still appear periodically in the literature. Several investment advisory services are based on the Dow Theory.

The theory is based on the existence of three types of price movements:

1. Primary moves, a broad market movement that lasts several years.
2. Secondary (intermediate) moves, occurring within the primary moves, which represent interruptions lasting several weeks or months.
3. Day-to-day moves, occurring randomly around the primary and secondary moves.

The Dow Theory focuses on the primary trend in the market, using the daily closing price of the DJIA. The term *bull market* refers to an upward primary move, whereas *bear market* refers to a downward primary move (in both cases, these are longer-term events, occurring over months or years). A major upward move is said to occur when successive rallies penetrate previous highs, whereas declines remain above previous lows. A major downward move is expected when successive rallies fail to penetrate previous highs, whereas declines penetrate previous lows.

As originally conceived, the Dow Jones Industrial and Rail Average (which was later replaced by the Transportation Average) must confirm each other for the movement to be validated. Therefore, a primary trend is bullish (bearish) when both the Industrials and the Transports are reaching significant highs (lows).

The secondary or intermediate moves give rise to the so-called technical corrections, which are often mentioned in the popular press. These corrections supposedly adjust for excesses that have occurred. These movements are of considerable importance in applying the Dow Theory.

Finally, the day-to-day "ripples" occur often and are of minor importance. Even ardent technical analysts do not usually try to predict day-to-day movements in the market.

Figure 16-2 illustrates the basic concept of the Dow Theory, although there are numerous variations. The primary trend, represented by the dotted line, is up through time Period 1. Although several downward (secondary) reactions occur, these "corrections" do not reach the previous low. Each of these reactions is followed by an upward movement that exceeds the previously obtained high. Trading volume continues to build over this period.

Although prices again decline after time Period 1 as another correction occurs, the price recovery fails to surpass the last peak reached. (This process is referred to as an abortive recovery.) When the next downward reaction occurs, it penetrates the previous low. This movement could suggest that a primary downturn or new bear market has begun, although it is subject to confirmation.

✓ The Dow Theory is intended to forecast the start of a primary movement, but it does not tell us how long the movement will last.

Another important consideration is that the confirmation referred to above is up to each user of the Dow Theory. The trend will continue as long as the averages confirm each other. Only these averages matter; extensive records are not required, chart patterns are not studied, and so on.

The Dow Theory is subject to a number of criticisms, and investors continue today debating its merits. Studies of its success rate have been disappointing; for example, some indicate that over periods of as much as 25 years, investors would have been more successful with a buy-and-hold policy in the same stocks. It is obvious that today's economy is vastly

Figure 16-2

The Basic Concept of the Dow Theory.

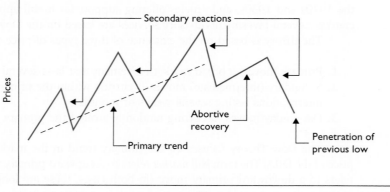

different from the one that existed when the theory was developed. In addition, confirmations are slow to arrive and are often unclear when they do. The amount of price movement needed for a confirmation is ambiguous.

✓ One problem associated with the Dow Theory is that several versions are available. Its users interpret the theory in various ways; therefore, it may predict different (and conflicting) movements at the same time.

CHARTS OF PRICE PATTERNS

Trendline A line on the chart of a security indicating the general direction in which the security's price is moving

Support Level A price range at which a technician expects a significant increase in the demand for a stock

Resistance Level A price range at which a technician expects a significant increase in the supply of a stock

To assess individual stock-price movements, technicians generally rely on charts or graphs of price movements and on relative strength analysis. The charting of price patterns is one of the classic technical analysis techniques. Technicians believe that stock prices move in trends, with price changes forming patterns that can be recognized and categorized. By visually assessing the forces of supply and demand, technicians hope to be able to predict the likely direction of future movements. The most basic measure of a stock's direction is the **trendline**, which simply shows the direction the stock is moving. If demand is increasing more rapidly than supply and the stock shows successively higher low points, it is in an uptrend. Consistently lower highs indicates that supply is increasing more rapidly, and the stock is in a downtrend. Obviously, investors seek to buy in an uptrend and sell on a downtrend.

Technicians seek to identify certain signals in a chart of stock prices, and use certain terminology to describe the events. A **support level** is the level of price (or, more correctly, a price range) at which a technician expects a significant increase in the demand for a stock—in other words, a lower bound on price where it is expected that buyers will act, supporting the price and preventing additional price declines. A **resistance level**, on the other hand, is the level of price (range) at which a technician expects a significant increase in the supply of a stock—in other words, an upper bound on price where sellers are expected to act, providing a resistance to any further rise in price.

Figure 16-3 illustrates support and resistance levels. As the stock approaches $10 per share, it encounters a resistance level and drops back below this price. Conversely, as it approaches slightly less than $6 per share, it gains supports and eventually rises. If the stock breaks through the resistance level on heavy volume, this is taken as a very bullish sign and is referred to as a *breakthrough*.

Support levels tend to develop when profit taking causes a reversal in a stock's price following an increase. Investors who did not purchase earlier are now willing to buy at this

Figure 16-3

Support and Resistance Level for a Stock and a Breakthrough.

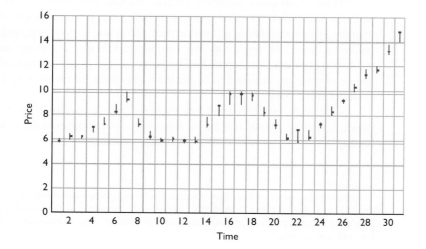

price, which becomes a support level. Resistance levels tend to develop after a stock declines from a higher level. Investors are waiting to sell the stocks at a certain recovery point. At certain price levels, therefore, a significant increase in supply occurs, and the price will encounter resistance moving beyond this level.

As noted, a trendline is a line drawn on a chart to identify a trend. If a trend exhibits support and resistance levels simultaneously that appear to be well defined, the trend lines are referred to as *channel lines*, and price is said to move between the upper channel line and the lower channel line. *Momentum* is used to indicate the speed with which prices are changing, and a number of measures of momentum exist, referred to as momentum indicators. When a change in direction occurs in a short-term trend, technicians say that a *reversal* has occurred. A correction occurs when the reversal involves only a partial retracing of the prior movement. Corrections may be followed by periods of *consolidation*, with the initial trend resuming following the consolidation.

Technical analysts rely primarily on line charts, bar charts and point-and-figure charts, although other types of charts are also used, such as candlestick charts.[6]

Bar Charts One of the most popular charts in technical analysis, **bar charts** are plotted with price on the vertical axis and time on the horizontal axis. Each day's price movement is represented by a vertical bar whose top (bottom) represents the high (low) price for the day. (A small horizontal tick is often used to designate the closing price for the day.) The bottom of a bar chart usually shows the trading volume for each day, permitting the simultaneous observation of both price and volume activity.

Figure 16-4 shows a daily bar chart for Cloud Services, Inc. The technician using charts will search for patterns in the chart that can be used to predict future price moves. Note in Figure 16-4 the strong uptrend occurring over a period of months. This trend ended with a rally on high volume (at point 1 in the figure) that forms part of the left shoulder of a famous chart pattern called a *head-and-shoulders pattern*.

The left shoulder shows initially strong demand followed by a reaction on lower volume (2), and then a second rally, with strong volume, carrying prices still higher (3). Profit taking again causes prices to fall to the so-called neckline (4), thus completing the left shoulder. (The neckline is formed by connecting previous low points.) A rally occurs, but this time on low volume, and again prices sink back to the neckline. This is the head (5). The last step is the formation of the right shoulder, which occurs with light volume (6). Growing weakness can be identified as the price approaches the neckline. As can be seen in Figure 16-4, a downside breakout occurs on heavy volume, which technicians consider to be a sell signal.

What about other patterns? Technicians have considered a very large number of such patterns. Some of the possible patterns include flags, pennants, gaps (of more than one type), triangles of various types (e.g., symmetrical, ascending, descending, and inverted), the inverted saucer or dome, the triple top, the compound fulcrum, the rising (and falling) wedge, the broadening bottom, the duplex horizontal, rectangles, and the inverted V. Figure 16-5 shows one set of price patterns said to be the most important for investors to recognize when reading charts of stock prices.

Obviously, numerous patterns are possible and can usually be found on a chart of stock prices. It is also obvious that most, if not all, of these patterns are much easier to identify in hindsight than at the time they are actually occurring.

Bar Chart A plot of daily stock price plotted against time

---

[6] Technicians also use a basic line chart, which uses only one number—usually the closing price for the day—to reflect the price movement. Another type of chart gaining some popularity in the United States is the candlestick chart. Developed in Japan, the candlestick is similar to the bar chart, although it shows the opening price as well as the high, low, and closing prices.

Figure 16-4

A Bar Chart for Cloud Services, Inc.

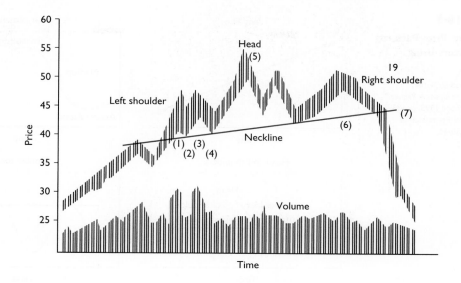

Point-and-Figure Charts Technicians also use **point-and-figure charts**. This type of chart is more complex in that it shows only significant price changes, and volume is not shown at all. The user determines what is a significant price change ($1, $2, etc.) and what constitutes a price reversal ($2, $3, $4, etc.). Although the horizontal axis still depicts time, specific calendar time is not particularly important—the passage of time is basically ignored. (Some chartists do show the month in which changes occur.)

Point-and-Figure Chart A plot of stock prices showing only significant price changes

An X is typically used to show upward movements, whereas an O is used for downward movements. Each X or O on a particular chart may represent $1 movements, $2 movements, $5 movements, and so on, depending on how much movement is considered significant for that stock. An X or O is recorded only when the price moves by the specified amount. Figure 16−6 illustrates the point-and-figure chart.

A point-and-figure chart is designed to compress many price changes into a small space. By doing so, areas of "congestion" can be identified. A congestion area is a compacted area of price fluctuations (i.e., a closely compacted horizontal band of Xs and Os). The technician studies a congestion area in search of a "breakout," which will indicate an expected upward or downward movement in stock price.

Some Evidence on Price Charts There are many chart patterns, some of which were mentioned earlier, and numerous technicians analyze and interpret these patterns. It is impossible to demonstrate conclusively the lack of predictive significance in charting. Very few scientific studies of the ability of chart patterns to predict the future direction of price movements have been conducted.

Levy studied the predictive significance of "five-point" chart patterns.[7] A five-point chart pattern is one with two highs and three lows, or two lows and three highs. As Levy noted, "The avid chartist will recognize, among the 32 patterns, several variations of channels, wedges, diamonds, symmetrical triangles, head and shoulders, reverse head and shoulders, triple tops, and triple bottoms. Each of these formations allegedly reflects underlying supply/demand and support/resistance conditions that have implications as to future price behavior. A common

---

[7] R. Levy, "The Predictive Significance of Five-Point Chart Patterns," *The Journal of Business*, 44 (July 1971): pp. 316−323.

Figure 16-5

Important Price Patterns for Investors Using Charts.

SOURCE: Jonathan Butler, "Technical Analysis: A Primer," *Worth*, October 1995, p. 133. Reprinted by Permission of Worth Magazine.

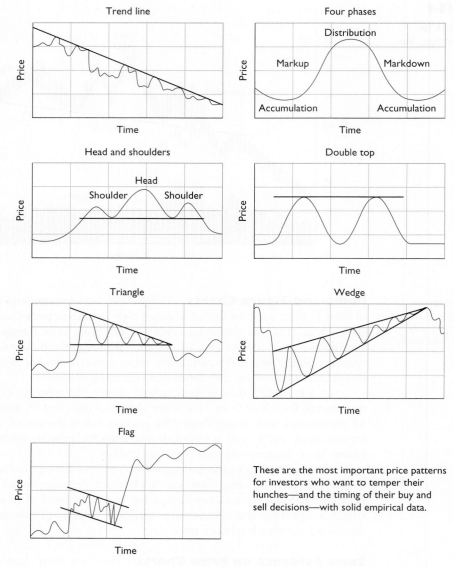

These are the most important price patterns for investors who want to temper their hunches—and the timing of their buy and sell decisions—with solid empirical data.

Figure 16-6

A Point-and-Figure Chart for Gigantic Computers. X = $1 Upward Price Change, O = $1 Downward Price Change (Numbers Indicate Months).

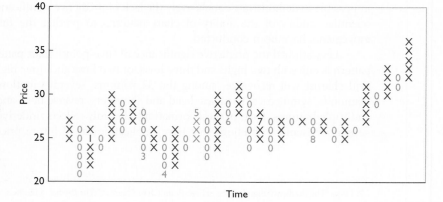

belief among chartists is that the appearance of certain patterns followed by a 'breakout' gives a profitable buy or sell signal."[8]

The results indicated that, although some patterns did produce better results than others, none performed very differently from the market. When brokerage commissions were deducted, none of the 32 patterns was found to have any "profitable forecasting ability in either [bullish or bearish] direction." The really surprising conclusion of this study, however, was that "the best-performing patterns would probably be characterized as bearish by most technicians, and conversely, the worst-performing patterns would, in two of the three cases, be characterized as bullish."

Opinions about charting vary widely. Since the evidence is not conclusive—at least to everyone's satisfaction—the controversy will continue.

Checking Your Understanding

3. Suppose someone tells you that they use the Dow Theory regularly, and that it provides them with valuable information. They urge you to do the same. What objections might you raise against doing this?
4. What are the implications of the efficient market hypothesis for technical analysts practicing the charting of stock prices?

Concepts in Action

Using Technical Analysis When Making Investing Decisions

The average investor today can easily access charts and graphs of individual stocks and the market as a whole. While numerous services provide this type of information at a cost, going into substantial detail, the average investor can probably find what he or she wants at no cost.

Start with Yahoo! Finance. Entering the stock symbol for a company, a page comes up with a small chart showing one day's price activity. The time period can be easily changed. The chart can be viewed as a bar chart, a line chart, or a candlestick chart. By clicking on "Technical Analysis" on the left, an investor can easily construct various moving averages around the stock's price movements. Furthermore, various indicators and overlays can be added. Taken together, the average investor

can probably accomplish what they want at this one site.

Another well-known source of charts for stocks can be found at www.bigcharts.com. One can construct various charts and also quickly link to analysts information, insider statistics, news about the company, and so forth.

Effective charts can be quickly assembled at www.stockcharts.com. This site has some interesting tools, among them its "Carpets" diagrams.

The bottom line for investors when it comes to looking at, or using, charts is that such data can be accessed on numerous sites. Most investors who wish to use this type of analysis would be well advised to select one or two such sites and become familiar with what they can offer.

MOVING AVERAGES

A moving average of prices is a popular technique for analyzing both the overall market and individual stocks and is used specifically to detect both the direction and the rate of change.

---

[8] Using daily prices for 548 NYSE stocks over a five-year period (1964–1969), Levy found 19,077 five-point patterns. Of these, 9,383 were followed by a breakout and were therefore studied.

Some number of days of closing prices is chosen to calculate a moving average. After initially calculating the average price, the new value for the moving average is calculated by dropping the earliest observation and adding the latest one. This process is repeated daily (or weekly). The resulting moving average line supposedly represents the basic trend of stock prices. Moving averages smooth data, tending to eliminate or soften outliers in price data.

Three major decisions have to be made in constructing a moving average; furthermore, each of the three involves several alternatives.

1. *The time period over which the average is calculated.* This decision has the greatest impact on the moving average. A well-known average for identifying major trends is the 200-day moving average (alternatively, a 10-week [50 day] average is used to identify intermediate trends). Shorter trends can be captured by 10-, 20-, and 50-day averages, as well as 100-day averages. The 200-day moving average will tend to be flatter and lower on the graph than over moving averages.
2. *The price used* Although closing prices are often used, sometimes the open, high, low, and close prices are used in different configurations.
3. *The type of moving average used* A simple moving average is often used, but alternatives include a weighted average and an exponential average (whether simple or weighted). The latter two place greater weight on recent price activity, while the simple moving average places equal weight on each day's price activity.

A comparison of the current market price to the moving average produces a buy or sell signal. The general buy signal is generated when actual prices rise through the moving average on high volume, with the opposite applying to a sell signal. Specific signals of an upper turning point (a sell signal) are the following:

1. Actual price is below the moving average, advances toward it, does not penetrate the average, and starts to turn down again.
2. Following a rise, the moving average flattens out or declines, and the price of the stock or index penetrates it from the top.
3. The stock price rises above the moving average line while the line is still falling.

Buy signals would be generated if these situations were turned upside down.

Figure 16-7 shows Coca-Cola plotted daily for a recent period, with both a 200-day moving average and a 50-day moving average included. Volume is shown at the bottom of the chart. Various publications and websites offer plots of a 200-day moving average, a 50-day moving average, and other moving averages, for both individual stocks and market indices.

Investors should remember that moving averages show what prices have already done, not what they will do. They indicate if prices, over a given time period, have gone up or gone down. Regardless of how it is constructed, the moving average is always reacting to what has happened.

A variation of the moving average popular on some websites is the moving average convergence divergence, or MACD. This involves a longer moving average (such as the 200-day) and a shorter moving average (such as the 50-day). As a stock price rises, a bullish signal is generated if the short-term average consistently is greater than the long-term average. A warning signal is generated when the short-term average falls below the long-term average.

Figure 16-7

A Full Screen Shot from Yahoo! Finance Showing a Chart of Coca-Cola with Two Moving Averages, a 50-day Average and a 200-day Average (the Smoother Line).

SOURCE: Reproduced with the Permission of YAHOO! Inc. Copyright © 2012 by YAHOO! Inc. YAHOO! and the YAHOO! Logo are Trademarks of YAHOO! Inc.

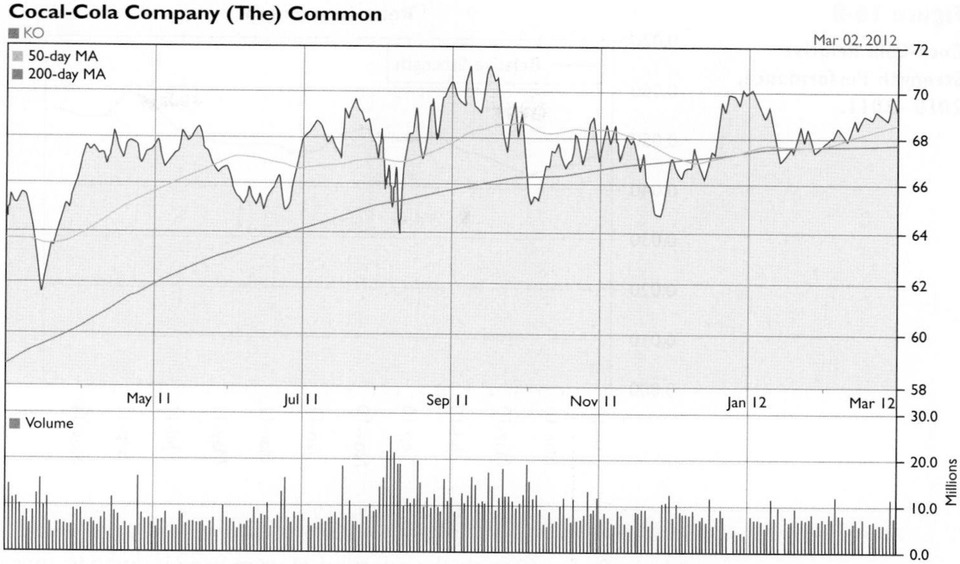

RELATIVE STRENGTH

Relative Strength The ratio of a stock's price to some market or industry index, usually plotted as a graph

A well-known technique used for individual stocks (or industries) is relative strength analysis. The **relative strength** for a given stock is calculated as the ratio of the stock's price to a market index, or an industry index, or the average price of the stock itself over some previous period. Relative strength could also be calculated as the ratio of an industry average relative to the market. These ratios can be plotted to form a graph of relative prices across time. In effect, the graph shows the strength of the stock relative to its industry, the market, or whatever. A chief market analyst at Merrill Lynch in New York has stated, "Very often changes in trend, from good to bad or from bad to good, will be preceded by a change in the stock's relative performance."[9]

The relative strength of a stock over time may be of use in forecasting.[10] Because trends are assumed to continue for some time, a rising ratio (an upward-sloping line when relative strength is plotted) indicates relative strength. That is, it indicates a stock that is outperforming the market and that may continue to do so. A declining ratio would have the same implications for the downside. One rule of thumb is that a stock is attractive when the relative strength has improved for at least four months, but as with most technical indicators, technicians interpret some of these signals in different ways.

Figure 16-8 shows relative performance for Coca-Cola in recent years by plotting the ratio of closing monthly prices for Coke to closing monthly prices for the S&P 500. Coca-Cola stock during this period generally increased, particularly toward the end of the period shown. The market also generally increased during this time period. However, Coca-Cola did better from beginning to end, and therefore had increasing relative strength.

Relative strength is often used by technicians to identify industry sectors that look attractive, prior to selecting individual stocks. This is in line with our analysis in Part IV which supports a top-down approach to security analysis, with industry analysis preceding company

[9] See Butler, p. 133.

[10] Some evidence supporting relative strength can be found in Narasimhan Jegadeesh and Sheridan Titman, "Returns to Buying Winners and Selling Losers: Implications for Stock Market Efficiency," *The Journal of Finance*, 48 (March 1993): pp. 65–91.

Figure 16-8

Coca-Cola Relative Strength Performance, 2010–2011.

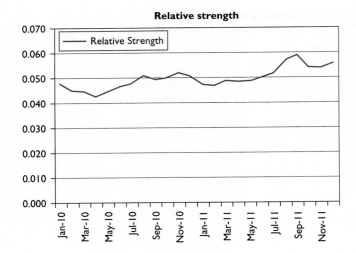

analysis. By focusing on the selection of promising industries, investors narrow the number of possibilities to be considered.

This group selection approach may be helpful in supporting the proposition that an individual stock showing relative strength is not an anomaly, but the technique does not protect an investor against the chance that the overall market is weak, and that one or more groups which currently appear strong are next in line to show weakness. Such a possibility once again supports the case for a top-down approach that begins with market analysis in order to assess the likelihood that now is a good time to be investing in stocks.

One of the problems with relative strength is that a stock or group could show increasing relative strength because it is declining less quickly than the market, not because it is, in fact, increasing. This suggests that relative strength is not a technique to be used in isolation.

Numerous investment information services provide information on relative strength. For example, *The Value Line Investment Survey*, discussed in Chapter 15, divides a stock's price by the Value Line Composite Average and plots this relative strength ratio for each company it covers at the top of the page. Relative strength analysis lends itself well to computerized stock analysis. This probably accounts for its popularity among institutional investors who own highly automated and sophisticated data analysis systems. The extent to which a number of institutional investors use relative strength techniques and have the means to observe changes at about the same time can affect the volatility of a stock.

USING THE COMPUTER FOR TECHNICAL ANALYSIS

Obviously, the widespread use of personal computers makes technical analysis much more accessible than previously. A few years ago, individual investors could either do the charting themselves or buy a subscription to a service that delivered hard copy of charts on a regular basis. In today's world one can buy a wide variety of software with programs and data.

The basic choice for those interested in technical analysis remains either obtaining software or using an online service. Software-based programs are more comprehensive, both with regard to charting and to technical indicators, which are discussed below. Software-based programs allow the user to select a trading system based on multiple technical indicators and backtest the system to determine what the profitability would have been. Few online services offer any type of trading system, and none allow significant historical backtesting.

Using technical analysis systems requires both a program and a data vendor, and costs can add up quickly. Data can be provided at the end-of-the-day, intraday delayed, or real-time. Most users will find web-based services sufficient.

Technical Indicators

The chart remains the technician's most important tool for making buy and sell decisions. However, in addition to looking at the plot of stock prices, technicians also like to examine the overall situation by analyzing such factors as breadth and market sentiment indicators.

BREADTH INDICATORS

The Advance-Decline Line (Breadth of the Market) The **advance-decline line** measures, on a cumulative daily basis, the net difference between the number of stocks advancing in price and those declining in price for a group of stocks such as those on the NYSE. Subtracting the number of declines from the number of advances produces the net advance for a given day (which, of course, can be negative). This measure may include thousands of stocks.

Advance-Decline Line A technical analysis measure that relates the number of stocks rising to the number declining

The advance-decline line, often referred to as the breadth of the market, results from plotting a running total of these numbers across time. The line can be based on daily or weekly figures, which are readily available from daily newspapers such as *The Wall Street Journal*.

The advance-decline line is compared to a stock average, in particular the Dow Jones Industrial Average, in order to analyze any divergence—that is, to determine whether movements in the market indicator have also occurred in the market as a whole. Technicians believe that divergence can signal that the trend is about to change.

The advance-decline line and the market averages normally move together. If both are rising (declining), the overall market is said to be technically strong (weak). If the advance-decline line is rising while the market average is declining, the decline in the market average should reverse itself. Particular attention is paid to a divergence between the two during a bull market. If the market rises while the line weakens or declines, this indicates a weakening in the market; the market would therefore be expected to reverse itself and start declining.

New Highs and Lows Part of the information reported for the NYSE and other stocks is the 52-week high and low prices for each stock. Technicians regard the market as bullish when a significant number of stocks each day hit 52-week highs. On the other hand, technicians see rising market indexes and few stocks hitting new highs as a troublesome sign.

Volume Volume is an accepted part of technical analysis. High trading volume, other things being equal, is generally regarded as a bullish sign. Heavy volume combined with rising prices is even more bullish.

SENTIMENT INDICATORS

Short-Interest Ratio The **short interest** for a security is the number of shares that have been sold short but not yet bought back. The short-interest ratio can be defined relative to shares outstanding or average daily volume, as in:

Short Interest The total number of shares in the market sold short and not yet repurchased

$$\text{Short-interest ratio} = \text{Total shares sold short}/\text{Average daily trading volume} \qquad \textbf{(16-1)}$$

The NYSE, AMEX, and NASDAQ report the short interest monthly for each stock. The NYSE and AMEX indicate those securities where arbitrage or hedging may be important, but the significance of these activities cannot be determined. For investors interested in the short interest, each month *The Wall Street Journal* reports NYSE and AMEX issues for which a short-interest position of at least 100,000 shares existed or for which a short-position change of 50,000 shares occurred from the previous month.[11] In effect, the ratio indicates the number of days necessary to "work off" the current short interest.[12] It is considered to be a measure of investor sentiment, and many investors continue to refer to it.

Investors sell short when they expect prices to decline; therefore, it would appear, the higher the short interest, the more investors are expecting a decline. A large short-interest position for an individual stock should indicate strong negative sentiment against a stock.

Many technical analysts interpret this ratio in the opposite manner, as a contrarian indicator (discussed below): a high short-interest ratio is taken as a bullish sign, because the large number of shares sold short represents a large number of shares that must be repurchased in order to close out the short sales. (If the ratio is low, the required purchases are not present.) In effect, the short seller must repurchase, regardless of whether or not his or her expectations were correct. The larger the short-interest ratio, the larger the potential demand that is indicated. Therefore, an increase in the ratio indicates more "pent-up" demand for the shares that have been shorted.

The short-interest ratio for a given month should be interpreted in relation to historical boundaries, which historically were in the range of 1.0 to 2.0 for the NYSE. The problem is that the boundaries keep changing. In the 1960s, 1970s, and 1980s, a ratio of 2.0 was bullish. More recently, the ratio has been in the 3.0 to 6.0 range regardless of the market.

Short-interest figures have been distorted by hedging and arbitrage techniques that have become more popular. For example, if a fund buys Delta and shorts American Airlines, how does this affect the interpretation of the short interest? Hedged short sellers are not likely to panic if their short position moves adversely, which otherwise might lead them to buy and push the price up.

Mutual Fund Liquidity Several indicators are based on the theory of *contrary investing*. The idea is to trade contrary to most investors, who supposedly almost always lose—in other words, to go against the crowd. This is an old idea on Wall Street, and over the years technicians have developed several measures designed to capitalize on this concept. As mentioned above, the short interest is often used as a contrarian indicator, with high short levels in a stock viewed as being overly pessimistic.

Mutual fund liquidity can be used as a contrary opinion technique. Under this scenario, mutual funds are viewed in a manner similar to odd-lotters; that is, they are presumed to act incorrectly before a market turning point.[13] Therefore, when mutual fund liquidity is low because the funds are fully invested, contrarians believe that the market is at, or near, a peak. The funds should be building up cash (liquidity); instead, they are extremely bullish and are fully invested. Conversely, when funds hold large liquid reserves, it suggests that they are bearish. Contrarians would consider this a good time to buy because the market may be at, or near, its low point.

The Opinions of Investment Advisory Newsletters *Investors Intelligence*, an investment advisory service, samples weekly the opinions of about 150 investment advisory services and calculates an index of investment service opinions. It has found that, on average, these services are most bearish at the market bottom and least bearish at the market top. This index, published since 1963, is now available weekly and is widely quoted in the investing community.

---

[11] A list of stocks with the largest short-interest ratios broken down by exchange can be found at www.trading-ideas.com.

[12] For example, a ratio of 1.0 means that the outstanding short interest approximates a day's trading volume.

[13] According to the odd-lot theory, small investors who often buy or sell odd lots (less than 100 shares of stock) are usually wrong in their actions at market peaks and troughs. Supposedly, such investors typically buy (sell) when the market is at or close to a peak (bottom). In particular, small investors do not get involved with short sales unless they are particularly bearish.

The "bearish sentiment index" is calculated as the ratio of advisory services that are bearish to the total number with an opinion. When this index approaches 55 or 60 percent, this would indicate a bearish attitude on the part of investment advisory services. As this ratio approaches 20 percent, the opposite occurs. Thus, a contrarian should react in the opposite direction of the sentiment this ratio is exhibiting. As the ratio nears 60 percent, the contrarian becomes bullish because a majority of the investment advisory services are bearish, and around 20 percent the contrarian becomes bearish because most of the investment advisory services are not bearish.

The reason for this seeming contradiction to logic—that investment advisory services are wrong at the extremes—is attributed to the fact that these services tend to follow trends rather than forecast them. Thus, they are reporting and reacting to what has happened rather than concentrating on anticipating what is likely to happen.

CBOE Put/Call Ratio   Speculators buy calls when they expect stock prices to rise, and they buy puts when they expect prices to fall. Because they are generally more optimistic than pessimistic, the put to call ratio is well below 1.0. The Puts/Calls Ratio (P/C Ratio) was developed as a sentiment indicator between the number of Puts to Calls on the Chicago Board Options Exchange. For example, a ratio of 0.60 indicates that only six puts are purchased for every 10 calls purchased.

This ratio was designed to capture the actions of unsophisticated investors trading options. A rise in this ratio indicates pessimism on the part of speculators in options. However, the P/C ratio is used as a contrarian indicator; therefore, when it reaches an excessive level, this is a buy signal to a contrarian. A low ratio would be a sell signal to a contrarian because of the rampant optimism such a ratio indicates.

Small changes are considered unimportant. Extreme readings are said to convey information. According to some sources, a ratio greater than 0.80 (based on a 10-day moving average) would be excessively bearish, and therefore a *buy* signal. A ratio less than 0.45 would be excessively bullish, and therefore a *sell* signal.[14] Like many technical indicators, the exact levels to trigger signals are open to debate. No one indicator should be used in isolation, but rather with other indicators as part of a total package.

Testing Technical Analysis Strategies

What constitutes a fair test of a technical trading rule? The adjustments that should be made include at least the following:

1. *Risk.* If the risk involved in two strategies is not comparable, a fair comparison cannot be made. As we know, other things being equal, a more risky strategy would be expected to outperform a less risky strategy.
2. *Transaction and other costs (e.g., taxes).* Several technical trading rules appeared to produce excess returns before transaction costs were deducted. After such costs were deducted, however, the rules were inferior to a buy-and-hold strategy, which generates little costs.
3. *Consistency.* Can the rule outperform the alternative over a reasonable period of time, such as five or 10 years? Any rule may outperform an alternative for a short period, but it will not be too useful unless it holds up over some longer term.
4. *Out-of-sample validity.* Has the rule been tried on data other than that used to produce the rule? It is always possible to find a rule that works on a particular sample if enough rules are tried—that is, it is possible to torture the data until it confesses.

---

[14] See Steven B. Achelis, *Technical Analysis from A to Z*, McGraw-Hill Professional Publishing, 2000.

Filter Rule A rule for
buying and selling stocks
according to the stock's
price movements

A well-known technical trading rule is the so-called **filter rule**. A filter rule specifies a breakpoint for an individual stock or a market average, and trades are made when the stock-price change is greater than this filter. For example, buy a stock if the price moves up 10 percent from some established base, such as a previous low, hold it until it declines 10 percent from its new high, and then sell it and possibly go short.

Several studies of filters have been conducted. Fama and Blume tested 24 filters (ranging from 0.50 percent to 50 percent) on each of the 30 Dow Jones stocks.[15] Before commissions, several of the filters were profitable, in particular the smallest (0.5 percent). After commissions, however, average returns were typically negative or very small. Brokerage commissions more than offset any gains that could be exploited. The low correlations found in the statistical tests were insufficient to provide profitable filter trading rules.

Many different variations of the relative strength technique can be tested by varying the time period over which the average price is calculated and the percentage of the top stocks selected. If we conduct enough tests, we can find a rule that produces favorable results on a particular sample. Therefore, before we conclude that a trading rule of this type is successful, we should conduct a fair test as outlined earlier. Risks must be comparable, and appropriate costs must be deducted. Finally, the rule should be tried on a different sample of stocks.

The Challenge of the Efficient Market Hypothesis

The efficient market hypothesis (EMH) discussed in Chapter 12 poses a major challenge to the usefulness of technical analysis. Virtually all statistical tests of the weak form of the EMH offer strong support for the weak form, thereby providing evidence against technical analysis which holds that stock price changes across time are dependent and that prices move in trends. Many tests of technical trading rules suggest that such rules do not generate superior risk-adjusted returns after all relevant costs have been deducted. The sum total of all of this evidence is the reason why many informed observers do not believe that technical analysis can really work on a consistent basis. Nevertheless, proponents of technical analysis claim that it can and does work, and certainly there is some supporting evidence, which we now examine.

Some Supporting Evidence on Technical Analysis

Many academic studies have been published which indicate that technical analysis does not work. That is why most academics (and textbooks) do not speak favorably about technical analysis. Nevertheless, some recent credible evidence does exist that supports technical analysis. The following articles have appeared in *The Journal of Finance*, one of the top journals in the field.

Jegadeesh found predictable patterns in stock prices based on monthly returns for the period 1934—1987, a long period of time.[16] His study showed that stocks with large losses in one month are likely to show a significant reversal in the following month, and that stocks with large gains in one month are likely to show a significant loss in the next month.

Brock, LeBaron, and Lakonishok published a paper titled "Simple Technical Trading Rules and the Stochastic Properties of Stock Returns."[17] This paper provides support for two basic technical indicators, moving averages and support and resistance. The period studied was 1897—1986, using the DJIA. Subperiods were also considered.

[15] E. Fama and M. Blume, "Filter Rules and Stock-Market Trading," *The Journal of Business: A Supplement*, 39 (January 1969): pp. 2—21.

[16] Narasimhan Jegadeesh, "Evidence of Predictable Behavior of Security Returns," *The Journal of Finance* (July 1990): pp. 881—898.

[17] William Baron, Josef Lakonishok, and Blake LeBaron, "Simple Technical Trading Rules and the Stochastic Properties of Stock Returns," *The Journal of Finance*, 47 (December 1992): pp. 1731—1764.

Regarding the moving average, the results of this study suggest it does pay to be in the market when the DJIA is above its 200-day moving average, and to be more cautious when it is below that average. The authors concluded that the results are "consistent with technical rules having predictive power."

Chordia and Swaminathan found that trading volume is a significant determinant of leads and lags observed in stock prices.[18] Returns on low volume portfolios respond more slowly to information in market returns than do the returns on high volume portfolios.

Lo, Mamaysky, and Wang at MIT developed a systematic and automatic approach to technical pattern recognition in order to bypass the subjective nature of technical analysis.[19] Testing a large number of stocks from 1962 to 1996, they found that several technical indicators provide incremental information and may have some practical value.

The Ebb and Flow of Technical Analysis

The 1990s was a great decade for common stocks, with most years showing strong performance. Accordingly, firms hired many fundamental analysts and technical analysts during that time, although most firms always have considerably more of the former than the latter. Following the market downturns in 2000 and 2001, however, several firms began to cut their analysts. Given that many more are fundamental analysts than technical analysts to begin with, the result was a distinctive decrease in technical analysis at some firms. This came as somewhat of a shock to the investment community in general and technical analysts in particular.

Some Conclusions about Technical Analysis

Technical analysis often appeals to those who are beginning a study of investments because it is easy to believe that stock prices form repeatable patterns over time or that certain indicators should be related to future market (or individual stock) price movements. Most people who look at a chart of a particular stock will immediately see what they believe to be patterns in the price changes and clear evidence of trends that should have been obvious to anyone studying it.

Consider a quote from John Allen Paulos, a mathematician who wrote *A Mathematician Plays the Stock Market*:[20]

> "People tend not to believe that markets move in random ways. Randomness is difficult to recognize. If you have people write down 100 *H*s and *T*s to simulate 100 flips of a coin, you will always be able to tell a sequence generated by a human from one generated by real coin flips. When humans make up the sequence, they don't put in enough consecutive *H*s and consecutive *T*s, and they don't make the lengths of these runs long enough or frequent enough. And that is one of the reasons people look at patterns in the stock market and ascribe significance to them."

---

[18] Taran Chordia and Bhaskaran Swaminathan, "Trading Volume and Cross-Autocorrelation in Stock Returns," *The Journal of Finance*, 55 (April 2000): pp. 913–935.

[19] Andrew Lo, Harry Mamaysky, and Jiang Wang, "Foundations of Technical Analysis: Computational Algorithms, Statistical Inference, and Empirical Implementation," *The Journal of Finance*, 55 (August 2000): pp. 1705–1770.

[20] *In The Vanguard*, © The Vanguard Group, Autumn 2003, p. 4.

How should we view this situation? Academicians (and numerous practitioners) are highly skeptical of technical analysis, to say the least. Most academic discussions at the college level dismiss, or seriously disparage, this concept. A primary reason is that thorough tests of technical analysis techniques typically fail to confirm their value, given all costs and considering an alternative, such as a buy-and-hold strategy.

✓ Efficient market theories, as typically presented, argue against the possibility of trading profits in speculative markets using technical analysis.

In addition to these reasons, other troubling features of technical analysis remain. First, several interpretations of each technical tool and chart pattern are not only possible but typical. One or more of the interpreters will be correct (more or less), but it is virtually impossible to know beforehand who these will be. After the fact, we will know which indicator or chart, or whose interpretation, was correct, but only those investors who used that particular information will benefit. Tools such as the Dow Theory are well known for their multiple interpretations by various observers who disagree over how the theory is to be interpreted. These types of problems come under various labels such as data snooping and ex post selection of trading rules and search methods.

Furthermore, consider a technical trading rule (or chart pattern) that is, in fact, successful. When it gives its signal on the basis of reaching some specified value (or forms a clear picture on a chart), it correctly predicts movements in the market or some particular stock. Such a rule or pattern, if observed by several market participants, will be self-destructive as more and more investors use it. Price will reach its equilibrium value quickly, taking away profit opportunities from all but the quickest. Some observers will start trying to act before the rest on the basis of what they expect to happen. (For example, they may act before a complete head and shoulders forms.) Price will then reach an equilibrium even more quickly, so that only those who act earliest will benefit. Eventually, the value of any such rule will be negated entirely.

Investments Intuition

No inherent reason exists for stock-price movements to repeat themselves. For example, flipping a fair coin 100 times should, on average, result in about 50 heads and 50 tails. There is some probability that the first 10 tosses could produce 10 heads. However, the chance of such a pattern repeating itself is very small.

As we saw in Chapter 12, strong evidence exists suggesting that stock-price changes over time are weak-form efficient. If this is the case, any patterns formed are accidental but not surprising.

Yet, it is impossible to test all the techniques of technical analysis and their variations and interpretations. In fact, technical analysis has not been tested thoroughly. The techniques of this approach are simply too numerous, and technical analysis is broader than the use of only price information. Therefore, absolutely definitive statements about this subject cannot be made. A good example of the omissions in this area is the use of volume in technical strategies. Although volume is a recognized part of technical analysis, at least until recently relatively few tests have been conducted on its use in conjunction with the rest of technical analysis.

Also, in recent years some more modern evidence has been presented that tends to support the basis of technical analysis. And, of course, other evidence has been presented. For example, Brown and Jennings have presented a different way of looking at technical analysis which provides a justification for technical analysis being useful to investors.[21] They construct a scenario that shows how each investor can learn something about what other investors know by observing the price at which a security trades. In effect, prices reveal information as well as simply convey information. Furthermore, today's behavioral models open up the possibility of profitable trading strategies using technical analysis because of noise in the markets or irrational behavior on the part of investors.

What can we conclude about technical analysis? On the basis of all available evidence, it is difficult to justify technical analysis. Until quite recently, the studies that have been done in support of this concept have produced relatively weak arguments in its favor. Studies done in support of the efficient market hypothesis, on the other hand, are much stronger in their conclusions that technical analysis does not work on a consistent, after-transactions-cost basis. Regardless of the evidence, technical analysis remains popular with many investors, at least to some degree.

Perhaps a recent quote from the popular press summarizes it best:

> Whether it works or not, TA is no quick road to riches. Even die-hard technical analysts say that the method works best when accompanied by fundamental research—for example, to time entry and exit points for a stock.[22]

Summary

▶ Technical analysis, the other approach to selecting securities, is the oldest approach available to investors and in many respects the most controversial.

▶ Technical analysis relies on published market data, primarily price and volume data, to predict the short-term direction of individual stocks or the market as a whole. The emphasis is on internal factors that help to detect demand-supply conditions in the market.

▶ The rationale for technical analysis is that the net demand (or lack thereof) for stocks can be detected by various technical indicators and that trends in stock prices occur and continue for considerable periods of time. Stock prices require time to adjust to the change in supply and demand.

▶ Price and volume are primary tools of the technical analyst, as are various technical indicators.

▶ Technical analysis involves the use of charts of price patterns to detect trends that are believed to persist over time. Technical analysis can be applied to both the aggregate market and individual stocks.

▶ Aggregate market analysis originated with the Dow Theory, the best-known technical theory. It is designed to detect the start of major movements.

▶ The most frequently used charts are line charts; bar charts, which show each day's price movement as well as volume; and point-and-figure charts, which show only significant price changes as they occur.

▶ Numerous chart "patterns" are recognizable to a technician. However, all patterns are subject to multiple interpretations, because different technicians will read the same chart differently.

▶ A very well-known tool of technical analysis is the moving average, which is used to detect both the direction and the rate of change in prices.

▶ Another well-known technique for individual stocks is relative strength, which shows the strength of a particular stock in relation to its average price, its industry, or the market.

▶ Technical indicators of the aggregate market include, but are not limited to, the following:

---

[21] See David Brown and Robert Jennings, "On Technical Analysis," *Review of Financial Studies*, 1989, pp. 527–552.
[22] See Hirson, op. cit., p. 98.

1. The advance-decline line (breadth of market), which is used to assess the condition of the overall market.
2. Mutual fund liquidity, which uses the potential buying power (liquidity) of mutual funds as a bullish or bearish indicator.
3. Short-interest ratio, which assesses potential demand from investors who have sold short.

4. Contrary opinion, which is designed to go against the crowd. Included here are the put-call ratio and the opinions of investment advisory services. The short-sale ratio can also be interpreted as a contrarian indicator, as can mutual fund liquidity.

Questions

16-1 Describe the rationale for technical analysis.

16-2 Differentiate between fundamental analysis and technical analysis.

16-3 What do technicians assume about the adjustment of stock prices from one equilibrium position to another?

16-4 What role does volume play in technical analysis?

16-5 What is the Dow Theory? What is the significance of the "confirmation" signal in this theory?

16-6 How does the Dow Theory forecast how long a market movement will last?

16-7 Using a moving average, how is a sell signal generated?

16-8 Why is the advance-decline line called an indicator of breadth of the market?

16-9 Why are the opinions of investment advisory services considered a contrary opinion signal?

16-10 What is the rationale for the theory of contrary opinion?

16-11 How is the odd-lot index calculated? How is it used as a buy or sell signal?

16-12 Why is a rising short-interest ratio considered to be a bullish indicator?

16-13 Distinguish between a bar chart and a point-and-figure chart.

16-14 What is relative strength analysis?

16-15 On a rational economic basis, why is the study of chart patterns likely to be an unrewarding activity?

16-16 Is it possible to prove or disprove categorically the validity of technical analysis?

16-17 Assume that you know a technical analyst who claims success on the basis of his or her chart patterns. How might you go about scientifically testing this claim?

16-18 How do the new contrarians differ from the more traditional contrarians?

16-19 Why do stock-price movements repeat themselves?

16-20 Look at the bar chart of the Dow-Jones Averages in section C1 of *The Wall Street Journal*. Does this chart cover a sufficient time period to apply the Dow Theory?

16-21 With reference to Question 16-20, why would this chart, or possibly several of these charts covering a number of months, be useful in trying to apply the Dow Theory?

16-22 What new financial instruments have caused the short-interest ratio to be less reliable? Why?

16-23 Describe a bullish sign when using a moving average; a bearish sign. Do the same for the advance-decline line.

Computational Problems

16-1 A technician supposedly bragged that he earned 30 percent a month for a 10-year period using his charts. Assuming he started with a $10,000 investment, determine how much money he would have at the end of the 10-year period if he did compound his investment at 30 percent per month.

Checking Your Understanding

16-1 A technical analyst need not know the name of a stock, because the analyst is not interested in the fundamental data for that company. Instead, the technical analyst is studying the price patterns of the stock over time, and to do this one need not know the name of the company.

16-2 Intrinsic value is of no use to a technical analyst. A stock is evaluated on the basis of its price patterns across time.

16-3 There are several versions of the Dow Theory. Even assuming someone is using this theory successfully (and you can't be sure of this without documentation), you might very well use a different version or interpretation if you tried to follow this approach. Furthermore, confirmation signals vary from user to user.

16-4 The weak form of the EMH is directly contra to the use of charts to predict stock prices. The weak form states that stock price changes are essentially independent; therefore, one cannot use them to predict future price changes. Technical analysis, in contrast, relies on stock price changes being dependent, moving in trends which are somewhat predictable.

chapter *17*

Fixed Income Securities Are Available Worldwide

Following your study of stocks, you realize you also need to understand the basics about bonds. After all, portfolio theory stresses the virtues of diversification, and that includes asset classes. A little math quickly tells you that $1 million invested in bonds returning 6 percent produces a *nominal* income stream of $60,000 a year, which seems like a significant annual annuity. By now, however, you have learned that when it comes to investing things are not always what they seem. Maybe bond returns are not as straightforward as they appear to be. Furthermore, you have heard people say that when interest rates rise, bond prices decline, and you wonder why. It becomes apparent to you that knowing something about bond prices and yields could be useful to you as you manage your inheritance.

Chapter 17 provides an analysis of bond yields and prices. Bond market participants use various yield measures unique to bonds when quoting potential returns to investors. However, these measures can mislead unwary investors who fail to understand the basis on which they are constructed. It is important to understand how bonds are valued and how bond prices change over time. We cover here the mechanics of bond calculations, an important part of an investor's toolkit.

AFTER READING THIS CHAPTER YOU WILL BE ABLE TO:

► Understand and calculate various bond yield measures, most importantly the yield to maturity.
► Calculate the price of a bond.

► Determine how bond prices change as the interest rate changes.

Introduction

You have decided to invest 40 percent of your $1 million in fixed income securities—specifically, bonds—at the outset in order to earn a return while you refine your equity strategy. How do you think the following variables would influence your decision as to the fixed income securities you will hold?

Maturity, Type of Bond, Credit Worthiness, Inflation, Yield, and Future Interest Rates.

Bond Yields and Interest Rates

For our purposes, bond yields and interest rates are interchangeable concepts. Therefore, we begin our discussion with a consideration of interest rates.

Interest rates measure the price paid by a borrower to a lender for the use of resources over some time period—that is, interest rates are the price for loanable funds. The price differs from case to case, based on the demand and supply for these funds, resulting in a wide variety of interest rates. The spread between the lowest and highest rates at any normal point in time could be as much 10 to 15 percentage points. In bond parlance, this would be equivalent to 1,000 to 1,500 basis points, since 1 percentage point of a bond yield consists of 100 **basis points**. During the financial crisis of 2008, the spread became much wider, exceeding 20 percentage points.

Basis Points 100 basis points is equal to 1 percentage point

✓ 100 basis points = 1 percentage point

Example 17-1

Assume the 10-year Treasury bond yield is 4.54 percent, compared to 4.39 percent a week earlier. The yield has increased 15 basis points in a week, or 0.15 percent.

It is convenient to focus on the one interest rate that provides the foundation for other rates. This rate is referred to as the short-term riskless rate (designated RF in this text) and is typically proxied by the rate on Treasury bills. All other rates differ from RF because of risk and time premiums.

THE BASIC COMPONENTS OF INTEREST RATES

Explaining interest rates is a complex task that involves substantial economics reasoning and study. Such a task is not feasible in this text.[1] However, we can analyze the basic determinants of nominal (current) interest rates with an eye toward recognizing the factors that affect such rates and cause them to fluctuate. The bond investor who understands the foundations of market rates can then rely on expert help for more details and be in a better position to interpret and evaluate such help.

The basic foundation of market interest rates is the opportunity cost of foregoing consumption, representing the rate that must be offered to individuals to persuade them to save rather than consume. This rate is sometimes called the **real risk-free rate of interest**, because it is not affected by price changes or risk factors.[2] We will refer to it simply as the *real rate* and designate it rr in this discussion.

Real Risk-Free Rate of Interest The opportunity cost of foregoing consumption, given no inflation

✓ Nominal (current) interest rates on Treasury bills consist of the real rate plus an adjustment for *expected inflation*.

A lender who lends $100 for a year at 10 percent will be repaid $110. But if inflation is 4 percent a year, the $110 that the lender receives upon repayment of the loan is worth, in terms of purchasing power, only (1/1.04)($110), or $105.60. Lenders therefore expect to be compensated for the *expected* rate of inflation in order to leave the real purchasing power

[1] Most texts on financial markets contain a good, concise discussion of interest rates.
[2] The real rate of interest cannot be measured directly. It is often estimated by dividing $(1.0 + MIR)$ by $(1.0 + EI)$, where MIR is the market interest rate and EI is expected inflation. This result can be approximated by subtracting estimates of inflation from nominal (market) interest rates (on either a realized or expected basis).

of wealth unchanged. *As an approximation for discussion purposes*, this inflation adjustment can be added to the real risk-free rate of interest. Unlike rr, which is often assumed by market participants to be reasonably stable with time, adjustments for *expected* inflation vary widely over time.

Thus, for short-term risk-free securities, such as three-month Treasury bills, the nominal interest rate is a function of the real rate of interest and the *expected* inflation premium. This is expressed as Equation 17-1, which is an approximation:[3]

$$RF \approx rr + ei \qquad\qquad (17\text{-}1)$$

where

$$RF = \text{short-term Treasury bill rate}$$
$$rr \; = \text{the real risk-free rate of interest}$$
$$ei \; = \text{the expected rate of inflation over the term of the instrument}$$

Equation 17-1 implies that the nominal rate on short-term risk-free securities rises point-for-point with expected inflation, with the real rate of interest remaining unaffected.[4] Turning Equation 17-1 around, estimates of the real risk-free rate of interest can be *approximated* by subtracting the *expected* inflation rate from the observed nominal interest rate.[5] Most market participants typically estimate the real rate to be in the range of 1−2 percent.

One of the best sources of expected inflation data is the Survey of Consumers by the University of Michigan. Participants are asked to predict how much prices will change over a horizon of one year and five to 10 years. The median expected price change for the next 12 months can be seen in graphical form at the St. Louis Fed website.[6] Some evidence suggests that the median response from this survey has been at least as accurate as forecasts of future inflation by professional forecasters.[7]

Building on Equation 17-1, we can formulate a statement for all interest rates, IR, as

$$IR = rr + ei + rp \qquad\qquad (17\text{-}2)$$

In this formulation, rp represents all risk premiums involved, including time to maturity and credit quality as well as differences among corporate bonds such as call features, collateral, and sinking fund provisions. However, in the discussion that follows, we will separate out the time element from the issuer characteristics.

---

[3] The correct procedure is to multiply (1 + the real rate) by (1 + the expected rate of inflation), and subtract 1.0. For purposes of our discussion, the additive relationship is satisfactory.

[4] Equation 17-1 is known as the *Fisher hypothesis*. Fisher believed that inflation expectations were based on past observations as well as information about the future and that inflation expectations were slow to develop and slow to disappear.

[5] While estimates of the real federal funds rate can be made by subtracting actual inflation for the same quarter because federal funds are of very short duration, estimates of real rates on instruments with longer maturities require measures of expected inflation over the term of the instrument.

[6] One source for viewing these data is http://research.stlouisfed.org/fred2/series/MICH/.

[7] N. G. Mankiw, R. Reis, and J. Wolfers, "Disagreement About Inflation Expectations," *NBER Macroeconomics Annual* 2003.

THE TERM STRUCTURE OF INTEREST RATES

Term Structure of Interest Rates The relationship between time to maturity and yields for a particular category of bonds

The **term structure of interest rates** refers to the relationship between time to maturity and yields for a specified category of bonds at a particular point in time. Ideally, other factors are held constant, particularly the risk of default. The easiest way to do this is to examine U.S. Treasury securities, which have no practical risk of default, have no sinking fund, and are taxable. By eliminating those that may have some special feature, a quite homogeneous sample of bonds is obtained for analysis.

Yield Curve A graphical depiction of the relationship between yields and time for bonds that are identical except for maturity

Yield Curves   The term structure is usually plotted in the form of a **yield curve**. The horizontal axis represents time to maturity, whereas the vertical axis represents yield to maturity. Yield curves were illustrated in Chapter 13.

✓ The yield curve is a graphical depiction of the relationship between yields and time for bonds of the same issuer, such as the U.S. Treasury, at a particular point in time.

Most observations about yield curves involve tendencies and not exact relationships. Forecasts from yield curves can vary from forecaster to forecaster.

Expectations Theory States that the long-term rate of interest is equal to an average of the short-term rates that are expected to prevail over the long-term period

Term Structure Theories   A theory of the term structure of interest rates is needed to explain the shape and slope of the yield curve and why it shifts over time. Theories traditionally advanced are the expectations theory, the liquidity premium theory, the preferred habitat theory, and the market segmentation theory.

The *pure or "unbiased"* **expectations theory** of the term structure of interest rates asserts that financial market participants determine security yields such that the return from holding an *n*-period security equals the average return expected from holding a series of one-year securities over the same *n* periods. In other words, the long-term rate of interest is equal to an average of the present yield on short-term securities plus the expected future yields on short-term securities that are expected to prevail over the long-term period. For each period, the total rate of return is expected to be the same on all securities regardless of time to maturity.

In effect, the term structure consists of a set of forward rates and a current known rate. **Forward rates** are rates that are expected to prevail in the future; that is, they are unobservable but anticipated future rates.

Forward rates
Unobservable rates expected to prevail in the future

✓ Under the expectations theory, long rates must be an average of the present and future short-term rates.

For example, a three-year bond would carry an interest rate that is an average of the current rate for one year and the expected forward rates for the next two years. The same principle holds for any number of periods; therefore, the market rate for any period to maturity can be expressed as an average of the current rate and the applicable forward rates. Technically, the average involved is a geometric rather than an arithmetic average.

For expositional purposes:

$_tR_n$ = the current known yield (i.e., at time *t*), on a security with *n* periods to maturity

$_{t+1}r_n$ = the yield expected to prevail one year from today (at time *t* + 1) for *n* periods—

these are forward rates

The rate for the three-year bond referred to above must be a geometric average of the current one-year rate ($_tR_1$) and the expected forward rates for the subsequent two years. Therefore, in equation form

$$(1 + {}_tR_3) = [(1 + {}_tR_1)(1 + {}_{t+1}r_1)(1 + {}_{t+2}r_1)]^{1/3} - 1.0 \qquad \textbf{(17-3)}$$

where

$(1 + {}_tR_3)$ = the rate on a three-year bond

$(1 + {}_tR_1)$ = the current known rate on a one-year bond

$(1 + {}_{t+1}r_1)$ = the expected rate on a bond with one year to maturity beginning one year from now

$(1 + {}_{t+2}r_1)$ = the expected rate on a bond with one year to maturity beginning two years from now

Example 17-2   Assume that the current one-year bond rate ($_tR_1$) is 0.07, and the two forward rates are 0.075 ($_{t+1}r_1$) and 0.082 ($_{t+2}r_1$). The rate for a three-year bond, $(1 + {}_tR_3)$, would be

$$
\begin{aligned}
1 + {}_tR_3) &= [(1.07)(1.075)(1.082)]^{1/3} - 1.0 \\
&= 1.0757 - 1.0 \\
&= 0.0757 \text{ or } 7.57\%
\end{aligned}
$$

The same principle applies for any number of periods. Any long-term rate is a geometric average of consecutive one-period rates.

Forward rates cannot be easily measured, but they can be inferred for any one-year future period. The expectations theory, however, does not say that these future expected rates will be correct; it simply says that there is a relationship between rates today and rates expected in the future.

Under this hypothesis, investors can expect the same return regardless of the choice of investment. Any combination of securities for a specified period will have the same expected return.

Example 17-3

A five-year bond will have the same expected return as a two-year bond held to maturity plus a three-year bond bought at the beginning of the third year.

The assumption under this hypothesis is that expected future rates are equal to computed forward rates. Profit-seeking individuals will exploit any differences between forward rates and expected rates, ensuring that they equilibrate.

The second theory, the **liquidity preference theory**, states that interest rates reflect the sum of current and expected short rates, as in the expectations theory, plus liquidity (risk) premiums. Because uncertainty increases with time, investors prefer to lend for the short run. Borrowers, however, prefer to borrow for the long run in order to be assured of funds. Investors receive a liquidity premium to induce them to lend long-term, while paying a price premium (in the form of lower yields) for investing short-term. The implication of this theory is that longer-term bonds should offer higher yields.

The difference between the liquidity preference theory and the expectations theory is the recognition that interest rate expectations are uncertain. Risk-averse investors seek to be compensated for this uncertainty. Forward rates and estimated future rates are not the same; they differ by the amount of the liquidity premiums.

The preferred habitat theory and the market segmentation theory are explained in Appendix 17-A.

RISK PREMIUMS (YIELD SPREADS)

Liquidity Preference Theory States that interest rates reflect the sum of current and expected short rates, as in the expectations theory, plus liquidity (risk) premiums

Yield Spread The relationship between bond yields and the particular features on various bonds such as quality, callability, and taxes

Risk premiums, or **yield spreads**, refer to the issue characteristics of the bonds involved. They are a result of the following factors:

1. Differences in quality, or risk of default. Clearly, all other things being equal, a bond rated BAA will offer a higher yield than a similar bond rated AAA because of the difference in default risk.
2. Differences in time to maturity. The longer the time period involved, the greater the uncertainty.
3. Differences in call features. Bonds that are callable have higher ytms than otherwise identical noncallable bonds. If the bond is called, bondholders must give it up, and they could replace it only with a bond carrying a lower ytm. Therefore, investors expect to be compensated for this risk.
4. Differences in coupon rates. Bonds with low coupons have a larger part of their ytm in the form of capital gains.
5. Differences in marketability. Some bonds are more marketable than others, meaning that their liquidity is better. They can be sold either more quickly or with less of a price concession, or both. The less marketable a bond, the higher the ytm.
6. Differences in tax treatments.
7. Differences between countries.

✓ Yield spreads are a function of the variables connected with a particular issue or issuer.

Other Factors Affecting Yield Spreads   Investors expect to be compensated for the risk of a particular issue, and this compensation is reflected in the risk premium. However, investors are not the only determining factor in yield spreads. The actions of borrowers also affect them. Heavy Treasury financing, for example, may cause the yield spreads between governments and corporates to narrow as the large increase in the supply of Treasury securities pushes up the yields on Treasuries.

The level of interest rates also plays a role in explaining yield spreads. As a general proposition, risk premiums tend to be high when the level of interest rates is high.

Yield Spreads over Time   Yield spreads among alternative bonds may be positive or negative at any time. Furthermore, the size of the yield spread changes over time. Whenever the differences in yield become smaller, the yield spread is said to "narrow"; as the differences increase, it "widens."

It seems reasonable to assume that yield spreads widen during recessions, when investors become more risk-averse, and narrow during times of economic prosperity. Since the probability of default is greater during a recession, investors demand more of a premium. Yield spreads were at their widest during the early 1930s, when the Great Depression was at its worst. In contrast, yield spreads narrow during boom periods because even financially weak companies have a good chance of surviving and paying their debt obligations.

Figure 17-1 shows the spread between 10-year Treasuries and Baa corporate bonds. Notice how much the spread widened in late 2008 (extreme left part of Figure 17-1) because of the recession and financial crisis occurring at the time.

✓ The yield spread varies inversely to the business cycle.

Figure 17-1

Yield Spreads between 10-Year Treasuries and Baa Corporate Bonds, 2008–2011.

Source: *Monetary Trends*, Federal Reserve Bank of St. Louis, February 2012, p. 9.

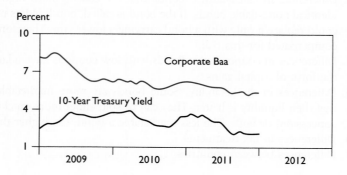

Figure 17-2

Some Measures of a Bond's Yield or Return.

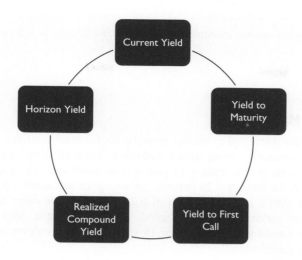

Measuring Bond Yields

Several measures of the yield on a bond are used by investors. It is very important for bond investors to understand which yield measure is being discussed, and what the underlying assumptions of any particular measure are. We will consider five different measures of a bond's return, as shown in Figure 17-2.

To illustrate the current yield and the yield to maturity measures, we will use as an example an AAA-rated corporate bond:

$$\text{Current price} = \$1,052.42;$$

Premium Bond A bond whose price is above the $1,000 face value

Discount Bond A bond whose price is below the face value of $1,000

Note that this is a **premium bond** because its price is greater than its par value of $1,000. For a **discount bond**, the price is less than par value.

Maturity = three years

Coupon = 10%, or $100 per year, with interest payments occurring exactly six months from now, one year from now, and so forth.

✓ Interest payments on bonds (i.e., the coupons) are typically paid semiannually—this is simply the actual payment mechanism that has existed for many years. Unless otherwise noted, we will always assume that coupons are paid semiannually.

CURRENT YIELD

Current Yield A bond's annual coupon divided by the current market price

The ratio of the coupon interest to the current market price is the **current yield**, which is clearly superior to simply citing the coupon rate on a bond because it uses the current market price as opposed to the face amount of a bond (almost always, $1,000). However, current yield is not a true measure of the return to a bond purchaser because it does not account for the difference between the bond's purchase price and its eventual redemption at par value.

Example 17-4   The current yield on our example bond is $100/$1,052.10 = 9.5 percent.

YIELD TO MATURITY

Assume you are interested in buying some bonds for your portfolio, and you talk with your registered representative about what's available in terms of safety, maturity, and yield. After a diligent search he or she finds a 15-year quality bond and tells you that the current yield to maturity on the bond is 6.25 percent. So, says your registered rep, buy this bond, hold to maturity and earn a nice safe return of 6.25 percent while other reasonable fixed income investments are yielding less. Sounds good, you say, I'll take it. After all, this is a no-brainer, wrapping up a good yield like this for 15 years. Are you as clever as you think, or perhaps misguided or misinformed?

Yield to Maturity (YTM) The promised compounded rate of return on a bond purchased at the current market price and held to maturity

✓ The rate of return on bonds most often quoted for investors is the **yield to maturity (YTM)**, a *promised* rate of return that occurs only under specific assumptions.

YTM is the compound rate of return an investor will receive from a bond purchased at the current market price if

1. The bond is held to maturity
2. The coupons received while the bond is held are reinvested at the calculated yield to maturity for that bond

In practice, YTM is thought of as the average annual return on the bond over its life.[8] However, an investor will actually earn this *promised* rate if, and only if, the two stated conditions are met. As we shall see, the likelihood of the second condition actually being met is extremely small. Thus, in our example above, your chances of earning exactly 6.25 percent over the 15-year life of this bond are almost zero.

The yield to maturity is based on Equation 17-4 where the market price, the coupon, the number of years to maturity, and the face value of the bond are known, and the discount rate or yield to maturity is the variable to be determined. *Note in the following discussion that lower case letters, ytm, c, and n, are used to denote semiannual variables, while capital letters, YTM, C, and N are used to denote annual variables.*

✓ Correct bond calculations in the United States usually involve semiannual periods, because bond interest is typically paid twice a year.

$$P = \sum_{t=1}^{n} \frac{c_t}{(1+\text{ytm})^t} + \frac{\text{FV}}{(1+\text{ytm})^n} \qquad \textbf{(17-4)}$$

---

[8] The yield to maturity is the IRR (internal rate of return) on the bond investment, similar to the IRR used in capital budgeting analysis (and subject to the same limitations).

where

P $\quad=$ the current market price of the bond

$n\quad=$ the number of semiannual periods to maturity

ytm $=$ the semiannual yield to maturity to be solved for

c $\quad=$ the semiannual coupon in dollars

FV $\quad=$ the face value (or maturity value or par value) which in this discussion is always $1,000

Since both the left-hand side of Equation 17-4 and the numerator values (cash flows) on the right side are known, the equation can be solved for ytm. Because of the semiannual nature of interest payments, the annual coupon on the bond, C, is divided in half (to obtain c) and the number of periods, N, is doubled (to obtain n). The discount rate, ytm, equates the inflows from the bond (coupons plus maturity value) with its current price (cost).

Example 17-5 Consider a 10 percent coupon bond with three years to maturity. The annual coupon is $100, which is paid $50 every six months, and the total number of semiannual periods is six. Assume that the bond is selling at a premium with a current market price of $1,052.42. Because of the inverse relation between bond prices and market yields, it is clear that yields have declined since the bond was originally issued, because the price is greater than $1,000. Using Equation 17-4, we can illustrate conceptually what is happening when we solve for ytm, although to actually solve for ytm we would use a calculator or computer.

$$\$1,052.42 = \sum_{t=1}^{6} + \frac{\$50}{(1 + \text{ytm})^t} + \frac{\$1,000}{(1 + \text{ytm})^6}$$

$\$1,052.42 = \$50 \times$ (present value of an annuity, 4 percent for six periods)
$\qquad\qquad + \$1,000 \times$ (present value factor, 4 percent for three periods)

$\$1,052.42 = \$50(5.242) + \$1,000(0.790)$

$\$1,052.42 = \$1,052.10$ (rounding error accounts for the differential)

$\qquad 4\% = $ semiannual ytm

$2 \times 4\% = 8\% = $ annual YTM (bond equivalent yield)

In Example 17-5, the solution is 4 percent on a semiannual basis, which we are calling ytm, and which by convention is doubled to obtain the annual YTM of 8 percent. A YTM calculated by annualizing in this manner is referred to as the **bond-equivalent yield**.

Bond-Equivalent Yield Yield on an annual basis, derived by doubling the semiannual compound yield

Using the Calculator: Using a HP 10B calculator, we enter the following values:

N	I/YR	PV	PMT	FV
6	?	−1052.42	50	100

Note that using the HP, PV (the price of the bond) is entered as a negative using the $+/-$ key. The values entered for N and PMT are semiannual values. The face or par value is almost always $1,000.

Pressing the I/YR key, we find the semiannual yield, ytm, to be 4 percent. We double this to obtain the bond-equivalent yield, 8 percent.

An investor who purchases a bond and holds it to maturity will earn the promised yield to maturity as calculated on the purchase date (barring default or failure to receive the cash flows in a timely manner) if, and only if, the cash flows are reinvested at the calculated yield to maturity rate. Thus, the rate(s) at which the cash flows are reinvested over the life of the bond will affect the actual outcome of every coupon-paying bond investment.

YTM for a Zero-Coupon Bond   Recall from Chapter 2 that a zero-coupon bond has no cash flows (coupons); instead, it is bought at a discount and held to maturity to earn a return. The yield to maturity calculation for a zero-coupon bond is based on the same process expressed in Equation 17-4—equating the current price to the future cash flows to find ytm, and then doubling this result to obtain the annual YTM. Because there are no coupons, the only cash flow is the face value of the bond to be received at maturity. We will always assume a $1,000 face value for all bonds discussed. The ytm calculation for a zero-coupon bond reduces to Equation 17-5, with all terms as previously defined:

$$\text{ytm} = [FV/P]^{1/n} - 1 \qquad\qquad \textbf{(17-5)}$$

multiply by 2 to obtain YTM, the bond equivalent yield.

Using the Calculator: Using a HP 10B, enter the following values:

N	I/YR	PV	PMT	FV
24		−300	0	100

Pressing the I/YR key, we find the semiannual yield, ytm, to be 5.1445 percent. The bond equivalent yield is 10.29 percent.

Example 17-6

A zero-coupon bond has 12 years to maturity and is selling for $300. Given the 24 semiannual periods, the power to be used in raising the ratio of $1,000/$300, or 3.3333, is 0.04167 (calculated as $1/(2\times12)$). Using a calculator with a power function produces a value of 1.05145. Subtracting the 1.0 and multiplying by 100 leaves a semiannual yield to maturity, ytm, of 5.145 percent. The bond equivalent yield is 10.29 percent.

YIELD TO FIRST CALL

Yield to First Call The promised return on a bond from the present to the date that the bond is likely to be called

Most corporate bonds, as well as some government bonds, are callable by the issuers, typically after some deferred call period. For bonds likely to be called, the yield-to-maturity calculation is unrealistic. A better calculation is the **yield to first call**. The end of the deferred call period, when a bond can first be called, is often used for the yield-to-first-call calculation. This is particularly appropriate for bonds selling at a premium (i.e., high-coupon bonds with market prices above par value).[9]

---

[9] That is, bonds with high coupons (and high yields) are prime candidates to be called.

✓ Premium bonds are vulnerable to a call as their price approaches the call price. Investors in premium bonds pay careful attention to the bond's yield to first call, particularly if they expect a further drop in interest rates.

To calculate the yield to first call, the ytm formula (Equation 17-4) is used, but with the number of periods until the first call date substituted for the number of periods until maturity and the call price substituted for face value. Issuers often pay a call premium for a specified period of time to call the bonds, and therefore the call price can differ from the maturity value of $1,000. These changes are shown in Equation 17-6.

$$P = \sum_{t=1}^{n} \frac{c_t}{(1 + yc)^t} + \frac{CP}{(1 + yc)^{fc}} \qquad (17\text{-}6)$$

where

fc	=	the number of semiannual periods until the first call date
yc	=	the yield to first call on a semiannual basis
CP	=	the call price to be paid by the issuer if the bond is called

Example 17-7

Assume a 15-year, 6 percent coupon bond is callable in five years at a price of $1,050. The bond currently sells for $1,075. The semiannual yield to call is calculated as

N	I/YR	PV	PMT	FV
10	?	−1,075	30	1050

I/YR, the semiannual yield to call, is 2.58 percent. The bond equivalent yield is 5.16 percent. The YTM on this bond is 5.51 percent bond equivalent.

Bond prices are calculated on the basis of the lowest yield measure. Therefore, for premium bonds selling above a certain level, yield to first call replaces yield to maturity, because it produces the lowest measure of yield.

REALIZED COMPOUND YIELD

Realized Compound Yield (RCY) Yield earned on a bond based on actual reinvestment rates during the life of the bond

After the investment period for a bond is over, an investor can calculate the **Realized Compound Yield (RCY)**. This rate measures the compound yield on the bond investment actually earned over the investment period, taking into account all intermediate cash flows and reinvestment rates. Defined in this manner, it cannot be determined until the investment is concluded and all of the cash flows are known. Thus, if you invest $1,000 in a bond for five years, reinvesting the coupons as they are received, you will have X dollars at the conclusion of the five years, consisting of the coupons received, the amount earned from reinvesting the coupons, and the $1,000 par value of the bond payable at maturity. You can then calculate your actual realized rate of return on the investment.

✓ The RCY for a bond can be calculated by dividing the total dollar return at the bond's maturity by the amount invested, and raising the result to the $1/n$ power, where n is the number of (semiannual) compounding periods. Next, subtract 1.0 from the result. Finally, because of the semiannual basis for bonds, multiply by 2 to obtain the bond equivalent rate.

The realized compound yield can be calculated using the following formula:

$$RCY = \left[\frac{\text{Total Dollar Return}}{\text{Purchase price of bond}} \right]^{1/n} - 1.0 \tag{17-7}$$

For our purposes, we define *Total Dollar Return* for a coupon bond held to maturity as the sum of the maturity value ($1,000), the coupons, and the interest earned by reinvesting the coupons.

Example 17-8   Assume an investor had $1,000 to invest three years ago. This investor purchased a 10 percent coupon bond with a three-year maturity at face value. The promised YTM for this bond was 10 percent.

Assume the investor reinvested each coupon at a semiannual rate, or ytm, of exactly 5 percent. At the end of the three years the investor has a total ending wealth of $1,340.10 which includes the initial investment of $1,000 (in other words, the investor earned $340.10 on the $1,000, given the compounding over time).

This $340.10 is a combination of the coupons and the interest earned on the coupons. Using the calculator,

N	I/YR	PV	PMT	FV
6	5	0	50	?

Solving for FV produces $340.10, which added to the maturity value of the bond gives us a total dollar return of $1,340.10.

The Realized Compound Yield on this investment, under the circumstances described, is 5 percent on a semiannual basis or 10 percent on a bond equivalent basis, calculated as

$$[\$1,340.10/\$1,000]^{1/6} - 1.0 = .05 \text{ semiannually, or } .10 \text{ on a bond equivalent basis.}$$

Now we are in a better position to understand the YTM calculation. The YTM on a bond assumes that all coupons are reinvested at an interest rate equal to the bond's YTM. If all coupons are reinvested at the calculated yield to maturity, the realized compound yield after the investment period ends will be equal to the rate promised to the investor at the time of purchase, the YTM. This is the case for the bond in Example 17–8. The promised YTM was 10 percent annually (bond equivalent basis), and the actual realized compound yield was 10 percent annually (bond equivalent basis).

If the coupons are reinvested at different rates, however, the RYC will not be equal to the promised YTM.

Assume in Example 17–8 that conditions changed immediately after the investor purchased the bond so that the coupons could be reinvested only at a rate of 9 percent. In this case, the value of the coupons and the interest earned on these coupons is $335.84.

N	I/YR	PV	PMT	FV
6	4.5	0	50	?

The total dollar return is $1,335.84. While the YTM was 10 percent when the investor purchased the bond, the RCY is now 9.89 percent.

$$[\$1,335.84/\$1,000]^{1/6} - 1.0 = .04944 \text{ semiannually, or } .0989 \text{ on an annual basis}$$

✓ For the typical bond investment, the YTM will seldom equal the RCY.

This is true because subsequent reinvestment rates will seldom equal the calculated YTM on the bond. Instead, they will vary over time, being higher than the calculated YTM at times and lower than the calculated YTM at other times.
Remember,

❏ The YTM is a promised rate, and is dependent upon the coupons being reinvested at the calculated YTM.
❏ The RCY is the actual return realized at the conclusion of the investment, and reflects exactly what was earned based on the reinvestment rates available.

Investments Intuition

Consider what happens when investors purchase bonds at high **YTMs**, such as the record levels reached in the summer of 1982. Some utilities issued bonds with an 18 percent coupon. Those investors expecting to actually earn 18 percent were disappointed unless they reinvested the coupons at these record YTMs; that is, investors did not actually achieve a realized compound yield equal to the calculated YTM. For the promised **YTM** to become a realized yield, coupons had to be reinvested over time at the record rates existing at the purchase date of the bond, an unlikely situation for a high-**YTM** bond with a long maturity. The subsequent decline in interest rates during the fall of 1982 illustrates the fallacy of believing that one has "locked up" record yields during a relatively brief period of very high interest rates. Investors in this situation are sometimes said to be subject to *yield illusion.*

This analysis highlights the importance of reinvestment rates to investors, and, therefore, reinvestment rate risk.

Checking Your Understanding

1. Agree or disagree with the following statement, and explain your reasoning. "Investors are routinely quoted the yield to maturity on a bond, but the chance of them actually earning this quoted yield at the termination of the investment is almost zero."
2. Explain why, for a bond selling at a discount, the coupon rate is less than the current yield, which is less than the yield to maturity.

Interest-on-Interest The process by which bond coupons are reinvested to earn interest

Reinvestment Risk   As noted, the YTM calculation assumes that the investor reinvests all coupons received from a bond at a rate equal to the computed YTM on that bond, thereby earning interest on interest over the life of the bond. **Interest-on-interest** is the income earned on the reinvestment of the intermediate cash flows, which for a bond are the coupon (interest) payments made semiannually.

Example 17-9   Given the bond in Example 17–8, with a 10 percent coupon and a three-year maturity, assume that the coupons are reinvested at a rate of 5 percent semiannually. The interest-on-interest from this bond is as follows: The first $50, received six months after buying the bond, is reinvested and earns $50 \times (1.05)^5 = \$63.81$, the second $50 received at the end of one year is reinvested and earns $50 \times (1.05)^4 = \$60.78$, the third $50 received at the end of one and a half years is reinvested and earns $50 \times (1.05)^3 = \$57.88$, the fourth $50 received at the end of two years is reinvested and earns $(1.05)^2 = \$55.13$, the fifth $50 received is reinvested and earns $50 \times (1.05) = \$52.50$, and the last $50 is received at the end of three years and cannot be reinvested. Adding all six numbers together produces a total of $340.10.

The YTM calculation assumes that the reinvestment rate on all cash flows during the life of the bond is the calculated yield to maturity for that bond. If the investor spends the coupons, or reinvests them at a rate different from the assumed reinvestment rate, the realized compound yield that will actually be earned when the bond matures will differ from the calculated YTM which is only a promised rate. And, in fact, coupons almost always will be reinvested at rates higher or lower than the computed YTM. This gives rise to an important bond risk.

Reinvestment Rate Risk
That part of interest rate risk resulting from uncertainty about the rate at which future interest coupons can be reinvested

✓ **Reinvestment rate risk** is the risk that future reinvestment rates will be less than the YTM at the time the bond is purchased.

The total dollar return on a bond consists of three components: (1) the coupons paid on the bond, (2) interest income from the reinvestment of the coupons, and (3) the maturity value of the bond, which is always assumed to be $1,000.

The interest-on-interest concept significantly affects the potential total dollar return from a bond investment. The exact impact is a function of coupon and time to maturity, with reinvestment becoming more important as either coupon or time to maturity, or both, rises. Specifically,

1. Holding everything else constant, the longer the maturity of a bond, the greater the reinvestment risk
2. Holding everything else constant, the higher the coupon rate, the greater the dependence of the total dollar return from the bond on the reinvestment of the coupon payments

Figure 17-3 illustrates the importance of the interest-on-interest in impacting the total dollar return from a bond. The total dollar return for this bond is $2,000 + $4,040 + $1,000 = $7,040. This is a 10 percent coupon, 20-year bond purchased at par ($1,000). All coupons are reinvested at 5 percent on a semiannual basis; that is, the ytm is 5 percent (10 percent on an annual basis). At the end of 20 years (40 semiannual periods), the total dollar return on this bond will be $7,040, consisting of

$1,000 received at maturity

+ $2,000 in coupons received over the life of the bond

+ $4,040 as a result of interest-on-interest (reinvesting each coupon at 5 percent semiannually)

Figure 17-3

The Three Components of a Bond's Total Dollar Return.

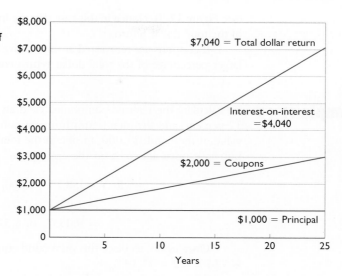

Table 17-1 Realized Compound Yields Using Different Reinvestment Rate Assumptions, for a 10 percent 20-Year Bond Purchased at Face Value

(1) Coupon Income[a] ($)	(2) Assumed Reinvestment Rate (%)	(3) Total Return from Coupons[b] ($)	(4) Amount Attributable to Reinvestment[c] ($)	(5) Realized Compound Yields[d] (%)
2000	0	2000	0	5.57
2000	5	3370	1370	7.51
2000	8	4751	2751	8.94
2000	9	5352	3352	9.46
2000	10	6040	4040	10.00
2000	11	6830	4830	10.56
2000	12	7738	5738	11.14

[a]Coupon income = total dollars received from coupons over 20 years (40 semiannual periods) = $50 coupon received semiannually × 40 periods. 10 percent coupon bond generates $100 income annually or $50 every six months.

[b]Total return from coupons = all coupons received plus all income earned from reinvesting the coupons over the life of the bond. Using a calculator: N = 40; I/YR = ½ of assumed reinvestment rate; PV = 0; PMT = 50; solve for FV.
Example: at an 8 percent reinvestment rate, N = 40; I/YR = 4; PV = 0; PMT = 50; FV = $4751.

[c]Amount attributable to reinvestment of coupons = total return from coupons minus coupon income. This is also known as the interest-on-interest. Notice that in each case it is $2,000 (the amount of the coupons) less than the Total Return from Coupons.

[d]Realized compound yield = [total dollar return/cost of the bond]$^{1/n}$ − 1, where total dollar return = total return from coupons + the maturity value of $1,000.

Example: at a 9 percent reinvestment rate, total dollar return is $5,352 + $1,000 = $6,352. Divide $6,352 by the cost of the bond; $6,352/$1,000 = 6.352.

Next, raise 6.352 to the 1/40: $(6.352)^{1/40}$ = 1.0473; 1.0473 − 1.0 = 0.0473 on a semiannual basis: (Note: 6.352 is the same value one would obtain by raising the semiannual rate of 0.0473 + 1.0 to the 40th power [which reflects semiannual compounding for 20 years]— that is, 1.0473^{40} = 6.352).

The result of this calculation is the realized yield on a semiannual basis. To put this on an annual basis, known as the bond equivalent yield, this number must be doubled. This has been done for the yields in Table 17-1. For this example, 4.73 × 2 = 9.46%.

To illustrate the importance of the reinvestment rate in determining the actual yields that will be realized from a bond, Table 17-1 shows the realized compound yields actually earned under different assumed reinvestment rates for a 10 percent noncallable 20-year bond purchased at face value—which has a YTM of 10 percent. If the reinvestment rate exactly equals the YTM of 10 percent, the investor earns a 10 percent RCY when the bond is held to maturity, with $4,040 of the total dollar return from the bond attributable to interest-on-interest (see Figure 17-3). Notice in this case that the interest-on-interest is the largest single component of the total dollar return.

If coupons are reinvested at rates above the calculated YTM, the RCY rises, and an even larger percentage of the total dollar return comes from interest-on-interest.

Example 17-10   To calculate the realized compound yield an investor would earn if the reinvestment rate is 12 percent, add the total return from coupons shown in Table 17-1, $7,738, to the maturity value of the bond, $1,000, to obtain the total dollar return of $8,738.[10] Then divide by the purchase price and raise to the appropriate power (take the 40th root). Therefore,

$$RCY = [\$8,738/1,000]^{1/40} - 1.0$$
$$= 1.0557 - 1.0$$
$$= 0.0557, \text{ or } 5.57\% \text{ on a semiannual basis}$$

Once again, to place this on a bond equivalent basis, multiply by two. The annual RCY is $5.57\% \times 2 = 11.14\%$.

Almost 75 percent of the total return comes from interest-on-interest ($5,738/$7,738).

On the other hand, with no reinvestment of coupons (spending them as received), the investor will achieve only a 5.57 percent RCY when the bond is held to maturity. This is calculated by adding the $2000 in coupons received over the life of the bond to the $1000 maturity value, for a total ending wealth of $3,000, and dividing by the purchase price of $1000 for a value of 3. The 40th root of 3 is 1.02785. Subtract out the 1.0 to obtain .02785, and multiply by 2 to obtain .0557 or 5.57 percent for a bond equivalent basis.

Clearly, the reinvestment portion of a bond's total dollar return is critical in determining the actual rate of return earned.

✓   For long-term bonds, when coupons are reinvested, the interest-on-interest component is typically the most important component of the bond's total dollar return.

One advantage of a zero-coupon bond is the elimination of reinvestment rate risk because there are no coupons to be reinvested. At the time of purchase investors know the RCY that will be earned when the bond is held to maturity—it is simply the YTM because there are no coupons to reinvest.

✓   A zero-coupon bond eliminates reinvestment rate risk.

Horizon Return   As we have seen, each of the yield measures has problems. Current yield is clearly not a correct measure of the return that will be received on a bond. Both the yield to maturity and the yield to first call have potential problems because of the reinvestment rate assumptions made, which are basically unrealistic. What can a bond investor do in these circumstances?

Bond investors today often make specific assumptions about future reinvestment rates in order to cope with the reinvestment rate problem illustrated earlier. This is sometimes referred to as *horizon analysis*. Given their explicit assumptions about the reinvestment rate, investors

---

[10] A common calculation in finance is to divide an ending amount by a beginning amount and take the root of the result to determine the compound growth rate over time. With bonds the root will be based on semiannual periods.

Horizon (Total)
Return Bond returns to
be earned based on
assumptions about
reinvestment rates

can calculate the **horizon (total) return** to be earned over a specified period based upon an assumed reinvestment rate.

The investor makes an assumption about the reinvestment rate expected to prevail over the planned investment horizon. The investor may also make an assumption about the yield to maturity expected to prevail at the end of the planned investment horizon, which in turn is used to estimate the price of the bond at that time. Based on these assumptions, the total future dollars expected to be available at the end of the planned investment horizon can be determined. The horizon return, or total return, is then calculated as the interest rate that equates the total future dollars to the purchase price of the bond.

Checking Your Understanding

3. Assume an investor holds a bond that is guaranteed not to default. Can the YTM on this bond be described as the actual return the investor will receive, rather than a promised return?

Bond Prices

THE VALUATION PRINCIPLE

What determines the price of a security? As we learned in Chapter 10, the answer is *estimated* value! A security's estimated value determines the price that investors place on it in the open market.

Recall from Chapter 10 that a security's *intrinsic value*, or estimated value, is the present value of the expected cash flows from that asset. Any security purchased is expected to provide one or more cash flows some time in the future. These cash flows could be periodic, such as interest or dividends, or simply a terminal price or redemption value, or a combination of these. Since these cash flows occur in the future, they must be discounted at an appropriate rate to determine their present value. The sum of these discounted cash flows is the estimated intrinsic value of the asset. Calculating intrinsic value, therefore, requires the use of present value techniques. Equation 17−8 expresses this concept, which is a repeat of Equation 10−1:

$$\text{value} = \sum_{t=1}^{n} \frac{\text{Cash flows}}{(1 + k)^t} \tag{17-8}$$

where

$\text{Value}_{t=0}$ = the estimated value of the asset now (time period 0)

Cash flows = the future cash flows resulting from ownership of the asset

k = the appropriate discount rate or rate of return required by an investor for an investment of this type

n = number of periods over which the cash flows are expected

BOND VALUATION

The price of a bond should equal the present value of its expected cash flows.[11] The coupons and the principal repayment of $1,000 are known, and the present value, or price, can be determined by discounting these future payments from the issuer at an appropriate required yield, r, for the

---

[11] An investor purchasing a bond must also pay to the seller the accrued interest on that bond.

issue. Equation 17-9 is used to solve for the price of an option-free coupon bond.

$$P = \sum_{t=1}^{n} \frac{c_t}{(1+r)^t} + \frac{FV}{(1+r)^n}$$

(17-9)

where

P = the present value or price of the bond today (time period 0)

c = the semiannual coupons or interest payments

FV = the face value (or par value) of the bond

n = the number of semiannual periods until the bond matures

r = the appropriate semiannual discount rate or market yield

In order to conform with the existing payment practice on bonds of paying interest semiannually rather than annually, the discount rate being used (r), the coupon (c_t) on the bond and the number of periods are all on a semiannual basis. Equation 17–9 is the equation that underlies standard bond practices.

The present value process for a typical coupon-bearing bond involves three steps, given the dollar coupon on the bond, the face value, and the current market yield applicable to a particular bond:

1. Determine the present value of the coupons (interest payments).
2. Determine the present value of the maturity (par) value of the bond; for our purposes, the maturity value will always be $1,000.
3. Add the present values determined in steps 1 and 2 together.

Example 17-11   Consider newly issued bond A with a three-year maturity, sold at par with a 10 percent coupon rate. Assuming semiannual interest payments of $50 per year for each of the next six periods, the price of bond A, based on Equation 17-9, is:

$$P(A) = \sum_{t=1}^{6} \frac{\$50}{(1+0.05)^t} + \frac{\$1,000}{(1+0.05)} = \$253.78 + \$746.21$$

$$= \$999.99, \text{ or } \$1,000$$

which, of course, agrees with our immediate recognition that the bond's price should be $1,000 since it has just been sold at par.

Now consider bond B, with characteristics identical to A's, issued five years ago when the interest rate demanded for such a bond was 7 percent. Assume that the current discount rate or required yield on bonds of this type is 10 percent on an annual basis, or 5 percent on a semiannual basis, and that the bond has three years left to maturity. Investors certainly will not pay $1,000 for bond B and receive the dollar coupon of $70 per year, or $35 semiannually, when they can purchase bond A and receive $100 per year. However, they should be willing to pay a price determined by the use of Equation 17-9.

$$P(B) = \sum_{t=1}^{6} \frac{\$35}{(1+0.05)^t} + \frac{\$1,000}{(1+0.05)} = \$177.65 + \$746.21 = \$923.85$$

Using the Calculator: Using a HP 10B, enter the following values:

N	I/YR	PV	PMT	FV
6	5		35	1000

Hitting the PV key, we find the price of the bond to be $923.86.

Thus, bond B is valued, as is any other asset, on the basis of its future stream of benefits (cash flows), using an appropriate market yield. Since the numerator is always specified for coupon-bearing bonds at time of issuance, the only issue in valuing a typical bond is to determine the denominator or discount rate.

✓ The appropriate discount rate is the bond's required yield.

The *required yield*, *r*, in Equation 17-9 is specific for each particular bond. It is the current market rate being earned by investors on comparable bonds with the same maturity and the same credit quality. (In other words, it is an opportunity cost.) Thus, market interest rates are incorporated directly into the discount rate used to solve for the fundamental value of a bond.

Since market interest rates fluctuate constantly, required yields do also. When solving for a bond price it is customary to use the yield to maturity. If the YTM is used, we can, for convenience, restate Equation 17–4 in terms of price and YTM, using the semiannual ytm.

$$P = \sum_{t=1}^{n} \frac{c_t}{(1+\text{ytm})^t} + \frac{FV}{(1+\text{ytm})^n} \tag{17-10}$$

Investments Calculation

Solving for the price of a bond is an easy procedure in today's financial world using either a financial calculator or personal computer. For example, by using a basic financial calculator such as the HP-10B, price can be solved for after entering the cash flows and required yield. Spreadsheet functions will also solve for the price of a bond.

Bond Price Changes

BOND PRICE CHANGES OVER TIME

We now know how to calculate the price of a bond, using the cash flows to be received and the YTM as the discount rate. Assume that we calculate the price of a 20-year bond issued five years ago and determine that it is $910. The bond still has 15 years to maturity. What can we say about its price over the next 15 years?

When everything else is held constant, including market interest rates, bond prices that differ from the bond's face value (assumed to be $1,000) must change over time. Why? On a bond's specified maturity date, it must be worth its face value or maturity value.

Figure 17-4

Bond Price Movements Over Time, Assuming Constant Yields for a 10 Percent Coupon 30-Year Bond.

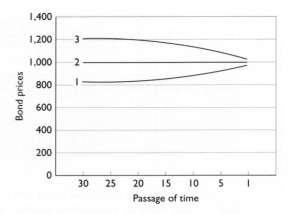

✓ Over time, holding all other factors constant, a bond's price must converge to $1,000 on the maturity date because that is the amount the issuer will pay to the bond holder on the maturity date.

After bonds are issued, they sell at discounts (prices less than $1,000) and premiums (prices greater than $1,000) during their lifetimes. Therefore, a bond selling at a discount will experience a rise in price over time, holding all other factors constant, and a bond selling at a premium will experience a decline in price over time, holding all other factors constant, as the bond's remaining life approaches the maturity date.

Figure 17-4 illustrates bond price movements over time assuming constant yields. Bond 2 in Figure 17-4 illustrates a 10 percent coupon, 30-year bond assuming that yields remain constant at 10 percent. The price of this bond does not change, beginning at $1,000 and ending at $1,000. Bond 1, on the other hand, illustrates an 8 percent coupon, 30-year bond assuming that required yields start, and remain constant, at 10 percent. The price starts below $1,000 because bond 1 is selling at a discount as a result of its coupon of 8 percent being less than the required yield of 10 percent. Bond 3 illustrates a 12 percent coupon, 30-year bond assuming that required yields start, and remain constant, at 10 percent. The price of bond 3 begins above $1,000, because it is selling at a premium (its coupon of 12 percent is greater than the required yield of 10 percent).

If all other factors are held constant, the price of all three bonds must converge to $1,000 on the maturity date. Before the maturity date, however, interest rates and bond prices are continually changing. An important issue is, how much do they change, and why.

The sensitivity of the price change is a function of certain variables, especially coupon and maturity. We now examine these variables.

BOND PRICE CHANGES AS A RESULT OF INTEREST RATE CHANGES

Bond prices change because interest rates and required yields change. Understanding how bond prices change given a change in interest rates is critical to successful bond management. The basics of bond price movements as a result of interest rate changes have been known for many years. For example, over 45 years ago Burton Malkiel derived five theorems about the relationship between bond prices and yields.[12] Using the bond valuation model, he showed the changes that occur in the price of a bond (i.e., its volatility), given a change in yields, as a

[12] Burton G. Malkiel, "Expectations, Bond Prices, and the Term Structure of Interest Rates," *Quarterly Journal of Economics*, May 1962, pp. 197–218.

result of bond variables such as time to maturity and coupon. We will use Malkiel's bond theorems to illustrate how bond prices change as a result of changes in interest rates.

Bond Prices Move Inversely to Interest Rates Investors must always keep in mind *the* fundamental fact about the relationship between bond prices and bond yields: *Bond prices move inversely to market yields*. When the level of required yields demanded by investors on new issues changes, the required yields on all bonds already outstanding will also change. For these yields to change, the prices of these bonds must change. This inverse relationship is the basis for understanding, valuing, and managing bonds.

Example 17-12

Table 17-2 shows prices for a 10 percent coupon bond for market yields from 6 to 14 percent and for maturity dates from one to 30 years. For any given maturity, the price of the bond declines as the required yield increases and increases as the required yield declines from the 10 percent level.

Figure 17-5 shows the convex relationship that exists between bond prices and market yields using data from Table 17-2 for a time of maturity of 10 years.

Table 17-2 Bond Prices at Different Market Yields and Maturities for a 10 Percent Coupon Bond

Time to Maturity	6%	8%	10%	12%	14%
1	$1,038.27	$1,018.86	$1000	$981.67	$963.84
5	1,170.60	1,081.11	1000	926.40	859.53
10	1,297.55	1,135.90	1000	885.30	788.12
15	1,392.01	1,172.92	1000	862.35	751.82
20	1,462.30	1,197.93	1000	849.54	733.37
25	1,514.60	1,214.82	1000	842.38	723.99
30	1,553.51	1,226.23	1000	838.39	719.22

Figure 17-5

The Relationship between Bond Prices and Market Yields.

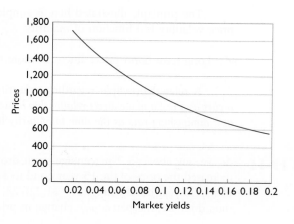

An interesting corollary of the inverse relationship between bond prices and interest rates is as follows: *Holding maturity constant, a decrease in rates will raise bond prices on a percentage basis more than a corresponding increase in rates will lower bond prices.*

Example 17-13   Table 17-2 shows that for the 15-year 10 percent coupon bond, the price would be $1,172.92 if market rates were to decline from 10 percent to 8 percent, resulting in a price appreciation of 17.29 percent. On the other hand, a rise of 2 percentage points in market rates from 10 percent to 12 percent results in a change in price to $862.35, a price decline of only 13.77 percent.

Obviously, bond price volatility can work for, as well as against, investors. Money can be made, and lost, in risk-free Treasury securities as well as more risky corporate bonds. Although the inverse relationship between bond prices and interest rates is the basis of all bond analysis, a complete understanding of bond price changes as a result of interest rate changes requires additional information.

✓   An increase (decrease) in interest rates will cause bond prices to decline (increase), but the exact amount of decline will depend on important variables unique to each bond such as time to maturity and coupon.

We will examine each of these in turn.

The Effects of Maturity   The effect of a change in yields on bond prices depends on the maturity of the bond. An important principle is that *for a given change in market yields, changes in bond prices are directly related to time to maturity.*

✓   As interest rates change, the prices of longer term bonds will change more than the prices of shorter term bonds, everything else being equal.

Example 17-14   Given two 10 percent coupon bonds and a drop in market yields from 10 percent to 8 percent, we can see from Table 17-2 that the price of the 15-year bond will be $1,172.92, while the price of the 30-year bond will be $1,226.23.

The principle illustrated here is simple but important. Other things being equal, bond price volatility is a function of maturity.

✓   Long-term bond prices fluctuate more than do short-term bond prices.

A related principle regarding maturity is as follows: *The percentage price change that occurs as a result of the direct relationship between a bond's maturity and its price volatility increases at a diminishing rate as the time to maturity increases.*

Example 17-15   As we saw above, a 2-percentage-point drop in market yields from 10 percent to 8 percent increased the price of the 15-year bond to $1,172.92, a 17.29 percent change, while the price of the 30-year bond changed to $1,226.23, a 26.23 percent change. Therefore, although the time doubled, the percentage change in price did not double.

This example shows that the percentage price change resulting from an increase in time to maturity increases, but at a decreasing rate. Simply stated, a doubling of the time to maturity will not result in a doubling of the percentage price change resulting from a change in market yields.

The Effects of Coupon   In addition to the maturity effect, the change in the price of a bond as a result of a change in interest rates depends on the coupon rate of the bond.

✓   Bond price fluctuations (volatility) and bond coupon rates are inversely related.[13]

The Implications of Malkiel's Theorems for Investors   Malkiel's derivations for bond investors lead to a practical conclusion: the two bond variables of major importance in assessing the change in the price of a bond, given a change in interest rates, are its coupon and its maturity. This conclusion can be summarized as follows: A decline (rise) in interest rates will cause a rise (decline) in bond prices, with the most volatility in bond prices occurring in longer maturity bonds and bonds with low coupons. Therefore,

1. A bond buyer, in order to receive the maximum price impact of an expected change in interest rates, should purchase low-coupon, long-maturity bonds.
2. If an increase in interest rates is expected (or feared), an investor contemplating his or her purchase should consider those bonds with large coupons or short maturities, or both.

These relationships provide useful information for bond investors by demonstrating how the price of a bond changes as interest rates change. Although investors have no control over the change and direction in market rates, they can exercise control over the coupon and maturity, both of which have significant effects on bond price changes. Nevertheless, it is cumbersome to calculate various possible price changes on the basis of these theorems. Furthermore, maturity is an inadequate measure of the sensitivity of a bond's price change to changes in yields because it ignores the coupon payments and the principal repayment.

Investors managing bond portfolios need a measure of time designed to more accurately portray a bond's "average" life, taking into account all of the bond's cash flows, including both coupons and the return of principal at maturity. Such a measure, called duration, is available and is widely used today. It is discussed in Chapter 18.

Checking Your Understanding

4. The price of a bond will not remain constant if it is selling for either a discount or a premium. Agree or disagree, and explain your reasoning.
5. We know that the prices of long-term bonds are more sensitive to interest rate changes than the prices of short-term bonds. Why, then, is maturity alone not sufficient to measure interest rate sensitivity?

---

[13] Note that we are talking about percentage price fluctuations; this relationship does not necessarily hold if we measure volatility in terms of dollar price changes rather than percentage price changes.

Summary

▶ The level of market interest rates for short-term, risk-free securities is a function of the real rate of interest and inflationary expectations. Inflationary expectations are the primary variable in understanding changes in market rates for short-term, default-free securities.

▶ Other interest rates vary from the short-term riskless rate as a result of risk premiums.

▶ The term structure of interest rates denotes the relationship between market yields and time to maturity. A yield curve graphically depicts this relationship with upward-sloping curves being the norm.

▶ None of the prevalent theories proposed to explain term structure—the expectations theory, the liquidity preference theory, the preferred habitat theory, and the market segmentation theory—is dominant.

▶ Yield spreads are the relationship between bond yields and particular bond features such as quality and callability. Differences in type, quality, and coupon account for most of the yield spreads.

▶ The yield to maturity is defined as the compound rate of return an investor will receive from a bond purchased at the current market price and held to maturity.

▶ The yield to call is the expected yield to the end of the deferred call period, when a bond first can be called.

▶ The horizon return is the total rate of return earned on a bond over some time period given a specified reinvestment rate of return.

▶ Bonds are valued using a present value process. The cash flows for a bond—interest payments and principal repayments—are discounted at the bond's required yield.

▶ Bond prices change over time independent of other factors because they must be worth their face value (typically, $1,000) on the maturity date.

▶ Bond prices move inversely with interest rates, with price increasing (decreasing) as the required yield decreases (increases).

▶ The two bond variables of major importance in assessing the change in price of a bond, given a change in interest rates, are its coupon and its maturity.

▶ Changes in bond prices are directly related to time to maturity and inversely related to bond coupons.

Questions

17-1 When a bond is issued, its coupon rate is set at approximately _____?

17-2 Why is current yield an incorrect measure of a bond's return?

17-3 Define YTM. How is YTM determined?

17-4 Why is YTM important?

17-5 What does it mean to say that YTM is a promised yield?

17-6 If YTM is merely a promised yield, why do investors not use some other measure of yield?

17-7 Yield to maturity can be thought of as the internal rate of return on a bond investment. Agree of disagree, and explain your reasoning.

17-8 Given two bonds with identical risk, coupons and maturity date, with the only difference between the two being that one is callable, which bond will sell for the higher price?

17-9 What is meant by interest-on-interest?

17-10 Which bond is more affected by interest-on-interest considerations?
  a. Bond A—12 percent coupon, 20 years to maturity
  b. Bond B—6 percent coupon, 25 years to maturity

17-11 Distinguish between YTM and RCY. How does interest-on-interest affect the RCY?

17-12 What two characteristics of a bond determine its reinvestment rate risk?

17-13 How can bond investors eliminate the reinvestment rate risk inherent in bonds?

17-14 What is meant by the intrinsic value of a bond?

17-15 How is the price of a bond determined? Why is this process relatively straightforward for a bond?

17-16 What effect does the use of semiannual discounting have on the value of a bond in relation to annual discounting?

17-17 The bond price curve is said to have a convex shape. What does this mean in terms of increases in interest rates relative to changes in bond prices

17-18 What are the implications of Malkiel's bond price theorems to bond investors? Which two bond variables are of major importance in assessing bond price changes?

17-19 When is a bond selling at a discount, based on coupon rate and current yield? A premium?

17-20 What assumptions are involved in calculating the horizon return?

17-21 Agree or Disagree: For the typical bond investment, the YTM will seldom equal the RCY.

17-22 Agree or Disagree: Holding everything else constant, the longer the maturity of a bond, the greater the reinvestment risk.

CFA
17-23 Two salespeople of analytical systems are making a presentation to you about the merits of their respective systems. One salesperson states that in valuing bonds the system first constructs the theoretical spot rates and then discounts cash flows using these rates. The other salesperson interjects that his firm takes a different approach. Rather than using spot rates, forward rates are used to value the cash flows; he believes this is a better approach to valuing bonds compared to using spot rates. How would you respond to the second salesperson's comment about his firm's approach?

CFA
17-24 Suppose a 10-year nine percent coupon bond is selling for $112 with a par value of $100. What is the current yield for the bond? What is the limitation of the current yield measure?

CFA
17-25 Determine whether the yield to maturity of a 6.5 percent 20-year bond that pays interest semiannually and is selling for $90.68 is 7.2 percent, 7.4 percent, or 7.8 percent.

CFA
17-26 Suppose that a 10-percent 15-year bond has the following call structure:

not callable for the next five years
first callable in five years at $105
first par call date is in 10 years

The price of the bond is $127.5880.

a. Is the yield to maturity for this bond 7.0 percent, 7.4 percent, or 7.8 percent?
b. Is the yield to first call for this bond 4.55 percent, 4.65 percent, or 4.85 percent?
c. Is the yield to first par call for this bond 6.25 percent, 6.55 percent, or 6.75 percent?

CFA
17-27 What is the value of a five-year 7.4 percent coupon bond selling to yield 5.6 percent, assuming the coupon payments are made semiannually?

CFA
17-28 A four-year 5.8 percent coupon bond is selling to yield 7 percent. The bond pays interest annually. One year later, interest rates decrease from 7 percent to 6.2 percent.

a. What is the price of the four-year 5.8 percent coupon bond selling to yield 7 percent?
b. What is the price of this bond one year later, assuming the yield is unchanged at 7 percent?
c. What is the price of this bond one year later if instead of the yield's being unchanged, the yield decreases to 6.2 percent?
d. Complete the following:
Price change attributable to moving to maturity (no change in discount rate) _____
Price change attributable to a decrease in the discount rate from 7 percent to 6.2 percent _____ Total price change _____

CFA
17-29 What is the value of a zero-coupon bond paying semiannually that matures in 20 years, has a maturity of $1 million, and is selling to yield 7.6 percent?

CFA
17-30 Consider the following two bond issues:
Bond A : 5 percent 15-year bond
Bond B : 5 percent 30-year bond

a. Neither bond has an embedded option. Both bonds are trading in the market at the same yield.
b. Which bond will fluctuate *more* in price when interest rates change? Why?

CFA
17-31 John Smith and Jane Brody are assistant portfolio managers. The senior portfolio manager has asked them to consider the acquisition of one of two option-free bond issues with the following characteristics:
Issue 1 has a lower coupon rate than Issue 2.
Issue 1 has a shorter maturity than Issue 2.
Both issues have the same credit rating

Smith and Brody are discussing the interest rate risk of the two issues. Smith argues that Issue 1 has greater interest rate risk than Issue 2 because of its lower coupon rate. Brody counters by arguing that Issue 2 has greater interest rate risk, because it has a longer maturity than Issue 1.

a. Which assistant portfolio manager is correct with respect to their selection of the issue with the greater interest rate risk?

b. Suppose that you are the senior portfolio manager. How would you suggest that Smith and Brody determine which issue has the greater interest rate risk?

Problems

17-1 Calculate the price of a 12 percent coupon bond with 18 years to maturity, given an appropriate discount rate of 15 percent, using both annual and semiannual discounting.

17-2 The YTM on an 8 percent, 15-year bond is 10 percent. Calculate the price of the bond.

17-3 Calculate the YTM for a 10-year zero-coupon bond sold at $450. Recalculate the YTM if the bond had been priced at $350.

17-4 Calculate the realized compound yield for a 10 percent bond with 20 years to maturity and an expected reinvestment rate of 8 percent.

17-5 A 7 percent coupon bond has five years remaining to maturity. It is priced to yield 8 percent. What is its current price?

17-6 Consider a junk bond with a 10 percent coupon and 20 years to maturity. The current required rate of return for this bond is 15 percent. What is its price? What would its price be if the required yield rose to 18 percent? 20 percent?

17-7 A five-year zero-coupon bond with a face value of $1,000 is priced to yield 6.5 percent. What is the price of this bond today?

17-8 Consider a 6 percent coupon bond with 15 years to maturity. Determine the YTM that would be necessary to drive the price of this bond to $500.

17-9 Calculate the yield to first call for a 12 percent, 10-year bond that is callable five years from now. The current market price is $980, and the call price is $1,020.

17-10 Calculate the YTM for the following bonds.
  a. A 12 percent, 20-year bond with a current price of $925
  b. A 6 percent, 10-year bond with a current price of $768
  c. A 9 percent, eight-year bond with a current price of $814

17-11 Texaco Oil's 10 percent coupon bonds are selling at 109 1/8. Exactly 15 years remain to maturity. Determine the
  a. Current yield
  b. Yield to maturity

17-12 Using Problem 17-11, assume that 30 years remain to maturity. How would the yield to maturity change? Does the current yield change?

17-13 A seven-year, 5 percent coupon bond is sold at par. However, soon after the bond is sold the going rate for this bond is 5.01 percent. What will be the price of this bond?

17-14 A 12 percent coupon bond has 10 years to maturity. It is currently selling for 15 percent less than face value. Determine its yield to maturity.

17-15   The Saxena Corporation sells a zero-coupon bond with a 7 percent yield to maturity and a maturity of 20 years. Assume interest rates remain constant for four years. What will be the price of this bond in four years?

Computational Problems

17-1   Consider a 6 percent 10-year bond purchased at face value. Based on Table 17-1 and assuming a reinvestment rate of 5 percent, calculate
  a. The interest-on-interest
  b. The total dollar return
  c. The realized compound yield

17-2   You need $60,000 five years from now to pay off a balloon payment on your house. You buy 30 bonds at face value with five-year maturities yielding 8.2 percent. Will you have enough to meet your obligation at the end of five years?

17-3   Some of your relatives wish to accumulate $100,000 as part of their retirement, which will occur 15 years from now. They can buy today 50 bonds at face value yielding 5.4 percent. These bonds have a maturity of nine years. They anticipate that at the end of nine years they can invest their accumulated wealth from the bonds in a 4.2 percent savings account with semiannual compounding. Can they achieve their goal of $100,000?

17-4   You are considering the purchase of an unusual corporate bond with a face value of $25,000, which matures in exactly eight years. The cost of this bond is $14,000. Based on semiannual interest, what bond equivalent rate of return will be earned on this investment?

17-5   A six-year bond with a 9 percent coupon is selling to yield 8 percent. If interest rates remain constant, one year from now will the price of this bond be lower or higher? Prove your answer.

Spreadsheet Exercises

17-1   The yield to maturity on a bond can be calculated using the IRR function. Enter the bond price as a negative number, and the coupons (on a semiannual basis) and maturity value as cash flows. Use the spreadsheet formula = IRR(A1:An) where n is the last cell with a cash flow.
    Calculate, using the spreadsheet, the ytm for a five-year, 7 percent coupon bond currently selling for $975.49.

17-2   Using the spreadsheet, calculate the yield to call for a 6 percent, 12-year bond callable in five years at a call price of $1,050.

17-3   YTM can also be calculated directly in the spreadsheet using the function=YIELD(A1, A2, An) where n is the last cell with inputs for the problem. The user inputs settlement date, maturity date, coupon rate, current bond price, maturity value (par value), and the number of coupons paid per year. You can set the settlement date as the current date, and the maturity date as the same month and day in the year of maturity (five years from now, eight years from now, etc.) Price is stated as a percentage of par (e.g., 100 = $1,000). The following format solved the ytm for the bond in Example 17-3.

1/1/2007	Settlement date = YEAR (year, month, day)*
1/1/2010	Maturity date = YEAR(year, month, day)*
0.1	Annual coupon rate
105.242	Bond price
100	Face value = par value
2	Coupon payments per year
0.08	Yield to maturity as a decimal

*Be sure under the Format settings for the spreadsheet (Format, Cells, Number) to select for Date the format *m/d/year*.
Note: Settlement date is not important—use the current date. Maturity date should reflect the number of years to maturity and the same month and day as the settlement date.

17-4 Using the same basic format as in Problem 17-3, we can solve for bond price be entering the settlement date, the maturity date, the annual coupon rate, the ytm, the par value of the bond expressed as a percentage (100), and the number of coupons per year. Use the function = PRICE(A1, A2, A3, A4, A5, A6). Problem—solve for the price of a six-year, 7 percent coupon bond if the ytm is 8.25 percent.

17-5 Use the spreadsheet format below, which illustrates the cash flows from a bond, to find its price. This bond has a 5.5 percent coupon, five years to maturity, and the required yield on the bond is 6 percent. The 10th cash flow should include both the maturity value and the last coupon payment. The cell for bond price, B9, should reflect the summation of all the present values of the cash flows.

Number of Periods										
Coupon per Period										
Maturity Value										
Required Rate of Return										
Period	0	1	2	3	4	5	6	7	8	9	10
Cash Flows										
PV of Cash Flows										
Bond Price										

Checking Your Understanding

17-1 Agree. The YTM is a promised yield, and to realize this yield an investor must hold the bond to maturity and reinvest the coupons at exactly the calculated yield to maturity. The chance of the reinvestment assumption occurring is practically zero.

17-2 A bond sells at a discount when interest rates rise, leading to declines in the bond price. The lower price raises the current yield above the coupon rate, which is fixed. The YTM will be higher because the bond is being purchased at a discount.

17-3 No. The actual return will depend upon the rate at which the coupons are reinvested. The YTM is still a promised rate.

17-4 The price of discount and premium bonds must move toward $1,000 as the bond approaches its maturity date. On the date the bond will be worth $1,000, because that is what the issuer will redeem it for.

17-5 Taking only maturity into account ignores the coupon on a bond, which also affects the bond's sensitivity to interest rate changes.

chapter *18*

Managing Bond Portfolios: Some Issues Affect All Investors

As you think about managing your inheritance, you may change your mind about the 40 percent bonds and convince yourself that at your age you should only be interested in equities. However, you also realize that it would be smart to at least learn something now about including and managing bonds in your portfolio. After all, you are familiar enough with sharp stock market declines, such as the ones in 2000–2002 and 2008, to understand that there are times you may wish not to have all your inheritance invested in stocks. Furthermore, you may have heard about the strong performance by bonds in recent years. And you now understand the importance of asset allocation and diversification. Once you learn some key principles about managing bonds, you will be in a much better position to evaluate recommendations from brokers, financial advisors, and others as to what you should buy and hold in your portfolio.

Chapter 18 concludes Part V on fixed-income securities by analyzing strategies and approaches to the management of a bond portfolio. We consider why investors buy bonds as well as the issues an investor should consider in managing a bond portfolio. Some basic strategies available to a bond investor are discussed. Investors must also grapple with the overall strategy issue of whether to be active or passive in their investment approach.

AFTER READING THIS CHAPTER YOU WILL BE ABLE TO:

▶ Analyze the reasons why investors buy bonds.
▶ Differentiate between the passive and active strategies for managing a bond portfolio.

▶ Understand the concept of duration, and how it can be used in managing bond volatility.

Why Buy Bonds?

Do stocks always outperform bonds over long periods of time, as many commentators on investing have stated? Are bonds always destined for a 2nd-place finish? Despite the fact that this statement is almost always true, exceptions do occur. Consider the 30 years ending September 30, 2011. A government long-term bond index beat the Standard & Poor's

500 stock index, 11.5 percent to 10.8 percent on a total return basis.[1] The major explanation for this was the long decline in interest rates over this period, from some 14 percent on Treasury bonds to less than 3 percent. Thus, investors enjoyed capital gains as well as interest income, and did not suffer the losses that stocks suffered in 2000–2002 and 2008. Unfortunately, such a dramatic decline in interest rates is a very rare event, and not likely to be repeated again anytime soon. Clearly, with the 10-year Treasury rate hovering around 1.4 percent, as it was in early 2012, there was little room for further decline.

Also, bonds outperform other asset classes for shorter periods of time. In 2011, for example, Treasury bonds outperformed both U.S. stocks and corporate bonds.

As noted in Chapter 6, the total return on bonds can be separated into two components, which helps to explain why bonds appeal to both conservative investors seeking steady income and aggressive investors seeking capital gains. A wide range of investors participate in the fixed-income securities marketplace, ranging from individuals who own a few government or corporate bonds to large institutional investors who own billions of dollars of bonds. Most of these investors are presumably seeking the basic *steady return-low risk* characteristics that most bonds offer; however, quite different overall objectives can be accomplished by purchasing bonds. It is worthwhile to consider these points.

Conservative investors view bonds as fixed-income securities that will pay them a steady stream of income. In most cases the risk is small, and Treasury issues have traditionally been regarded as having no practical risk of default. These investors tend to use a buy-and-hold approach. Investors following this strategy seek to maximize their current income subject to the risk they are willing to assume: corporates should return more than Treasury issues, BAA should return more than A or AA or AAA, longer maturities should return more than short maturities, and so on.

The *promised* yield on a bond held to maturity is known at the time of purchase. Barring default by the issuer, the buyers will have the bond's principal returned to them at maturity. By holding to maturity, investors can escape the risk that the price of the bonds will be lower when they go to sell them, although other risks (such as inflation risk and reinvestment rate risk) may not be eliminated.

✓   As fixed-income securities, bonds are desirable to many investors because they offer a steady stream of interest income over the life of the obligation and a return of principal at maturity.

Example 18-1   As an illustration of the return and risk situation for this type of investor, who is seeking steady returns, consider long-term Treasury securities for the period 1926–2010 as discussed in Chapter 6. There is little or no practical risk of default. At the end of 2010, investors in these government bonds would have earned an average annual compound rate of return of 5.4 percent. Over the same period corporate bonds earned an average annual compound return of 5.9 percent. The standard deviations for these two series were less than half that of stocks. Thus, government bonds, as well as corporate bonds, offer a stream of steady returns over long periods of time, with relatively small risks as measured by the standard deviation.

While most investors buy "standard" coupon-paying bonds where the payoffs are known in advance, other types of bonds are available. Some bonds have yields that depend upon a specified index or are tied to a specific Treasury yield. Some floating rate bonds have yields tied

---

[1] This information is based on Cordell Eddings and Evan Applegate, "Bonds Notch a Rare Win over Stocks," *Bloomberg Businessweek*, November 7–November 13, 2011, pp. 46, 48.

to LIBOR (London Interbank Offered Rate) plus some percentage yield amount. Still others may have yields that are pegged to inflation. We can think of these as structured income-producing products.

Investments Insight

Of Course, Not Everything Goes as Expected

Despite the typical steady performance of coupon-paying bonds over time that produce a positive nominal and real return barring unusual inflation, the situation can be reversed during unusual conditions such as the recent financial crisis. Consider an investor around 1985 holding 10-year Treasuries. The coupon was 10 percent, and inflation was about 4 percent, leaving a real return of approximately 6 percent. Now consider an investor in late 2011 holding 10-year Treasuries. The coupon was 2 percent, which was approximately equal to the annual estimated inflation. Thus, the real return was zero. If you did not hold these securities in a tax-deferred account, you paid taxes on the interest. Therefore, on a real basis you were paying the government to hold these securities and earning a negative real return. This helps to illustrate that even conservative bond investors face a wide range of situations in today's world.

Other investors are interested in bonds exactly because bond prices will change as interest rates change. If interest rates rise (fall), bond prices will fall (rise). These investors are interested not in holding the bonds to maturity, but rather in earning the capital gains that are possible if they correctly anticipate movements in interest rates.

Aggressive investors are interested in capital gains that arise from a change in interest rates. There is a substantial range of aggressiveness, from the really short-term speculator to the somewhat less aggressive investor who is willing to realize capital gains over a longer period while receiving a stream of interest income.

The short-term speculator studies interest rates carefully and moves into and out of securities on the basis of interest rate expectations. If rates are expected to fall, this investor can buy long-term, low-coupon issues and achieve maximum capital gains if the interest rate forecast is correct. Treasury bonds can be bought on 10 percent margin to further magnify gains (or losses). The speculator often uses Treasury issues (the highest quality bond available) or high-grade corporates in doing this kind of bond trading. It is not necessary to resort to low-quality bonds.

Example 18-2   To obtain some idea of the total returns that can result from changes in interest rates, consider again Treasury bonds. Some of the total annual returns have been very large, far beyond the yield component alone. In 1982, for example, the total return was approximately 42 percent; in 1985, 32 percent; in 1995, 31 percent; in 2000, 20 percent; and in 2011, approximately 35 percent for 30-year bonds. Clearly, successful bond speculation in each of those years resulted in very large returns.

Of course, losses also occur as a result of interest rate changes, both for longer periods and for short periods.

In the past, bonds were viewed as very stable instruments whose prices fluctuated very little in the short run. This situation changed drastically in the 1980s, however, when the bond

Example 18-3 From November 1, 2001, to April 1, 2002, the 10-year Treasury bond rate went from 4.2 percent to 5.4 percent, and the face value of these bonds went down more than 9 percent. Thus, in only five months holders of this security could have experienced a negative price change of 9 percent on a bond instrument typically considered default-free.

markets became quite volatile. Interest rates in the early 1980s reached record levels, causing large changes in bond prices.

Bond speculators encompass a wide range of participants, from financial institutions to individual investors. All are trying to take advantage of an expected movement in interest rates. Thus, investors seeking the income component from bonds as well as investors attempting to speculate with bonds are keenly interested in the level of interest rates and any likely changes in the level. A critical part of bond strategy and management, therefore, must involve these interest rate considerations.

BUYING FOREIGN BONDS

How important are foreign bonds in the total investing environment? Foreign bond markets account for approximately 60 percent of the fixed-income investment opportunities available today on a global basis; in 1990, they accounted for only one-third. Therefore, U.S. investors should be considering foreign bonds for their portfolios.

Why do U.S. investors consider foreign bonds for possible inclusion in their portfolios?

1. Foreign bonds may offer higher returns at a given point in time than alternative domestic bonds. Investors can sometimes make a good case for buying foreign bonds on the basis of potentially attractive returns.

Example 18-4 Foreign bond funds had average returns that were more than double U.S. taxable bond fund returns in 2004.

2. Foreign bonds can expand diversification possibilities. Diversification is extremely important, both in a stock portfolio and a bond portfolio.

Individual investors have often found it difficult to invest directly in European bonds. Some brokerage firms do not offer foreign bonds to individual investors, while most that do require a minimum investment of at least $50,000. Selling foreign bonds that are directly owned also can be a problem. Secondary markets in Europe are not comparable to the huge U.S. Treasury markets. This means that individual investors selling small amounts of foreign bonds abroad will typically incur significant price concessions. In addition, these investors face transaction costs. Dollars must be converted into the foreign currency to make purchases, and receipts from the foreign bonds must be converted back into dollars. On small transactions, these costs can significantly impact returns.

✓ Given the difficulties involved, most investors buying foreign bonds do so with mutual funds or ETFs.

Some Practical Advice

Investors pursuing foreign bonds can always buy managed funds, counting on the expertise of the portfolio managers. There are also world bond-index mutual funds such as the Vanguard Global Bond Index Fund which will have lower expense ratios. Furthermore, since late 2007 investors can buy a world bond ETF.

What About Currency Risk?   Investors in foreign bonds (or any other security) face exchange rate risk, which can be favorable or unfavorable. The euro strengthened against the dollar for several years of the new decade, providing a currency gain to U.S. investors. Of course, the opposite can happen. If the euro weakens instead of strengthens, a U.S. investor's dollar-denominated return suffers.

Investors buying mutual funds can choose world-bond funds that hedge their currency exposure. When a fund does this, a U.S. investor earns a return close to what local investors would earn on bonds. On the other hand, investors seeking currency exposure in the bond area can choose unhedged funds.

Example 18-5   The T. Rowe Price International Bond Fund provides U.S. investors with diversification away from U.S. markets. The fund invests heavily in government bonds from developed countries, although it will also invest modestly in foreign corporate issues and emerging market debt. Because the fund is exposed to currency risk, it is more volatile than it otherwise would be. This exposure to currency risk can work for or against investors for any time period.

Important Considerations in Managing a Bond Portfolio

UNDERSTANDING THE BOND MARKET

The first consideration for any investor is to understand the relationship between the bond market and the economy as a whole. It has been commonplace to talk about the bond market benefiting from a weak economy. If the economy is growing slowly, interest rates may decline, and bond prices rise. In effect, a decline in economic growth may lead to fewer investment opportunities, inducing savers to increase their demand for bonds, which pushes bond prices up and bond yields down. Talk of a rapidly growing economy is thought to frighten bond investors, because strong economic activity is likely to push interest rates up, and bond prices down.

Another important relationship is between bond yields and inflation. As we know from Chapter 17, interest rates reflect expected inflation. If investors anticipate a rise in inflation, they demand more from a bond to compensate for the expected decline in the purchasing power of their cash flows from the bond investment. An increase in expected inflation will tend to depress bond prices and increase yields.

✓   While the bond market appears to like a weak economy with its lower interest rates, *the bond market clearly dislikes inflation*.

Bond investors fear inflation because of its negative effect on fixed-income securities, and they favor Fed actions that temper economic growth and reduce inflation. Bond investors may react quite favorably to a tightening of monetary policy, because this helps to calm inflation fears.

Not surprisingly typical relationships between economic data and bond prices and yields do not always hold. In December 2011, economic data came in better than expected. This would normally suggest rising interest rates. Instead, the 10-year Treasury bond yield ended the year below 2 percent. Fears about the European debt crisis and doubts about the U.S. economy led investors to seek the safety of Treasury debt, even at record low yields.

GLOBAL FACTORS AND THE U.S. BOND MARKETS

A stronger dollar increases the value of dollar-denominated assets to foreign investors. Other events of a global nature affect the U.S. bond market. When the Brazilian crisis erupted around the end of 1998, there was a flight to safety in the form of purchases of Treasuries. As the crisis diminished, this demand for Treasuries decreased. On the other hand, with Japanese interest rates on the rise, bond investors feared that Japanese investors would liquidate their holdings of Treasuries in order to buy their own government bonds. Such a movement decreases the demand for Treasuries and hence their prices.

The most notable impact of foreign factors on U.S. bond prices, particularly Treasuries, occurred during the European sovereign debt and bond crisis in 2011. With Greece on the brink of bankruptcy, and Italy facing a major debt problem, along with some other countries such as Spain and Portugal, a flight to safety was common. Investors sought the relative safety of Treasury securities given all the turmoil. As one source noted on the Internet on September 12, 2011: "Investors continued to pile into Treasuries Monday as the intensifying debt crisis in Europe sparked a broad flight to safety."[2] Yields on 10-year Treasuries went below 2 percent and finished 2011 below 2 percent.

Checking Your Understanding

1. During the first several years of the 21st century, the euro typically strengthened relative to the dollar. How did this affect U.S. investors in European bonds?
2. Bond investors are often said to react favorably to a Federal Reserve movement to tighten monetary policy. What is the explanation for this?
3. What are the two most important reasons for a U.S. investor to buy foreign bonds?
4. Given an economy that is growing better than expected, is it rational for bond holders to sell?

Bond Strategies and Techniques

Bond investing has become increasingly popular, no doubt as a result of record low interest rates in recent years. Unfortunately, bond portfolio management has not received the same amount of attention as common stocks. A majority of investors are simply more interested in owning stocks than in owning bonds. Stocks are more "glamorous," and more attention has been devoted to them. Furthermore, more data exist for common stocks, undoubtedly because the most prominent stocks trade on the New York Stock Exchange where detailed prices can be collected and analyzed. The same is not true for bonds. Even today investors may have difficulty obtaining instantaneous, current quotes on many bonds.

Despite the lesser emphasis on bond portfolio management, investors must manage their bond portfolios and make investment decisions. Different bond investors have adopted different strategies, depending on their risk preferences, knowledge of the bond market, and

---

[2] Ben Rooney, "Treasury yields hit record lows on Euro turmoil," *money.cnn.com*, September 12, 2011.

investment objectives. Two broad strategies that any investor can follow with any type of portfolio are the passive and active strategies.

We know that bond prices change as interest rates change. Investors need to be able to make reasonable estimates of the change in a bond's price if interest rates change by a specified amount. Therefore, as part of our consideration of bond strategies and management techniques, we will analyze how investors can accurately assess bond price volatility. We will also consider how investors can protect a bond portfolio against interest rate movements.

Passive Management Strategies

Many investors agree that securities are fairly priced in the sense that the expected return is commensurate with the risk taken. Passive bond strategies are based on the proposition that bond prices are determined rationally, leaving risk as the portfolio variable to control. These strategies have a lower cost than do active strategies. As we know from Chapter 3, costs are the most important determinant in determining a fund's success over time, and this is particularly true for bonds because bond returns are typically lower than stock returns.

✓ Passive management strategies are based on inputs that are known at the time, rather than expectations.

Passive management does not mean that investors accept changes in market conditions, securities, and so on, if these changes cause undesirable modifications in the securities they hold. They must still monitor the status of their portfolios in order to match their holdings with their risk preferences and objectives. Conditions in the financial markets change quickly, and investors must also make fast changes when necessary. Thus, a passive investment strategy does not mean that investors do nothing.

The passive approach to bond investing is supported by evidence for various periods of years showing that the performance of bond managers during the years examined failed to equal that of a market index. For example, reporting on a five-year period when the managers of fixed-income portfolios had an annualized total return of 14.4 percent compared to 14.5 percent for a bond index (and this was before fees) *Forbes* magazine noted that "The average pension fund would have done better with its bond money in a passive index fund."[3]

A comprehensive study examining the performance of bond mutual funds, using two samples of bond funds, found that such funds underperformed relevant indexes from the fixed-income area.[4] The results were robust across a wide choice of models. For the most part, this underperformance approximated the average management fees; therefore, before expenses, funds performed about as well as the indexes. There was no evidence of predictability using past performance to predict future performance.

Other evidence indicates that about two-thirds of bond investors could not outperform the fixed-income market over the period 1990–2005, whether investing for the short term or the long term. This evidence was based on all taxable fixed-income funds for the period.[5]

Strategies for investors following a passive bond management approach include buy and hold and indexing.

---

[3] Taken from Steve Kichen, "The *Forbes*/TUCS Institutional Portfolio Report," *Forbes*, August 21, 1989, p. 112.

[4] Christopher Blake, Edwin Elton, and Martin Gruber, "The Performance of Bond Mutual Funds," *The Journal of Business*, July 1993, pp. 371–403.

[5] As reported in "Investing in Bonds: Myths and Realities," *Balance: Quarterly News and Tools for Tiaa-Cref*, TIAA-CREF, Winter, 2006, p. 21.

BUY AND HOLD

An obvious strategy for any investor interested in nonactive trading policies is simply to buy and hold. Such an investor carefully chooses a balanced and diversified portfolio of bonds and does not attempt to trade them in a search for higher returns. An important part of this strategy is to choose the most promising bonds that meet the investor's requirements. Making this selection requires some knowledge of bonds and markets. Simply because an investor is following a basic buy-and-hold strategy does not mean that the initial selection is unimportant. This strategy works best with very high-quality, noncallable bonds, regardless of issuer. Such bonds minimize the risk associated with changes in the cash flows attributable to embedded options which remain with the bonds during their life.

The buy-and-hold investor must have knowledge of the yield advantages of various bonds (for example, agency securities over U.S. Treasuries), the default risk, call risk, the marketability of a bond, any current income requirements, and taxes.

One alternative for the buy-and-hold investor is to try to duplicate the overall bond market by purchasing a broad cross-section of bonds. Another is to selectively build a portfolio of bonds based on characteristics that match those that the investor is seeking, whether a high level of safety, an intermediate maturity, large coupons, and so forth.

Regardless of the bonds sought, individual investors have traditionally faced a very difficult job because the bond market caters to institutional investors, using real-time data bases not available to individuals. Therefore, traditionally individual investors could not easily determine current prices. However, this situation has changed dramatically in recent years with the introduction of websites providing current price information on numerous bonds.

Bond Ladders   One approach for those who do not wish to be active in the market but instead want to protect themselves from some risk is the *ladder approach*. Under a laddering approach, investors protect themselves to some degree against rises in interest rates by purchasing bonds with different maturity dates (think of these as the rungs of the ladder). The investor chooses dates that mesh with his or her own situation. Any type of bond can be used in a laddering strategy.

Example 18-6   With $100,000 to invest, an investor could put approximately $20,000 in each of five bonds, with the first bond maturing two years from now, the second one maturing three years from now, and so forth. Thus, if interest rates rise, the investor will have some principal returned periodically which can be reinvested in new bonds with a higher yield. If interest rates decline, some of the previous higher yields are locked up until those bonds mature.

INDEXING

If investors decide that they are unlikely to outperform a market index, they may opt to buy a portfolio that closely matches the performance of a well-known bond index such as the Barclays Capital Aggregate Bond Index.[6] As we know from Chapter 3, mutual funds designed to match the performance of some index are known as index funds, and such funds are

---

[6] In practice, it is not feasible to exactly replicate a broad bond index. For example, the Barclays Capital Aggregate Bond Index covers more than 6,000 securities. This index was formerly known as the Lehman Brothers Aggregate Bond Index, and was taken over by Barclays. Most bond-index funds use a sampling approach to replicate the index as closely as possible.

available for both bonds and stocks (stock-index funds as a passive strategy were discussed in Chapter 11). While the typical actively managed bond fund has an expense ratio of almost 1 percent, the average expense ratio of bond-index funds is half that, and some are less. Vanguard is well known for having very low expense ratios on bond-index funds. ETFs are another alternative, and often have very low expense ratios.

Example 18-7 The *Vanguard Total Bond Market Index* is one of the largest bond-index funds. Its expense ratio is a mere 0.22 percent, which Vanguard states is on average 76 percent lower than other bond funds with similar holdings.[7] Vanguard also offers Vanguard Total Bond Market ETF with similar holdings and an expense ratio of 0.11 percent, an expense ratio said to be 88 percent lower than other funds with similar holdings.

How important are expense ratios for bond funds? Very important! With high-grade corporates often yielding 5 or 6 percent and Treasuries even less, the impact of a 0.2 percent expense ratio subtracted from these returns versus about 1 percent subtracted from these returns is obvious.

Some Practical Advice

As we know from Chapter 3, some ETFs focus on bonds. Barclays offers several iShares ETFs concentrating on both corporate and Treasury bonds such as iShares Barclay U.S. Aggregate Bond Fund. Vanguard offers the Vanguard Total Bond Market ETF and the Vanguard Short-Term Bond ETF and Long-Term Bond ETF. As with other ETFs, annual costs are extremely low relative to most alternatives.

Active Management Strategies

Although bonds are often purchased to be held to maturity, frequently they are not. Many bond investors use active management strategies. These strategies have traditionally sought to profit from active management of bonds by activities such as[8]

1. Forecasting changes in interest rates, because we know that bond prices will change as well
2. Identifying abnormal yield spreads between bond sectors and acting to take advantage of these discrepancies
3. Identifying relative mispricing between various fixed-income securities

Notice that, unlike the passive strategy, the key inputs are not known at the time of the analysis. Instead, investors have expectations about interest rate changes and yield spreads and mispricings among securities.

We will consider each of these alternatives in turn. This is a nonexhaustive list of active strategies.

---

[7] This expense ratio is for the Investor Shares. For the Admiral Shares, which require a higher initial investment, the expense ratio is only 0.11 percent. This portfolio is also available as an ETF.

[8] This is not necessarily a complete list of active strategies. Different sources of bond information list varying numbers of strategies.

FORECASTING CHANGES IN INTEREST RATES

Changes in interest rates are the chief factor affecting bond prices because of the inverse relationship between changes in bond prices and changes in interest rates. When investors project interest rate declines, they should take action to invest in bonds, and the right bonds, for price appreciation opportunities. When interest rates are expected to rise, the objective is to minimize losses by not holding bonds or holding bonds with short maturities.

How does an investor forecast interest rates? Not very well, on a consistent and accurate basis, because interest rate forecasting is a notoriously difficult proposition. Consider this quote on the Internet at the beginning of 2012 concerning the yield on 10-year Treasury bonds: "Strategists at Credit Suisse predicted the yield will tumble to as low as 1.5% during the first half of 2012. But analysts at Nomura expect the yield to rise to 2.4% in the next few months."[9]

Reasonable forecasts can sometimes be made about the likely growth rate of the economy and the prospects for inflation, both of which affect interest rates and, therefore, bond investors. Assuming that an investor has a forecast of interest rates, he or she should lengthen (shorten) the maturity of a bond portfolio when interest rates are expected to decline (rise).

It is important to be aware of the tradeoffs in strategies involving maturity.

1. Short maturities sacrifice price appreciation opportunities and usually offer lower coupons (income), but serve to protect the investor when rates are expected to rise.
2. Longer maturities have greater price fluctuations; therefore, the chance for bigger gains (and bigger losses) is magnified. However, longer maturities may be less liquid than Treasury bills.

✓ An important component in forecasting interest rates is the yield curve. The shape of the yield curve at any point in time contains potentially valuable information about the future course of interest rates. Bond market participants in particular, and investors in general, pay close attention to yield curves as an aid in forecasting interest rates and as part of deciding what segments of the bond market to invest in.

Example 18-8   A report from Fidelity's Investment Grade Bond Fund made the following observation: "Yield curve positioning was a solid contributor to fund performance during the year while the yield curve flattened. The fund benefited from the barbell style yield curve positioning it employed with investments concentrated to a higher degree on the short and long ends of the yield curve and to a lesser degree in between."

One form of interest rate forecasting, *horizon analysis*, involves the projection of bond performance over a planned investment horizon. The investor evaluates bonds that are being considered for purchase over a selected holding period in order to determine which will perform the best. To do this, the investor must make assumptions about reinvestment rates and future market rates and calculate the *horizon returns* for the bonds being considered based on that set of assumptions. Note that this concept is different from the yield-to-maturity concept, which does not require expectations to be integrated into the analysis. Horizon analysis requires users to make assumptions about reinvestment rates and future yields but allows them to consider how different scenarios will affect the performance of the bonds being considered. Horizon analysis was discussed in Chapter 17.

---

[9] Min Zeng, "Treasurys End Year Below 2% for the First Time Since '77," *The Wall Street Journal* online, December 30, 2011.

Some Practical Advice

Assume that you expect interest rates to decline over the next year or two and you want to invest in bonds based on this scenario. A good way would be to use Treasury bonds, which are default-free, exempt from state and local taxes, and not callable. You could buy zero Treasuries for maximum price change. Or you could buy long-term Treasuries, such as the original 30-year maturity bond issued in 2001, or the 30-year bond issued in February 2006. If you are right in your interest rate forecast, percentage returns could be large.

✓ Always remember that interest rate forecasts are notoriously inaccurate across time. While a particular forecaster may get it right one time, the same forecaster probably will not the next time.

Example 18-9   The Fed started raising short-term interest rates in June 2004, and raised them 14 times through early 2006. When the raises started, the 10-year Treasury note yielded about 4.6 percent. In mid-February 2006, the 10-year note yielded 4.54 percent. Thus, long-term rates did not follow the rise in short-term rates as many expected. Even the chairman of the Fed called the failure of long-term rates to rise a "conundrum."

YIELD SPREAD ANALYSIS

In Chapter 17 we discussed the risk premiums which help to explain why rates differ between different bond issues or segments of the bond market. We can categorize the differences between two segments of the bond market as a yield spread. As we know, the bond market comprises different sectors based on issuer (the Treasury, corporations, and so forth), quality (treasury, government agency, AAA, AA, A, BBB, below investment grade), or call feature (callable or noncallable).

Yield spread analysis involves analyzing the differences in promised yields between various segments of the bond market at a point in time, and trying to capitalize on this analysis.

✓ Yield spread strategies seek to profit from an expected change in the yield spreads between bond sectors, based on an assumption that there exists some normal yield spread level between sectors.

Therefore, investors would monitor the yield relationships between various types of bonds and look for abnormalities, based on what they believe the normal spreads are. In these strategies, investors sell bonds in one sector and buy bonds in another sector in the hopes of profiting as the yield spread moves from its current level to its "normal" level.

During periods of economic expansion, the spread between Treasury issues and corporate issues generally narrows, reflecting corporate bonds' decreased credit risk. Conversely, during recessions, the Treasury-corporate yield spread generally widens, reflecting the increased credit risk due to a weakening economy. Thus, if an expansion is forecast, a manager would purchase corporates and sell treasuries in anticipation of greater price appreciation or less price erosion due to the spread narrowing. On the other hand, if the economy is expected to weaken the manager would sell corporates and buy treasuries to reduce the price loss due to the spread widening.

Example 18-10   Consider 10-year Treasury rates and corporate Baa rates for recent years. A very wide spread occurred in 2008 between the two because of the economic turmoil in the economy. Investors rushed to Treasury securities (a "flight to safety"), pushing the price up and the yield down. The result was a wide gap between Treasury yields and the yields on lower quality corporates.

If a spread were thought to be abnormally high, investors would trade to take advantage of a return to a normal spread. The objective is to invest in the sector or sectors that will display the strongest relative price movements. Historical records of yield spreads are available from brokerage firms.

What can cause corporate yield spreads (relative to Treasuries) to widen?

- A financial crisis, such as occurred in 2008, when the spread between high-yield bonds and Treasuries reached 2,000 basis points
- Accounting debacles, such as those in 2002 involving WorldCom, Enron, and Tyco
- Litigation problems, such as Halliburton and other companies involved in asbestos exposure
- Excessive debt levels, which increase the risk of default and bankruptcy
- Weak earnings, which increase the risk that the companies cannot service their debt

Smart bond investors understand that not all corporate yield spreads are justified. Markets sometimes overreact to particular issuers by being caught up in a current environment of despair or panic. Some investors look for such opportunities.

IDENTIFYING MISPRICING AMONG BONDS

Managers of bond portfolios attempt to adjust to the constantly changing environment for bonds. They seek to improve the rate of return on the bond portfolio by identifying temporary mispricings in the bond market, which do occur.

Bond swaps An active bond management strategy involving the purchase and sale of bonds in an attempt to improve the rate of return on the bond portfolio

Bond swaps refer to selling one bond and simultaneously buying a different bond. There are various types of swaps, but all are designed to improve the investor's portfolio position. Some swaps are relatively straightforward, simple transactions, while others are very complex. Various inputs are required to do the analysis for a swap, including most importantly predictions about future interest rates. Also, a time horizon is needed as an input, with a typical time horizon in the range of six months to a year.

Some active mutual fund managers have been able to outperform their bond benchmarks over respectable periods of time as a result of mispricings or inefficiencies in the bond market. According to Morningstar, 37 out of 338 funds in the intermediate-term category outperformed the Aggregate Bond Index's gain over a 10-year period.[10] Pimco Total Return is often cited as an outstanding actively managed bond fund that frequently outperforms its index.

Investments Intuition

The Best Laid Plans of Mice and Men Can Backfire

Even the best active managers of bond funds make incorrect guesses about bond prices and interest rates, particularly in turbulent times such as those experienced in recent years. In late 2011 some of

---

[10] This information is available on Morningstar's website.

the top managers were making positive bets on emerging market debt securities and negative bets on Treasury securities. However, the Euro-zone's sovereign debt crisis, which dominated the news in late 2011, turned these bets upside-down.

Investors rushed to the perceived safety of Treasury bonds, providing one of the largest price rallies seen in Treasuries, and relatively poor returns in more risky assets such as emerging markets debt.

NEW TOOLS FOR INDIVIDUAL INVESTORS

Traditionally, the bond market has been an institutional market, and one not friendly to individual investors. Up-to-date price information was not easily available, and investors could not be sure that the prices they paid were fair because they were not transparent. This situation has changed dramatically with the Internet.

Consider Fidelity Investments, which has a new set of online tools and research for investors.[11] Investors can search through approximately 30,000 bonds, bond funds, and CDs and sort them in various ways. Transaction costs are extremely low and transparent. Investors can use a bond ladder tool to construct a steady stream of income. Considerable research on both bonds and bond funds are available.

Managing Price Volatility

We know from Chapter 17 that coupon and maturity are the primary factors affecting bond price volatility. Both maturity and coupon affect bond price changes for a given change in yields. When yields change, these are the two variables that investors can control. The problem is that a given change in interest rates can result in very different percentage price changes for the various bonds that investors hold. Furthermore, in our previous analysis the effects of these two variables were considered separately. To properly manage bond price volatility, we need a measure that combines these variables. Duration is such a measure. It combines the properties of maturity and coupon and allows investors to estimate the change in a bond's price for any estimated change in interest rates.

DURATION

Although maturity is the traditional measure of a bond's lifetime, it is inadequate, because it focuses only on the return of principal at the maturity date. Two 20-year bonds, one with a 4 percent coupon and the other with a 9 percent coupon, do not have identical economic lifetimes. An investor will recover the original purchase price much sooner with the 9 percent coupon bond compared to the 4 percent coupon bond. Therefore, a measure is needed that accounts for the entire pattern (both size and timing) of the cash flows over the life of the bond—the effective maturity of the bond. Such a concept, called duration (or Macaulay duration), was conceived many years ago by Frederick Macaulay.

Duration is a present-value weighted average of the number of years over which investors receive cash flows from a bond.[12] It measures the economic life of a bond rather than simply its time to maturity.

Figure 18-1 illustrates the concepts of both time to maturity and duration for a bond with five years to maturity, a 10 percent coupon, and selling for $1,000. As the figure indicates, the stream of cash flows generated by this bond over the term to maturity consists of $50 every

Duration A measure of a bond's economic lifetime that accounts for the entire pattern of cash flows over the life of the bond; a measure of bond price sensitivity to interest rate movements

[11] Fidelity.com/fixedincome.

[12] This discussion applies only to option-free bonds.

Figure 18-1

Illustration of the Cash Flow Pattern of a 10 Percent Coupon, Five-Year Maturity Bond Paying Interest Semiannually and Returning the Principal of $1,000 at Maturity.

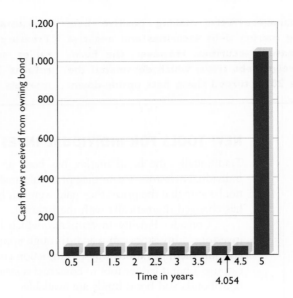

six months, or $100 per year, plus the return of principal of $1,000 at the end of the five years. The last cash flow combines the interest payment of $50 with the principal repayment of $1,000, which occurs at the maturity date.

Although the term to maturity for the bond illustrated in Figure 18-1 is five years, its duration is only 4.054 years, as indicated by the arrow. This means that the time-value-of-money weighted average number of years needed to recover the cost of this bond is 4.054. In effect, the arrow indicates the point where the weights, which are the cash flows, are in balance on either side.

As illustrated by Figure 18-1, while the bond has five years to maturity, interest payments are received in each of the first four years. Therefore, describing the bond as a five-year bond is not totally accurate because the average time to receipt of each of the cash flows is clearly less than five years. Duration describes the weighted average time to each payment.

It is very unusual for a coupon-paying bond to have a duration greater than 10 years, regardless of its maturity date. This is because cash flows far in the future have small present values today. Because the only payment from a zero-coupon bond is its maturity value, this amount has a weight of one.

✓ A zero-coupon bond has a duration equal to its maturity, because there are no coupons.

Calculating Duration To calculate duration, it is necessary to calculate a weighted time period because duration is stated in years. The time periods in which the cash flows are received are expressed in terms of years (or semiannual periods) and denoted by t in this discussion. Weighting and summing these t's produces the duration measure, which is stated in years.

✓ Duration is a concept stated in years.

The present values of the cash flows, as a percentage of the bond's current market price, serve as the weighting factors to apply to the time periods. Each weighting factor shows the relative importance of each cash flow to the bond's total present value, which is simply its current market price. The sum of these weighting factors will be 1.0, indicating that all cash flows have been accounted for. The sum of all the discounted cash flows from the bond will equal the bond's price.

The equation for duration is shown as Equation 18-1:

$$\text{Macaulay duration} = D = \sum_{t=1}^{n} \frac{PV(CF_t)}{\text{Market price}} \times t \qquad \textbf{(18-1)}$$

Example 18-11

Table 18-1 provides an example of calculating the duration for a 5 percent, five-year bond. The bond is currently priced at $974.17 because interest rates are assumed to have risen so that the current YTM is 5.6 percent (semiannual yield, ytm, is 2.8 percent).[13]

The cash flows, column 2, consist of ten $25 coupons (the annual coupon is $50) plus the return of principal at the end of the fifth year. Column 3 shows the present value of the cash flows using 2.8 percent as the discount rate. Column 4 shows the weights, or the present value of the cash flows as a percentage of the bond's price, which in this example is $974.17. Notice that the final cash flow of $1,025 ($25 coupon plus $1,000 return of principal) accounts for 79.8 percent of the value of the bond on a weighted average basis. Column 5 is calculated by multiplying the weights in column 4 (which sum to 1.0) by the time periods in column 1, and summing these products. The end result, 4.48 years, is the present-value weighted average number of years over which investors receive cash flows from the bond, which is the bond's duration.

The duration of 4.48 years is approximately one-half year less than the term to maturity of five years.

Table 18-1 An Example of Calculating the Duration of a Bond with a 5 Percent Coupon, Five-Year Maturity, Currently Priced at $974.17 for a YTM of 5.6 Percent

(1) Periods	(2) Cash Flow (CF)	(3) PV of CFs	(4) Weighted PV of CFs (weighted by price) (3) / Price of the Bond	(5) Weighted Average of Time Periods (1) × (4)
0.5	25	24.319	0.025	0.012
1	25	23.657	0.024	0.024
1.5	25	23.012	0.024	0.035
2	25	22.386	0.023	0.046
2.5	25	21.776	0.022	0.056
3	25	21.183	0.022	0.065
3.5	25	20.606	0.021	0.074
4	25	20.044	0.021	0.082
4.5	25	19.499	0.020	0.090
5	1025	777.665	0.798	3.991
			1.000	4.477

---

[13] A shortcut formula can be used for coupon bonds selling at face value:

$$\text{Duration} = \frac{1 + YTM}{YTM}[1 - (1/(1 + YTM)^n)]$$

Using the semiannual rate and doubling the number of periods, we must divide the answer by 2.0 to put it on an annual basis.

where

t = the time period at which the cash flow is expected to be received

n = the number of periods to maturity

$PV(CF_t)$ = present value of the cash flow in period t discounted at the yield-to-maturity

Market price = the bond's current price or present value of all the cash flows

As Equation 18-1 shows, duration is obtained by multiplying the weighted present value of each period's cash flow by the number of periods when each is to be received, and summing. Note that duration is expressed in years because we are calculating a weighted average of the number of years.

✓ Duration will always be less than time to maturity for bonds that pay coupons. For zero-coupon bonds, duration will be equal to time to maturity.[14]

Understanding Duration   How is duration related to the key bond variables previously analyzed? An examination of Equation 18-1 shows that the calculation of duration depends on three factors:[15]

- ❑ The final maturity of the bond
- ❑ The coupon payments
- ❑ The yield to maturity
  1. Duration expands with time to maturity but at a decreasing rate (holding the size of coupon payments and the yield to maturity constant, particularly beyond 15 years time to maturity). Even between five and 10 years time to maturity, duration is expanding at a significantly lower rate than in the case of a time to maturity of up to five years, where it expands rapidly.[16] Note once again that for all coupon-paying bonds, duration is always less than maturity. For a zero-coupon bond, duration is equal to time to maturity.[17]
  2. Yield to maturity is inversely related to duration (holding coupon payments and maturity constant).
  3. Coupon is inversely related to duration (holding maturity and yield to maturity constant). This is logical because higher coupons lead to quicker recovery of the bond's value, resulting in a shorter duration, relative to lower coupons.

Duration and Bond Management   Why is duration important in bond analysis and management? First, it tells us the difference between the effective lives of alternative bonds. Bonds A and B, with the same duration but different years to maturity, have more in

---

[14] For a zero-coupon bond, the modified duration (explained later) is less than its maturity.

[15] The duration of a bond can change significantly if there is a sinking fund or a call feature.

[16] The duration of a perpetuity is $(1 + YTM)/YTM$. This indicates that maturity and duration can differ greatly since the maturity of a perpetuity is infinite, but duration is not. That is, perpetuities have an infinite maturity but a finite duration.

[17] Deep discount bonds are an exception to the general rule. Their duration first increases with time to maturity, up to some distant point, and then decreases in duration beyond this point. This is because deep discount bonds with very long maturities behave like perpetuities.

common than bonds C and D with the same maturity but different durations. For any particular bond, as maturity increases the duration increases at a decreasing rate.

Example 18-12   Consider a 10 percent coupon bond with a yield to maturity of 10 percent and a five-year life. This bond has a duration of 4.054 years, approximately one year less than maturity. However, if the maturity of this bond was 10 years, it would have an effective life (duration) of 6.76 years, and with a 20-year maturity it would have an effective life of only 9.36 years. Furthermore, under these conditions, a 50-year maturity for this bond would change the effective life to only 10.91 years. The reason for the sharp differences between the term to maturity and the duration is that cash receipts received in the distant future have very small present values and therefore add little to a bond's value.

Second, the duration concept is used in certain bond management strategies, particularly immunization, as explained later.

Third, and most importantly for bond investors, duration is a measure of bond price sensitivity to interest rate movements; that is, it is a direct measure of interest rate risk. Malkiel's bond price theorems are inadequate to examine all aspects of bond price sensitivity. This issue is considered in some detail below because of its potential importance to bond investors.

Estimating Price Changes Using Duration   The real value of the duration measure to bond investors is that it combines coupon and maturity, the two key variables that investors must consider in response to expected changes in interest rates. As noted earlier, duration is positively related to maturity and negatively related to coupon. However, bond price changes are directly related to duration; that is, the percentage change in a bond's price, given a change in interest rates, is proportional to its duration. Therefore, duration can be used to measure interest rate exposure.

✓   Duration measures the approximate percentage change in the price of a bond for a 1-percentage-point (100 basis points) change in interest rates. This can be implemented by using modified duration.

Modified Duration Duration divided by 1 + ytm

The term **modified duration** refers to Macaulay's duration in Equation 18-2 divided by $(1 + \text{ytm})$.[18]

$$\text{Modified duration} = D^* = D/(1 + \text{ytm}) \qquad \textbf{(18-2)}$$

Where

  D^* = modified duration

  ytm = the bond's semiannual yield to maturity (we divide YTM by the number of discounting periods, which for semiannual bond payments is 2)

Example 18-13   Using the duration of 4.054 years from Example 18-12 and the YTM of 10 percent, the modified duration based on semiannual interest would be

$$D^* = 4.054/(1 + 0.05) = 3.861$$

----

[18] This applies to bonds paying semiannual interest because ytm as used here is the semiannual yield to maturity.

The modified duration can be used to calculate the percentage price change in a bond for a given change in the yield; that is, for small changes in yield, the price movements of most bonds will vary proportionally with modified duration. This is shown by Equation 18-3, which is an approximation.[19]

$$\text{Percentage change} \atop \text{In bond price} \approx -D^* \times \text{Yield change} \qquad \text{(18-3)}$$

or

$$\Delta P/P \approx -D * \Delta r \qquad \text{(18-4)}$$

where

ΔP = change in price

P = the price of the bond

$-D^*$ = modified duration with a negative sign (the negative sign occurs because of the inverse relation between price changes and yield)

Δr = the instantaneous change in yield in decimal form

Example 18-14

Using our same bond with a modified duration of 3.861, assume an instantaneous yield change of 20 basis points (+0.0020), from 10 percent to 10.20 percent. The approximate change in price, based on Equation 18-4 would be:

$$\Delta P/P = -3.861 \times (+0.0020) \times 100 = -0.772\%$$

Given that the original price of the bond is $1,000, this percentage price change would result in an estimated bond price of $992.28. For very small changes in yield, Equation 18-4 produces a good approximation.[20]

The steps involved in calculating the approximate price change in the bond are illustrated in Figure 18-2, using the information in Example 18-14.

In summary, for small changes in a bond's required yield, modified duration shows the bond's percentage change in price for a 1-percentage-point change (100 basis points) in its yield. It can be used to measure the price risk of a bond or a bond portfolio since the same holds true for a portfolio of bonds.

Concepts in Action

Using Duration in Managing Bond Portfolios

Let's see how these concepts are used in practice. According to a popular financial magazine, the Nuveen

Select Tax Free Income 2 closed-end fund had an average duration of 5.4 years in Spring, 2008. "That

---

[19] This formula can provide an exact estimate of the percentage price change if the change in yield is very small and the security does not involve embedded options.

[20] To prove this, we could solve for the price of this bond using a YTM of 10.20 percent. If we did, we would find that the price should decline to $992.32, a percentage decline of .768 percent as compared to our estimate of .772 percent. For larger changes in yield, such as 100 or 200 basis points, the approximate percentage price change is less good.

suggests that the fund's NAV per share would fall about 5.4% if interest rates rose by 1 percentage point."[21]

Investors in bond funds can obtain information about the fund's duration directly from the fund company. For example, if you own a Fidelity bond fund, call a Fidelity representative. Or, go to the fund's website and look up the particular fund of interest. Alternatively, Morningstar's website provides duration information for bond funds.

Figure 18-2

Calculating the Approximate Price Change for a Bond.

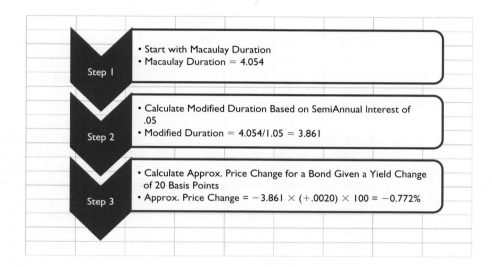

Step 1
• Start with Macaulay Duration
• Macaulay Duration = 4.054

Step 2
• Calculate Modified Duration Based on SemiAnnual Interest of .05
• Modified Duration = 4.054/1.05 = 3.861

Step 3
• Calculate Approx. Price Change for a Bond Given a Yield Change of 20 Basis Points
• Approx. Price Change = −3.861 × (+.0020) × 100 = −0.772%

Convexity Although Equation 18-3 generally provides only an approximation, for very small changes in the required yield the approximation is quite close and at times could be exact. However, as the changes in required yield become larger the approximation becomes poorer. The problem is that modified duration produces symmetric percentage price change estimates using Equation 18-3 (if r had decreased 0.20 percent, the price change would have been +0.772 percent) when, in actuality, the price-yield relationship is not linear. This relationship is, in fact, curvilinear.

We refer to the curved nature of the price-yield relationship as the bond's convexity (the relationship is said to be convex because it opens upward). More formally, **convexity** is a term used to refer to the degree to which duration changes as the yield to maturity changes. The degree of convexity is not the same for all bonds. Calculations of price changes should properly account for this convexity in order to improve the approximation of a bond's price change given some yield change.[22]

To understand the convexity issue, Figure 18-3 repeats the analysis from Chapter 17, which showed a 10 percent coupon bond at different market yields and prices. We can think of duration graphically as the slope of a line that is tangent to the convex price-yield curve of Figure 18-3 at the current price and yield of the bond, which is assumed to be $1,000 and 10 percent.[23] In effect, we are using a tangent line to measure the slope of the curve that

Convexity A measure of the degree to which the relationship between a bond's price and yield departs from a straight line

---

[21] Elizabeth Ody, "Buy Munis at a Discount," *Kiplinger's Personal Finance*, May 2008, p. 46.

[22] An in-depth discussion of convexity is beyond the scope of this text.

[23] Technically, the slope of the tangent line in Figure 18-3 is equal to the negative of modified duration multiplied by the bond's current market price.

Figure 18-3

Convex Relationship Between Yields and Prices and Tangent Line Representing Modified Duration for a 10 Percent 10-Year Bond.

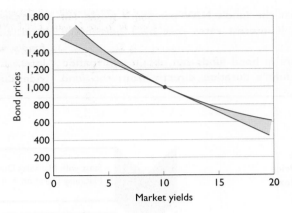

depicts bond prices as a function of market yields. For a very small change in yield, such as a few basis points, the slope of the line—the duration—provides a good approximation for the rate of change in price given a change in yield. As the change in yield increases, the error that results from using a straight line to estimate a bond's price behavior as given by a curve increases.[24]

As we move away from the point of tangency in Figure 18-3 in either direction, we underestimate the change in price of the bond using duration; that is, the price change is always more favorable than suggested by the duration. Notice that the shaded area in Figure 18-3 captures the convexity areas both above and below the starting point of 10 percent and $1,000. If yields decrease, prices increase, and the duration tangent line fails to indicate the true higher price, which is given by the curve. Conversely, when yields increase, prices decrease, but the duration tangent line overstates the amount of the price decrease relative to the true convex relationship. This helps to illustrate what is meant by the term positive convexity.

Convexity is largest for low-coupon bonds, long-maturity bonds, and low yields to maturity. A zero-coupon, long-term bond would have a large amount of convexity. If convexity is large, large changes in duration are implied, with corresponding inaccuracies in forecasts of price changes.

Convexity calculations can be made similar to those with modified duration discussed earlier. These calculations produce an approximate percentage price change due to convexity, which can be added to the approximate percentage price change based on duration discussed earlier. This total percentage price change is still an approximation, but it is considerably improved over that using only duration.

Checking Your Understanding

5. Holding maturity constant, a bond with a larger coupon will have a shorter duration than a bond with a smaller coupon. Agree or disagree, and explain your reasoning.
6. Using the duration concept, if you expect a decline in interest rates, and you want to use this decline to your advantage, how should you adjust your bond portfolio?

---

[24] As the yield changes, the tangency line and slope also change; that is, modified duration changes as yield changes.

MANAGING PRICE VOLATILITY

What does this analysis of price volatility mean to bond investors? The message is simple—to obtain the maximum (minimum) price volatility from a bond, investors should choose bonds with the longest (shortest) duration. If an investor already owns a portfolio of bonds, he or she can act to increase the average modified duration of the portfolio if a decline in interest rates is expected and the investor is attempting to achieve the largest price appreciation possible. Fortunately, duration is additive, which means that a bond portfolio's modified duration is a (market-value) weighted average of each individual bond's modified duration.

How popular is the duration concept in today's investment world? This concept has become widely known and referred to in the popular press. Investors can find duration numbers in a variety of sources, particularly with regard to bond funds.

Although duration is an important measure of bond risk, it is not necessarily always the most appropriate one. Duration measures volatility, which is important but is only one aspect of the risk in bonds. If an investor considers volatility an acceptable proxy for risk, duration is the measure of risk to use along with the correction for convexity.

Immunization

Immunization The strategy of immunizing (protecting) a portfolio against interest rate risk by canceling out its two components, price risk and reinvestment rate risk

Because interest rates change over time, investors face uncertainty about the realized returns from bonds. This, of course, is the nature of interest rate risk. The strategy of immunizing (protecting) a portfolio against interest rate risk (i.e., changes in the general level of interest rates) is called **immunization**. This is one form of a structured portfolio strategy, which aims to have a portfolio achieve the performance of a benchmark that has been specified beforehand.

To see how such a strategy works, think of interest rate risk as being composed of two parts:

1. The price risk, resulting from the inverse relationship between bond prices and required rates of return.
2. The reinvestment rate risk, resulting from the uncertainty about the rate at which future coupon income can be reinvested. As discussed in Chapter 17, the YTM calculation assumes that future coupons from a given bond investment will be reinvested at the calculated yield to maturity. If interest rates change so that this assumption is no longer operable, the bond's realized YTM will differ from the calculated (expected) YTM.

Notice that these two components of interest rate risk move in opposite directions:

- ❏ If interest rates rise, reinvestment rates (and therefore income) rise, whereas the price of the bond declines.
- ❏ If interest rates decline, reinvestment rates (and therefore income) decline, whereas the price of the bond rises.

In effect, the favorable results on one side can be used to offset the unfavorable results on the other.

✓ Immunization involves protecting a bond portfolio against interest rate risk by canceling out the two components of interest rate risk, reinvestment rate risk and price risk.

A portfolio is said to be immunized (the effects of interest rate risk are neutralized) if the duration of the portfolio is made equal to a preselected investment horizon for the portfolio.

EXHIBIT 18-1

Understanding the Concept of Immunization

Immunization

Seeks to

Protect a Portfolio Against Interest Rate Risk

by

Playing the Two Components of Interest Rate Risk

Against Each Other

The Objective Is to Have the Portfolio Earn a Prespecified

Rate of Return

With an Immunized Portfolio:

If Interest Rates Go UP ⇑

Reinvestment Rates ↑

While

The Prices of the Bonds ↓

If Interest Rates Go DOWN ⇓

Reinvestment Rates ↓

While

The Prices of the Bonds ↑

The Key to Immunization Is Duration

Note carefully what this statement says. An investor with, say, a 10-year horizon does not choose bonds with 10 years to maturity but bonds with a duration of 10 years—quite a different statement. The duration strategy will usually require holding bonds with maturities in excess of the investment horizon in order to make the duration match the investment horizon.

✓ The duration concept is the basis for immunization theory.

Exhibit 18-1 outlines the concept of immunization, showing the essential points.

✓ Immunization is a strategy to protect against the adverse consequences of interest rate risk, thereby allowing the portfolio holder to achieve a prespecified rate of return over a selected period of time.

For an example of the immunization concept, consider Table 18-2, which illustrates for a portfolio consisting of one bond what ideally could happen with a portfolio of several bonds.[25] Assume an investor has a five-year investment horizon after which she wishes to liquidate her bond portfolio and spend the proceeds. The current yield to maturity for AAA-rated bonds, the only investment grade our investor is willing to consider, is 7.9 percent for

---

[25] We assume here that the yield curve is flat and that any changes in the yield curve are parallel changes.

Table 18-2 Ending Wealth for a Bond Following a Change in Market Yields with and without Immunization

Bond A: Purchased for $1,000, five-year maturity, 7.9% coupon, 7.9% yield to maturity

Bond B: Purchased for $1,000, six-year maturity, 7.9% coupon, 7.9% yield to maturity, duration = 5.00 years

Part A: Ending Wealth for Bond A if Market Yields Remain Constant at 7.9%

Years	Cash Flow	Reinvestment Rate (%)	Ending Wealth
I	$ 79	—[a]	$ 79.00
2	79	7.9	164.24
3	79	7.9	256.22
4	79	7.9	355.46
5	79	7.9	462.54
5	1,000	—	1,462.54

Part B: Ending Wealth for Bond A if Market Yields Decline to 6% in Year 3

Years	Cash Flow	Reinvestment Rate (%)	Ending Wealth
I	$ 79	—	$ 79.00
2	79	7.9	164.24
3	79	6.0	253.10
4	79	6.0	347.29
5	79	6.0	477.13
5	1,000	—	1,447.13

Part C: Ending Wealth for Bond B if Market Yields Decline to 6% in Year 3 (Bond B has a duration of five years.)

Years	Cash Flow	Reinvestment Rate (%)	Ending Wealth
I	$ 79	—	$ 79.00
2	79	7.9	164.24
3	79	6.0	253.10
4	79	6.0	347.29
5	79	6.0	477.13
5	1,017.92[b]	—	1,465.05

[a]Cash flows are received at the end of the year.
[b]The price of bond B with one year left to maturity and a market yield of 6% is $1,017.92.

both five-year and six-year bonds because of the flatness of the yield curve. In order to simplify the calculations, we will assume that interest is paid annually so that we can concentrate on the immunization principle.

Because the YTM is 7.9 percent, our investor, understanding the reinvestment rate implications of bonds, expects that her investment should yield, after five years, an ending wealth ratio of $(1.079)^5$, or 1.46254, or $1.46254 per dollar invested today. That is, if she invests $1,000 in a bond today and the intermediate coupons are reinvested at 7.9 percent each, as the YTM calculation assumes, the ending wealth for this investment in a bond that can be purchased for face value should be $1,000 \ (1.079)^5$, or $1,462.54.

Our investor can purchase bond A, with a 7.9 percent coupon and a five-year maturity, or bond B, with a 7.9 percent coupon, a six-year maturity, and a duration of five years. The top panel of Table 18-2 illustrates what happens if bond A is purchased and market yields remain constant for our investor's five-year investment horizon. Because the intermediate cash flows are reinvested at exactly 7.9 percent each year, the ending amounts cumulate toward the final ending wealth of $1,462.54, or a wealth ratio of 1.46254. Notice in these examples that we separate year 5 from the other four because of the return of principal ($1,000) at the end of year 5; obviously, no compound interest is earned on the return of this $1,000 at the end of the year. In a similar manner, no interest is earned on the first year's cash flow of $79, which is assumed to occur at the end of the year.

Now consider what would happen if our investor bought bond A and in the third year of its five-year life market yields for this and comparable bonds declined to 6 percent and remained at that level for the remainder of the five-year period. As a result, the intermediate cash flows in the last three years of the bond's life would be reinvested at 6 percent rather than at 7.9 percent. Therefore, the reinvestment rate risk present in bond investments has a negative impact on this particular bond investment.

The results of a drop in the reinvestment rate are shown in the middle panel of Table 18-2, using the same format as previously. As this panel shows, at the end of year 5 the ending amount of wealth for bond A now is only $1,447.13, representing a shortfall for the investor's ending-wealth objective. This result occurred because she did not immunize her bond portfolio against interest rate risk, but instead purchased a bond based on matching the maturity of the bond with her investment horizon. As explained above, to protect against this interest rate risk it is necessary to purchase a bond whose duration is equal to the investor's investment horizon.

Assume that a $1,000 bond with a coupon rate of 7.9 percent and a five-year maturity could have been purchased at the same time. The duration of this bond, which we call bond B, is exactly five years, matching the investor's investment horizon. In this case, the bond would be immunized against interest rate risk, because any shortfall arising from a declining reinvestment rate would be offset by a higher price for the bond at the end of the investment horizon because the drop in interest rates produces an increase in the price of the bond. Note that at the end of five years, which is our investor's investment horizon, bond B has one year left to maturity and could be sold in the market.

The bottom panel of Table 18-2 illustrates the same process as before for bond B. Notice that the ending cash flows are the same for the first four years as they were for the previous situation with the five-year bond. At the end of year 5, the bond still has one year to go to maturity. Its price has risen because of the drop in interest rates. As the analysis in Table 18-2 demonstrates, the ending wealth is more than enough to meet the investor's objective of $1,462.54 per $1,000 invested.

✓ By choosing a bond or a portfolio of bonds with a duration equal to a predetermined investment horizon, it is possible, in principle, to immunize a portfolio against interest rate risk.

Immunization is only one of the structured portfolio strategies. These strategies occupy a position between passive strategies and active strategies. Although the classical immunization discussed here could possibly be thought of as a passive strategy, we must be aware of the real-world problems involved in implementing such a strategy. In truth, this strategy is not easy to implement, and it is not a passive strategy in application. To achieve immunization as discussed here requires frequent rebalancing because duration should always be equal to the investment horizon. An investor simply cannot set duration equal to investment horizon at the beginning of the process and ignore the bond, or portfolio, thereafter.[26]

Summary

▶ A wide range of investors are interested in bonds, ranging from those who seek a steady stream of interest income and return of principal to those seeking capital gains by speculating on future interest rate movements.

▶ In understanding what drives the bond market, fears of inflation play a key role.

▶ Passive bond strategies, whereby the investor does not actively seek out trading possibilities in an attempt to outperform the market, include buy and hold and indexing.

▶ Active management strategies include, but are not limited to, forecasting changes in interest rates, yield spread analysis, and identifying relative mispricings in fixed-income securities.

▶ Duration, stated in years, is the weighted average time to recovery of all interest payments plus principal repayment.

▶ Duration expands with time to maturity but at a decreasing rate, and it is inversely related to coupon and yield to maturity.

▶ The modified duration can be used to calculate the approximate percentage price change in a bond for a given change in the bond's yield to maturity.

▶ Convexity refers to the degree to which duration changes as the yield to maturity changes. The degree of convexity is not the same for all bonds.

▶ Immunization is the strategy of protecting (immunizing) a portfolio against interest rate risk by attempting to have the two components of interest rate risk, reinvestment rate risk and price risk, cancel each other out.

▶ A portfolio is said to be immunized (the effects of interest rate risk are neutralized) if the duration of the portfolio is made equal to a preselected investment horizon for the portfolio.

▶ Immunization is only one of the structured portfolio strategies, which occupy a position between passive strategies and active strategies.

Questions

18-1 Describe two different types of investors interested in bonds as an investment.

18-2 List two of the most important reasons for U.S. investors to purchase foreign bonds.

18-3 Assume a U.S. investor buys French bonds. If the Euro weakens, how does that affect the U.S. investor's dollar-denominated return?

18-4 A U.S. investor buying foreign bonds is selling the dollar. Agree or disagree and explain your reasoning.

18-5 When would bond yields be expected to move in the same direction as nominal GDP?

18-6 When would an expected increase in inflation negatively impact bond investors?

---

[26] There are several variations of the basic immunization strategy. The most popular variation is called *horizon-matching*, or combination matching. This involves a portfolio that is duration-matched and also cash-matched in the first few years. An alternative variation is *contingent* immunization, which involves active management plus a lower floor return that is ensured for the horizon period. The portfolio manager must act to earn the floor return by immunizing the portfolio if necessary. Otherwise, the manager can actively manage the portfolio or some portion thereof.

18-7 Why would the Fed's multiple increases in the federal funds rate be expected to lead to increases in the long-term bond rate?

18-8 What is the key factor in analyzing bonds? Why?

18-9 Under the expectations theory, long rates must be an average of the present and future short-term rates. Explain.

18-10 What is the difference between the expectations theory and the liquidity preference theory?

18-11 Why are yield spreads important to an investor?

18-12 Identify and explain at least two passive bond management strategies.

18-13 Identify and explain two specific active bond management strategies. Are the two related?

18-14 How does duration differ from time to maturity? What does duration tell you?

18-15 How is duration related to time to maturity? to coupon? the yield to maturity? Do the same relationships hold for a zero-coupon bond?

18-16 Assume that a bond investor wishes to maximize the potential price volatility from a portfolio of bonds about to be constructed. What should this investor seek in the way of coupon, maturity, and duration?

18-17 Is duration a complete measure of bond risk? Is it the best measure?

18-18 Explain the concept of immunization. What role, if any, does duration play in this concept?

18-19 Assume you have correctly forecast that interest rates will soon decline sharply. Also assume that you will invest only in fixed-income securities, and that your time horizon is one year; how would you construct a portfolio?

18-20 When would investors find bonds with long maturities, selling at large discounts, particularly unattractive as investment opportunities?

18-21 What is meant by the term "bond mispricings?"

18-22 How can horizon analysis be used to manage a bond portfolio?

18-23 Consider some Canadian government bonds that are currently yielding 2 percentage points more than comparable Treasury securities. Now suppose you have projected that the Canadian economy will slow down. How would this impact your decision to purchase the Canadian bonds? How would you go about deciding whether to hedge this position?

CFA
18-24 Sam Stevens is the trustee for the Hole Punchers Labor Union (HPLU). He has approached the investment management firm of IM Associates (IMA) to manage its $200 million bond portfolios. IMA assigned Carol Peters as the portfolio manager for the HPLU account. In their first meeting, Mr. Stevens told Ms. Peters: "We are an extremely conservative pension fund. We believe in investing only in investment grade bonds so that there will be minimal risk that the principal invested will be lost. We want at least 40% of the portfolio to be held in bonds that will mature within the next three years. I would like your thoughts on this proposed structure for the portfolio."

How should Ms. Peters respond?

CFA
18-25 A British portfolio manager is considering investing in Japanese government bonds denominated in yen. What are the major risks associated with this investment?

CFA
18-26 A portfolio manager wants to estimate the interest rate risk of a bond using duration. The current price of the bond is 82. A valuation model found that if interest rates decline by 30 basis points, the price will increase to 83.50; if interest rates increase by 30 basis points, the price will decline to 80.75. What is the duration of this bond?

CFA
18-27 A portfolio manager purchased $8 million in market value of a bond with a duration of 5. For this bond, determine the estimated change in its market value for the change in interest rates shown below:

(a) 100 basis points

(b) 50 basis points

(c) 25 basis points

(d) 10 basis points

CFA

18-28   James Smith and Donald Robertson are assistant portfolio managers for Micro Management Partners. In a review of the interest rate risk of a portfolio, Smith and Robertson discussed the riskiness of two Treasury securities. Following is the information about these two Treasuries:

Bond	Price	Modified Duration
A	90	4
B	50	6

Smith noted that Treasury bond B has more price volatility because of its higher modified duration. Robertson disagreed noting that Treasury bond A has more price volatility despite its lower modified duration. Which manager is correct?

CFA

18-29   Explain why you agree or disagree with the following statement:

If two bonds have the same duration, then the percentage change in price of the two bonds will be the same for a given change in interest rates.

CFA

18-30   What is the difference between an active and a passive bond portfolio strategy?

CFA

18-31   What is the objective of a bond immunization strategy?

CFA

18-32   What is the basic underlying principle in the immunization strategy?

CFA

18-33   A portfolio manager is contemplating the implication of an immunization strategy. He believes that one advantage of the strategy is that it requires no management of the portfolio once the initial portfolio is constructed. That is, it is simply a "buy-and-hold strategy." Explain whether or not you agree with the portfolio manager's assessment of the immunization strategy as a "buy- and-hold strategy."

CFA

18-34   A portfolio manager is considering an immunization strategy for a client. The portfolio manager is concerned that the portfolio must be rebalanced very frequently in order to match the duration of the portfolio each day to the time remaining in the investment horizon. Comment on this portfolio manager's concern.

CFA

18-35   "I can immunize a portfolio by simply investing in zero-coupon bonds." Comment on this statement.

Problems

18-1   Determine the point at which duration decreases with maturity for a 4 percent bond with an original maturity of 15 years. Use increments in maturity of five years. The market yield on this bond is 10 percent.

18-2   Consider a 6.5 percent bond with a maturity of 10 years. The price of this bond is $972.50. The Macaulay duration is 5.9 years. What is the modified duration for this bond?

18-3   Assume a 7 percent, eight-year bond has a Macaulay duration of 5.6 years and a YTM of 8 percent. Calculate the approximate price change for this bond if interest rates decline 50 basis points.

18-4   A 5.8 percent, 15-year bond is currently priced at $924.55. The required yield is 6.6 percent. The yield immediately changes to 6.7 percent. What will be the new price of the bond?

18-5   Assuming you do earn the stated YTM, which bond would you rather own, if all other things are equal? Bond A, YTM = 12 percent, 10-year maturity; Bond B, YTM = 11 percent, nine-year maturity.

Computational Problems

18-1 Given a 10 percent, three-year bond with a price of $1,025.42 with a market yield of 8 percent, calculate its duration using the format illustrated in Table 18-1.

18-2 Using the duration from Problem 18-1, determine

   a. The modified duration

   b. The percentage change in the price of the bond if r changes 0.25 percent.

18-3 Calculate the duration of a 12 percent coupon bond with 10 years remaining to maturity and selling at par. Use annual interest rates.

   Given the duration calculated, calculate the percentage change in bond price if the market discount rate for this bond declines by 0.50 percent.

Spreadsheet Exercises

18-1 Duration can be calculated using spreadsheet formulas. Data must be entered as follows:

Settlement date	Date is entered as DATE(year, month, day)
Maturity date	Date is entered as DATE(year, month, day)
Coupon as a decimal	
Required yield as a decimal	
Frequency of Payments	

Use the formula = DURATION(A1,A2,A3,A4,A5) for duration and = MDURATION(A1,A2, A3,A4,A5) for modified duration.

   Example—Calculate the duration and modified duration for a 6 percent, seven-year bond with a required yield of 5 percent. This is done as follows:

   (note that dates are seven years apart, resulting in the format as illustrated)

2/16/2006	Settlement date =DATE(year,m,d)
2/16/2013	Maturity date =DATE(year,m,d)
0.06	Coupon rate as decimal
0.05	Required yield as decimal
2	Frequency of coupons
5.86	Macaulay duration
5.71	Modified duration

   Problem—Using this format, calculate the duration for the bond in Table 18-1.

18-2 Calculate the duration of a bond using the cash flow approach shown in the spreadsheet below. This bond has a current price of $974.47, a coupon of 5.5 percent, and a maturity of five years. The YTM on this bond is 6.10 percent.

Use three decimal places for the last two rows of the spreadsheet. Refer to the example for calculating duration in Chapter 18. Note that the duration of this bond is the sum of the values found on the last row of the spreadsheet.

Annual Coupon	55										
YTM	6.10%										
Current Price	974.47										
Maturity Value	1000										
Period	0	1	2	3	4	5	6	7	8	9	10
Time in Years	0	0.5	1	1.5	2	2.5	3	3.5	4	4.5	5
Cash Flows											
PV of Cash Flows											
Weighted PV of Cash Flows											
Wgtd. Av of Time Periods											
Duration = Sum of Row 13											

Checking Your Understanding

18-1   U.S. investors were helped as the euro strengthened relative to the dollar, because they could buy back more dollars when they cashed in their investment. Therefore, U.S. investors benefited from a favorable currency movement.

18-2   The Fed may tighten monetary policy in order to dampen inflationary pressures. Bond investors should react favorably to such actions, other things being equal.

18-3   The two most important reasons for U.S. investors to buy foreign bonds are the possibility of higher returns relative to U.S. bonds, and the diversification benefits for the portfolio.

18-4   Agree. There is more of a risk of increased inflation in an economy growing faster than expected, which would lower the real return on bonds. Also, the Fed may try to check inflation by raising interest rates, which would lower bond prices.

18-5   Agree. More of the cash flows come earlier in the form of interest payments, reducing the duration of the higher-coupon bond.

18-6   You should adjust your portfolio by increasing the average duration of the portfolio, which will increase its interest rate sensitivity.

chapter *19*

Understanding Derivative Securities: Options

Having heard about options from several sources, you decide this is one of those topics that you at least have to be able to talk about. If you are going to manage your inheritance without interference, you don't want to be left standing there looking foolish when someone asks you about writing calls or buying a put to protect against market declines. Even the popular press talks about calls and puts on a regular basis. Therefore, you see no alternative but to plow ahead and learn enough about derivatives in general, and options in particular, to let you hold your own. And, besides, this may turn out to be very valuable information you can use in the future when investing.

Derivatives are contracts between two parties, a buyer and a seller, that have a price and trade in specific markets. Note that derivative contracts are simply agreements to transfer ownership of the asset involved under specified conditions.

The importance of derivative securities lies in the flexibility they provide investors in managing investment risk. Derivative instruments can also be used to speculate in various markets. This chapter analyzes one of these derivative contracts, options, while Chapter 20 analyzes another, futures.

AFTER READING THIS CHAPTER YOU WILL BE ABLE TO:

▶ **Understand why investors use options in their investment strategies.**

▶ **Describe the option alternatives available to investors and how the options markets operate.**

▶ **Analyze basic option strategies.**

▶ **Understand the valuation of options.**

This chapter focuses on put and call equity options.[1] Equity options give the holder the right to receive or deliver shares of stock under certain specified conditions. We concentrate mostly on options on individual stocks but also consider index options. We

---

[1] The reason for this is that these options are of most interest to the typical individual investor.

concentrate our discussion in both Chapters 19 and 20 on *financial derivatives* as opposed to derivatives involving commodities such as gold and oil.

The emphasis here is on how puts and calls work, and on their importance to portfolio managers. As derivative securities, options are innovations in *risk management*, not in risk itself, and are used by both individual investors and portfolio managers.

Why Have Derivative Securities?

Over the years some people have asked why we have derivative instruments such as options and futures, which allow investors to speculate on securities and indexes. Investors can easily lose their entire investment in the derivative security by speculating, and they always have as an alternative buying the underlying security or index (typically, via an ETF or index mutual fund).

One important reason for the existence of derivatives is that they contribute to market completeness. A *complete market* is one where all identifiable payoffs can be obtained by trading the securities that are in that market. Incomplete markets occur as a result of investors not being able to exploit all opportunities that may exist.

Derivatives offer an opportunity to limit the risk faced by both individual investors and firms. They can also be used as a substitute for the underlying positions, and may offer lower transaction costs as well as more liquidity. Finally, derivatives allow investors to speculate, which involves taking a market position when a change in prices or interest rates is expected.

✓ Financial derivatives have several important applications, including risk management, trading efficiency, and speculation.

WHY OPTIONS MARKETS?

An investor can always purchase shares of common stock if he or she is bullish about the company's prospects, or sell short if bearish. Why, then, should we create these indirect claims on a stock as an alternative way to invest? Several reasons have been advanced, including the following:

1. Puts and calls expand the opportunity set available to investors, making available risk-return combinations that would otherwise be impossible or that improve the risk-return characteristics of a portfolio.[2]
2. An investor can establish a position with options for a much smaller investment than required with the security itself. The buyer's maximum loss is known in advance. If an option expires worthless, the most the buyer can lose is the cost (price) of the option.
3. Options provide leverage—the chance to magnify percentage gains.
4. Using options on a market index such as the S&P 500, an investor can participate in market movements with a single trading decision.

Introduction to Options

Options Rights to buy or sell a stated number of shares of a security within a specified period at a specified price

Options on common stocks, representing short-term claims on the underlying stock, are created by investors and sold to other investors. The corporation whose common stock underlies these claims has no direct interest in the transaction, and is not responsible for creating, terminating, or executing put and call contracts.

---

[2] Many stocks do not have puts and calls available in the organized options markets.

An option is created when someone writes (sells) it. Options can be created and destroyed; therefore, there is no predefined number of puts and calls.

Call An option to buy a specified number of shares of stock at a stated price within a specified period

✓   A **call** option on a stock gives the holder the right to buy (or "call away") 100 shares of a particular common stock at a specified price any time prior to a specified expiration date.[3]

Investors purchase calls if they expect the stock price to rise because the price of the call and the common stock will move together. Therefore, calls permit investors to speculate on a rise in the price of the underlying common stock without buying the stock itself.

Example 19-1   A Coca-Cola six-month call option at $55 per share gives the buyer the right (an option) to purchase 100 shares of Coke at $55 per share from a writer (seller) of the option anytime during the six months before the specified expiration date. The buyer pays a premium (the price of the call) to the writer for this option.

Put An option to sell a specified number of shares of stock at a stated price within a specified period

✓   A **put** option on a stock gives the buyer the right to sell (or "put away") 100 shares of a particular common stock at a specified price prior to a specified expiration date.

Investors purchase puts if they expect the stock price to fall, because the value of the put will rise as the stock price declines. Therefore, puts allow investors to speculate on a decline in the stock price without selling the common stock short.

Example 19-2   A writer (seller) of a Coca-Cola six-month put at $55 per share is obligated, under certain circumstances, to receive from a holder of this put 100 shares of Coke for which the writer will pay $55 per share. The writer receives a premium (the price of the put) for selling this option.

LONG-TERM OPTIONS

Long-Term Equity Anticipation Securities (LEAPS) Puts and calls with longer maturity dates, up to two years

Long-term options known as **Long-Term Equity Anticipation Securities (LEAPS)** were introduced in 1990. These long-term options are available on several hundred stocks and several indexes.

Example 19-3   Equity LEAPS are available on stocks such as Dell and Adobe and Index LEAPS are available on indexes such as the S&P 100 and S&P 500.

LEAPS have maturities longer than one year, and up to three years. They typically are considerably more expensive than short-term options, but with a longer maturity they may cost less per share when calculated on a daily basis. Like other options, they can be used to hedge or speculate.[4]

---

[3] It is important to remember throughout this discussion that the standard option contract on the organized exchanges is for 100 shares of the underlying common stock; therefore, when we speak of buying or selling *a* call or *a* put, we mean one contract representing an option on 100 shares of stock.

[4] Information on LEAPS can be found at www.cboe.com/products/leaps.aspx.

WEEKLYS^{SM} OPTIONS

A relatively new trend in options is to list very short-term options called Weeklys. These options are listed on Thursdays and expire on the following Friday. New Weeklys are listed each week.[5] These options can provide investors with more targeted trading opportunities. For example, if on Monday an investor expects a company to announce good unexpected earnings on Thursday, the investor could buy a Weekly at a lesser cost than a regular option.

Weeklys are available on individual stocks, indexes, and exchange traded funds.[6] By early 2012 Weeklys were accounting for about 8 percent of total options trading.

Understanding Options

OPTIONS TERMINOLOGY

To understand puts and calls, one must understand the terminology used in connection with them. Our discussion here applies specifically to options on the organized options exchanges.[7] Important options terms include the following:

Exercise (Strike) Price The per-share price at which the common stock may be purchased from (in the case of a call) or sold to a writer (in the case of a put)

Expiration Date The date an option expires

Option Premium The price paid by the option buyer to the seller of the option

1. *Exercise (strike) price.* The **exercise (strike) price** is the per-share price at which the common stock may be purchased (in the case of a call) or sold to a writer (in the case of a put). Most stocks in the options market have options available at several different exercise prices, thereby providing investors with multiple alternatives.[8]
2. *Expiration date.* The **expiration date** is the last date at which an option can be exercised.[9] Every option has an expiration date. All puts and calls are designated by the month of expiration. The expiration dates for options contracts vary from stock to stock but do not exceed nine months for regular options (LEAPS have longer expiration dates).
3. *Option premium.* The **option premium** is the price paid by the option buyer to the writer (seller) of the option, whether put or call. The premium is stated on a per share basis for options on organized exchanges, and since the standard contract is for 100 shares, a $3 premium represents $300, a $15 premium represents $1500, and so forth.

✓   Option premium = option price

Checking Your Understanding

1. Why might an investor prefer to buy a put on a particular stock rather than sell it short?
2. What does it mean to say a call buyer has a right but not an obligation? What about the call seller?
3. Suppose you buy car insurance that can be renewed annually. Thinking in general terms, can this be considered an option? If so, which type?

---

[5] Weeklys are not listed if they would expire on the Friday of the expiration week for regular options.

[6] A listing of the Weeklys currently available for trading can be found at http://www.cboe.com/micro/weeklys/availableweeklys.aspx.

[7] Puts and calls existed for many years before these organized exchanges. They could be bought or sold in the over-the-counter market through brokers who were part of the Put and Call Dealers and Brokers Association. Members of this association endeavored to satisfy investor demands for particular options on a case-by-case basis. The terms of each individual contract (price, exercise date, etc.) had to be negotiated between buyer and seller. This was clearly a cumbersome, inefficient process.

[8] Options sold on these exchanges are protected against stock dividends and stock splits; therefore, if either is paid during the life of an option, both the exercise price and the number of shares in the contract are adjusted as necessary.

[9] American-style options can be exercised any time prior to expiration; European-style options can be exercised only at expiration.

HOW OPTIONS WORK

As noted, a standard call (put) contract gives the buyer the right to purchase (sell) 100 shares of a particular stock at a specified exercise price any time before the expiration date. Both are created by sellers, either individuals or institutions, who seek to profit from their beliefs about the underlying stock's likely price performance.

✓   The buyer and the seller of a particular option have opposite expectations about the likely performance of the underlying stock, and therefore the performance of the option.

  ❏ The call writer expects the price of the stock to remain roughly steady or perhaps move down.
  ❏ The call buyer expects the price of the stock to move upward, and relatively soon.
  ❏ The put writer expects the price of the stock to remain roughly steady or perhaps move up.
  ❏ The put buyer expects the price of the stock to move down, and relatively soon.

Example 19-4   Consider an individual named Carl who is optimistic about Coca-Cola's prospects. Carl instructs his broker to buy a March call option on Coca-Cola at a strike price of $40. Assume that the stock price is $41.15 and the premium is $1.60. Carl pays this premium, a total cost of $160 since 100 shares are involved, plus brokerage commissions.

Three courses of action are possible with any option:

1. *The option may expire worthless.* Assume the price of Coke fluctuates up and down but is at $39.25 on the expiration date. The call gives the buyer (owner) the right to purchase Coke at $40, but this would make no sense when Coke can be purchased on the open market at $39.25. Therefore, the option will expire worthless.
2. *The option may be exercised.* If Coke appreciates, Carl could exercise the option by paying $4,000 (the $40 exercise price multiplied by 100 shares) and receiving 100 shares of Coke.[10]
3. *The option can be sold in the secondary market.* If Coke appreciates, the value (price) of the call will also appreciate. Carl can easily *sell the call in the secondary market* to another investor who wishes to speculate on Coke, because listed options are traded continuously. Most investors trading puts and calls do not exercise those that are valuable; instead, they simply sell them on the open market, exactly as they would the common stock if they owned it.[11]

Puts work the same way as calls, except in reverse. A writer creates a particular put contract and sells it for the premium that the buyer pays. The writer believes that the underlying common stock is likely to remain flat or appreciate, while the buyer believes that the stock price is likely to decline.

---

[10] Assume the price has appreciated to $50 before expiration. Carl now owns 100 shares of Coca-Cola worth $50 per share, for which he paid $40 per share (plus the $1.60 per share for the call option itself). An immediate sale of the stock in the market would result in a $840 *gross profit* (brokerage costs are not included here), or [$5,000 − ($4,000 + $160)].

[11] One of the implications of the option-pricing model to be considered later is that American calls on stocks that do not pay a cash dividend should never be exercised before the expiration date. Calls on stocks paying a cash dividend might be exercised before the expiration date.

✓ Unlike a buyer, who is not obligated to act, a writer may be assigned to take action in the form of making or taking delivery of the stock.

Example 19-5

Assume a writer sells a March Coca-Cola put at an exercise price of $45 when the stock price is $41.15. The premium is $3.70, or $370 for 100 shares, which the buyer of the put pays and the seller (writer) receives (brokerage costs would be involved in both cases). Suppose the price of Coke declines to $35 near the expiration date.

The put owner (buyer), who did not own Coke stock previously, could instruct the broker to purchase 100 shares of Coke in the open market for $3,500. The buyer could then exercise the put, which means that a writer chosen randomly must accept the 100 shares of Coke and pay the put owner $45 per share, or $4,500 total (although the current market price is only $35). The put buyer grosses $630 ($4,500 received less $3,500 cost of 100 shares less the $370 paid for the put). The put writer suffers an immediate *paper* loss of $1,000 because the 100 shares of Coke are worth $35 per share but have a cost of $45 per share, although the premium received by the writer reduces this loss by $370. (Brokerage costs have once again been omitted in the example.)[12]

As in the case of a call, two other courses of action are possible in addition to the exercise of the put. The put may expire worthless because the price of the common did not decline enough to justify exercising the put. Far more likely, however, the put owner can sell the put in the secondary market for a profit (or a loss).

What actually happens to puts and calls?

✓ Most call and put investors simply sell their options in the open market. Therefore, they close out their positions before the expiration date.

THE MECHANICS OF TRADING

The Options Exchanges   There are several options exchanges, such as: the Chicago Board Options Exchange (CBOE), the American, NASDAQ OMX PHLX, the International Securities Exchange (ISE) in New York, BATS Exchange Options Market, and the NYSE Arca.[13] The American is part of the NYSE Euronext group, as is NYSE Arca.

The options markets provide liquidity to investors, which is a very important requirement for successful trading. Investors know that they can instruct their broker to buy or sell whenever they choose to do so at a price set by the forces of supply and demand.

---

[12] With stock options, the transactor must pay the brokerage commission for buying or selling the stock.

[13] In addition, the Options Clearing Corporation reports trading for the Boston Options Exchange (BOX) and the NSDQ (NASDAQ) market. Volume for the latter is very small compared to the other trading forums. For more details, see http://www.optionsclearing.com/market/vol_data/main/exchange_volume.jsp.

✓ Options exchanges make puts and calls a success by standardizing the exercise date and exercise price of contracts. One Coca-Cola May 45 call option is identical to every other Coca-Cola May 45 call option.

The same types of orders discussed in Chapter 5, in particular, market, limit, and stop orders, are used in trading puts and calls.[14] Certificates representing ownership are not used for puts and calls; instead, transactions are handled as bookkeeping entries. Option trades settle on the next business day after the trade.

The secondary markets for puts and calls have worked well in the years since the Chicago Board Options Exchange (CBOE) started operations in 1973. Trading volume has been large, and the number of puts and calls available has expanded.

Options Clearing Corporation (OCC)
Stands between buyers and sellers of options to ensure fulfillment of obligations

The Clearing Corporation   The **options clearing corporation (OCC)** performs a number of important functions that contribute to the success of the secondary market for options. It functions as an intermediary between the brokers representing the buyers and the writers. That is, once the brokers representing the buyer and the seller negotiate the price on the floor of the exchange, they no longer deal with each other, but with the OCC.

Through their brokers, call writers are effectively contracting with the OCC itself to deliver shares of the particular stock, and buyers of calls actually receive the right to purchase the shares from the OCC.

✓ The OCC becomes the buyer for every seller and the seller for every buyer, guaranteeing that all contract obligations will be met. This prevents the problems that could occur as buyers attempted to force writers to honor their obligations.

The net position of the OCC is zero, because the number of contracts purchased must equal the number sold.

Investors wishing to exercise their options inform their brokers, who in turn inform the OCC of the exercise. The OCC randomly selects a broker on whom it holds the same written contract, and the broker randomly selects a customer who has written these options to honor the contract. Writers chosen in this manner are said to be assigned an obligation or to have received an assignment notice. Once assigned, the writer cannot execute an offsetting transaction to eliminate the obligation; that is, a call writer who receives an assignment must sell the underlying securities, and a put writer who receives an assignment must purchase them.

One of the great advantages of a clearinghouse is that transactors in this market can easily cancel their positions prior to assignment. Since the OCC maintains all the positions for both buyers and sellers, it can cancel out the obligations of both call and put writers wishing to terminate their position.[15]

✓ A writer of a put or call can buy the exact same option and cancel the position at any time (except in the case of assignment).

With regard to puts and calls, margin refers to the collateral that option *writers* provide their brokers to ensure fulfillment of the contract in case of exercise. Options cannot be

---

[14] Although available, the manner in which some types of orders are executed on some of the options exchanges varies from that used on the stock exchanges.

[15] For example, a call writer can terminate the obligation to deliver the stock any time before the expiration date (or assignment) by making a "closing purchase transaction" at the current market-determined price of the option. The OCC offsets the outstanding call written with the call purchased in the closing transaction. A put writer can also close out a position at any time by making an offsetting transaction.

purchased on margin. Buyers must pay 100 percent of the purchase price.[16] Margin requirements are important to sellers. However, these requirements are often complex, differ between instruments, and are subject to frequent adjustments. Therefore, an option seller needs to be sure he or she understands all of the current requirements.

Checking Your Understanding

4. Assume an investor buys a put on a stock. Describe three different outcomes that could occur for the investor holding this put.
5. How does the clearinghouse help to ensure the fulfillment of put and call contracts?

Payoffs and Profits from Basic Option Positions

We can better understand the characteristics of options by examining their potential payoffs and profits. The simplest way to do this is to examine their value at expiration.

❑ At expiration, an option's *payoff* is simply the greater of $0 or the proceeds from the transaction.
❑ The *profit* takes into account the cost of the transaction.

We consider both variables because option traders are obviously interested in their net profits, but option valuation is perhaps better understood by focusing on payoffs. We use letters to designate the key variables:

$$S_T = \text{the value of the stock at expiration}$$
$$E = \text{the exercise price of the option}$$

✓ Options graphs showing their payoffs and profits are distinguished by the two-line segments needed to describe the payoffs and profits.

CALLS

Buying a Call   Consider first the buyer of a call option. At expiration, the investment value or *payoff* to the call holder is

> Payoff to call buyer at expiration :
> $= S_T - E$ if $S_T > E$
> $= 0$ if $S_T \le E$

This payoff to a call buyer is illustrated in Figure 19-1. The payoff is $0 until the exercise price is reached, at which point the payoff rises as the stock price rises.

---

[16] To protect itself, the OCC requires that its member firms whose customers have written options provide collateral to it in order to protect the OCC against defaults by writers. The member firms, in turn, require its customers who have *written* options to provide collateral for their written positions.

Figure 19-1

Payoff Profiles for Call
and Put Options at
Expiration.

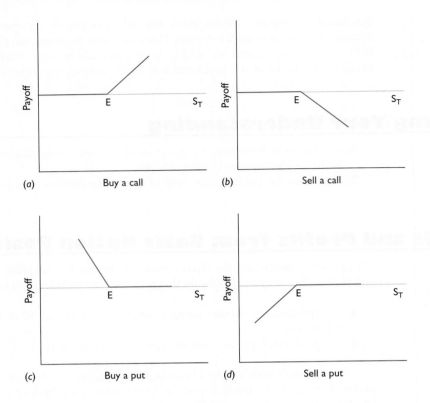

(a)   Buy a call

(b)   Sell a call

(c)   Buy a put

(d)   Sell a put

Example 19-6

Assume an investor buys a Coca-Cola three-month call with an exercise price of $50. The payoff for the call at expiration is a function of the stock price at that time. For example, at expiration the value of the call relative to various possible stock prices would be calculated as in the following partial set of prices:

Coca-Cola stock price at expiration	$40	45	50	55	60
Coca-Cola call price at expiration	$0	0	0	5	10

Notice that the payoff is not the same as the net profit to the option holder or writer. For example, if Coca-Cola is at $60 per share, the payoff to the option buyer is $10, but the net profit must reflect the cost of the call. In general, the profit to an option holder is the value of the option less the price paid for it.

Example 19-7

Figure 19-2 illustrates the *profit* situation for a call buyer. The stock price is assumed to be $48, and a six-month call with an exercise price of $50 has a premium of $4 (i.e., $400). Up to the exercise price of $50, the loss is $4 (which is the maximum loss). The breakeven point for the investor is the sum of the exercise price and the premium, or $50 + $4 = $54. If the price of the stock rises above $54, the value of the call will increase with it, at least point for point, as shown by the two parallel lines above the $0 profit-loss line.

Figure 19-2

Profit and Loss to the Buyer of a Call Option.

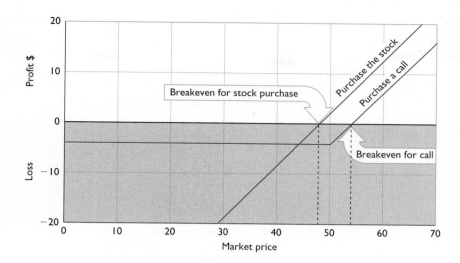

Selling (Writing) a Call   A call writer of an uncovered (naked) call incurs losses if the stock's price increases, as shown by the payoff profile in part (b) of Figure 19-1 (note carefully that we are not talking here about covered call writing—writing a covered call is a different situation, as explained below). The payoff is flat at the amount of the premium until the exercise price is reached, at which point it declines as the stock price rises. The uncovered call writer loses if the stock price rises, exactly as the call buyer gains if the stock price rises.[17]

> **Payoff to call writer at expiration:**
> $$= -(S_T - E) \text{ if } S_T > E;$$
> $$= 0 \qquad\quad \text{if } S_T \leq E$$

The net *profit* line in Figure 19-3 shows a similar pattern to that of the call buyer, except now the profit is positive up to the exercise price because the call writer is receiving the premium. The horizontal axis intercept in Figure 19-3 occurs at the breakeven point for the option writer—the sum of the exercise price and the option premium received (note that the breakeven point is identical to that of the call buyer). As the stock price exceeds the breakeven point, the uncovered call writer loses.

The mirror images of the payoff and net profit profiles for the call buyer (Figure 19-2) and the call writer (Figure 19-3) illustrate an important point.

✓   Options trading is *a zero-sum game*. What the option buyer (writer) gains, the option writer (buyer) loses.

PUTS

Buying a Put   A put buyer makes money if the price of the stock declines. Therefore, as part (c) of Figure 19-1 illustrates, the payoff pattern is flat at the $0 axis to the right of the exercise price; that is, stock prices greater than the exercise price result in a $0 payoff for the put buyer. As the stock declines below the exercise price, the payoff for the put option increases. The larger the decline in the stock price, the larger the payoff.

---

[17] The author is indebted to William Dukes for helpful comments in this discussion.

Figure 19-3

Profit and Loss to the Writer of a Call Option.

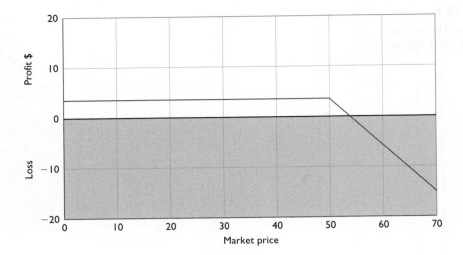

Figure 19-4

Profit and Loss to the Buyer of a Put Option.

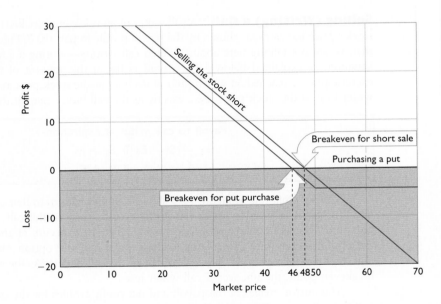

Payoff to put buyer at expiration:

$= 0$ if $S_T \geq E$

$= E - S_T$ if $S_T < E$

Once again, the profit line parallels the payoff pattern for the put option at expiration. As Figure 19-4 illustrates, the investor breaks even (no net profit) at the point where the stock price is equal to the exercise price minus the premium paid for the put. Beyond that point, the net profit line parallels the payoff line representing the investment value of the put.

Selling (Writing) a Put   The payoff pattern for the put writer is the mirror image of that for the put buyer as shown in part (d) of Figure 19-1. The put writer retains the premium if the stock price rises, and loses if the stock price declines. The put writer exchanges a fixed payoff for unknown losses.

Figure 19-5

Profit and Loss to the Writer of a Put Option.

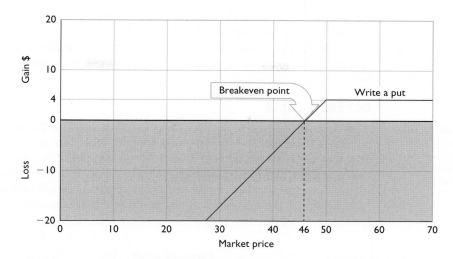

Payoff to put writer at expiration:

$$= 0 \qquad \text{if } S_T \geq E$$
$$= -(E - S_T) \text{ if } S_T < E$$

Writers (sellers) of puts are seeking the premium income exactly as call writers are. The writer obligates him- or herself to purchase a stock at the specified exercise price during the life of the put contract. If stock prices decline, the put buyer may purchase the stock and exercise the put by delivering the stock to the writer, who must pay the specified price.

Note that the put writer may be obligated to purchase a stock for, say, $50 a share when it is selling in the market for $40 a share. This represents an immediate paper loss (less the premium received for selling the put). Also note that the put writer can cancel the obligation by purchasing an identical contract in the market.

Example 19-8   Figure 19-5 illustrates the profit-loss position for the seller of a put. Assume a six-month put is sold at an exercise price of $50 for a premium of $4. The seller of a naked put receives the premium and hopes that the stock price remains at or above the exercise price. The seller begins to lose money below the breakeven point ($50 − $4 = $46). Losses could be substantial if the price of the stock declines sharply. The price of the put will increase point for point as the stock price declines.

Some Observations on Buying and Selling Options   Options are attractive because of the small investment required and the potentially large payoff. According to the studies that have been done, the odds favor the sellers. Writing calls produces steady, although not extraordinary, returns. Call buying is often unprofitable. When buying options investors should generally avoid options that expire in a few weeks—about 75 percent of the option premium disappears in the last three weeks of the option's life. Selling uncovered options can be very risky. In effect, the reward (premium) does not justify the risk for most investors.

Some Basic Options Strategies

In the previous section we examined the payoffs, and profit/losses, for basic "uncovered" positions involving options (and their underlying stocks). The six uncovered positions are: long stock, short stock, buy call, write call, buy put, and write put. In this section we analyze "covered" positions involving hedges.[18]

Hedge A strategy using derivatives to offset or reduce the risk resulting from exposure to an underlying asset

A **hedge** is a combination of an option and its underlying stock designed such that the option protects the stock against loss or the stock protects the option against loss. We consider below the more popular hedges.

COVERED CALLS

Covered Call A strategy involving the sale of a call option to supplement a long position in an underlying asset

A **covered call** involves the purchase of stock and the sale of a call on that stock; that is, it is a long position in the stock and a short position in a call.[19] The position is "covered" because the writer owns the stock and could deliver it if called to do so as a result of the exercise of the call option by the holder. In effect, the investor is willing to sell the stock at a fixed price, limiting the gains if the stock rises in exchange for cushioning the loss, by the amount of the call premium, if the stock declines.

Using our previous notation, the payoff profile at expiration is

	$S_T < E$	$S_T > E$
Payoff of stock	S_T	S_T
Payoff of call	-0	$-(S_T - E)$
Total payoff	S_T	E

Figure 19-6 illustrates the *payoffs* on the covered call hedge by showing all three situations: purchase of the stock, writing a call, and the combined position. The sale of the call truncates the combined position if the stock price rises above the exercise price. In effect, the writer has sold the claim to this gain for the call premium. At expiration, the position is worth, at most, the exercise price and the profit is the call premium received by selling the call.

As Figure 19-6 shows, if the stock price declines, the position is protected by the amount of the call premium received. Therefore, the breakeven point is lower compared to simply owning the stock, and the loss incurred as the stock price drops will be less with the covered call position by the amount of the call premium.

Example 19-9

Assume that an investor purchased 100 shares of Coca-Cola last year for $40 per share and this year, with the stock price at $48, writes a (covered) six-month call with an exercise price of $50. The writer receives a premium of $4. This situation is illustrated in Figure 19-7.

If called on to deliver his or her 100 shares, the investor will receive $50 per share, plus the $4 premium, for a gross profit of $14 per share (since the stock was purchased at $40 per share). However, the investor gives up the additional potential gain if the price of this stock rises above $50—shown by the flat line to the right of $50 for the covered call position in Figure 19-7. If the price rises to $60 after the call is sold, for example, the investor will gross $14 per share but could have grossed $20 per share if no call had been written.

Writing a naked call is also illustrated (by the broken line) in Figure 19-7. If the call is not exercised, the writer profits by the amount of the premium, $4. The naked writer's breakeven point is $54. This position will be profitable if the price of the stock does not rise above the breakeven point. While the potential gain for the naked writer is limited to $4, the potential loss is large. If the price of the stock were to rise sharply, the writer could easily lose an amount in excess of what was received in premium income.

---

[18] Spreads and combinations, which are also covered positions, are discussed in Appendix 19-A.

[19] If the stock is purchased at the same time as the call is written, it is called a "buy-write." If the shares are already owned, it is sometimes called an "overwrite."

Figure 19-6

Payoff Profiles for a Covered Call.

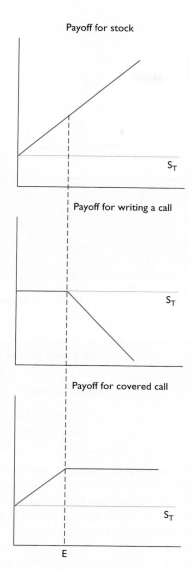

✓ Writing a covered call is typically regarded as a conservative strategy because it reduces the cost of owning the stock.

PROTECTIVE PUTS

Protective Put A strategy involving the purchase of a put option as a supplement to a long position in an underlying asset

A **protective put** involves buying a stock (or owning it already) and a put for the same stock; that is, it is a long position in both the stock and a put. The put acts as insurance against a decline in the underlying stock, guaranteeing an investor a minimum price at which the stock can be sold. In effect, the insurance acts to limit losses or unfavorable outcomes. The largest profit possible is infinite.

Figure 19-7

Profit and Loss for a Covered Call Position.

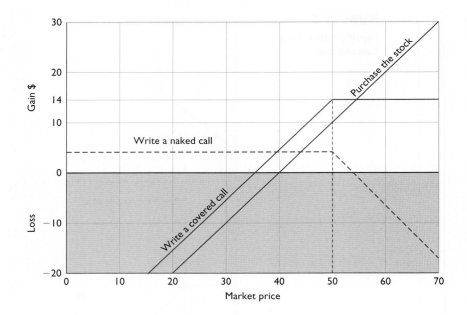

The payoff profile is :

	$S_T < E$	$S_T > E$
Payoff of stock	S_T	S_T
+ Payoff of put	$(E - S_T)$	0
Total payoff	E	S_T

Above the exercise price, the payoff reflects the increase in the stock price. Below the exercise price, the payoff is worth the exercise price at expiration.

Figure 19-8 shows the protective put versus an investment in the underlying stock. As always, the payoff for the stock is a straight line, and the payoff for the option strategy is an asymmetrical line consisting of two segments. The payoff for the protective put clearly illustrates what is meant by the term *truncating* the distribution of returns. Below a certain stock price (the exercise price), the payoff line is flat or horizontal. Therefore, the loss is limited to the cost of the put. Above the breakeven point, the protective put strategy shares in the gains as the stock price rises. This is the true benefit of derivative securities and the reason for their phenomenal growth—derivatives provide a quick and inexpensive way to alter the risk of a portfolio.

✓   A protective put offers some insurance against a decline in the stock price. The cost if the insurance turns out not to be needed is the cost of the put.

The protective put is identical to purchasing a call except for a different intercept on the vertical axis. This position illustrates a well-known concept called portfolio insurance, which is explained below.

PORTFOLIO INSURANCE

Portfolio Insurance An asset management technique designed to provide a portfolio with a lower limit on value while permitting it to benefit from rising security prices

The potential return-risk modification properties of options, and particularly the insurance aspects discussed above, are well illustrated by the technique known as **portfolio insurance**. This term

Figure 19-8

**Payoff Profile and Profit/
Losses for a Protected
Put Position.**

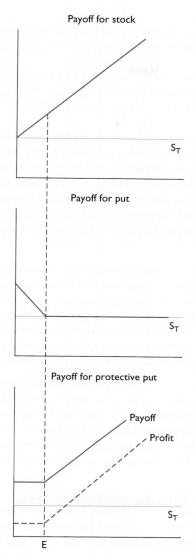

Payoff for stock

S_T

Payoff for put

S_T

Payoff for protective put

Payoff

Profit

S_T

E

refers to investment strategies designed to hedge portfolio positions by providing a minimum return on the portfolio while simultaneously providing an opportunity for the portfolio to participate in rising security prices. This asset management technique became very popular in the 1980s, with many billions of dollars of assets insured.

There are several methods of insuring a portfolio, including options, futures, and the creation of **synthetic options**. In practice, it is common to use futures contracts on market indexes (as discussed in Chapter 20). However, in principle options can be used in portfolio insurance strategies, and their use illustrates the basic nature of a hedge.

The idea behind portfolio insurance as regards options is simple. A protective put can be purchased that allows the portfolio to be sold for an amount sufficient to provide the minimum return. The remaining portfolio funds are invested in the usual manner. The protective put provides insurance for the portfolio by limiting losses in the event stock prices decline. The portfolio's value at the end of the period must equal or exceed the exercise price of the put.

Synthetic Options
Created by a combination
of two options or
an option and shares

Example 19-10   An investor wishes to ensure a minimum return of 5 percent. For simplicity, we assume that the investor starts with $1.[20] The investor buys a stock index and a put.

- ❏ One unit of a stock market index sells for $0.9097.
- ❏ A European put on this index can be bought for $0.0903.
- ❏ The put has a strike price of $1.05.

The investor has used portfolio insurance to ensure a 5 percent minimum return. If the value of the stock index exceeds $1.05 by the end of the investing period, the investor is ahead that much and allows the put to expire worthless. If the value of the index is less than $1.05 by the end of the period, the investor can exercise the option and sell the stock index for $1.05, thereby earning the required 5 percent minimum return on the initial investment of $1.00. Portfolio insurance has provided protection against the downside while allowing the investor to participate in stock price advances.

This example illustrates the conceptual use of puts in portfolio insurance strategies. In practice, however, puts and calls are not used to insure portfolios because those typically available to investors are American and not European. The exercise-at-any-time feature of American options makes them not only more valuable than corresponding European options but also more costly for portfolio insurance purposes. Furthermore, it generally is not possible to find puts and calls with the exact time to expiration, exercise price, and so on that matches a particular portfolio.

It should also be noted that portfolio insurance is not costless. The costs include:

- ❏ The *cost of the option* itself. In our example, the put cost is $0.0903. Obviously, if stocks advance and the put expires worthless, the cost of the put has been lost relative to an uninsured strategy. This can be thought of as the insurance premium.
- ❏ An *opportunity cost*. An investor who places 100 percent of investment funds in the stock index would participate fully in any market rise. In our example, the insured investor would participate in only 90.97 percent of any market rise.

Checking Your Understanding

6. In terms of payoff and profit profiles, what is the distinguishing characteristic for the various options positions? How does this differ from simply buying a stock, or shorting a stock?
7. Why is covered call writing considered a conservative strategy?

Option Valuation

A GENERAL FRAMEWORK

In this section we examine the determinants of the value of a put or call. Special terminology is used to describe the relationship between the exercise price of the option and the current stock price. If the price of the common stock, S, exceeds the exercise price of a call, E, the call is said to be *in the money* and has an immediate exercisable value. On the other hand, if the price of the common is less than the exercise price of a call, it is said to be *out of the money*. Finally, calls that are *near the money* are those with exercise prices slightly greater than current market price, whereas calls that are *at the money* are those with exercise prices equal to the stock price.

---

[20] This example is based on Richard J. Rendleman and Richard W. McEnally, "Assessing the Costs of Portfolio Insurance," *Financial Analysts Journal* (May–June 1987): pp. 27–37.

These same definitions also apply to puts, but in reverse. In summary,

If S > E,   a call is in the money and a put is out of the money.
If S < E,   a call is out of the money and a put is in the money.
If S = E,   an option is at the money.

Example 19-11 Consider a stock currently selling at $40. We will analyze an exercise price that is $5 on either side of the stock price.

Exercise Price	_____stock price = 40_____	
$45	in the money put	out of the money call
$40	at the money put	at the money call
$35	in the money call	out of the money put

INTRINSIC VALUES AND TIME VALUES

The price of a call option can be dichotomized in the following manner. If a call is in the money (the market price of the stock exceeds the exercise price for the call option), it has an *immediate* value equal to the difference in the two prices. This value will be designated as the *intrinsic value* of the call; it could also be referred to as the option's minimum value, which in this case is positive. If the call is out of the money (the stock price is less than the exercise price), the intrinsic value is zero; in this case, the price of the option is based on its speculative appeal. Summarizing, where S_0 = current stock price:

$$\text{Intrinsic value of a call} = \text{Maximum } (S_0 - E), 0 \qquad (19\text{-}1)$$

Example 19-12 Assume that on February 10 Pfizer closes at $25.70, and that a March call option with a strike price of 25 is available on that day for a price of $1.15. This option is in the money because the stock price is greater than the exercise price.

$$\text{Intrinsic value of March 25 call} = \$25.70 - \$25 = \$0.70$$

Puts work in reverse. If the market price of the stock is less than the exercise price of the put, the put is in the money and has an intrinsic value. Otherwise, it is out of the money and has a zero intrinsic value. Thus,

$$\text{Intrinsic value of a put} = \text{Maximum } (E - S_0), 0 \qquad (19\text{-}2)$$

Example 19-13 Assume there is a Pfizer March put available on February 10 with a strike price of $27.50. The current market price of the stock is $25.70. The price of the put on that day is $1.90.

$$\text{Intrinsic value of Pfizer } \$27.50 \text{ March put} = \$27.50 - \$25.70 = \$1.80$$

✓ An option's premium almost never declines below its intrinsic value.

The reason is that market arbitrageurs, who constantly monitor option prices for discrepancies, would purchase the options and exercise them, thus earning riskless returns. **Arbitrageurs** are speculators who seek to earn a return without assuming risk by constructing riskless hedges. Short-lived deviations are possible, but they will quickly be exploited.

Arbitrageurs Investors who seek discrepancies in security prices in an attempt to earn riskless returns

✓ Option prices almost always exceed intrinsic values, with the difference reflecting the option's potential appreciation typically referred to as the *time value*.[21]

Because buyers are willing to pay a price for potential future stock-price movements, time has a positive value—the longer the time to expiration for the option, the more chance it has to appreciate in value. However, when the stock price is held constant, options are seen as a *wasting asset* whose value approaches intrinsic value as expiration approaches. In other words, as expiration approaches, the time value of the option declines to zero.[22]

The time value can be calculated as the difference between the option price and the intrinsic value:

$$\text{Time value} = \text{Option price} - \text{Intrinsic value} \qquad (19\text{-}3)$$

Example 19-14 For the Pfizer options referred to earlier:

$$\text{Time value of Mar \$25 call} \quad = \$1.15 - \$0.70 = \$0.45$$
$$\text{Time value of Mar \$27.50 put} = \$1.90 - \$1.80 = \$0.10$$

We can now understand the premium for an option as the sum of its intrinsic value and its time value, or

$$\text{Premium or Option price} = \text{Intrinsic value} + \text{Time value} \qquad (19\text{-}4)$$

Example 19-15 For the Pfizer options:

$$\text{Premium for March 25 call} \quad = \$0.70 + \$0.45 = \$1.15$$
$$\text{Premium for March 27.50 put} = \$1.80 + \$0.10 = \$1.90$$

Notice an important point about options based on the preceding discussion. An investor who owns a call option and wishes to acquire the underlying common stock will always find it preferable to sell the option and purchase the stock in the open market rather than exercise the option (at least if the stock pays no dividends). Why? Because otherwise, he or she will lose the speculative premium on the option.

---

[21] This is somewhat of a misnomer because the actual source of value is volatility in price. However, price volatility decreases with a shortening of the time to expiration—hence the term time value.

[22] For an American option, time value cannot be zero because the option can be exercised at any time.

Example 19-16   Consider the Pfizer 25 call option, with the market price of the common at $25.70. An investor who owned the call and wanted to own the common would be better off to sell the option at $1.15 and purchase the common for $25.70, for a net investment of $24.55. Exercising the call option, the investor would have to pay $25 per share for shares of stock worth $25.70 in the market, but at a cost of $26.15 per share. (Brokerage commissions are ignored in this example.)

On the other hand, it can be optimal to exercise an American put early (on a nondividend-paying stock). A put sufficiently deep in the money should be exercised early because the payment received at exercise can be invested to earn a return.

Some Practical Advice

The time to maturity is clearly a major determinant of the value of an option. Most investors should generally avoid deep in-the-money options, because they are expensive and their profit potential is limited. Similarly, most investors should generally avoid deep out-of-the-money options. Although the premium is low, the chances of a large return are also low. Most investors will generally be better served with slightly in-the-money or out-of-the-money options, or options that are at the money.

BOUNDARIES ON OPTIONS PRICES

In the previous section we learned what the premium, or price, of a put or call consists of, but we do not know why options trade at the prices they do and the range of values they can assume. In this section we learn about the boundaries for option prices, and in the next section we discuss the exact determinants of options prices.

The value of an option must be related to the value of the underlying security. The basic relationship is most easy to understand by considering an option immediately prior to expiration, when there is no time premium. If the option is not exercised, it will expire immediately, leaving the option with no value. Obviously, investors will exercise it only if it is worth exercising (if it is in the money).

Figure 19-9(a) shows the values of call options at expiration, assuming a strike price of $50. At expiration, a call must have a value that is the maximum of 0 or its intrinsic value. Therefore, the line representing the value of a call option must be horizontal at $0 up to the exercise price and then rise as the stock price exceeds the exercise price. Above $50, the call price must equal the difference between the stock price and the exercise price, or its intrinsic value.

For puts the situation is reversed. At expiration, a put must have a value that is the maximum of 0 or its intrinsic value. Therefore, the line in Figure 19-9(b) representing the value of a put option must be horizontal beyond the exercise price. Below $50, the put price must equal the difference between the exercise price and the stock price. Note that a put option has a strict upper limit on intrinsic value, whereas the call has no upper limit.

✓   A put's strike price is its maximum intrinsic value.

What is the maximum price an option can assume? To see this think of a call. Since the call's value is derived from its ability to be converted into the underlying stock, it can never sell

Figure 19-9

Determining the
Boundaries on
Option Prices.

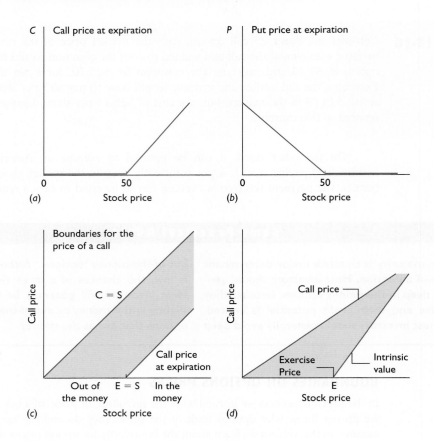

for more than the stock itself. It would not make sense to pay more for a call on one share of stock than the price of the stock itself.

✓   The maximum price for a call is the price of the underlying stock.

Based on the preceding, we can establish the absolute upper and lower boundaries for the price of a call option as shown in Figure 19-9(c). The upper boundary is a 45 degree line from the origin representing a call price equal to the stock price.[23] The lower boundary is represented by a 45 degree line starting at the exercise price. This lower boundary can be interpreted as the value of the call at the moment the call is exercised, or its intrinsic value.

✓   The lower boundary for a call is the price of the option at expiration, which must be either zero or its in-the-money value.

Finally, Figure 19-9(d) illustrates more precisely and realistically the variation in price for a call option by illustrating how the price of a call varies with the stock price and the exercise price. The call price is always above intrinsic value and rises as the stock price increases beyond the exercise price. The time value, represented by the shaded area in Figure 19-9(d), decreases beyond the exercise price.

---

[23] Think of this as a call with a zero exercise price and an infinite maturity.

To understand fully the price of a call option, we can use a formal model of call prices, the Black–Scholes model. The price of a put can also be found from this model because of a parity relationship between puts and calls.

THE BLACK–SCHOLES MODEL

Fischer Black and Myron Scholes have developed a model for the valuation of call options that is widely accepted and used in the investments community.[24] The formula itself is mathematical and appears to be very complex, but it is widely available on calculators and computers. Numerous investors estimate the value of calls using the **Black–Scholes model**.

Black–Scholes model A widely used model for the valuation of call options

The Black–Scholes model uses five variables to value the call option of a *nondividend-paying stock*.[25] These five variables, all but the last of which are directly observable in the market, are as follows:

1. The price of the underlying stock
2. The exercise price of the option
3. The time remaining to the expiration of the option
4. The interest rate
5. The volatility of the underlying stock

The first two variables are of obvious importance in valuing an option, because, as noted before, they determine the option's intrinsic value—whether it is in the money or not. If it is out of the money, it has only a time value based on the speculative interest in the stock.

Time to expiration (measured as a fraction of a year) is also an important factor in the value of an option because value generally increases with maturity. The relationship between time and value is not proportional, however.

✓ The time value of an option is greatest when the market price and the exercise price are equal.[26]

The interest rate affects option values, but the reasoning behind this is often ambiguous. Furthermore, different sources give different reasons for the relationship between interest rates and option premiums. Suffice it to say that increases in interest rates increase call premiums and decrease put premiums.

The last factor, and the only one not directly observable in the marketplace, is the stock's volatility. The greater the volatility, the *higher* the price of a call option because of the increased potential for the stock to move up. Therefore, a positive relation exists between the volatility of the stock and the value of the call option.[27]

---

[24] F. Black and M. Scholes, "The Pricing of Options and Corporate Liabilities," *The Journal of Political Economy*, 81 (May–June 1973): pp. 637–654.

[25] Options traded on organized exchanges are not protected against cash dividends, and this can have significant effects on option values. When a cash dividend is paid, the stock price should decline to reflect this payment. Any event that reduces the stock price reduces the value of a call and increases the value of a put.

[26] If the option is already in the money, a rise in the stock price will not result in the same percentage gain in the option price that would occur in the previous situation. For out-of-the-money options, part of the time remaining will be used for the price of the stock to reach the exercise price.

[27] "Volatility" as used in the options model is not the same concept as a stock's beta as used in Chapter 9. Volatility is used here as a measure of the variability in the stock price as opposed to sensitivity to market movements.

The Black–Scholes option-pricing formula can be expressed as[28]

$$C = S[N(d_1)] - \frac{E}{e^{rt}}[N(d_2)]$$ (19-5)

where

C	=	the price of the call option
S	=	current market price of the underlying common stock
$N(d_1)$	=	the cumulative density function of d_1
E	=	the exercise price of the option
e	=	the base of natural logarithms = approximately 2.71828
r	=	the continuously compounded riskless rate of interest on an annual basis
t	=	the time remaining before the expiration date of the option, expressed as a fraction of a year
$N(d_2)$	=	the cumulative density function of d_2

To find d_1 and d_2, it is necessary to solve these equations:

$$d_1 = \frac{\ln(S/E) + (r + 0.5\sigma^2)t}{(\sigma[(t)^{1/2}])}$$ (19-6)

$$d_2 = d_1 - (\sigma[(t)^{1/2}])$$ (19-7)

where

$\ln(S/E)$	=	the natural log of (S/E)
σ	=	the standard deviation of the annual rate of return on the underlying common stock

The five variables previously listed are needed as inputs. Variables 1–4 are immediately available. Variable 5 is not, however, because what is needed is the volatility expected to occur in the stock's rate of return.

Although historical data on stock returns are typically used to estimate this standard deviation, volatility does change over time. A formula user should try to incorporate expected changes in the volatility when using historical data. To do so, the user should examine any likely changes in either the market's or the individual stock's volatility. Empirical studies have shown that estimates of the variance obtained from other than historical data are more valuable than the estimates based on historical data.

Because the price of an option can be observed at any time, it is possible to solve the Black–Scholes formula for the implied volatility of the stock's return.[29] The **implied volatility** is the volatility level for the stock implied by the option price. By using the observed call price, one can solve the Black–Scholes model for the volatility level implied by that price.

Implied Volatility The volatility of an option based on the other parameters determining its value

---

[28] This version of the model applies to nondividend-paying stocks. Adjustments can be made for stocks that pay dividends.

[29] H. Latane and R. Rendleman, Jr., "Standard Deviations of Stock Price Ratios Implied in Option Prices," *The Journal of Finance* (May 1976): pp. 369–382.

Example 19-17   The following is an example of the use of the Black–Scholes option-pricing formula:
Assume

$$S = \$40$$
$$E = \$45$$
$$r = 0.10$$
$$t = 0.5 \text{ (six months)}$$
$$\sigma = 0.45$$

Step 1: Solve for d_1.

$$d_1 = \frac{\ln(40/45) + \left[0.10 + 0.5(0.45)^2\right]0.5}{0.45\left[(0.5)^{1/2}\right]}$$

$$= \frac{-0.1178 + 0.1006}{0.3182}$$

$$= -0.054$$

Step 2: Use a cumulative probability distribution table to find the value of $N(d_1)$.[30]

$$N(d_1) \quad = 0.4785$$
$$\text{where } d_1 = -0.054$$

Step 3: Find d_2.

$$d_2 = -0.054 - \left[0.45\left((0.5)^{1/2}\right)\right]$$
$$= -0.372$$

Step 4: Find $N(d_2)$.

$$N(d_2) = 0.3549$$

Step 5: Solve for C.

$$C = S[0.4785] - E[\text{antilog} - (0.1)(0.5)][0.3549]$$
$$= 19.14 - 45(0.9512)(0.3549)$$
$$= 19.14 - 15.19$$
$$= \$3.95$$

The theoretical (fair) value of the option, according to the Black–Scholes formula, is $3.95. If the current market price of the option is greater than the theoretical value, it is overpriced; if less, it is underpriced.

Investors can use knowledge gained from understanding the Black–Scholes valuation model in their trading activities.

Doing the Calculations   There are multiple sources that can be used to calculate the price of a call. Spreadsheet programs have helpful steps. An example of doing so is illustrated in the *Spreadsheet Exercises* at the end of the chapter. Option price calculators can be found at www.cboe.com and www.schaefferresearch.com (Quotes & Tools).

---

[30] Using *Excel*, we can use the formula = NORMSDIST(value) to determine $N(d_1)$. Therefore, we would place into a cell the following: = NORMSDIST($-.054$) which results in a value of .4785.

PUT OPTION VALUATION

To establish put prices, we can take advantage of the principle of put-call parity. The **put-call parity** principle expresses the relationship between the prices of puts and calls on the same stock that must hold if arbitrage is to be ruled out.[31] In other words, unless the price of the put and the call bear a certain relationship to each other, there will be opportunities for earning riskless profits (arbitrage).

Put-Call Parity The formal relationship between a call and a put on the same item which must hold if no arbitrage is to occur

Ultimately we can express the put-call parity relationship as:[32]

$$P = C - S + E/(e^{rt}) \tag{19-8}$$

where all terms are as defined before and P is the price of the put.

Example 19-18

Consider the information for the call given earlier. Since the Black–Scholes model uses continuous interest, the discount factor is expressed in continuous form.[33] It is equal to e^{rt}, or $e^{10(.5)}$. Using a calculator, this value is 1.051. Therefore,

$$\text{Price of put} = 3.95 - 40 + 45/1.051 = \$6.77$$

SUMMARIZING THE FACTORS AFFECTING OPTIONS PRICES

If we allow for stocks that pay dividends, we can summarize the factors affecting options prices into a table with six elements, as shown in Table 19-1. The + sign indicates a direct relation, and a negative sign a negative relation. The assumption behind Table 19-1 is that all other variables remain fixed as we consider any of the six variables individually.

HEDGE RATIOS

A key concept with options is their use as a hedging device. Although risky assets themselves, options can be used to control risk. In particular, options can be used to control the riskiness inherent in common stocks.

Table 19-1 Effects of Various Variables on Options Prices

Variable	Calls	Puts
Stock price	+	−
Exercise price	−	+
Time to expiration	+	+
Stock volatility	+	+
Interest rates	+	−
Cash dividends	−	+

[31] We are considering European options with the same exercise price and time to expiration.
[32] If investors could own a stock, write a call, and buy a put and make money, arbitrage possibilities would exist.
[33] The value e^k is the equivalent of $(1+r)$ in continuous compounding. If r is 5 percent, the value of e^k is $e^{.05}$, or 1.051.

Hedge Ratio The ratio of options written to shares of stock held long in a riskless portfolio

Delta A measure of how much the theoretical value of an option should change for a $1.00 change in the underlying stock

To hedge a long stock position with options, an investor would write one call option while simultaneously buying a certain number of shares of common. This number is given by the **hedge ratio**, or **delta**, which is $N(d_1)$ from the Black–Scholes model.[34]

✓ The hedge ratio for an option, commonly referred to as the option's *delta*, indicates the change in the price of the option for a $1 change in the price of the common.

Since the hedge ratio with a call option is $N(d_1)$, for a put option it is $N(d_1) - 1$.

Example 19-19

In the preceding example, $N(d_1)$ was 0.48; therefore, for every call option written, 0.48 share of the common would be required to hedge the position. For a standard 100-share option contract, 48 shares of stock would be required. A $1 increase in the price of the stock should produce a $0.48 change in the price of the option. The loss on the call options written is $100 \times \$0.48$, or $48, which is offset by the gain on the 48 shares of stock of $48. A perfectly hedged position leaves total wealth unchanged.

The fact that hedge ratios are less than 1.0 indicates that option values change with stock prices on less than a one-for-one basis. That is, dollar movements in options prices are smaller than dollar movements in the underlying stock. However, *percentage* price changes on the option generally will be greater than percentage price changes on the stock.

USING THE BLACK–SCHOLES MODEL

Development of the Black–Scholes model was a significant event and has had a major impact on all options investors, both directly and indirectly. This model has been the basis of extensive empirical investigations into how options are priced. How well does this model work?

The numerous studies that have been conducted offer general support for the Black–Scholes model and the proposition that options are efficiently priced by the market. Some deficiencies have been noted.[35] The original Black–Scholes model is based on some simplifying assumptions, such as the payment of no dividends, a constant variance, and continuous stock prices. The standard deviation cannot be observed and must be estimated. Therefore, any observed discrepancies could reflect errors in the estimation of the stock's volatility, or other noise in the data.

Checking Your Understanding

8. Why does an option's price almost always exceed its intrinsic value?
9. What are the boundaries for the price of a call?

An Investor's Perspective on Puts and Calls

WHAT PUTS AND CALLS MEAN TO INVESTORS

Earlier we examined some simple strategies using puts and calls and briefly considered some more sophisticated strategies. It is important for investors to have an overall perspective on puts and calls and consider what they really add to the investment process.

---

[34] Technically, the hedge ratio is the slope of the functional relationship between the value of the option (vertical axis) and the value of the stock (horizontal axis), evaluated at the current stock price.

[35] See Dan Galai, "A Survey of Empirical Tests of Option-Pricing Models," in Menachem Brenner, ed., *Option Pricing: Theory and Applications* (Lexington, Mass.: Lexington Books, 1983), pp. 45–80.

Options contracts are important to investors in terms of the two dimensions of every investment decision that we have emphasized throughout this book—the return and risk from an asset or portfolio. Options can be used for various types of hedging, which are concerned with risk management. Options also offer speculators a way to leverage their investment with a strict limit on downside risk.

The return-risk modification properties of puts and calls vary significantly from other derivative instruments such as futures contracts, which we consider in Chapter 20. In the case of buying a call the most the investor can lose is the premium, regardless of what happens to the stock price; that is, the distribution of payoffs or profits is truncated. The same is true when buying a put—relative to the profit-loss line when selling short—the distribution of possible profits and losses from buying a put is truncated. If the stock price continues to rise, adversely affecting the investor, the most that can be lost from the put purchase is the premium.

✓ The important point about options and their impact on portfolio return and risk is that the impact is not symmetrical. The distribution of payoffs is *truncated*.

Some Practical Advice

Investors who consider buying options as a way to trade in securities should remember the following important points:

☐ With options, you have a significant chance of losing your entire investment. Thus, speculating in options can be risky.

☐ With options, there is a small chance of making a large profit, often five to 10 times the original investment, and sometimes more.

Given these two points, options may be attractive to some investors, and very unattractive to others.

THE EVOLUTIONARY USE OF OPTIONS

Puts and calls on *organized* options exchanges have been available to investors since 1973, although financial derivatives were being used long before then. Puts and calls have been popular with individual investors since the beginning of CBOE trading, although the manner in which they are viewed has changed somewhat. At first, options were viewed more or less as speculative instruments and were often purchased for their leverage possibilities. Covered option writing was used to enhance portfolio yields. During the 1980s many investors were selling puts in order to capitalize on the rising trend in stock prices. This strategy worked well until the famous market crash in October 1987. Market conditions always change—the market does not continue to go up and up without corrections, nor down and down without corrections.

The current emphasis by the options markets and the brokerage industry is on educating investors as to how options can be used efficiently as part of their portfolio. Investors have continued to learn how to hedge their risk using derivatives.

Example 19-20 The CBOE has a nice tutorial on options for investors, starting with the basics and going to more advanced topics—see www.cboe.com. In December 2008, the ISE announced a new options trading education section on its website. Included are webcasts, podcasts, and YouTube videos.

Options today are increasingly valued in strategic portfolio management because they allow investors to create strategies that expand the set of outcomes beyond what could be achieved in the absence of options. In other words, investors and investment managers sometimes need the nonsymmetric distributions of returns that options can provide. Options strategies increase the set of contingencies that can be provided for.[36]

At some brokerage firms, such as E-Trade, options volume has increased significantly and now accounts for a sizeable percentage of the firm's revenues. The online brokerage firms have made options trading much easier, and options information, recommendations, and strategies much more accessible. Meanwhile, some investors with a strong interest in options use so-called "options boutiques" that cater to options traders. These specialized brokers, such as OptionsXpress by Charles Schwab and Wall Street Access, offer complex trades at lower prices than regular brokerage firms, specialized risk-assessment tools, and a staff specifically trained in options.

Stock-Index Options

Stock-Index Options
Option contracts on a stock market index such as the S&P 500

For many investors, an important part of the options market is **stock-index options**. Rather than concentrate on options for individual securities, investors can buy puts and calls on various market indexes, thereby taking a position on broad market movements or market segments.

THE BASICS OF STOCK-INDEX OPTIONS

Stock-index options are available on more than 50 stock indexes, such as the S&P 100 Index, the S&P 500 Index, the DJIA Index, the Russell 2000 Index, and the NASDAQ-100 Index. Index options are also available on some industry sectors, including Technology, Oil, the Internet, Gold, and Semiconductors. Index options are also available on foreign markets such as Korea, Germany, Hong Kong, Japan, and the United Kingdom. In addition, long-term index options (LEAPS) are available for several market indexes.[37]

Stock-index options enable investors to trade on general stock market movements or industries in the same way that they can trade on individual stocks. Thus, an investor who is bullish on a market index such as the S&P 500 can buy a call on this index, and an investor who is bearish on the same index can buy a put.

✓ An investor in stock-index options can make market decisions rather than individual stock decisions.

Overall, stock-index options are similar to equity options on individual stocks. As usual, the exercise price and the expiration date are uniformly established. Investors buy and sell them through their broker in the normal manner. Index option information is read in the same manner as that for stock options.

---

[36] This discussion is based on Richard Bookstaber, "The Use of Options in Performance Structuring," *Journal of Portfolio Management* (Summer 1985): pp. 36–37.

[37] In 1986 the S&P 500 Index option was converted to a European-style contract, meaning it cannot be exercised until the contract expires. The predictable exercise date appeals to institutional investors when they attempt to hedge their portfolios against losses in volatile markets. Hedgers using standard index options may find their hedges exercised before the contracts expire, thereby giving an edge to the European-style contracts. The Institutional Index is also European-style.

✓ Unlike stock options which require the actual delivery of the stock upon exercise, buyers of index options receive cash from the seller upon exercise of the contract.

The amount of cash settlement is equal to the difference between the closing price of the index and the strike price of the option multiplied by a specified dollar amount, generally $100.

Example 19-21

Assume an investor holds an S&P 100 Index option™ (OEX)—the S&P 100 Index consists of 100 stocks (capitalization weighted) from a broad range of industries.[38] The strike price is 580, and the investor decides to exercise the option on a day that the S&P 100 Index closes at 588.5. The investor will receive a cash payment from the assigned writer equal to $100 multiplied by the difference between the option's strike price and the closing value of the index, or

$$
\begin{aligned}
\text{S\&P 100 Index close} &= 588.5 \\
\text{S\&P 100 Index option strike price} &= \frac{580.0}{8.5} \\
8.5 \times \$100 &= \$850
\end{aligned}
$$

The multiplier for this index option is $100—one point = $100. The multiplier performs a function similar to the unit of trading (100 shares) for a stock option in that it determines the total dollar value of the cash settlement. Since options on different indexes may have different multipliers, it is important to know the multiplier for the stock index being used.

STRATEGIES WITH STOCK-INDEX OPTIONS

The strategies with index options are similar to those for individual stock options. Investors expecting a market rise buy calls, and investors expecting a market decline buy puts. The maximum losses from these two strategies—the premiums—are known at the outset of the transaction. The potential gains can be large because of the leverage involved with options.

Example 19-22

In early April, an investor expects the stock market to rise strongly over the next two to three months. This investor decides to purchase an S&P 100 Index May 590 call, currently selling for 24, on a day when the S&P 100 Index closed at 588.5. Note that the performance of the S&P 100 Index consistently has a high correlation with the S&P 500 Index.

Assume that the market rises, as the investor expected, to a mid-May level of 623.81 (a 6 percent increase). The investor could exercise the option and receive a cash settlement equal

---

[38] OEX designates an American-style option while XEO designates an European-style option.

to the difference between the index close (623.81) and the exercise price of 590, multiplied by $100, or[39]

$$623.81 \text{ S\&P 100 Index close}$$
$$\underline{- 590.00 \text{ S\&P 100 Call exercise price}}$$
$$= 33.81 \times \$100 = \$3,381$$

The leverage offered by index options is illustrated in this example by the fact that a 6 percent rise in the index leads to a 40.9 percent profit on the option position [($3,381 − $2,400)/$2,400 = 40.88 percent]. Obviously, losses can occur. If the market declined or remained flat, the entire option premium of $2,400 could be lost unless the buyer of this option sold at some point before expiration.

✓ As with any option, the investor buying an index option has a limited loss of known amount—the premium paid.

Investors can use stock-index options to hedge their positions. For example, an investor who owns a diversified portfolio of stocks may be unwilling to liquidate his or her portfolio but is concerned about a near-term market decline. Buying a put on a market index will provide some protection to the investor in the event of a market decline. In effect, the investor is purchasing a form of market insurance. The losses on the portfolio holdings will be partially offset by the gains on the put. If the market rises, the investor loses the premium paid but gains with the portfolio holdings. A problem arises, however, in that the portfolio holdings and the market index are unlikely to be a perfect match. The effectiveness of this hedge will depend on the similarity between the two.

Example 19-23 Assume an investor has a portfolio of NYSE blue-chip common stocks currently worth $60,000. It is early April, and this investor is concerned about a market decline over the next couple of months. The S&P 100 Index is currently at 588.5, and an S&P 100 Index May 590 put is available for 10. In an attempt to protect the portfolio's profits against a market decline, the investor purchases a put, which represents an aggregate exercise price of $59,000, calculated as (590 × 100 = $59,000).[40]

Assume that the market declines about 10 percent by the May expiration. If the OEX Index is 530 at that point,

$$\text{Put exercise price} = 590$$
$$\text{OEX Index price} = 530$$
$$60 \times \$100 = \$6,000$$

If the value of the investor's portfolio declines approximately 10 percent, the loss on the portfolio of $6,000 will be somewhat offset by the net gain on the put contract of $6,000 − $1,000 premium paid for the put. It is important to note, however, that a particular portfolio's value may decline more or less than the overall market as represented by one of the market indexes such as the S&P 100 or 500 Index.

---

[39] Before exercising, the investor should determine if a better price could be obtained by selling the option.

[40] The exercise value of an index option, like any stock option, is equal to 100 (shares) multiplied by the exercise price.

As before, if the option is held to expiration and a market decline (of a significant amount) does not occur, the investor could lose the entire premium paid for the put(s). In our example, the investor could lose the entire $1,000 paid for the put. This could be viewed as the cost of obtaining "market insurance."

Stock index options can be useful to institutional investors (or individuals) who do not have funds available immediately for investment but anticipate a market rise. Buying calls will allow such investors to take advantage of the rise in prices if the market rise does occur. Of course, the premium could be lost if the investor's expectations are incorrect.

Investors can sell (write) index options, either to speculate or to hedge their positions. If the seller is correct in his or her beliefs, the profit is limited to the amount of the premium; if incorrect, the seller faces potential losses far in excess of the premiums received from selling the options. It is impractical (or impossible) to write a completely covered stock-index option because of the difficulty of owning a portfolio that exactly matches the index at all points in time. Although the writer of an individual stock call option can deliver the stock if the option is exercised, the writer of a stock-index call option that is exercised must settle in cash and cannot be certain that gains in the stock portfolio will *fully* offset losses on the index option.[41]

THE POPULARITY OF STOCK-INDEX OPTIONS

Stock index put options allow a portfolio manager to hedge equity market risk by limiting a portfolio's downside exposure while retaining the upside potential. If the index rises while the puts are held, the cost of the puts can be thought of as the cost of insuring the portfolio against a loss. If the index declines, the protective puts will limit the portfolio's downside, and could offset the decline almost entirely in some cases.

Stock-index options appeal to speculators because of the leverage they offer. A change in the underlying index of less than one percent can result in a change in the value of the contract of 15 percent or more. Given the increased volatility in the financial markets in recent years, investors can experience rapid changes in the value of their positions, both up and down.

Introduced in 1983, stock index options quickly became a popular investment in the United States. Much of the initial volume was accounted for by professional speculators and trading firms. As familiarity with index options increased, individual investors have assumed a larger role in this market.

Summary

▶ Equity-derivative securities consist of puts and calls, created by investors, and warrants and convertible securities, created by corporations.

▶ A call (put) is an option to buy (sell) 100 shares of a particular stock at a stated price any time before a specified expiration date. The seller receives a premium for selling either of these options, and the buyer pays the premium.

▶ Advantages of options include a smaller investment than transacting in the stock itself, knowing the maximum loss in advance, leverage, and an expansion of the opportunity set available to investors.

▶ Buyers of calls expect the underlying stock to perform in the opposite direction from the expectations of put buyers. Writers of each instrument have opposite expectations from the buyers.

▶ The basic strategies for options involve a call writer and a put buyer expecting the underlying stock price to decline, whereas the call buyer and the put writer expect it to rise. Options may also be used to hedge against a portfolio position by establishing an opposite position in options on that stock.

▶ More sophisticated options strategies include combinations of options, such as strips, straps, and straddles

[41] Writers of index options are notified of their obligation to make a cash settlement on the business day following the day of exercise.

and spreads, which include money spreads and time spreads.

▶ Options have an intrinsic value ranging from $0 to the "in-the-money" value. Most sell for more than this, representing a speculative premium.

▶ According to the Black–Scholes option valuation model, value is a function of the price of the stock, the exercise price of the option, time to maturity, the interest rate, and the volatility of the underlying stock.

▶ The available empirical evidence seems to suggest that the options market is efficient, with trading rules unable to exploit any biases that exist in the Black–Scholes or other option-pricing models.

▶ Interest rate options and stock-index options are also available to investors.

▶ Stock-index options are a popular innovation in the options area that allows investors to buy puts and calls on broad stock market indexes and industry subindexes.

▶ The major distinction with these options contracts is that settlement is in cash.

▶ In effect, stock-index options allow investors to make only a market decision and to purchase a form of market insurance.

▶ The strategies with index options are similar to those for individual stock options. Investors can both hedge and speculate.

Questions

19-1 State three justifications given for the existence of options.

19-2 Distinguish between a call and a warrant.

19-3 What does it mean to say an option buyer has a right but not an obligation?

19-4 Explain the following terms used with puts and calls:
   a. Strike price
   b. Naked option
   c. Premium
   d. Out-of-the-money option

19-5 What is the difference between option premiums and option prices?

19-6 Who writes puts and calls? Why?

19-7 What role does the options clearing corporation play in the options market?

19-8 How can the writer of a call option cancel his or her obligation?

19-9 What is the relationship between option prices and their intrinsic values? Why?

19-10 What is meant by the time premium of an option?

19-11 Explain the factors used in the Black–Scholes option valuation model. What is the relationship between each factor and the value of the option?

19-12 State three reasons why an investor might purchase a call.

19-13 Why do investors write calls? What are their obligations?

19-14 Why is the call or put writer's position considerably different from the buyer's position?

19-15 What is an index option? What index options are available?

19-16 What are the major differences between a stock option and an index option?

19-17 How can a put be used to protect a particular position? A call?

19-18 How does writing a covered call differ from writing a naked call?

19-19 Which is greater for an option relative to the underlying common, dollar movements or return volatility? Why?

19-20 What is the significance of the industry subindex stock index options?

19-21 Assume that you own a diversified portfolio of 50 stocks and fear a market decline over the next six months.
   a. How could you protect your portfolio during this period using stock-index options?
   b. How effective would this hedge be?
   c. Other things being equal, if your portfolio consisted of 150 stocks, would the protection be more effective?

19-22 Assume that you expect interest rates to rise and that you wish to speculate on this expectation.

How could interest rate options be used to do this?

19-23 What does it mean to say that an option is worth more alive than dead?

19-24 Is it possible for two calls identical in their characteristics except for the time to expiration to have approximately the same price?

19-25 When might it pay to exercise an American call early? Would it pay to exercise an American put early?

19-26 You are considering a particular put. You calculate its value using the put-call parity relationship. You find that the price of this put exceeds the calculated value. What action would you take to profit from this? Assume a European put.

19-27 How do higher interest rates affect call option prices? Put option prices?

CFA
19-28 What is the maximum amount the buyer of an option can lose?

CFA
19-29 Suppose an investor purchases a call option on a Treasury bond futures contract with a strike price of $91.

  a. If at the expiration date the price of the Treasury bond futures contract is $96, will the investor exercise the call option; if so, what will the investor and the writer of the call option receive?

  b. If at the expiration date the price of the Treasury bond futures contract is $89, will the investor exercise the call option; if so, what will the investor and the writer of the call option receive?

CFA
19-30 Suppose an investor purchases a put option on a Treasury bond futures contract with a strike price of $97.

  a. If at the expiration date the price of the Treasury bond futures contract is $99, will the investor exercise the put option; if so, what will the investor and the writer of the put option receive?

  b. If at the expiration date the price of the Treasury bond futures contract is $91, will the investor exercise the put option; if so, what will the investor and the writer of the put option receive?

CFA
19-31 Why would a bond portfolio manager employ a protective put buying strategy?

CFA
19-32 The investment guidelines of the Wycoff Pension Fund prohibit the fund's external bond managers from using options in any capacity. At a meeting between the trustees of the Wycoff Pension fund, its consultant, and one of its external portfolio managers, the issue of relaxing this restriction was discussed.

One trustee agreed that its external managers should be permitted to use options. However, the trustee was adamant that the manager only be allowed to write options on bonds in the portfolio. The trustee felt that in contrast to buying options a strategy of writing call options would not result in a loss to the fund if options expired unexercised, nor would the fund have wasted the option premium. In the case of writing call options, the trustee argued that even if the option is exercised, there is no loss to the fund, because it collected the option premium; besides, it is just taking out of its portfolio a bond that it already owns.

The portfolio manager responded that he was uncomfortable with such a restrictive policy, because it is not a true hedging strategy. Moreover, he believes that there are costs associated with the strategy.

The consultant was asked to comment on the statements made by the trustee and the portfolio manager. How should the consultant respond?

Problems

19-1 The common stock of Teledyne trades on the NYSE. Teledyne has never paid a cash dividend. The stock is relatively risky. Assume that the beta for Teledyne is 1.5 and that Teledyne closed at a price of $162. Hypothetical option quotes on Teledyne are as follows:

Strike	Call			Put		
Price	Apr	Jul	Oct	Apr	Jul	Oct
140	23 1/2	s	s	3/8	s	s
150	16	21	25	1	3 3/4	r
160	8 7/8	14	20	3	7	9
170	3	9	13 1/4	9	10	11
180	1 1/4	5 1/4	9	r	20	r

r=not traded; s=no option offered.

Based on the Teledyne data, answer the following questions:

a. Which calls are in the money?

b. Which puts are in the money?

c. Why are investors willing to pay 1 1/4 for the 180 call but only 1 for the 150 put, which is closer to the current market price?

19-2 Based on the Teledyne data answer the following:

a. Calculate the intrinsic value of the April 160 and the October 180 calls.

b. Calculate the intrinsic value of the April 160 and the October 180 puts.

c. Explain the reasons for the differences in intrinsic values between a and b.

19-3 Using the Teledyne data, answer the following:

a. What is the cost of 20 October 150 call contracts in total dollars? From the text, what is the commission? Total cost?

b. What is the cost of 10 October 160 put contracts in total dollars? What is the commission? Total cost?

c. On the following day, Teledyne closed at $164. Which of the options would you have expected to increase? Decrease?

d. The new quote on the October 150 call was 26. What would have been your one-day profit on the 20 contracts?

e. The new quote on the October 160 put was 7 1/2. What would have been your one-day profit on the 10 contracts?

f. What is the most you could lose on these 10 contracts?

19-4 You are considering some put and call options and have available the following data:

	Call ABC	Call DEF	Put ABC
Time to expiration (months)	3	3	3
Annual risk--Free rate	8%	8%	8%
Exercise price	$40	$50	$40
Option price	$ 3		$ 4
Stock price	$45	$45	$45

a. Comparing the two calls, should DEF sell for more or less than ABC? Why?

b. What is the time value for ABC?

c. Based on the information for the call and the put for ABC, determine if put-call parity is working.

Computational Problems

19-1 Assume that the value of a call option using the Black–Scholes model is $8.94. The interest rate is 4 percent, and the time to maturity is 90 days. The price of the underlying stock is $47.35, and the exercise price is $45. Calculate the price of a put using the put-call parity relationship.

19-2 Calculate, using the Black–Scholes formula, the value of a call option given the following information:

Interest rate   = 8%
Time to expiration = 90 days
Stock price   = $50
Exercise price   = $40
Standard deviation = 0.3

What is the price of the put using the same information?

19-3 Using the information in Problem 19-2, determine the sensitivity of the call value to a change in inputs by recalculating the call value if

  a. The interest rate doubles to 16 percent, but all other values remain the same

  b. The standard deviation doubles to 0.6, but all other values remain the same

  c. Which change causes the greatest change in the value of the call? What can you infer from this?

19-4 Given the following information, determine the number of shares of stock that must be purchased to form a hedged position if one option contract (covering 100 shares of stock) is to be written.

Stock price   = $100
Exercise price   = $90
Interest rate   = 4%
Time to expiration = 180 days
Standard deviation = 0.6

19-5 Given the information in Problem 19-4, determine how the value of the call would change if

  (a) The exercise price is $110
  (b) The time to expiration is 30 days (use the original exercise price of $90)
  (c) The time to expiration is 8 days

19-6 Determine the value of Ribex call options if the exercise price is $40, the stock is currently selling for $2 out of the money, the time to expiration is 90 days, the interest rate is 0.08, and the variance of return on the stock for the past few months has been 0.49.

19-7 Using the information in Problem 19-6, decide intuitively whether the put or the call will sell at a higher price, and verify your answer.

Spreadsheet Exercises

19-1 There are various ways to calculate the price of a call option using the Black–Scholes model. Below is a spreadsheet that breaks the required formulas into pieces to make it easy to work with. Column (1) shows the various inputs. The first five cells are the required inputs for a nondividend-paying stock. The remainder of the cells are the formula parts. Column (2) shows a solved problem for a stock selling for $50, with an exercise price of $45, an interest rate of 6 percent, 90 days (one-quarter of a year), and a standard deviation of .235. Column (3) shows how the cell values in Column (2) were calculated.

Once you have this set up in the spreadsheet, you can calculate the price of any call option by substituting the correct values in the first five cells of column (2). Spreadsheet begins in row 2.

Calculating a Call Price Using the Black–Scholes Model

S	50	
X	45	
R	0.06	
T	0.25	
S	0.235	
ln(S/X)	0.105361	LN(B2/B3)
$r+0.5\sigma^2$	0.087613	B4+(.5)*(B6)^2
$\sigma(t)^{1/2}$	0.1175	B6*((B5)^0.5)
d1	1.083095	(B7+(B8*B5))/B9
d2	0.965595	B10-B9
N(d1)	0.860617	NORMSDIST(B10)
N(d2)	0.832877	NORMSDIST(B11)
S*N(d1)	43.03084	B2*B12
E	2.7183	
e^{-rt}	0.985112	B15^−(B4*B5)
Call Price	6.109398	B14−(B3*B16*B13)

Given a stock price of $42, an exercise price of $40, an interest rate of 6 percent, a time to expiration of 90 days, and a standard deviation of .65, solve for the call price.

19-2 Consider a Pfizer call and put purchased on July 28. Exercise price of call = $17.5, and for the put, $20. Price of call = $1.41, and for the put $1.51.

a. Calculate the dollar gain or loss for each of following August 16 possible closing prices: $0, 5, 10, 12, 14, 16, 18, 20, 22, 24, 26, 28, 30, 32.

b. Graph the possible dollar gain or loss for both positions as calculated in part (a).

Checking Your Understanding

19-1 To sell a stock short, an investor must have a margin account, meet margin requirements, pay interest, make up any dividends on the stock sold short, and worry about possible large losses if the stock price rises sharply. Buying a put, an investor has a maximum loss that is known at the outset. No other requirements have to be met. On the other hand, the put has a relatively short maturity and could expire worthless.

19-2 A call buyer has a right to exercise the call, but does not have an obligation. Even if the buyer forgets about the option, the worse that can happen is that it will expire worthless. The writer, on the other hand, could be assigned to deliver the stock. Once assigned, the writer must carry out the contract.

19-3 Car insurance in this case can be thought of as an American put option, with the insurance company as the writer of the option. The insured is long the put option and can choose to exercise or not in case of an accident.

19-4 The buyer of a put has three alternatives: let it expire worthless, exercise it, or sell it in the options market to another investor. Most investors simply sell their options to another investor.

19-5 The clearinghouse stands between buyers and sellers. It keeps the books on all transactions. Therefore, a seller can offset the position by buying the same option because the clearinghouse can simply cancel the seller's position.

19-6 Options positions truncate the distribution of returns available to investors. This reflects the fact that most profiles involve two different line segments. In contrast, buying a stock or shorting a stock involves a straight line profile which investors move up or down on.

19-7 Writing covered calls is considered a conservative strategy, because it reduces the cost of stock ownership by the amount of the premium received for writing the calls.

19-8 An option's price generally exceeds its intrinsic value because of the speculative (time) value. Investors are willing to pay an additional amount for the chance that the option will have value.

19-9 The upper boundary for a call option is the price of the underlying stock. The lower boundary for a call is the price of the option at expiration, which must be either zero or its in-the-money value.

chapter *20*

Understanding Derivative Securities: Futures

Q uick —there is a freeze in Florida, so buy orange juice futures! You have probably heard this one before, but you never thought about doing it because you know nothing about futures contracts. Furthermore, given all that you have had to learn lately as part of your investments education, you are not enthused about learning too much about futures contracts at this time. Nevertheless, it would be helpful to understand what people are talking about when they discuss futures, and even to mull them over in your mind in case one day you want to use futures as part of your portfolio strategy. Therefore, you realize a little effort in this area might be worthwhile. At the very least, you will be able to talk the talk.

Chapter 20 covers futures, the other derivative security of importance to many investors. Although our discussion pertains in general to all futures markets, our primary interest is financial futures as opposed to commodity futures. As with options, futures allow investors to manage investment risk and to speculate in the equity, fixed-income, and currency markets.

AFTER READING THIS CHAPTER YOU WILL BE ABLE TO:

► Understand why financial futures have been developed for use by investors.
► Describe the alternatives available to investors in the futures markets as well as how futures markets operate.

► Analyze basic strategies involving futures contracts.

An Overview of Futures Markets

WHY FUTURES MARKETS?

Physical commodities and financial instruments typically are traded in *cash markets*. A cash contract calls for immediate delivery and is used by those who need a commodity now (e.g., food processors). Cash contracts cannot be canceled unless both parties agree. The current cash prices of commodities and financial instruments can be found daily in various sources.

There are two types of cash markets, spot markets and forward markets: (1) *Spot markets* are markets for immediate delivery.[1] The spot price refers to the current market price of an item available for immediate delivery. (2) *Forward markets* are markets for deferred delivery. The forward price is the price of an item for deferred delivery. The asset is delivered in the future at a price that is agreed upon today.

Example 20-1

Suppose that a manufacturer of high school and college class rings is gathering orders to fill for this school year and wishes to ensure an established price today for gold to be delivered six months from now, when the rings will actually be manufactured. The spot (current) price of gold is not the manufacturer's primary concern, because the gold will not be purchased until it is needed for the manufacturing process. However, to reduce the risk involved with the future price of gold, the manufacturer wishes to contract now for gold to be delivered in six months at a price established today. This will allow the manufacturer to price its rings more accurately, having locked in the price of gold.

Our manufacturer could find a gold supplier who was willing to enter into a forward commitment or contract, which is simply a commitment today to transact in the future. The other party to the contract, such as a mining company, agrees to deliver the gold six months from now at a price negotiated today. Both parties have agreed to a deferred delivery at a sales price that is currently determined. No funds have been exchanged. Both parties have reduced their risk in the sense that the mining company knows what it will receive for the gold when it is sold six months from now, and the ring manufacturer knows what it will pay for the gold when it actually needs to take delivery six months from now.

Investments Intuition

Obviously, one of the parties may be disappointed six months later, when the price of gold has changed, but that is the advantage of hindsight. If investors could foresee the future, they would know what to do to start with and would not have to worry about risk. The forward and futures markets were developed to allow individuals to deal with the risks they face because the future is uncertain.

Forward contracts are centuries old, traceable to at least the ancient Romans and Greeks. Organized futures markets in the United States, on the other hand, effectively go back to the mid-19th century in Chicago. Futures markets are, in effect, organized and standardized forward markets.

✓ An organized futures exchange standardizes the nonstandard forward contracts, establishing such features as contract size, delivery dates, and condition of the items that can be delivered. Only the price and number of contracts are left for futures traders to negotiate.

Individuals can trade without personal contact with each other because of the centralized marketplace. Performance is guaranteed by a clearinghouse, relieving one party to the transaction from worry that the other party will fail to honor its commitment.

---

[1] "Immediate" means in the normal course of business. For example, it may normally take two days for an item to be delivered after being ordered.

An important economic function performed by futures markets is price discovery; that is, developing information about future cash market prices. The price of a futures contract reflects current expectations about values at some future date, which in effect is a forecast of the price at a specific time in the future.

Some people or companies have a preexisting risk exposure of some type that they want to reduce. They do this by hedging their position. The futures markets serve a valuable economic purpose by allowing hedgers to shift price risk to speculators. The risk of price fluctuations is shifted from participants unwilling to assume such risk to those who are. From a societal standpoint, hedging is the most important rationale for futures markets.

✓   Price discovery and hedging (price risk management) are the primary functions of futures markets.

WHAT IS TRADED IN THE FUTURES MARKETS?

To most people, futures trading traditionally has meant trading in commodities such as wheat, gold, and oil. However, money can be thought of simply as another commodity, and financial futures have become a particularly viable investment alternative for numerous investors. Therefore, futures contracts currently traded on U.S. futures exchanges can be divided into two broad categories:

1. Commodities: agricultural, metals, and energy-related
2. Financials: foreign currencies and debt and equity instruments

Although financial futures are relatively new (compared to commodity futures), they now account for about two-thirds of all futures traded in the United States. Thus, the futures market to a large extent is a financial futures market.

Each category can be further subdivided as shown in Exhibit 20-1. As we can see, the futures markets involve trading in a variety of both commodities and financials. Note that Exhibit 20-1 is a *nonexhaustive* list of items that trade on the futures exchanges.

For each type of contract, such as corn or silver, different delivery dates are available. Each contract will specify the trading unit involved and, where applicable, the deliverable grade necessary to satisfy the contract. Investors can also purchase options on futures contracts.

Concepts in Action

Yes, You Can Do Something About the Weather

Futures contracts exist on a variety of commodities and financial instruments. One of the most interesting is the weather contract, trade on the CME, which can be used to manage the risk associated with unexpected weather events. Known as weather derivatives, these futures allow one to both hedge and speculate on the weather in 47 U.S. cities and several foreign countries. The underlying index can be based on temperatures, snowfalls, frost, and hurricanes (in the United States). These contracts have many potential uses, particularly in agriculture. Other examples include ski resorts that rely on snowfall for skies and coastal resorts that fear hurricanes during the peak season for vacation renters.

EXHIBIT 20-1

Futures Contracts Traded in the United States, by Category

The major futures contracted traded in the United States can be classified into the following categories (this is not an all-inclusive list):

I. Commodities

Grains and oilseeds	Wheat, corn, oats, soybeans, soybean oils, soybean meal, flaxseed, rye, canola, rough rice
Livestock and meats	Cattle (both live and feeders), pork bellies, and hogs
Foods	Cocoa, coffee, orange juice, and sugar
Fibers	Cotton
Metals	Copper, gold, platinum, silver, and palladium
Oil	Gasoline, heating oil, crude oil, gas oil, propane, ethanol
Wood	Lumber

II. Financials

Interest rates	Treasury bills, Treasury notes, Treasury bonds, municipal bond index, 30-day federal funds, 10-year swap, five-year swap, Eurodollar, one-month Libor, Sterling, Long Gilt, Euromark, EuroSwiss, EuroLira, German Government Bond, Italian Government Bond, French Government Bond, Canadian Government Bond
Stock indexes	S&P 500 Index, S&P MidCap 400, NYSE Composite Index, Major Market Index, KR-CRB Index, KC Value Line Index, Russell 2000, CAC 40, Nikkei 225 Index, GSCL FT-SE 100 Index, Toronto 35 Index
Foreign exchange	Japanese yen, German mark, Canadian dollar, British pound, Swiss franc, Australian dollar, Mexican peso, Chinese renminbi, Russian ruble

The Structure of Futures Markets

U.S. FUTURES EXCHANGES

As noted, futures contracts are traded on an organized futures exchange. While U.S. exchanges were nonprofit associations for many years, exchanges now are often for-profit corporations. Although multiple futures exchanges are in operation, most trading occurs on the Chicago Mercantile Exchange (CME), the Chicago Board of Trade (CBOT), and the New York Mercantile Exchange (NYNEX). The CME is the most active exchange. The CME and CBOT merged to form the CME Group, which later acquired NYNEX. However, these exchanges continue to operate separately.

Unlike stocks, there are no specialists on futures exchanges. U.S. futures exchanges have traditionally operated with a trading floor (a "pit") where traders and brokers come together in an auction-style, open-outcry market. This means that they communicate with each other verbally and with hand signals. A futures customer submits an order which goes to a floor broker on the trading floor to be executed with other floor brokers representing other customers or with floor traders trading for their own accounts.

Electronic order matching has developed rapidly in the United States after a slow start. The major futures exchanges in the United States use both methods of trading—open-outcry trading and electronic trading—for at least some of the instruments they trade. Included here are the CBOT, the CME, and NYMEX. Firms can now offer customers 24-hour futures trading.

Example 20-2   The Chicago Board of Trade (CBOT®) is a leading futures and futures-options exchange that is part of the CME Group. According to the CBOT, "more than 3,600 CBOT member/ stockholders trade 50 different futures and options products at the CBOT by open auction and electronically."

The Chicago Mercantile Exchange (CME) bills itself as the world's largest and most diverse financial exchange. It offers futures and options on futures on commodities as well as on finance-related items—interest rates, stock indexes, and foreign exchange. The CME acts as an international marketplace with its open-outcry platform and trading floor systems linked to its Globex® electronic trading platform. As noted, it is now part of the CME Group.

Investments Intuition

As noted above, futures markets are valuable because they allow those with a preexisting risk position to reduce their risk exposure, or even eliminate it. Everyone is aware of the European sovereign debt and banking crises that so dominated the news in the latter half of 2011 and into 2012. We should reasonably expect that many people with financial risk exposures would be drawn to the futures market. Sure enough, CME's futures market, with a 163-year history, had its busiest August ever. Its third quarter revenue set a record, as did its operating margin.

✓ Think of futures exchanges as business firms that create markets. They compete for the exclusive right to trade specific contracts.[2]

Futures brokerage firms, known as futures commission merchants (FCMs), act as agents for the general public, for which they receive commissions. Thus, a customer can establish an account with an FCM, who, in turn may work through a floor broker at the exchange. FCMs can be full service firms or discount firms, and they can be standalone firms (doing business only in futures) or part of a financial services firm offering securities and other services (for example, a national or regional brokerage firm).

FOREIGN FUTURES MARKETS

European futures exchanges are very competitive. Most of these systems are now fully automated order-matching systems. Euronext was the first pan-European exchange. It was created in 2000 by the merger of the Amsterdam, Brussels, and Paris markets. In 2002 it acquired the London International Financial Futures and Options Exchange (LIFFE). This makes Euronext a cross-border market with multiple products traded on a single platform.

Japan, which banned financial futures until 1985, has been very active in developing futures exchanges. Commodity futures markets account for most of the futures trading. Japan has several commodity futures exchanges, each of which trades specific contracts.

---

[2] These statements are indebted to Robert W. Kolb and James A. Overdahl, *Futures, Options and Swaps*, 5th edition. Malden, Mass. Blackwell Publishing, 2007, p. 54.

THE CLEARINGHOUSE

The clearinghouse, a corporation separate from, but associated with, each exchange, plays an important role in every futures transaction. Since all futures trades are cleared through the clearinghouse each business day, exchange members must either be members of the clearinghouse or pay a member for this service.

Essentially, the clearinghouse for futures markets operates in the same way as the clearinghouse for options, which was discussed in some detail in Chapter 19. Buyers and sellers settle with the clearinghouse, not each other. The clearinghouse is the seller to the buyer, and the buyer to the seller. It stands ready to fulfill a contract if either buyer or seller defaults, thereby guaranteeing performance and helping to facilitate an orderly market in futures.

The clearinghouse makes the futures market impersonal, which is the key to its success because any buyer or seller can always close out a position and be assured of payment. The first failure of a clearing member in modern times occurred in the 1980s, and the system worked perfectly in preventing any customer from losing money.[3]

✓ The clearinghouse, and not another investor, is on the other side of every futures transaction and ensures that all payments are made as specified.

Finally, as explained below, the clearinghouse allows participants to easily reverse a position (take the opposite position) before maturity because the clearinghouse keeps track of each participant's obligations. Thus, an investor who is short a gold contract can easily cancel this position by buying (going long) the same gold contract.

Checking Your Understanding

1. Given the development of futures markets, and the disadvantages of forward contracts, what advantage does a forward contract offer?
2. Assume you buy several futures contracts that, at the expiration date, are worth considerably more than when purchased so that you have a large gain. How can you be assured that the losers on these same positions will make good on their obligations?

The Mechanics of Trading

FUTURES CONTRACTS

Forward Contract A commitment today to transact in the future at a price that is currently determined, with no funds having been exchanged

Swap An agreement between parties to exchange streams of cash flows over some future period

As noted earlier, a **forward contract** is an agreement between two parties that calls for delivery of a commodity (tangible or financial) at a specified future time at a price agreed upon today. Each contract has a buyer and a seller. Forward markets have grown primarily because of the growth in swaps, which in general are similar to forward contracts. A **swap** is an agreement between parties to exchange streams of cash flows over some future period.

✓ Forward contracts involve credit risk—either party can default on their obligation.

---

[3] The clearinghouse deals only with clearing members, and not individual investors, making each clearing member completely responsible for every position it carries on its books. Because the clearinghouse has nothing to do with individual customers, it depends entirely on the clearing member's carrying and guaranteeing individual customer accounts when it comes to margin requirements and payments.

These contracts also involve liquidity risk because of the difficulties involved in getting out of the contract. On the other hand, forward contracts can be customized to the specific needs of the parties involved.

Futures Contract Agreement providing for the future exchange of a particular asset at a currently determined market price

A **futures contract** is a standardized, transferable agreement providing for the deferred delivery of either a specified grade and quantity of a designated commodity within a specified geographical area or of a financial instrument (or its cash value). Futures contracts are very well specified commitments. Market participants know exactly what is involved in the transaction, which in fact helps to promote liquidity in these markets.

✓ A futures contract locks in a price for delivery on a future date. The futures price at which this exchange will occur at contract maturity is determined today.

The trading of futures contracts means only that commitments have been made by buyers and sellers; therefore, "buying" and "selling" do not have the same meaning in futures transactions as they do in stock and bond transactions. Although these commitments are binding because futures contracts are legal contracts, a buyer or seller can eliminate the commitment simply by taking an opposite position in the same commodity or financial instrument for the same futures month. This is referred to as offset.

Futures contracts are not securities and are not regulated by the Securities and Exchange Commission. The Commodity Futures Trading Commission (CFTC), a federal regulatory agency, is responsible for regulating trading in all domestic futures markets. In practice, the National Futures Association, a self-regulating body, has assumed some of the duties previously performed by the CFTC. In addition, each futures exchange has a supervisory body to oversee its members.

BASIC PROCEDURES

Because the futures contract is a commitment to buy or sell at a specified future settlement date, a contract is not really being sold or bought, as in the case of buying and selling Treasury bills, stocks, or CDs, because *no money is exchanged at the time the contract is negotiated*. Instead, the seller and the buyer simply are agreeing to make and take delivery, respectively, at some future time for a price agreed upon today. As noted above, the terms *buy* and *sell* do not have the same meanings with futures. It is more accurate to think in terms of

Short Position An agreement to sell an asset at a specified future date at a specified price

Long Position An agreement to purchase an asset at a specified future date at a specified price

- A **short position** (seller), which commits a trader to deliver an item at contract maturity at a price agreed upon today
- A **long position** (buyer), which commits a trader to purchase an item at contract maturity at a price agreed upon today

Selling short in futures trading means only that a contract not previously purchased is sold. For every futures contract, someone sold it (thereby establishing a short position) and someone else bought it (thereby establishing a long position).

✓ Like options, futures trading is a zero-sum game. The gains and losses on all positions net to zero.

Whereas an options contract involves the *right* to make or take delivery on the part of the buyer, a futures contract involves an *obligation* to take or make delivery. Delivery, or settlement of the contract, occurs in months that are designated by the various exchanges for each of the items traded. However, futures contracts can be settled by delivery or by offset, and most are settled by offset.

✓ A futures contract involves an obligation—either offset occurs, or delivery occurs.

Indeed, about 95 percent of futures contracts are closed by offset before the contract expires. Holders liquidate a position by arranging an offsetting transaction. This means that buyers sell their positions, and sellers buy in their positions sometime prior to delivery. When an investor offsets his or her position, it means that their trading account is adjusted to reflect the final gains (or losses) and their position is closed.

Offset Liquidation of a futures position by an offsetting transaction

✓   **Offset** is the typical method of settling a contract.

Thus, to eliminate a futures market position, the investor simply does the reverse of what was done originally. As explained above, the clearinghouse makes this easy to accomplish. It is critical to remember that if a futures contract is not offset, it must be closed out by delivery.

Each exchange establishes price fluctuation limits on the various types of contracts. Typically, a minimum price change is specified. In the case of corn, for example, it is 0.25 cents per bushel, or $12.50 per contract. A daily price limit is in effect for all futures contracts except stock-index futures. For corn it is 10 cents per bushel ($500 per contract) above and below the previous day's settlement price.

Long stock positions can literally be held forever. Even many short positions can be held indefinitely as long as certain conditions are met. However, futures positions must be closed out within a specified time, either by offsetting the position or by making or taking delivery.

Brokerage commissions on commodities contracts are paid on the basis of a completed contract (purchase and sale), rather than each purchase and sale, as in the case of stocks. As with options, no certificates exist for futures contracts.

The *open interest* indicates contracts that are not offset by opposite transactions or delivery. That is, it measures the number of unliquidated contracts at any point in time, on a cumulative basis.[4] The open interest increases when an investor goes long on a contract and is reduced when the contract is liquidated.

MARGIN

Recall that in the case of stock transactions the term margin refers to the down payment in a transaction in which money is borrowed from the broker to finance the total cost. **Futures margin**, on the other hand, is not a down payment because ownership of the underlying item is not being transferred at the time of the transaction.[5] Futures margin refers to the "good faith" (or earnest money) deposit made by both buyer and seller to ensure the completion of the contract. These funds serve as a performance bond to help ensure that traders will fulfill their contract obligations.

Futures Margin The earnest money deposit made by a transactor to ensure the completion of a contract

Unlike stock trading, futures margin is required of all participants. All futures markets participants, whether buyers or sellers, must deposit minimum specified amounts in their futures margin accounts to guarantee contract obligations.

Initial Margin In dollar terms, the initial equity an investor has in a margin transaction

Each clearinghouse sets its own minimum **initial margin** requirements (in dollars). Furthermore, brokerage houses can require a higher margin and typically do so. The margin required for futures contracts, which is small in relation to the value of the contract itself, represents the equity of the transactor (either buyer or seller). It is not unusual for the initial margin to be only a few thousand dollars while the value of the contract is much larger. As a

---

[4] The open interest can be measured using either the open long positions or the open short positions, but not both.

[5] Because no credit is being extended, no interest expense is incurred on that part of the contract not covered by the margin as is the case when stocks are purchased on margin. With futures, customers often receive interest on margin money deposited. A customer with a large enough requirement (roughly, $15,000 and over) can use Treasury bills as part of the margin.

generalized approximation, the margin requirement for futures contracts is about 6 percent of the value of the contract. Since the equity is small, the risk to the transactor is magnified.

Example 20-3

Assume the initial margin is equal to 5 percent of the total value and an investor holds one contract in an account. If the price of the contract changes by 5 percent because the price of the underlying commodity changes by 5 percent, this is equivalent to a 100 percent change in the investor's equity. This example shows why futures trading can be so risky!

Maintenance Margin The amount of funds that must be on hand at all times as equity

Margin Call A demand from the broker for additional cash or securities as a result of the actual margin declining below the maintenance margin

Marked To The Market The daily posting of all profits and losses in an investor's account

In addition to the initial margin requirement, each contract requires a **maintenance margin** below which the transactor's equity cannot drop without action being taken. If the market price of a futures contract moves adversely to the owner's position, the equity declines. A **margin call** occurs when the price goes against the transactor, requiring the deposit of additional cash (the variation margin).[6] The transactor must restore the account back to the initial margin level (not the maintenance margin level).

To understand how the margin process for futures contracts works, we must first understand how profits and losses from futures contracts are debited and credited daily to a participant's account. All futures contracts are **marked to the market** daily, which means that all profits and losses on a contract are credited and debited to each account every trading day.[7] Those contract holders with a profit can withdraw the gains, whereas those with a loss will receive a margin call when the equity falls below the specified maintenance margin. This process is referred to as daily resettlement, and the price used is the contract's settlement price.[8]

Example 20-4

Table 20-1 illustrates how accounts are marked to the market daily. Consider an investor who buys a stock-index futures contract on the Dow Jones Industrial Average using the Chicago Board of Trade's CBOT® DJIA℠ futures contract.[9] Assume that the investor's brokerage firm requires an initial margin of $7,000. The maintenance margin is $4,000 per contract.

This contract has a multiplier of $10. Price quotes are in points ($10), and the tick size is $10. The value of a CBOT DJIA Index futures contract is equal to $10 times the current index level. For example, if the index is trading at 10,000, one of these futures contracts is equivalent to investing $100,000 in the DJIA portfolio. The seller of such a contract (the short position) is agreeing to sell $10 times the index and the buyer (the long position) is agreeing to buy $10 times the index on the expiration date of the contract. On the settlement day of this futures contract, the final settlement price is $10 times the Special Opening Quotation of the index.

Assume investor A buys a contract with the DJIA at 10,000 while investor B, believing the DJIA will decline, sells (goes short) one contract at the same time. After day one the settlement price is 9,925. The buyer will have a debit in his/her account of 75 × $10 = $750 because the price declined and the buyer was long. Conversely, the seller will have a credit of the same

[6] The variation margin must be paid in cash.

[7] This is not true of forward contracts, where no funds are transferred until the maturity date.

[8] The settlement price does not always reflect the final trade of the day. The clearinghouse establishes the settlement price at the close of trading.

[9] Information about futures contracts on the Dow Jones Industrial Average can be found at the Chicago Board of Trade's website, www.cbot.com.

amount in his/her account because the seller was short and the price declined. At the end of day 1 the value of the buyer's account is $7,000 − $750 = $6,250, while the value of the seller's account is $7,000 + $750 = $7,750. In effect, both accounts have been marked to the market.

Now assume that two weeks have passed, during which time each account has been marked to the market daily (we also assume there have been no margin calls).[10] The settlement price on this contract has reached 10,400, with a move on the last day of this two-week period of 150 points. The aggregate change in market value for each investor is the difference between the current price and the initial price multiplied by $10, the value of one point in price. This will be

$$10,400 − 10,000 = 400 \times \$10 = \$4,000$$

As shown in Table 20-1, this amount is currently credited to the buyer because the price moved up as the buyer expected. Conversely, this same amount is currently debited to the seller, who is now on the wrong side of the price movement. Therefore, starting with an initial equity or margin of $7,000, after two weeks the cumulative mark to the market is $4,000. This results in a current equity of $11,000 for the buyer and $3,000 for the seller. The buyer has a withdrawable excess equity of $4,000 because of the favorable price movement, whereas the seller now faces a margin call because the maintenance margin for this contract is $4,000.[11] In this example, the market declined sharply on the last day of the two-week period, bringing the seller's equity below the required maintenance level. The seller would now have to put up funds to return the account to the initial margin requirement level of $7,000.

Table 20-1 An Example of Investor Accounts, Using Stock-Index Futures, Marked to the Market

	Buyer (Long)	Seller (Short)
Account after one day		
Original equity (initial margin)	$7,000	$7,000
Day I mark to the market	(750)	750
Current equity	$6,250	7,750
Account after two weeks		
Original equity	$7,000	$7,000
Cumulative mark to the market	4,000	(4,000)
Current equity	$11,000	$3,000
Withdrawable excess equity	$4,000	
Margin call		$4,000

Investments Intuition

This example illustrates what is meant by the expression that futures trading, like options trading, is a zero-sum game. The aggregate gains and losses net to zero. The aggregate profits enjoyed by the winners must be equal to the aggregate losses suffered by the losers. This also means that the net exposure to changes in the commodity's price must be zero.

[10] We are condensing the time element here for the sake of simplicity. The account would be marked to the market each day of this two-week period, and therefore each investor's equity would change every single day.

[11] If the investor's current equity drops below the maintenance level required (which in this case is $4,000), he or she receives a margin call and must add enough money to restore the account to the initial margin level.

Checking Your Understanding

3. The short position's loss is equal to the long position's gain. Explain.
4. The maturity date of a contract does not dictate realization of an investor's gains and losses. Explain.

Using Futures Contracts

Who uses futures, and for what purpose? Traditionally, participants in the futures market have been classified as either hedgers or speculators. Because both groups are important in understanding the role and functioning of futures markets, we will consider each in turn. The distinctions between these two groups apply to financial futures as well as to the more traditional commodity futures.

HEDGERS

Hedgers are parties at risk with a commodity or an asset, which means they are exposed to price changes. They buy or sell futures contracts in order to offset their risk. In other words, hedgers actually deal in the commodity or financial instrument specified in the futures contract.[12]

✓ By taking a position opposite to that of one already held, at a price set today, hedgers plan to reduce the risk of adverse price fluctuations—that is, to hedge the risk of unexpected price changes. In effect, this is a form of insurance.

In a sense, the real motivation for all futures trading is to reduce price risk. With futures, risk is reduced by having the gain (loss) in the futures position offset the loss (gain) on the cash position. A hedger is willing to forego some profit potential in exchange for having someone else assume part of the risk. Figure 20-1 illustrates the hedging process as it affects the return-risk distribution. Notice that the unhedged position not only has a greater chance of a larger loss, but also a greater chance of a larger gain.

✓ The hedged position has a smaller chance of a low return but also a smaller chance of a high return. Thus, hedging reduces the variance in the outcome.

Figure 20-1

Return Distribution for Hedged and Unhedged Positions.

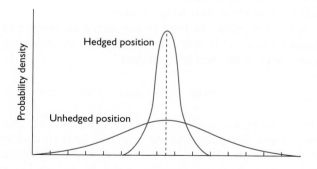

---

[12] The cash position may currently exist (a cash hedge) or may be expected to exist in the future (an anticipatory hedge).

HOW TO HEDGE WITH FUTURES

The nature of the cash market position determines the hedge in the futures market. A commodity or financial instrument held (in effect, in inventory) represents a long position because these items could be sold in the cash market. On the other hand, a transactor who sells a futures position not owned has created a short position.

✓   The key to any hedge is that a futures position is taken opposite to the position in the cash market.

Because transactors can assume two basic positions with futures contracts, long and short, there are two basic hedge positions: the short (sell) hedge and the long (buy) hedge.

Short Hedge A transaction involving the sale of futures (a short position) while holding the asset (a long position)

1. The short (sell) hedge. A cash market inventory holder must sell (short) the futures. For example, investors should think of short hedges as a means of protecting the value of their portfolios. Since they are holding securities, they are long on the cash position and need to protect themselves against a decline in prices. A **short hedge** reduces, or possibly eliminates, the risk taken in a cash market (long) position.

Long Hedge A transaction where the asset is currently not held but futures are purchased to lock in current prices

2. The long (buy) hedge. An individual who currently holds no cash inventory (holds no commodities or financial instruments) is, in effect, short in the cash market; therefore, to hedge with futures requires a long position. Someone who is not currently in the cash market but who expects to be in the future and who wants to lock in current prices and yields until cash is available to make the investment can use a **long hedge** which reduces the risk of a short position.

Hedging is not an automatic process. It requires more than simply taking a position. Hedgers must make timing decisions as to when to initiate and end the process. As conditions change, hedgers must adjust their hedge strategy.

One aspect of hedging that must be considered for hedging to be successful is "basis" risk. The **basis** for financial futures often is defined as the difference between the cash price and the futures price of the item being hedged:[13]

Basis The difference between the futures price of an item and the spot price of the item

$$\text{Basis} = \text{Cash price} - \text{Futures price}$$

The basis must be zero on the maturity date of the contract. That is, the futures price and the cash price must be equal, resulting in a zero basis (transaction costs can cause discrepancies). In the interim, the basis fluctuates in an unpredictable manner and is not constant during a hedge period. Basis risk, therefore, is the risk hedgers face as a result of unexpected changes in basis.

---

[13] The typical definition for basis is the cash price minus the futures price. For financial futures, the definition is often reversed.

In hedging, the buyer benefits from a weakening basis (cash price weakens relative to futures.) The seller benefits from a strengthening basis (cash price strengthens relative to futures.) It is important to note that the basis can strengthen or weaken when price levels are falling or rising.

Although changes in the basis will affect the hedge position during its life, a hedge will reduce risk as long as the variability in the basis is less than the variability in the price of the asset being hedged. The significance of basis risk to investors is that risk cannot be entirely eliminated. Hedging a cash position will involve basis risk.

SPECULATORS

In contrast to hedgers, speculators buy or sell futures contracts in an attempt to earn a return. Unlike hedgers, speculators typically do not transact in the physical commodity or financial instrument underlying the futures contract. In other words, they have no prior market position. Some speculators are professionals who do this for a living; others are amateurs, ranging from the very sophisticated to the novice.[14]

✓ Speculators are willing to assume the risk of price fluctuations, hoping to profit from them.

Speculators are essential to the proper functioning of the futures market, absorbing the excess demand or supply generated by hedgers and assuming the risk of price fluctuations that hedgers wish to avoid. Speculators contribute to the liquidity of the market and reduce the variability in prices over time.

Why speculate in futures markets? After all, one could speculate in the underlying instruments. For example, an investor who believed interest rates were going to decline could buy Treasury bonds directly and avoid the Treasury bond futures market. The potential advantages of speculating in futures markets include

1. Leverage. The magnification of gains (and losses) can easily be 10 to 1.
2. Ease of transacting. An investor who thinks interest rates will rise will have difficulty selling bonds short, but it is very easy to take a short position in a Treasury bond futures contract.
3. Transaction costs. These are often significantly smaller in futures markets.

By all accounts, an investor's likelihood of success when speculating in futures is not very good. The small investor is up against stiff odds when it comes to *speculating* with futures contracts. Futures should be used for hedging purposes by most individuals.

CALCULATING THE RATE OF RETURN ON FUTURES CONTRACTS

Throughout this text we use Total Return to measure the rate of return on most financial assets because it relates the cash flows received by an investor to the purchase price of the asset. With futures contracts, there is no income component, only a price change or capital gain (loss). Furthermore, the investor does not put up the full amount of the contract, but only the margin

---

[14] Although most speculators are not actually present at the futures markets, floor traders (or locals) trade for their own accounts as well as others and often take very short-term (minutes or hours) positions in an attempt to exploit any short-lived market anomalies.

required, which is typically very small. What matters when we calculate a rate of return is to relate the cash flows received to the actual cash investment made by the investor.

The return on investment can be stated as

$$\frac{\text{Selling price of contracts(s)} - \text{Purchase price of contact(s)}}{\text{Margin deposit made by investor}} \qquad \text{(20-1)}$$

Example 20-5

Assume in December a speculator buys two May wheat contracts at 624'0 ($6.24 per bushel). The margin requirement for each is $1,700, and the contract size is 5,000 bushels. Sometime later the contract is quoted at 645'0 ($6.45 per bushel). The gain is $0.21 × 5000 × 2 = $2,100. The rate of return on the speculator's actual cash outlay (the total margin requirement) is

$$(64,500 - \$62,400)/\$3,400 = 61.8\%$$

This high rate of return comes about because the price of wheat did rise, and futures contracts have a lot of leverage. Note that the total margin requirement of $3,400 is only 5.4 percent of the value of the two wheat contracts on the day the futures are bought. Of course, there is always a downside. Had wheat prices declined, the entire margin could have been lost.

Checking Your Understanding

5. What is the essential difference between a hedger and a speculator when it comes to owning the underlying asset involved in a futures contract?

Financial Futures

Financial Futures Futures contracts on financial assets

Financial futures are futures contracts on equity indexes, fixed-income securities, and currencies. They give investors greater opportunity to fine-tune the risk-return characteristics of their portfolios. In recent years, this flexibility has become increasingly important as stock prices have become much more volatile and as investors have sought new techniques to reduce the risk of equity positions.

✓ There are three broad types of financial futures: currency futures, interest rate futures, and equity futures.

The procedures for trading financial futures are the same as those for any other commodity, with few exceptions. At maturity, stock-index futures settle in cash because it would be impossible or impractical to deliver all the stocks in a particular index.[15] Unlike traditional futures contracts, stock-index futures typically have no daily price limits (although they can be imposed).

We will analyze each of the three broad types of financial futures. Hedging and speculative activities within each category are discussed separately.

---

[15] Gains and losses on the last day of trading are credited and debited to the long and short positions in the same way—marked to the market—as was done for every other trading day of the contract. Therefore, not only is there no physical delivery of securities, but also the buyer does not pay the full value of the contract at settlement.

FOREIGN CURRENCY FUTURES

Foreign currency trading has existed for many years, and has become increasingly important in the global economy that now exists. Foreign currencies are traded in both a forward market and a futures market, with the forward market the larger of the two.

Every exchange rate (price) is a relative price because every pair of foreign exchange rates are related to each other as reciprocals. For example, a Euro rate of $1.3833 indicates that one Euro will buy $1.3833 of U.S. currency. Conversely, one U.S. dollar will buy $(1/1.3833 = .7229)$ Euros.[16]

Traders need information about individual contracts, including prices, size of contract, expiration dates, maximum daily movements, and so forth. This information can be found at the various exchanges where the contracts are traded, such as www.cmegroup.com.

Hedging with Foreign Currency Futures   Companies often use currency futures when they are exposed to foreign exchange risk. Investors can use currency futures to protect their positions in foreign securities, thereby earning what the foreign securities offer without being adversely affected by exchange rate movements.

Example 20-6   Let's consider the Euro/Dollar (EUR/USD) futures. Assume a U.S. investor bought $350,000 of French notes in January because of their much higher yields relative to U.S. notes and plans to sell them in December. We abstract from margin requirements and assume the yield curve remains flat for that time period. The investor wants to collect the higher yield without taking much exchange rate risk, which could reduce her overall return.

The contract size is €125,000, with expirations in March, June, September, and December. At a price of $1.3833, one contract is worth $1.3833 × 125,000, or $172,912.50. To protect against adverse currency movements, the investor sells two futures contracts with a total value of $172,912.50 × 2 = $345,825. Now assume the dollar rises against the Euro so that one dollar in December will buy .7435 Euros instead of the previous .7229 (calculated as 1/1.3833). The Euro contract is now quoted at (1/.7435 = $1.345), and each contract is worth 125,000 × $1.345 = $168,125, or a total of $336,250 for two.

The investor makes a profit on the two futures contracts of ($345,825− $336,250 = $9,575) because she sold the contracts and the dollar price of the Euro declined. However, when she sells the proceeds of the notes and buys dollars back, she loses on the transaction. The original $350,000 was worth, in Euros, $350,000 × .7229 = 253,015. Now the 253,015 is worth only 253,015 × 1.345 = $340,305 in dollars. Therefore, the investor has a loss in dollars on the investment of $9,695, and a gain on the futures of $9,575. Although the investor takes a small loss on the conversion, she is able to collect the high yields that the French notes were offering. Without the hedge, her return from this investment would have been significantly different.

Speculating with Foreign Currency Futures   Investors can speculate on the differences in exchange rates between two countries, based on their beliefs about what is going to happen. For example, the dollar fell against the Euro for a period of years recently. The Japanese yen appreciated against most currencies during the same time period. A speculative strategy depends upon accepting additional price risk because the speculator believes that the move will be profitable.

---

[16] The daily exchange rates can be found at several places including wsj.com, "Markets," "Currencies."

It is extremely important to remember that futures contracts can have large payoffs, but also staggering losses. Because of the small amount of margin required, if an investor's position works out well, the percentage gains can be very large. On the other hand, the margin can be wiped out.

INTEREST RATE FUTURES

Bond prices are highly volatile, and investors are exposed to adverse price movements. Interest rate futures, in effect, allow bondholders and others who are affected by volatile interest rates to transfer the risk. One of the primary reasons for the growth in financial futures is that portfolio managers and investors are trying to protect themselves against adverse movements in interest rates. An investor concerned with protecting the value of fixed-income securities must consider the possible impact of interest rates on the value of these securities.

Today's investors have the opportunity to consider several different interest rate futures contracts that are traded on various exchanges.[17] The Chicago Mercantile Exchange trades contracts on Treasury bills, agency notes, Eurodollars, and the one-month LIBOR rate, among others. The Chicago Board of Trade (CBT) specializes in longer-maturity instruments, including Treasury notes (two-year, five-year, and 10-year maturities) and Treasury bonds. The CBOT also trades contracts on 30-day Federal Funds as well as swaps.

Exhibit 20-2 describes some futures contracts (not an exhaustive list) on fixed-income securities. Contracts are available on various maturities of U.S. Treasury notes in trading units of $100,000 and $200,000, on Treasury bonds in units of $100,000, and on Treasury bills in trading units of $1 million.

Reading Quotes   As an example consider the 10-year Treasury note shown on the CME website. The face value of the contract at maturity is $100,000, and the price quotations are percentages of par, with 32nds, and halves of 32nds, shown. Since one point is $1,000, 1/32 is worth $31.25. Thus, in late 2011 the March 2012 quote was 129'120. This represents a price of 129 and 12/32nds percent of par, or $129,375.

EXHIBIT 20-2

Characteristics of Interest Rate Futures Contracts

	Where Traded[a]	Contract Size or Trading Unit	Minimum Fluctuations
Treasury bonds	CBT	$100,000 per value 8% coupon[b]	1/32 or $31.25
10-year Treasury notes	CBT	$100,000 par value	1/32 or $31.25
Treasury bills	CME	$1 million face value	1 point = .005 or $12.50
Five-year & two-year Treasury notes	CBT	$100,000 & $200,000 par value	1/32 or $31.25

[a]CBT=Chicago Board of Trade; CME—Chicago Mercantile Exchange.
[b]Bonds with other coupons are usable with price adjustments.

---

[17] The Chicago Board of Trade launched financial futures trading in 1975 by opening trading in Government National Mortgage Association (GNMA or Ginnie Mae) bonds. The concept accelerated in 1976, when the International Monetary Market started trading in Treasury bills. Treasury bond futures appeared in 1977.

Hedging with Interest Rate Futures   We now consider an example of using interest rate futures to hedge an investment position. Obviously, other examples could be constructed involving various transactors, such as a corporation or financial institution; various financial instruments, such as a portfolio of Treasury bills; and various scenarios under which the particular hedger is operating. Our objective is simply to illustrate the basic concepts. Here we concentrate on the short hedge since it is by far the more common; we discuss the concept of the long hedge below.

Short Hedge   Suppose an investor has a bond portfolio consisting of $1 million in two-year Treasury notes that mature at the end of 2014. This money is to be used to pay an obligation at that time. The investor fears that a rise in interest rates would leave her short in terms of paying the obligation. If, for example, the Fed raised the federal funds target rate, the two-year Treasury note rate would rise a comparable amount, and the price of these notes would decline.

This investor could take a short position in the two-year Treasury note futures. If done properly, the short position in the futures should gain as much as the actual Treasury notes held lose in value as a result of the interest rate rise. What if yields drop? In this case, the investor will lose on the futures position but will gain on the value of the Treasury notes held. Therefore, the investor should be able to meet the upcoming obligation regardless of what interest rates do.

The actual mechanics of executing a short hedge such as this (also called an inventory hedge) require the hedger to determine the hedge ratio, or the number of contracts to be sold. This is a function of the value of the long position in the asset and the value of each futures contract.

Long Hedge   An alternative hedge is the *anticipatory hedge*, a long hedge, whereby an investor purchases a futures contract as an alternative to buying the underlying security. At some designated time in the future, the investor will purchase the security and sell the futures contract. This results in a net price for the security position at the future point in time which is equal to the price paid for the security minus the gain or loss on the futures position.

Consider an investor who would like to purchase an interest rate asset now but will not have the cash for three months. If rates drop, the asset will cost more at that point in time. By purchasing a futures contract on the asset now, as a hedge, the investor can lock in the interest rate implied by the interest rate futures contract. This may be a good substitute for not being able to lock in the current interest rate because of the lack of funds now to do so. At the conclusion of this transaction, the investor will pay a *net* price that reflects the ending cash price minus the gain on the futures contract. In effect, the gain on the futures increases the rate of return earned on the interest rate asset.

Concepts in Action

Using Futures to Manage Your Bond Portfolio

Suppose investors are concerned about the possibility of rising interest rates. What if you own a substantial portfolio of bonds at this time, and the duration of this portfolio is moderately long—let's say six and a half years? We know that if interest rates rise, bond prices fall, and we know we can use the duration of the portfolio as an approximate guide to the percentage decreases that will occur.

Assume you want to shorten the duration of your portfolio—let's say to five years. If interest rates rise, the prices of your bonds will still decline, but with a shorter duration they will decline less than with your original position. An obvious way to shorten the duration of your portfolio is to sell longer-maturity bonds and replace them with shorter-maturity bonds.

However, this involves transaction costs, and has possible tax implications.

An alternative is to use futures to sell duration. This strategy will have lower transaction costs, and you can always reverse a futures position quickly and easily. Thus, you could use **CBOT** Treasury futures to lower the duration of your bond portfolio.

A simple way to sell duration is to sell 1.5 years of duration by going short in **CBOT** 10-year Treasury note futures. You would need to determine how many contracts to use. If you were to hedge completely, the duration would be zero. Instead, you wish to achieve a 23 percent hedge, reducing your duration from six and a half years to five years (1.5/6.5=23 percent). The details of such a transaction can be worked out with a little effort.

Although there are some complications in this transaction, such as whether the yield curve shifts in a parallel manner when rates go up, or whether it flattens, the concept is the same. Futures contracts can be used in innovative ways when it comes to managing a portfolio.

Speculating with Interest Rate Futures Investors may wish to speculate with interest rate futures as well as to hedge with them. To do so, investors make assessments of likely movements in interest rates and assume a futures position that corresponds with this assessment. If the investor anticipates a rise in interest rates, he or she will sell one (or more) interest rate futures, because a rise in interest rates will drive down the prices of bonds and therefore the price of the futures contract. The investor sells a contract with the expectation of buying it back later at a lower price. Of course, a decline in interest rates will result in a loss for this investor, since the price will rise.

Example 20-7 Assume that in November a speculator thinks interest rates will rise over the next two weeks and wishes to profit from this expectation. The investor can sell one December Treasury bond futures contract at a price of, say, 90−20. Two weeks later the price of this contract has declined to 88−24 because of rising interest rates. This investor would have a gain of 1 28/32, or $1,875 (each 1/32 is worth $31.25), and could close out this position by buying an identical contract.

The usefulness of interest rate futures for pursuing such a strategy is significant. A speculator who wishes to assume a short position in bonds cannot do so readily in the cash market (either financially or mechanically). Interest rate futures provide the means to short bonds easily.

In a similar manner, investors can speculate on a decline in interest rates by purchasing interest rate futures. If the decline materializes, bond prices and the value of the futures contract will rise. Because of the leverage involved, the gains can be large; however, the losses can also be large if interest rates move in the wrong direction.

STOCK-INDEX FUTURES

Stock-index futures trading was initiated in 1982 with several contracts quickly being created. Investors can trade futures contracts on major market indexes such as the DJIA and the S&P 500 Index. Contracts are also available on a "mini" S&P Index, the NASDAQ 100, the Russell 2000, and the Nikkei 225 Stock Average (Japanese market). Other indexes also are available.[18]

The S&P 500 contract is the most popular stock-index futures contract, accounting by far for the bulk of trading in stock-index futures. The value of an S&P 500 contract is determined by using a multiplier of $250. The minimum tick is 0.10, or $25.

---

[18] There is also a futures contract on the S&P Midcap 400 Index. It has a value of $500 times the index.

Delivery is not permitted in stock-index futures because of its impracticality. Instead, each remaining contract is settled by cash on the settlement day by taking an offsetting position using the price of the underlying index.[19]

Stock-index futures offer investors the opportunity to act on their investment opinions concerning the future direction of the market. They need not select individual stocks, and it is easy to short the market. Furthermore, investors who are concerned about unfavorable short-term market prospects but remain bullish for the longer run can protect themselves in the interim by selling stock-index futures.

Hedging with Stock-Index Futures   Common stock investors hedge with financial futures for the same reasons that fixed-income investors use them. Investors, whether individuals or institutions, may hold a substantial stock portfolio that is subject to the risk of the overall market, that is, systematic risk. A futures contract enables the investor to transfer part or all of the risk to those willing to assume it. Stock-index futures have opened up new, and relatively inexpensive, opportunities for investors to manage market risk through hedging.

Chapter 8 pointed out the two types of risk inherent in common stocks: systematic risk and nonsystematic risk. Diversification will eliminate most or all of the nonsystematic risk in a portfolio, but not the systematic risk. Although an investor could adjust the beta of the portfolio in anticipation of a market rise or fall, this is not an ideal solution because of the changes in portfolio composition that might be required.

Investors can use financial futures on stock market indexes to hedge against an overall market decline. That is, investors can hedge against systematic or market risk by selling the appropriate number of contracts against a stock portfolio. In effect, stock-index futures contracts give an investor the opportunity to protect his or her portfolio against market fluctuations.

To hedge market risk, investors must be able to take a position in the hedging asset (in this case, stock-index futures) such that profits or losses on the hedging asset offset changes in the value of the stock portfolio. Stock-index futures permit this action, because changes in the futures prices themselves generally are highly correlated with changes in the value of the stock portfolios that are caused by marketwide events. The more diversified the portfolio, and therefore the lower the nonsystematic risk, the greater the correlation between the futures contract and the stock positions.

A comparison of the price of the S&P 500 Index futures to the value of a portfolio that is essentially completely diversified (that is, the portfolio has only market risk) would show that the two track each other very closely. This indicates that stock-index futures can be very effective in hedging the market risk of a portfolio.

Short Hedges   Since so much common stock is held by investors, the short hedge is the natural type of contract for most investors. Investors who hold stock portfolios hedge market risk by selling stock-index futures, which means they assume a short position.

A short hedge can be implemented by selling a forward maturity of the contract. The purpose of this hedge is to offset (in total or in part) any losses on the stock portfolio with gains on the futures position. To implement this defensive strategy, an investor would sell one or more index futures contracts. Ideally, the value of these contracts would equal the value of the stock portfolio. If the market falls, leading to a loss on the cash (the stock portfolio) position, stock-index futures prices will also fall, leading to a profit for sellers of futures.

The reduction in price volatility that can be accomplished by hedging is shown in Figure 20-2, which compares the performance of a well-diversified portfolio (the unhedged portfolio)

---

[19] The final settlement price is set equal to the closing index on the maturity date.

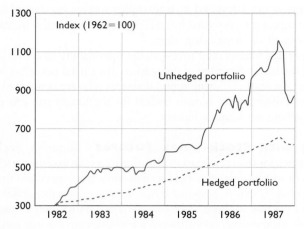

Figure 20-2

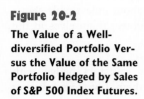

The Value of a Well-diversified Portfolio Versus the Value of the Same Portfolio Hedged by Sales of S&P 500 Index Futures.

SOURCE: Charles S. Morris, "Managing Stock Market Risk with Stock Index Futures," *Economic Review* (June 1989); 10.

with the same portfolio hedged by sales of the S&P 500 Index futures. To test the power of the hedge as much as possible, we focus on a period of time in the 1980s when the market suffered its greatest one day decline in history, October 1987.

Clearly, there is much less variability in the value of the hedged portfolio as compared to the value of the unhedged portfolio. In fact, the volatility of the returns is 91 percent lower.[20] Notice in particular what happened in the great market crash of October 1987. The value of the unhedged portfolio fell some 19 percent, whereas the value of the hedged portfolio fell only 6 percent.

Table 20-2 (top) illustrates the concept of a short hedge using the Standard & Poor's Index when it is at 1,140. Assume that an investor has a portfolio of stocks valued at $290,000 that he or she would like to protect against an anticipated market decline. By selling one S&P stock-index future also priced at 1,140, the investor has a short position of $285,000, because the value of the contract is $250 times the index quote. As the table illustrates, a decline in the stock market of 10 percent results in a loss on the stock portfolio of $29,000 and a gain on

Table 20-2 Examples of Short and Long Hedges Using Stock-Index Futures

	Short Hedge		
	Current Position	Position after a 10% Market Drop	Change in Position
(Long position) $ value of portfolio	$290,000	$261,000	$(29,000)
(Short position) sell one S&P 500 futures contract at 1140	285,000	256,500	28,500
Gain or loss from hedging			(500)
	Long Hedge		
	Current Position	Position or Cost Following a 10% Market Rise	Change in Position or Cost of Position
Buy three S&P 500 futures contracts at 1140 each	$855,000	$940,500	$85,500
Cost of stock position	850,000	935,000	(85,000)
Gain or loss from hedging			500

[20] See ibid.

the futures position of $28,500 (ignoring commissions). Thus, the investor almost makes up on the short side what is lost on the long side.

Long Hedges The long hedger, while awaiting funds to invest, generally wishes to reduce the risk of having to pay more for an equity position when prices rise. Potential users of a long hedge include the following:

1. Institutions with a regular cash flow that use long hedges to improve the timing of their positions.
2. Institutions switching large positions who wish to hedge during the time it takes to complete the process. (This could also be a short hedge.)

Example 20-8 Assume an investor with $850,000 to invest believes that the stock market will advance but has been unable to select the stocks he or she wishes to hold. The S&P stock-index future is at 1140. By purchasing three S&P 500 Index futures, each representing an aggregate dollar value of $1140 \times \$250 = \$285,000$, the investor will gain if the market advances. As shown in Table 20-2, a 10 percent market advance will increase the value of the futures contract $28,500 ($11.40 \times 1.10 = 1254$; $1254 \times \$250 = \$313,500$; $\$313,500 - \$285,000 = \$28,500$). With three contracts, the total gain is three times larger, or $85,500. Even if the investor has to pay 10 percent more (on average) for stocks purchased after the advance, he or she still gains because the net hedge result is positive.

Limitations of Hedging with Stock-Index Futures Although hedging with stock-index futures can reduce an investor's risk, typically risk cannot be eliminated completely. As with interest rate futures, basis risk is present with stock-index futures. It represents the difference between the price of the stock-index futures contract and the value of the underlying stock index. A daily examination of stock-index values and stock-index futures prices will show that each of the indexes quoted under the respective futures contracts differs from the closing price of the contracts.[21]

Basis risk as it applies to common stock portfolios can be defined as the risk that remains after a stock portfolio has been hedged.[22] Note here that stock-index futures hedge only systematic (market) risk. That is, when we consider a stock portfolio hedged with stock-index futures, the basis risk is attributable to unsystematic (nonmarket or firm-specific) risk.

Figure 20-3a illustrates the effects of basis risk by comparing the value of a relatively undiversified portfolio with the price of the S&P 500 futures contract. In contrast to Figure 20-2, where the portfolio was 99 percent diversified, this portfolio is only 66 percent diversified. Although the two series are related, the relationship is in no way as close as that illustrated in Figure 20-2. Therefore, stock-index futures will be less effective at hedging the total risk of the portfolio, as shown in Figure 20-3b. In this situation, the variance of returns on the hedged portfolio is only 27 percent lower than the unhedged position. Note that in the crash of October 1987 both portfolios fell sharply, demonstrating that the hedge was relatively ineffective. (It did better than the unhedged position, but not by much.)

---

[21] Futures prices are generally more volatile than the underlying indexes and therefore diverge from them. The index futures tend to lead the actual market indexes. If investors are bullish, the futures are priced at a premium, with greater maturities usually associated with greater premiums. If investors are bearish, the futures are normally priced at a discount, which may widen as maturity increases.

[22] This discussion is based heavily on Morris, "Managing Stock Market Risk with Stock Index Futures," pp. 11–13.

Figure 20-3

(*a*) **The Value of a Relatively Undiversified Stock Portfolio and the Price of the S&P Index Futures Contract.** (*b*) **The Value of the Unhedged Portfolio and the Same Portfolio Hedged by Sales of S&P 500 Futures Contracts.**

SOURCE: Charles S. Morris, "Managing Stock Market Risk with Stock Index Futures," *Economic Review* (June 1989); 12,13.

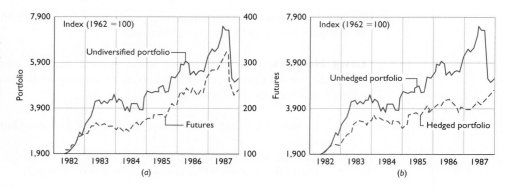

From this analysis we can conclude that stock-index futures generally do not provide a good hedge for relatively undiversified portfolios.

Index Arbitrage and Program Trading   A force of considerable magnitude hit Wall Street in the 1980s. Program trading (defined in Chapter 4) captured much attention and generated considerable controversy. It leads to headlines attributing market plunges at least in part to program trading, as happened on October 19, 1987, when the Dow Jones Industrial Average fell over 500 points. Because program trading typically involves positions in both stocks and stock-index futures contracts, we consider the topic within the general discussion of hedging.

Index Arbitrage Exploitation of price differences between stock-index futures and the index of stocks underlying the futures contract

The terms *program trading* and **index arbitrage** often are used together. In general terms, index arbitrage refers to attempts to exploit the differences between the prices of the stock-index futures and the prices of the index of stocks underlying the futures contract. For example, if the S&P 500 futures price is too high relative to the S&P 500 Index, investors could short the futures contract and buy the stocks in the index. In theory, arbitrageurs should be able to build a hedged portfolio that earns arbitrage profits equaling the difference between the two positions. If the price of the S&P 500 futures is deemed too low, investors could purchase the futures and short the stocks, again exploiting the differences between the two prices.

If investors are to be able to take advantage of discrepancies between the futures price and the underlying stock-index price, they must be able to act quickly. Program trading involves the use of computer-generated orders to coordinate buy and sell orders for entire portfolios based on arbitrage opportunities. The arbitrage occurs between portfolios of common stocks, on the one hand, and index futures and options, on the other.

Large institutional investors seek to exploit differences between the two sides. Specifically, when stock-index futures prices rise substantially above the current value of the stock index itself (e.g., the S&P 500), they sell the futures and buy the underlying stocks, typically in "baskets" of several million dollars. Because the futures price and the stock-index value must be equal when the futures contract expires, these investors are seeking to "capture the premium" between the two, thereby earning an arbitrage profit. That is, they seek high risk-free returns by arbitraging the difference between the cash value of the underlying securities and the prices of the futures contracts on these securities. In effect, they have a hedged position and should profit regardless of what happens to stock prices.

Normally, program traders and other speculators "unwind" their positions during the last trading hour of the day the futures expire. At this time, the futures premium goes to zero, because, as noted, the futures price at expiration must equal the stock-index value.

The headlines about program trading often reflect the results of rapid selling by the program traders. For whatever reason, traders decide to sell the futures. As the price falls, stock prices also fall. When the futures price drops below the price of the stock index, tremendous selling orders can be unleashed. These volume sell orders in stocks drive the futures prices even lower.

Speculating with Stock-Index Futures   In addition to the previous hedging strategies (and others not described), investors can speculate with stock-index futures if they wish to profit from stock market volatility by judging and acting on the likely market trends. Stock-index futures are effective instruments for speculating on movements in the stock market because:

1. Minimal costs are involved in establishing a futures position.
2. Stock-index futures mirror the market, offering just as much risk.

We can refer to one group of speculators as "active traders." These individuals are willing to risk their capital on price changes they expect to occur in the futures contracts. Such individuals are often sophisticated investors who are seeking the opportunity for large gains and who understand the risk they are assuming.

The strategies of active traders basically include long and short positions. Traders who expect the market to rise buy index futures. Because of the high leverage, the profit opportunities are great; however, the loss opportunities are equally great. The same is true for traders expecting a market decline who assume a short position by selling a stock-index futures contract. Selling a contract is a convenient way to go short the entire market. It can be done at any time.

Another form of speculation involves spreaders, who establish both long and short positions at the same time. Their objective is to profit from changes in price relationships between two futures contracts. Spreads include the following:

1. The intramarket spread, also known as a calendar or time spread. This spread involves contracts for two different settlement months, such as buying a March contract and selling a June contract.
2. The intermarket spread, also known as a quality spread. This spread involves two different markets, such as buying a NYSE contract and selling a S&P contract (both for the same month).

Spreaders are interested in relative price as opposed to absolute price changes. If two different contracts appear to be out of line, the spreader hopes to profit by buying one contract and selling the other and waiting for the price difference to adjust. This adjustment may require the spread between the two contracts to widen in some cases and narrow in others.

Single Stock Futures

A more recent innovation in financial futures is the single stock futures (SSFs). These are futures contracts on individual stocks as well as on the exchange traded fund for the DJIA, called DIAMONDS®. These futures are traded on a newer exchange, OneChicago, a joint venture of the Chicago Board Options Exchange, the Chicago Mercantile Exchange, and the Chicago Board of Trade. It is a wholly electronic futures exchange.

Like other futures contracts, SSFs are standardized agreements between two parties to buy or sell 100 shares of a specified stock in the future at a price determined today. The minimum price fluctuation ("tick") is one cent per share, or $1 per contract (contracts are for 100 shares). There are no daily price limits. The initial margin requirement is 20 percent, providing substantial leverage for these contracts. Note that SSFs settle to physical delivery rather than cash. The contract cannot be exercised early. Of course, a contract can be offset prior to expiration.

Using SSFs   As we would expect from what we have learned, an investor buys or "goes long" a SSF contract if he or she believes that the price of a particular stock will rise, and sells or "goes short" a SSF contract if the price is expected to decline. Shorting is easily accomplished. As always with a futures contract, both a buy and sell are involved, and which is done first really does not matter in terms of the process working smoothly.

Example 20-9   Assume an investor buys 10 contracts on Microsoft at $50, and sells them two months later at $60. The profit on this position would be

$$[\$60 - \$50] \times 100 \text{ shares} \times 10 \text{ contracts} = \$10,000$$

The primary advantages of SSFs may be the low cost and ease with which short selling can be accomplished. Some investors will view the 20 percent margin requirement as an advantage, but it can also be a significant disadvantage if the price moves against the investor, particularly when multiple contracts are involved.

Example 20-10   Assume an investor shorts 10 contracts on Microsoft at $50, and buys them back at $57. The loss on this position would be

$$[\$50 - \$57] \times 100 \text{ shares} \times 10 \text{ contracts} = -\$7,000.$$

How SSFs Differ from Stocks and Options   SSFs have price and risk profiles that are similar to stocks. For example, if the stock price goes up, the futures price will also go up in all but the most unusual circumstances. On the other hand, the payoff profile for options is often nonlinear, consisting of two or more different segments. Options truncate the returns distribution, while futures do not. There are several variables that affect the prices of options, while futures prices are more straightforward.

On the other hand, SSFs are like any other futures in some respects, and therefore differ from stocks. Margin for futures represents funds to ensure that obligations are met, not funds to finance part of the purchase or short sell of the stock. There is no interest to pay on the loan as in the case of margin with stocks. Profits and losses are credited to an investor's account daily. SSF prices are often higher than the actual stock because the price of the SSF includes the cost of interest.

The Future of SSFs   Because SSFs are a relatively recent innovation, it is difficult to say how successful they will be, and the total impact they will have on investors. They clearly offer investors one more tool in hedging risk and constructing specific return-risk profiles. At their introduction, some critics immediately questioned their necessity, or even desirability. However, it is worthwhile to remember that foreign-currency futures, exchange traded funds, and stock-index futures were also attacked by some critics at their introduction. Each has gone on to be quite successful. ETFs, for example, started slowly, but total volume today is very respectable.

Summary

▶ Futures markets play an important role in risk management.

▶ Spot markets are markets for immediate delivery. Forward markets are markets for deferred delivery.

▶ An organized futures exchange standardizes the nonstandard forward contracts, with only the price and number of contracts left for futures traders to negotiate.

▶ A futures contract designates a specific amount of a particular item to be delivered at a specified date in the future at a currently determined market price.

▶ Buyers assume long positions and sellers assume short positions. A short position indicates only that a contract not previously purchased is sold.

▶ Most contracts are settled by offset, whereby a position is liquidated by an offsetting transaction. The clearinghouse is on the other side of every transaction and ensures that all payments are made as specified.

▶ Contracts are traded on designated futures exchanges, which set minimum price changes and may establish daily price limits.

▶ Futures positions must be closed out within a specified time. There are no certificates and no specialists to handle the trading. Each futures contract is traded in an auction market process by a system of "open-outcry."

▶ Margin, the norm in futures trading, is the "good faith" deposit made to ensure completion of the contract.

▶ All futures contracts are marked to the market daily; that is, all profits and losses are credited and debited to each investor's account daily.

▶ Hedgers buy or sell futures contracts to offset the risk in some other position.

▶ Speculators buy or sell futures contracts in an attempt to earn a return and are valuable to the proper functioning of the market.

▶ Interest rate futures, one of the two principal types of financial futures, allow investors to hedge against, and speculate on, interest rate movements. Numerous contracts are available on both domestic instruments and foreign instruments.

▶ Investors can, among other transactions, execute short hedges to protect their long positions in bonds.

▶ Stock-index futures are available on the NYSE Composite Index, the S&P 500 Index, and numerous other indexes, both domestic and foreign.

▶ Investors can use stock-index futures to hedge the systematic risk of common stocks—that is, broad market movements.

▶ Short hedges protect a stock position against a market decline, and long hedges protect against having to pay more for an equity position because prices rise before the investment can be made.

▶ Index arbitrage refers to attempts to exploit the differences between the prices of the stock-index futures and the prices of the index of stocks underlying the futures contract.

▶ Single stock futures are standardized agreements between two parties to buy or sell 100 shares of a specified stock in the future at a price determined today.

Questions

20-1 Carefully describe a futures contract.

20-2 How do forward contracts differ from futures contracts?

20-3 Explain how futures contracts are valued daily and how most contracts are settled.

20-4 Describe the role of the clearinghouses in futures trading.

20-5 What determines if an investor receives a margin call?

20-6 Describe the differences between trading in stocks and trading in futures contracts.

20-7 What does it mean to say that futures trading is a zero-sum game?

20-8 How do financial futures differ from other futures contracts?

20-9 Explain the differences between a hedger and a speculator.

20-10 What is meant by basis? When is the basis positive?

20-11 Which side benefits from a strengthening basis? A weakening basis?

20-12 Given a futures contract on Treasury bonds, determine the dollar price of a contract quoted at 80−5, 90−24, and 69−2.

20-13 When might a portfolio manager with a bond position use a short hedge involving interest rate futures?

20-14 Is it possible to construct a perfect hedge? Why or why not?

20-15 Why would an investor have preferences among the different stock-index futures?

20-16 Which is the most popular stock-index futures contract? Where is it traded?

20-17 Which type of risk does stock-index futures allow investors to hedge? Why would this be desirable?

20-18 Explain how a pension fund might use a long hedge with stock-index futures.

20-19 When would an investor likely do the following?
a. Buy a call on a stock index.
b. Buy a put on interest rate futures.

20-20 What is program trading? How does it work?

CFA
20-21 Explain why you agree or disagree with the following statement: "One difference between futures and forward contracts is that futures contracts are marked to market while forward contracts are not."

CFA
20-22 Explain why you agree or disagree with the following statement: "Futures and forward contracts expose the parties to the same degree of counterparty risk."

CFA
20-23 Mr. Dawson is a portfolio manager who is responsible for the account of the Pizza Delivery Personnel Union (PDPU). At this time, the trustees have not authorized Mr. Dawson to take positions in Treasury bond futures contracts. At his quarterly meeting with PDPU's board of trustees, Mr. Dawson requested that the board grant him authorization to use Treasury bond futures to control interest rate risk. One of the trustees asked whether it was necessary to use Treasury bond futures contracts to control risk. The trustee noted that Mr. Dawson already had authorization by the investment guidelines to short Treasury securities, and that should be sufficient to control interest rate risk when combined with the opportunity to buy Treasury securities. What advantages could Mr. Dawson present to the trustee for using Treasury futures contracts to control risk, rather than using Treasury securities?

Problems

20-1 Assume that an investor buys one March NYSE Composite Index futures contract on February 1 at 67.2. The position is closed out after five days. The prices on the four days after purchase were 67.8, 68.1, 68, and 68.5. The initial margin is $3,000.
a. Calculate the current equity on each of the next four days.
b. Calculate the excess equity for these four days.
c. Calculate the final gain or loss for the week.
d. Recalculate (a), (b), and (c) assuming that the investor had been short over this same period.

20-2 Given the information in Problem 20-1, assume that the investor holds until the contract expires. Ignore the four days after purchase and assume that on the next to last day of trading in March the investor was long and the final settlement price on that date was 70.2. Calculate the cumulative profit.

Computational Problems

20-1 Calculate the dollar gain or loss on Treasury bond futures contracts ($100,000) per contract for the following transactions. In each case the position is held six months before closing it out.

a. Sell 10 T-bond contracts at a price of 82−18 and buy 10 at 76−20.

b. Sell 10 T-bond contracts at a price of 78−14 and buy 10 at 75.

c. Buy 15 T-bond contracts at 62−20 and sell 15 at 65−24.

d. Sell one T-bond contract at 70−10 and buy one at 78−48.

20-2 Assume a portfolio manager holds $1 million of 5.2 percent Treasury bonds due 2010−2015. The current market price is 76−2, for a yield of 6.95 percent. The manager fears a rise in interest rates in the next three months and wishes to protect this position against such a rise by hedging in futures.

a. Ignoring weighted hedges, what should the manager do?

b. Assume T-bond futures contracts are available at 68, and the price three months later is 59−8. If the manager constructs the correct hedge, what is the gain or loss on this position?

c. The price of the Treasury bonds three months later is 67−12. What is the gain or loss on this cash position?

d. What is the net effect of this hedge?

Checking Your Understanding

20-1 Forward contracts can be tailored to individual requirements in terms of quantities, time, etc. Futures contracts are specified and fixed as to characteristics such as those, and may not match a buyer or seller's requirements.

20-2 The clearinghouse acts as the seller to every buyer, thereby assuring the performance of the contracts. The clearinghouse, in turn, will look to its clearing members to make good on all obligations. Finally, the clearing members will have to deal with any individual customers who may have shortages in their accounts. Of course, by marking to the market, most of the gains and losses have been settled prior to the expiration date.

20-3 Futures trading is a zero-sum game. The aggregate gains must equal the aggregate losses. Futures contracts are marked to the market daily. The buyer's gains (losses) must equal the seller's losses (gains).

20-4 With a forward contract, the gains and losses involved are settled at contract expiration. No money changes hands until then. With a futures contract, each account is marked to the market daily; therefore, gains and losses are recorded daily. On the last day of the contract's life, there is only one day of gains and losses to account for.

20-5 A hedger typically owns the underlying asset—he or she is said to be long the cash position, or asset. Therefore, the hedger is trying to reduce risk by selling a futures contract. A speculator, on the other hand, does not typically have a position in the asset. He or she is simply trying to profit by anticipated price changes in the underlying item.

chapter 21

All Investors Must Consider Portfolio Management

As you near the end of your study of investing tools and techniques, which will help you handle your inheritance, you realize that you have covered a number of important topics. However, it sometimes seems that you are seeing the trees, but not the forest. It strikes you that all of this might make more sense if there was a clear framework for thinking about all the issues you need to consider when investing and managing your assets. And, in fact, there is. You can do some financial planning and manage your portfolio in an orderly, sensible manner. By doing this, you see where the various pieces fit, and you are less likely to overlook one or more important issues.

Chapter 21 considers how investors should go about actually planning the management of their financial assets. We consider why and how financial planning should be thought of as an ongoing, systematic process. Having a framework within which to make financial decisions in general, and portfolio decisions in particular, allows investors to be more consistent in managing their portfolios. We also analyze some personal financial planning issues, such as taxes, protection against inflation, potential market returns, the life cycle of investors, and other related issues.

AFTER READING THIS CHAPTER YOU WILL BE ABLE TO:

▶ Organize the management of your portfolio in a logical, systematic manner.

▶ Better understand some personal financial planning issues.

▶ Better assess some issues of major importance, such as asset allocation.

A Perspective on Investing in Financial Assets

The investment of funds in various assets is only part of the overall financial decision making and planning that most individuals must do. Before investing, each individual should develop an overall financial plan. Such a plan should include the decision on whether to purchase a house, which for most individuals represents a major investment. This has never been more important than today, given the collapse of the housing market in the last few years. Tax planning is an ongoing important activity because most financial decisions involve taxes one way or the other. Mistakes in tax planning can be very costly. In addition, decisions must be made about insurance of various types—life, health, disability, and protection of business and property. Finally, the plan should provide for emergency reserve funds.[1]

Managing Your Financial Assets

The management of your assets should be viewed within an organized framework regardless of how active or not investors plan to be in selecting and holding their financial assets. As we saw when we examined portfolio theory, the relationships among the various investment alternatives that are held as a portfolio must be considered together if an investor is to hold an optimal portfolio and achieve his or her investment objectives.

Financial planning can be thought of as an ongoing process. Good financial planning calls for an organized, systematic framework. When we consider our financial assets, we can examine detailed models for managing these assets. For example, the **portfolio management process** has been described by Maginn, Tuttle, McLeavey, and Pinto in a book on managing investment portfolios as part of the CFA Institute Investment Series.[2] CFA Institute, the successor organization to the Association for Investment Management and Research, awards the CFA designation and acts as the professional organization for the investment industry. It advocates the highest levels of professional standards and ethical conduct, and takes positions on issues of importance to the capital markets.

Managing your portfolio in a systematic manner is an important development because of its contrast with the past, where it was typically done by matching investors with portfolios on an individual basis, one investor at the time. However, investors should arrange the management of their portfolios such that they can execute a thoughtful, organized plan on an ongoing basis rather than react to events and be forced to make ad hoc decisions. Furthermore, if an individual investor chooses to work with a financial planner or financial advisor, having an organized plan will provide a basis for a clear understanding between the two parties. Conflicts often arise because the parameters involved, such as the client's risk tolerance and return expectations, have not been clearly spelled out and agreed to by both parties.

As part of their financial planning, investors can view the management of their portfolios within the following framework.

Portfolio Management Process The second step in the investment decision process, involving the management of a group of assets (i.e., a portfolio) as a unit.

1. Decide what objectives you wish to accomplish and any constraints you may face, along with any particular preferences you have. For example, some investors won't buy the "sin" stocks (alcohol, tobacco, gambling, etc.). Or an investor could feel the need to have a certain amount of liquidity always available.
2. Determine your expectations for the economy and its sectors. Try to assess the outlook for the economy and for the financial markets. Study individual stocks if you are going to be an active investor.
3. Develop a strategy and implement it. This involves asset allocation, portfolio optimization, and selection of securities.
4. Keep up with what is going on with your portfolio on an ongoing basis and be prepared to make changes. An economy moving into deflation has very different implications for

---

[1] Personal finance decisions of this type are discussed in personal finance texts.

[2] See John L. Maginn, CFA, Donald L. Tuttle, CFA, Dennis W. McLeavey, CFA, and Jerald E. Pinto, CFA, eds., *Managing Investment Portfolios: A Dynamic Process*, CFA Institute Investment Series. John Wiley & Sons, Publishers, 2007. This chapter is indebted to this book and earlier editions for the overall format of much of the discussion. While this discussion centers on individual investors and changes the terminology somewhat, it is clearly indebted to the investment process outlined in Maginn et al.

Figure 21-1

The Portfolio Construc-tion, Monitoring, and Revision Process.

Source: Figure 1-1 from "Chapter 1—The Portfolio Process and Its Dynamics" by John L. Margin and Donald L. Tuttle from *MANAGING INVESTMENT PORTFOLIOS: A DYNAMIC PROCESS*, 2/e. Copy-right © CFA Institute. Repro-duced and Republished from Managing Investment Portfolios: A Dynamic Process, 2/e with Per-mission from CFA Institute. All Rights Reserved.

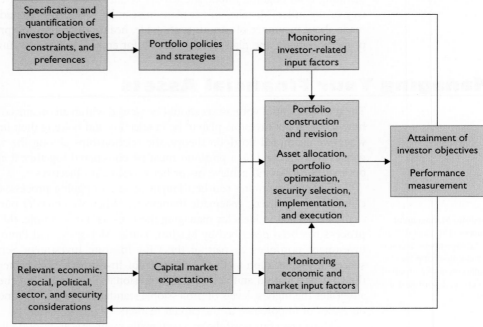

investors than the normal situation. Changes in the current tax laws can have a sig-nificant impact on investors.

5. Rebalance the portfolio as necessary. For example, if you want at least 40 percent bonds in the portfolio and stocks become too large a percentage of the portfolio, rebalance.

6. As part of their financial planning, investors need to know how they are doing as investors. Portfolio performance must be measured and evaluated.

Figure 21-1 illustrates this framework. Notice that it begins with the specification of investor objectives, constraints, and preferences. This should lead investors to articulate what they hope to accomplish when they invest, and how.

INDIVIDUAL INVESTORS VARY WIDELY

Significant differences exist among investors as to objectives, constraints, and preferences. Individual investors may engage in direct investing, indirect investing, or a combination of the two. Investors use differing approaches to the valuation of securities. Some may believe in efficient markets, while others may attempt to use the principles of behavioral finance in their investing activities. Individual investors may find it useful to think of a life-cycle approach, as people go from the beginning of their careers to retirement. Taxes often are a very important consideration for individual investors.

Because each individual's financial profile may be different, individual investors must incorporate their unique factors into their financial planning. Nevertheless, investors should attempt to orient their financial planning toward an organized, logical framework within which they will make and execute decisions. We will refer to this as the **investment strategy**.[3]

Investment Strategy An organized, logical framework within which to make and execute portfolio decisions.

----

[3] This is similar to what Maginn et al. call the *investment policy statement*.

Checking Your Understanding

1. If proper financial planning calls for a framework as described above, do all investors need to structure themselves in a similar manner?
2. If individuals are to a large extent free to act as they choose, why do they need to be explicit in stating their investment strategy?

Formulate an Appropriate Investment Strategy

Along with, or perhaps after, investors work on their financial planning as it pertains to matters such as housing and insurance, they will typically turn to their investments. Many of their tax issues will come up within the confines of investing. The first thing investors need to do in managing their portfolios is to carefully think about what they are trying to achieve, and determine if their investing goals are reasonable. For example, attempting to earn a compound average rate of return of 15 percent annually from a portfolio of stocks over a long period of time is not consistent with the known history of stock returns, as discussed in Chapter 6.

Investors can do this on an informal basis or on a more formal basis. An example of the latter is the approach recommended by Maginn et. al. in formulating an investment strategy which is simply to provide information, in the following order, for an investor.

- OBJECTIVES:
  - return requirements
  - risk tolerance

followed by

- CONSTRAINTS AND PREFERENCES:
  - liquidity
  - time horizon
  - laws and regulations
  - taxes
  - unique preferences and circumstances

Investor Objectives

Return and risk are the basis of all investing decisions.

✓ Portfolio objectives are always going to center on return and risk, because these are the two aspects of most interest to investors, and return and risk are the basis of financial decisions.

Investors seek returns, but must assume risk in order to have an opportunity to earn the returns. A good starting point here is to think in terms of the return-risk tradeoff developed in Chapter 1 and emphasized throughout the text. Expected return and risk are related by an upward-sloping tradeoff, as shown in part (a) of Figure 21-2.

Alternatively, the life-cycle approach can be depicted as shown in part (b) of Figure 21-2. Here we see four different phases in which individual investors view their wealth, although it is important to note that the boundaries between the stages are not necessarily clear cut and can require years to complete. Furthermore, an individual can be a composite of these stages at the same time. The four stages are as follows:

1. *Accumulation Phase* In the early stage of the life cycle, net worth is typically small, but the time horizon is long. Investors can afford to assume large risks.

Figure 21-2

Risk-return position at various life-cycle stages.

SOURCE: Figures 3-5 and 3-6 from "Chapter 3—Individual Investors" by Ronald W. Kaiser in *MANAGING INVESTMENT PORTFOLIOS: A DYNAMIC PROCESS*, 2/e. Copyright © CFA Institute. Reproduced and Republished from Managing Investment Portfolios: A Dynamic Process, 2/e with permission from CFA Institute. All Rights Reserved.

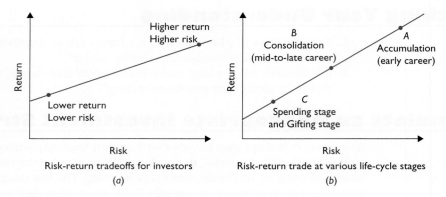

2. *Consolidation Phase* In this phase, involving the mid-to-late career stage of the life cycle when income exceeds expenses, an investment portfolio can be accumulated. A portfolio balance is sought to provide a moderate tradeoff between risk and return.

3. *Spending Phase* In this phase, living expenses are covered from accumulated assets rather than earned income. While some risk-taking is still preferable, the emphasis is on safety, resulting in a relatively low position on the risk-return tradeoff.

4. *Gifting Phase* In this phase, the attitudes about the purpose of investments changes. The basic position on the tradeoff remains about the same as in Stage 3.

ESTABLISHING YOUR RETURN EXPECTATIONS

We know from Chapter 7 that investors must think in terms of expected returns, which implicitly or explicitly involves probability distributions. The future is uncertain, and the best that investors can do is to make probabilistic estimates of likely returns over some holding period, such as one year. Because the future is uncertain, mistakes are inevitable, but this is simply the nature of investing decisions. Estimates of expected returns must be made regardless of the uncertainties, using the best information and investment processes available.

An investor whose portfolio consists only of stocks must ensure that the portfolio is well diversified. The investor who has an asset allocation model must consider how the various asset classes go together to affect the likely outcomes for the expected return of a portfolio.

Inflation Considerations Inflation should be a concern for investors when thinking about the return requirements for a portfolio. The inflation rate of 13 percent in 1979–1980 speaks for itself in terms of the significantly negative impact it had on investors' real wealth. Inflation typically persists steadily across time, at varying rates, eroding values. Over the long run, as we saw in Chapter 6, inflation has compounded at an annual rate of 3 percent. Even at this rate the damage to investors' real wealth is substantial.

Example 21-1 At a 3 percent inflation rate, the purchasing power of a dollar is cut in half in less than 25 years. Therefore, someone retiring at age 60 who lives to approximately 85 and does not protect his or herself from inflation will suffer a drastic decline in purchasing power over the years. According to the Bureau of Labor Statistics, a basket of goods that cost $100 in 1970 cost $583.07 in December 2011.

Some Practical Advice

What, Me Worry About Inflation?

Most investors need to think about the long run when investing. While inflation may have been low in recent years, for the last 80 plus years, the compound annual average rate of inflation has been approximately 3 percent. To bet against this long-run average in favor of recent inflation levels is foolhardy, and will lead to disappointments. Think of someone working for 30 years and inflation averaging a compound rate of 3 percent a year. In today's terms, a dollar will be worth only 41 cents at that time. With 4 percent inflation, it will be worth only 31 cents. Long-run portfolio management without consideration for inflation is a very bad bet—actually, it is irresponsible.

Contrary to some people's beliefs, common stocks are not always an inflationary hedge. In the 1970s, for example, inflation more than doubled to an average annual rate of about 7.5 percent, and the average stock showed a return of slightly less than 6 percent. Nevertheless, common stocks have been one of the best major asset classes to own in terms of maintaining purchasing power over long periods. Historically, inflation has severely damaged bond performance over long periods of time.

The very low inflation rates of the late 1990s and early 2000s, along with talk of deflation in 2008–2011, may have lulled many investors into thinking that inflation is no longer a serious problem, and that they need not consider this issue as very important. It is reasonable to assume that inflation will be higher in the second decade of the 21st century than it was in the first decade of the 21st century; regardless, this is not an issue that investors should ignore. Good financial planning requires investors to always be aware of inflationary possibilities and plan accordingly.

ASSESSING YOUR RISK TOLERANCE

Investors should establish a portfolio risk level that is suitable for them, and then seek the highest returns consistent with that level of risk. We will assume here that investors have a long-run horizon. If not, they should carefully consider the risks that stocks entail, and perhaps hold modest equity positions.

Assuming you are a long-term investor, and that you own an S&P 500—type portfolio, ask yourself what is the worst that is likely to happen to you as an investor in stocks. Ignoring the Great Depression, consider the worst events that have occurred. During the bear market of 1973–1974, investors could have lost about 37 percent of their investment in S&P 500 stocks. During the bear market of 2000–2002, investors could have lost over 40 percent. In 2008, the total return on the S&P 500 was −37 percent. Therefore, it is reasonable to assume that with a long time horizon, investors will face one or more bear markets with approximately 40 percent declines. This is consistent with the long-term standard deviation of S&P 500 returns of about 20 percent—with two standard deviations on either side of the mean return encompassing 95 percent of all returns.

If an investor can accept a loss (at least on paper) of approximately 40 percent once or twice in an investing lifetime, and is otherwise optimistic about the economy and about stocks, the investor can assume the risk of U.S. stocks. On the other hand, if such a potential decline is unacceptable, an investor will need to construct a portfolio with a lower risk profile. For example, a portfolio of 50 percent stocks and 50 percent Treasury bills would cut the risk roughly in half. Other alternatives consisting of stocks and bonds would also decrease the risk.

✓ Perhaps the best way to think about investor objectives is to think about an investor's risk tolerance. Investors decide how much risk they are willing to take, and then attempt to maximize expected return given this level of risk.

Checking Your Understanding

3. Assume you believe that inflation will be higher in the future than it has been in the past, averaging 3.5 percent on a compound annual basis. How can you determine the impact of such an inflation rate on your purchasing power?

What Issues Do Investors Face in Their Financial Planning?

Investors deal with any constraints and preferences they have as the circumstances warrant. Since investors vary widely in their constraints and preferences, these details may vary widely also. Investors should do some careful financial planning to deal with these issues, some of which are analyzed below.

LIQUIDITY NEEDS

Good financial planning requires individuals to consider how they would raise cash in an emergency, or in the event that cash was urgently needed for some purpose. As noted in Chapter 2, liquidity is the ease with which an asset can be sold without a sharp change in price as the result of selling. Obviously, cash equivalents (money market securities) have high liquidity, and are easily sold at close to face value. Many stocks also have great liquidity, but the price at which they are sold will reflect their current market valuations.

Investors must decide how likely they are to sell some part of their portfolio in the short run. As part of the asset allocation decision, they must decide how much of their funds to keep in cash equivalents.

An important consideration in financial planning is the establishment of an emergency fund that will carry you for some period of time if a crisis arises, such as a loss of your job. Individuals have often been advised to build a six-month emergency fund that can be immediately accessed without loss of principal. Building such a fund can be easily incorporated into the overall framework for the management of your assets.

The financial crisis in 2008 gave a whole new emphasis and perspective on liquidity considerations and the importance of considering liquidity when doing financial planning. Borrowing became much more difficult to do, and the cost of borrowing, when available, was considerably higher. Investors wanted liquid positions, and safe positions, as evidenced by the "flight to safety" to Treasury securities. Yields on these securities were extremely low by historical standards, and in the case of Treasury bills even negative for short periods.

TIME HORIZON

Investors need to think about the time period involved in their investment plans. The objectives being pursued may require a strategy that speaks to specific planning horizons. In the case of an individual investor, for example, this could well be the investor's expected lifetime.

It is important to note that investors' time horizons have been shortened in today's world more than they have ever been. Computer-generated models emphasize the short term, and turnover rates for portfolios are at record levels. It appears that many investors are focused on short-term performance, often to their detriment.

As we saw in Chapter 1, investing a sum of money each year for many years can result in a very large ending wealth. This is due to the power of compounding. All individuals, as part of their financial planning, should try to avail themselves of the benefit afforded from compounding. It is indeed a powerful force.

TAX CONSIDERATIONS

Individuals must carefully consider the impact of taxes in their financial planning. The treatment of ordinary income as opposed to capital gains is an important issue because typically there is a differential tax rate. Estates can face taxation, depending upon the current regulations in effect. Even the cash surrender value of whole life insurance can be taxable under certain circumstances.

The tax laws in the United States have been changed several times, making it difficult for investors to forecast the tax rates that will apply in the future. It appears that Americans can count on more changes in the tax code in the future.

Example 21-2

In recent years, dividends have been taxed at 15 percent, the lowest tax rate on dividends in modern history. Furthermore, long-term capital gains have been taxed at a maximum of 15 percent. Ordinary income, on the other hand, could be taxed at a federal rate as high as 35 percent.

In addition to the differential tax rates and their changes over time, the capital gains component of security returns benefits from the fact that the tax is not payable until the gain is realized. This tax deferral is, in effect, a tax-free loan that remains invested for the benefit of the taxpayer. Some securities become "locked up" by the reluctance of investors to pay the capital gains that will result from selling the securities. For example, think about a stock bought for, say, $2 per share 40 years ago that today, after stock splits and growth, is worth $150 per share. Almost the entire proceeds from the sale of such a stock will be taxable if the security is sold—even with a favorable capital gains rate, the tax bill will be sizable.

Retirement programs offer tax sheltering whereby any income and/or capital gains taxes are avoided until such time as the funds are withdrawn. Investors with various retirement and taxable accounts must grapple with the issue of which type of account should hold stocks as opposed to bonds (given that bonds generate higher current income). Many investors must also decide whether to open standard tax-deferred accounts, with a tax savings for the year of opening, or open Roth accounts that will provide tax-free income when withdrawals are made.

Some Practical Advice

One of the easiest and most effective ways for an individual to add value to their portfolio is to be aware of the differences in taxes. Holding a security for more than 12 months, and thereby qualifying for a long-term capital gain, allows the investor to keep 85 percent of the gain since the capital gains tax in this case is 15 percent. In contrast, ordinary income can be taxed at a marginal rate as high as 35 percent. Therefore, one could be giving up an additional 20 percent of the gain to taxes solely as a result of the holding period. Making up such a difference could be difficult to do.

Marginal Tax Rate The tax rate on the last dollar of income

Average Tax Rate Total tax divided by taxable income

In doing their financial planning, investors should be aware of the terminology involved with taxes. Individuals often confuse marginal tax rates and average tax rates, both of which are progressive. Your **marginal tax rate** is the highest tax rate at which your income is taxed. Only part of your income is taxed at a marginal tax rate. Your **average tax rate**, or effective tax rate, on the other hand, is calculated by dividing the actual amount of taxes you pay by all income you receive.

Example 21-3 An investor with a 10 percent rate of return would have an 8.5 percent after-tax rate of return with a long-term capital gain. The same rate of return taxed at the top federal marginal tax rate of 35 percent would result in a 6.5 percent rate of return, which is 31 percent less.

REGULATIONS

Investors must obviously deal with the rulings and regulations of state and federal agencies. Individuals are subject to relatively few such requirements, while a particular institutional portfolio, such as an endowment fund or a pension fund, is subject to several legal and regulatory requirements.[4,5]

Investors must deal with a number of regulations when it comes to tax-deferred accounts such as IRAs, Keoghs, SEPs, and so forth. There are strict rules on contribution amounts, and the timing of these contributions, as well as on withdrawals. Financial planning is very important in this area as mistakes—both omission and commission—can be costly.

UNIQUE INDIVIDUAL CIRCUMSTANCES

Investors often face a variety of unique circumstances. Therefore, there are many paths that financial planning can take. An individual who is 40 may plan to retire in 10 more years. Or an individual may feel that their life span is threatened by illness, and wish to benefit within a certain period of time. Individuals may be able to count on inheritances down the road, thereby taking some of the financial pressures off of them.

Almost regardless of the various circumstances that individuals may face, having a carefully thought out financial plan is important. Objectives need to be clearly specified, and contingencies planned for.

Investor Expectations as a Part of Financial Planning

RATE OF RETURN ASSUMPTIONS

Most investors base their actions on some assumptions about the rate of return expected from various assets. Obviously, it is important for investors to plan their investing activities based on realistic rate of return assumptions.

As a starting point, investors should study carefully the historical rates of return available in such sources as the data provided by Ibbotson Associates or the comparable data discussed in Chapter 6. We know the historical mean returns, both arithmetic and geometric, and the standard deviation of the returns for major asset classes such as stocks, bonds, and bills.

Having analyzed the historical series of returns, there are several difficulties in forming expectations about future returns. For example, how much should investors be influenced by recent stock market returns, particularly when they are unusually good or bad returns?

---

[4] With regard to fiduciary responsibilities, one of the most famous concepts is the Prudent Man Rule. This rule, which concerns fiduciaries, goes back to 1830, although it was not formally stated until more than 100 years later. Basically, the rule states that a fiduciary, in managing assets for another party, shall act like people of "prudence, discretion, and intelligence" act in governing their own affairs.

[5] One of the important pieces of federal legislation governing institutional investors is the Employment Retirement Income Security Act, referred to as ERISA. This act, administered by the Department of Labor, regulates employer-sponsored retirement plans. It requires that plan assets be diversified and that the standards being applied under the act be applied to management of the portfolio as a whole.

Example 21-4

The cumulative gain on the S&P 500 Index for 1995 and 1996 was 69.2 percent, the best two-year period in a generation and one of the best in the history of stock market returns for this index (only four other consecutive two-year periods were better as measured by the S&P 500). The geometric mean of approximately 30 percent a year for the years 1995 and 1996 was slightly more than three times the annual average gain for common stocks over many years.

Do investors form unrealistic expectations about future returns as a result of such activity? In the four previous cases of two-year cumulative returns averaging 30 percent per year or more (comparable to 1995–1996), the average annual return for the next five years was negative in two cases (−7.5 percent and −11.2 percent), and less than 9 percent in two cases of positive returns. Moreover, most observers believe that stock returns tend to "revert toward the mean" over time—that is, periods of unusually high returns tend to be followed by periods of lower returns (although not necessarily losses), and the opposite is also true.

Following the bottom that was reached in the stock market in August 1982, the S&P 500 Composite Index showed a compound annual average return of approximately 18.5 percent a year for the years 1982–1999. This is almost double the long-run average return of about 9.5 percent a year for the years 1926–2011. And the return was negative in only one year, 1990, and this was relatively small. However, the years 2000–2002 brought substantial losses in the stock market, followed by five years of positive stock returns, one of which (2003) was 28 percent. Therefore, we need to ask how investor expectations about stock returns are influenced by these unusually good, and bad, returns in recent years? How are investors, particularly relatively new investors, affected by this history as they form expectations about future returns?

What about 2008, one of the most extraordinary years in market history in terms of volatility, violent daily fluctuations in market indexes, and stock market losses? Investment banks failed (Lehman Brothers), others were reorganized (Goldman Sachs), short sale restrictions were imposed, massive bailouts of financial institutions occurred, and government intervention in the economic system took place on an unprecedented scale. Should 2008 be recognized as an anomaly, not likely (hopefully) to reoccur, or should it be included in future planning when assessing likely market returns?

Investors should recognize some key points about future rates of return. In estimating the expected return on stocks (as proxied by the S&P 500), we can combine the riskless rate and the expected risk premium for large company stocks. The expected equity risk premium to be used in this calculation is based on the *arithmetic mean* of equity risk premiums and not the geometric mean because this is an additive relationship.

A second key point that investors should recognize in thinking about expected rates of return, and the returns they can realistically expect to achieve, is that common stock returns involve considerable risk. While we know that the annual average compound rate of return on common stocks for the period 1926–2010, according to Table 6-6, was 9.6 percent, that does not mean that all investors can realistically expect to achieve this historical rate of return. To see this, we can analyze the probabilities of actually realizing various compound rates of return over time.

Jones and Wilson have analyzed data for the S&P 500 index using "corrected" S&P observations.[6] The differences in this mean and that provided by Ibbotson Associates and others stems from a difference in the data used for the earlier years of the S&P 500. Ibbotson Associates uses 90 companies from 1926 to 1957, while Jones and Wilson use a larger number of companies.

---

[6] See Charles P. Jones and Jack W. Wilson, "Probabilities Associated with Common Stock Returns," *The Journal of Portfolio Management* (Fall 1995): pp. 21–32.

Jones and Wilson determined from a statistical analysis of the data that the historical returns on the S&P 500 Index are lognormally distributed, which means that we can use compound rates of return to estimate probabilities based on the mean and standard deviation of the logs of annual total returns. These probabilities are calculated and reported as the probabilities of achieving any specifierd *compound* annual average rate of return over any specified holding period. It is important to note that these are probabilities of achieving *at least* the stated compound rate of return or more.

Table 21-1 shows the probabilities of achieving at least a specified compound rate of return, or *more*, based on the history of the S&P 500 Index over the period 1926–2011 (updated from Table 6-6). In analyzing this table, note that the approximate geometric mean for the revised S&P 500 for this period was 9.5 percent. These probabilities should be interpreted in the following manner: "Based *solely* on the entire history of annual returns on the S&P Index for the period 1926–2011, where the geometric mean was approximately 9.5 percent, what are the probabilities of achieving *at least* a specified *compound* rate of return over various holding periods ranging from one to 40 years?"

As Table 21-1 shows, the probability of achieving approximately 9.5 percent or more on a compound basis is (essentially) 50 percent, regardless of the holding period. Note that for rates of

Table 21-1 Estimated Probabilities of Receiving a Specified Compound Annual Average Rate of Return, or Greater, for Various Holding Periods for the S&P 500 Stocks Based on Data for 1926–2011

Per annum return %	Years											
	1	2	3	4	5	10	15	20	25	30	35	40
40	0.09	0.03	0.01	0.00	0.00	0.00	0.00	0.00	0.00	0.00	0.00	0.00
35	0.13	0.05	0.02	0.01	0.01	0.00	0.00	0.00	0.00	0.00	0.00	0.00
30	0.17	0.09	0.05	0.03	0.02	0.00	0.00	0.00	0.00	0.00	0.00	0.00
29	0.18	0.10	0.06	0.04	0.02	0.00	0.00	0.00	0.00	0.00	0.00	0.00
28	0.20	0.11	0.07	0.04	0.03	0.00	0.00	0.00	0.00	0.00	0.00	0.00
27	0.21	0.13	0.08	0.05	0.03	0.01	0.00	0.00	0.00	0.00	0.00	0.00
26	0.22	0.14	0.09	0.06	0.04	0.01	0.00	0.00	0.00	0.00	0.00	0.00
25	0.23	0.15	0.10	0.07	0.05	0.01	0.00	0.00	0.00	0.00	0.00	0.00
24	0.25	0.17	0.12	0.09	0.06	0.02	0.00	0.00	0.00	0.00	0.00	0.00
23	0.26	0.18	0.14	0.10	0.08	0.02	0.01	0.00	0.00	0.00	0.00	0.00
22	0.28	0.20	0.15	0.12	0.09	0.03	0.01	0.00	0.00	0.00	0.00	0.00
21	0.29	0.22	0.17	0.14	0.11	0.04	0.02	0.01	0.00	0.00	0.00	0.00
20	0.31	0.24	0.19	0.16	0.13	0.06	0.03	0.01	0.01	0.00	0.00	0.00
19	0.33	0.26	0.22	0.18	0.16	0.08	0.04	0.02	0.01	0.01	0.00	0.00
18	0.34	0.28	0.24	0.21	0.18	0.10	0.06	0.03	0.02	0.01	0.01	0.01
17	0.36	0.31	0.27	0.24	0.21	0.13	0.08	0.05	0.04	0.02	0.02	0.01
16	0.38	0.33	0.29	0.27	0.24	0.16	0.11	0.08	0.06	0.04	0.03	0.02
15	0.40	0.35	0.32	0.30	0.28	0.20	0.15	0.12	0.09	0.07	0.06	0.05
14	0.41	0.38	0.35	0.33	0.31	0.25	0.20	0.17	0.14	0.12	0.10	0.09
13	0.43	0.41	0.39	0.37	0.35	0.30	0.26	0.23	0.20	0.18	0.16	0.14
12	0.45	0.43	0.42	0.41	0.39	0.35	0.32	0.30	0.28	0.26	0.24	0.23
11	0.47	0.46	0.45	0.44	0.44	0.41	0.39	0.38	0.36	0.35	0.34	0.33
10	0.49	0.49	0.49	0.48	0.48	0.47	0.47	0.46	0.46	0.46	0.45	0.45
9	0.51	0.52	0.52	0.52	0.53	0.54	0.55	0.55	0.56	0.57	0.57	0.58
8	0.53	0.55	0.56	0.56	0.57	0.60	0.62	0.64	0.66	0.67	0.68	0.70

Table 21-1 Continued

Per annum return %	Years											
	1	2	3	4	5	10	15	20	25	30	35	40
7	0.55	0.57	0.59	0.60	0.62	0.66	0.70	0.72	0.75	0.77	0.78	0.80
6	0.57	0.60	0.63	0.64	0.66	0.72	0.76	0.79	0.82	0.84	0.86	0.88
5	0.59	0.63	0.66	0.68	0.70	0.77	0.82	0.85	0.88	0.90	0.92	0.93
4	0.61	0.66	0.69	0.72	0.74	0.82	0.87	0.90	0.93	0.94	0.96	0.97
3	0.63	0.69	0.72	0.75	0.78	0.86	0.91	0.94	0.96	0.97	0.98	0.98
2	0.65	0.71	0.75	0.79	0.81	0.89	0.94	0.96	0.98	0.98	0.99	0.99
1	0.67	0.74	0.78	0.82	0.84	0.92	0.96	0.98	0.99	0.99	1.00	1.00
0	0.69	0.76	0.81	0.84	0.87	0.94	0.97	0.99	0.99	1.00	1.00	1.00
−1	0.71	0.79	0.83	0.87	0.89	0.96	0.99	0.99	1.00	1.00	1.00	1.00
−2	0.73	0.81	0.86	0.89	0.92	0.97	0.99	1.00	1.00	1.00	1.00	1.00
−3	0.75	0.83	0.88	0.91	0.93	0.98	1.00	1.00	1.00	1.00	1.00	1.00
−4	0.77	0.85	0.90	0.93	0.95	0.99	1.00	1.00	1.00	1.00	1.00	1.00
−5	0.78	0.87	0.91	0.94	0.96	0.99	1.00	1.00	1.00	1.00	1.00	1.00
−6	0.80	0.88	0.93	0.95	0.97	1.00	1.00	1.00	1.00	1.00	1.00	1.00
−7	0.82	0.90	0.94	0.96	0.98	1.00	1.00	1.00	1.00	1.00	1.00	1.00
−8	0.83	0.91	0.95	0.97	0.98	1.00	1.00	1.00	1.00	1.00	1.00	1.00
−9	0.85	0.93	0.96	0.98	0.99	1.00	1.00	1.00	1.00	1.00	1.00	1.00
−10	0.86	0.94	0.97	0.99	0.99	1.00	1.00	1.00	1.00	1.00	1.00	1.00
−15	0.92	0.98	0.99	1.00	1.00	1.00	1.00	1.00	1.00	1.00	1.00	1.00
−20	0.96	0.99	1.00	1.00	1.00	1.00	1.00	1.00	1.00	1.00	1.00	1.00
−25	0.98	1.00	1.00	1.00	1.00	1.00	1.00	1.00	1.00	1.00	1.00	1.00
−30	0.99	1.00	1.00	1.00	1.00	1.00	1.00	1.00	1.00	1.00	1.00	1.00
−35	1.00	1.00	1.00	1.00	1.00	1.00	1.00	1.00	1.00	1.00	1.00	1.00

return of 9.5 percent or more, the probabilities of achieving that rate of return *decrease* over time, contrary to assertions of many market observers that the risk of owning common stocks decreases over time. On the other hand, the probabilities of achieving at least a 9 percent rate of return, or an 8 percent rate of return, or any lower return, increase over time because these rates of return are below the geometric mean return for the period. Nevertheless, after 40 years the probability of earning a compound rate of return of 9 percent or more on the S&P 500, based on this long history, is only .58—thus, investors have almost a 40 percent chance of earning 9 percent or less if the future is like the past. Even for a compound rate of return of 8 percent or more, the probability after 40 years is only 70 percent, which means there is a 30 percent chance of earning 8 percent or less.

The message from Table 21-1 is important. Based on the known history of stock returns, the chance that an investor will actually achieve some compound rate of return over time from owning common stocks may not be as high as he or she believes. Common stocks are risky, and expected returns are not guaranteed.

Checking Your Understanding

4. The geometric mean for the S&P 500 for the period 1926–2011 was 9.5 percent. What was the probability, based on the returns data, of earning 9.5 percent or more for any holding period?

Implementing Investing Strategies

Portfolio construction can be viewed from a broad perspective as consisting of the following steps (again, given the investor's investing strategy and capital market expectations):

1. Define the universe of securities to be considered for inclusion in a particular portfolio. This step is really the asset allocation decision, probably the key decision made by investment managers.
2. Utilize an optimization procedure to select securities and determine the proper portfolio weights for these securities.

Both of these steps are discussed in more detail following.

ASSET ALLOCATION

As discussed in Chapter 8, the asset allocation decision involves deciding the percentage of investable funds an investor will place in asset classes such as stocks, bonds, cash equivalents, and so forth. While multiple asset classes are available, for discussion purposes we can think of the asset allocation decision in terms of stocks, bonds, and safe assets (Treasury bills), because most investors hold some or all of these three asset classes.[7]

Within an asset class, highly diversified portfolios will tend to produce similar returns over time. However, different asset classes are likely to produce results that are quite dissimilar. Therefore, differences in asset allocation will be the key factor over time causing differences in portfolio performance.

William Sharpe, a winner of the Nobel prize in Economics, has stated that when he breaks down the performance results of pension fund managers, including not only the major asset classes but also growth and value stocks, "asset allocation accounts for 98 percent or more of the returns." As Sharpe noted, "those are really profound numbers."

Example 21-5   To appreciate the importance of the asset allocation decision, think of an investor with a five-year investment horizon making this decision at the beginning of 1995. If this investor had placed all of his or her portfolio funds in stocks, the investor would have enjoyed great success as the market compounded at 20 over percent for the next five years. On the other hand, think of this investor making the decision at the beginning of 2000, with a three-year horizon. A 100 percent commitment to stocks would have resulted in large losses as the market declined sharply. In contrast, the investor who placed all of his or her funds in bonds at the beginning of 2000 would have been spared this debacle, and enjoyed nice returns.

✓ Asset allocation is the most important investment decision made by investors because it is the basic determinant of the return and risk taken. Having allocated funds to asset classes, an investor's fate is largely determined assuming adequate diversification.

---

[7] Strategic asset allocation is usually done once every few years, thereby establishing a long-run, or strategic, asset mix. Tactical asset allocation is performed routinely, driven by changes in predictions concerning asset returns. In effect, tactical asset allocation is a market timing approach to portfolio management intended to increase exposure to a particular market when its performance is expected to be good, and decrease exposure when performance is expected to be poor.

The Asset Allocation Decision Important considerations in making the asset allocation decision include the investor's return requirements (current income versus future income), the investor's risk tolerance, and the time horizon. This is done in conjunction with the investment manager's expectations about the capital markets and about individual assets, as described above.

How asset allocation decisions are made by investors remains a subject that is not fully understood. It is known that actual allocation decisions often differ widely from how investors say they will allocate assets.

According to some analyses, asset allocation is closely related to the age of an investor. This involves the so-called life-cycle theory of asset allocation. This makes intuitive sense because the needs and financial positions of workers in their 50s will differ on average from those who are starting out in their 20s. According to the life-cycle theory, for example, as individuals approach retirement they become more risk-averse.

Table 21-2 illustrates the asset allocation decision by presenting two examples to show how major changes during life can affect asset allocation. One investor is "conservative," and one "aggressive." They begin their investment programs with different allocations and end with different allocations, but their responses to major changes over the life cycle are similar. Both investors have a minimum of 50 percent allocated to stocks at all stages of the life cycle because of the need for growth.

Table 21-2, published in *AAII Journal*, a magazine for individual investors, is illustrative only. Different investors will choose different allocations. Lifestyle changes could cause investors to move from one stage to the other, or changes in life may not cause a change in the allocation percentages. Moreover, even among similar age groups, goals can vary substantially. Overall, asset allocation decisions may depend more upon goals than age. The important point is that all investors must make the asset allocation decision, and this decision will have a major impact on the investment results achieved.

It seems reasonable to assert that the level of risk tolerance affects the asset allocation decision. Some research has been done on the risk preferences of U.S. households using available financial data. The definitions of risk used varied, but a reasonable measure is, investors' tolerance for risk relative to wealth. Not surprisingly, differences in relative risk-aversion across groups of individuals based on age and levels of wealth. As we might expect, income and wealth affect asset allocation decisions in a positive manner.

Table 21-2 How Major Changes Can Affect Your Asset Allocation.

	Conservative			Aggressive		
Asset Category	Early Career (%)	Late Career (%)	Retirement (%)	Early Career (%)	Late Career (%)	Retirement (%)
Cash	10	10	10	10	10	10
Bonds	20	30	40	0	10	10
Large-Cap Stocks	40	40	40	30	40	50
Small-Cap Stocks	15	10	5	30	20	15
International Stocks	15	10	5	30	20	15

SOURCE: Maria Crawford Scott. "How Major Changes in Your Life Can Affect Your Asset Allocation," *AAII Journal*, October 1995, p. 17. Copyright © 1995 by the American Association of Individual Investors. Reprinted by permission.

Investments Intuition

All Investors Are Asset Allocators

All investors make asset allocation decisions, whether they realize it or not. If you choose to put your investment funds under the mattress, you have allocated your funds 100 percent to cash. If you use all your funds to buy a CD, you have made an asset allocation decision to hold fixed-income securities. Quite simply, when it comes to asset allocation, doing nothing is actually doing something—holding cash, earning no return, taking no risk, but ultimately at the very least losing to inflation.

PORTFOLIO OPTIMIZATION

Stated at its simplest, portfolio construction involves the selection of securities to be included in the portfolio and the determination of portfolio funds (the weights) to be placed in each security. As we know from Chapter 7, the Markowitz model provides the basis for a scientific portfolio construction resulting in efficient portfolios. An efficient portfolio, as discussed in Chapter 8, is one with the highest level of expected return for a given level of risk, or the lowest risk for a given level of expected return.

On a formal basis, the Markowitz model provides an organized framework for portfolio optimization, which allows investors to construct portfolios that are efficient. The basic concepts pioneered by Markowitz are widely known and used today by money managers and investors to varying degrees.

Financial Planning on an Ongoing Basis

It is important for individuals to monitor their circumstances on an ongoing basis. As they go through the life cycle, different aspects will assume differing degrees of importance. For example, retirement may not seem important to someone who is starting out their career, but for most people it will become an item of significant interest. As for investing, this is an ongoing and dynamic process, and changes occur rapidly and frequently.

An investor's circumstances can change for several reasons. These can be easily organized in a systematic manner and include:

- *Change in Wealth* A change in wealth may cause an investor to behave differently, possibly accepting more risk in the case of an increase in wealth, or becoming more risk-averse in the case of a decline in wealth.
- *Change in Time Horizon* Traditionally, we think of investors aging and becoming more conservative in their investment approach.
- *Change in Liquidity Requirements* A need for more current income could increase the emphasis on dividend-paying stocks, while a decrease in current income requirements could lead to greater investment in mid-cap and small stocks whose potential payoff may be years in the future.
- *Change in Tax Circumstances* An investor who moves to a higher tax bracket may find municipal bonds more attractive. Also, the timing of the realization of capital gains can become more important.
- *Change in Regulations* Laws affecting investors change regularly, whether tax laws or laws governing retirement accounts, annuities, and so forth.

TAX-ADVANTAGED INVESTING

As mentioned previously, a significant part of personal financial planning has to do with taxes. After all, for investors what is important is not what they make on an investment, but what they get to keep after taxes.

For taxable investors, the impact of taxes should play an important part in their portfolio management strategy. Too often tax considerations are an after-thought, or are handled on an ad hoc basis. Taxes can easily have a larger impact than any other costs associated with a portfolio of securities.

A simple approach to tax-advantaged investing traditionally was to choose a portfolio of growth stocks that would be held for a multiple year period. These stocks generally pay minimal or no dividends, thereby escaping the higher taxation associated with dividends.

The 2003 tax cuts allowed investors to more easily construct a diversified portfolio with a low tax impact. The capital-gains rate for long-term gains was cut to 15 percent, with the same rate applied to dividends issued by domestic stocks and mutual funds. Note that payouts from foreign stocks and REITs (real estate investment trusts) do not qualify for the dividend tax break. Of course, tax rates are subject to change, and do change, being a product of the political process.

We know from Chapter 2 that many municipal bonds are not subject to federal taxation. Tax-free money market accounts are also available. Investors holding corporate bonds, particularly the high-yield variety, typically should do so in tax-advantaged accounts; otherwise, the interest will be taxed at full income tax rates.

Some mutual funds strive for tax efficiency. Of course, index funds by nature are tax efficient because their only portfolio changes occur when the underlying index changes. Some actively managed funds also seek to be tax efficient by keeping turnover low, minimizing the capital gains that are realized. Others try to match realized gains by selling those positions with losses, thereby offsetting the gains with losses.

Some of the tax efficient mutual funds can be identified by their names, such as Vanguard's Tax-Managed Balanced fund, which invests in both stocks and bonds. Others can be found by doing some research on such sites as Morningstar. For example, Third Avenue Value is well known for having a low tax impact on investors.

ETFs, typically being passively managed portfolios, tend to have extremely low expenses. They also typically have little turnover, few or no capital gains distributions and low dividend yields; therefore, they tend to be tax efficient.

MONITORING MARKET CONDITIONS

Individuals should monitor market conditions to the extent possible. Financial decisions are made in a dynamic marketplace where change occurs on a continuing basis. Key macro variables, such as inflation and interest rates, should be tracked on a regular basis. Whether individuals plan to buy a house, borrow money for various purposes, invest in various assets, and so forth, they need to be aware of what is going on in the financial marketplace.

A good example of how financial plans can go astray is to consider the Fed's actions between 2009—2014 to hold short-term interest rates down. Those who planned to steadily build up wealth through safe investments such as CDs and money market funds found themselves earning tiny interest rates, some close to zero. Individuals had to decide whether to accept these low rates in the name of safety, or try to earn more by taking more risk.

We now have enough market history to understand that financial crises are inevitable in a capitalistic economy where market participants are more or less free to act. Certainly the subprime meltdown and its aftershocks in 2008 presented a real challenge to the economy. Before that, we saw the Internet bubble in the late 1990s, and before that, the savings and loan crisis in the 1980s. The real question individuals face is not if there will be another financial crisis or major event in the economy in the future, but when.

Some Practical Advice

How might investors spot a future problem in the economy? One good tipoff is very large sums of money flowing to one sector, such as subprime and related securities, or dotcom companies in the late 1990s. Such imbalances have to be corrected, sooner or later.

Checking Your Understanding

5. Why do most market observers view asset allocation as the most important decision an investor makes? Explain your answer in the context of the 2008 financial crisis.

Rebalancing a Portfolio of Financial Assets

Even the most carefully constructed financial plan is not intended to remain intact without change. This is particularly true when it comes to one's portfolio of financial assets. It is important to monitor a portfolio and rebalance as necessary. The key is to know when and how to do such rebalancing, because a tradeoff is involved: the cost of trading versus the cost of not trading.[8]

The cost of trading involves commissions, possible impact on market price, and the time involved in deciding to trade. The cost of not trading involves holding positions that are not best suited for the portfolio's owner, holding positions that violate the asset allocation plan, holding a portfolio that is no longer adequately diversified, and so forth.

One of the problems involved in rebalancing is the "lockup" problem. This situation arises in taxable accounts subject to capital gains taxes. Even at low levels of turnover, the tax liabilities generated can be larger than the gains achieved by the active management driving the turnover. In the absence of taxes, such as with tax-deferred IRA and 401-k plans, investors would simply seek to hold those securities with the highest risk-adjusted expected rates of return. With a lockup problem, however, investors may be reluctant to rebalance the portfolio because of the capital gains taxes that will result on the accrued appreciation which, until realized, remains untaxed.

Individual investors, having taken the time to make the asset allocation decision, need to recognize that their chosen asset allocation percentages will likely get out of alignment over time. They often forget to rebalance their portfolios. This means that they may lose the benefits of having an asset allocation plan. Rebalancing reduces the risks of sharp losses—in general, a rebalanced portfolio is less volatile than one that is not rebalanced.

Investors should concentrate on keeping their chosen asset allocation percentages in line over the long run. There is no one correct formula for when to rebalance. One rule of thumb with a reasonable following is to rebalance when asset allocations vary by 10 percent or more, barring unusual circumstances.

Rebalancing is difficult for many investors because it represents a contrarian strategy. To rebalance, investors are selling those asset classes that have appreciated, and reinvesting the

---

[8] This discussion is indebted to Robert D. Arnott and Robert M. Lovell, Jr., "Monitoring and Rebalancing the Portfolio," in *Managing Investment Portfolios*, 2nd edition, edited by John L. Maginn and Donald L. Tuttle. New York: Warren, Gorham and Lamont, 1990.

funds in those that have not. This is very difficult to do psychologically. During the stock market bubble in the late 1990s, it was almost impossible to do as the market continued to rise and rise. Ultimately, of course, the benefits of rebalancing emerged as stocks plummeted and bonds appreciated.

Determining the Success of Your Financial Planning

The financial planning process is designed to facilitate making investment decisions in an organized, systematic manner. Clearly, it is important to evaluate the effectiveness of the overall decision-making process. One very important part of this is to measure the performance of the portfolio of financial assets. This allows investors to determine the success of both their direct investments and their indirect investments in mutual funds and ETFs. It is a key part of monitoring one's overall financial planning.

Performance measurement is important to both those who employ a professional portfolio manager on their behalf as well as to those who invest personal funds. It allows investors to evaluate the risks that are being taken, the reasons for the success or failure of the investing program, and the costs of any restrictions that may have been placed on the investment manager. This, in turn, could lead to revisions in an individual's financial plans. It is a critical part of the investment management process, and the logical capstone in its own right of the entire study of investments. We therefore consider this issue next as a separate and concluding chapter of the text.

Minimize Costs and Effort, and Improve Performance, When Managing a Portfolio of Financial Assets

We have now considered how investors can carry out their financial planning in a systematic, rational manner. Having an orderly process identifies the issues that are of importance to investors such as expectations about the future, taxes, portfolio rebalancing, and so forth. Let's now consider how investors can deal with some of these issues by employing some options available to today's investors.

An issue of Standard & Poor's *The Outlook* contained the following statement: "Evidence suggests that most investors' portfolios significantly underperform both the stock market and the mutual funds in which they invest."[9] If this is really true, what can the average investor do to improve the performance of their portfolio?

In earlier chapters we considered issues involved with passive portfolio management. Chief among these perhaps is the use of index funds and ETFs. Such funds offer investors diversification and very low costs, allowing them to come close to earning the returns available on some index of assets, such as the S&P 500 Index or an international stock index.

Passive investing in the form of index funds and some ETFs is the way to go for most investors. Take a long-run approach, make a reasonable asset allocation decision, use index funds and ETFs, and enjoy the benefits of low costs, low taxes, and diversification. Plan to match the performance of the overall markets in which you are invested. Surprising as it may be to many people, such a strategy would allow most investors to outperform their friends and contemporaries over a long period of time.

Jack Bogle, the founder of Vanguard and a persistent critic of actively managed mutual funds, perhaps said it best: Just "buy right and sit tight."

---

[9] Standard & Poor's *The Outlook*, Vol. 80, No. 17, April 30, 2008, p. 1.

Summary

▶ Good financial planning should be thought of by investors as a process.

▶ A portfolio management process can be applied to each investor to produce a set of strategy recommendations for accomplishing a given end result.

▶ The entire process as it applies to investing consists of: developing explicit investment policies, consisting of objectives, constraints, and preferences, determining and quantifying capital market expectations, constructing the portfolio, monitoring portfolio factors and responding to changes, rebalancing the portfolio when necessary, and measuring and evaluating portfolio performance.

▶ As part of their financial planning, investors should develop a policy statement consisting of carefully stated objectives, constraints, and preferences.

▶ The portfolio construction process can be thought of in terms of the asset allocation decision and the portfolio optimization decision.

▶ Asset allocation is the most important investment decision made by investors.

▶ It is important to monitor market conditions, the relative asset mix, and the investor's circumstances. Investing is an ongoing and dynamic process, and changes occur rapidly and frequently.

▶ Portfolio managers spend much of their time monitoring their portfolios and doing portfolio rebalancing. The key is to know when and how to do such rebalancing, because a tradeoff is involved: the cost of trading versus the cost of not trading.

▶ The measurement of portfolio performance allows investors to determine the success of investing program.

▶ Today's investors can take advantage of recommended asset allocations from financial firms, life-cycle funds, tax-advantaged investing, and, very simply, index funds and ETFs.

Questions

21-1 Should most individuals do financial planning?

21-2 How does the investment management process relate to financial planning?

21-3 What are some of the differences between individual investors and institutional investors?

21-4 What are the objectives of an investment strategy? Do these objectives have equal status?

21-5 How can a well-specified investment strategy facilitate the job of investment managers in managing portfolios?

21-6 Why is the asset allocation decision the most important decision made by investors?

21-7 What is meant by portfolio optimization?

21-8 What rule of thumb might investors follow when considering portfolio rebalancing?

21-9 In forming expectations about future returns from stocks, to what extent should investors be influenced by the more recent past (e.g., the previous 15 years) versus the history of stock market returns starting, for example, in 1926?

CFA
21-10 Why are tax considerations important in developing an investment policy?

CFA
21-11 **a.** A treasurer of a municipality with a municipal pension fund has required that its in-house portfolio manager invest all funds in the highest investment grade securities that mature in one month or less. The treasurer believes that this is a safe policy. Comment on this investment policy.

b. The same treasurer requires that the in-house portfolio municipality's operating fund (i.e., fund needed for day-to-day operations of the municipality) follow the same investment policy. Comment on the appropriateness of this investment policy for managing the municipality's operating fund.

CFA

21-12 James Stephenson Investment Profile

Case Facts

Type of investor	Individual; surgeon, 55 years of age, in good health
Asset base	$2 million
Stated return desire or investment goal	10 percentage points above the average annual return on U.S. small-capitalization stocks
Annual spending needs	$150,000
Annual income from nonportfolio sources (before tax)	$350,00 from surgical practice
Other return factors	Inflation is 3%
Risk considerations	Owns large concentration in U.S. small-capitalization stocks
Specific liquidity requirements	$70,000 charitable donation in 10 months
Time specifications	Retirement at age 70
Tax concerns	Income and capital gains taxed at 30 percent

Questions

1. Underline the word at right that best describes the client's:

A. Willingness to accept risk	Below average	Above average
B. Ability to accept risk	Below average	Above average
C. Risk tolerance	Below average	Above average
D. Liquidity requirement	Significant	Not significant
E. Time horizon	Single stage	Multistage
F. Overall time horizon	Short to intermediate term	Long-term
G. Tax concerns	Significant	Not significant

2. Discuss appropriate client objectives:
   A. Risk
   B. return

CFA

21-13 Foothill College Endowment Fund

Case Facts

Type of investor	Institutional; endowment
Purpose	Provide annual scholarships currently totaling $39.5 million
Asset base	$1 billion
Stated return desire	6 percent, calculated as spending rate of 4 percent plus previously expected college tuition inflation of 2 percent
Other return factors	Revised expectation of college tuition inflation is 3 percent
Tax concerns	Tax exempt

Questions

1. Underline the word at right that best describes the client's:

A. Risk tolerance	Below average	Above average
B. Liquidity requirement	Significant	Not significant
C. Time horizon	Single stage	Multistage
D. Overall time horizon	Short- to intermediate-term	Long-term
E. Tax concern	Significant	Not significant

2. Discuss appropriate client objectives:
   A. Risk
   B. return

CFA

21-14 Vincenzo Donadoni Investment Profile (adapted from 1998 CFA Level III Exam)

Case Facts

Type of investor	Individual; 56-year-old male in good health
Asset base	13.0 million Swiss francs (CHF)
Stated return desire or investment goal	Leave a trust fund of CHF 15.0 million for three children
Annual spending needs	CHF 250,000 rising with inflation
Annual income from other sources (after tax)	CHF 125,000 consulting income for next two years only
Ability to generate additional income	No
Willingness to accept risk	Impulsive, opinionated, successful, with large bets as a businessman, believes success depends on taking initiative
Specific liquidity requirements	CHF 1.5 million immediately to renovate house
	CHF 2.0 million in taxes due in nine months
Time specifications	Long-term except for liquidity concerns
Legal and regulatory factors	None
Unique circumstances	None

Questions

1. Underline the word at right that best describes the client's:

A. Willingness to accept risk	Below average	Above average
B. Ability to accept risk	Below average	Above Average
C. Risk tolerance	Below average	Above Average
D. Liquidity requirement	Significant	Not significant
E. Time horizon	Single stage	Multistage
F. Overall time horizon	Short- to intermediate-term	Long-term

2. Discuss appropriate client objectives:
   A. Risk
   B. return

CFA

21-15 For the following types of investors, appraise the importance of using the specified asset class for strategic asset allocation.

    a. Long-term bonds for a life insurer and for a young investor

    b. Common stock for a bank and for a young investor

    c. Domestic tax-exempt bonds for an endowment and for a midcareer professional

    d. Private equity for a major foundation and for a young investor

CFA

21-16 Hugh Donovan is chief financial officer (CFO) of LightSpeed Connections (LSC), a rapidly growing U.S. technology company with a traditional defined-benefit pension plan. Because of LSC's young workforce, Donovan believes the pension plan has no liquidity needs and can thus invest aggressively to maximize pension assets. He also believes that Treasury bills and bonds, yielding 5.4 percent and 6.1 percent, respectively, have no place in a portfolio with such a long time horizon. His strategy, which has produced excellent returns for the past two years, is to invest the portfolio as follows:

- 50 percent in a concentrated pool (15 to 20 stocks) of initial public offerings (IPOs) in technology and Internet companies, managed internally by Donavan.
- 25 percent in a small-cap growth fund.
- 10 percent in a venture capital fund.
- 10 percent in an S&P 500 index fund.
- 5 percent in an international equity fund.

(Working with LSC's Investment Committee, the firm's president, Eileen Jeffries, had produced a formal investment policy statement, which reads as follows:

The LSC Pension Plan's return objective should focus on real total returns that will fund its long-term obligations on an inflation-adjusted basis. The "time-to-maturity" of the corporate workforce is a key element for any defined pension plan; given our young workforce, LSC's Plan has a long investment horizon and more time available for wealth compounding to occur. Therefore, the Plan can pursue an aggressive investment course and focus on the higher return potential of capital growth. Under present U.S. tax laws, pension portfolio income and capital gains are not taxed. The portfolio should focus primarily on investments in business directly related to our main business to leverage our knowledge base.

Jeffries takes an asset-only approach to strategic asset allocation. She is considering three alternative allocations, shown in Exhibit 21-1 along with the portfolio's current asset allocation.

Select and justify the portfolio that is most appropriate for LSC's pension plan.

EXHIBIT 21-1

Alternative Asset Allocations and Current Portfolio

Asset	Portfolio A	Portfolio B	Portfolio C	Current Portfolio
S&P 500 Index	25%	16%	35%	10%
IPO/tech portfolio	20	40	10	50
Small-cap growth fund	26	10	19	25
International equity fund	0	16	15	5
Venture capital fund	10	5	5	10
Money market fund	7	7	2	0
Corporate bond fund	12	6	14	0
Total	100%	100%	100%	100%
Expected return	16.6%	22.1%	13.3%	26.2%
Standard deviation	26.7%	38.4%	19.8%	55.2%

Spreadsheet Exercises

21-1 Assume you are doing some personal planning for the management of your portfolio. It is early 2012. You have decided to build a portfolio that is either 40 percent bonds/60 percent stocks or 30 percent bonds/70 percent stocks. However, at this time an Aggregate U.S. bond index is yielding only 2.2 percent. In order for you to make a judgment as to your likelihood of success, you will need to determine how much stocks will have to return to provide an overall portfolio return ranging from 6 percent to 10 percent, as shown in the spreadsheet below.

  a. Fill in the spreadsheet below by determining what equity return will (approximately) provide you with the portfolio objective shown.

  b. Which portfolio combination would you choose, based on what you now know about likely equity returns?

Pf Objective	40% bonds	60% stocks	Pf Return	30% bonds	70% stocks	Pf Return
6%	0.022			0.022		
7%	0.022			0.022		
8%	0.022			0.022		
9%	0.022			0.022		
10%	0.022			0.022		

21-2 In order to see the effects of inflation, fill out the following spreadsheet given that the compound annual average rate of inflation has been 3 percent.

Annual Inflation Rate	2.5%
Cumulative Inflation after 10 years	
Value of $1 after 10 years	
Cumulative inflation after 20 years	
Value of $1 after 20 years	
Cumulative inflation after 30 years	
Value of $1 after 30 years	
Cumulative inflation after 40 years	
Value of $1 after 40 years	

21-3 Use the spreadsheet below to calculate the federal taxes owed on the taxable income shown. Determine the average and marginal tax rates.

2011 IRS Tax Brackets		
Over	**But not over**	**Tax Rate on Bracket**
0	8,500.00	10%
8,500.00	34,500.00	15%
34,500.00	83,600.00	25%
83,600.00	174,400.00	28%
174,400.00	379,150.00	33%
379,150+		35%
Taxable Income	12,350	
Total Tax Owed		
Average Tax Rate		
Marginal Tax Rate		

Checking Your Understanding

21-1 Individuals have differences and these should be accounted for within the financial planning framework. Each investor should decide how best to carry out activities, consistent with viewing portfolio management as a process.

21-2 Individual investors need to be explicit in stating their investment strategy in order to avoid conflicts and inconsistencies that often arise. For example, an investor may say that he or she wants a 10 percent after-tax return while maintaining a very low tolerance for risk. Such an objective is very unlikely, based on the history of asset returns, and by having to work through an explicit investment strategy the investor can be shown why such a statement is a problem.

21-3 The rule of 72 tells us how many years it will take for $1 to double, given some compound rate of return. This can be reversed to ask how many years does it take for the purchasing power of money to be cut in half, because doubling and halving are related concepts. Using the rule of 72 and a 3.5 percent compound growth rate, it would take approximately 20.6 years for the purchasing power to be cut in half ($72/3.5 = 20.57$ years).

21-4 Because 9.5 percent is both the mean and the median of the S&P 500 returns for the period 1926–2011, the probability of earning more than 9.5 percent for any holding period was 50 percent. The probability of earning 9.5 percent or less for any holding period was also 50 percent.

21-5 Having made the asset allocation decision for some holding period, an investor has largely determined his or her fate. Given the 2008 financial crisis, stocks declined sharply. Investors with a 100 percent portfolio allocation to stocks, or a large allocation percentage, suffered sharp losses (at least on paper). Conversely, investors with portfolios largely in cash avoided these losses. So, having made their asset allocation decisions prior to the sharp decline in stock prices in Fall 2008, investors who took no subsequent actions had largely determined their portfolio performance outcomes.

chapter 22

Evaluation of Investment Performance: A Global Concept

A t long last you have arrived at the end of your quest to learn enough about investing to manage your inheritance sensibly. Now that you know some basics about how to invest, what your alternatives are, and what to expect, you must consider how well you are doing as an investor over time. Measuring portfolio performance is the bottom line of investing. Everyone wants to know how they are performing as investors, either in managing their own portfolios or entrusting their money to others to manage for them. Furthermore, if they use others to manage their money, or read investing newsletters, they should be aware of what to look for when investment results are presented to them.

Chapter 22 explains what is involved in the evaluation of investment performance. While it might seem like a straightforward process to determine how well an investor's portfolio has performed, such is not always the case. Chapter 22 covers well-known measures of portfolio performance such as the Sharpe measure and also discusses style investing, performance benchmarks, and performance presentation standards.

AFTER READING THIS CHAPTER YOU WILL BE ABLE TO:

▶ Understand the issues involved in evaluating portfolio performance.

▶ Evaluate popular press claims about the performance of various portfolios, such as mutual funds, available to investors.

▶ Understand concepts such as performance attribution and style analysis.

W e have now discussed, in an organized and systematic manner, the major components of the investing process. One important issue that remains is the "bottom line" of the investing process: evaluating and understanding the performance of a portfolio. This is important regardless of whether an individual investor manages his or her own funds or invests indirectly through investment companies. Direct investing can be time-consuming and has high opportunity costs. If the results are inadequate, why do it (unless the investor simply enjoys it)? On the other hand, if professional portfolio managers (such as mutual fund managers) are employed, it is necessary to know how well they perform. If manager A consistently outperforms manager B, other things being equal, investors should prefer manager A. Alternatively, if neither A nor B outperforms an index fund, other things being equal, investors may prefer neither. The obvious point is that performance has to be evaluated before intelligent decisions can be made about existing portfolios.

Currently, thousands of mutual funds are operating, with several trillion dollars under management. More than 90 million individuals own mutual funds. The pension fund universe is also very large. The majority of all U.S. pension plans with assets of several billion employ multiple managers. In addition to these money managers, trusts, discretionary accounts, and endowment funds have portfolios that must be evaluated. Professional portfolio management is an unforgiving profession, with managers hired and fired regularly because of their performance, both absolute and relative to other managers.

Portfolio evaluation techniques have become more sophisticated, and the demands by portfolio clients more intense. The broad acceptance of modern portfolio theory has changed the evaluation process and how it is viewed.

A Framework for Evaluating and Assessing Portfolio Performance

We will consider four broad issues in evaluating portfolio performance:

1. **Performance Measurement Issues**—The critical concern for most investors is to correctly determine how a portfolio performed over some period of time. Thus, the portfolio's results have to be correctly measured and analyzed.
2. **Well-Known Measures of Performance**—Several risk-adjusted measures of portfolio performance have been available for many years. One or more of these are often referred to in discussions of portfolio performance, and therefore investors need to be aware of them.
3. **Performance Attribution and Style Analysis**—Going beyond measuring a portfolio's performance, the concept of performance attribution seeks to determine why a portfolio had the rate of return it did over some specified period of time. This relates to style analysis, which describes a portfolio manager's investing style.
4. **Portfolio Presentation Standards**—How should the actual results of a portfolio be presented to those directly affected by that portfolio—in other words, from investment manager to client? Fifteen years ago there were few standards or guidelines. Now there are a clearly stated set of standards to be followed when presenting portfolio results.

We consider each of these issues in turn.

Performance Measurement Issues

If you read financial press magazines and newspapers, you will be exposed to claims from various mutual fund companies touting the performance of at least some of their funds. This is an ongoing process, and therefore it may pay you to learn to quickly spot the deficiencies in such ads.

You would expect to see, over time, a changing set of fund companies promoting their funds that have performed well. Why does this happen? As one or more of their funds achieve good ratings, based on the latest measurement periods, companies hurry to put out ads proclaiming these new stellar ratings. Investors are attracted to top performing funds, and start to buy the ones that are rated highly. The problem is that the ratings reflect past performance, not future performance. Often the fund happened to be in the right sectors, or the right stocks, for the time period involved. These stocks and sectors typically do not continue to perform strongly, and investors end up disappointed because they buy into the funds when it is too late.

Or consider an excerpt from an ad placed by a well-known mutual fund company in one recent year. This ad listed five funds said to be "peer-beating funds." It highlighted five of its funds that were in the first quartile of Lipper Quartile rankings for one year, three years, and the life of the fund. How should you react to this information?

In this case the fund's average annual returns are not shown. What if, for a one-year period, one of these funds achieved a first-quartile ranking although it had a 2 percent positive return, less than you could have earned in Treasury bills? What about the fund's risk—would you want to know something about it? Why are five-year and 10-year returns not highlighted, as they often are in other ads? Although the information presented is totally legitimate, one might wonder if it is selectively presented to put these funds in the best light.

Or consider another ad placed at the same time by a large company that featured only one of its funds. The only real message was that this fund has a four-star overall rating out of 300 over funds in the same category. There was no mention of returns, risk, benchmark returns, or anything else.

In order to correctly measure portfolio performance, certain factors must be considered. We discuss below the most important factors that must be accounted for in order to correctly assess a portfolio's performance.

To initiate our discussion about measuring portfolio performance, assume that you are evaluating the GoGrowth mutual fund, a domestic equity fund in the category of large growth (it emphasizes large-capitalization growth stocks). This fund earned a total return of 19 percent for its shareholders for 2012. It claims in an advertisement that it is the number one performing mutual fund in its category. As a shareholder, what can you conclude about GoGrowth's performance, both absolutely and relatively?

THREE QUESTIONS TO ANSWER IN MEASURING PORTFOLIO PERFORMANCE

The first question to be answered is obvious: Was the return on a portfolio, less all expenses, adequate, all things considered? Every investor is primarily concerned with this issue because, after all, the objective of investing is to increase or at least protect financial wealth. Unsatisfactory results must be detected so that changes can be made.

The second question to be answered is related to the first. How much risk did the investor, or portfolio manager, take in creating and managing a particular portfolio? We have stressed throughout this text that we must always think in terms of both return and risk, because they are opposite sides of the same coin.

Given the risk that all investors face, it is totally inappropriate to consider only the returns from various investment alternatives. Although all investors prefer higher returns, rational investors are also risk-averse. To evaluate portfolio performance properly, we must determine whether the returns are large enough given the risk involved. If we are to assess portfolio performance correctly, we must evaluate performance on a risk-adjusted basis.

The third question concerns comparisons, or benchmarks. What return should have been earned on the portfolio, given the risk taken and the alternative returns available to be earned from other investments over the same period? This issue is so important that when someone asks you how your portfolio performed compared to the market, the proper response is to say, "We need to compare my portfolio's performance to the proper benchmark."

As noted in Chapter 4, the Dow Jones Industrial Average is arguably the most famous stock market index in the world, widely reported and widely recognized by most investors. Very few investors, however, use it as a performance benchmark—this is almost universally true for money managers. Why? The Dow's 30 blue-chip stocks are not as good an indicator of the breadth of today's stock market as are some other indexes.

It is critical in evaluating portfolio performance to compare the returns obtained on the portfolio being evaluated with the returns that could have been obtained from a comparable alternative. The measurement process must involve relevant and obtainable alternatives; that is, the **benchmark portfolio** must be a legitimate alternative that accurately reflects the objectives of the portfolio being evaluated. One might assume that, unlike the Dow, the S&P 500 Index would be a widely accepted benchmark portfolio because it is typically cited by institutional investors. And indeed it is often used as a benchmark, but as we shall see it may not adequately capture the various dimensions of a portfolio.

Benchmark Portfolio An alternative portfolio against which to measure a portfolio's performance

Example 22-1

Over a recent five-year period small-cap value funds significantly outperformed large cap value funds. Therefore, the typical owner of a small-cap value fund during that period should expect to have outperformed the S&P 500 Index and should not compare his or her results to the S&P 500, but instead to the Russell 2000 or a category average of small-cap value funds.

The S&P 500 has been the most frequently used benchmark for evaluating the performance of institutional portfolios such as those of pension funds and mutual funds. However, many observers now agree that multiple benchmarks are more appropriate to use when evaluating portfolio returns. Customized benchmarks, explained later in the chapter, also can be constructed to more accurately evaluate a manager's style.

Given these three questions, what can we say about the performance of GoGrowth Fund as described above? Based on our discussion throughout this text of the risk-return tradeoff that underlies all investment actions, we can legitimately say relatively little about GoGrowth's performance. If we know nothing about the risk of this fund, little can be said about its performance. After all, GoGrowth's managers may have taken twice the risk of comparable portfolios to achieve this 19 percent return. Furthermore, even if we know GoGrowth's risk, its 19 percent return is meaningful only when compared to a legitimate benchmark. Obviously, if the average-risk large growth fund returned 23 percent in 2008, and GoGrowth is an average-risk fund, we would rate its performance unfavorable. Therefore, we must make *relative* comparisons in performance measurement, and an important related issue is the benchmark to be used in evaluating the performance of a portfolio.

Finally, note that it is not unusual to pick up a publication from the popular press and see two different mutual funds of the same type—for example, small-capitalization growth funds or balanced funds—advertise themselves as the number one performer. How can this occur?

The answer is simple. Each of these funds is using a different time period over which to measure performance. For example, one fund could use the 10 years ending December 31, 2012, while another fund uses the five years ending June 30, 2012. Mutual fund sponsors may emphasize different time periods in promoting their performance. Funds can also define the group or index to which comparisons are made differently.

Mark Hulbert publishes the *Hulbert Financial Digest*, which has tracked the performance of investment advisors for more than 30 years. Consider this quote from him, made in 2012:

"I am constantly bombarded with questions about investment advisors that my Hulbert Financial Digest (HFD) has not been monitoring. Inevitably, the inquiries focus on alleged performance that is tantalizingly good—so good, in fact, that even if actual performance were only half as good, it still would justify our immediately allocating all our investment portfolios to following the advisor or strategy in question. My reply is always the same: don't believe it."[1]

Some Practical Advice

Buyer Beware

Performance evaluation extends to the evaluation of money managers and investment newsletters. A large number of newsletters offering investment advice and model portfolios compete for readers. Think of a newsletter charging $75 a year, or $125 a year, or more, and the marginal cost of producing and mailing one more newsletter, and it is easy to understand why these newsletters work hard at attracting readers.

Unfortunately, publishers of financial newsletters are not regulated by the SEC. Therefore, subscribers or potential subscribers might be caught unaware. Consider one newsletter endorsed by a well-known personal finance celebrity. A mutual fund managed by the same company claimed a strong annual average return from 2002 to 2011, but the fund was not started until December 31, 2009. After questions arose, this was said to be the result of a misunderstanding.

The same newsletter reported that in 2009 one of the company's portfolios outperformed the S&P 500, which was stated to have a return of 19.79 percent. The actual S&P return for that year, as officially declared by Standard & Poor's, was 26.46 percent. In fact, the newsletter understated the performance of the S&P 500 in nine of the 10 years cited. Some of the company's other newsletters have made the claim "Ranked #1 & Recommended by Hulbert Financial Digest!" The publisher of the Digest, Mark Hulbert, states that his publication does not make recommendations.[2]

Bottom line—investors must be particularly diligent when evaluating the claims of investment newsletters.

RETURN CALCULATIONS

Performance measurement begins with portfolio valuations and transactions translated into rate of return. When portfolio performance is evaluated, the investor should be concerned with the total change in wealth. As discussed throughout this text, a proper measure of this return is the total return (TR), which captures both the income component and the capital gains (or losses) component of return.[3]

The market value of a portfolio can be measured at the beginning and ending of a period, and the rate of return can be calculated as

$$R_p = \frac{V_E - V_B}{V_B} \tag{22-1}$$

where V_E is the ending value of the portfolio and V_B is its beginning value.

This calculation assumes that no funds were added to or withdrawn from the portfolio by the client during the measurement period. If such transactions occur, the portfolio return as

---

[1] Mark Hulbert, "Believing Performance Claims: A Triumph of Hope over Experience," *AAII Journal*, 2012.

[2] This entire paragraph is based on Jason Zweig, "Meet Suze Orman's Newsletter Guru," *The Wall Street Journal*, January 21–22, 2012, pp. B1, B2.

[3] The Global Investment Performance Standards developed by CFA Institute require the use of total return to calculate performance.

calculated, R_p, may not be an accurate measure of the portfolio's performance. For example, if the client adds funds close to the end of the measurement period, use of Equation 22-1 would produce inaccurate results, because the ending value was not determined by the actions of the portfolio manager. Although a close approximation of portfolio performance might be obtained by simply adding any withdrawals or subtracting any contributions that are made very close to the end of the measurement period, timing issues are a problem.

Dollar-Weighted Returns   Traditionally, portfolio measurement consisted of calculating the **Dollar-Weighted Rate of Return (DWR)**, which is equivalent to the *internal rate of return (IRR)* used in several financial calculations. The IRR measures the actual return earned on a beginning portfolio value and on any net contributions made during the period.

Dollar-Weighted Rate of Return (DWR) Equates all cash flows, including ending market value, with the beginning market value of the portfolio

The DWR equates all cash flows, including ending market value, with the beginning market value of the portfolio. Because the DWR is affected by cash flows to the portfolio, it is inappropriate to use when making comparisons to other portfolios or to market indexes, a key factor in performance measurement.

✓   *The DWR measures the rate of return to the portfolio owner;* that is, it accurately measures the investor's return.

To reemphasize, the DWR is a misleading measure of the manager's ability because the manager does not have control over the timing of the cash inflows and outflows. Clearly, if an investor with $1,000,000 allocates these funds to a portfolio manager by providing half at the beginning of the year and half at mid-year, the portfolio value at the end of the year will differ from another manager who received the entire $1,000,000 at the beginning of the year. This is true even if both managers had the same two six-month returns during that year.

Time-Weighted Rate of Return (TWR) Measures the actual rate of return earned by the portfolio manager

Time-Weighted Returns   The **Time-Weighted Rate of Return (TWR)** is unaffected by any cash flows to the portfolio and measures the actual rate of return earned by the portfolio manager.

✓   In order to evaluate a manager's performance properly, we should use the time-weighted rate of return.

Example 22-2

A portfolio manager begins with $1,000. Halfway through the year $200 is withdrawn by the client. The value of the portfolio at the end of the year, reflecting the performance of the portfolio, is $910. Clearly, the portfolio manager did not decrease the value of the portfolio by $90. Therefore, we cannot simply look at the beginning and ending values for the portfolio. Instead, we must measure the rate of return on the amount of money invested during the period before the cash flow occurred, and during the period after.

We wish to determine how well the portfolio manager performed regardless of the size or timing of the cash flows. Generally, the portfolio manager has no control over the deposits and withdrawals made by the clients. The time-weighted rate of return links together the subperiod rates of return during the evaluation period, assuming that all income and realized gains are reinvested at each subperiod interval. The time-weighted rate of return is often annualized.

Example 22-3 Assume a client provides a portfolio manager with $500,000 which is invested at the beginning of the year. At year-end the account is worth $545,000. At the beginning of year two, the client provides the manager with another $55,000. At the end of year two the value of the portfolio is $630,000. How well did the manager perform; that is, what is the time-weighted return?

During year one, the portfolio rate of return is ($545,000 − $500,000)/$500,000, or 9 percent. During year two, the portfolio rate of return is ($630,000 − $600,000)/$600,000, or 5 percent. The TWR for the two-year period $= [(1.09)(1.05)] − 1.0 = 14.45$ percent. Annualized, TWR $= [(1.09)(1.05)]^{1/2} = (1.1445)^{1/2} = 1.0698 − 1.0 = 6.98$ percent

Which Measure to Use? The dollar-weighted return and the time-weighted return can produce different results, and at times these differences are substantial. In fact, the two will produce identical results only in the case of no withdrawals or contributions during the evaluation period, and with all investment income reinvested.

✓ The time-weighted return captures the rate of return actually earned by the portfolio *manager*, while the dollar-weighted return captures the rate of return earned by the portfolio *owner*.

As we will see later in the chapter, the Global Performance Presentation Standards now used by many money managers require that returns be computed using the TWR approach.[4]

RISK CONSIDERATIONS

Why can we not measure investment performance on the basis of a properly calculated rate of return measure? After all, rankings of mutual funds are often done this way in the popular press, with one-year, three-year, and, sometimes, five-year returns shown. Are rates of return, or averages, good indicators of performance?

As stated in Chapter 1 and restated above, we must consider risk when making judgments. The two prevalent measures of risk used in investment analysis are total risk and nondiversifiable, or systematic, risk. Total risk is measured by calculating the standard deviation, and systematic risk—that part of total risk that cannot be diversified away—is assessed by considering the beta for the portfolio. Differences in risk will cause portfolios to respond differently to changes in the overall market and should be accounted for in evaluating performance. We will consider three dimensions of risk in this discussion. The first two are the same risk measures we have used throughout the text, standard deviation and beta.

We now know that the standard deviation for a portfolio's set of realized returns can be calculated easily with a calculator or computer and is a measure of total risk. A spreadsheet program can quickly calculate the standard deviation for a set of portfolio returns.

Recall that the beta for the market as a whole is 1.0. For a large, diversified portfolio of domestic stocks, we would typically expect the beta of the portfolio to be close to 1.0.

[4] The Global Investment Performance Standards (GIPS®), associated with CFA Institute, were preceded in North America by the AIMR Performance Presentation Standards (AIMR-PPS) created in 1993 by AIMR, the predecessor to CFA Institute.

Example 22-4   At the beginning of 2012 Fidelity's Equity Income Fund had a beta of 1.18 while T. Rowe Price's Growth and Income Fund had a beta of .93.

Beta, a relative measure of systematic risk, can be calculated with any number of software programs. However, we must remember that betas are only estimates of systematic risk. Betas can be calculated using weekly, monthly, quarterly, or annual data, and for different periods of time, and each will produce a different estimate. Such variations in this calculation could produce differences in rankings which use beta as a measure of risk. Furthermore, betas can be unstable, and they change over time.

Although not strictly a measure of risk, we can also consider a third measure that directly relates to the risk of a portfolio. This measure of risk arises from the process of fitting a characteristic line whereby the portfolio's returns are regressed against the market's returns. The square of the correlation coefficient produced as a part of the analysis, called the **coefficient of determination**, or R^2, is used to denote the degree of diversification.

Coefficient of Determination The square of the correlation coefficient, measuring the percentage of the variance in the dependent variable that is explained by the independent variable

✓   The coefficient of determination indicates the percentage of the variance in the portfolio's returns that is explained by the market's returns.

If the fund is totally diversified, the R^2 will approach 1.0, indicating that the fund's returns are completely explained by the market's returns. The lower the coefficient of determination, the less the portfolio's returns are attributable to the market's returns. This indicates that other factors, which could have been diversified away, are being allowed to influence the portfolio's returns.

Example 22-5   Using the Russell 3000 Index, Fidelity's Equity Income fund has an R^2 of .98, while Fidelity's Contrafund has an R^2 of .93 using the S&P 500.

All three of these measures—standard deviation, beta, and the coefficient of determination—are readily available for mutual funds from such sources as *Morningstar*.

Checking Your Understanding

1. Assume you have a portfolio that you wish to evaluate. When would you use the TWR for this portfolio? The DWR?
2. Assume you own a portfolio that turns out to have an R^2 of 1.0 when measured against the S&P 500. What would you conclude about the performance of this portfolio?

PERFORMANCE BENCHMARKS AND PERFORMANCE UNIVERSES

As noted earlier, the third question to be answered in measuring a particular portfolio's performance concerns the benchmarks to use as a comparison. The two primary standards in use are performance universes and performance benchmarks.

What constitutes a good universe or benchmark for the evaluation of portfolio performance? Characteristics that have been identified include the following:

❏ Unambiguous
❏ Specified in advance

- ❏ Appropriate
- ❏ Investable
- ❏ Measurable

As we will see below, it can be difficult to find benchmarks that meet these criteria.

PERFORMANCE UNIVERSES

Performance Universe Constructed by aggregating market valuations and income accruals for a large number of portfolios that are managed individually

A **performance universe** is constructed by aggregating market valuations and income accruals for a large number of portfolios that are managed individually. The data to do this come from various portfolio managers such as bank trust departments, brokerage firms, and investment advisory firms. A large universe allows subuniverses to be constructed that in principle more closely match the portfolio being evaluated.

Example 22-6

Russell/Mellon is a leading provider of investment information services to more than 3,000 institutional investors such as pension funds, asset managers, and consultants. This company is able to develop and offer some 800 universes based on monitoring of about 2,000 pension funds, 1,400 asset managers and 75,000 portfolios. Russell/Mellon also offers performance attribution services, allowing a client to analyze how a return was achieved.

Problems can arise when using manager universes to evaluate portfolio performance. First, they usually are broadly defined, and therefore may not accurately reflect the portfolio of a particular manager. Second, since they represent someone else's portfolios, they are not investable. Third, they are not specified in advance. Fourth, manager universes are subject to survivorship bias, whereby the poor performing managers may drop out (or be merged with other funds that are performing better).[5]

PERFORMANCE BENCHMARKS

Performance Benchmarks Unmanaged, passive portfolios that reflect a manager's investment style

Unlike universes, **performance benchmarks** are unmanaged, passive portfolios that reflect a manager's investment style. They can be specified in advance—the S&P 500, Russell 3000, the Wilshire Index, and so forth. They are also unambiguous, measurable, and investable. Ideally, a benchmark explains all of a manager's returns resulting from systematic factors such as market movements, as well as the manager's style involving factors such as the sectors chosen. This means that if the portfolio performs above or below the benchmark, such performance can be attributed to the manager's skill.

A potential problem is that except for portfolios holding large stocks such as those found in the DJIA and S&P 500, broad market indexes may be too broad to reflect a particular portfolio's style. If a benchmark has this problem, we cannot be sure if the manager outperformed (or underperformed) a benchmark because of skill (or lack thereof) or because the benchmark did not adequately capture the manager's "style." Even so-called style indexes designed to reflect a narrower segment of the market—may not be appropriate for many portfolios. These style indexes include the Russell 1000 Growth and 1000 Value Indexes, and the Russell 2000 Growth and 2000 Value Indexes. On the other hand, these style indexes sometimes explain the performance of a particular fund better than the typically cited market index.

---

[5] See Chapter 3 for a discussion of the survivorship bias.

A STRAIGHTFORWARD APPROACH TO PERFORMANCE EVALUATION

Let's consider a simple, straightforward approach to evaluating performance that many investors can use. Numerous investors today hold various combinations of domestic and foreign stocks, large-cap stocks and small-cap stocks, different varieties of bonds, TIPS, and other assets. Each of these asset classes should be evaluated relative to a proper benchmark. ETFs and index funds can be used effectively in many cases as benchmarks. Let's focus on ETFs because of their low expense ratios and their tradability.

There are several choices among the various fund companies for ETFs that could be used; because Vanguard ETFs often have extremely low expenses, we will cite several of their funds. Keep in mind there are multiple alternative in most cases. If you hold Treasury and corporate bonds, you can use Vanguard's Total Bond Market ETF as a benchmark. If your bond holdings are limited to one or the other, Vanguard has ETFs devoted to each, which can be further broken down to long-term and short-term corporate or Treasury ETFs. If you hold emerging markets stocks or funds, Vanguard's MSCI Emerging Market ETF could serve as a benchmark, as could Fidelity's Emerging Markets Fund. European stocks or funds can be benchmarked against Vanguard's MSCI European ETF. Alternatively, for a fund holding mostly European blue chip companies, you could use International Dividend Achievers ETF. For REITS, you could use iShares Cohen and Steers Realty Majors ETF or Vanguard's U.S. Real Estate Investment Trust.

For stocks, there are many choices depending on how exacting you wish to be. Vanguard has available the Total Stock Market ETF (symbol = VTI). It also has a small-cap ETF and other stock ETFs like the S&P 500 and mid-cap-growth and mid-cap-value ETFs. Obviously, other investment companies offer stock ETFs that could be used as benchmarks.

As an example of this approach, assume in 2012 your portfolio consisted of 15 percent REITs, 30 percent long-term Treasury bonds, 10 percent emerging markets funds, and 45 percent S&P 500 stocks. Using the returns for 2012 for four appropriate ETFs that concentrate on these asset classes, calculate the weighted average return. Compare this to your portfolio return for 2012. As noted earlier, the dollar-weighted return correctly measures the portfolio's return to the owner.

Risk-adjusted Measures of Performance

Based on the concepts of capital market theory, and recognizing the necessity to incorporate both return and risk into the analysis, several measures of risk-adjusted performance have been advanced over the years. Some of these go back many years, while others are more recent. These measures are often still used. For example, *Morningstar*, perhaps the best-known source of mutual fund information, reports the Sharpe ratio, explained below.

THE SHARPE RATIO

Sharpe Ratio A measure of portfolio performance calculated as the ratio of excess portfolio return to the standard deviation

William Sharpe, who has made several important contributions to portfolio theory, introduced a risk-adjusted measure of portfolio performance in the 1960s. The so-called **Sharpe ratio** uses a benchmark based on the ex-post capital market line (the capital market line, CML, was discussed in Chapter 9).[6] This measure, sometimes called the Reward to Variability (RVAR) Ratio, can be defined as

$$\text{Sharpe Ratio} = [\overline{TR}_p - \overline{RF}]/SD_p$$
$$= \text{Excess return/Risk}$$

(22-2)

---

[6] Sharpe used it to rank the performance of 34 mutual funds over the period 1954–1963.

$$\overline{TR}_p = \text{ the average TR for portfolio } p \text{ during some period}$$
$$\text{of time (we will use annual data)}$$
$$\overline{RF} = \text{ the average risk-free rate of return during the period}$$
$$SD_p = \text{ the standard deviation of return for portfolio } p \text{ during the}$$
$$\text{period}$$
$$\overline{TR}_p - \overline{RF} = \text{ the excess return (risk premium) on portfolio } p$$

The numerator of Equation 22-2 measures the portfolio's excess return, or the return above the risk-free rate. (RF could have been earned without assuming risk.) This is also referred to as the risk premium. The denominator uses the standard deviation, which is a measure of the total risk or variability in the return of the portfolio. Note the following about the Sharpe ratio:

1. It measures the excess return per unit of total risk (standard deviation).
2. The higher the calculated value, the better the portfolio performance.
3. Portfolios can be ranked using the Sharpe ratio.

As an example of calculating the Sharpe ratio, consider actual data for five equity mutual funds for a 15-year period: we will refer to these funds as D, I, K, M, and W. Table 22-1 shows annual shareholder returns, the standard deviation of these returns, the average return for the S&P 500 Index for those years, and the average yield on Treasury bills as a proxy for RF. On the basis of these data, Sharpe's ratio can be calculated using Equation 22-2, with results as reported in Table 22-2.

Table 22-1 Return and Risk Data for Five Equity Mutual Funds, 15-Year Period

Mutual Fund	Average Return	Standard Deviation	Beta	R^2
D	15.86	22.85	1.46	.64
I	18.10	13.44	.96	.79
K	18.59	21.68	1.45	.69
M	22.09	17.27	1.24	.79
W	18.39	11.82	.60	.39
S&P 500	16.35	12.44		
RF	7.96			

Table 22-2 Risk-Adjusted Measures for Five Equity Mutual Funds, 15-Year Period

Mutual Fund	RVAR	RVOL	Jensen's Alpa
D	.35	5.40	−3.95
I	.75	10.54	2.67
K	.49	7.33	−1.04
M	.82	11.42	4.21
W	.88	17.38	5.35*
S&P 500	.67		

Significant at the 5% level

✓ Based on these calculations, we see that three of these five funds—I, W, and M—outperformed the S&P 500 Index on an excess return-risk basis during this period, although the average return exceeded that for the S&P 500 for four of the funds. Since this is an ordinal (relative) measure of portfolio performance, different portfolios can easily be ranked on this variable. In addition, a Sharpe ratio for the appropriate market index can also be calculated and used for comparison purposes.

✓ Using only the Sharpe ratio as our measure of portfolio performance, we would judge the portfolio with the highest calculated value best in terms of ex post performance.

As we can see, W, I, and M have ratios that exceed the ratio of 0.67 for the S&P 500 for the period. The average return for three of these funds—I, K, and W—were very close together—18.10 percent, 18.59 percent, and 18.39, respectively. However, their standard deviations were very different—13.44 percent, 21.68 percent, and 11.82 percent, respectively. Therefore, their Sharpe ratios differed significantly. In effect, K's risk was very high in relation to its average return as compared in particular to W, which showed slightly less average return but with a much lower standard deviation.

Sharpe's measure for these funds is illustrated graphically in Figure 22-1. The vertical axis is rate of return, and the horizontal axis is standard deviation of returns. The vertical intercept is RF.

Investments Intuition

In Figure 22-1 we are drawing the capital market line (CML) when we plot the market's return against its standard deviation and use RF as the vertical intercept. Based on the discussion in Chapter 9, all efficient portfolios should plot on this line, and an investor with the ability to borrow and lend at the rate RF should be able to attain any point on this line. Of course, this is the ex post and not the ex ante CML.

As Figure 22-1 shows, the Sharpe ratio measures the slope of the line from RF to the portfolio being evaluated. The steeper the line, the higher the slope and the better the performance. The arrow indicates the slope for the S&P 500 and for W, the fund with the greatest slope.

Because of their better performance, W, M, and I have the higher slopes, whereas K's and D's slopes are lower than that of the S&P 500. Because the Sharpe ratio for these three portfolios is greater than that for the market measure (in this case the S&P 500), these portfolios lie above the CML, indicating superior risk-adjusted performance. The other two lie below the CML, indicating inferior risk-adjusted performance.

TREYNOR'S REWARD TO VOLATILITY

At approximately the same time as Sharpe's measure was developed (the mid-1960s), Jack Treynor presented a similar measure.[7] Treynor, however, distinguished between total risk and systematic risk, implicitly assuming that portfolios are well diversified; that is, he ignored any diversifiable risk. Thus, Treynor's measure has the same numerator as the Sharpe ratio, but uses beta in the denominator as the measure of risk. He used as a benchmark the ex post security market line. Treynor's measure, sometimes called the reward to volatility measure, is explained in an appendix. Results for the Treynor measure for the same five funds used before are shown in Table 22-2.

[7] J. Treynor, "How to Rate Management of Investment Funds," *Harvard Business Review* (January–February 1965), pp. 63–75.

Figure 22-1

Sharpe's Measure of Performance (RVAR) for Five Mutual Funds, 15-year period.

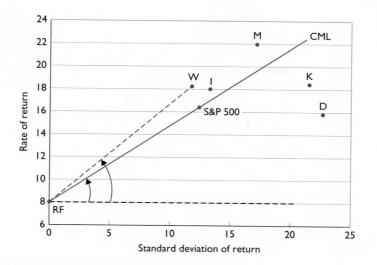

Checking Your Understanding

3. Can the numerator of the Sharpe ratio be described as the portfolio's risk premium? If so, what does this mean?

JENSEN'S ALPHA

Alpha The difference between an independently determined expected rate of return on a stock and the required rate of return on that stock.

Jensen's **alpha**, a measure of the portfolio manager's performance, is based on the CAPM. The expected one-period return for any security (i) or, in this case, portfolio (p) is given as

$$E(R_p) = RF + \beta_p[E(R_M) - RF] \qquad (22\text{-}3)$$

with all terms as previously defined.

Notice that Equation 22-3 can be applied to ex post periods if the investor's expectations are, on the average, fulfilled. Empirically, Equation 22-3 can be approximated as Equation 22-4.

$$R_{pt} = RF_t + \beta_p[R_{Mt} - RF_t] + E_{pt} \qquad (22\text{-}4)$$

where

$$
\begin{aligned}
R_{pt} &= \text{the return on portfolio } p \text{ in period } t \\
RF_t &= \text{the risk-free rate in period } t \\
R_{Mt} &= \text{the return on the market in period } t \\
E_{pt} &= \text{a random error term for portfolio } p \text{ in period } t \\
[R_{Mt} - RF_t] &= \text{the market risk premium during period } t
\end{aligned}
$$

Equation 22-4 relates the realized return on portfolio p during any period t to the sum of the risk-free rate and the portfolio's risk premium plus an error term. Given the market risk premium, the risk premium on portfolio p is a function of portfolio p's systematic risk—the larger its systematic risk; the larger the risk premium.

Equation 22-4 can be written in what is called the risk premium (or, alternatively, the excess return) form by moving RF to the left side and subtracting it from R_{pt}, as in Equation 22-5:

$$R_{pt} - RF_t = \beta_{RE}[R_{Mt} - RF_t] + E_{pt} \qquad (22\text{-}5)$$

Figure 22-2

Jensen's Measure of Performance for Three Hypothetical Funds.

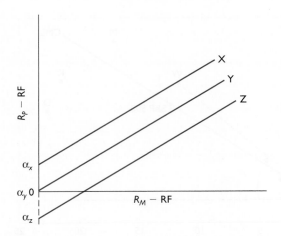

Where

$$R_{pt} - RF_t = \text{the risk premium on portfolio } p$$

Equation 22-5 indicates that the risk premium on portfolio p is equal to the product of its beta and the market risk premium plus an error term. In other words, the risk premium on portfolio p should be proportional to the risk premium on the market portfolio if the CAPM model is correct and investor expectations were generally realized (in effect, if all assets and portfolios were in equilibrium).

A return proportional to the risk assumed is illustrated by Fund Y in Figure 22-2. This diagram shows the characteristic line in excess return form, where the risk-free rate each period, RF_t, is subtracted from both the portfolio's return and the market's return.[8]

Equation 22-5 can be empirically tested by fitting a regression for some number of periods. Portfolio excess returns (risk premiums) are regressed against the excess returns (risk premiums) for the market. If managers earn a return proportional to the risk assumed, this relationship should hold. That is, there should be no intercept term (alpha) in the regression, which should go through the origin, as in the case of Fund Y in Figure 22-2.

Given these expected findings, Jensen argued that an intercept term, alpha, could be added to Equation 22-5 as a means of identifying superior or inferior portfolio performance. Therefore, Equation 22-5 becomes Equation 22-6 where α_p is the alpha or intercept term:

$$R_{pt} - RF_t = \alpha_p + \beta_p[R_{Mt} - RF_t] + E_{pt} \tag{22-6}$$

The CAPM asserts that equilibrium conditions should result in a zero-intercept term. Therefore, the alpha should measure the contribution of the portfolio manager since it represents the average incremental rate of return per period beyond the return attributable to the level of risk assumed. Specifically,

1. If alpha is significantly positive, this is evidence of superior performance (illustrated in Figure 22-2 with portfolio X, which has a positive intercept).
2. If alpha is significantly negative, this is evidence of inferior performance (illustrated in Figure 22-2 with portfolio Z, which has a negative intercept).
3. If alpha is insignificantly different from zero, this is evidence that the portfolio manager matched the market on a risk-adjusted basis (as in the case of portfolio Y).

---

[8] This version is usually referred to as a characteristic line in risk premium or excess return form.

Note that Equation 22-6 can be rearranged to better demonstrate what α_p really is. Rearranging terms, Equation 22-6 (assuming a zero-error term) becomes

$$\alpha_p = (\overline{R}_p - \overline{RF}) - \beta_p(\overline{R}_M - \overline{RF}) \tag{22-7}$$

where the bars above the variables indicate averages for the period measured.

Equation 22-7 states that α_p is the difference between the actual excess return on portfolio p during some period and the risk premium on that portfolio that should have been earned, given its level of systematic risk and the use of the CAPM. It measures the constant return that the portfolio manager earned above, or below, the return of an unmanaged portfolio with the same (market) risk. As noted, this difference can be positive, negative, or zero.

✓ It is important to recognize the role of statistical significance in the interpretation of Jensen's measure. Although the estimated alpha may be positive or negative, it may not be significantly different (statistically) from zero. If it is not, we would conclude that the manager of the portfolio being evaluated performed as expected.[9]

Jensen's performance measure can be estimated by regressing excess returns for the portfolio being evaluated against excess returns for the market (in effect, producing a characteristic line in excess return form). When this was done for the five mutual funds evaluated earlier, the results are as shown in Table 22-2.

Three of the funds showed positive alphas, and reasonably high ones given the alphas typically observed for mutual funds. In this example, the 5.35 for W is significant, indicating that this fund, on average, earned an annual risk-adjusted rate of return that was more than 5 percent above the market average. In other words, W earned a positive return attributable to factors other than the market, presumably because of the ability of its managers. However, the standard errors for the other funds indicate that the alphas are not significantly different from zero.[10] Therefore, we cannot conclude that these funds exhibited superior performance. As in any regression equation, the coefficients must be statistically significant for any conclusions to be drawn. The larger the number of observations, the more likely we are to find statistical significance.

✓ Portfolios often fail to meet this statistical significance test because of the variability in security returns. This means that if the manager does actually add value, it cannot be detected statistically.

Superior and inferior portfolio performance can result from at least two sources. First, the portfolio manager may be able to select undervalued securities consistently enough to affect portfolio performance. Second, the manager may be able to time market turns, varying the portfolio's composition in accordance with the rise and fall of the market. Obviously, a manager with enough ability may be able to do both.

A computational advantage of the Jensen measure is that it permits the performance measure to be estimated simultaneously with the beta for a portfolio. That is, by estimating a characteristic line in risk premium form, estimates of both alpha and beta are obtained at the

---

[9] That is, the manager earned an average risk-adjusted return, neither more nor less than would be expected given the risk assumed.

[10] A general rule of thumb is that a coefficient should be twice its standard error in order to be significant at the 5 percent level. Alternatively, t values can be examined in order to test the significance of the coefficients. For a reasonably large number of observations, and therefore degrees of freedom, t values of approximately 2.0 would indicate significance at the 5 percent level.

same time. However, unlike the Sharpe and Treynor measures, each period's returns must be used in the estimating process, rather than an average return for the entire period. Thus, if performance is being measured on an annual basis, the annual returns on RF, RM, and R$_p$ must be obtained.

M2

A newer measure of risk-adjusted performance is called M2, named after its developers, Franco Modigliani and Leah Modigliani. It is a return adjusted for volatility that allows returns between portfolios to be compared. Since it is measured in percentage terms, it is easier to understand than the Sharpe and Jensen measures, which are not intuitive.

Essentially, M2 equates the volatility of the portfolio whose performance is being measured with the market. It does this by using Treasury bills and the portfolio being evaluated. If the risk of the portfolio being evaluated is less than that of the market, leverage can be used to increase the volatility. If risk is greater than that of the market, part of the funds can be placed in Treasury bills—the fund can be delivered to match the lower volatility of the market. After adjusting the portfolio for leverage to be comparable to the market, its return can be compared to the market, or some benchmark.

✓ A big advantage of M2 is that the results are stated in decimal or percentage form.

M2 can be calculated as:

$$M2 = RF + \sigma_M / \sigma_p + (R_p - RF) \qquad \text{(22-8)}$$

where

σ_M = standard deviation of the market

σ_p = standard deviation of the portfolio being measured

R_p = the return on the portfolio whose performance is being measured

Example 22-7   Assume you wish to evaluate the performance of a portfolio that had a 14 percent average return for a period of time, with a standard deviation of 23 percent. The market for the same period had an average return of 10.5 percent, with a standard deviation of 20 percent. The average risk-free rate was 5 percent.

$$
\begin{aligned}
M2 &= RF + \sigma_M / \sigma_p + (R_p - RF) \\
&= 5 + 20/23 + 5.5 \\
&= 11.37\%
\end{aligned}
$$

This portfolio had better risk-adjusted performance than did the market.

A Comparison of Performance Measures   The Sharpe ratio, which uses the standard deviation, evaluates portfolio performance on the basis of both the portfolio's return and its diversification.[11] Although the Sharpe ratio ranks portfolios, it does not tell us in percentage terms how much a fund outperformed (or underperformed) some benchmark.

M2 produces a percentage return which can be easily understood. It produces the same rankings as the Sharpe measure.

---

[11] Treynor's measure considers only the systematic risk of the portfolio and, like the Sharpe measure, can be used to rank portfolios on the basis of realized performance.

Jensen's alpha uses beta as the measure of risk. Jensen's measure is not suitable for ranking portfolio performance, but it can be modified to do so. The Jensen and Treynor measures can produce, with proper adjustments, identical relative rankings of portfolio performance.[12]

If a portfolio is completely diversified, all of these measures will agree on a ranking of portfolios. The reason for this is that with complete diversification, total variance is equal to systematic variance. When portfolios are not completely diversified, the Treynor and Jensen measures can rank relatively undiversified portfolios much higher than the Sharpe measure does. Since the Sharpe measure uses total risk, both systematic and nonsystematic components are included.

USING THE SHARPE RATIO TODAY

The Sharpe measure of portfolio performance is a widely known, and frequently cited, measure of portfolio performance. The user can compare the Sharpe ratio for the fund of interest to other funds and/or to market indexes. However, an important issue has arisen in recent years concerning the use of this ratio. A number of observers have claimed that because hedge funds and other nontypical types of funds often generate returns that are not normally distributed, the Sharpe ratio cannot be used to measure performance. This, in turn, has led to the development of several new measures of performance designed to get around this problem.

In a recent study, Eling tested a large number of funds investing in a variety of assets and found that "the choice of performance measure does not affect the ranking of hedge funds and mutual funds."[13] The author concluded that the Sharpe ratio is adequate for the job of evaluating the returns of hedge funds and mutual funds.

Checking Your Understanding

4. Assume you examine five completely diversified portfolios. Will the Sharpe, Treynor, and Jensen measures agree on how the managers should be ranked? Why, or why not?

Style Analysis and Performance Attribution

Style Analysis A classification reflecting a portfolio manager's "style" characteristics

Performance Attribution A part of portfolio evaluation that seeks to determine why success or failure occurred

Most of this chapter is concerned with how to measure a portfolio manager's performance. However, a complete evaluation of portfolio performance also involves style analysis and performance attribution. **Style analysis** seeks to determine the detailed investment style adopted by a money manager. **Performance attribution** analyzes the reasons why a manager did better or worse than a properly constructed benchmark with complete risk adjustment; in effect, it seeks to determine, after the fact, why a particular portfolio had a given return over some specified time period and, therefore, why success or failure occurred.

STYLE ANALYSIS

In Chapter 3 we considered *Morningstar's* style box for mutual funds. A style box classifies a fund into one of nine cells in the box depending upon the market capitalization of the portfolio's stocks and whether they are growth or value stocks, or a blend. Such a classification

---

[12] Jensen's alpha divided by beta is equivalent to Treynor's measure minus the average risk premium for the market portfolio for the period.

[13] Martin Eling, "Does the Measure Matter in the Mutual Fund Industry?" *Financial Analysts Journal*, Vol. 64, No. 3, pp. 54–66.

reflects a portfolio manager's "style" characteristics. For example, a manager who invests in small growth stocks would be classified at the intersection of these two characteristics (small cap and growth) in the style box. The style box provides an analysis of the stocks in the portfolio based on their size and value/growth characteristics.

The style box does not resolve all issues. This is because almost all portfolios differ from each other with regard to securities held and/or the proportion of the portfolio invested in each security. For example, among equity funds, a fund may describe itself as a large growth fund and still show a performance that differs from other funds in that same category. Style analysis can be used to determine why these funds differ in their results.

A portfolio manager constructs the portfolio based on his or her investment philosophy, resulting in a unique portfolio. This causes the portfolio's returns to behave accordingly. We can describe this behavior as the style of the portfolio. Style analysis seeks to identify the investing style of a portfolio in terms of asset classes, equity styles, or index returns.

Example 22-8

Consider a mid-cap stock fund whose manager emphasizes stocks that currently are out of favor with investors. The manager believes that recent events have caused these stocks to sell for less than their intrinsic value. To identify these stocks, the manager screens the mid-cap database for stocks with low price to book ratios and low P/E ratios. These value criteria will cause the portfolio to have a unique returns behavior that relates directly to the manager's style. Such a style would differ from that of another mid-cap fund manager who emphasized growth when selecting stocks.

There are two approaches to style analysis, returns-based and holdings-based:

- *Holdings-based style analysis* uses the stocks in a portfolio to describe a fund's allocation among asset classes or equity styles. As noted, *Morningstar* uses a holdings-based approach to style analysis.
- *Returns-based style analysis* compares a portfolio's return to the returns generated by a set of market indexes, each of which tracks a specific investment style such as large-cap growth or small-cap value.

Sharpe developed returns-based style analysis using an asset class factor model (think of it as similar to a regression model).[14] His analysis used multiple asset classes, ranging from Treasury bills to several bond indexes to even more stock indexes, and also a mortgage-related securities index.[15] Equities are divided into four mutually exclusive groups using the indexes developed: large-cap value stocks, large-cap growth stocks, medium-cap stocks, and small-cap stocks. This type of style analysis typically requires at least 20—36 months of returns data.

✓ Using a returns-based style analysis, a manager's style reflects only an analysis of the components of a portfolio's actual return behavior, making it an objective method for determining risk exposure.

---

[14] Sharpe has noted that the term "factor analysis" is not a good term to use to describe this process. He prefers "factor model."

[15] William F. Sharpe, "Asset Allocation: Management Style And Performance Measurement," *The Journal of Portfolio Management*, Winter 1992, pp. 7—19.

Sharpe's analysis produces a "style benchmark", or customized benchmark which reflects an individualized weighting of a set of indexes that document the manager's style. Many portfolio managers prefer style benchmarks to single index benchmarks.

Example 22-9   Consider a domestic large-cap equity fund manager who gradually shifts more of the portfolio's assets to international stocks. Furthermore, the manager tends to inadvertently focus on mid-cap stocks. A single index would be unlikely to best reflect what this manager is now doing, whereas a customized index could do that.

As Sharpe himself said in an interview, "Before I would invest in a fund I would want to read the *Morningstar* material and whatever else I could find." In other words, style analysis does not resolve all issues for an investor. Furthermore, some experienced users of returns-based style analysis claim there can be problems referred to as "noise in the data." These problems could include a lack of diversification, selection of inappropriate style indexes and market changes in asset allocation.

One problem with style analysis is style "consistency." One estimate is that over a five-year period less than half the domestic mutual funds maintain their style consistency. Standard & Poor's conducted a study of consistency and found that large cap growth funds maintained a consistency level of about 70 percent over a five-year period while small-cap blend funds maintained a consistency of only 18 percent. All mid-cap funds had a consistency of only 31 percent, and all small-cap funds had a consistency of less than 40 percent. Taken together, all large-cap funds had a consistency over five years of only 54 percent.

PERFORMANCE ATTRIBUTION

The purpose of **performance attribution** is to decompose the total performance of a portfolio into specific components that can be associated with specific decisions made by the portfolio manager.

Typically, performance attribution is a top-down approach; it looks first at the broad issues and progresses by narrowing the investigation. It often begins with the policy statement that guides the management of the portfolio. The portfolio normally would have a set of portfolio weights to be used. If the manager uses a different set, this will account for some of the results. In effect, we are looking at the asset allocation decision referred to in Chapters 8 and 21. If the manager chooses to allocate portfolio funds differently than the weights that occur in the benchmark portfolio, what are the results?

After this analysis, performance attribution might analyze sector (industry) selection and security selection. Did the manager concentrate on, or avoid, certain sectors, and if so what were the results? Security selection speaks for itself.

Part of this process involves identifying a benchmark of performance (bogey) to use in comparing the portfolio's results. This bogey is designed to measure passive results, ruling out both asset allocation and security selection decisions. Any differences between the portfolio's results and the bogey must be attributable to one or more of these decisions made by the portfolio manager. We consider the issue of benchmarks later in the chapter.

Another way to think about performance attribution is to recognize that performance different from a properly constructed benchmark comes from one of two sources, or both:

1. Market timing
2. Security selection

Techniques are available to decompose the performance of a portfolio into these two components.[16]

Money Managers and Performance Presentations

Up until the early 1990s, investment managers had great freedom in presenting their performance results to the public. This generated considerable confusion when investors tried to compare results among money managers. Naturally, money managers tried to put the best light they could on their own performance, knowing that their success in attracting money, and possibly even their jobs, depended on their performance. Is it any wonder that misrepresentations of that performance were not unusual?

In 1993 the Association for Investment Management and Research, based on years of discussion, issued *minimum* standards for presenting investment performance.[17] These Performance Presentation Standards (PPS) were a set of guiding ethical principles with two objectives:

1. To promote full disclosure and fair representation by investment managers in reporting their investment results.
2. To ensure uniformity in reporting in order to enhance comparability among investment managers.

AIMR's PPS dealt primarily with the performance composites that money managers present. A composite is a set of managed accounts (portfolios) that are managed in essentially the same way. PPS required a manager to present a composite in compliance with the PPS to the public as the record of the firm's accomplishments. This significantly aided clients and potential clients in making valid evaluations of the firm's performance, and comparisons among different money managers. Basically, the standards provided for full disclosure of information, and eliminate abusive practices.

Note that the requirement for members to adhere to a set of standards is not limited to the United States. In order to "level the playing field" with regard to performance presentation among firms competing globally, and to aid investors in making comparisons among global firms, CFA Institute (the successor to AIMR) created the **Global Investment Performance Standards (GIPS)**®. The objective of GIPS® is to obtain global acceptance of a standard for fair presentation of performance and ensure accuracy and consistency of data in record keeping, marketing, and presentation. Its introduction recognized the fact that investment management is increasingly a global industry.

GIPS® requirements include:

Global Investment Performance Standards (GIPS)® A global standard used for the fair presentation of portfolio performance and for ensuring accuracy and consistency of data in record keeping, marketing, and presentation

- ❏ Uniformity in certain performance calculations and disclosures
- ❏ Inclusion of all actual fee-paying discretionary portfolios in composites that have a similar objective
- ❏ Compliant history for at least five years, or since inception if less than five years.

---

[16] R. Henriksson, "Market Timing and Mutual Fund Performance: An Empirical Investigation," *Journal of Business* (1984): pp. 73–96.

[17] Association for Investment Management and Research, *Performance Presentation Standards 1993*, Charlottesville, Va. 1993.

Checking Your Understanding

5. Assume you are the manager of an investment management firm that has a good record of portfolio performance that is fairly presented to its clients. Will the introduction of GIPS® improve the performance results of your firm? If not, how will its introduction help you as a firm?

An Overview on Performance Evaluation

Although it seems obvious when one thinks about it, investors tend not to be careful when making comparisons of portfolios over various time periods. One popular press article summarized the extent of the problem by noting that "most investors . . . don't have the slightest idea how well their portfolios are actually performing." Even when investors are aware of their portfolio's performance, they should understand that in today's investment world of computers and databases, exact, precise universally agreed-upon methods of portfolio evaluation remain an elusive goal.

As we have seen, investors can use several well-known techniques to assess the actual performance of a portfolio relative to one or more alternatives. In the final analysis, when investors are selecting money managers to turn their money over to, they evaluate these managers only on the basis of their published performance statistics. If the published "track record" looks good, that is typically enough to convince many investors to invest in a particular mutual fund. However, the past is no guarantee of an investment manager's future. Short-term results may be particularly misleading.

Finally, note that a long evaluation period is needed to successfully determine performance that is truly superior. Over short periods, luck can overshadow all else, but luck cannot be expected to continue unabated.

Summary

▶ Evaluation of portfolio performance, the bottom line of the investing process, is an important aspect of interest to all investors and money managers.

▶ The framework for evaluating portfolio performance consists of measuring both the realized return and the risk of the portfolio being evaluated, determining an appropriate benchmark portfolio to use to compare a portfolio's performance, and recognizing any constraints that the portfolio manager may face.

▶ The time-weighted, as opposed to the dollar-weighted, return captures the rate of return actually earned by the portfolio manager. Total returns are used in the calculations.

▶ The two prevalent measures of risk are total risk (standard deviation) and systematic risk (beta).

▶ The coefficient of determination, or R^2, is used to denote the degree of diversification.

▶ Risk-adjusted (composite) measures of portfolio performance combine return and risk together in one calculation.

▶ The Sharpe and Treynor measures can be used to rank portfolio performance and indicate the relative positions of the portfolios being evaluated. Jensen's measure is an absolute measure of performance. M2 is a variant of the Sharpe measure.

▶ Both the Sharpe and Treynor measures relate the excess return on a portfolio to a measure of its risk. Sharpe's RVAR uses standard deviation, whereas Treynor's RVOL uses beta. Portfolio rankings from the two measures can differ if portfolios are not well diversified.

▶ Jensen's differential return measures the difference between what the portfolio was expected to earn, given its systematic risk, and what it actually did earn.

By regressing the portfolio's excess return against that of the market index, alpha can be used to capture the superior or inferior performance of the portfolio manager.

▶ Based on capital market theory, alphas are expected to be zero. Significantly positive or negative alphas are used to indicate corresponding performance.

▶ M2 is a newer measure of performance that gives rankings identical to the Sharpe measure but states results in percentage terms.

▶ A good universe or benchmark for evaluating portfolio performance should be unambiguous, specified in advance, appropriate, investable, and measurable.

▶ Style analysis seeks to identify the characteristics of a portfolio.

▶ Sharpe developed returns-based style analysis using an asset class factor model (think of it as similar to a regression model)

▶ Performance attribution is concerned with why a portfolio manager did better or worse than an expected benchmark. It involves decomposing performance to determine why the particular results occurred.

▶ CFA Institute (the successor to AIMR) created GIPS® as a way to obtain global acceptance of a standard for fair presentation of performance results by investment management firms.

Questions

22-1 Outline the framework for evaluating portfolio performance.

22-2 Why can the evaluation of a portfolio be different from the evaluation of a portfolio manager?

22-3 Explain how the three composite measures of performance are related to capital market theory and the CAPM.

22-4 What role does diversification play in the Sharpe and Treynor measures?

22-5 How can one construct a characteristic line for a portfolio? What does it show?

22-6 How can portfolio diversification be measured? On average, what degree of diversification would you expect to find for a typical equity mutual fund holding large-cap stocks?

22-7 For what type of mutual fund discussed in Chapter 3 could you expect to find complete diversification?

22-8 In general, when may an investor prefer to rely on the Sharpe measure? The Treynor measure?

22-9 Explain how Jensen's differential return measure is derived from the CAPM.

22-10 Why is the Jensen measure computationally efficient?

22-11 What role does statistical significance play in the Jensen measure?

22-12 How does Roll's questioning of the testing of the CAPM relate to the issue of performance measurement?

22-13 Illustrate how the choice of the wrong market index could affect the rankings of portfolios.

22-14 In theory, what would be the proper market index to use?

22-15 Explain why the steeper the angle, the better the performance in Figure 22-1.

22-16 Do the Sharpe and Jensen measures produce the same rankings of portfolio performance?

22-17 How do the Global Performance Investment Standards help investors?

22-18 What does the term "performance attribution" mean?

22-19 What does style analysis seek to accomplish?

22-20 Identify a major problem when using style analysis.

CFA
22-21 Paul Joubert retired from his firm. He has continued to hold his private retirement investments in a portfolio of common stocks and bonds. At the beginning of 2002, when he retired, his account was valued at €453,000. By the end of 2002, the value of his account was €523,500. Joubert made no contributions to or withdrawals from the portfolio during 2002. What rate of return did Joubert earn on his portfolio during 2002?

CFA
22-22 Compare and contrast the time-weighted rate of return with the money-weighted rate of return.

In general terms, how is each calculated? Are there certain situations that would cause the two methods to have drastic differences in the calculated rates of return?

CFA
22-23 John Wilson buys 150 shares of ABM on 1 January 2002 at $156.30 per share. A dividend of $10 per share is paid on 1 January 2003. Assume that this dividend is not reinvested. Also, on January 1, 2003 Wilson sells 100 shares at a price of $165 per share. On January 1, 2004, he collects a dividend of $15 per share (on 50 shares) and sells his remaining 50 shares at $170 per share.

    a. Write the formula to calculate the money-weighted rate of return on Wilson's portfolio.

    b. Using any method, compute the money-weighted rate of return.

    c. Calculate the time-weighted rate of return on Wilson's portfolio.

    d. Describe a set of circumstances for which the money-weighted rate of return is an appropriate return measure for Wilson's portfolio.

    e. Describe a set of circumstances for which the time-weighted rate of return is an appropriate return measure for Wilson's portfolio.

CFA
22-24 Briefly discuss the properties that a valid benchmark should have.

CFA
22-25 Kim Lee Ltd., an investment management firm in Singapore managing portfolios of Pacific Rim equities, tells you that its benchmark for performance is to be in the top quartile of its peer group (Singapore managers running portfolios of Pacific Rim equities) over the previous calendar year. Is this a valid benchmark? Why, or why not?

CFA
22-26 The Reliable Performance Management firm was retained by a client. The investment objective specified by the client was to outperform a broad-based bond market index by at least 50 basis points. In the first year, Reliable was able to earn more than 80 basis points over the benchmark index. However, the client was dissatisfied with the performance of Reliable because the client was not able to meet its liabilities. Ms. Florez of

Reliable is responsible for client accounts. How should Ms. Florez respond to the client's dissatisfaction with the performance of Reliable?

CFA
22-27 A client retained the Conservative Management Company to manage funds on an indexed basis. The benchmark selected was the Lehman Brothers U.S. Aggregate index. In each of the first four quarters, the management company outperformed the benchmark by a minimum of 70 basis points. In its annual review, a representative of the management company stressed its company's superior performance. You are a consultant who has been retained by the client. Comment on the claim of the management company representative.

CFA
22-28 **a.** What is the difference between performance measurement and performance evaluation?

    b. What are the two issues that performance evaluation seeks to address?

CFA
22-29 The following table repeats the annual total returns on the MSCI Germany Index previously given (see CFA Question 6-2) and also gives the annual total returns on the JP Morgan Germany five- to seven-year government bond index (JPM 5–7-Year GBI, for short). During the period given in the table, the International Monetary Fund Germany Money Market Index (IMF Germany MMI, for short) had a mean total return of 4.33 percent. Use that information and the information in the table to answer Problems A through C.

Year	MSCI Germany Index	JPM Germany 5–7-Year GBI
1993	46.21%	15.74%
1994	−6.18%	−3.40%
1995	8.04%	18.30%
1996	22.87%	8.35%
1997	45.90%	6.65%
1998	20.32%	12.45%
1999	41.20%	−2.19%
2000	−9.53%	7.44%
2001	−17.75%	5.55%
2002	−43.06%	10.27%

Source: Ibbotson EnCorr Analyzer.

a. Calculate the annual returns and the mean annual return on a portfolio 60 percent invested in the MSCI Germany Index and 40 percent invested in the JPM Germany GBI.

b. Using the IMF Germany MMI as a proxy for the risk-free return, calculate the Sharpe ratio for

i. the 60/40 equity/bond portfolio described in Problem A.

ii. the MSCI Germany Index.

iii. the JPM Germany 5−7-Year GBI.

c. Contrast the risk-adjusted performance of the 60/40 equity/bond portfolio, the MSCI Germany Index, and the JPM Germany 5−7-Year GBI, as measured by the Sharpe ratio.

Problems

22-1 Consider the five funds shown below:

	α	β	R^2
1	0.9[a]	1.20	0.60
4	2.0	1.0	0.98
3	1.6[a]	1.1	0.95
5	3.5	0.9	0.90
2	1.2	0.8	0.80

[a] Significant at 5 percent level.

a. Which fund's returns are best explained by the market's returns?

b. Which fund had the largest total risk?

c. Which fund had the lowest market risk? The highest?

d. Which fund(s), according to Jensen's alpha, outperformed the market?

22-2 Draw a diagram showing characteristic lines in risk premium form for two portfolios, A and B. A's line is steeper than B's, with a lower intercept. Both alphas are significant.

a. Label each axis.

b. Which fund has the larger beta?

c. Based on a visual inspection, which fund has the larger alpha?

d. Which fund outperformed the market?

22-3 Given the following information:

Period	Market Ret.	RF	Portfolio 1	Portfolio 2
1	−0.40	.07	−0.25	−0.30
2	0.10	.07	0.18	0.20
3	0.02	.08	0.06	0.04
4	0.20	.08	0.30	0.26
5	0.18	.07	0.21	0.21
6	−0.03	.08	−0.04	−0.06
7	−0.05	.07	−0.02	−0.01
8	0.13	.07	0.	0.12
9	0.30	.08	0.28	0.32
10	−0.15	.09	−0.20	−0.25

  a. Rank the portfolios on RVAR.

  b. Rank the portfolios on RVOL.

  c. Rank the portfolios on alpha.

  d. Which portfolio had the smaller nonsystematic risk?

  e. Which portfolio had the larger beta?

  f. Which portfolio had the larger standard deviation?

  g. Which portfolio had the larger average return?

  h. How are the answers to (f) and (g) related to the results for the composite performance measures?

22-4 Given the following information for three portfolios for a six-year period:

Period	Market Return	RF	Portfolio 1	Portfolio 2	Portfolio 3
1	0.10	.05	0.17	0.16	0.15
2	0.02	.06	0.13	0.11	0.09
3	0.20	.08	0.18	0.28	0.26
4	0.30	.09	0.42	0.36	0.34
5	−0.04	.08	−0.16	−0.03	−0.02
6	0.16	.07	0.17	0.17	0.16

Answer (a) through (d) without doing the calculations.

  a. Which portfolio would you expect to have the largest beta?

  b. Which portfolio would you expect to have the largest standard deviation?

  c. Which portfolio would you expect to have the largest R^2?

  d. Which portfolio would you expect to rank first on the basis of RVAR?

  e. Determine the rankings of the three portfolios on RVAR and RVOL.

  f. How did the portfolios rank in terms of R^2?

  g. Which portfolio had the largest alpha?

  h. Which portfolio exhibited the best performance based on the composite measures of performance?

22-5 The following information is available for two portfolios, a market index, and the risk-free rate:

Period	Market Return	RF	1	2
1	0.10	.06	0.10	0.20
2	0.12	.08	0.12	0.24
3	0.20	.08	0.20	0.40
4	0.04	.08	0.04	0.08
5	0.12	.08	0.12	0.24

  a. Without doing calculations, determine the portfolio with a beta of 1.0.

  b. Without doing calculations, determine the beta of portfolio 2.

    c. Without doing calculations, determine the R^2 for each portfolio.

    d. Without doing calculations, what would you expect the alpha of portfolio 1 to be?

    e. What would you expect the RVAR and RVOL to be for portfolio 1 relative to the market?

Computational Problems

22-1 The following data are available for five portfolios and the market for a recent 10-year period:

	Average Annual Return (%)	Standard Deviation (%)	β_P	R^2
2	14	21	1.15	0.70
3	16	24	1.1	0.98
5	26	30	1.3	0.96
4	17	25	0.9	0.92
1	10	18	0.45	0.60
S&P 500	12	20		
RF	6			

    a. Rank these portfolios using the Sharpe measure.

    b. Rank these portfolios using the Treynor measure.

    c. Compare the rankings of portfolios 2 and 3. Are there any differences? How can you explain these differences?

    d. Which of these portfolios outperformed the market?

22-2 Annual total returns for nine years are shown below for eight mutual funds. Characteristic lines are calculated using annual market returns. The *ex post* values are as follows:

Fund	(1) R_p(%)	(2) σ_P(%)	(3) α_P	(4) β_P	(5) R^2
A	17.0	20.0	7.53	0.88	0.82
B	19.0	17.8	11.70	0.65	0.57
C	12.3	25.0	3.12	0.83	0.47
D	20.0	24.5	9.00	1.00	0.72
E	15.0	17.4	6.15	0.79	0.88
F	19.0	18.0	10.11	0.83	0.89
G	8.6	19.0	−1.37	0.91	0.95
H	20.0	21.5	9.52	0.93	0.78

where

$$R_p = \text{mean annual total return for each fund}$$
$$\sigma_P = \text{standard deviation of the annual yields}$$
$$\alpha_P = \text{the constant of the characteristic line}$$
$$\beta_P = \text{the slope}$$

Using an 8.6 percent risk-free return,

a. Calculate Sharpe's RVAR for each of these eight funds and rank the eight funds from high to low performance.

b. Calculate Treynor's RVOL for each fund and perform the same ranking as in part a.

c. Use the R^2 in column 5 to comment on the degree of diversification of the eight mutual funds. Which fund appears to be the most highly diversified? Which fund appears to be the least diversified?

d. The returns, standard deviations, and characteristic lines were recalculated using the annual Treasury bill rate. The results are shown in the following table in excess yield form:

Fund	R_P	σ_P	SE(α)	β_P	t Values
A	8.60	20.00	(3.53)	0.87	−2.15
B	10.30	16.90	(4.78)	0.61	−2.23
C	3.70	25.50	(7.37)	0.86	−0.24
D	11.50	25.00	(5.23)	1.03	−1.96
E	6.30	18.09	(2.51)	0.81	−1.91
F	10.80	18.20	(2.40)	0.83	−4.21
G	−0.02	19.80	(1.65)	0.92	−1.49
H	11.30	23.40	(4.20)	0.95	−2.40

In the column to the right of the α_P is the calculated standard error of alpha [SE(α)]. The critical value of t for 7 degrees of freedom (number of observations minus 2) for a two-tailed test at the 5 percent level is 2.365. With a large number of degrees of freedom, the critical value of t is close to 2.00. If the absolute value in that column exceeds 2.365, that fund's alpha is significantly different from zero. Which funds exhibit above, or below, average performance?

e. Compare the values of α and β calculated in excess yield form with those calculated initially.

Spreadsheet Problems

22-1 The spreadsheet below has annual returns for three mutual funds—Capital Appreciation, High Return, and Total Return—for 10 years. A market return and a risk-free rate are provided, along with the beta for each of the three funds.

a. Calculate the average return and standard deviation for each of the three funds and for the market.

b. Calculate the Sharpe and Treynor measures for each of the three funds and for the market based on your part (a) answers and the betas provided. Which fund performed best according to each measure?

c. Calculate Jensen's alpha in the indicated cells by subtracting the required return as given by the CAPM equation from the average return. Alpha is the difference between what the fund actually returned and what it was expected to return based on the CAPM equation.

d. Determine the amount of diversification for each fund.

	Cap Appr	Hi Growth	Total Ret	Mk. Ret	Risk-Free
2012	6.78%	11.30%	14.15%	10.45%	1.56%
2011	2.00%	−3.40%	5.14%	2.30%	1.25%
2010	9.80%	12.79%	21.24%	9.65%	2.40%
2009	16.30%	14.30%	12.45%	11.23%	2.10%
2008	−28.56%	−20.78%	−36.78%	−37%	3.10%
2007	11.78%	8.50%	9.56%	8.89%	3.50%
2006	14.20%	12.44%	13.56%	17.56%	4.20%
2005	11.80%	5.67%	12.34%	12.45%	4.34%
2004	14.67%	9.13%	9.89%	6.45%	4.87%
2003	−3.40%	6.37%	−4.56%	8.76%	4.98%
Aver					
St Dev					
Beta	0.96	0.92	1.15		
Sharpe					
Treynor					
Jensen					
R2					

Checking Your Understanding

22-1   The time-weighed return is the correct measure of the portfolio manager's performance because it takes into account cash contributions and withdrawals. Use the dollar-weighted return to measure the return to the portfolio itself.

22-2   A portfolio with an R^2 of 1.0 is a perfectly diversified portfolio whose returns are completely explained by the returns of the market as a whole.

22-3   The numerator of these measures is the portfolio's risk premium. It measures the excess return (above the risk-free rate) per unit of risk. For the Sharpe measure, this means per unit of total risk. For the Treynor measure, this means per unit of systematic risk.

22-4   All three measures will agree on how managers should be ranked when the portfolios being evaluated are completely diversified. This is because the total risk (variance) of a completely diversified portfolio is equivalent to its systematic risk.

22-5   GIPS® is a set of guidelines for the presentation of portfolio performance results. As such, it cannot help a firm improve upon its performance—that is up to the firm itself. However, by requiring other firms to fairly present their performance results, clients and potential clients can fairly judge a firm's performance, and hopefully those firms that might choose to slant their performance results will not easily be able to do so.

Glossary

A

Abnormal Return Return on a security beyond that expected on the basis of its risk

Active Management Strategy A strategy designed to provide additional returns by trading activities

Advance-Decline Line A technical analysis measure that relates the number of stocks rising to the number declining

Alpha The difference between an independently determined expected rate of return on a stock and the required rate of return on that stock.

American Depository Receipts (ADRs) Securities representing an ownership interest in the equities of foreign companies

Arbitrage Pricing Theory (APT) An equilibrium theory of expected returns for securities involving few assumptions about investor preferences

Arbitrageurs Investors who seek discrepancies in security prices in an attempt to earn riskless returns

Asset Allocation Decision The allocation of a portfolio's funds to classes of assets, such as cash equivalents, bonds, and equities

Asset-Backed Securities (ABS) Securities issued against some type of asset-linked debts bundled together, such as credit card receivables or mortgages

Average Annual Total Return A hypothetical rate of return used by mutual funds that, if achieved annually, would have produced the same cumulative total return if performance had been constant over the entire period

Average Tax Rate Total tax divided by taxable income

B

Balance Sheet A summary of a company's assets, liabilities, and owner's equity at a specific point in time

Bar Chart A plot of daily stock price plotted against time

Basis The difference between the futures price of an item and the spot price of the item

Basis Points 100 basis points is equal to 1 percentage point

Bear Market A downward trend in the stock market

Behavioral Finance (BF) The study of investment behavior, based on the belief that investors do not always act rationally

Benchmark Portfolio An alternative portfolio against which to measure a portfolio's performance

Beta A measure of volatility, or relative systematic risk, for a stock or a portfolio

Black–Scholes Model A widely used model for the valuation of call options

Blocks Transactions involving at least 10,000 shares

Blue-Chip Stocks Stocks with long records of earnings and dividends—well-known, stable, mature companies

Bond-Equivalent Yield Yield on an annual basis, derived by doubling the semiannual compound yield

Bond Ratings Letters assigned to bonds by rating agencies to express the relative probability of default

Bonds Long-term debt instruments representing the issuer's contractual obligation

Bond Swaps An active bond management strategy involving the purchase and sale of bonds in an attempt to improve the rate of return on the bond portfolio

Book Value The accounting value of the equity as shown on the balance sheet

Broker An intermediary who represents buyers and sellers in securities transactions and receives a commission

Bubble When speculation pushes asset prices to unsustainable highs

Business Cycle The recurring patterns of expansion, boom, contraction, and recession in the economy

Buy-Side Analysts Analysts employed by money management firms to search for equities for their firms to buy as investing opportunities

C

Call An option to buy a specified number of shares of stock at a stated price within a specified period

Call Provision Gives the issuer the right to call in a security and retire it by paying off the obligation

Capital Asset Pricing Model (CAPM) Relates the required rate of return for any security with the risk for that security as measured by beta

Capital Gain (Loss) The change in price on a security over some period

Capital Market The market for long-term securities such as bonds and stocks

Capital Market Line (CML) The tradeoff between expected return and risk for efficient portfolios

Cash Flow Statement The third financial statement of a company, designed to track the flow of cash through the firm

Characteristic Line A regression equation used to estimate beta by regressing stock returns on market returns

Chartered Financial Analyst (CFA) A professional designation for people in the investments field

Closed-End Investment Company An investment company with a fixed capitalization whose shares trade on exchanges

Coefficient of Determination The square of the correlation coefficient, measuring the percentage of the variance in the dependent variable that is explained by the independent variable

Common Stock An equity security representing the ownership interest in a corporation

Composite Economic Indexes Leading, coincident, and lagging indicators of economic activity

Consensus Forecast Most likely EPS value expected by analysts

Constant (Normal) Growth Rate Case A well-known scenario in valuation in which dividends are expected to grow at a constant growth rate over time

Contrarian Investing The theory that it pays to trade contrary to most investors

Convexity A measure of the degree to which the relationship between a bond's price and yield departs from a straight line

Corporate Bonds Long-term debt securities of various types sold by corporations

Correlation Coefficient A statistical measure of the extent to which two variables are associated

Covariance An absolute measure of the extent to which two variables tend to covary, or move together

Covered Call A strategy involving the sale of a call option to supplement a long position in an underlying asset

Cumulative Abnormal Return (CAR) The sum of the individual abnormal returns over the period under examination

Cumulative Wealth Index Cumulative wealth over time, given an initial wealth and a series of returns on some asset

Currency Risk (Exchange Rate Risk) The risk of an adverse impact on the return from a foreign investment as a result of movements in currencies

Current Yield A bond's annual coupon divided by the current market price

Cyclical Industries Industries most affected, both up and down, by the business cycle

D

Data Mining The search for apparent patterns in stock returns by intensively analyzing data

Debenture An unsecured bond backed by the general worthiness of the firm

Defensive Industries Industries least affected by recessions and economic adversity

Delta A measure of how much the theoretical value of an option should change for a $1.00 change in the underlying stock

Derivative Securities Securities that derive their value in whole or in part by having a claim on some underlying security

Direct Investing Investors buy and sell securities themselves, typically through brokerage accounts

Discount Bond A bond whose price is below the $1,000 face value

Discount Broker Brokerage firms offering execution services at prices typically significantly less than full-line brokerage firms

Dividend Reinvestment Plan (DRIPs) A plan offered by a company whereby stockholders can reinvest dividends in additional shares of stock at no cost

Dividend Yield Dividend divided by current stock price

Dollar-Weighted Rate of Return (DWR) Equates all cash flows, including ending market value, with the beginning market value of the portfolio

Dow Jones Industrial Average (DJIA) A price-weighted series of 30 leading industrial stocks, used as a measure of stock market activity

Dow Jones World Stock Index A capitalization-weighted index designed to be a comprehensive measure of worldwide stock performance

Dow Theory A technique for detecting long-term trends in the aggregate stock market

Duration A measure of a bond's economic lifetime that accounts for the entire pattern of cash flows over the life of the bond; a measure of bond price sensitivity to interest rate movements

E

Earnings Surprises The difference between a firm's actual earnings and its expected earnings

Efficient Frontier The Markowitz tradeoff between expected portfolio return and portfolio risk (standard deviation) showing all efficient portfolios given some set of securities

Efficient Market (EM) A market in which prices of securities quickly and fully reflect all available information

Efficient Market Hypothesis (EMH) The proposition that securities markets are efficient, with the prices of securities reflecting their economic value

Efficient Portfolio A portfolio with the highest level of expected return for a given level of risk or a portfolio with the lowest risk for a given level of expected return

Efficient Set The set of portfolios generated by the Markowitz portfolio model

Electronic Communication Network (ECN) A computerized trading network for buying and selling securities electronically

Equity Risk Premium The difference between stock returns and the risk-free rate

Event Study An empirical analysis of stock price behavior surrounding a particular event

Exchange-Traded Fund (ETF) Generally an index fund priced and traded on exchanges like any share of stock

Exercise (Strike) Price The per-share price at which the common stock may be purchased from (in the case of a call) or sold to a writer (in the case of a put)

Expectations Theory States that the long-term rate of interest is equal to an average of the short-term rates that are expected to prevail over the long-term period

Expected Return The ex ante return expected by investors over some future holding period

Expense Ratio The annual charge by a mutual fund to its shareholders as a percentage of assets under management

Expiration Date The date an option expires

F

Factor Model Used to depict the behavior of security prices by identifying major factors in the economy that affect large numbers of securities

Filter Rule A rule for buying and selling stocks according to the stock's price movements

Financial Assets Pieces of paper evidencing a claim on some issuer

Financial Futures Futures contracts on financial assets

Financial Statements The principal published financial data about a company, primarily the balance sheet and income statement

Fixed-Income Securities Securities with specified payment dates and amounts, primarily bonds

Forward Contract A commitment today to transact in the future at a price that is currently determined, with no funds having been exchanged

Forward Rates Unobservable rates expected to prevail in the future

Free Cash Flows to Equity (FCFE) Model It differs from the DDM in that FCFE measures what a firm *could* pay out as dividends, rather than what they actually do pay out

Full Service Broker A brokerage firm offering a full range of services, including information and advice

Fund Supermarkets Offered by brokerage firms, these allow the firm's customers to choose from a large set of mutual funds through their brokerage accounts

Futures Contract Agreement providing for the future exchange of a particular asset at a currently determined market price

Futures Margin The earnest money deposit made by a transactor to ensure the completion of a contract

G

Generally Accepted Accounting Principles (GAAP) Financial reporting requirements establishing the rules for producing financial statements

Geometric Mean The compound rate of return over time

Global Dow^{SM} Index A stock market index designed to reflect the global stock market as it actually exists in terms of industries and regions

Global Funds Mutual funds that keep a minimum of 25 percent of their assets in U.S. securities

Global Industry Classification Standard (GICS) Provides a complete, continuous set of global sector and industry definitions using 10 economic sectors

Global Investment Performance Standards GIPS® A global standard used for the fair presentation of portfolio performance and for ensuring accuracy and consistency of data in record keeping, marketing and presentation

Government Agency Securities Securities issued by federal credit agencies (fully guaranteed) or by government-sponsored agencies (not guaranteed)

Gross Domestic Product (GDP) The basic measure of a country's output used in National Income accounts

Growth Industries Industries with expected earnings growth significantly above the average of all industries

Growth Stocks Stocks that emphasize expectations about future growth in earnings

H

Hedge A strategy using derivatives to offset or reduce the risk resulting from exposure to an underlying asset

Hedge Funds Unregulated companies that seek to exploit various market opportunities and thereby earn larger returns than are ordinarily available to investment companies

Hedge Ratio The ratio of options written to shares of stock held long in a riskless portfolio

Homogeneous Expectations Investors have the same expectations regarding the expected return and risk of securities

Horizon (Total) Return Bond returns to be earned based on assumptions about reinvestment rates

I

Immunization The strategy of immunizing (protecting) a portfolio against interest rate risk by canceling out its two components, price risk and reinvestment rate risk

Implied Volatility The volatility of an option based on the other parameters determining its value

Income Statement An accounting of a company's income and expenses over a specified period of time

Index Arbitrage Exploitation of price differences between stock-index futures and the index of stocks underlying the futures contract

Index Funds Mutual funds holding a bond or stock portfolio designed to match a particular market index

Indifference Curves Curves describing investor preferences for risk and return

Industry Life Cycle The stages of an industry's evolution from pioneering to stabilization and decline

Initial Margin In dollar terms, the initial equity an investor has in a margin transaction

Initial Public Offering (IPO) Common stock shares of a company being sold for the first time

Interest on Interest The process by which bond coupons are reinvested to earn interest

Interest Rate Risk The variability in a security's returns resulting from changes in interest rates

International Funds Mutual funds that concentrate primarily on international stocks

International Investing Investing in the securities of other countries

Intrinsic Value The estimated value of a security

Investment The commitment of funds to one or more assets that will be held over some future period

Investment Banker Firm specializing in the sale of new securities to the public, typically by underwriting the issue

Investment Company A company engaged primarily in the business of investing in, and managing, a portfolio of securities

Investments The study of the investment process

Investment Strategy An organized, logical framework within which to make and execute portfolio decisions

J

January Effect The observed tendency for small-company stock returns to be higher in January than in other months

Junk Bonds Bonds that carry ratings of BB or lower, with correspondingly higher yields

L

LEAPS Puts and calls with longer maturity dates, up to two years

Limit Order An order to buy or sell at a specified (or better) price

Liquidity The ease with which an asset can be bought or sold quickly with relatively small price changes

Liquidity Preference Theory States that interest rates reflect the sum of current and expected short rates, as in the expectations theory, plus liquidity (risk) premiums

Listed Securities The securities of companies meeting specified requirements of exchanges and marketplaces

Load Funds Mutual funds with a sales charge or load fee, a direct cost to investors

Long Hedge A transaction where the asset is currently not held but futures are purchased to lock in current prices

Long Position An agreement to purchase an asset at a specified future date at a specified price

M

Maintenance Margin The percentage of a security's value that must be on hand at all times as equity

Margin The investor's equity in a transaction; margin can apply to both securities and to futures contracts

Marginal Tax Rate The tax rate on the last dollar of income

Margin Borrowing Borrowing from a brokerage firm to finance a securities transaction

Margin Call A demand from the broker for additional cash or securities as a result of the actual margin declining below the maintenance margin

Marked to Market The daily posting of all profits and losses in an investor's account

Marketable Securities Financial assets that are easily and cheaply traded in organized markets

Market Anomalies Techniques or strategies that appear to be contrary to an efficient market

Market Data Price and volume information for stocks or indexes

Market Data Primarily stock price and volume information

Market Makers (Dealers) An individual (firm) who makes a market in a stock by buying from and selling to investors

Market Model Relates the return on each stock to the return on the market, using a linear relationship with intercept and slope

Market Order An order to buy or sell at the best price when the order reaches the trading floor

Market Portfolio The portfolio of all risky assets, with each asset weighted by the ratio of its market value to the market value of all risky assets

Market Risk The variability in a security's returns resulting from fluctuations in the aggregate market

Market Risk Premium The difference between the expected return for the equities market and the risk-free rate of return

Modified Duration Duration divided by 1 + ytm

Momentum Investing on the basis of recent movements in the price of a stock

Money Markets The market for short-term, highly liquid, low-risk assets such as Treasury bills and negotiable CDs

Money Market Funds (MMFs) A mutual fund that invests in money market instruments

Mortgage-Backed Securities Securities whose value depends upon some set of mortgages

MSCI EAFE Index The Europe, Australia, and Far East Index, a value-weighted index of the equity performance of major foreign markets

Multiple Growth Rate Case One of three possible forms of the dividend discount model, involving two or more expected growth rates for dividends.

Municipal Bonds Securities issued by political entities other than the federal government and its agencies, such as states and cities

Mutual Fund Prospectus A document designed to describe a particular mutual fund's objectives, policies, operations, and fees

N

NASDAQ Composite Index Measures all NASDAQ domestic-and international-based common type stocks listed on the NASDAQ Stock Market

NASDAQ Stock Market^{SM} (NASDAQ) An electronic marketplace providing instantaneous transactions as its market makers compete for investor orders.

Net Asset Value (NAV) The per share value of the securities in an investment company's portfolio

New York Stock Exchange (NYSE) The major secondary market for the trading of equity securities

No-Load Funds Mutual funds with no sales charge

Nominal Return Return in current dollars, with no adjustment for inflation

Nonsystematic Risk Risk attributable to factors unique to a security

North American Industry Classification System (NAICS) A company classification system that uses a production-oriented conceptual framework

O

Offset Liquidation of a futures position by an offsetting transaction

Open-End Investment Company An investment company whose capitalization constantly changes as new shares are sold and outstanding shares are redeemed

Operating Earnings Net income adjusted for nonrecurring or unusual items

Option Premium The price paid by the option buyer to the seller of the option

Options Rights to buy or sell a stated number of shares of a security within a specified period at a specified price

Options Clearing Corporation (OCC) Stands between buyers and sellers of options to ensure fulfillment of obligations

P

Par Value (Face Value) The redemption value of a bond paid at maturity, typically $1,000

Passive Management Strategy A strategy whereby investors do not actively seek out trading possibilities in an attempt to outperform the market

Payout Ratio Dividends divided by earnings

PEG Ratio The P/E ratio divided by the short-term earnings growth rate

Performance Attribution A part of portfolio evaluation that seeks to determine why success or failure occurred

Performance Benchmarks Unmanaged, passive portfolios that reflect a manager's investment style

Performance Universe Constructed by aggregating market valuations and income accruals for a large number of portfolios that are managed individually

P/E Ratio (Earnings Multiplier) The ratio of stock price to earnings, using historical, current or estimated data

Point-and-Figure Chart A plot of stock prices showing only significant price changes

Portfolio The securities held by an investor taken as a unit

Portfolio Insurance An asset management technique designed to provide a portfolio with a lower limit on value while permitting it to benefit from rising security prices

Portfolio Management Process The second step in the investment decision process, involving the management of a group of assets (i.e., a portfolio) as a unit.

Portfolio Rebalancing Periodically rebalancing a portfolio to maintain some specified or desired asset allocation decision

Portfolio Weights Percentages of portfolio funds invested in each security, summing to 1.0.

Preferred Stock An equity security with an intermediate claim (between the bondholders and the stockholders) on a firm's assets and earnings

Premium Bond A bond whose price is above the face value of $1,000

Primary Market The market for new issues of securities, typically involving investment bankers

Program Trading Involves the use of computer-generated orders to buy and sell securities based on arbitrage opportunities between common stocks and index futures and options

Prospectus Provides information about an initial public offering of securities to potential buyers

Protective Put A strategy involving the purchase of a put option as a supplement to a long position in an underlying asset

Put An option to sell a specified number of shares of stock at a stated price within a specified period

Put-Call Parity The formal relationship between a call and a put on the same item which must hold if no arbitrage is to occur

R

Random Walk A theory from the 1960s stating that stock prices wander randomly across time

Realized Compound Yield (RCY) Yield earned on a bond based on actual reinvestment rates during the life of the bond

Realized Return Actual return on an investment for some previous period of time

Real Returns Nominal (dollar) returns adjusted for inflation

Real Risk-Free Rate of Interest The opportunity cost of foregoing consumption, given no inflation

Regulation FD Regulates communications between public companies and investment professionals

Reinvestment Rate Risk That part of interest rate risk resulting from uncertainty about the rate at which future interest coupons can be reinvested

Relative Strength The ratio of a stock's price to some market or industry index, usually plotted as a graph

Reported Earnings GAAP earnings, the "official" earnings of a company as reported to stockholders and the SEC

Required Rate of Return The minimum expected rate of return necessary to induce an investor to purchase a security

Resistance Level A price range at which a technician expects a significant increase in the supply of a stock

Return on Assets (ROA) The accounting rate of return on a firm's assets

Return on Equity (ROE) The accounting rate of return on stockholders equity

Return Relative The total return for an investment for a given period stated on the basis of 1.0

Risk The chance that the actual return on an investment will be different from the expected return

Risk-Averse Investor An investor who will not assume a given level of risk unless there is an expectation of adequate compensation for having done so

Risk-Free Rate of Return The return on a riskless asset, often proxied by the rate of return on Treasury securities

Risk Premium That part of a security's return above the risk-free rate of return

Risk Tolerance An investor's willingness to accept risk when investing

S

Secondary Markets Markets where existing securities are traded among investors

Securities and Exchange Commission (SEC) A federal government agency established by the Securities Exchange Act of 1934 to protect investors

Security Analysis The first part of the investment decision process, involving the valuation and analysis of individual securities

Security Analysts Market professionals whose job it is to study, evaluate and recommend stocks to investors, either institutions or individuals

Security Market Line (SML) The graphical depiction of the CAPM

Sell-Side Analysts "Wall Street" analysts who cover stocks and make recommendation on them to investors

Semistrong Form That part of the efficient market hypothesis stating that prices reflect all publicly available information

Senior Securities Securities, typically debt securities, ahead of common stock in terms of payment or in case of liquidation

Separation Theorem The idea that the decision of which portfolio of risky assets to hold is separate from the decision of how to allocate investable funds between the risk-free asset and the risky asset

Sharpe Ratio A measure of portfolio performance calculated as the ratio of excess portfolio return to the standard deviation

Short Hedge A transaction involving the sale of futures (a short position) while holding the asset (a long position)

Short Interest The total number of shares in the market sold short and not yet repurchased

Short-Interest Ratio The ratio of total shares sold short to average daily trading volume

Short Position An agreement to sell an asset at a specified future date at a specified price

Short Sale The sale of a stock not owned in order to take advantage of an expected decline in the price of the stock

Single-Country Fund Investment companies, primarily closed-end funds, concentrating on the securities of a single country

Single Index Model A model that relates returns on each security to the returns on a market index

Size Effect The observed tendency for smaller firms to have higher stock returns than large firms

Standard & Poor's 500 Composite Index (S&P 500) Market value index of stock market activity covering 500 stocks

Standard Deviation A measure of the dispersion in outcomes around the expected value

Standard Industrial Classification (SIC) system A classification of firms on the basis of what they produce using census data

Standardized Unexpected Earnings (SUE) A variable used in the selection of common stocks, calculated as the ratio of unexpected earnings to a standardization factor

Stock Dividend A payment by the corporation in shares of stock rather than cash

Stock Index Options Option contracts on a stock market index such as the S&P 500

Stock Split The issuance by a corporation of shares of common stock in proportion to the existing shares outstanding

Stop Order An order specifying a certain price at which a market order takes effect

Strong Form That part of the efficient market hypothesis stating that prices reflect all information, public and private

Style Analysis A classification reflecting a portfolio manager's "style" characteristics

Support Level A price range at which a technician expects a significant increase in the demand for a stock

Survivorship Bias The bias resulting from the fact that analyzing a sample of investment companies at a point in time reflects only those companies that survived, ignoring those that did not

Sustainable Growth Rate A firm's expected growth rate in earnings and dividends, often calculated as the produce of ROE and the retention rate of earnings

Synthetic Options Created by a combination of two options or an option and shares

Systematic Risk Risk attributable to broad macro factors affecting all securities

Swap An agreement between parties to exchange streams of cash flows over some future period

T

Technical Analysis The use of specific market data for the analysis of both aggregate stock prices and individual stock prices

Term Structure of Interest Rates The relationship between time to maturity and yields for a particular category of bonds

Time-weighted Rate of Return (TWR) Measures the actual rate of return earned by the portfolio manager

Total Return (TR) Percentage measure relating all cash flows on a security for a given time period to its purchase price

Treasury Bill A short-term money market instrument sold at discount by the U.S. government

Treasury Bond Long-term bonds sold by the U.S. government

Treasury Inflation-Indexed Securities (TIPS) Treasury securities fully indexed for inflation

Treasury Notes Treasury securities with maturities up to 10 years

Trendlines A line on the chart of a security indicating the general direction in which the security's price is moving

U

Underwrite   The process by which investment bankers purchase an issue of securities from a firm and resell it to the public

V

Value Stocks   Stocks whose prices are considered "cheap" relative to earnings, book value, and other measures thought indicative of value

Variance   A statistical term measuring dispersion—the standard deviation squared

W

Warrant   A corporate-created option to purchase a stated number of common shares at a specified price within a specified time (typically several years)

Weak Form   That part of the efficient market hypothesis stating that prices reflect all price and volume data

Wrap Account   A new type of brokerage account where all costs are wrapped in one fee

Y

Yield   The income component of a security's return

Yield Curve   A graphical depiction of the relationship between yields and time for bonds that are identical except for maturity

Yield Spreads   The relationship between bond yields and the particular features on various bonds such as quality, callability, and taxes

Yield to First Call   The promised return on a bond from the present to the date that the bond is likely to be called

Yield to Maturity (YTM)   The promised compounded rate of return on a bond purchased as the current market price and held to maturity

Z

Zero Coupon Bond   A bond sold with no coupons at a discount and redeemed for face value at maturity

Zero Growth Rate Case   One of three growth rate cases of the dividend discount model, when the dollar dividend being paid is not expected to change

Index